The Big Fella

ALSO BY JANE LEAVY

Nonfiction

*The Last Boy: Mickey Mantle
and the End of America's Childhood*

Sandy Koufax: A Lefty's Legacy

Fiction

Squeeze Play

The Big Fella

Babe Ruth
and the World
He Created

Jane Leavy

HARPER LUXE

An Imprint of HarperCollinsPublishers

HarperCollins books may be purchased for educational, business, or sales promotional use. For information please e-mail the Special Markets Department at SPsales@harpercollins.com.

FIRST HARPERLUXE EDITION

ISBN: 978-0-06-286025-5

HarperLuxe™ is a trademark of HarperCollins Publishers.

Library of Congress Cataloging-in-Publication Data is available upon request.

18 19 20 21 22   ID/LSC   10 9 8 7 6 5 4 3 2 1

For Emma
Here's Looking at You, Kid

Give me the child for the first seven years and I'll give you the man.

—Jesuit maxim

Babe Ruth is the king of kings, the ace of aces, the what of what-not.

—*Lima News* (Ohio)

Babe Ruth is as much a part of the daily life and thought of this nation as the milkman, pay day, Prohibition, the Bible and evolution.

—*New York Evening Post*

Contents

Introduction

Twenty-five years ago, when I took my son to visit the Babe Ruth Birthplace and Museum in Baltimore, I was already trying to decide how to write about the Babe. Nick was seven years old, George Herman Ruth Jr.'s age when his parents sent him away to live at St. Mary's Industrial School for Orphans, Delinquent, Incorrigible, and Wayward Boys on the western edge of the city.

The minimalist, redbrick row house at 216 Emory Street where he was born on February 6, 1895, was the home of his maternal grandparents. Just twelve feet wide, sixty feet deep, and three squat stories high, it had four fireplaces but no running water or indoor plumbing, no gas or electricity.

Four adjoining row houses, the only homes fronting on the two-block side street, shared a pump located in the alley that ran behind them. Runoff collected in the center of the banked cobblestone street. There were no sewers.

The house, built in 1880, was situated in a working-class neighborhood with a grand name, Ridgely's Delight, which dated back to the mid-seventeenth-century plantation built by Colonel Charles Ridgely. By the late 1800s, the plantation was gone, and the area on the southwest cusp of downtown Baltimore was heavily industrial. The lightning rod shop operated by George Ruth Sr.'s father was just around the corner.

Museum curators had carefully appointed the dollhouse-size bedroom in which George Jr. came into the world in period antiques. Angels perched on the whitewashed mantel above an impossibly small wooden cradle. A marble washstand with a pink-and-white porcelain basin and pitcher, lace curtains, and brass wall sconces on either side of a double bed with an ornate mahogany headboard filled out the room, set off from the public by velvet ropes and stanchions—reminiscent of a presidential birthplace.

Katie Ruth told her son that he was born on February 7, 1894, which was untrue. Odd that she should have gotten the year wrong, arriving as he did in the middle of the February Freeze of '95, when it seemed hell might just freeze over, as had the Baltimore harbor.

The bollixed birth date wasn't the only incongruity I took away from our visit to the museum. There was something unsettling about the whole tableau, at odds with the well-worn tropes about Ruth's impoverished beginnings and guttersnipe childhood on the Baltimore waterfront.

It would take the better part of twenty-five years for me to put my finger on the precise nature of the disconnect: the myths and misconceptions about Babe Ruth *begin* at his birthplace. Only the dimensions of the familial still life and the outsized man Ruth became were incontrovertible. Everything else was conjecture.

Something different was bothering my son. He lingered at the threshold far longer than boys that age linger anywhere, trying to reconcile the life-size image of the Babe that greeted us at the museum entrance with the petite set piece of family life on the border of Victorian Pigtown.

Finally, he said, "Babe Ruth fit in here?"

His confusion was understandable. The Babe is a priori: too big ever to have been that small. No one thinks of him as Little George, his nickname in the family that banished him in June 1902. In part, that's a function of the sheer size of the man he grew to be, six foot two and 215 pounds when he was in trim and made everyone else in uniform look like the boys who now play in youth leagues named for him. In part, it is because so little is known about the boyhood of the man Casey Stengel called "the big feller." And in part, it is an expression of the huge place he still occupies in the American imagination.

Jim Murray, the late Pulitzer Prize–winning sports columnist for the *Los Angeles Times*, defined that place in an introduction to a 1991 children's book, *Babe Ruth*:

"A star is not something that flashes through the sky. That's a comet. Or a meteor. A star is something you can steer ships by. It stays in place and gives off a steady glow; it is fixed, permanent."

More than a century after his major-league debut, and seventy years after his death, Babe Ruth remains the lodestar of American fame. And that star has not diminished.

Curator Greg Schwalenberg rewarded my son's patience with a visit to the storage closet that then housed the museum's archives. The metal shelves were stocked with Cal Ripken bobbleheads, expired packs of baseball cards, and a cascade of bats thrown together on wire and steel shelving. "Here, try this," Schwalenberg said, extricating a hunk of swarthy, tapered ash from the heap of bats that fell against each other with the echo of falling timber in the small, enclosed space.

Dinged and gouged, rubbed and boned, with black, oblong splotches where baseballs had left their mark, the 35-inch-long and 38-ounce bat spoke to effort, ambition, history, and idiosyncrasy. Just as Nick got the thing balanced over his shoulder and assumed his stance, Schwalenberg said, "That's one of the bats the Babe used in 1927."

Nick struggled manfully to maintain his composure and his equilibrium, staggering under the weight of the moment. As soon as he got himself right, Schwalenberg exchanged Babe's bat for a more manageable Cal Ripken model, a practical maneuver intended to protect the museum's most precious asset and ensure a teachable moment.

"You should see the major leaguers who come here," longtime museum director Mike Gibbons told me later. "They have the same reaction."

Chris Davis, the Baltimore Orioles first baseman, for one. He arrived in a sports coat and tie with a solemn expression for his meeting with Babe's bat. Like Nick, he noticed the slim taper of the wood—more like a fungo bat than today's balloon-headed lumber— and that it was weighted so differently than bats used today. And the seven razor-thin slashes Babe had made in the shaft, spaced at irregular intervals—the first is 2¾ inches from the knob, then 3, 2¾, 3½, 3⅛, 6¾, 4½ inches apart—cutting across the grain, the way Ruth cut across convention.

"Women, hot dogs, or home runs," Gibbons speculated.

"I would go with the latter," said Davis, a God-fearing man.

Davis also noticed an odd bow in the ash, a gentle curve of the sort a tree might acquire after too many hard winters in the wind. "It's hard to believe a bat would bend over time just from swinging it," Davis said, "but with him you never know."

On Friday, June 13, 2014, the National Baseball Hall of Fame and Museum in Cooperstown celebrated the hundredth anniversary of Babe Ruth's major-league debut by unveiling its first new Babe Ruth exhibit in three decades. It was designed by senior curator Tom Shieber as a scrapbook journey through Ruth's life and as an historical corrective, baseball's first institutional attempt to bring human dimension to the Big Fella, a decision symbolized by the life-size mannequin stationed at the entrance. Only its calves are larger than life: a necessity mandated by stabilizing brass rods within its pinstriped uniform.

Attendance at the ribbon cutting was sparse: two Hall of Famers; one Babe Ruth impersonator, who grumped that "Babe Ruth had to pay to get into his hall today"; one very pregnant great-granddaughter representing the Ruth family; and one flustered docent, who told a group of fifth graders from Albany, New York, how lucky they were to be there visiting the Babe on opening day.

"Can anybody tell me what Babe Ruth was known for?"

"He made thousands of pitches," one little boy said.

"I don't know if he pitched," she corrected in her best schoolmarm voice. "Anybody know how many home runs he hit?"

"Seven hundred and fourteen!" chimed a chorus of certainty.

"Yes!" she said, clearly relieved at the unanimity of response. "He held the record until, until—it's not coming to me right now—until someone else broke it."

When I was their age, Ruth's shiny red metal locker, donated to the Hall of Fame in 1949—where he had dressed and undressed for fourteen major-league seasons, exchanging silk shirts for Yankee pinstripes—stood alone, as he did, its doors flung open wide in welcome. The silver crown fashioned for him after he hit fifty-nine home runs in 1921, and studded with fifty-nine silver baseballs, perched atop the locker, almost grazing the ceiling.

He was the tops.

In the Babe's new digs upstairs on the second floor, his locker functions as a display case, its doors with his name and number stenciled in white, subsumed in museum cabinetry. Inside: his 1932 jersey; a 1923 bat he gave to New York governor Al Smith; a loving cup from students in Philadelphia; and Nat Fein's Pulitzer Prize–winning photograph taken on June 13, 1948, after he posed before that locker for the last time.

The archival clutter leaves no room to imagine him lighting up a stogie, putting on white duck pants for a night on the town, ignoring a stack of mail with checks that would go uncashed. No room to imagine what it was like to be Babe Ruth—to be *with* Babe Ruth—when he was young and full and powerful and so incandescent he lit up the world.

The 180-square-foot gallery, with its black ceilings and dim museum lighting, feels just too claustrophobic for the Babe, containing him behind glass in a way he could never be contained in life. He needs fresh air, and running room, great green expanses of outfield grass where he could track down hard-hit balls and inhale deeply the helium-like giddiness of being him.

By the fall of 1927, Babe Ruth had completely re-shaped the game of baseball, bending it to his will. Little ball and the shortsighted micromanagement of his outsized talent and personality were things of the past.

Subtlety was banished. Clout was all.

Ruth had taught America to think big—expect big.

"Watch my dust," the Babe said.

He kicked up a whole lot of it in 1927, rounding the bases sixty times, while breaking his 1921 home-run record.

This was a year of outsized events. In January, the Harlem Globetrotters debuted. In April, the Great Mississippi Flood caused over $400 million in damage, precipitating the great migration of southern blacks to northern cities.

In May, Charles Lindbergh crossed the Atlantic in the *Spirit of St. Louis*. An earthquake killed two hundred thousand people in China and the last of 15 million Tin Lizzies rolled off Henry Ford's assembly line.

In June, the Cyclone roller coaster made its maiden run in Coney Island, a 110-second primal scream of ups, downs, and hairpin turns around tilted curves—which is one way to describe the decade—and Shipwreck Kelly spent twelve days on top of a flagpole in New Jersey.

In August, the execution of Sacco and Vanzetti, the Italian anarchists exonerated fifty-seven years later for a murder they always claimed they didn't commit, briefly deflected attention from the Bustin' Twins, Babe Ruth and Lou Gehrig, whose home-run binge was the talk not just of baseball but of headline writers across the nation. On September 14, Isadora Duncan's scarf made news when it became entangled in the rear axle of a car, breaking her neck.

Then, in the breathless space of thirty days, Ruth hit his sixtieth home run, led the Yankees to a four-game sweep in the World Series, and completed a twenty-one-day victory lap of the country with Gehrig in tow, kicking up more dust in bandboxes across the American heartland.

It was the best month of his life.

This, I realized, twenty-five years after the fact, was the way to write about the Babe. I would re-create that month: round the bases with him in his jaunty Bustin' Babes jersey; follow him to Western League Park in Omaha; fill in the empty scorecard from Firemen's Park in Fresno, on display in a glass cabinet beside his jersey.

I wanted to be on the field when the stands emptied and marauding mobs waylaid him on the base paths, tackling, besieging, and occasionally holding him hostage to a new kind of love. I figured if I could do that, readers might forgive me for not documenting every pitch he threw, or home run he hit, or season he played in twenty-one years in the major leagues, which has been done admirably and thoroughly by previous biographers.

"C'mere," a voice said.

Cal Ripken Jr. dragged me by the elbow across the room to a display case housing Ruth's blue-and-black paisley Ebonite N29918 bowling ball. The Babe did a lot of bowling after he retired and baseball couldn't find any use for him.

Bald, verging on stout, Cal Ripken bears little resemblance to the lithe Rookie of the Year I covered for the *Washington Post* in 1983. But his boyish enthusiasm and baby blues haven't changed. Nose pressed against the glass, Cal expressed his ardent desire to put his fingers in Babe's ball, which wasn't as odd as it sounds.

This was a great athlete, the man who surpassed Lou Gehrig's record for tenacity, wanting to get a grip on the greatness that was Babe Ruth. "I'd like to put my fingers in the holes. See how wide his hand is, how big the spread is."

Growing up in Aberdeen, Maryland, the son of a baseball lifer, he had hefted a couple of Babe-size bats his dad, Cal Sr., had brought home for him to try. As the star and anchor of the Baltimore Orioles for twenty-one years, he, too, had had a chance to swing the bat Ruth's family donated to the Birthplace and Museum. "How big was it? Only thirty-eight?" he said, shaking his head.

Cal was in Cooperstown to celebrate the Hall of Fame's seventy-fifth anniversary and to celebrate the Babe. The foundation he created in his father's name had contracted with Saint Agnes Hospital, across the road from St. Mary's, to rehabilitate the baseball field where Ruth learned the game. Now he was fixated on the Babe's sixteen-pound bowling ball with its custom-drilled holes and the tantalizing but elusive opportunity it offered to take the full measure of the man, to gauge the size and strength of his hands and the power they had unleashed.

In the interest of history, and with Tom Shieber's aid, I arranged for Mark Rathbun of the Perfect Game Pro Shop in nearby Oneonta to measure Babe's balls for Cal—the Ebonite ball on display and the homely black one in storage in the basement of the Hall of Fame.

How big was the spread of Babe's hand?

The distance from the edge of his thumb hole to the middle-finger hole on his Ebonite ball is just shy of four inches; and the distance from the thumb to the pointer finger is just a quarter inch less than that. Plenty big for a big man, Rathbun said, but not unheard of.

It's the diameter of those finger holes that made the bowling man quake and remeasure: Babe Ruth's thumb was $1\frac{3}{32}$ inches wide at the knuckle. That's the approximate width of an unshelled walnut.

Diagram *that*.

His fingers were huge, which explains, in part, his ability both to control a major-league baseball thrown from a distance of sixty feet, six inches, and to wallop one with a 54-ounce bat. In 1918 and 1919, his last two seasons with the Boston Red Sox, when he was making the transition from starting pitcher to everyday out-fielder, he batted .312 with 40 home runs and 174 RBI and had a 2.55 ERA in just under 300 innings pitched.

"He was the original natural," observed Mike Rizzo, general manager of the Washington Nationals. "He picked up a ball at St. Mary's and became one of the best left-handed pitchers ever. Then he said, 'Screw it, I'd rather hit,' and became the best hitter ever."

By any standard or metric, ancient or modern, Ruth remains the best, most remarkable player in baseball history. He is still ranked first in slugging percentage (.690), and is also first in the newer, chic modern metrics of on-base + slugging (OPS, 1.164) and wins above replacement (WAR, 182.5).

He exploded notions of the doable. He swung the heaviest bat, earned the most money, and incurred the biggest fines. He had altered the dimensions of the game, its architecture and equipment. And every ball hit over every fence altered baseball's relationship with those seated behind it, a revolutionary change noted by Waldo Frank, writing under the nom de plume Searchlight, in the May 16, 1925, edition of the *New Yorker*: "The Babe's home run is an effort on the part of the machine to *connect* with the crowd. When the ball reaches the bleachers, contact is established. The game and the watchers of the game for that instant have the ball in common."

"He was a trailblazer," Bill James has said. "A man who had the courage to escape the fictions and falsehoods that constrained other men's talents and show them what could be done."

He was synonymous with undiluted American power and unbridled appetite. Playing the role of the Babe in the 2014 New York production of *Bronx Bombers*, the actor C. J. Wilson literally gagged at the prospect of eating two cold hot dogs—with buns—at every performance, especially on matinee days.

He was a symbol of the new American obsession

with mobility. John Kieran, a sports columnist for the *New York Times*, recalled one spring training when Ruth decided to motor north from camp and bought a car for the trip. "An hour later the garage at which he had bought the car received a telephone call," Kieran wrote. "'This is Babe Ruth. You know that car you sold me? Well, it's off the road upside down in a culvert out there. It's busted up plenty.'

"'We'll be right out to fix it, Mr. Ruth.'

"'Fix nothing,' Babe replied. 'Send me another car.'"

He was a symbol of the power of self-invention. The dirty-faced street urchin of myth morphed into a man of style, even elegance, and underappreciated dignity. Call it the triumph of couth. He got regular manicures (buff, no polish) and never shaved his own face if he could help it, a gentleman's prerogative.

But what made him "the complete American," as the *New York Herald Tribune* would describe him in his obituary, was not that rags-to-riches mythology, but his restlessness and energy. Winking, swinging, mincing, sliding, he seemed always to be going somewhere, doing something, usually over the speed limit.

What is most striking about Ruth at this remove is how thoroughly modern he was, not just in the way he attacked a baseball, but also in the creation, manipulation, and exploitation of his public image at the precise moment in history when mass media was redefining what it meant to be public. He challenged the prevailing ethos that great athletes must pay for their success with asceticism. He challenged the salary structure of the sport, and the authority of the baseball commissioner to dictate where and how players made money in the off-season. He challenged the notion that stardom was the sole province of saints and movie stars. He challenged the autonomy of team owners by hiring Christy Walsh, the first sports agent, to promote and protect his interests.

Under Walsh's management, Ruth became the first sports star to avail himself fully of the machinery of fame that roared to life as the Babe ascended the national stage.

He sought refuge in the blaze of notoriety, in the persona he created, in the diversions of a lavish and profligate public life; in the attentions of the famous, the infamous, the ballyhooed, the know-it-alls, and oh-so-many boys hungry for attention, who must have reminded him of himself.

Bad boy Ruth—that was me. Don't get the idea that I'm proud of my harum-scarum youth. I'm not. I simply had a rotten start in life, and it took me a long time to get my bearings. Looking back to my youth, I honestly don't think I knew the difference between right and wrong. I spent much of my early boyhood living over my father's saloon, in Baltimore—and when I wasn't living over it, I was in it, soaking up the atmosphere.

Like so many of the words attributed to him, the statement at the entrance to the exhibition, written as a farewell message to Catholic youth as he lay dying in Memorial Hospital in August 1948, was not his own. Below it hung the photo of Little George that my son, Nick, and I had seen in Baltimore all those years earlier. He still looked sad, his cumbrous eyebrows punctuating the glum set of his brow. But his being was so animated, his face so mobile, it was easy to miss its downcast mien. The Italian artist Paulo Garretto captured the look in a 1929 caricature for the New York *World*. With five strokes of his lithographer's crayon—eyes, nose, mouth, cap—he evoked the sadness in Ruth's bloated cartoon features.

The caricature, featured in a 2016 "One Life: Babe Ruth" exhibit at the National Portrait Gallery in Washington, D.C., was unique in that Garretto gave him no lower body, no underpinning. What some view as a portrait of buoyancy, I have come to see as a depiction of rootlessness and disconnection.

By the time Garretto's drawing appeared on September 22, 1929, the received wisdom had congealed into hard fact, like the Babe's thickening middle. "A big likeable kid," the *Sporting News* said in 1922. "Well named, Babe."

"The Babe is a boy—moody, clever, tangible, and human," Waldo Frank noted in the *New Yorker*.

"A child of nature," Red Smith eulogized.

Everyone agreed he never grew up. Never provided "a noble example for the youth of the nation," Bill Veeck observed, "which is undoubtedly why the youth of the nation loved him."

"Appealing and appalling," the actress Teresa Wright concluded after meeting him on the set of *The Pride of the Yankees* in 1942.

Appealing.

The doting dad who collected his daughter Dot at her best friend's apartment after school, settling his large self on a delicate, Duncan Phyfe–style side chair while helping himself to another handful of homemade chocolate chip cookies—and remembering to praise the lady of the house, who looked on in dismay as her most valuable possession teetered under his grateful bulk.

Appalling.

Steve Wulf, the longtime baseball writer and editor for *Sports Illustrated* and then *ESPN the Magazine*, was sitting at a picnic table in the Yankee locker room back in the eighties when the ancient clubhouse man, Pete Sheehy, hired in 1927, came and sat down across from him. "You knew the Babe, what was he really like?" Wulf asked. "He looked around to make sure nobody was really listening. He said, 'He never flushed.'

"It was like a secret he'd been holding in for sixty years."

So, when Wulf's brother-in-law, a building contractor in Sudbury, Massachusetts, was hired to renovate Ruth's former farmhouse, Home Plate Farm, and called offering the Babe's bathtub or toilet as a souvenir, Wulf opted for the tub. "Of course, the bathtub was probably no better," he said.

But no one asked, or succeeded in eliciting much from him, about the childhood they said he never outgrew. And he volunteered very little, even to his daughter Julia Ruth Stevens. Of his years at St. Mary's, he told her only: "I never felt full."

Little George is a spectral presence, when he is present at all, in the Ruth oeuvre and at the Birthplace and Museum, where shards from an untold family story are preserved behind glass. A copy of the misdated birth certificate that misspells his mother's maiden name and omits the name of the newborn. A picture of baby George looking glum in a frilly collar. A photo taken at a family reunion with Little George in Katie's lap, the only picture of mother and son. A hymnal found under floorboards at St. Mary's.

If Mickey Mantle was the last boy to function under a set of rules that Babe Ruth created for athletic celebrities, then the Babe is a boy lost in his own life story. Without that boy, it is impossible to grasp the full dimensions of the man he became and the complex relationship between public and private, between the persona and the person, between "the Big Fella" and Little George. If I wanted to write about the Babe, I had to find a way to allow Little George to tell his story.

I had to hear his voice, not one scripted by Christy Walsh's ghostwriters, or one running on an endless loop of newsreel clips in the Hall of Fame exhibit, but that of an authentic, unguarded, unimproved human being.

I found it downstairs in the Hall of Fame's research library, in a dog-eared Xerox copy of a 1963 *Sport* magazine article by Jhan Robbins, stuffed among decades of unscanned Babe Ruth newspaper clippings. It figures that Ruth would allow himself to be heard by a fourteen-year-old boy reporter trying to play the part of a grown-up.

Ruth was in his last year with the Yankees when Robbins showed up for his interview on Saturday afternoon, June 25, 1934. Yankee owner Jacob Ruppert had personally approved the request from Jhan's English teacher, who called him "a serious student of journalism."

Ruth was standing in a pair of striped undershorts by his shiny red locker inhaling mouthfuls of peanuts and soda pop when Jhan arrived in the clubhouse. After taking a moment to regain his equilibrium, Jhan formulated his first question. "To what do you owe your success?"

Ruth laughed. "Good, clean living."

Robbins recorded his answers faithfully on yellow copy paper that schoolkids used back then, and which would provide the basis for his story published on the fifteenth anniversary of Ruth's last visit to the Stadium in June 1948.

They talked about Ruth's prize bull terrier—Ruth said manager Joe McCarthy looked like one and made a point of telling the boy, "You can print that." Everyone knew he hated McCarthy.

He said his greatest thrill in baseball was the 29⅔ scoreless innings he'd pitched for the Red Sox in the

World Series and a 587-foot home run he'd hit in spring training in Tampa, Florida, in 1919. He'd said those things plenty of times before.

He talked about his childhood, trotting out familiar lines he'd repeated so often he could no longer distinguish fact from fiction—but then again neither could anyone else. How his father ran a bar and he began chewing tobacco when he was seven and drinking whiskey when he was ten. He said that his mother, who didn't remember his birth date, died when he was fifteen, when actually he was seventeen.

He talked about St. Mary's Industrial School, where he learned what it meant to be on his own and how to make the best of it. The brothers taught him how to make a shirt collar and how to stave off loneliness in the crucible of competition. Daily confrontations with a man sixty feet, six inches away left little room for rumination or regret, as Jhan learned when he asked what the Babe thought about in the batter's box. It was a question no adult writer I've read ever thought to ask.

"Well, you're all alone out there," the Babe said. "You're expected to belt it. You don't want to let anybody down. But I don't worry about how I'm going to hit. I don't bother trying to outguess the field. I think about the pork chops I had the night before and if there should have been more salt in the barbecue sauce."

He didn't have long to think about being a disappointment or to remember the self-consciousness that predated the glamorous reinvention of Little George, who suspected that he was too ugly to merit visitors at St. Mary's. There was always another pitch to focus his mind on the present. A hard, round ball that obliterated everything but the moment.

"The second the pitcher rears back everything goes out of my mind but the ball," he told Jhan. "What I see is the heart of it and that's what I lean into."

That insight, elicited by a boy from Brooklyn, was what I leaned on as I followed the ball from Ruth's hand on the mound at Fenway Park to the batter's box at Yankee Stadium, tracing the trajectory of a life that transformed Little George into the Big Fella.

The Big Fella

Prologue
June 13, 1902 / Baltimore

I

Friday the thirteenth was a fortunate day for most of the residents of Baltimore City. Thundershowers and cooler temperatures had temporarily paroled H. L. Mencken's "wicked seaport" from unseasonable 94-degree heat and humidity that had reached 82 percent at 8:00 A.M. the previous day and was no lower when Oliver Fassig at the United States Weather Bureau recorded it twelve hours later.

"Sunshine of the most powerful sort" had put the city on notice, the *Baltimore Sun* declared. The front page was full of advertisements for summer rentals and excursions leaving from the Light Street Wharf.

Perched on the fall line between the Piedmont Plateau and the Atlantic Coastal Plain, Baltimore City was divided by geology into an upper and a lower city, where George Herman Ruth Jr. awoke in the apartment above his father's saloon at 426 West Camden Street, a half mile from the waterfront.

For all its growth and municipal improvements in the Progressive Era, Baltimore was also the largest unsewered city in the country: every lower-city privy—the post office, in local parlance—and every upper-city cesspool drained into the back basin and percolated into sea-level streets. Cobblestones were laid at an angle to the curb to facilitate drainage. But the indolent tide, fed by Gwynns Falls, a twenty-five-mile stream descending from the hills of western Baltimore County into the Patapsco River, kept the human detritus close. A "mephitic" municipal stench blossomed every spring, a smell Mencken likened to "a billion polecats" in summer.

For Baltimore residents, nothing in the morning headlines seemed as pressing as making plans to get out of town. President Theodore Roosevelt had reluctantly postponed a weekend at his Long Island estate in Oyster Bay to deal with pressing business on Capitol Hill, where additional funding for the continued dredging of Baltimore harbor had just been approved.

A delegation of colored Baltimoreans had visited

the Washington office of Republican senator Louis E. McComas to discuss the efforts of Democrats to deprive them of their franchise, while in Virginia Robert E. Lee's daughter Mary Custis Lee had been arrested for sitting in the colored section of an Alexandria streetcar. She claimed ignorance of the law.

The Baltimore Orioles game in Detroit had been called after seven innings on account of a cyclone, with the Orioles ahead 9–3. A "Remarkable Baseball Fatality" had occurred in Charlottesville, Virginia, when the shortstop for the city team was struck in the throat by an opposing batter's ground ball; he died three minutes after throwing the man out.

Also, the creation of a new American League baseball club, the first to call New York home, was announced in Manhattan.

The sun rose at 4:39 A.M., a half hour after the city's new electric streetlights went dark, and would set at 7:33 P.M.—one of the longest days of the year and surely the longest day of any year in the life of the boy his family called Little George.

He was seven years old but he thought he was eight.

In the spring of 1902, what George Washington had dubbed "the risingest town in America" in 1789 was the country's sixth-largest city, home to 509,000 residents, 34,000 of whom, including George and Katie

Ruth and their two children, George and Mamie, were of German descent.

It was the era of "good government" Republicanism, the Democratic machine having been swept out of power in 1895. The city had tripled in size with the 1888 annexation of portions of Baltimore County, and facilitated growth into this new southwest territory with the consolidation and extension of a maze of streetcar lines into the United Railways and Electric Company. George Sr. had tried his hand as a gripman among other occupations before settling on the saloon business. For a nickel you could go anywhere.

Health consciousness had prompted the purchase of 391 acres of public parkland in Gwynns Falls, the creation of a Free Public Bath Commission, and a city-wide campaign initiated by the state against tuberculosis. The second of two public bathhouses funded by philanthropist Henry Walters, Walters Bath House Number 2, in its second month of operation, charged three cents for soap and towels for adults and a penny for children. Users were restricted to a twenty-minute shower. For a few cents more, you could wash your laundry in one of its eighteen tubs.

Innovation and optimism also prevailed in the state capital in Annapolis, where that year the progressive Maryland legislature passed the first workers' compensation law in the country, enacted mine safety regulations, voted to permit female attorneys to practice in state courts, and guaranteed pensions for public-school teachers. New legislation allocated funding for public libraries, outlawed child labor under the age of twelve, created kindergarten classes, and made school attendance compulsory for all children age eight to twelve. An attempt, Mencken observed with asperity, to rid the state of "dirt pedagogy."

That new law, passed in April, was scheduled to go into effect when the school year commenced in September—an unwelcome development for Little George. The closest white public school, at the corner of Barre and Warner Streets, was a third of a mile walk from the Ruths' home. Primary School No. 12, a gloomy pre–Civil War brick building, had been rated "very defective"—one step from unacceptable—in the school administration's 1900 survey of its facilities. Two years later, none of the recommended repairs had been made.

The Ruths were new to the neighborhood, having relocated in April 1901, when George Sr. was granted a liquor license to operate a saloon at the corner of South Paca and West Camden Streets, in the industrial heart of the city. It was a world of grit and bustle and thirst and crowds: the locus of a city in transit and transition.

It was also home to Camden Station, the principal terminal of the B&O Railroad, to tradesmen and traveling salesmen, and to back alleys where horses grazed on the grass growing between the cobblestones. A vast Italianate structure that stretched five city blocks, the station dictated the rhythm, character, sound, and history of the neighborhood. Abraham Lincoln had to be smuggled into the station en route to his 1861 inauguration; the first Union casualties of the Civil War occurred two months later when Massachusetts troops were attacked by Confederate sympathizers as they made their way through the city to board a train for Washington.

In the spring of 1902, the B&O was expanding its operations, building a thousand-foot-long warehouse adjacent to the station with a capacity of a thousand carloads of freight. It was the longest brick structure in the United States.

Train whistles announcing arrivals and departures vied for attention with jackhammers and the hollers of oystermen and "arabbers" (pronounced *ay-rabbers*), street hucksters who patrolled the streets in pony-drawn carts laden with fresh produce, each announcing their wares with jangling bells and singsong cries. The air was filled with the screech and gong of streetcar motormen braking for slower traffic under the windows of the Ruths' second-story apartment.

Their neighbors included a chemical company and a shipping outfit that handled all the freight that came through the station. Directly across the street: William J. Tickner and Sons, Undertakers. Down the block: Charles G. Summers & Co., dealers in canned goods, and Swift & Co., meatpackers. The 1900 census described neighborhood residents as "poor white." They lived in tenements squeezed between factories; African Americans survived in cramped alleys that bisected the main streets.

There were two rival saloons on the same side of the block, and seven doors down, the Baltimore branch of Jacob Ruppert's New York Brewery. The Ruppert family was not yet in the baseball business.

Baltimore was a thirsty city—twenty breweries had been consolidated by the so-called beer trust into the Maryland Brewing Company four years earlier. George Sr. was counting on the unquenchable thirst of traveling salesmen and local laborers to keep his saloon busy. Katie prepared crab cakes and hot German potato salad in the kitchen.

George Sr. joined a Bohemian social club, Spolek Veselych Hochu—the Jolly Brothers—where he served on the dance committee. He looked plenty jolly posing with his new brothers in a bow tie and a Panama hat worn by all Baltimore gentlemen after May 15. And he looked prosperous in a top hat and tails at the Christmas party held at the Germania Maennerchor Hall on Lombard Street, just a couple of blocks from the saloon. Being a Jolly Brother was good for business.

A twenty-round boxing match was scheduled to take place at the Germania on the evening of June 13.

Eleven days after opening for business on West Camden Street, George Ruth had been fined ten dollars and costs by Judge Poe for "allowing minors to play billiards and pool in his place." That was one consequence of his decision to uproot his young family from a stable, working-class neighborhood to an apartment above a bar. The minors were not named in the complaint. But a local beat cop named Harry C. Birmingham, who patrolled the streets he and George Sr. had prowled as boys, had already concluded it was no place for seven-year-old George Jr.

Legend would hand down a bill of particulars against him and history would presume him guilty on all counts: stealing one dollar from his father's till to buy ice cream for his pals; filching vegetables from arabbers and hurling them through shop windows;

knocking over vegetable baskets and running home to hide; chewing and smoking tobacco; emptying glasses left behind on the tables in his father's saloon.

"When I wasn't living over it, I was living in it," Ruth once said.

And, everyone agreed, he just wouldn't go to school.

Of course, in June 1902 he wasn't yet of school age. And children who were enrolled were just getting out for the summer.

A patron told George Sr. he had parked his own unruly son at St. Mary's Industrial School for Boys, a Catholic-run institution on the southwestern edge of the city for white boys deemed "incorrigible or vicious, or beyond the control" of their parents.

St. Mary's unique quasi-public status was granted by the state in 1874 when the school was publicly incorporated and local courts were authorized to institutionalize "any destitute white boy, or any white boy convicted before such court or magistrate of any offence against any law or laws of this State; provided, that the parent or guardian of said boy or boys shall request that they be committed."

The school also accepted orphans and boarders whose parents paid tuition.

George Sr. sought Harry Birmingham's advice. Birmingham, who worked out of the Western District on

Pine Street, was a familiar and formidable presence in his Keystone Copper's cap and brilliantined mustache. It was his job to know every barkeep's business. He didn't drink, his great-granddaughter would say, and liked telling others not to. Nosiness, an asset for a beat cop, came naturally to him.

The liquor situation, as it was sometimes called in Christian publications, was much in the news. Enforcement of hundred-year-old blue laws banning the sale of liquor on Sunday was an ongoing battle and topic of newspaper conversation. On June 13, 1902, the *Sun* reported new charges had been brought against six tavern operators "upon testimony furnished by agents of the Anti-Saloon League."

One of the other saloons on West Camden Street had been cited twice that spring. Birmingham had participated in a March undercover raid on Charles Bradley's establishment around the corner on South Eutaw, entering the premises through the back gate while posing as a customer.

Birmingham, officially Patrolman 469, agreed that St. Mary's was a good solution for George Sr.'s highspirited son and offered to escort him there. Harry's great-granddaughter recalled hearing that he came to collect the boy in a police car, which the force wouldn't have until 1911. They might have taken a police cart or the Lombard Street trolley, recently extended to the city line just past St. Mary's.

Whether Birmingham volunteered to transport the boy, as his obituary recounted fifty years later, or was asked to do so as a favor to an old family friend, the fact remains that Little George left home in police custody on June 13, 1902.

II

There was only one route: straight out Wilkens Avenue, the boulevard named for, and endowed by, the industrialist William Wilkens, proprietor of William Wilkens & Co., Manufacturers of Steam-Curled Hair and Bristles, which occupied fifteen acres in a natural hollow between his eponymously named thoroughfare and Frederick Avenue, where Little George had spent the first two years of his life in the home of his paternal grandparents.

Wilkens Avenue extended south and west from downtown Baltimore into farmland acquired in the 1888 annexation. It had been expanded as part of the one hundredth anniversary of the Revolutionary War, and at the urging of local businessmen, including Wilkens, to facilitate the increasing traffic on this rapidly industrializing portion of U.S. Route 1. Wilkens, who came to America with eighteen cents in his pocket in 1836, donated thirty-three acres of land to the city to erect what he envisioned as a grand boulevard for the immigrant laborers, most of them German, who serviced the stockyards, brickyards, coal yards, breweries, lime kilns, butcher shops, and slaughterhouses—not to mention his own factory, where pig bristles and horsehair were turned into paintbrushes and stuffing for mattresses and chignons for the chic matrons of the town.

Wilkens had in mind a broad avenue on a par with Charles Street in downtown Baltimore. He built a seven-block promenade, planted with hyacinths and tulips. Among the flowering white maple and poplar trees stood pewter urns and cupids—the Wilkens statuary—and a fountain of a chubby little boy holding an umbrella over a chubby little girl to protect her from the manufactured rain. George Jr. and his younger sister, two-year-old Mamie, were protective of each other that way, shielding each other from cloudbursts of parental rage.

"Daddy had a powerful big hand," Mamie would say later. "When he walloped you, you knew you were walloped."

There was a natural bottleneck near the promenade at the foot of Wilkens Avenue, where cars and horse carts

THE BIG FELLA · 13

and Streetcar Number 9 had to slow while negotiating an acute right turn from South Gilmor Street. Looking back over the basin of Baltimore Harbor, George Jr. would have had an unobstructed view of the B&O warehouse under construction just a block from home, and the twin smokestacks of the Baltimore Cold Storage Company poking through a scrim of cloud and omnipresent coal dust.

A century later his statue would be erected on that spot.

The avenue had been terraced in expectation of urban development. Vacant lots on Mill Hill would be transformed into the longest continuous block of houses in Baltimore—neat, brick proletarian structures with electric wiring and gas heat built for Mr. Wilkens's workers with clay that came out of the surrounding hills. For generations of boys who grew up in those houses, the reform school at the top of the hill would become a threat and a caution. *Behave—or you'll get sent where the Babe went when he was bad.*

By streetcar, the two-mile ascent of the Gwynns Falls valley would have taken perhaps twenty minutes, depending on how many horse-drawn wagons were also riding the rails, built to the same wide gauge of carts delivering livestock to the Union Stockyards just south of Brunswick Street. Old-timers told of seeing herds of pigs and cattle driven through the streets en route to market and slaughter. Discarded pig bladders, washed and inflated like balloons, were fashioned into footballs by neighborhood boys, who according to legend were barred from wearing red in case a bull got anxious en route to his fate.

The stockyards, a sprawling split-rail, four-legged municipality large enough to house five thousand cattle, eight thousand sheep, and thirteen thousand hogs, was the culmination of the effort by city fathers and railroad officials to remove the messy business of slaughtering animals from the city's downtown. New track had been laid, allowing for the consolidation of the Pennsylvania and B&O Railroad stockyards in 1891. "Every hoof under one roof" was the motto. The property was practically adjacent to St. Mary's, where the brothers, who fed the boys three hot dogs each Sunday, the only meat in their diet, were fattening up sixty-six head of cattle for export.

The avenue crossed lower Gwynns Falls and a railroad spur Mr. Wilkens had laid to facilitate deliveries to his plant in Snake Hollow, where slithering reptiles lived in a stream that powered the plant and carried away the residue of its success. "The hair mines," local boys called it. Scalded pigskins and horsehides were laid out on Hog Hair Hill to dry in the sun; when the wind turned southwesterly, as it had on June 13, 1902, the stench rivaled poison gas, Mencken said.

The "branch," as locals called it, coursed downhill, rejoining the falls below the stockyard's abattoir, adding momentum and detritus to its flow. The waste city fathers had sought to banish was re-deposited in the back bay. Epidemics were common and virulent. Babies died. Little George had seen plenty of that.

He was eight blocks from St. Mary's. Up, up, up, they climbed, ascending Mr. Wilkens's Avenue to God's country. Life as he knew it receded from view.

St. Mary's Industrial School stood 124 feet above sea level. From that elevation, Little George could see the spire of the Baltimore Basilica, the first Catholic cathedral built in the United States, and the emerging skyline of Baltimore's business district, a great steel and granite mass of Progressive Era commerce—the Maryland, Union, and Continental Trust buildings, as well as the Equitable and Calvert buildings, all of which would be gutted in the Great Fire of 1904. The Fidelity Building at 210 North Charles Street, on the northwest edge of the burnt district, would survive the conflagration. Two years later, at that address, depositions would be taken in the Second Baltimore City Circuit Court, Case No. 8862, *George H. Ruth v. Katie Ruth.*

III

At the corner of Wilkens and Caton Avenues, Harry Birmingham delivered George Jr. into the care of the Xaverian Brothers who ran St. Mary's. He was a minim now, the name given to the youngest of the boys—"the least of the little fellows," they were called in the school's 1902 annual report. He went to sleep that night in a dormitory organized in rows of wrought-iron cots as straight as pinstripes. A bentwood chair was stationed beside each starched pillow. No bed was more than two feet away from its neighbor. The boys slept head to toe, with just enough room between them to get down on their knees and pray.

It was as impersonal and as orderly as a hospital ward, an ethos in keeping with the description of St. Mary's as a "moral hospital" in the 1880 Baltimore Sesquicentennial Memorial Volume. The Church called them "young unfortunates."

They called themselves inmates.

He would join the other solemn, sullen boys lined up to be photographed in fussy collars and bows (produced in the tailor shop by older boys) for annual reports prepared for state and city authorities, upon whom the brothers were dependent for financial support. They stared gravely into the camera's lens and an uncertain future.

Birmingham would continue to walk his west Baltimore beat throughout George Ruth's tenure at St. Mary's. He closed bars on Sundays, broke up craps games, locked up drunks, chased shoplifters, and broke two ribs jumping from a moving train in an effort to catch an escaping prisoner. He also won a commendation for saving a family of four from a house fire and always made time to check up on young George.

He was the first—though hardly the last—of a series of father figures who would enter his life at crucial moments when he most needed their counsel and advice. He would visit George in the "Little Yard" the brothers had set aside for the minims, and later in the "Big Yard" reserved for the older fellows, chasing him down when he ran away, taking him back up the hill as often as he had to, with a stern admonishment that he had no place else to go.

He felt sorry for the boy, living above a bar like that, he later told his children and grandchildren. And he told anyone who would listen what he told Baltimore sportswriter Rodger Pippen in 1947, when reports of Ruth's failing health reached his hometown. "I remember that Babe was a little rascal. Although he was not a bad boy—just mischievous, and no more so than any other boys his age. He certainly never gave the police any trouble. But his father decided to send him to St. Mary's because he just couldn't make him mind at home. Babe had a will of his own and was never one to take orders."

Even if he had filched vegetables and hurled them, chewed tobacco, and stolen a dollar from his daddy's cash register—how bad could he have been? He was seven years old.

Of all the many journeys of Babe Ruth's life—from uncouth to couth, spartan to spendthrift, abandoned to abandon and back again; from the dead ball era to power baseball; from Baltimore to Boston to New York, and back to Boston for a finale with the only team that would have him; from grand tours of Europe and the Orient to barnstorming tours of the American heartland; not to mention 714 trips around the bases—the trip from home to the home, fateful and formative, was the most important one of all.

Chapter 1
October 10 / Providence

HOME RUN KING AND CROWN PRINCE HERE TODAY

—PROVIDENCE JOURNAL

BOTH STARS PITCH IN WEIRD CONTEST AS AUTOGRAPH-SEEKERS SWARM AROUND PLAYERS AT ALL TIMES

SCORE OF TILT IS MYSTERY.

—PROVIDENCE JOURNAL

I

Jean Bedini, a vaudeville star known in the trades as "the Turnip Catcher" for his ability to apprehend root vegetables dropped from skyscrapers with a fork clenched between his teeth, met Babe Ruth at home plate at Kinsley Park in Providence at 2:30 P.M. Bedini had canceled the opening performance of his new burlesque show, "Cock-a-Doodle-Doo," to present his pal with a large floral tribute.

No one could have anticipated when Bedini's troupe was booked into the Empire Theatre that the Babe would be in town—an impromptu one-day engagement organized just twenty-four hours earlier, after he put a premature end to the World Series, leaving an unexpected hole in his schedule.

There was no percentage in opening up against the Babe and plenty of advantage to be had in appearing with him. So Bedini brought the entire cast of "the peppiest, jazziest show on earth" to home plate, all sixty of them, one for every home run the Babe had hit that season. There were chorines and choristers, dancing girls and jugglers, comedians, acrobatic dancers and eccentric buffoons, Harry Reser's ten-piece orchestra, straight from the Folies Bergère in Atlantic City, as well as a radio artist and phonograph recorder.

Also waiting for the Big Bam at home plate was Lou Gehrig, otherwise known as the Little Bam, as well as the promoters of the game, the first stop on a barnstorming tour their agent Christy Walsh billed as "A

Symphony of Swat." In their fedoras and business suits, the promoters stood out among the leggy lovelies: Judge James E. Dooley, who, having served a single year on Rhode Island's Eighth District Court, earned a title for life; Tim O'Neill, the "sandlot baseball king"; and Peter Laudati, who had built Kinsley Park as a home for the current iteration of the Providence Grays.

Hasty as the arrangements were, the advertisement in the morning *Journal* promising that "Babe Ruth, King of Swat, and Lou Gehrig, Fence Buster, Will Positively Appear" proved persuasive. Five thousand "hilarious fans of all sexes and conditions" showed up, among them "2222 yelling, romping, tumbling kids," each of them intent upon joining the scrum at home plate.

This was two days after Murderers' Row had done in the Pittsburgh Pirates in four straight with Ruth as chief executioner. He batted .400, drove in seven of the Yankees' nineteen runs, and hit the only two home runs of the series, ensuring each of his teammates a $5,709 check for four days' work.

It was four days after the first talkie, *The Jazz Singer*, opened at the Warners' Theatre in New York. Six days after sculptors began chiseling George Washington's nose on Mount Rushmore. And twelve days after the Big Fella had made good on his New Year's pledge to Yankee owner Colonel Jacob Ruppert, which had been bannered across the top of the *New York Telegram*: "I promise 60 homers to Jake."

It was an audacious promise, considering he hadn't hit as many as fifty since 1921, one he made while living it up in Hollywood between vaudeville engagements and movie negotiations—and, most notably, before coming to terms with Ruppert on a 1927 contract.

But the Babe made good. Circling the bases on the afternoon of September 30, doffing his cap, bowing, grinning, winking, Ruth crowed: "Sixty! Count 'em, sixty. Let's see some other sonofabitch do that!"

Bedini, who put an end to his vegetable-catching days after sacrificing all his front teeth to a one-pound turnip, had a particular appreciation for the showman Ruth had become, the sheer gameness of the man. More than anyone, Bedini was in a position to grasp the difficulty of the stunt Ruth pulled off on behalf of Citizens' Military Training Camps the previous July, when Christy Walsh stationed him on a dusty Long Island airfield to try to set a world record for catching a baseball dropped from an airplane—a record Walsh invented for Ruth to break.

Walsh would do just about anything to align his Rabelaisian charge with what he called "pure Americanism of the horse and buggy sort" and divert attention from his less savory ways. He posed the Babe in a lot of woolen military garb, in this instance at high noon on the same airfield where Lucky Lindy would take off for Paris ten months later. It took seven tries, with Ruth darting about the empty field in a blistering sun, and the propellers kicking up tornadoes of dust that obfuscated everything but the man on the ground and the plane in the sky.

Walsh "really put one over" for the Babe that day, as he liked to say of his best PR stunts. The *Daily News* showed up as well as a newsreel cameramen. The *New York Times* played the story on page 1.

There was no suggestion in the unsigned *Times* dispatch, datelined July 22, 1926, that Ruth intentionally ducked the first two balls bombed at him from a thousand feet up, which Major General Benjamin Foulois, chief of the U.S. Army Air Corps, claimed "knocked him flat."

The newsreel cameras missed that.

Then the pilot descended to three hundred feet and Ruth gloved the ball. There he was, down on one knee in the grass, making eye contact with the lens as the plane soared out of the frame. He looked like a supplicant, asking for what? Attention? Approval? Or maybe just to get the hell out of there?

"Gee, it's like trying to stop a bullet," Ruth told the military men, who may or may not have appreciated the analogy.

After dutifully turning over the record-setting ball to Foulois, signing a bat for the best athlete at each of the Citizens' Military Training Camps, and enjoying a much-needed bath in the Officers' Club, Ruth had returned to Yankee Stadium in time for a 3:00 P.M. game in which he went 2 for 5 with a triple and a stolen base.

Sonofabitch.

On October 10, 1927, he was the most famous man in America—who wanted to be famous, that is. Charlie Chaplin and Charles Lindbergh could give him a run for his money. But the Little Tramp, with whom Babe was known to play an occasional game of tennis on his court in Hollywood, wasn't homegrown. And Lindy preferred higher altitudes to the fleshy business of being loved at field level.

For Ruth, the visit to Providence that afternoon was a homecoming and a measuring stick of just how much had changed since the summer of 1914, when he'd spent six weeks with the Grays, pitching them to the International League championship and hitting his first professional home run. He was nineteen then and just five months removed from his final parole from St. Mary's.

This was a different Babe. "More portly, more famous but no less genial," the *Journal* attested. "As a matter of fact, between the boys and the chorus girls gathered about him at the plate, the Babe seemed to give preference to the boys."

They knew all about him, or thought they did.

He was an orphan. (He grew up in an orphanage, didn't he?) Or an incorrigible sentenced to St. Mary's, where the courts sent boys to straighten out. The brothers and baseball had imposed order on his rowdy soul.

He was the guy who ate so many hot dogs he ended up in the hospital. The guy who drove Packards into ditches and climbed out smiling. The guy arrested for speeding who got a police escort from jail in time to bat in the sixth inning at the Polo Grounds.

He was the Babe, the Bam, the Big Bam, the Great Bambino (or Slambino).

The Bazoo of Bang and Bash. Behemoth of Biff, Bust, and Bangs. Blunderbuss. The Bulky Monarch and the Monarch of Swatdom.

Caliph of Clout, Colossus of Club (and vice versa). The Circuit Smasher.

Demon Swatter. Diamond-Studded Ball-Buster. His Eminence, the Priest of Swat.

G. Herman Hercules and Pan Hercules. The Goliath of Grand Slam and Great Keagle of Klout.

Hedjaz of Hit, Herman the Great, and Homeric Herman.

Infant of Swategy.

Kid of Crash, King of Clout, King of Swing.

The Home Run King.

The Maharajah and Mauler of Mash. The Mauling Menace, Monarch, and Mastodon. Also, the Mandarin of Maul and Mastodonic Mauler.

The Modern Beowulf.

Paladin of Punch. Prince of Ash and Potentate of Pounders.

Rajah of Rap.

Sheik of Slam, Sachem of Slug, the Sampson and Sultan of Swat. The Swattingest Swatter of Swatdom.

The Terrible Titan and the Titan of Thump. Whazir of Wham, Wali of Wallop and Wizard of Whack.

Jidge, Jedge, George.

The Big Fella.

And all the names put together were still not enough to encompass the idea of him. Maybe a few of the older men in the crowd had caught a glimpse of him in 1914 when he was young and lithe and just growing into his name. Maybe some of the younger ones had tried one of his candy bars. Or worn one of his Babe Ruth Sweaters for Boys. Or seen one of his movies. Or heard his voice on the new radio set in the living room.

All summer long in American League cities boys played hooky, jumped turnstiles, scaled lumberyards, and otherwise evaded flat-footed coppers, pleading with indulgent fathers to let them see for themselves. Roger Angell, who grew up to be the Babe Ruth of baseball writers, was one of the lucky ones, whose father took him to see the Great Bambino at Yankee Stadium. "I had heard about Babe Ruth," he said. "I read about Babe Ruth. I remember looking for him and there he was. He was instantly verified. It was stunning. The creature I'd heard about. He didn't look like anybody else in the whole world. The monkey swollen body tapering down to the ankles—I once called them debutante ankles.

"Everything about him was absolutely extraordinary, starting with his name. The first name was a baby and the second name was a girl's, which suggested to me the complexity of the world. He was so available. You got on the subway, paid a nickel, and there he would be in right field. The other thing I remember is not him hitting a home run but him swinging and missing. His whole body swiveled to face the first base stand."

Here was a man who kept promises, who exulted in making them and daring himself to keep them. It would take until the second to last day of the season to make good on his New Year's pledge to Jake Ruppert but make good he did.

II

All season he and Gehrig had chased each other and the home-run record few thought would ever be broken: Ruth's fifty-nine home runs in 1921. Newspapers charted "The Great American Home Run Derby," as the *Times* called it, with hyperbole, charts, and diagrams. The *World* measured "The Fence Busting Heat" against an illustration of a bulb thermometer accompanied by mug shots of the two protagonists.

Gehrig refused to wilt in the heat of August. Then, in September, Ruth remembered who he was, hitting seventeen home runs in twenty-nine days. In Philadelphia, on September 2, he hit number forty-four; Gehrig hit numbers forty-two and forty-three and tied him three days later in the first game of a Monday doubleheader in Boston on Labor Day. Something, or someone, had to give. They played another doubleheader on Tuesday, and twenty thousand people took another day off in hopes of seeing who it would be. Ruth hit two home runs in the first game and another in the second; Gehrig managed just one. He would never come close again.

Ruth's splurge continued with two more homers the next day. He left Boston with forty-nine home runs; Gehrig wouldn't hit another until September 27. Numbers fifty-one and fifty-two came in a doubleheader against the Cleveland Indians on September 13, the day the Yankees clinched the pennant, freeing him, he said later, to turn his attention to the record. Number fifty-six came on September 22 in the bottom of the ninth inning with a man on and the Yankees trailing the Detroit Tigers by a run. It was the Yankees' 105th win.

As he made his way around the bases, carrying his bat as he often did, a boy bounded out of the stands and chased him down between home and third, pounding the Babe's back and grabbing ahold of his wood. "At last sight," the Times reported, "in a swirling crowd of other juveniles, the youngster was like the tail of a flying comet, holding onto the bat for dear life and being dragged into the dugout by the Babe, who raced to escape the rush."

Ruth had three more games to outdo himself. Number fifty-seven was a grand slam off Lefty Grove in Philadelphia. Numbers fifty-eight and fifty-nine came at home against the Washington Senators. The record-tying home run—a grand slam!—came off a rookie pitcher, Paul Hopkins, making his major-league debut. His catcher told him to throw only curves, so that's what he did. The one Ruth hit, Hopkins told *Sports Illustrated* in 1998, was "so slow Ruth started to swing and then hesitated, hitched on it and brought the bat back. And then he swung, breaking his wrists as he came through it. What a great eye he had! He hit it at the right second. Put everything behind it."

Hopkins struck out Gehrig to end his misery, then retreated to the dugout and cried.

"Once he had that 59, that Number 60 was as sure as the setting sun," declared Paul Gallico in the *Daily News*.

Luckless Tom Zachary was on the mound for the luckless Washington Senators the next day, September 30, 1927. He had helped the Senators to their only world championship, winning two games in the 1924 World Series, but had been shipped to the St. Louis Browns in 1926. The Nats had reacquired him in July, in hopes that his left-handed junk might stymie the Yankees' left-handed hitting.

Old Tom, as the baseball writers called him, wasn't any older than the Babe—a year younger, in fact. But he pitched old before he got old, crafty like the college graduate he was, and as slow as a summer afternoon in his native North Carolina. He was a shuffling, drawling, knock-kneed country boy who threw slop as thick as molasses and stayed employed through nineteen major-league seasons by making others look foolish. "He hasn't got a muscle in his arm," Casey Stengel said of him. "His pulse carries the ball to the plate."

One out, one on in the bottom of the eighth inning, the score 2–2. Zachary's first pitch was a strike and Ruth took it. Umpire Bill Dinneen, the pitching star of the 1903 World Series, called the second pitch high. Ruth stood at the plate awaiting the next delivery, his left foot slightly behind his right, his toes turned inward. He had hit number fifty-nine with the bat he called Black Betsy. This time, he brought Beautiful Bella to the plate. He held it back, behind him, as if playing hard to get.

By 1927, fans were accustomed to the size of the man and the size of the swing and had forgotten, perhaps, how revolutionary a thing it was, this weight shift that, in concert with his exquisite timing, generated such unprecedented power. It was a model of biomechanical efficiency, though no one possessed the language or the technology to understand it then. They saw the big chest, like an accordion with its bellows full, turning with the swing, and called him an upper-body hitter: a tornado on chopsticks. It would take decades to fully appreciate the modernity of his approach and technique.

The third pitch was a screwball that broke down and into the trajectory of Ruth's swing; he caught it flush. By the time he hit the ball, he had taken a long stride forward and had "turned his shoulders and ass and wrists into it," Shirley Povich of the *Washington Post* told *Sports Illustrated* in 1998. His upturned chin and chest, canted toward right field, were already moving out of the batter's box as if yanked by the thrust of the ball. Dinneen rose out of his crouch and Muddy Ruel, the Senators' catcher, rose, too, following with their eyes and their body language the trajectory of inevitability.

The ball crashed into the right field bleachers, fifteen rows from the top, and fair by just six inches. Old Tom threw his glove down in disgust, protesting loudly that the ball was foul.

There was history between Dinneen and the Big Fella. So perhaps Zachary thought he would get a sympathetic hearing. Five years earlier, Ruth had been suspended after charging in from left field to protest a call, scalding Big Bill with obscenities and challenging him to a fistfight in the dugout the next day. And it was Dinneen who called Ruth out, trying to steal second, to end the 1926 World Series.

Dinneen saw the ball fair; Ruth pranced around the bases. "I threw him a curve, but I made a bad mistake,"

Zachary would write in a letter to a fan decades later. "I should have thrown a fast one at his big fat head."

Returning to right field for the top of the ninth, Ruth was greeted with an array of white handkerchiefs, waving in abject surrender to his omnipotence. He saluted his troops in Ruthville with bows and military aplomb, then caught the final out—a fly ball off the bat of Walter Johnson, making his final major-league appearance as a pinch-hitter for Zachary.

Upstairs in the press box, Gallico typed new orders for readers of the *Daily News*: "succumb to the power and romance of this man."

The *Times* recorded the score: Ruth 4, Senators 2.

The Babe himself professed to be unimpressed and unsurprised. "I knew I was going to hit it," he said.

What delighted him most was the sight of Charlie O'Leary's bald head shining in the falling sun. Now *that* was something. O'Leary was a Yankees coach and Ruth's longtime pal. He had been in the car when Ruth drove off the road outside Philadelphia in 1920 en route home from a game in Washington, D.C., prompting headlines that Ruth was dead. O'Leary was thrown from the car and knocked out cold—the first thing he said after returning to consciousness was "Where's my hat?" But he had remained as partial to the Babe as he was unhappy with his pate. He always managed to disappear on those rare occasions when "The Star-Spangled Banner" was played. But when Dinneen signaled "fair ball," O'Leary threw his cap in the air in jubilation.

Ruth was chased back to the dugout and down the tunnel toward the clubhouse by a tumult of humanity that seemed much greater than it was. Only eight thousand fans attended the game, among them Joe Forner, a Yankee Stadium regular, who had situated himself strategically—and successfully—in the right field grandstand after learning that a cash reward was in the offing for the sixtieth home-run ball.

Albert "Truly" Warner, a haberdasher with a flagship store on Forty-second Street and fifty or so others around the country, had spread some cash around the grandstand, paying vendors to apprise the tenants of Ruthville of a one-hundred-dollar reward, a mighty sum in the embryonic world of sports memorabilia. Clutching the ball, Forner made his way through the joyous tumult to the Yankee locker room where Truly was waiting and Ruth was admitting to Arthur Mann of the *New York Evening World* that he had been kicking himself for batting right-handed in the second game of a doubleheader on May 31.

Forner relinquished the ball and Ruth autographed it for Truly though oddly not on the sweet spot and not with the quotation marks he customarily used to set "Babe" apart from Ruth. He owned the name now.

Truly had photo enlargements made for display in each of his showroom windows, further amortizing his investment with newspaper ads that ran in Boston, Pittsburgh, Chicago, Philadelphia, and New York throughout the World Series. Sales would soar.

Arriving home that evening, Ruth was greeted with a profusion of floral arrangements—mixed bouquets and long-stemmed roses. "Where did these all come from?" he said. "What's going on?"

It was almost like somebody died. Then he saw the notes of congratulations.

There is no official record of how he celebrated that evening. But it was Saturday night. And, tellingly, he went hitless the next day, the last of the regular season.

He was a one-man antidote to the grimness of Prohibition. He had arrived in New York ten days before the Eighteenth Amendment went into effect, fleeing puritanical New England for the joie de vivre of Broadway. He was a beer man and drank lots of it. Later he had a tap installed in the sink of his Riverside apartment. Some called him a lush and a drunk, "a carousing bum," as his friend and teammate Waite Hoyt wrote in rebutting the assertion. "He drank no more than an insurance agent—and less than many sports writers during the prohibition era—when everone [*sic*] it seems took advantage of an opportunity."

Fact is: he imbibed whatever life had to offer. He indulged in excess, guzzling it down with a chaser of more.

III

While Ruth was in Providence accepting postseason plaudits and more floral arrangements as his due, the righteous baseball commissioner Kenesaw Mountain Landis and club owners Colonel Jacob Ruppert and Barney Dreyfuss were counting their losses. The net result of the attenuated World Series was this: receipts had failed to reach $1 million for the first time in five years. The Babe giveth and the Babe taketh away. Ruppert and Dreyfuss were compelled to refund some $350,000 in ticket sales, including $200,000 for the Sunday game at the Stadium.

Christy Walsh, sometimes known in the sports pages as the Impresario of Swat, and other times as "the man who relieves Babe of his burden of thinking," functioned not only as Ruth's agent, but as his manager, promoter, factotum, amanuensis, conscience, and mythmaker. On Saturday night, while everyone else had been celebrating the Yankees' World Series triumph, he was in his Seventh Avenue office trying to figure out what to do with the Babe. Murderers' Row was hell on pitching and planning.

On September 26, Walsh had announced plans for a twelve- to fifteen-game barnstorming tour featuring the "Home Run Hitting Twins." The carefully worded press release noted that permission had been obtained from Colonel Ruppert. This was a nod to the cranky commissioner who had suspended Ruth for the first six weeks of the 1922 season for having had the audacity to insist upon his right to make a living in the off-season doing what he did best, traveling from town to town with a bat in his hands.

As it turned out, Ruth made as much money touring in vaudeville that winter as he lost in salary and fines and got the idiot rule changed. So now he was allowed to barnstorm as long as he said pretty please and promised not to play after Halloween.

Walsh billed the tour as a competition for "the Copper Cup"—a continuation of the season's home-run chase. It was a victory lap across America for the Babe, a chance to showcase Gehrig, who had never been west of St. Louis—which was as far as big-league baseball would venture until 1958—and a chance to generate some coin. Walsh printed the promotional brochure on yellow tour stationery in bold red ink:

AFTER THE SEASON CLOSES!
AFTER THE WORLD SERIES ENDS!
THE BATTLE FOR THE HOME RUN TITLE CONTINUES

RUTH VS. GEHRIG
A SERIES OF POST-SEASON GAMES FROM NEW YORK
TO CALIFORNIA

BABE RUTH AND LOU GEHRIG
THE GREATEST DOUBLE-BARREL BOX OFFICE
ATTRACTION IN BASEBALL HISTORY—GOING OUT TO
THOUSANDS THAT CANNOT COME TO THEM.
TERMS: GUARANTEE WITH PRIVILEGE OF PERCENTAGE

Walsh posed them behind home plate at the Stadium, one on either side of him in the uniforms he had designed for the tour: Ruth in a black Bustin' Babes uniform with a white cap and Lou in his white Larrupin' Lous costume with a black hat. Walsh wore his customary double-breasted suit. The caption on the wirephoto might as well have said: For sale to the highest bidder.

But when the World Series ended prematurely, the only dates in place were those he'd arranged in Los Angeles, the Bay Area, and Kansas City. Walsh scrambled to fill the Babe's dance card.

The Lincoln Giants of the Eastern Colored League quickly made themselves available for a Sunday doubleheader at the Catholic Protectory Oval in the Bronx. The Negro Leaguers were always happy to see the Babe and the guaranteed payday he brought, but the weather wasn't promising.

Walsh claimed that more than fifty cities were vying for their services. He had received feelers from Toledo and Lima, Ohio; El Paso, Texas; and Portland, Maine, where the Twins were wanted for a Tuesday-afternoon game. He grandly offered the Knights of Columbus in Oxnard, California, "the opportunity to underwrite an exhibition game" for their community. Ruth had been a member of the Catholic organization since his Red Sox days, and the Knights came through with multiple sponsorships, though not one in Oxnard.

Ruth got other offers, too, forty telegrams a day begging him to attend this banquet and that luncheon. Leaving the Stadium in the company of a police guard during the World Series, he had been engulfed by three thousand fans, among them Joe Plumeri, a Sicilian immigrant who had a small real estate business in Trenton, New Jersey, and ten $100 bills in his outstretched hand. "What do you got there?" Ruth asked.

"This is for you if you'll come and barnstorm," came the reply.

So much for Portland.

Gehrig announced the game in Trenton during a Sunday-evening radio interview broadcast from the new Fifth Avenue studios of WJZ, the flagship station of the NBC Blue Network, which had debuted on New Year's Day. The 50,000-watt signal overwhelmed local stations for miles around and reached as far as Decatur, Illinois, where the local newspaper reported that Gehrig had given "a very nice radio talk. To many listeners it appeared that Gehrig is a sincere friend and respecting pupil of the Big Fellow, and is thankful to be playing on the same team."

Listeners in Trenton were startled by the announcement and by their good fortune.

Meanwhile, Walsh was negotiating with Judge Dooley, a fixer and sports promoter in Providence, who called with an invitation to play on Monday afternoon. Dooley was a classic Irish pol in every way except that he was a Republican. He importuned Tim O'Neill, a former sportswriter for the *Providence Journal* who knew Ruth from his time with the Grays, to recruit a supporting cast for the Diamond Busters. O'Neill was known around town as the "Caliph of Kids," one of whom, Andy Coakley, was Gehrig's coach at Columbia, thus his other moniker—"the man who discovered the man who discovered Lou Gehrig." He enlisted the top two teams from his best amateur league to provide competition.

Peter Laudati supplied the location. Tucked between the Nicholson File Company and the New York, New Haven, and Hartford Railroad tracks, just south of the Woonasquatucket River on the western edge of the city, Kinsley Park was at times home to the Providence Gold Bugs, the local professional soccer team, and the local National Football League franchise called the Steam Roller, of which Laudati was co-owner. He was nothing if not hands-on—he moved first-down markers himself during the 1928 season when the Roller beat the Frankford Yellow Jackets for the NFL championship. A year later, Kinsley Park would host the first night game in league history—with the pigskin painted the color of egg whites.

Ruth wired Judge Dooley on Sunday night: "Christy Walsh tells me Lou Gehrig and myself are booked for Providence Monday. Believe me, I am glad to come back to Providence where the fans treated me great when I was a green kid with the Grays. Lou Gehrig is a wonderful boy and a real home-run champion. The

Providence fans will like him. Will arrive in Providence tomorrow morning."

He detrained at Union Station at noon and was whisked to City Hall, where he was greeted on the steps by Mayor James E. Dunne, Judge Dooley, and Ruth's onetime teammate Jean Dubuc, now coach of the Brown University baseball team, who, while pitching for the Detroit Tigers, had surrendered Ruth's fifth major-league home run, the longest ever hit at Navin Field.

Gehrig took a later train, having stayed behind at his mother's bedside at St. Vincent's Hospital, where she was recovering from goiter surgery.

Ruth retired to the Biltmore Hotel, where he met with reporters and dressed for the game. He answered their baseball questions but was far more interested in hearing how his movie *Babe Comes Home* had fared in local theaters than in reviewing the abbreviated World Series. "That was a lotta fun making that picture. It was funny!" he said. "I saw it about eight times myself and laughed my head off."

He predicted they'd repeat in 1928 as American League champions. "It'll be tough to keep us out because we're getting more young fellows all the time," he told the *Evening Bulletin.* "It's going to be a real club for three or four years, at least."

Yep, the Yankees were an intimating bunch. Seeing a photograph of the young Pittsburgh Pirate stars, Paul and Lloyd Waner, prior to the Series, Ruth harrumphed, "Why, they're just kids. If I was that little, I'd be afraid of getting hurt."

Legend had it that the Pirates quaked before the first pitch of Game 1 after seeing the Yankees take batting practice. Or so Ruth's paid propagandist, Ford Frick, wrote in the *New York Evening Journal,* a notion that went unchallenged until the eve of the 1960 World Series, when former Pirate great Pie Traynor declared that none of them had even watched batting practice.

Ruth's estranged wife and daughter, Helen and Dorothy, rarely seen or mentioned in public anymore, attended Games 3 and 4 in New York, occupying a field box just beyond the Yankee dugout along the left field line. Dorothy abandoned her seat, announcing, "I'm going down to see Daddy," just as he strode to the plate in the bottom of the seventh of Game 3 and drove an opposite field home run into the left field bleachers.

They posed for a series of family photos. In one particularly awkward shot, used, among other places, in the *Sioux City Journal* after the Yankees won the series, little Dorothy was draped around her mother's neck, her back turned to her unsmiling father. The caption read: "Ruth Family Happy It's Ended."

Not that there hadn't been moments of anxiety for Yankee manager Miller Huggins, especially in the ninth inning of the final game. The score was tied 3–3 when Donie Bush, the Pirates manager, brought in Johnny Miljus to face Earle Combs. Combs walked. Mark Koenig bunted safely for a single, sending Combs to second. A wild pitch—an unsettling harbinger in the Pirates dugout—advanced the runners. Up stepped the Babe, who, having brushed off a car accident en route to the ballpark the way he brushed off all his vehicular mishaps, had driven in all three of the Yankees' runs, the last two on a two-run homer in the fifth inning.

Bush had vowed not to pitch around Ruth but ultimately lacked the courage of his convictions. Ruth cursed him all the way down the first base line. The oaths and imprecations were not audible to the 35 million Americans listening to the first national broadcast of the World Series, which was carried on fifty-seven stations by the new networks of CBS and NBC.

As Gehrig stepped to the plate, Huggins, the Mighty Mite manager—"the only man that could walk straight up in the dugout"—began to pace. Unable to watch, he relied on utility man Mike Gazella to tell him what happened, squeezing the scrub's thigh between pitches until it turned black and blue.

Gehrig struck out. Then, Bob Meusel struck out. The count went to 2 and 2 on Tony Lazzeri. "Huggins never saw a single pitch," Gazella recalled. "On the two-two pitch, Miljus's curveball didn't break. The catcher Johnny Gooch didn't reach up high enough. The ball hit the tip of his glove and rolled away and Earle Combs scored and the World Series was over. I looked around for Huggins and I thought he was dead. All that excitement could have killed him."

Ruth celebrated in the locker room with Dorothy and his teammates. "Yes, Dorothy, the man gave your daddy a low curve on the inside this time. Yesterday the other man curved the ball on the outside. Yes, Dorothy, those were the two that landed in the stands."

Forty-eight hours later, Huggins was alive and well and Ruth and Gehrig were conducting a pregame home-run hitting contest in Providence, a staple of their barnstorming games. At the plate, Tim O'Neill reviewed the ground rules with umpires Tim Ferrick and Dan Burke: pitchers would not be allowed to walk Ruth or Gehrig.

Gehrig batted cleanup and played first base for the pennant-winning team from the Universal Winding Company, known as the Universals. Ruth batted cleanup and played the outfield for the runner-up team from the Immaculate Conception Institute, known as the ICI. A bushel basket of balls and a crate of fountain pens were provided for the occasion; he tucked one of the pens into his back pocket the next day in Trenton to facilitate signing autographs on the field. It provided added incentive to hit the ball far enough to ensure he wouldn't have to slide.

The game resembled baseball for five innings. Special rules be damned. When Ruth asked the opposing catcher Emilio "Cappy" Cappalli what to expect from the kid on the mound, Cappy said: "The straightball, no curves." The kid struck him out on three straight curves.

Decorum broke down. All that stood between Ruth and 2,222 boys was a score of overdressed Providence city cops and a flimsy railing marking the boundary between propriety and jubilation. They poured out of the grandstand and leaped from the box seats. They flew to him, climbed on him, clung to him.

Soon the kids began to storm the field between at-bats, and between pitches, accosting Ruth and Gehrig at their positions, and in the batter's box, racing each other—and outracing the cops—for every batted ball. "After a few stray notes, the orchestra jumped the fracas," the *Evening Bulletin* reported, the spooked musicians scrambling pell-mell for shelter from the mob.

Ruth and Gehrig accommodated everyone, signing schoolbooks, pocketbooks, diaries, handkerchiefs, order slips, collars, and cuffs, "everything but blank checks, which earned them a 10,000 batting average in the signing department," the paper said.

In the seventh inning, Ruth decided to take a turn on the mound, an ill-advised decision that yielded the only home run of the day, a majestic thing that sailed off Gehrig's bat and over the center field fence.

In the eighth, Ruth meandered to the plate, two batters out of turn, to face Gehrig, who hadn't pitched since his days on Morningside Heights. "Here began the greatest battle between a pitcher and a batter in the history of baseball," the *Providence Journal* declared. "Gehrig struck him out three times and walked him at least once oftener than that."

Ruth refused to leave the batter's box. Gehrig kept pitching. Ruth kept swinging. The last of seven pecks of balls disappeared. Still the Babe refused to budge. Time was called. Tim O'Neill was compelled to surrender the last available ball in the ballpark—one signed by Ruth and Gehrig that he had sequestered in his jacket pocket.

"Babe waved the outfielders back and then on the

25th or 26th pitch . . . history being forever in the dark as to the exact number . . . The Babe hit the ball into right for a single and two men went over."

A hundred kids fell on O'Neill's souvenir. The umpires called Ruth out for batting out of turn and called the game on account of no more baseballs. The final score was either 13–7 or 13–9, depending on whether you counted the last two men to cross the plate.

Before catching a late train back to New York, Ruth advised Joe Plumeri not to expect them in Trenton in time for lunch with the governor the next day; their train wouldn't arrive until an hour and a half before the first pitch. He had business to clear up in the city before leaving on the barnstorming tour that was getting longer each day. He would have to miss Tim O'Neill's testimonial dinner at the Biltmore in Providence on October 18, too. They'd be in Sioux City, Iowa, by then. He would telegraph his regrets and send a letter of praise to be read in his absence.

Chapter 2

October 10 / Aboard the New York Central to Manhattan

**THE WORLD SERIES HAS NOTHING ON
BABE COMES HOME**

SEE HIM "SOCK" HIS GREATEST HOME RUN

—*WINNIPEG EVENING TRIBUNE*

**BABE RUTH LOSES FILM JOB BECAUSE
HE CHEWS**

CHICAGO CENSOR SEES NO INHERENT VIRTUE IN
USE OF TOBACCO

—ASSOCIATED PRESS

I

*B*abe *Comes Home* was no longer showing in Providence or many of the grand movie palaces on the East Coast. It had premiered at the Friars Club in New York on April 27 at a screening Ruth and Walsh hosted for five hundred editors, publishers, and sportswriters, and opened to the general public at Broadway's Longacre Theatre on July 25. Unfortunately, the newly installed Vocafilm system, which was to supply sound effects though no dialogue, malfunctioned, emitting piercing noises throughout the movie. Half the audience had quit the theater by the time the Babe got the girl.

Billed as a romantic comedy, the plot required a lot of spitting and chewing, not a stretch for the Babe; nor was his role as a ballplayer named Babe Dugan, who falls for a pretty young laundress but nearly loses her, thanks to his offensive habits of mastication. Ruth was known at St. Mary's to carry about a glass inkwell in lieu of a cuspidor.

First National Pictures had lined up support from a national association of laundrymen in advance of the premiere, *Motion Picture World* reported, in exchange for filming certain scenes on location at the American Laundry in Los Angeles. This did not assuage the concerns of Mrs. Albert Stevenson, the high-minded censor responsible for maintaining the high moral standards of Highland Park, Illinois, a tony suburb of Chicago. "Babe Ruth cannot spit tobacco juice on the screens of Highland Park theaters and get away with it," she declared in banning the film from her jurisdiction, thus causing the Babe to "lose a job," as the Associated Press put it. "We do not wish the children of Highland Park to believe that one must chew to achieve fame."

First National Pictures vowed to take legal action. Leading lady Anna Q. Nilsson objected to his performance on other grounds. "He didn't have any emotional scenes," she sniffed. "He was just Babe Ruth."

The studio made sure the movie played in every American League city during the baseball season. The Olympia Theatre on Broadway near Columbia University had booked it to run during the World Series, figuring on local interest in the Lions' former first baseman. But now the series was over. Football season had begun and all anyone could talk about was Al Jolson in *The Jazz Singer.*

The Babe's silent rom-com was big now only in smaller towns—Zanesville and Coshocton, Ohio; Alexandria, Indiana; Decatur and Thomson, Illinois; Greene, Iowa; Helena, Montana; Tucson, Arizona; Eugene, Oregon.

It was also playing in a few national league cities, black theaters in the "chitlin district," and in Melbourne, Australia, and Winnipeg, Canada, where it was the feature attraction at the Province Theater, the lights dimming for the first show as Ruth headed home from Providence on the New York Central.

The astute and uncredited reviewer for the *Winnipeg Evening Tribune* saw something in his performance that escaped the notice of others: the hurts of childhood projected and magnified in the dark on a big screen. "A childish pathos is still in his eyes, and neither fame nor fortune have given him excessive assurance," the critic observed. "His natural gestures are the tentative ones of a child not quite sure that a rebuff is not waiting somewhere. Something is there which never fails to rouse the maternal instinct."

Except, it seems, in his own mother.

Death, disease, discord, and dislocation had been constants in the marriage of George Herman Ruth and Catherine Schamberger. She was seven weeks pregnant with their first child, George Jr., when they married on June 25, 1894. Both were the children of German immigrants. Both came from large, extended families. He was Lutheran. She was Catholic. They were married in a Baptist church.

They lived with George's family on the western edge of the city, across the street from Mount Olivet Cemetery. Katie gave birth to her first child two miles away, in her parents' bed on Emory Street, a dead-end side street in a neighborhood that was a rabbit warren of brick and cobblestone meeting at irregular angles. The Schambergers lived around the corner from the saloon her father, Pius, ran before going into the upholstery business, which was located across the street from the former site of John Ruth's lightning rod shop. Perhaps that's how George and Katie met.

The baby arrived in the midst of a great continental freeze that began with a blizzard just after Christmas and spread across the country and up the Eastern Seaboard from Palm Beach, Florida, where the 35-degree temperature—the highest recorded in the United States at the time—killed all the royal palms and citrus trees. The temperature in Baltimore was just one degree above zero at 8:00 A.M. on February 6, a cold so fierce that water pumped from hoses at a store fire less than a mile away froze, encasing several firemen in ice. It is highly unlikely that Katie Ruth hiked to her parents' house that day, as legend had it in recounting the miraculous birth of George Herman Ruth Jr.

Not that she lacked resolve. She had her baby boy baptized on March 1, 1895, by Father J. T. O'Brien at

St. Peter the Apostle Church, a Catholic church that served Irish immigrants, eight blocks from Emory Street, and managed to keep it secret from George Sr. Katie's sister Lena Fell was named as godparent. "His father hated Catholics so much—he hated everyone so much—they had to hide it from him," recalled Father Michael Roach, who served at St. Peter's for fourteen years. "They had to sneak the little one in." (This might explain why there are no baptismal records for any of George and Katie's other children on file at St. Mary's Seminary in Baltimore, where church records are maintained.)

George Jr. spent the first two years of his life in the home of his paternal grandparents, John Antone Ruth and Mary Strodtman Ruth, two miles from the grit and bustle of the Baltimore waterfront. John's family was well regarded and well established in Baltimore City. Two brothers, Francis J. and Jacob A.—John Antone's father—had emigrated from Germany in December 1832. Baltimore was second only to New York's Ellis Island as a point of entry into the United States. By 1850, there were 20,000 German-born residents of the city. By the beginning of the Civil War, that number had grown to 32,613, not counting the American-born descendants of those first-generation immigrants. The

B&O Railroad facilitated the arrival of German citizens through an agreement with the Norddeutscher Lloyd (North German Lloyd) shipping line that brought immigrants into the city at Locust Point.

In immigration records, Francis J. Ruth was listed as a carpenter and his brother Jacob, nine years his junior, as a farmer. The brothers settled in the Fells Point area of east Baltimore, a neighborhood of merchants and mariners where Harriet Tubman hid the first slave she rescued via the Underground Railroad. The brothers married quickly and fruitfully, proudly giving their children and their children's children the same Christian names—a frustration to later generations of genealogists attempting to reconstruct the history of Babe Ruth's family in Baltimore.

Francis prospered and diversified. He was a tinner, a canner, and an oysterman—employing two hundred men at his cannery—at a time when Baltimore was the largest oyster supplier in the world and a leader in canned fruits and vegetables. He opened an oyster house, which he supplied with catch brought in on the schooner *Francis J. Ruth*, until it ran aground on Christmas Day 1885.

He was wealthy enough to tithe liberally, donating enough money to St. Michael the Archangel Roman Catholic Church, descendants say, to have an assigned pew in the church that served the German population of east Baltimore.

Jacob became a cabinetmaker in Ward 17, also home to Fort McHenry. He had six children, three of whom he named John. John Antone, born in 1844, would become Babe Ruth's grandfather. He spent his earliest years, as would his grandson, surrounded by aunts and uncles and cousins in a tight-knit—some said clannish—community that worshipped in churches where services were conducted in German, read German-language newspapers, and attended German-speaking schools.

When John Antone registered for the draft in 1863, he listed his occupation as a carpenter. By then, he had relocated to an alley address in southwest Baltimore. The family was now divided east from west by the Baltimore harbor. The split widened further when John Antone married into the Lutheran faith. His marriage to Mary Strodtman, daughter of a bank night watchman, was performed by the renegade Lutheran pastor Leonhard Frederick Zimmerman, who that year sued his former congregation at St. Stephen's German Evangelical Lutheran Church for reinstatement.

John Antone and Mary would settle in Ridgely's Delight, on the cusp of Pigtown, home to many African Americans pushed out of their houses during the construction of Camden Station. John Antone was inventive and ambitious. He became a lightning rod manufacturer and received kudos from the *Baltimore Sun* in 1871 after removing a broken 50-pound weather vane atop the cupola of the G. W. Gail and Ax's Tobacco Works—165 feet off the ground. "A Lofty Performance," the paper called it.

A savvy businessman, he made sure to advertise his services in the same edition of the newspaper. When Baltimore celebrated its 150th anniversary nine years later, he sponsored a float in the parade featuring a house with a steeple surrounded by lightning rods and a picture of Ben Franklin flying his kite.

He received patents for a lightning rod insulator, a wagon, and a clothes fastener to use with heavy-duty outerwear, which he advertised to motormen, conductors, and policemen in the *Sun*: "It is like a stove in front of your clothing. Make your tailor put it on for you."

He ran his lightning rod business from a building on Haw Street around the corner from Schamberger's saloon. When the building was demolished in the early 1890s as part of an initial effort to build a city sewer system (construction of a comprehensive system was not begun until after the 1904 fire that destroyed seventy city blocks), he moved his family and business to a house on the western outskirts of town that also functioned as a kind of saloon.

Incorporated by John Antone, his son John Jr., and several associates as the 21st Ward Industrial and Social Club in 1893, it was outfitted with tables and chairs, buffets, decanters, and spittoons. The club employed John Ruth Sr. as caretaker, paid the rent on the building, and allowed his family to occupy the living quarters. John Jr. and his brother George Herman lived at home and worked with their father in the lightning rod shop, in the club, and in the grocery store the family managed across the street. The brothers had tried to make a go of it in the tinning business as so many of their east Baltimore relatives had done, but their bid to secure a contract to provide license plates for Baltimore City was rejected.

It was here on Frederick Avenue that George, Katie, and Little George were living when she became pregnant again in 1896; here that John Antone died of cirrhosis of the liver on January 31, 1897; here that the child was born less than two months later.

In birth and death records maintained in the Maryland State Archives in Annapolis, the child is identified as a female named Augusta. In Loudon Park Cemetery records, the child is identified as Augustav. A paid obit-

THE BIG FELLA · 59

uary notice in the *Baltimore Sun* described the baby as "an adored son Augustus."

By the time the baby died of pneumonia and spinal meningitis on March 16, 1898, five days after its first birthday, George and John Ruth Jr. had moved their families and the business they inherited from their father to adjoining row houses at 339 and 341 South Woodyear Street in southwest Baltimore. The child was buried in a family plot, large enough to accommodate future tragedies, purchased by the brothers a day after the unexpected death.

II

The 300 block of South Woodyear Street was an unlikely idyll. It backed up to the Mount Clare Yards, the sprawling industrial complex where the B&O Railroad built, maintained, and repaired its locomotives, freight cars, and passenger carriages; and where many of the men who lived on Woodyear Street found employment as iron molders and forgers, carpenters and boilermakers, cabinetmakers and machinists for the railroad.

Each morning at 7:00, families were summoned from sleep by a shrill whistle calling husbands and fathers to work. The blacksmith shop, seventy-five feet wide and a tenth of a mile long—longer than the 300 block of South Woodyear Street—lay just on the other side of the Ruths' backyard. And beyond that, the octagonal roundhouse that looked like it should have housed a merry-go-round.

Loud and industrial as it may have been, Woodyear Street was also a kind of working-class refuge. Secure, stable, and self-enclosed, it was blockaded by two coal yards and railroad tracks at the south end of the street and by a row of adjoining brick houses to the north on McHenry Street. True, coal dust soiled clean clothes as quickly as Katie hung them out to dry. But the back-yard oven of William Plimpster, a baker who lived just five doors down the block, added the sweet smell of fresh bread and a patina of flour to the coal-dusted air.

Neighborhood grocers to whom a child could be sent on errands occupied each of the block's four corners. Though one of the residents identified himself as a sa-loonkeeper in the 1900 census, there was no tavern on the block. There were plenty of those on the waterfront two and a half miles away.

Most of the 254 residents were of German descent, including the aunts, uncles, and cousins in Little George's extended family; 107 of them, according to the 1890 census, were children between the ages of two months and twenty-six years. Playmates were as plentiful as adult supervision. Uncle John had five children, all within five years of George Jr.'s age. George and Katie shared their home with his sister Annie and her husband, Milton C. Brundige. Two other uncles, an aunt, and two cousins born within a year of George Jr. lived two blocks away.

The fifty-six attached row houses on South Woodyear Street were small—just twelve feet wide—but also less than five years old. Downstairs there was a living room, a dining room, and a kitchen with a coal stove. Upstairs, three bedrooms, a tub, and a sink. There were flush toilets in the backyard, and coal chutes at street level that fed a bin in the basement. In better Baltimore neighborhoods, the front stoop would have been marble. The Ruths' house had wooden steps. Mothers like Katie saw to it they were whitewashed every spring.

The lots were deep; some houses had back porches; others had garages that exited onto South Carey Street opposite the Mount Clare Yards. George and his brother John ran the lightning rod business out of a shop in the backyard. Like their father before them, they advertised prolifically and were considered experts in their field. When a violent lightning storm struck the city in July 1900, killing ten people and eight head of livestock, George was interviewed by the *Sun* for a story headlined "Death from the Skies."

"Mr. Geo. H. Ruth of the Baltimore Lightning Rod Works, speaking upon the subject yesterday, said, 'Lightning rods should be placed upon country houses and tall buildings in the city. An unpainted metal roof with down spouting and good connection throughout is sufficient, provided the highest points, as the chimney for instance, are also coppered. I do not think that painted roofs will do as well.'"

A month later, on August 2, 1900, Katie gave birth to a set of female twins: Mary Margaret, whom her older brother would call Mamie, and Anna, named for George's sister. Mamie was a sickly baby and not expected to survive. It was a surprise then when Anna, who had seemed so healthy, died three months later of "broncho-pneumonia and asthma."

Little George was five years old.

Mamie Ruth Moberly, the only one of his siblings to survive into adulthood, was the primary source of family history in the decades after her brother's death. Though her memory faltered near the end of her life—she died at age ninety-one in 1992—and she sometimes confused names and dates, she consistently claimed that Katie bore eight children and buried six of them. "There were four boys and four girls, with two sets of twins, one set of boys, and one set of girls," she wrote Ruth's biographer Marshall Smelser in 1972.

The Maryland State Archives has no record of a set of male twins born to George and Katie. The births of six children and the deaths of four of them have been verified. In the 1972 letter, Moberly said she believed she was Katie's fifth or sixth child. A fragment of her 1900 birth certificate, which is all that remains on file in Annapolis, attributes five births to Katie Ruth.

How many babies George Jr. saw die by the time he turned five is unknown. How the legacy of death and disease and grief would have affected him is easily guessed. How much time and attention his mother would have had for him is an open question.

But Woodyear Street also offered distraction and solace. His aunt Annie, to whom he would turn for shelter later in childhood, gave birth to a healthy baby, Ellen, in 1898. And Carroll Park, twenty acres of public parkland purchased from the Mount Clare estate in 1890, was within walking distance. There were open fields where games of baseball were played. H. L. Mencken, who lived a half mile away in the gilded sanctuary of Union Square, would later write how he and his uptown crew would be harassed by "brigandish fellows from the neighborhood" who "in a mild mood would chase" them from the field, or worse, "cabbage their bats and balls." Which might account for his lifelong antipathy for the game, which, he said, stimulated "a childish and orgiastic local pride, a typical American weakness."

At age two, when the Ruths arrived on Woodyear Street, George Ruth Jr. was too young to harass anyone. He was six—a boy in full—by the time the family left, and full of boyish mischief. Nellie Ruth, one of Uncle John's daughters, never forgave him for one prank he pulled. "She was out in the backyard with her mother," according to her grandson Tony Brady. "Her mother was hanging clothes up, and he sneaked up behind her and dropped a snake down the back of her dress and was laughing and laughing. It was a black snake. It scared her to death. She didn't like him at all. He was a hellion. Typical boy."

Magdalena Henrietta Freudenberger, who was two years his senior, lived down the block on the other side of the street. She wouldn't leave Woodyear Street until 1961, when she moved in with her children and shared a bedroom with her granddaughter Dotty Schluepner, to whom she would tell stories about growing up with George Herman Ruth Jr. He was her favorite playmate, the only boy who would play with girls: "They played softball or whatever it was called. They had to go to the field because they couldn't break windows. Many times, she'd come home dirty; and her mother would say, 'What were you doing?'

"She said, 'Well, we played ball.'

"Later, when she turned school age, her mother told her she needed to quit playing with the boys. Her dress was getting dirty playing ball in the field at Carroll Park."

By then, the Ruths had left Woodyear Street, which was just as well as far as Magdalena's mother was concerned. Reports about George Jr. being sent to St. Mary's filtered back to the old neighborhood. "The word of mouth came back that it was a good thing they weren't playing anymore," Schluepner said. "And her mother believed everything that went around."

Nor was Schluepner's grandmother well disposed to George Sr.'s new line of work. "They were very possessive of their values, and they wanted their values to be passed on. One of their values was not to have friends that run saloons. That was frowned upon; it wasn't a good occupation."

On April 13, 1901, George Sr. filed a petition for a liquor license for an existing saloon at 426 West Camden Street. Five months later, he sold the family house on Woodyear Street for forty-two dollars and quit the lightning rod business. It was surprising because he had acquired an enviable reputation in the field. It was equally surprising that he sold the house to someone other than his brother, who would buy it back from

George's purchaser two years later—indeed, John Ruth would live on South Woodyear until his death in 1932, and the houses would remain in the family for another thirty-five years. Surprising, too, that George would deprive Katie, who was pregnant again, of the helping hands open to her on Woodyear Street.

Gussie Ruth was born above the saloon at 426 West Camden Street on August 25, 1901. She lived less than four months. The cause of death cited on her death certificate was marasmus, a severe form of malnutrition that led to progressive emaciation. In infants less than a year old, the disease was characterized by thinness, dry skin, poor muscle development, and irritability. Physicians of the era believed the causes to include unsuitable food, chronic vomiting, chronic diarrhea, and inherited syphilis.

Little George was six years old.

Gussie was buried with her siblings in the family plot purchased two and a half years earlier. Her uncle John was named as father on her birth certificate.

There are many innocent and plausible explanations; a clerical error is most likely. (John is also identified as a saloonkeeper on her birth certificate.) But given the apparent rupture between the brothers, it is worth wondering exactly what caused George to sever business ties with John as abruptly as he did.

III

George and Katie remained on West Camden Street for two tumultuous years, during which they buried one child and sent another away. A turbulent and itinerant period of family life ensued. In April 1903, George applied for a liquor license at a new location on Hanover Street, a few blocks southeast of Camden Yards. A year later, he put that bar up for sale, advertising in the *Sun*: "Doing good business; License Granted."

They moved next to East Clement Street, a mile from Camden Yards, where they stayed just long enough for Katie to give birth to another son, William E., on August 25, 1905. Within three months, the family had yet another new address.

Construction on the B&O warehouse adjacent to Camden Station was nearing completion when George Sr. opened a new saloon at 406 West Conway Street, now center field at Oriole Park at Camden Yards. He would remain in business at that address from 1905 until 1912, years Mamie Moberly would recall as "tough on occasion" but in "the majority, they were pretty good."

From her window, she could see trains loading and unloading their wares, and trucks backing up to the loading docks. "The neighborhood was mostly colored," she told Mike Gibbons, director emeritus of the Babe Ruth Birthplace and Museum. "There was white but not right up on the block where we lived. We had colored and factories. We were surrounded by factories."

How much time George Jr. spent at home with his peripatetic family after June 13, 1902, is uncertain. His records were destroyed in an April 24, 1919, fire that demolished much of St. Mary's and all of its written history. The only remaining documentation is a handwritten ledger in the archives of Catholic Charities of Baltimore. "Your grandfather just took up one line of the page," Ellen Warnock, associate administrator, informed Ruth's grandson, Tom Stevens, in an email in 2014. "It shows when he was admitted and discharged from St. Mary's. The record is completely bare except for the dates."

June 13, 1902–February 27, 1914.

The duration of his initial commitment is unknown. The time line given in his 1948 authorized autobiography, *The Babe Ruth Story*, written with Bob Considine, is factually suspect; among other things, the year of his mother's death and the spelling of her family name are incorrect.

Considine, a national columnist who did not know Ruth well, was working under deadline pressure imposed by the publisher and Ruth's terminal illness. He hired his own ghostwriter, sportswriter Fred Lieb, who had the advantage of having covered Ruth for more than a quarter of a century. But Ruth, always a reluctant and unreliable narrator of his own history, was unable to contribute much.

According to *The Babe Ruth Story*, he was in and out of St. Mary's twice in 1902, staying a month each time; at home from Christmas 1902 until sometime in 1904; and committed again from 1904 to 1908. His second wife, Claire, adopted those dates in her later memoir, but they are unconfirmed.

Church records do show that he was baptized for a second time at St. Mary's on August 7, 1906, received his First Communion "as a convert" one week later, and was confirmed the following spring, on May 7, 1907. The brothers weren't taking any chances with his soul.

He was still there on Thanksgiving 1908, appearing in blackface in a school minstrel show called "One Thousand Smiles in One Thousand and Twenty Minutes," while downtown his father and other members of the dance committee at his social club were supervising a holiday ball for children of the membership at Maennerchor Hall. The mention of G. Ruth among the named cast members in the next morning's *Sun* was likely the first time his name appeared in print.

Considine has George Jr. living at home again in 1911–12, at which point his father returned him to St. Mary's and left him there until his final discharge.

The first and most formative account of his childhood, published in August 1920, was the handiwork of an unsentimental young reporter named Westbrook Pegler, just breaking into the business with the United News Service when he was charged with the responsibility of confecting an 80,000-word, twelve-part newspaper serial in Ruth's voice, without the benefit of hearing it for more than fifteen minutes.

His George is forthright, admitting in the first sentence that St. Mary's was a reform school, which, in Pegler's account, he was to leave only once in twelve years, at Christmas 1902.

"After about six months I was given a holiday leave of absence to go home," Pegler has Little George say. "I think father was pleased with the change the brothers had already worked in me. It seemed he and I had come to think alike. . . . At any rate, when we talked together we had an understanding which we had not had before and were more like good friends and companions than father and son."

Mamie Ruth Moberly, the only member of the family who survived long enough to bear witness to events in the Ruth household, always maintained her brother was committed to St. Mary's because he wouldn't go to school. Truancy was an issue in the city, especially after the new law mandating compulsory attendance went into effect in the fall of 1902. With that law came a new, highly motivated corps of attendance officers.

But he was too young for school when he was first consigned to St. Mary's in June 1902. And city schools were just letting out for the summer. He was no truant then. Moberly said it was her job to walk him through the school door and make sure he didn't walk right back out. But she was just two years old, far too young to remember those events, much less to act as an enforcer.

In her last interview with Gibbons in March 1992, she said her brother came home mostly on holidays and as an occasional reward for good behavior in the years that George Sr. ran the bar on Conway Street. On those occasions good behavior was not sustained. Brother Paul, St. Mary's superintendent, would remind the adult Babe about a time when he was released at his father's request but immediately "hooked" school, as Mamie put it, getting her in lots of trouble.

"They said, 'He either has to go to school or we're going to put him in the state thing,'" Moberly told Gibbons. "Daddy said, 'You're not going to put him in a state thing. If he's going anywhere I'm going to put him in St. Mary's.'"

The home that he returned to was hardly a peaceable one. "He wouldn't listen to my father," Moberly said. "My father would talk to him and talk to him. And it'd go in one ear and out the other. Oh, I'll never forget one time—my father was beating him. He was a big boy. As a boy, he was big. My father'd get him across the knee and beat his butt. I says, 'Don't hit him like that. You're hurting him.'"

Little George escaped from his father and she went to him. "My father said, 'If you don't get away from him I'll give you some of it,'" Moberly said. "I knew he wasn't going to touch me. But I thought I better get away. Babe stood at the kitchen door. If my father had gotten ahold of him, there wouldn't have been a Babe Ruth.

"He said, 'You dirty old SOB, I hate you.'

"If my father had got him, he would have beat him 'til there wasn't any life left in him. They both had vicious tempers."

Little as she was—Katie was no bigger than four foot ten—"she didn't mind boxing your ears either," Moberly said. "She was something. I'd say, 'Mother, why did you hit me?' She said, 'You ran the last time you were supposed to be corrected.' That's the Germans for you."

Mamie did not escape unscathed the anger and violence in the home. When she ran away to get married at age sixteen, she left with a trousseau of emotional problems, compounded by the death of two infant sons before she gave birth at age nineteen to her only surviving child. She would suffer episodes of instability throughout her life, her granddaughter Jan McNamee said. "She had a happy life except for her demons."

Pegler's fanciful summation of Ruth's childhood is an insult to credulity, ascribing to seven-year-old George Jr. a degree of insight that he never possessed as an adult. But there is truth, if not fact, in Pegler's conclusion. At the end of the Christmas holiday in 1902, Pegler's Little George resists the temptation to ask permission to stay at home lest he risk his father's newfound faith in him, and heads back to St. Mary's for the better part of his childhood. "As the months multiplied into years the arrangement seemed to become the natural disposition of the family."

IV

Seven-month-old William and five-year-old Mamie would have been asleep in their beds in the early morning of March 12, 1906, when George Sr. confronted his wife, telling her he had evidence that she had been sleeping with his bartender, George Sowers.

"I the under sign fucked Mrs Geo. H, Ruth March 12 1906 on her dinging room floor whitch She ask me to do Geo Sowers."

The next morning, George Sr. swore out a warrant against Katie, charging her with drunkenness and infidelity.

Magistrate Daniel Loden at the Western District police station issued a warrant for their arrest and took statements from each of the parties. Katie told Loden that Sowers had "taken advantage of her." She said, "her husband and other people were in the house but . . . she had made no attempt to make an outcry," Loden noted in his report.

She refused to confirm or deny her husband's accusations and declined to press charges against Sowers.

Loden noted that Sowers had told the magistrate, in Katie's presence, that "Mrs. Ruth was continually after him and that Mr. Ruth had accused her from time to time of being unfaithful to him, and that if he continued to accuse her, she would in reality commit the deeds that he had accused her of, whereupon Sowers remarked, 'When you make up your mind, I hope you let me have the first crack at you.'

"She continually followed Sowers around the bar

where he was employed as bar-tender. . . . From that time on Sowers said she seemed to look for it as regularly as she did her meals, and of course he liked it and was ready to accommodate her."

Katie was found guilty of violating Section 5 of Article 27 of Public General Laws, "having unlawful sexual intercourse with another man not her husband," and fined $10.00 and costs, according to court records. But the fine was remitted, and the case dismissed on costs of $1.70 when she told the authorities she had an infant and no means of support.

On March 17, George Sr. filed for divorce, seeking custody of all three children, and posted a legal notice in the *Sun* notifying creditors that he was no longer responsible for his wife's debts.

At a preliminary hearing on April 6, her attorney argued that she was destitute and asked for twenty dollars for legal fees and ten dollars a week in permanent alimony in order to be able to support the children—the only indication in the paperwork that she might have had custody of them at the time. In court papers, Katie said that George Sr. cleared thirty dollars a week after expenses at the West Conway Street bar.

The judge ordered George Sr. to pay Katie three dollars a week in alimony through the duration of the case and fifteen dollars in legal fees.

Depositions in the case of *George H. Ruth Sr. v. Katie Ruth* were scheduled for April 11 at the Fidelity Building. Katie failed to appear. No one testified on her behalf.

Sowers did not appear either. George Sr. said his attorneys had been unable to locate Sowers since the night he had kicked him out of the house. "I think he has skipped for good," George said.

Ward Baldwin Coe, a Standing Examiner of the Circuit Courts of Baltimore City, presided over the depositions. The only two witnesses were Magistrate Loden and George Sr. himself.

In his deposition, George came across as well spoken and well coached by his attorney, Frank V. Moale. He affected the righteous tone of the cuckold as he testified that he had long suspected his wife of infidelity, which was the reason he had moved his family so often. He charged her with the crime of adultery with one George Sowers, of Baltimore City, and "with other men whose names are to your orator unknown."

He said that he had not spoken to Katie, who had gone to live with her sister Lena a half mile away on Portland Street, since she had come to collect her clothes, and had not seen her except when she passed by in the street as she did every day.

Q. What has been your conduct toward your wife during all your married life?

A. I always was faithful to my family, and cared for them in every way, shape, and form. I always treated her kindly. Sometimes she got drunk and I would tear up a little with her, but I never beat her or anything of that kind. I was always kind and affectionate. Just three weeks before this thing happened, I gave her $45.00 to buy clothes, which put the business in a bad way.

Q. How did your wife treat you?

A. Well, outside of her drinking, she was alright, but she was always drunk. The children were lousy, and she was lousy herself, when she got drunk she would lay in a stupor. Drink was the cause of it all.

Q. When did you first have occasion to suspect your wife of being unfaithful to you?

A. On Monday morning, March 10, 1906, I came down stairs and found my wife under the influence of liquor, and I asked her if she had been out and she said, "No." I had seen my wife and Sowers in close conversation, under suspicious circumstances. I went into the bar and asked the bar-tender, Sowers, if he gave my wife any whiskey, and he denied it at first but afterward said that when he had slipped out into the yard and came back in he saw my wife take a cup full of whiskey. I said no more that day, and the next night I went to bed with my wife and I asked her if Sowers ever made any improper propositions to her. She got excited, which aroused my suspicions and I told her then that I had accused Sowers down stairs, and that he had confessed to everything. I did this to see what she would say, and I said, "How many times did you have sexual intercourse with Sowers?" She said, "Once." I then asked her when this occurred, and she said it was last week. This settled it in my mind and I then got out of bed and went into Mr. Sowers' room, which is the adjoining room next to mine, and pulling the bed clothes off of him, I grabbed him by the neck and accused him of being intimate with my wife. I took him into my room in the presence of my wife, and got her by the clothes, and got them together, and asked him what he had done to that woman, my wife. At first he said nothing, and I hit him once, and he said, "For God's sake don't hit me again, and I will tell you everything. I was going to tell you before." (This all occurred in my wife's presence.)

Well, when he got his clothes on, I took him down
stairs, into the bar, and got pen and ink and made
him write what had happened.

George's attorney submitted as evidence two statements signed by Sowers, the second in George's hand, because Sowers was shaking so badly. (The chief difference
between them is that *dining room* is spelled correctly in
George's version.) Initially, Sowers acknowledged only
that he had "staid with Mrs. Ruth," but ultimately confessed that they had been intimate for five weeks.

The cross-examination by Katie's attorney proved
ineffective, despite Sowers's statement to police that
George was pointing a pistol at him.

George responded with indignation. No one was
going to challenge his manhood again.

Q. Mr. Sowers testified at the Station House,
according to the testimony of Justice Loden, that
you had a pistol in your hand. Did you have any
such weapon?

A. No, not in my hand. I had a pistol in my coat
pocket which I put in there when I closed the bar,
and which I did not remember. Every night when
I closed up I took that pistol and put it in my coat
pocket. I never gave the pistol a thought, I was so

excited. I had forgotten all about it. I didn't need the pistol for the simple reason that it was man to man, and I was not afraid of him.

Notice of the divorce of George and Catherine Ruth appeared in the *Baltimore Sun* on May 15, 1906, just two months after she was arrested. The grounds were drunkenness and infidelity.

George Sr. was awarded custody of all three minor children. The final decree did not award Katie any alimony.

IV

Baby William died on August 29, 1906, four days after his first birthday.

The cause of death was marasmus, the same diagnosis of infant malnutrition cited on Gussie's death certificate. Unlike Gussie, William did not die at home. He was a patient at the Thomas Wilson Sanitarium for the Sick Children of Baltimore, a summer hospital located ten miles northwest of downtown. The Thomas Wilson Sanitarium was a progressive and philanthropic organization established in 1879 to treat infants suffering from gastrointestinal disorders during the summer heat when, in the years before pasteurization, milk supplies were most likely to be tainted. (Pasteurization would not become mandatory in Baltimore until 1917.)

Staff members operated four free milk stations within the city limits to help nourish babies unable to get pure milk in overheated, crowded neighborhoods. Nurses volunteered their services and paid follow-up visits after babies were discharged. Mothers were allowed to stay with their children throughout treatment at the sanitarium.

It is impossible to know whose custody William was in at the time of his death, or, in fact, whether either parent was with him. Though George had been granted legal custody, it was his brother William, for whom the baby was named, who was listed on the death certificate as "father and informant."

Two of the four Ruth children for whom death records could be located in the Maryland State Archives succumbed to a combination of diseases that had no treatment in turn-of-the-century Baltimore—asthma, pneumonia, and spinal meningitis.

Two others, Gussie and William, died of malnutrition, a preventable condition.

The infant mortality rate in Baltimore in 1900 was approximately 10 percent, according to Christopher

Boone, dean and professor at the School of Sustain-ability at Arizona State University. By that standard, he said, the losses suffered by George and Katie Ruth were disproportionately high.

Babe's daughter Julia said he never spoke about his dead siblings. The Considine autobiography quotes him as saying he had an older brother John who died "be-fore he could be any help to me," but there is no docu-mentation in state archives of a child by that name, and Mamie Moberly claimed her brother was mistaken.

Shelby Fell Daugherty, a direct descendant of Ka-tie's sister Lena, has tried to research her family his-tory in an effort to fill in genealogical gaps for her father. She has been frustrated by a lack of documen-tation and a familial tendency to keep things "hush-hush." "There's a lot of alcoholism on that side of the family," she said. "Seems like [Katie] was a serious alcoholic."

George and Katie reunited for William's funeral—at least for appearances. The death announcement in the *Sun* read: "William E., aged 1 year, beloved son of George H. and Catherine Ruth. Funeral from his parents residence, No. 406 W. Conway St, this (Friday) afternoon at 3 o'clock."

William was buried in the family plot in Loudon

Park Cemetery, his coffin stacked on top of those of his siblings. The cemetery was just up the road from St. Mary's, where two weeks earlier his brother had received his First Communion.

He was eleven years old, not so little anymore, old enough surely to understand this death, at least the fourth he had known in his young life. He never acknowledged their existence much less their loss or the divorce of his parents. Why would he? He never posed, publicly, the question that begs asking: What parents give up one of their two surviving children?

"I don't think he wanted to remember his childhood," Julia said. "With both parents alive, I would have thought that he would have resented that neither of them wanted him."

In Considine's telling, Ruth says, "I hardly knew my parents."

In the hundredth-anniversary book published by the Birthplace and Museum, he says, "I think my mother hated me."

Whatever the ins and outs of his institutional life may have been, one fact remains incontrovertible: each summons home and each subsequent commitment reprised the pain of the first repudiation.

Parental abandonment would become the defining

and unacknowledged biographical fact of his life. It is the lens that clarifies; the mystery he would never explain.

That is what the movie critic for the *Winnipeg Evening Tribune* saw in his eyes projected on the big screen at the Province Theater where the lights were going down as Ruth hurtled through the night toward Manhattan. In the dark, it was there for anyone to see.

Chapter 3
October 11 / Trenton

HOME RUN KING AND LOU HERE FOR GAME AT HIGH SCHOOL FIELD

WILL NOT ARRIVE IN TIME FOR LUNCHEON

—TRENTON EVENING TIMES

HOME RUN TWINS CALL ON MOORE

STATE HOUSE "STENOGS" IN TURMOIL AS
RUTH AND GEHRIG ARRIVE

—TRENTON EVENING TIMES

I

Babe Ruth swept into the great hall of Manhattan's Pennsylvania Station either with or without two ladies of the night prominently clinging to his arm. He had or had not spent the night before in their company. Did or did not pat them on the derrière and tip them effusively, calling out to a pal among the assembled scribes, photogs, hangers-on, autograph addicts, and redcaps gathered to see him off: "Coupla beauts, eh?"

Christy Walsh thrust himself into the scrum. Among other things, it was his job to make sure the story remained an either/or—either it wouldn't find its way into print until long after they were all dead or it would be forgotten in a blitz of favorable mentions of the visits Walsh had arranged to hospitals and orphanages, where Babe would be photographed being his best self.

Most Americans still thought the Babe was a happily married man—the photos of Dorothy and Helen in the stands at Games 3 and 4 helped. Walsh could count on the discretion of the beat guys on the payroll of the Christy Walsh Syndicate who doubled as Ruth's ghosts, but not on their editors. Not anymore. Not since Joe Patterson, publisher of the *New York Daily News*, America's first tabloid, plastered photos of Babe's mistress, Claire Hodgson, on page 1 in August 1925. And not with Bernarr Macfadden of *True Story* fame bankrolling New York's newest scandal sheet, the *New York Evening Graphic*—known around town as the Porno-Graphic.

Walsh's immediate task was to extricate Ruth from

the mob that attached to him like an appendage. They had a train to catch. There was a ball game, a mayor, and a governor waiting for them in Trenton.

The station occupied seven acres of Manhattan real estate, stretching two city blocks along Seventh Avenue. With its two grand carriage entrances evoking Berlin's Brandenburg Gate, a main waiting room fashioned of pink granite and modeled on the Baths of Caracalla—the biggest indoor space in the city—and a soaring concourse with a greenhouse ceiling confected of iron and glass, Penn Station was Ruthian in proportion. It was also a landmark in the professional relationship between Ruth and Walsh: it was here, on February 21, 1921, that he secured Ruth's signature on their first contract.

Walsh wasn't exactly a kid on the come. He was twenty-nine years old and out of a job, having been fired again, this time by the Van Patten advertising agency. It was hard to fail at that when all of New York was in thrall to the new art of propaganda. Walsh couldn't have imagined when he signed the Big Fella to that one-year deal—fifteen minutes before Babe and Helen boarded the 4:50 P.M. train for Hot Springs, Arkansas, where Babe went to boil out before spring training—that Ruth would get this big. That the money would get this big. That the job would get this big.

Ruth was the first athlete to be as famous for what he did off the field (or what people thought he did) as he was for what he did on it. And in 1927, with Walsh's help, he would become the first ballplayer to be paid as much for what he did off the field as what he did on it. What began six years earlier as an agreement to syndicate ghostwritten stories under the Babe's byline had become not only big business but an entirely new kind of business: the management, marketing, and promotion of athletic heroism. Together they were inventing a new way for athletes to be famous—and to profit from that fame.

The sports world had begun to take notice. Even the inveterate curmudgeon Westbrook Pegler, the former ghostwriter responsible for the treacle serialized under Ruth's name in 1920, had been forced to admit they were onto something new. Now a syndicated columnist for the *Chicago Tribune*, Pegler had given Walsh his grudging due in a February 11, 1927, column, played as a scoop by the *Washington Post*: "Babe Ruth Now an Industry and Has Acquired a Manager."

Which was particularly sweet coming from Pegler, who had dismissed the syndicate's offerings as "journalistic chitterlings" and "rhetorical offal."

Radical as it was to think of an athlete as an entity to be capitalized, the headline was new only to the news-

paper's editors—Walsh had been in complete control
of Ruth's affairs for more than a year. In fact, he had
signed him to a new five-year contract in July. He gave
the story to *New York Telegram* columnist Joe Williams, who reciprocated with a fawning profile titled
"Christy Walsh, the Man Behind Mr. Babe Ruth." He
now controlled every aspect of Ruth's financial life: investments, annuities, insurance policies, endorsements,
personal appearances, and taxes. And he was involved
in every aspect of Ruth's personal life, too. He would
say later, "I did everything but sleep with him." And
one night, when only a single unoccupied berth was
available on their overbooked Pullman, he even tried
that. Ruth kicked him out of bed.

The Big Fella didn't set out to be a revolutionary. But
in his anti-authoritarian soul, he understood the injustice of ownership holding all the cards. He thumbed
his nose at the pooh-bahs in every front office of every
major-league franchise by authorizing Walsh to represent and protect his interests, making him the first
sports agent in industry history. Why shouldn't he
get his?

He thumbed his nose at the autocrats of the dugout,
managers like John McGraw, who exerted complete
control of the game, moving men around the bases like

chess pieces until the Babe came along, took the game into his own hands, and remade it in his image. Who said bunt and slash was the only way to play baseball? Who said you can't swing away?

He thumbed his nose at baseball commissioner Kenesaw Mountain Landis every time he barnstormed against Negro Leaguers and other touring black ball clubs as he had since 1918, and as they would that afternoon at a high school field in Trenton against the Brooklyn Royal Giants, and again in Asbury Park. True, Ruth wasn't the only white player to compete against Negro Leaguers. But he was the Babe.

He thumbed his nose at Landis in 1921 when he defied the capricious ban on World Series participants barnstorming in the off-season. In his own unlettered way, Ruth understood something the big shots in the commissioner's office wouldn't get for decades about showcasing the national pastime and creating a market west of the Mississippi: "I think we are doing something that is in the interest of baseball. I do not see why we are singled out when other big players, members of second and third place clubs in the World Series money, are permitted to play post-season games. I am out to earn an honest dollar, and at the same time give baseball fans an opportunity to see the big players in action."

Ruth had other lawyers and secretaries and "winter managers" before Walsh came along. He'd had a press agent since 1919, he bragged to the *Brooklyn Daily Eagle.* Connie Savage organized the early barnstorming tours. Harry Weber, a theatrical agent, booked the vaudeville tour in the winter of 1921–22. Johnny Igoe, a Boston pharmacist pal, was in charge when Ruth signed on to tour Cuba with the John McGraw All-Stars in October 1920. Everyone knew how that turned out: with Ruth locked in a train toilet with Giants' pitcher Rosy Ryan and a gallon of rum on their way back to Havana, where the Babe got stranded, having been swindled out of everything he'd bankrolled by gamblers and con men.

Walsh was first to merge all aspects of representation into a single agency. After signing Ruth to initial one-year syndication deals, he had acquired power of attorney and complete control of Ruth's money when the Big Fella got himself in a financial hole. Now, thanks to Ruth, Walsh was sole proprietor of two companies: the Christy Walsh Syndicate, which spit out hundreds of thousands of words over the telegraph wires during the 1927 World Series and brought in $43,252; and Christy Walsh Management, which he had created to handle Ruth's and now Gehrig's financial affairs. "He made the Ruthian bankroll what it is today," Williams wrote.

In short, Ruthian.

Gehrig's signing had been revealed in an August 18 story by Henry L. Farrell of the United Press, who took the opportunity to chide Jake Ruppert—he'd have to do better by Lou than his 1927 $7,500 salary, now that he had demonstrated Ruth's power and hired his agent.

"Until Christy Walsh came along, Babe didn't know how to make use of his by-products," Dan Parker opined in the *New York Mirror*. "But what Armour did to the pig and the cow, Christy did for Babe."

Cleaned up and packaged right, Ruth also made Walsh a wealthy man. Parker called it "the most equitable partnership ever established in athletics."

Since signing Ruth, Walsh had expanded his sphere of influence into college football, establishing the "All American Board of Football" in 1924, the year before Walter Camp's death, no doubt in hopes of replacing Camp's annual All-America team. He packed the board with his clients—Knute Rockne at Notre Dame, Tad Jones at Yale, Howard Jones at the University of Southern California, and Glen "Pop" Warner at Stanford—and packaged their opinions of each other in ghostwritten columns.

He created a board for the Babe to chair as well—"The All America Board of Baseball"—and loaded that up with sportswriter pals from every major-league city. Babe's All-Stars received a personally autographed certificate and a red, white, and blue woolen sweater.

II

They were an unlikely pair.

Ruth was all id; Walsh was all superego. Everybody knew Ruth; Walsh made it his business to know everybody it was important to know. What they shared was a kinetic restlessness. Walsh traveled twenty-five thousand miles a year selling Ruth. Ruth traveled at least that much during the baseball season being himself.

Born in St. Louis on December 2, 1891, Walsh was only four years Ruth's senior, but now found himself acting in loco parentis, legally and otherwise. Yes, it could be frustrating "handling these children dressed as adults," he would confide to his son in future correspondence. "But as long as they need you, you're safe. You make them believe they can't go on without you."

He looked like he was born responsible. His birthday suit was probably three-piece. His slicked-back black hair might have been parted with a nun's ruler. A devout Catholic and son of Ireland, he pined for the old sod though he had never set foot on it.

Walsh was a teetotaler and, to be polite about it, extremely careful with his money—and Ruth's. Ruth wasn't careful about anything.

Walsh favored pinstriped, double-breasted suits that made him look older and squarer than he was, filling out his otherwise slim five-eleven frame. He wore shamrocks and Kelly green ties in solidarity with the movement for Irish independence, having adopted the cause of his paternal grandparents, from Cork. Ruth favored silk shirts of every hue, tossed away after a single wearing, and $225 handmade suits from his downtown Italian tailor, Carloni.

Walsh was Hollywood by way of middle America, extolling the conservative "horse and buggy" values of his maternal grandparents, who had arrived in Los Angeles in the mid-1880s by covered wagon. In temperament and frugality, he was closer to Gehrig than Ruth; he, too, was a mama's boy.

In his thinking and rah-rah sensibility, he was closest to Knute Rockne. But no one doubted that Ruth was his meal ticket. And one thing about the Big Fella: unlike Rockne, who dallied with other agents, he was loyal.

Walsh had married well and touted the arrival of his son in a ghostwritten birth announcement under

Christy Jr.'s byline, identifying himself as "a chip off the old Syndicate." His wife, Madeline—Mada to the family—was the daughter of Oscar M. Souden, president of the U.S. National Bank. Daddy built them an impressive home in the hills above Griffith Park with a view from the Pacific Ocean to downtown Los Angeles. Walsh dubbed it Walshchateau. Mada called it Villa Cypress. Among its twenty rooms, there were five bedrooms, six baths, and an entertaining space capable of holding one hundred to one hundred fifty guests, according to his grandson Bob Walsh. The foyer, where guests left their cards, was paved with black-and-white squares of marble, brought over from Europe.

A circular banister graced a grandiose staircase accented by arched stained-glass windows. A sideboard in the dining room held a white-and-gold Limoges service for forty or fifty, each plate inscribed with a prominent W.

The Walshes entertained strategically: clients mingled with gossip columnists Hedda Hopper, Louella Parsons, and Walter Winchell. Walsh knew everyone from the Little Rascals and silent-movie star Harold Lloyd to New York Democratic boss Jim Farley and New York governor Al Smith, for whom he would corral a glittering roster of supporters, including Ruth and

Gehrig, under the banner "Champions of the World, Champions of Al Smith" during the 1928 presidential campaign.

"Mada told me Einstein was there," Bob's wife, Katie Walsh, said. "She wasn't impressed with Einstein because all he talked about was fish," Bob said. "He liked to catch them, eat them, and talk about them."

They also owned a summer place on a rocky out-cropping called Hemlock Point, situated on Lake Oscawana, forty miles north of New York City, where Walsh brought his most favored clients, and sports-writers he wanted to coddle. He had Gehrig pho-tographed perched on a photogenic rock and Ruth photographed rowing on the lake with Army football coach Biff Jones. Walsh saw to it that both photo-graphs made the papers, the first underscoring Geh-rig's ruggedness and the second aligning Ruth with military conformity.

A corny Walsh cartoon tying Ruth's home-run hit-ting spree to passage of the Volstead Act, which made Prohibition the law of the land, appeared in the *Detroit Free Press* on June 6, 1920, nominating in the caption "The Hon. Babe Ruth, People's Choice on the Home Run Ticket (He Does Not Favor a 2¾% Batting Aver-age)." He surrounded Ruth with a slate of candidates for baseball immortality—McGraw, Johnson, Huggins.

He placed Ruth's cap at a jaunty angle with an errant lock of hair (to suggest boyishness) pasted to his wrinkled brow. But he also gave him a deeply shadowed cheek, downcast eyes, and a downturned mouth. Walsh *got* him. He drew the sadness behind the caricature.

As an artist, the best you could say about Walsh was that he was self-taught. He honed his skills by making his own Christmas cards and valentines. He had paid for his board at St. Vincent's College in Los Angeles by trading cartoons for food at a local restaurant. With help from his father, he landed a job as a daily cartoonist for the *Los Angeles Express*, a position that paid twelve dollars a week. He framed the eventual letter of termination from the managing editor telling him he was overpaid and hung it on the wall of his New York office.

He hooked on with the *Los Angeles Herald* as a cartoonist and cub reporter chasing hotel arrivals and taking copy over the phone, when he learned that Christy Mathewson, baseball's greatest pitcher, would be spending the winter in Southern California. He got the address of the rented bungalow on the outskirts of the city where the Mathewson family would be staying and cased the joint in advance of their arrival. The day of the interview, January 20, 1912, Walsh arrived early, and waited for the great man to awake. He was all set for first scoop. Only problem: he forgot to bring a pencil and paper.

By the time he returned from the nearest store, Matty was surrounded by seven baseball writers and one female reporter seeking "heart interest."

Unable to think of anything to ask, he dutifully scribbled the answers to questions posed by others and hustled back to the newsroom, where the editor said what editors always say: "Whaddya got?"

Walsh produced his rumpled notes (with unseemly bravado), which the editor appropriated, along with the story, handing it to the new gal reporter in town, Adela Rogers—later known as the World's Greatest Girl Reporter for her celebrity interviews for *Photoplay*.

Walsh retreated to his desk to draw a cartoon to accompany her story: Matty, golf club in hand, standing in front of the bungalow that was the site of his reportorial humiliation. "That, young man, is your first lesson in the art of ghostwriting," quipped fellow cub reporter William Ivan St. Johns, who would soon become Rogers's first husband.

That was how Walsh would eventually make his mark: syndicating the confected bons mots of the famous through what he liked to call the "ancient and honorable craft of literary make-believe."

Fired in what he described as a general shake-up

at the *Herald*, he solicited for telephone directories, and drifted into advertising, representing Los Angeles car dealerships while studying law at night at USC to please his father, a traveling salesman. He passed the California bar in 1915 and bragged he was never retained by a single client. After a brief stint covering the United States Military Training Camp in Monterey for the *Herald*, he resolved to cast his lot, and his powers of persuasion, with the emerging industry of public relations. "He was selling air, concept and heart," his grandson said.

In 1916, he was hired as the Pacific Coast representative of Chalmers Motor Car Company, according to an October profile in the *Fourth Estate*. That year Chalmers unveiled a revolutionary concept in auto design—a "one-man" convertible top allegedly manageable by a single red-blooded American male. Walsh decided he was that man. He organized a demonstration in front of Los Angeles City Hall for the boss, Hugh Chalmers, and an audience of former Southern California mayors in town for a convention. Alas, it required the combined strength of twelve former mayors to free Walsh when his sleeve got caught in the one-man top. The car went to a garage for repairs; several mayors sought treatment for lacerations; and Walsh went back to work, without a sleeve, hoping to recoup the boss's good favor.

Two weeks later, on opening day of the Pacific Coast League, Walsh arranged for a parade of baseball players in Chalmers cars. This earned him a job in the company's advertising department in San Francisco, which he lost almost immediately when a new division chief decided he wanted his own man. Walsh went around the new chief and got rehired to the same position at the same salary but with a new title. In his spare time, he began syndicating a series of his cartoons called "Coast Stars in the Big Leagues" to California newspapers.

From San Francisco, he went to Detroit, hired by the New York advertising agency Van Patten, Inc., to edit *The Punch*, the house organ of the newly merged Maxwell-Chalmers Automobile Company. There he met the World War I flying ace Eddie Rickenbacker, newly engaged in the manufacture of automobiles. Walsh would later write and sell Rickenbacker's coverage of the 1919 Indianapolis 500 to sixty newspapers across the country. His first foray into newspaper syndication fetched $874, which they would split two ways.

When the war came, he enlisted in the Army Motor Transport Corps and wrote heartfelt stories from Fort Custer, Michigan, and Fort Johnston in Carrabelle, Florida, about military vehicles on parade, making sure to highlight those manufactured by Maxwell-Chalmers.

He mailed his copy along with personal letters written on Van Patten stationery to General John J. Pershing in France.

Dear Sir and General:

Having used your name to symbolize the clean-fisted fighting American youth now adding glorious chapters to our history of uninterrupted victories I am taking the liberty of handing you herewith a newspaper clipping containing the article referred to.

Assuring of the pride and everlasting cooperation of those at home and with application for immediate induction now in the mail I am looking forward to the honor of being one of your valiant over-sea legion before many months.

He got as far as Florida.

He proved adept at ingratiating himself with power, making and keeping important contacts. He parlayed the perfunctory functionary's letter of thanks into an excuse for continued correspondence, which would lead to Ruth's involvement with the Citizens' Training Camps and, much later, an opportunity to seek Pershing's help with a movie about Eddie Rickenbacker's career.

When released from his arduous tour of duty in 1919, Lieutenant Walsh returned to his job editing *The Punch*, successfully placing several columns in auto trade magazines touting the excellence of his own work. He had a knack for getting his name in print. Sometimes all he had to do was show up. Or quit. When he left the editing job in June 1920 to join the Van Pattens' New York office as national account manager for Maxwell-Chalmers, his friends at the *Oakland Tribune* hailed his new career move with a headline: "Christy Walsh Given Gold Fountain Pen." The gold fountain pen also found its way into the pages of *Advertising & Selling* and the *Fourth Estate*.

III

Arriving in New York at the dawn of the age of advertising and consumerism, Walsh saw himself as part of the vast migration of aspiration that F. Scott Fitzgerald evoked in his short stories and that Walsh would describe more floridly in his brief 1937 memoir, *Adios to Ghosts*. His was "the story of thousands of young dreamers anxious to escape the fetters of the smaller hometown and hie for the city on the Hendrik Hudson, where the rainbow of opportunity is alleged to terminate and be within the grasp of all who reach high enough."

The rainbow of his ambition led to "a blend of sport-cartooning, peddling publicity and working for an advertising agency," at the end of which he hoped to find the proverbial pot of gold.

He decamped for New York at a propitious moment. Advertising revenues in the United States would climb from $682 million in 1914 to $3 billion in 1929. By the mid-1920s the number of advertising agencies had grown from twelve hundred before World War I to five thousand.

Van Patten was a boutique agency—without either an art or copy department—specializing in automobile accounts. "Out of some 1,500 firms in the same line of business, it ranks in number of accounts somewhere near the bottom of the list," reported the October 16, 1920, edition of *Automobile Topics*. "Yet in size of volume, per account, Van Patten, Inc., ranks among the first ten to fifteen."

Walsh believed deeply in two things: Irish independence and the power of advertising. In the late winter of 1921, he took it upon himself to write, print, publish, and distribute a special issue of *The Punch* dedicated to the cause that was inimical to the beliefs of his immediate superior, a Scot violently opposed to Sinn Fein. Walsh bribed the printers to keep his opus a secret and had it delivered to Boston in time for the annual convention of Maxwell-Chalmers agents. It was liberally decorated with green shamrocks and gold harps. The lead article was written by Eamon de Valera, political leader in the Irish War of Independence and founder of the upstart Republican Party, Fianna Fáil. Walsh paid the waiters to hand copies around with the meal. "Before the first course was over," the *New Yorker* later reported, "Walsh's usefulness to the Maxwell-Chalmers organization was ended."

Walsh put a happier spin on it. "Alas my rainbow dissolved abruptly, the alluring colors faded into a murky smear, the salary stopped, the jig was up and the red light went on, just where Opportunity Boulevard runs into Success."

But he stumbled upon that most elusive form of American currency: a great idea. His initial plan was to syndicate ghostwritten copy for entertainers, giving a public voice to the still silent stars of Hollywood movies, and the strong, silent hero types like Rickenbacker. He quickly sized up the competition in the syndication racket and concluded it might be wiser to specialize in something they didn't offer: columns from clients who made daily headlines instead of one movie a year.

He told so many versions of how he met Babe Ruth that it was hard to keep track of them all. There was the version he told his brother Matt: how he found out the floor and room number of the hotel where Ruth was staying, climbed the fire escape, clambered through the window (magically open a crack), found Ruth in bed with a blonde, slapped the Babe on the butt, and said, "I want to represent you."

If it wasn't true, it should have been.

There was the one he told for attribution in *Adios to Ghosts*, in which he staked out Ruth's apartment at the Ansonia Hotel on the West Side of Manhattan. Time was running out.

Four days before Ruth was scheduled to leave for Hot Springs, Arkansas, to steep his suety self in 108-degree sitz baths, Walsh was at the local deli where the Babe bought his beer, when the counterman got a telephone call. "Baby Root vants a case of beer. Right avay, right avay, and mine boy is gone. *Yoi. Yoi. Yoi.*"

Ten minutes later, Walsh was unloading beer in the Babe's kitchen and inquiring how much Ruth was paid for the ghostwritten accounts of each of his fifty-four home runs in 1920 published by the United News Service.

Five bucks, said the Babe.

That came to $270 for the season—which was

about all they were worth. His literary input, according to Westbrook Pegler, amounted to baseball haiku. "Socked one today. Fast ball. High outside."

Walsh said, "I can get you five hundred dollars."

Now he had the Babe's attention.

Years later, Walsh would tell Joe Williams off the record that he bribed the deliveryman with a fiver to let him make the delivery.

In all the tellings—written and oral—handed down to successive generations of Walshes, one part of the story never changed. Having traded his suit jacket for a delivery boy's pocketless white coat, Walsh didn't have the contract with him when he talked his way into Ruth's apartment and got him to agree to a one-year syndication deal.

His grandson Bob, an L.A. guy—who calls his grandfather Walsh—tells it like a scene from a Hollywood screenplay. Ruth tells Walsh to meet him on the platform at Penn Station. Young Christy, his life disappearing in front of his eyes, stays up all night and gets to the station early, which was unlike him. (He would grow accustomed to trains being held for him.) "He waits on the platform," Bob Walsh said. "Then out of nowhere, through the steam, like an Inspector Poirot–type thing, there comes Ruth, beaming in a belted camel hair coat with an oversized cigar all aglow."

While Helen Ruth diverted her husband's many admirers, Walsh secured his signature on the wrinkled contract he had typed out in letter form, a copy of which would sell for $21,510 in 2010.

Walsh announced the creation of the Christy Walsh Syndicate in the March 19, 1921, edition of *Editor & Publisher*. Two weeks later, he placed a full-page ad in the same publication, touting the "greatest array of talent and genius ever offered American newspapers, names whose combined annual services would cost half a million dollars, whose work and deeds are known to newspaper readers through $5,000,000 worth of personal advertising."

That great array of talent he claimed to represent included filmmaker D. W. Griffith, whose secretary never actually let Walsh through the front door; Gene Buck, who was too busy running the Ziegfeld Follies to write the proposed Broadway column, "A Buck a Day"; opera diva Mary Garden, who boarded a ship for Europe without crafting a single word; historian Hendrik Willem van Loon, who wrote his own stuff; and Jack Dempsey's fight manager, Jack "Doc" Kearns, who had the virtue of being available, which the Manassa Mauler was not. And of course, Babe Ruth, who had agreed to write two articles a week.

The editorial response to Walsh's initial pitch was

less than underwhelming; his only employee quit two weeks later.

He persuaded a charitable printer to print five hundred circulars on credit, hauled them to the post office, and waited. The next morning, Bradford Merrill, general manager of the Hearst Syndicate, ordered the Babe Ruth feature for the entire Hearst string. Merrill re-upped for the Babe's World Series coverage and for the entire 1922 season.

Walsh didn't invent ghostwriting. It was known as "the player-author evil" when Ban Johnson, president of the American League, threatened to ban Eddie Collins and Frank "Home Run" Baker from the 1913 World Series because of contracts they had signed with John Wheeler's Bell Syndicate.

But, as Joe Williams put it, Walsh "harnessed this Niagara of writing genius and turned it into artistically useful channels. Other hardy pioneers had dabbled in this unique literary field on earlier occasions, but it remained for Walsh, a tall, dark-haired Irishman in his middle thirties, to put the proposition on a sound, systematic basis, by which the reading public was assured the best thoughts of the best athletic minds in the best manner."

Once he had Ruth under contract, other big names quickly followed: John McGraw, Walter Johnson, Ty

Cobb, Miller Huggins, Rogers Hornsby, and Gehrig, whose life story he had been aggressively peddling since August. Then came the gridiron greats. Soon he was bragging that the Christy Walsh Syndicate was the only one in the country "dealing exclusively in sport page material."

Walsh was selling a kind of fool's gold, whose value peaked in the golden age of sports: bright, shiny words with little mettle that generated lots of cold, hard cash for author, subject, and the syndicate man, casting a gauzy glow over the putative authors while offering readers the illusion of being in the know. Paul Gallico, upon exiting the sporting stage, expressed astonishment at "how much of the hogwash was taken as gospel."

But in an era before radio delivered pregame, postgame, and in-game interviews, Walsh's fables were as close as baseball fans could get to hearing voices of faraway stars. No one knew what they sounded like anyway. So what if reading them required a willing suspension of disbelief?

On opening day at the Polo Grounds in 1921, ninety days before he was contractually obliged to do so, Walsh handed Ruth a check for a thousand dollars— borrowed at 6 percent interest. "I shall never forget the expression on Babe Ruth's face when I handed him the check," he wrote. "Here's a fellow who had been skinned so many times by strangers that I felt the way to win his confidence was to pay in advance."

What Walsh didn't know, according to Matt Cwieka, Christy Walsh Jr.'s son-in-law, was that Mada's father, the bank president, had arranged for the loans. "Mada was on the phone with him telling him, 'You can do this,'" said Cwieka.

At the end of that first year, he had $8.90 in his bank account.

Broke as he may have been, Walsh was a visionary. He saw that a new kind of stardom was emerging, one grounded in personality and amplified by marketing and technology, by the repetition and dissemination of images in the new tabloid press, by the transmission of the human voice through what the Babe called "the ether."

He also saw the opportunities and the dangers that awaited when Ruth reported to Manhattan traffic court at 9:00 A.M. on June 8, 1921, having been arrested for speeding for the second time in three months—by a cop who held motorcycle racing records! Ruth expected the crowd of press and well-wishers that greeted him at the courthouse at 300 Mulberry Street. He also expected leniency. His lawyer had told him to check the part in the magistrate's hair for a clue to the judge's mood.

He left his car, the 12-cylinder maroon torpedo

roadster in which he'd been arrested—known fondly to his teammates as the ghost of Riverside Drive—in the care of a couple of boys. He didn't figure to be gone long. He confidently and remorsefully pleaded guilty, submitted to fingerprinting, paid his hundred-dollar fine, and was sentenced to a day in the slammer despite the encouraging part in his honor's hair.

Having observed the C-note with which he had ostentatiously paid his fine, Ruth's cellmates—chauffeurs found guilty of the same crime—demanded he join them in a jailhouse game of craps. Ruth sought refuge by the window.

"I see a shadow!" bellowed a news photographer who'd mounted a fire escape on a building across the street.

"Snap the shadow!" came the fevered reply from the reporter on the pavement below.

Even the slightest intimation of the Babe was news.

Ruth used his one telephone call to ask for his uniform, which he donned under his street clothes, a dove gray suit. "I'm going to run like hell to get to the game," he told his cellmates. "Keeping you late like this makes a speeder of you."

At 3:57 P.M., three minutes before the end of his sentence, Ruth was ushered out a side door. He covered the nine miles between the jail and the Polo Grounds in eighteen minutes flat, thereby exceeding the speed for which he had been arrested by four miles an hour. Trailing scribes lost him and the motorcycle police escorting him at 110th Street, where he exited Central Park. He arrived in time to bat in the bottom of the sixth inning, slowing down, finally, enough to walk. Then, according to the Associated Press, "he stole second and was not arrested."

The story made the front page of the *Times* and the *Daily News*, which ran a full-page photograph of the Babe signing his confession. The *Times* earnestly included figures cited by the sentencing magistrate comparing the ninety-one thousand fatalities that occurred on American highways during a nineteen-month period with the forty-eight thousand U.S. soldiers who lost their lives on the killing fields of France.

One American soldier, according to legend, Captain Joe Patterson, returned home from a decisive encounter with his cousin Robert McCormick in a manure pile in Mareuil-en-Dôle, France, during the Second Battle of the Marne, with a mission. Patterson had been to London on furlough and witnessed the stunning success of Lord Northcliffe's new "picture paper," the *Daily Mirror*. During Patterson's serendipitous farmyard meeting with his cousin, publisher of the *Chicago Tribune*, he secured familial support for the *Daily News*.

The first edition of the *Illustrated Daily News* went to press less than a year later, on June 26, 1919. In the eight years since, Patterson's cheeky tab had completely reinvented the way news was covered in the city, giving, among other things, more space and prominence to sports, especially baseball.

It was the first flower of jazz journalism in America, a sassy bouquet of sex and money, heavy on gossip and local crime with lots of contests for readers to enter. Patterson wanted riffs rather than ruminations, punctuated with as many illustrations and photographs as his editors could cram on the page.

"We can't make it too clear and easy for our readers," Patterson wrote in a memo to his editorial staff seven weeks before the first edition went to press. He reinforced that message in the June 19 paper, promising readers that no story would be continued on a jump page.

The birth of tabloid journalism marked the beginning of an inexorable shift from word to image and from information to entertainment. If the mandate was to entertain, it followed that sports, the entertainment of the masses, would become central to tabloid journalism. Ruth would descend on New York six months later, bludgeon in hand, in a "burst of dazzle and jingle," *New York Post* columnist Jimmy Cannon wrote some years later.

He was the perfect story for a publisher whose mandate to his sports editor, Marshall Hunt, was to produce "very biff, bang, boom stuff."

Sportswriting—and baseball coverage in particular—had been on the rise since the first known box score was published in 1845, which evolved under Henry Chadwick's stewardship in the *New York Clipper* in the late 1850s. By 1860, Chadwick was compiling season totals for teams and players in *Beadle's Dime Base-Ball Player.*

The rise of yellow journalism in New York City twenty years later and the circulation war between Joseph Pulitzer and William Randolph Hearst also proved a boon for sportswriting. Pulitzer created the first newspaper sports department at the *New York World* in 1883. Hearst countered with the first separate sports section in the *New York Journal* two years later. The *Sporting Life* and the *Sporting News* were born in the same period.

In 1887, the *New York Tribune* published a handbook of sports with rules for various games because the editors said they had detected a widespread interest—and market—in athletics and had themselves printed eighty columns of sports news during the previous year.

Rough Rider Teddy Roosevelt's embrace of manly pursuits, and the movement for muscular Christianity, prompted the nation's dailies to bulk up their skeletal sports coverage from less than half a percent of the news hole in the 1880s to 4 percent by the turn of the century. By 1914 the *Readers' Guide to Periodical Literature* listed 249 publications devoted to baseball.

This rise coincided with the golden age of newspapering. As general readership increased from 32 million in 1920 to 40 million in 1929, the percentage of space allotted to sports went up right along with it. Not everyone rejoiced. Concerned about the upward tick in crime and sports reporting, the American Society of News Editors commissioned a study in 1926 that confirmed the worst: the average newspaper dedicated ten columns daily to sports and twice that on Sunday. By 1927, even the sober broadsheets were devoting twenty-five or more columns a day to sports.

Sports coverage proliferated. In the years before World War II, when newsprint shortages curtailed available space, "twelve-to-fourteen-page sports sections were not uncommon," Stanley Woodward wrote in his primer for the business, *Sports Page*, and many papers "printed eighty pages of sports on a single Sunday."

Joe Patterson put sports out front, on page 1, within two weeks of the first edition. The occasion was the July 4, 1919, heavyweight title fight in Toledo, Ohio, between Jack Dempsey and Jess Willard. Christy Walsh covered the fight for the *San Francisco Chronicle*, complaining to his editor that all ringside seats had been reserved for New York scribes, while he was assigned a seat fifty feet from the action. Enterprising as always, he rushed along with the crowd for unoccupied seats by the ropes, snapping a few unauthorized photographs with a camera he had hidden in his jacket pocket.

Even as he drew the cartoon that accompanied his story, Walsh knew that the era of pen and ink was coming to an end. Patterson would sign its death warrant when he removed "Illustrated" from his newspaper's name between the first and second editions of the November 19 paper. (The *Daily News* officially became "New York's Picture Newspaper"—with a camera prominently featured in the paper's logo—ten months later.)

Patterson's choice for managing editor was Arthur Clarke, who began his career as a sportswriter in Omaha, Nebraska, and was hired away from the *Evening World*, the New York repository of yellow journalism. Clarke's tenure at the *News* was brief. He stayed only seven months, but during that time instituted one of the most significant developments in sports reporting: converting the back page into a front page for sports.

He broke readers in gently on November 3 and 4 with stories about Boston terriers and foxhounds. But, on Wednesday November 5, the back page featured real sports, the college football game of the week between Syracuse and Rutgers.

Sports editors would never surrender that turf. The back page—and its "Socko! No. 60! O, BABE!" headlines—would become a staple of sports journalism, as well as a measuring stick employed by agents following in Christy Walsh's footsteps to argue on behalf of their clients. (In January 2017, representatives for Mets slugger Yoenis Céspedes calculated that fifty back-page mentions in 2016 were worth $3.2 million to the team.)

Clarke didn't create the back page for the Babe, but he might as well have. The sale of the Bambino was announced on January 5, 1920. Ruth made his back-page debut two days later.

BABE RUTH, HOME RUN KING, NOW WITH YANKEES

Three Ruthian photographs filled the top half of the page. The images were static in the manner of the era: the perfect finish to his swing; detraining with Helen in Seattle prior to the sale; and his Red Sox team photo. But the quality of the photos was less important than their placement and the amount of space allotted to them.

Ruth fully grasped the power of the press to reinforce the legend he and Walsh were creating, but Marshall Hunt doubted he was ever aware of how concerted Patterson's strategy was in using him to build circulation. Patterson consciously cultivated neon names, stars "we could latch onto and sort of cultivate and make our own and have exclusive stuff on," Hunt told Jerome Holtzman for his 1974 oral history of American sportswriters, *No Cheering in the Press Box*. "We recognized the Babe as a guy we could really do business with."

And so, "the Babe became sort of a *Daily News* man."

Hunt became Patterson's full-time Babe Ruth man. His mandate was to follow him everywhere, before, during, and after the season, on the road and at home, a precursor of today's 24/7 coverage. He was the first reporter from a morning paper to travel with the Yankees and the only beat reporter whose paper insisted upon paying his way. Ruth called Hunt his shadow, which may explain why he detested him, the Babe's daughter says—always following him around with a photographer "trying to ambush him and catch him at his worst." An early intimation of gotcha journalism and a very modern complaint.

Hunt was also the first reporter for a morning paper to travel with the team and the only Yankees reporter whose paper insisted upon paying its own way.

In June 1924, Hearst belatedly launched the *New York Daily Mirror*, his entry into the tabloid market Patterson had created, followed three months later by Bernarr Macfadden's snarky evening tab, the *New York Evening Graphic*. The tabloid wars were on.

Arthur Brisbane, who managed the Hearst empire, chose the path of least resistance and produced a tabloid very much in Joe Patterson's image. After seeing sixty thousand people turn out to see Red Grange play football at the Polo Grounds, he summoned Ford Frick from his duties at the *Evening Journal*—where he doubled as Babe Ruth's ghost—and ordered him to follow the Galloping Ghost wherever he went. Frick called his wife and said he wouldn't be home for dinner for a month.

Macfadden's scandal sheet featured howling headlines and plunging décolletage. Shamelessly and gleefully unscrupulous, the *Graphic* was known for splashing salacious "cosmographs"—fake photos—across its pink front page. The most notorious was an elaborate depiction of Rudolph Valentino's corpse with an accompanying story about his ascension to heaven.

The paper launched the career of the legendary Walter Winchell, whose three-dot gossip column, the first in the nation, sold seventy-five thousand to a hundred thousand newspapers a day and, with its advice column to lovelorn New Yorkers, inspired Nathanael West's novel *Miss Lonelyhearts*.

Macfadden, who was far ahead of his time in his zealousness for diet and nutrition, also discovered and promoted Charles Atlas. He filled his pages with columns extolling the virtues of bodybuilding—with lots of grainy photos of scantily clad versions of Mr. America. He attempted to polish his tawdry image at the annual sports banquet he hosted, honoring the person "who, during the past year, has contributed most to the cause of clean sport"—a source of amusement to some readers but a see-and-be-seen event for governors and mayors and champions of every ilk. The festivities were carried live on radio; Ed Sullivan, the *Graphic*'s pickle-faced sports columnist, honed his skills as the future host of Sunday-night television by serving as emcee. Ruth would win the award in 1929 and 1930.

In 1927, New York's shanty newsstands sagged under the weight of twelve daily papers—not including the *Brooklyn Eagle, El Diario,* and the Jewish *Daily Forward,* and the three dailies that published A.M. and P.M. papers—and all those thick new magazines arranged in racks and dangling from clothespins. The city consumed 3.5 million newspapers a day, and every broadsheet and tabloid, morning and afternoon, had a big-name sports columnist who made his bones in printer's ink—much of it quite purple. No one was more vivid or more widely syndicated than Grantland Rice, who draped Ruth in "a purple toga of royalty" in a 1921 column, and had cast his resurrection after hitting bottom in 1922 as a return from Elba.

The gilded names of New York sportswriting—Damon Runyon, Ring Lardner, Paul Gallico, Bill McGeehan, Dan Daniel, Fred Lieb, Heywood Broun, and John Kieran—were usually the highest-paid men in the newsroom. They dined out daily on Babe Ruth. "A Sunday buffet every day of the week," one writer called him.

By Hunt's estimation, "two-thirds of the front page of every afternoon paper in New York City" was devoted to Ruth. Gallico said he had more talent for staying on the front page than your average earthquake.

Ruth posed a daily challenge to skepticism; every home run was an act of hyperbole. "You can't exaggerate an exaggeration," wrote W. O. McGeehan of the *New York Tribune*. A man not given to exaggeration, he said of one of Ruth's home runs that the ball sailed so high it came down coated with ice.

Ruth's relationship with New York's sporting press was cozy, complex, and complicit. Rice was his golfing companion. Paul Gallico, Bill Slocum, and Richards Vidmer dined at his apartment. Hunt's fishing and hunting excursions, ostensibly arranged in order to generate copy, were always off the record. Fred Lieb acted as an intermediary between Ruth and Yankee co-owner Colonel Tillinghast L'Hommedieu Huston the night the Babe set out on his ill-conceived 1921 barnstorming trip.

And then there were Walsh's unholy ghosts, beat reporters like Frick and Slocum, who were richly remunerated to write under the byline of the Big Fella while also filing copy under their own names. One way or another, Ruth was responsible for the livelihood of every sportswriter who covered him, who wrote for him, or who took a pay cut because his editor spent the extra money in the budget to buy his syndicated columns.

In 1927, the *News* rode Ruth's coattails to a circulation just shy of a million, nearly three times that of the then very gray *New York Times*. Gallico, who had succeeded Hunt as sports editor, having impressed Patterson with a composite photograph of "the Ideal Athlete"—an amalgam of Babe Ruth's eyes, Jack Dempsey's torso, Bill Tilden's wrists, and Bobby Jones's arms—created the Golden Gloves amateur boxing tournament, putting the paper in the sports promotion racket. It was so successful that Patterson rewarded him with a month's vacation in Europe.

The paper's ascendancy was also facilitated by technology created in the photo department. The bulky Speed Graphic had long been the tool of the sports photographers' trade, until the fall of 1920 when Marlborough Sylvester (Lou) Walker began tinkering with his equipment in an effort to find something that would allow readers to get closer to the action. That something was Big Bertha, a camera named for a fat German howitzer that debuted on the eve of World War I. Walker attached an extra-long base and an extra-long bellows to his 5 x 7-inch Graflex and fitted it with a lens of 24-inch focal length—more than three times the length of a standard lens—and headed for Ebbets Field for Game 1 of the World Series between the Dodgers and the Cleveland Indians. While the paper's gal reporter was enjoying free hot dogs and coffee, Walker was taking panoramic photographs that allowed him to capture the action at three bases simultaneously.

The *News* trumpeted its get on the front page of its October 6 editions with a photo and headline: "Something New in Baseball." Editors devoted two full inside pages to the photos. "Crouched in the stand of Ebbets Field, Walker made pictures of plays on all bases of the diamond which were large enough on the negative plate to permit astonishing enlargement," John Chapman explained in *Tell It to Sweeney: The Informal History of the New York Daily News*. The *News* featured a double spread of these pictures daily and made a mystery of its coup, querying on page 1, "HOW DOES THE NEWS DO IT?"

The competition quickly figured it out. There was no hiding Big Bertha.

Patterson ordered expanded sports coverage and demanded more and better pictures, exhorting his editors to "publish them before anyone else." Another pioneering *News* photographer, Henry Olen, was busy mixing chemicals and improvising ways to increase the light sensitivity of the glass plates used to take action shots in darkened arenas and at nighttime outdoor events. His experiment worked. The image he captured at the Polo Grounds on September 14, 1923, during round 1 of the

Jack Dempsey–Luis "Angel" Firpo fight, remains one of the most significant sports photos ever taken. *News* readers could see in the dark as Dempsey fell backward through the ropes, landing on the typewriter of a ringside reporter. (Christy Walsh claimed Dempsey landed in his lap.)

As image gained ascendency over word, one author lamented in *Harper's Magazine*, "We can no longer see the ideas for the illustrations." But newspapers were still limited to printing next-day photos of events within the delivery range of daredevil motorcycle drivers and carrier pigeons. Engineers had been experimenting with how to send pictures by wire since the mid-1880s, but it wasn't until 1920 that Bell Laboratories invented the first fax machine, capable of transmitting an image; it was used to send fingerprints of a suspect wanted in a crime from New York to Cleveland in 1924—and as a result the coppers got their man. AT&T debuted the first commercial "telephotography system" in 1925, with sending and receiving stations in eight major cities. Transmission was unreliable due to breaks in telephone connections, however, and the venture proved commercially unviable.

On January 2, 1925, the *Chicago Tribune* trumpeted the debut of its Telepix system with a front-page story: "Telepix Beats Time, Space with Pictures." Photos from Notre Dame's victory over Stanford appeared on the back page that had been transmitted through telegraph wires as a series of dots and filled in by artists at the other end of the line.

Seven months later, a photograph of Babe Ruth's mistress was sent via Telepix from New York to Chicago to Los Angeles and beyond. In May, 1927, the *Daily News* filled six inside pages with photos of Lindbergh's landing in Paris sent across the ocean with the same technology.

And yet it wasn't until January 1, 1935, when the Associated Press unveiled its Wirephoto service, transmitting an aerial photograph of a plane crash in upstate New York to forty-seven papers in twenty-five states, that images became instantly and reliably available.

The quality of those images had improved, too, thanks to more manageable equipment and more sensitive film. The age of miniaturization had dawned in 1925 with the arrival of a 35mm Leica camera small enough to fit in your pocket but capable of producing newspaper-quality enlargements. It was followed three years later by a miniature from Ermanox that allowed sports photographers to capture fast-moving action.

Daily News photographer Tom Howard, a wartime comrade of Joe Patterson's, strapped one of those miniature cameras to his ankle and used it to capture the death of the notorious murderess Ruth Brown Snyder in the electric chair at Sing Sing in 1928.

The *News* printed an extra edition with a photo of the newly deceased and a one-word headline: "DEAD!"

If the twenties roared, it was in large part because of new means of amplification: bylined sports columns, screaming tabloid headlines, and radio frequencies that broadcast voices with unforeseen clarity from sea to shining sea, and beyond. Fame got bigger, louder, more personal.

That's why the story about ladies of the evening accompanying the Babe to Penn Station on the morning of October 11, 1927, would have legs whether or not it was true. Paul Gallico said as much in his September 3 column in the *Daily News*. "Ruth without temptations might be a pretty ordinary fellow. Part of his charm lies in the manner with which he succumbs to every temptation that comes his way. . . . Ruth is either planning to come loose, is cutting loose, or is repenting the last time he cut loose. He is a news story on legs going about looking for a place to happen."

Because Ruth made it his business to make the unbelievable believable, everyone believed everything they read and heard about him. Teammates who weren't at Penn Station that morning would recount the scene to sportswriters who weren't there who would write it anyway because it sounded true and surely could have been true. Those writers would add details like an early-morning departure, which it was not, and the cloud of cigar smoke curling above the Babe's head, which there might well have been, and the inevitable polo coat, which he wasn't wearing, and the big squeeze he gave Mama Gehrig, who was, in fact, still recuperating from goiter surgery at St. Vincent's Hospital, promising to make sure her son wrote home every day.

As if her Louie needed to be told.

Besides, they'd be on their way back to the city an hour after the game, which left plenty of time to visit the hospital before playing the Bushwicks on Wednesday afternoon at Dexter Park, on the border between Brooklyn and Queens.

IV

This was the third postseason tour Walsh had organized for the Babe and by far the most ambitious—twenty-one cities in less than three weeks. By now he had the formula down. At every stop, Ruth and Gehrig would visit hospitals and orphanages, attend luncheons and banquets—hosted most often by the Elks or the

Knights of Columbus, organizations to which Ruth belonged—give speeches (written by Walsh), praise local dignitaries, sign autographs (including baseballs left behind as prizes for the winners of student essay-writing contests), conduct pregame hitting exhibitions, and captain teams composed of local semi-pros, bush leaguers, and a few big leaguers in games between the Bustin' Babes and Larrupin' Lous, for which Walsh demanded a guaranteed flat fee. Up front. And never in cash.

In some towns, Walsh recruited newspapers that bought Ruth's columns to sponsor the games, generating this front-page headline in the *Tacoma Ledger* in 1924: "5000 Killed in Battle for Shanghai, *Ledger* Brings Babe Ruth to Tacoma."

"Barnstorming" was an aviator's term. But like the circus and vaudeville and the national pastime, too, Walsh's barnstorming tours derived from the oldest model of communal entertainment—the traveling troubadour. That said, Walsh was doing everything he could to modernize the tour, arranging for still and newsreel cameramen to show up at as many stops as possible, preferably with marching bands and a throng of clamoring boys. He booked radio interviews wherever he could. He sent dispatches to favored writers back in New York who could be counted on to write a column or place an item. He sold *Collier's* magazine on an exclusive story of the tour, inviting its writer John B. Kennedy to join the traveling caravan. *Collier's* would run the story in April, at the beginning of the 1928 season.

He gave exclusives to "girl reporters," whom he could count on for feminine fawning and teary-eyed puffery to round out the Babe's rougher edges. In 1926, he got Lorena Hickok, one of the first women to cover a sports beat for a major newspaper and later the first to receive a byline in the *New York Times*, to coo over Ruth in the society column of the *Minneapolis Tribune*. "What you most notice, after you have become accustomed to his size, are his eyes. Instead of being cold and keen and sharp, they are warm and amber colored and heavy-lidded, as clear and as soft as the eyes of a child."

The train pulled into Trenton's Clinton Street Pennsylvania Railroad Station at 1:00 P.M. Walsh, Gehrig, and Ruth were met by the enterprising promoters: George Giasco, described in the press as a prominent Trenton athlete, and Joe Plumeri, the businessman who had slipped those ten $100 bills into Ruth's paw outside Yankee Stadium. They had recruited Nat Strong's Brooklyn Royal Giants of the Eastern Colored League to oppose

Ruth and Gehrig, who would play with a collection of locals. The featured matchup was: the Babe versus Cannonball Dick Redding, the player-manager of the Royal Giants, who at age thirty-six was far past his prime but still capable of throwing a no-hitter, as he had in August. Redding had Chino Smith, the league's batting champion, on his roster, but not much else. The Royal Giants had finished last in their league with a record of 15-31. And they came cheap.

Giasco would talk to Cannonball before the game about ensuring a good show: "Now look, you know why all these people are here. You know what they came to see. They're out here to see Ruth hit home runs, right?"

"Right."

"Now, when the Babe comes to bat, no funny business."

"Got ya. Right down the pike."

Ruth had faced Redding for the first time seven years earlier at Shibe Park in Philadelphia at the end of his first season with the Yankees, when both were at the height of their powers. Ruth went 2 for 4, "walloping the leather over the right-field wall into the Twentieth Street in the seventh inning," Baltimore's *Afro-American* reported.

The next time was in Red Bank, New Jersey, five

years later in a barnstorming game between the Royal Giants and a local team featuring two ringers named Ruth and Gehrig. Giants second baseman Dick Seay, a rookie then, told Negro League historian John Holway: "Ninth inning. We had them by one run. A man got on, and Ruth was up. They said, 'Walk Ruth,' but he didn't listen. He threw one to Ruth, tried to get it by him, and Ruth hit it into the next county, I think."

They met again in 1926 in an exhibition game matching the Royal Giants against the Babe and eight of his Yankee teammates. Ruth got three hits, but his boys lost 3–1.

These intermittent confrontations played on uneven playing fields with uneven rosters offer a kind of historical amuse-bouche, a taste of what might have been had the best African American players been allowed to compete on an even playing field in major-league baseball. No matter how many home runs Ruth hit off Redding that afternoon—three!—on pitches that either were or were not grooved, nothing was going to change Ruth's opinion, which he shared with the *Pittsburgh Courier* when Cannonball finally retired in 1933: "Cannonball Dick Redding could have graced the roster of any big-league club."

The game was scheduled for 3:30 P.M., which left just enough time for a handshake and a photo at the

State House with Governor A. Harry Moore, where 150 stenographers formed an impromptu receiving line, then off to the Knights of Columbus headquarters to change into uniforms.

Cameras and moving-picture machines waited for them on the steps of the capitol's west wing.

"Meet Lou Gehrig, Gov," Ruth said by way of introduction.

Gehrig blushed. "The kid don't say much," Ruth explained.

In the photo, Ruth stood front and center, clasping the governor's hand. Gehrig, who was named the Most Valuable Player in the major leagues that very afternoon, was relegated to the side.

The caption identified the dapper gentleman standing behind Moore as "the business manager" of the Home Run Twins' barnstorming tour. That was where Walsh wanted to be, occupying the role he had created for himself, unnamed but acknowledged, presiding over the fray. But he wasn't the man in the picture. The editors got it wrong, a case of mistaken identity—which can happen when you're the fella behind the Big Fella. Walsh made sure it wasn't a regular occurrence.

Chapter 4
October 12 / Cityline

FANS' RUSH ON RUTH AGAIN HALTS GAME
RUTH'S ATTEMPT TO ATONE FOR DISAPPOINTMENT
BY APPEARING IN BOX CAUSES STAMPEDE
—NEW YORK TIMES

**INSTINCTIVE KNOWLEDGE OF MOB
PSYCHOLOGY IS SECRET OF RUTH SUCCESS**
—BROOKLYN DAILY EAGLE

I

On Columbus Day, the 435th anniversary of the discovery of the New World, the outfield at Dexter Park was roped off in anticipation of a standing-room-only crowd. Banks and schools and the stock exchanges were closed. Max Rosner, Hungarian immigrant, former butcher and cigar roller, now owner of the ballpark and the team that inhabited it, knew to expect a big turnout. Rosner had been fielding teams at Dexter Park, the Brooklyn ballpark that wasn't really in Brooklyn, since 1911.

Before Dexter Park became home to the Bush-wicks, the semi-pro baseball team Rosner named for his Brooklyn neighborhood, and home to Nat Strong's Brooklyn Royal Giants; before it became a playground for skeet and pigeon shooters; before the beer baron William Ulmer arrived to quench the thirst of picnick-ers who filled the taverns, hotels, ballrooms, and dance halls on the premises and bowled and rode the carousel in the amusement park where thoroughbreds once ran; before Union soldiers encamped on the grounds; before all that there was a racetrack at the intersection of El-dert Lane and Jamaica Avenue, just east of the Brook-lyn city line in the borough of Queens, where racing was legalized (and betting tolerated) in 1821. On the map, they called the neighborhood Woodhaven. Regu-lar people called it Cityline.

The Union Race Course was the first dirt track in the nation and home to Dexter, a four-legged nineteenth-century superstar known for setting records and defying convention. The big bay with four socks, a blaze on his nose, and a lot of flash was trained by the great Hiram Woodruff, who operated a hotel on the premises. Currier & Ives memorialized their feats in a series of lithographs: "The Celebrated Horse Dexter, 'The King of the Turf,'" "Going to the Trot," and "Coming from the Trot." Daniel Webster had frequented the place; Oliver Wendell Holmes composed odes to its steeds.

Unlike the genial Babe, who drew people to him, Dexter's disposition was "so wicked that he had to be gelded," the *New York Times* noted in his obituary. Also, unlike the Babe, Dexter had objected to trivial exhibitions of prowess. One September day in 1869, between races at another Long Island course, Dexter had been called on to entertain the crowd. Breaking away from his young handler, he dashed across the field at world-record speed, crashing into the stable with such force that he split the doors and wrecked the sulky he was dragging behind him. He then proceeded to circle the mile-long track in 2:21.

According to legend, this son of Hambletonian was buried beneath an incline in the outfield of the ballpark that bore his name. Locals called it Horse Heaven.

By game time on the afternoon of October 12, there were five to six thousand people jockeying for position in Horse Heaven. The gates had opened at noon. When Ruth and Gehrig emerged from the dugout wearing their spanking new Bustin' Babes and Larrupin' Lous uniforms for the first time in competition, every seat in the sixty-five-hundred-seat concrete-and-steel grand-stand was taken. The bleachers, with room for two thousand more fans, were packed. Even the old dance pavilions on the grounds were overflowing.

Newspapers variously estimated the crowd at between 20,000 and 26,000. It was the biggest crowd at Dexter Park since 60,000 spectators showed up for a match race at the old Union Course in 1823. Special ground rules would be needed.

Dexter Park was no bandbox. The outfield dimensions were major league: 430 feet in left field, 418 in left center, 431 in center field, 443 in right center, and 310 feet in right field. Beyond the left field wall lay Cypress Hills Cemetery, where Hiram Woodruff, Piet Mondrian, Mae West, and Jack Roosevelt Robinson would find their final resting places. Beyond the right field fence houses with front porches afforded a fine view of the action; their windows offered prime targets during batting practice. Rosner happily paid for the broken glass.

He and Strong offered something you couldn't see in major-league ballparks—the best African American players of their time in competition against Rosner's big-time semi-pro outfit—"Big League Baseball at Workingman's Rates." They made Dexter Park into a multi-sport venue, hosting football games and soccer matches and boxing cards. Just the night before, the cancellation of a fight between welterweights K. O. Phil Kaplan and Lew Chester resulted in a near riot requiring the intervention of thirty-five of New York's Finest.

By the time batting practice ended, Tommy Holmes reported in the *Eagle*, the "standees and sittees on the greensward" were already straining against the ropes separating them from the outfielders trying to assume their positions. "Sorties beyond the limit prescribed by the gallant but insufficient police" began as soon as the umpire cried, "Play ball."

Pitch by pitch, inning by inning, the mass inched forward, encroaching on the field, on the players, on batted balls, drawn by the irresistible force stationed at first base for the Bustin' Babes. Surveying the jostling mass of humanity, Holmes realized he was witnessing something new. Ruth exerted a magnetic pull. It was no longer enough to see him, Holmes observed. "They wanted to get within 'touching' distance of him."

The day before, in Trenton, where the crowd was smaller—thirty-five hundred officially, plus another three thousand or so schoolboys—Ruth twice circled the bases with children clinging to his arms and wrapped around his legs. "Oh, you Babe! Oh, you Babe!" they cried.

It had taken him ten minutes to make it around the bases and at least that long for the police to clear the field. After his third home run off Dick Redding, an army of boys chased him into the dugout, where he fell, heaving and sweating, into the laps of sportswriters and Mayor Donnelly of Trenton, who was attending his first game in thirty years in hopes of persuading Ruth to return for a Halloween celebration.

"My God, they scared me stiff," Ruth said, taking a minute to catch his breath and regain his equanimity. He wasn't afraid for himself, he explained quickly. "I was afraid I would trample one of them—these spiked shoes would cut a kid's shoes off."

Two spectators were injured in the melee: Thomas Margino, fifteen, and Frank Carkowsky, forty-eight, were treated at St. Francis Hospital.

It was a feature of a new kind of celebrity sweeping the nation. Just a year earlier, seventy-five mourners were injured in the swollen mob—a hundred thousand strong—that gathered outside Frank E. Campbell's Funeral Parlor on Broadway after Rudolph Valentino's death. Two women attempted suicide at the hospital where he died; two European fans succeeded in their attempts.

But the really extraordinary thing in Ruth's case, Holmes realized, was his élan in the face of the onslaught. In fact, he appeared to *welcome* the claustrophobia of his particular fame. "It's an old story in Babe Ruth's life. He's been mobbed before and learned years ago how to receive an over-enthusiastic crowd," Holmes wrote. "Crowds can't annoy the Babe. Nothing can annoy him down on the field. The mob may be with him in a manner to drive another ball player crazy, but the Babe never loses his good humor."

He wondered just what it was Ruth had learned under the tutelage of the good brothers of St. Mary's. He doubted they had offered classes in mass psychology or French, though he hailed Ruth's "noblesse obliges." "Somewhere and somehow, Babe has learned how to make people, whether individuals or in mass formation, like him. Instinctively, perhaps, the home-run king is a consummate showman and one who never fails to give his idolizing followers a real run for their dough."

It was a seminal column, perhaps the first to explore in depth how Ruth and Walsh devised a new template for how to be famous in America. A happy confluence of factors—timing, technology, economics, personality, unprecedented skill, and the fierce determination to exploit it fully on and off the field—conspired to transform Ruth into what the *New Yorker*'s Roger Angell called "the model for modern celebrity."

And he was uniquely qualified to fill the role just as he filled every ballpark in America. The boy who had created a life for himself at St. Mary's already had plenty of practical experience in creating a public life and *persona*—a word that entered the lexicon of fame when he was a teenager.

When he left St. Mary's in 1914 to enter the public realm, reporters made much of the fact that he had never ridden a bike or an elevator or eaten a steak. They missed the point. At St. Mary's he had never gone to the bathroom without company, never slept in a room by himself. Being public was all he knew. It was his norm. And as a result, his daughter Julia would say decades later, he could not stand to be alone.

II

St. Mary's Industrial School stood sentinel at the top of a gentle rise where Baltimore City ended and Baltimore County began. A large circular drive led to the front entrance and intruded on the avenue, forcing a deviation in its otherwise straight path, one indication of the power of the Church in the city and in the lives of the boys who crossed St. Mary's threshold.

Victorian in attitude and architecture, the impregnable structure with a mansard roof and a 120-foot Empire tower, adorned with a 45-foot flagpole and crowned by a cross, was at odds with the pastoral setting that greeted George Ruth on June 13, 1902. The rural campus was three miles and a world away from his scruffy urban home. Occupying a hundred verdant acres donated to the archdiocese by Miss Emily Caton McTavish, granddaughter of Charles Carroll, one of the signers of the Declaration of Independence, the buildings, constructed with stone quarried from the surrounding fields, erupted from an otherwise placid landscape where cattle grazed, wheat defied a spring drought, and boys played baseball.

The dour gray granite building stood five stories high and 136 feet wide. It spoke to seriousness of purpose, a solidity that was both reassuring and intimidating— penal in affect. What one newly ordained member of the Xaverian Order, Brother Arcadius Alkonis, would remember about arriving there on his first night was the bars on the windows.

Newly installed electric lights in the common rooms illuminated the austerity of the place. The crystal chandeliers added to brighten the premises failed to dilute its bleakness. To enter St. Mary's was to surrender freedom and light.

George Ruth never shared his first impressions of St. Mary's with his family. He never spoke about what it was like to go from being one of two surviving children in a family defined by loss to being one of the many, what it was to go to bed that night wondering when or if he'd see that family again. He never said what it was like to sleep in ordered rows and dress in matching clothes, to share sinks and stalls in a communal washroom, to surrender to a system predicated on uniformity and routine.

It couldn't have been easy. Even then he had within him the makings of distinction. He couldn't help standing out. He was younger than he knew, his mother having confused the year of his birth, but bigger than everyone else, an awkward, gawky, hollow-cheeked boy with a toothy grin presumably not much in evidence that day, a grin that always looked as if he had happiness clenched between his teeth.

"If you ever wanted to see a bone out of joint or one of nature's misfits, you should have seen him," Brother Gilbert told sportswriter Frank Graham.

His ears stuck out. Like handles on a loving cup, one writer said. His hair stuck up. His nostrils spread wide. His lips were as full as the rest of him would become. He was dark complected, having inherited his olive skin from his mother's side of the family. In the rough tongue of the playground, he quickly acquired a nickname: Nigger Lips, or Nig, for short.

The only account of the day he arrived was the one young Westbrook Pegler had confected out of thin air in a New York City apartment. By the time he got around to admitting twenty-five years later that he had made it all up, the myth had morphed into bedrock.

Pegler imagined a boy escorted to the institution by his father, not a beat cop. He imagined that boy awash in tears and his unrequited pleas to go home. He imagined a family that didn't exist and a magical savior who appeared deus ex machina at his bedside that first night, offering the salvation of baseball.

I was a pretty homesick kid along sundown. I could see the family gathered about the table for supper and my chair empty, and I was wondering whether they missed me as much as I missed them. . . .

I went to bed in the strange dormitory feeling as though I had been sold out by my best friends.

"What's the matter, Babe?"

I looked up from my pillow in the darkness there, to see a great six-foot-six man standing over me. He said it in a whisper because he knew that one kid would be sensitive about having the others know him to be homesick. . . .

Anyway, he told me he was coach of the ball club and advised me to come out and try for a place on the team. I knew I was going to like this kindly, understanding big friend. But I couldn't foresee, of course, that he was going to coach me along into the big leagues and make [me] the home run champion.

III

On August 17, 1866, four members of the Congregation of St. Francis Xavier, a Belgian lay teaching order, arrived in southwest Baltimore to find a hundred acres of untamed woodlands with a single, unfinished wooden shanty abandoned by Federal troops. They had been invited by Archbishop Martin Spalding to build a school for boys orphaned during the Civil War.

The brothers were industrious. They cleared the land and tilled the soil, hoping for a self-sufficiency that would never be achieved. They built dormitories where the boys would learn to do without privacy, and classrooms where they would learn their ABCs and perfect their handwriting—a skill that would serve George Ruth well.

By the time he arrived, the brothers had added a hennery, a piggery, and two libraries. They had acquired musical instruments and paraded members of the nationally recognized St. Mary's band in Johnny Reb uniforms in front of a brigade of '61 veterans in Theodore Roosevelt's inaugural parade.

In 1902, they built three new greenhouses so that they could cultivate and sell carnations and chrysanthemums all year round. They constructed a new 110-foot-long stone barn big enough to house fifty-six steers. Four years later, they added ten more steers and a four-story concrete building for manual training, where George Ruth learned to become a tailor. The window looked down on home plate.

St. Mary's was one of nine orphanages and two reformatories created by the Catholic Church in Baltimore between 1850 and 1890. It was unique among the religious institutions created to care for what Baltimore industrialist Alex Brown called "the broken wreckage of industrial society," because it was funded by Baltimore City and the state of Maryland. Founded by the archbishop as a refuge for Catholic boys who faced bias in public institutions, St. Mary's became a nondenominational public charity eight years later, when it was incorporated by the city and state as a place to settle vagrant and homeless boys.

The state and city were given three seats each on the school board in exchange for public funding. In 1882, when the legislature expanded St. Mary's purview to allow parents to apply to a justice of the peace to commit a child they deemed beyond their control, they were required, as a condition of admission, to designate the school superintendent as legal guardian.

The boys, who were allowed to go home for ten days at Christmas, adopted the language of incarceration to describe themselves. After 1937, when the state of Maryland designated St. Mary's as the repository for youthful offenders sentenced by the courts and the school accepted no other students, the language caught up with the reality of the place. Until 1940, the rate of parole violators was less than 5 percent. Twenty thousand boys were processed through St. Mary's by the time the state withdrew its support in 1950, having concluded that the institution violated separation of church and state.

Because St. Mary's accepted orphans, and perhaps because the adult George Ruth said so little about his parents, many writers, teammates, and friends assumed he was an orphan, an assumption he did his best to quell. He had a good mother and father, he protested, having forgotten which parent had died when. "Get me right now, I'm no orphan!" he barked at Harry T.

Brundidge of the *St. Louis Star* in May 1929. "All that stuff about my being an orphan kid, too tough for my aunts and uncle to handle, and about being shoved into a reform school for bringing up are a lot of boloney, just plain, every-day applesauce and hooey."

His protestations were to no avail. His visage can be seen today on highway billboards and airport video screens, courtesy of the Foundation for a Better Life, a nonprofit organization dedicated to creating inspirational public service campaigns, hailing the drive that propelled him "from orphanage to the Hall of Fame."

Because St. Mary's accepted "incorrigibles"—and perhaps because George Ruth was delivered to the moral hospital in the custody of a Baltimore City police officer—others would conclude he had been committed to the institution by court order. Although multiple biographies refer to a friendly, unnamed magistrate who provided the legal basis for his commitment, no documentation of such an order has ever been produced. None was found among the writs of habeas corpus on file at the Maryland State Archives. No public notice was published in the *Baltimore Sun*, customary when underage offenders were sent by the courts.

More to the point, his sister Mamie Ruth Moberly was adamant that George Ruth Sr. paid tuition, making his son one of 110 boarding students admitted to

St. Mary's in 1902. "Daddy had to pay for Babe to be out there," she said. "Orphans was different. Babe was different. He still had a daddy."

The single handwritten ledger to survive the 1919 St. Mary's fire did not note whether George Ruth paid tuition for his son, which the archivist at Catholic Charities said was the norm. In the absence of definitive information, history rendered its verdict: "I was a bad kid" is the first line of his *The Babe Ruth Story*. That would become the subtext of his life.

"They told him he was a bad boy, so he grew up thinking he was a bad boy," his daughter Julia recalled.

"When I was small I suppose I was raising the devil more or less," he would tell a reporter two years after his release from St. Mary's. "At least that is what *they* said."

His occasional protestations and frustrations fell on deaf reportorial ears. "All that stuff about my being a tough kid is boloney, too," he told Brundidge. "I was a pretty good kid when my old man decided I would be better off in St. Mary's Industrial Home, a Catholic school in Baltimore, because the fathers would keep an eye on me better than he could. I was just six years old when I went to that place, and it wasn't a reform school either. It was a good place. There's been a lot of talk about my being a hell-raiser in St. Mary's and that the brothers were glad to get rid of me, but you can put it down in your paper that some of the brothers cried when I left there. I'd been there so long. I didn't get in any more trouble than any other boy, although I didn't fall for all the rules and regulations but nobody else did."

IV

For the ancients—that is, anyone born before the twenties—gods and saints were celebrities. In the twenties, celebrities became gods. Virtue was passé. Celebrity was no longer predicated on skill but, as Tommy Holmes observed in the *Eagle* on personality:

"Commonly described as a red-necked, strong-arm guy who might be driving a truck were he not freighted with the ability of hitting a baseball harder than any other living man, Ruth nevertheless has personality—an attractive, vivid, compelling personality—to everyone who comes into the slightest contact with him. The Ruthian personality as much as the Ruthian wallop is responsible for the Babe being the greatest figure baseball ever had."

Ruth occupied a unique position in the pantheon of the new American elect. He was a willing, even joyful collaborator in the construction and marketing of his public persona, "the first athlete to be sold as much for his color, personality and crowd appeal" in the words of Grantland Rice, unofficial mythologist of the golden age of sports.

And he was the first athlete to be recognized as an entertainer who transcended and expanded the parameters of athletic fame. The usually understated W. O. McGeehan compared him favorably to Chaplin in a June 1927 column in the *New York Tribune*, writing, "If there were any way of appraising the drawing power of the Babe I think that he would be shown to be the greatest money maker as an entertainer for all time."

This marked a profound shift in the perception of athletes as performers. If, as the historian Ann Douglas argues in *Terrible Honesty: Mongrel Manhattan in the 1920s*, Ruth was responsible for the annexation of sports "by the burgeoning entertainment industry," then why shouldn't they be able to argue, as Walsh prompted Ruth to do, that he should be paid not just for what he did at the ballpark but for who he brought to the ballpark? He was creating a whole new fan base. People who didn't know or care where first base was needed to see and be seen with Babe Ruth. He was the reason Jake Ruppert had just announced that seven thousand new seats would be added to the ballpark by opening day.

People like Vin Scully's mother, a redheaded Irish girl just off the boat whose new beau took her to Yankee Stadium to learn about America. "One of the first things he said was, 'You must see Babe Ruth,'" said her son, who would become a defining voice of the game. "She had no idea what baseball was about. But that's how important it was. One of the first things this American wanted to show an immigrant was Babe Ruth."

Ruth always envisioned for himself a bigger kind of stardom than baseball afforded. When he didn't like Red Sox owner Harry Frazee's salary offer for 1920, he took himself to Hollywood and allowed his winter secretary to let it be known that he might just abandon baseball for the soundstage. In 1922, "Ruthing" became a verb in *Motion Picture News* reviews touting "box office home runs." In 1923, Heywood Broun of the *New York World* cast him as a fictional left fielder named Tiny Tyler, whose only weakness is "a fast blond on the outside corner of the park," a line far less remembered than his lede after Game 2 of the 1923 World Series: "The Ruth Is Mighty and Shall Prevail."

Ruth was the perfect hero for an unprecedented time because he, too, was unprecedented. He was unexplainable by any precedent other than himself. And in the 1920s, newness was everything and everything seemed new: IQ tests and opinion polls; sex ed, sex appeal, and birth control clinics; neon signs and skywriting; social X-rays, and acting out, a Freudian term of art that might have been invented for Babe Ruth.

Like all the newfangled consumer gadgets then flooding the marketplace—radios, Victrolas, automatic clothes washers, vacuum cleaners, pop-up toasters, do-it-yourself television kits—Ruth expanded notions of the possible.

It was his good fortune to become famous at the precise moment in history when mass media was redefining and amplifying what it meant to be public, and when societal upheaval was creating a new caste system for celebrity. Among the casualties of the Great War were old money and the old aristocracy; out of the ashes rose consumerism and marketing and a new, more equitable American star system featuring rags-to-riches heroes: Babe Ruth, Jack Dempsey, Clara Bow, and Rudolph Valentino. Their ascendance from lower stations, palpable need for public approbation, personal tragedies, and failings—and, critically, their triumphs over those tragedies and failings—affirmed the animating principle of the American dream.

If the twenties were a monument to modern man's creative capacity for mischief, as E. B. White wrote, Ruth was the chief mischief-maker. In a city of rule breakers—everyone who bent an elbow in 1927 was breaking the law of the land—he was rule breaker in chief. He never embodied the traditional public virtues that defined ancient celebrity, and he didn't have to. Instead, he gave the public glimpses of a bad boy having the time of his life. Hadn't they told him he was a bad boy? He did his adult best to fulfill the mandate: punching out umps, chasing after boobirds in the grandstand, driving the wrong way up a one-way street ("I'm only going one way!"), sleeping with other men's wives but ignoring his own. Everybody loved, forgave, and maybe envied the Babe for being himself.

"Babe was an internationally innovative figure in the new twentieth-century stardom precisely because he was never qualified to fulfill the expectation of virtue," explained Hans Gumbrecht, the author of *In 1926: Living at the Edge of Time,* a panoramic study of life on the cusp of the twentieth century's most transformative year. "This made the non-virtuous side of his private life interesting and authentic. Unlike a saint he was somebody whose life people could compare themselves to. He could sail through weaker seasons because of the interest in who he slept with, how much he ate, what he lost gambling, what caused his stomachaches. This was a first."

In virginal, tightfisted Columbia Lou, Ruth—and

Walsh—had the perfect foil. He was a mama's boy; Ruth was the motherless man-child who gratefully guzzled the pickled eels Mom Gehrig prepared for her Louie and his pal Babe. Though eight years Ruth's junior, Gehrig represented a passé kind of fame— "pre-stardom," Gumbrecht called it. "There was little interest in the Ironman's private life in part because he didn't have much of one until disease gave him some charisma."

The *New Yorker* dismissed him with the cruelest cut a celebrity-conscious magazine could muster: as unfit "in any way to have a public."

"The Bambino," on the other hand, John Kieran opined in the *New York Times*, "does not have to step out of character to be what he is—an appealing, swashbuckling, roistering, boisterous figure who is as natural a showman as the late Phineas T. Barnum."

Visionary though he was, Christy Walsh couldn't have foreseen that a century after the fact historians would be analyzing, hailing, and occasionally bemoaning his precedent-setting partnership with Ruth. But what Walsh did understand was this: stars were no longer marketed just for their specific skills, but for themselves.

The 1926 promotional flyer he drew advertising his services featured a halo of stars with the names of his celestial clients inscribed within—Frank Carideo, Hunk Anderson, Pop Warner, John McGraw, Tad Jones, A. A. Stagg, Connie Mack, Babe Ruth, Nick Altrock, We Mean Well (a thoroughbred), Lou Gehrig, and Dean Crowell:

> Stars available for personal appearance, Merchandise Endorsements, Exhibition Baseball Games, Vaudeville, Moving Pictures, Radio and All Forms of Commercial Contracts, under Christy Walsh Management.

Walsh recognized the public's desire to know the people behind the flickering images and the crackling voices, to be near them, to be like them, to experience their "personal appearance." Notions of stardom—and what it meant to be famous in America—were evolving as quickly as the technology of mass communication. The vocabulary of fame hustled to keep up: "celeb" was becoming slang just as Ruth was leaving St. Mary's. The United Press anointed him "a star" two months before his major-league debut. Grantland Rice elevated him to the rank of a "superstar in an age of stars" in 1919, four years after the superlative was coined by hockey innovators Frank and Lester Patrick for their superstar wingman, Cyclone Taylor. Ruth's home-run spree in September 1927 prompted Paul Gallico to advocate the retirement of the word "super"—Ruth had made it superfluous. "These supers don't last," Gallico lamented in the *Daily News*.

It was a speeded-up time: the dawn of hectic and hurry. The city was changing at breakneck speed, which is how Ruth lived, setting a pedal-to-the-metal example for the rest of the country. Walter Winchell popularized "the Big Apple" in a column proclaiming the city as "the pot of gold at the end of a drab and somewhat colorless rainbow." The city even smelled different—modern. The first espresso machine in the city perked up Greenwich Village. Carbon monoxide flooded the streets, replacing the earthy odor of manure. The clip-clop of horseshoes on cobblestones was drowned out by the honking horns of cars—27 million of which would be on American roads by 1929.

Returning to New York after an absence of three years, F. Scott Fitzgerald described the change in his 1932 short story "My Lost City": "The restlessness of New York in 1927 approached hysteria. The parties were bigger . . . the pace was faster—the catering to dissipation set an example to Paris; the shows were broader, the buildings were higher, the morals were looser, and the liquor was cheaper."

No one lived bigger, faster, or looser than Ruth. Take the week of September 11, 1927:

On Monday, September 12, his only day off, Ruth appeared in court to face charges that he had assaulted a cripple at the corner of Seventy-second Street and Broadway. On Tuesday, the Yankees clinched the pennant and Ruth hit his fifty-first and fifty-second home runs. On Wednesday, he hit his fifty-third home run. On Thursday morning, he filmed a cameo at the Hebrew Orphan Asylum in Upper Manhattan for Harold Lloyd's final silent film, *Speedy*, an homage to the last horse-drawn taxicab in New York.

Lloyd was a baseball fan and one of Walsh's Hollywood connections. He paid Ruth $5,750 for a morning's work, featuring a harrowing ride to the Bronx in a half-cab created to allow for tracking shots.

Delivered somewhat safely to the stadium, Ruth went 1 for 4 with a double and a run scored.

The next day, Ruth was cleared of charges in the assault case and carried from the courtroom on the shoulders of his ardent admirers.

It wasn't just the tempo of the city that had changed. The tempo of change itself had accelerated. It was as revolutionary a moment in technology and perception as the advent of the computer age would be seventy-five years later. Electrified, the countryside outshone the stars. Aviation and radio altered the fundamental experience of time and space. The world seemed to be getting at once bigger and smaller every day.

When Ruth was a Red Sox rookie in 1914, stardom was local, a small print story, circumscribed by distribution of the daily newspaper and the 11.94 words of the average telegram. Fame for the most part was historical, after the fact. Seven years later, communications were still so low tech that fans living on the East Side of Manhattan persuaded Charles Farbizo, a neighborhood resident, to take his flock of carrier pigeons to the Polo Grounds and send inning-by-inning dispatches from the four-game series between the Yankees and the Cleveland Indians that would decide the 1921 American League pennant. Ruth was photographed releasing one of the pigeons on September 26. Farbizo promised to make himself available for the World Series, Ruth's first as a Yankee.

By 1927, pigeons were has-beens. Airmail was in the wind. Voices were in the ether. The first words of the commercial radio age were uttered at 6:00 P.M. on November 2, 1920, from the Pittsburgh studio of station KDKA: "Is anyone listening out there?" Seven years later, Leo Rosenberg's question was answered with a resounding yes. The NBC radio network went live on New Year's Day 1927 at a gala at the Waldorf-Astoria with a signal that reached as far as Kansas City. Everybody who was anybody was there—except Ruth, who was starring in a vaudeville show at the Pantages Theater in San Francisco with boxer James J. Corbett.

That month, the first telephone call between London and New York was placed from the AT&T building at 195 Broadway. (It cost seventy-five dollars for a three-minute call.) And Philo T. Farnsworth filed patent application no. 1,773,980 for an "image dissector tube" he called a "television system."

On April 7, the smiling image of Secretary of Commerce Herbert Hoover was beamed from Washington, D.C., to AT&T headquarters on a 2 by 2½-inch screen, the first demonstration of television technology. "Human genius has now destroyed the impediment of distance in a new respect," Hoover told the company execs and scribes gathered to witness the event.

The Yankees opened their season at the Stadium on April 12 with Graham McNamee, the father of play-by-play, interviewing Ruth from a bunting-draped field box—a first in what would become ubiquitous pregame radio shows. The Yankees allowed the game against the Philadelphia A's to be broadcast, the only one that season. Unlike their counterparts in Chicago, which began broadcasting Cubs and White Sox games daily in 1924, the Yankees were slow to grasp the advantages of building a radio audience and the advertising revenues that would come with it. Their season would conclude with the first coast-to-coast broadcast of the World Series, carried by two national radio networks, NBC and CBS.

Although thousands of baseball fans still craned their necks to follow the games on newspaper scoreboards in Times Square, the new locus of the printed word, thousands more brought traffic to a standstill on Radio Row on Cortlandt Street on the Lower West Side, home to a growing stretch of radio shops.

The ink-stained wretches in the press box furiously feeding copy into the newest teletype machines—capable of transmitting forty words a minute—were too busy and too self-involved to realize that this marked the end of their dominion. Nearly 250 daily newspapers would fold in the ten years following the birth of network radio in 1927. The future was at hand. Now on sale from Brush Research Laboratories in Zanesville, Ohio: the "Mystic" Radio Bug and headset, a miniature, ceramic crystal radio made to look like an insect with prototypical earbuds that required neither batteries nor electrical current to operate.

In May, Fox Movietone used newly acquired

sound-on-film technology to produce the first of two special talking newsreels devoted to Charles Lindbergh: coming attractions for the future. Footage of his May 20 takeoff for Paris premiered five days later at the Sam Harris Theatre in New York. Their cameramen were also on hand to film his welcome home ceremony at the foot of the Washington Monument when he received the first Distinguished Flying Cross from President Coolidge. The ten-minute newsreel, narrated by McNamee, was distributed to theaters throughout the country for the benefit of those who'd been unable to listen to NBC's live broadcast of the event—a first in broadcast history, which required linking eighty-two radio stations and twelve thousand miles of telephone cable.

Three months later, McNamee spoke to an even larger audience, an estimated 50 million people who tuned in to hear his blow-by-blow account of the Dempsey-Tunney heavyweight fight in Chicago on September 22. His voice was heard at sheep stations in the Australian outback, on an iceberg in Greenland, in the United States Marine Corps regiment headquarters in Shanghai, and in Babe Ruth's living room in Manhattan.

Ruth, who had hit his fifty-sixth home run that afternoon, missed the "long count" in the seventh round when Dempsey failed to return to a neutral corner and gave Tunney time to recover from the knockdown. He had skipped out on his own party to fulfill a promise that his friend Harry M. Stevens, the Yankee concessionaire, had made to bring Ruth to a charity bazaar for a Catholic church in Westchester. He got back just in time to hear he had lost his bet on Dempsey.

According to *Radio Digest*, 127 listeners dropped dead while listening to the fight.

Sales soared. In the seven years between 1922 and 1929, the number of radio sets in American homes increased from one in every four hundred homes to a third of all American homes. A 1927 survey of listeners in Philadelphia and Buffalo conducted by H. S. Hittinger revealed that more than 60 percent of men and women liked to listen to sports on the radio.

Regularly scheduled radio programming and movie showtimes required daily listings, which became prominent features in every American newspaper. They also required listeners and viewers to be *on time* and *in time*. Grandpa's ponderous pocket watch was relegated to safekeeping with other family heirlooms. The times necessitated—and technology allowed for—a closer relationship with the clock. New quartz wristwatches made time available at the flick of the wrist. A temporal language emerged: buying, spending, borrowing, stealing, marking, wasting, doing, passing, and killing time, the latter being the one thing Ruth rarely did.

Walsh was quick to position Ruth as a man of the moment, signing him to annual endorsement deals for Benrus watches. "It's Jar-Proof!" World Series advertisements in Pennsylvania and Ohio newspapers proclaimed. With "Rustless Steel" parts and "Radiolite dials," the Babe Ruth model, priced at only $37.50, was guaranteed to hug your wrist.

"From the beginning fame has required publicity," Leo Braudy wrote in *The Frenzy of Renown*, the definitive study of fame in America. "In great part the history of fame is the history of the changing ways by which individuals have sought to bring themselves to the attention of others and, not incidentally, have thereby gained power over them."

For Alexander the Great, that meant stamping his visage on the coin of the realm, where only gods had gone before. In the twenties, technology was producing what the historian Warren Susman called "new ways of knowing" almost as quickly as Ruth hit home runs. That also meant new ways of being known.

Everywhere, there were new genres of information. Walsh made it his business to harness all of them in his bid to stamp Ruth's mug on the American consciousness: the back pages of the tabloids, syndicated sports and editorial columns, three-dot gossip columns, and ghostwritten sports columns that fostered the illusion that heroes were talking directly to their fans.

Comic strips, Sunday rotogravure sections, weekly magazines such as *Vanity Fair, The Smart Set,* and the *New Yorker,* whose editors called the city for which it was named a "gymnasium of celebrities."

Radio talk shows and gangster movies and chic urban comedies, book clubs, bestseller lists, and quickie books—Lindbergh's autobiography, *"We,"* published just two months after he landed in Paris, sold 190,000 copies and earned him $200,000.

Hit single records and record charts, neon signs and skywriting, advertising layouts and the packaged public personas of the new celebrities, actors, literary lights, pols, and sports heroes.

Fox Movietone premiered its first biweekly talking newsreels in New York in October 1927 and around the rest of the country in December, with highlights of the Army-Yale football game and a New York City rodeo—a prototype of the sports highlight packages that would dominate TV sports news and fill time between innings at the ballpark. With them came changes in memory. Spectators began to seek verification in the projection and repetition of imagery rather than trust their own recall.

Walsh saw to it that Ruth filled (and occasionally filled in for the authors of) those gossip columns and the ever-expanding airwaves. He would make bad romantic comedies, yak on talk shows, create comic strips to hawk breakfast cereal, and cut gramophone records for the 44 percent of American households with Victrolas. Ruth carried a portable record player with him on every road trip and sometimes staged impromptu concerts. One day in the fall of 1926, he held a barn dance beside a water tank when his train stopped to take on water in Montana.

Ruth and Gehrig recorded a corny six-minute comedy sketch released by Perfect Records, a Pathé label for cheap American 78s, during the 1927 World Series. The writer wisely chose to remain anonymous. Gehrig's Noo Yawk accent and squeaky high voice were so at odds with his corporeal self that people refused to believe he was doing the talking. Ruth's basso profundo was equally surprising. He managed to sound dignified, if not exactly smooth, while engaged in the stilted repartee. He didn't come off at all like the illiterate guttersnipe described in the newspapers.

And he flourished in the camera's lens, lighting

up with the explosion of each magnesium flare. The camera magnified every ridge and invaded every pore, revealing the tobacco stains on his uneven teeth and the crooked bite behind the famous grin. Each blast of powder made his face seem even bigger than it was, which was plenty.

The images were static, setup shots; the paparazzi were still decades in the future. Each of the "exclusive" photographs that Walsh orchestrated—and released to clients of the Christy Walsh Syndicate and stamped "No charge to Babe Ruth papers, not available to others"—was purposeful, intended to create what Gumbrecht calls "a motif of privacy" that fed the public desire to connect with him.

What readers wanted in the twenties—and what newspaper editors needed to fill all those new column inches that Ruth inspired—was freshness. "What is it that is not already known?" said Gumbrecht. "The private life. I think the Babe was probably the first star in the sense that the persona became increasingly fascinating and continued to be fascinating after retirement. . . . Performance triggered the initial interest. But, then at a certain point you began to care."

Walsh made sure Ruth was photographed with every Tinseltown celeb that crossed his path or train platform—Marion Davies, for instance, old man

Hearst's girlfriend, when they changed trains at the same time in Chicago. Her new flick was playing on the same bill with *Babe Comes Home* in Kansas City. Though Walsh had met Hearst only once, his newspaper chain was the Christy Walsh Syndicate's biggest account. No harm staying on his good side.

Not surprisingly, Hollywood was first to recognize the value of marketing a private life as part of a public persona. And Walsh was a Hollywood guy. He saw to it that Ruth's name was dropped liberally in the pages of *Variety*, Hollywood's paper of record, and in movie fan-magazines whose reporters breathlessly recounted his initiation into the biz on the set of *Babe Comes Home*. How the cast and crew (lovingly) tricked him into chasing a wax mouse—Ruth called it a rat—under small pieces of furniture, and (not so amusingly) tricked him into shoving a young boy as part of a scene in order to see if they could make the Big Fella cry. And he did!

Oh, the human interest!

In both his Hollywood features, *Headin' Home*, released in 1920, and *Babe Comes Home*, based on a sportswriter's short story "Said with Soap," he played ballplayers remarkably like himself, the only role he could play, star turns that further eroded the line between public and private and furthered the notion that he was knowable. One month after the release of

Headin' Home, Current Opinion magazine named him "the Most Talked About American."

Every magazine in America—*Time, Vanity Fair, Liberty, Popular Science, American Boy,* and even *Hardware Age*—found a reason to put him on the cover. He was so much in the public domain that a brief retreat in the summer of 1929 set off an anxious search by newspaper photographers and this relieved headline: "Ruth Found After Evading Camera for a Week."

There was no frame he couldn't or wouldn't fill. No pose he wouldn't assume. No one he wouldn't pose with. Posing was the only time he stood still.

He posed with athletes: Dempsey, Tilden, Zaharias, and Ed "the Strangler" Lewis. Generals: Alphonse Jacques of Belgium (outside the Palace Theatre in New York between vaudeville performances in 1921), Marshal Foch of France ("I suppose you were in the war?"), and John J. Pershing. Animals: chimp, greyhound, pigeon, turkey (dead and alive), tortoise, and lobster (on National Lobster Day). Royalty: King Prajadhipok of Siam and Queen Marie of Romania (he told her he was a king, too). Presidents: Coolidge, Harding, Franklin Roosevelt, George H. W. Bush as Yale's first baseman, and Hoover, albeit reluctantly. ("A matter of politics," he said.)

He posed in camel hair, coonskin, camouflage, raccoon coats, and two-piece bathing suits sunbathing on the beach at the Hotel del Coronado, taking his ease before the 1927 season; in silk Sulka ties made especially for him because his neck was too big to buy off the rack, and in an editor's green eyeshade; in monogrammed shirtsleeves and braces, whispering to a white sheet meant to evoke one of his many ghostwriters. In football helmets with Rockne, plus fours with Al Smith, and tennis whites with Bill Tilden.

He welcomed photographers into his home, seated beside his first wife, Helen, at the keyboard of a pump organ he couldn't play; wrestling on the grass with their daughter, Dorothy; and in later years, lying on a hospital gurney beside daughter Julia, donating blood for her when strep throat threatened her life; reclining in his Riverside Drive apartment in his paisley smoking jacket and red silk slippers; and subsumed by thousands and thousands of unnamed children: boys in ball caps and girls in baseball skirts, children on crutches and in wheelchairs, orphans, incorrigibles, and unfortunates, the dying and those who were said to be.

Walsh made sure there were photographers at every orphanage and tubercular asylum they visited. Not that the Babe needed encouragement to pay these calls. At the Glen Lake Sanatorium in Minnesota in 1926, a photographer for the *Minnesota Daily Star* took what may be the least known and most affecting photograph of those visits: the Babe, surrounded by a tribe of sick children clothed only in loincloths. Ruth, who wore "the world as a loose garment," biographer Tom Meany would say later, betrayed no hint of discomfort with their appearance or condition.

Later, on the same tour, at the Firland Sanatorium in Seattle, he assumed his stance in an imaginary batter's box with a young boy perched precariously on a folding chair behind him. Ruth looks toward an imaginary hurler, waiting for an imaginary pitch; the boy, all hollows and ridges, wearing an oversized catcher's glove, an ill-fitting mask, a pair of white shorts, and nothing else, hunches forward, hands out, as if the Babe might actually swing and miss. There is nothing between them, no opportunity for eye contact, just their collusion in creating the odd tableau featuring a boy with a concave chest and a barrel-chested man clothed in the vestments of fame: silk shirt, expensive cuff links, and the Benrus watch he had been paid five hundred dollars to wear.

The photo was intended to document the Babe's good works and good heart, which it did, but it also revealed something far more interesting and far more human, which Marion Badcon, a reporter for the *Seattle Post-Intelligencer*, captured in her description of "a big kid with a lot of smaller ones—a big kid who was a little awkward, a little hesitant, a little touched and very silent before the hundreds of youngsters whom he visited on his round of the children's homes and hospitals."

His moment of timidity—the fraction of a pause before assuming the garrulous persona expected of him—was endearing and authentic. "But he grinned," Badcon wrote. "And the kids grinned back. And then a baseball appeared."

"Deeds put a shine on him—always," Roger Angell would say.

He knew how far he had come from the boy he had been and how fast it had all happened. When it was time to fill out his 1927 application for *Who's Who in America*, he refused to fill in the blank for occupation. "If they don't know," he said, "let them have their best guess."

The evolving technology of illumination and focus, the pop and hiss of every flashbulb exploding in his face, documented how surprised and perhaps grateful he was to be the center of so much attention. Only in the public embrace would he feel completely full.

On those gala evenings when he got all dressed up in a tux with his white silk scarf to greet his public at some banquet or other, his daughter Julia recalled, he would stop at the front door to the apartment to allow for a moment's inspection, asking the women in his life:

"Am I a handsome fella or not?"

Or not.

In that question, in the patent need for approbation beneath the homely mug, people saw themselves, or somebody they knew. They couldn't get close enough to him. But, oh, how they tried.

V

"The first hundreds broke through the ropes in the fifth inning," Tommy Holmes reported.

The precipitating event: Ruth doubled, one of two that cleaved the crowd in Horse Heaven.

Boisterous crowds were nothing new at Dexter Park. Rosner and Strong were savvy promoters and longtime baseball men, each having served the game in various capacities for forty years. They had major-league ambitions and would, six months later, declare their intention to purchase the Dodgers, whom they routinely outdrew, and move them to a new 125,000-seat stadium in Queens. They would install a system for night games, designed by Rosner's electrical engineer son, five years before anything comparable in the major leagues existed.

Strong's teams showcased Oscar Charleston, John Henry Lloyd, Dick Redding, Cristobal Torriente, John Beckwith, Chino Smith, and Smokey Joe Williams. Rosner's teams featured minor leaguers on their way up and major leaguers on their way down—Dazzy Vance and Lefty Grove among them. He bragged he had the best semi-pro talent in the area, though he had turned away a shy young high school first baseman named Lou Gehrig in 1920 when he showed up for a tryout with his baseball gear in a beach bag.

Ruth arrived by cab an hour early for his first visit one November Sunday in 1923 to find Rosner alone in his office in his empty ballpark. He had offered Ruth a choice between a flat fee or a percentage of the gate. "I want to be paid now," Ruth said.

"Wait a while, Babe," Rosner said. "My crowd always comes late."

"Now," boomed the Babe.

Rosner gave him the promised nineteen-hundred-dollar flat fee and Ruth went off to get lunch. By the time he returned, a mob had formed, the stands were full, and he was short the additional four hundred dollars he would have earned had he taken Rosner's offer of a percentage. When the game ended in the gloaming of that late November afternoon, Ruth made his escape, according to a special dispatch in the *Chicago*

Tribune, by seizing the tail of a mounted police horse, which towed him through two thousand celebrants to safety.

That was nothing compared to the free-for-all he faced now, four years later, which was enough to rattle whatever was left of Dexter's bones. "It became so bad that unless an outfielder fielded a ball cleanly the crowd gobbled up the ball," wrote Tommy Holmes. "Every time a fly or grounder went past the infield there was a race between the outfielder and the spectators on the fringe of the crowd. Once Dean, the Bushwicks' right fielder, fumbled and the ball was plucked from under his feet by one of the spectators before he could reach it."

Stan Baumgartner, the Bushwicks' starting pitcher, who played eight years in Philadelphia for the Phillies and A's, pretty much had his way with Ruth and Gehrig, as well as their Yankee teammate Joe Dugan, who was in left for the Babes, and Al Moore, a Brooklyn boy who did time with the Giants in 1925 and 1926.

After Ruth grounded out in the seventh inning, the crowd bellowed its disappointment, realizing they had seen his last turn at bat. They had come to see him hit a home run—and he hadn't been able to manage even one in fifteen batting practice swings.

"Ruth, master showman that he is, made up for

this disappointment by going on the mound to pitch," Holmes wrote.

It was the safest place in the ballpark. Though he hadn't pitched in a major-league game since throwing four innings of relief against the Philadelphia A's on October 1, 1921—one of five games he would pitch for the Yankees, all of which he won—Ruth often sought refuge on the mound during barnstorming games. If he couldn't give the crowd at Dexter Park what they had come to see, he would give them a glimpse of the great left-handed pitcher he had been during the first five years of his career.

Back in Boston, when he was known as "the speed boy," he twice threw more than 320 innings in a 154-game season. He had a lifetime 2.28 ERA and surrendered only 10 home runs in 1,221.1 innings pitched. His glittering pitching line over ten years: 94 wins, 46 losses, for a winning percentage of .671, higher than Christy Mathewson, Roger Clemens, and Sandy Koufax. Of his 23 wins in 1916, 9 were shutouts, all were complete-game victories. He threw 13 scoreless innings in the 1916 World Series, then added 16⅔ more when he beat the Chicago Cubs twice in the World Series two years later.

He possessed an offhanded motion so fluid that it looks graceful even in the skittish footage that survives from his Boston days. "It didn't have too much extra motion to it," observed Arnold Hano, a future sportswriter who was just a boy when he saw Ruth pitch his last major-league game. "A simple slow windup. He was fast but not Lefty Grove fast. It was not much more than one would have expected if you were throwing batting practice."

As he told the young women featured in one of his later instructional films: "Just follow your arm right through." Which is what he did when he went to the mound at Dexter Park, his upper body leading the way for his lower half. Though the crowd may not have appreciated it, Ruth was giving them a demonstration of why he would be forever considered the best—and most complete—baseball player ever. "Beethoven *and* Cezanne," as the baseball historian Daniel Okrent would say a century later.

When he climbed the mound for the bottom of the eighth inning, the multitudes advanced on the diamond, a Pickett's Charge of Babe Ruth partisans, now just a few feet from the infield dirt. Nonetheless the Babe retired all three batters he faced, two on infield grounders and a third "with a curve that broke more than a foot," the Brooklyn *Standard-Union* reported.

He went to the bench with the Babes leading the Bushwicks 3–1.

The stampede began in the middle of the ninth. In the mayhem, bats, balls, bases, certainty, and safety disappeared. His was an "endangering fame," a writer for the *San Francisco Call* observed.

Press accounts of the riot diverged. In one story, Ruth's attempt to return to the mound for the bottom of the ninth precipitated the melee. Another writer contended that Ruth was minding his own business, having taken a seat in a field box, when the crowd charged.

"Two fans were trampled and slightly injured and several others are sporting black eyes as the result of a boisterous riot which followed the last out of the exhibition game between Babe Ruth's touring ball troupe and the local Bushwick nine today," the United Press Transcontinental Wire reported. "Milling and mauling, the fans swirled around the field, fistfights starting, and men and boys caught in the crush, shouting hysterically."

The *Times* reported that Ruth was carried to the clubhouse by the mob that engulfed him.

Tommy Holmes saw it differently. Becalmed in the throng, unable to push his way "through the jostling, shrieking, hysterical mob," Ruth was rescued when "finally, three or four policemen constructed a flying wedge before him and charged."

Everyone agreed he was smiling.

Chapter 5
October 13 / Asbury Park

**BABE AND LOU TALK IT OVER
AT ASBURY PARK**

—ASSOCIATED PRESS

RUTH AND GEHRIG PLAY HERE TODAY

DIAMOND BEING PUT IN SHAPE AFTER DOWNPOUR—
POLICE MAY HAVE HANDS FULL

—*ASBURY PARK PRESS*

I

While untold thousands of the good citizens of Asbury Park, New Jersey, and its entire police force waited impatiently in the raw wood bleachers at the new high school stadium, city fathers convened an urgent meeting by the grandstand. Their goal: to extricate the stars of that afternoon's performance from their room at the swank Berkeley-Carteret Hotel, where at game time Lou Gehrig was flexing his muscles for reporters and Babe Ruth was lounging in his underwear.

The issue at hand was money: specifically, the twenty-five-hundred-dollar appearance fee they had been promised by promoter William H. Truby, who had changed the date and location of the game three days earlier, moving it from Bradley Beach to the larger high school field, adjacent to Deal Lake, where baseball had never been played and where, as of the previous morning, there was no baseball diamond.

Truby was a local wheeler-dealer, manager of the Bradley Beach semi-pro baseball team, secretary of the New Jersey State Athletic Commission, and former secretary (and only named official) of the short-lived American Party, a party of America-Firsters that served mostly to get Truby's name in the papers. He was known to Christy Walsh from Ruth's visit to Bradley Beach the previous fall. Unknown to Walsh, to the city fathers, and to the reported seven thousand foot-stomping, catcalling fans, Truby was also the defendant in a lawsuit brought by one Umberto Grieco, who arrived at the ballpark in hopes of collecting a three-year-old judgment for $466.73, which had been issued in connection with subletting the beach chair concession at the annual bathing beauty parade.

Realizing that Truby was about to come into some money, Grieco seized the opportunity to have the sheriff's office seize the funds from gate sales.

"Out of an abundance of caution," as the court would later put it, and an apparent awareness of Truby's reputation for not paying up, the money was being held by a representative of the Asbury Park school board, which was to receive 10 percent of the take. Said representative would not relinquish the funds to any of the concerned parties, including the undersheriff, the school board president, two city commissioners, Monmouth County Surrogate Joseph L. Donahay, Grieco, or Truby.

Thus, Ruth and Gehrig remained in seclusion in their finely appointed beachside hotel suite dressing for a game no one was sure they would play. Keeping them company were Walsh, busy writing a press release announcing that Fresno had been added to the tour, and Edward J. Neil, a young reporter in the newly established Associated Press sports department, who had arrived to interview Gehrig about being named baseball's Most Valuable Player.

He found Gehrig "stripped to a mere breech cloth, the bulging muscles of his broad physique knotting as he stepped about assembling the uniform of the Larrupin' Lous."

Ruth was similarly attired but not at all cut from the same cloth. "The Babe is huge through the shoulders, pudgy of waist, with the legs of a welterweight bearing his 225-pound bulk, while Lou has the build of a four-square Dutchman, wide of shoulder and hips, with the legs of a heavyweight wrestler."

Neil, sometimes known as Mike and other times Eddie, had joined the AP in Baltimore in 1926 and made a name for himself as a boxing writer dictating running copy from the Dempsey-Tunney fight in Chicago in September—the AP had just begun putting author bylines on its stories. Neil had gotten to know Ruth and Gehrig while gathering clubhouse gossip during the 1927 World Series. He became Ruth's card-playing buddy, would cover his second wedding in 1929, and write a five-part World Series retrospective on his career in 1932, the same year Neil became the first sportswriter to be acknowledged by the Pulitzer Prize jury, for a feature about a bobsled crash at Lake Placid.

Relaxing with Ruth and Gehrig at the hotel, Neil quickly realized he had more than he bargained for in an otherwise routine assignment. So he ran with it. The resulting story appeared in hundreds of newspapers across the country. "Here was a peek at the Babe at his ease," he wrote, and at the uncomplicated, easy, fraternal relationship that existed between what sportswriters liked to call the two Bams.

Any baby fat was long gone from Henry Louis Gehrig's now chiseled visage and physique. He had grown into his body and his potential since newsreel cameras caught him lounging on the Yankee bench on June 1, 1925, the day Ruth returned to the lineup after missing the first two months of the season due to the most famous stomachache in the history of professional sports. It also marked the beginning of Gehrig's 2,130 consecutive-game streak when he pinch-hit in the eighth inning.

The next day first baseman Wally Pipp took himself out of the lineup with what would become known as the most famous headache in the history of professional sports, ceding his position to Gehrig, who would not relinquish it until terminal illness compelled him to do so in 1939.

Ruth and Gehrig would become inextricably linked in the public imagination: number 3 and number 4. Their numbers, assigned in 1929, were signifiers of their place in the lineup but were suggestive, too, of a Yankee birth order. The Babe always came first. Back then, Lou was happy to defer.

They played bridge together and fished together and spoke German together and brought out the best in each other. Their admiration and affection were reciprocal.

Unclad, Gehrig seemed particularly uninhibited, insisting that he'd had no idea that Ruth was ineligible to repeat as Most Valuable Player. "'All through the year I thought that Babe would get it,' he said. 'I never knew that he wasn't eligible because he won it in 1923.'

"About that time, the Bambino cut himself into the conversation. 'Listen kid, you were a cinch,' he said. 'You'd have won it anyway even if I wasn't out, now act your age and climb into that sweatshirt.'"

Everywhere they went, and in every interview Walsh granted, he was quick to promote Ruth in the unaccustomed role of wise elder, teaching Buster about the perils of celebrity, urging him to save his money for the future, and coaching him on how to avoid the nuisance lawsuits that were like so many bugs drawn to the flypaper of fame. "You've got to be careful who you talk to and what you say," Ruth would tell him, reminding him about the guy who had dragged him into court in September, claiming Ruth had slapped him on his way out of the ballpark. "You've got to be careful about some of these birds."

Yes, Gehrig said, it was a real education traveling around with the Big Bam. "Ruth taught me how to act while on parade," he would confide to John B. Kennedy. "We'd have been to jail more than once if Ruth didn't know how to talk to traffic cops."

Neil was happy to collaborate in the construction of Walsh's narrative, describing Gehrig's good-natured acceptance of the Babe's affectionate joshing, and Ruth's role as the "teacher, guide and clubbing mentor of his young teammate," but Ruth made it a hard sell.

Unperturbed, "Larrupin" Lou' stalked over to the Babe and said almost accusingly: "You know, that big hitting freak there taught me more about batting this season than all the rest of the people that have worked on me put together. He showed me how to line a ball into right field for two and three bases this spring after Miller Huggins taught me to loft pokey flies out that way for cheap singles.

"He tries to teach me to swing free and clean like he does but I can't even get a foul. All I can do is stand there and swing with my arms alone. Just my arms."

As Lou stretched at full length a pair of forearms that would shame a safe-mover, Babe bestirred himself, pulled on a pair of stockings, and then entered into the fascinating task of inserting himself backwards into the pants of his uniform.

First Babe turned the pants inside out and laid them on the floor. He then pulled each trouser leg on up to the knee and left the waist of the garment dangling, still inside out, around his ankles. After rolling stocking tops and pants knees together securely, he reached down and successfully peeled the garment up about his ample waist, adjusted the belt and grunted. "There's one pair of pants that won't get loose from my stockings in a hurry."

This act of astonishing athletic dexterity—worthy of a kindergartner learning to put on a winter coat—was interrupted by an urgent summons from an *Asbury Park Press* reporter, telling them to get ready quick. Joseph Donahay, who was up for reelection, having served five terms as county surrogate, and whose photo graced the souvenir scorecard, had stepped into the breach with a personal check for twenty-five hundred dollars. Donahay, Truby, and assorted city officials had been downtown to a bank to exchange the surrogate's personal check for currency acceptable to Walsh and were now en route to the Berkeley-Carteret with police sirens wailing. Ruth pulled up his pants and Gehrig grabbed their lumber.

"Remember, Babe, we've got to catch a train west at 5:30 P.M. and it's three o'clock now," Gehrig said as they exited the hotel. "Hit a couple out of the park about the sixth inning and I'll sic the kids on you and break up the ball game."

II

Much had transpired in the tumultuous and profitable year since Ruth last accepted an invitation from William Truby to barnstorm on the Jersey Shore. Then he was in hock to his agent and his wife. Then he was the hero of the 1926 World Series—hitting three home runs in Game 4 against the St. Louis Cardinals—as well as its goat, having tried and failed to steal second base with two outs in the ninth inning of Game 7, with the Yankees trailing by a run. The only "dumb play" of Ruth's career, Yankee general manager Ed Barrow called it.

Ruth was quickly forgiven in part because of his otherwise spectacular performance in the series and because of his thoroughly unanticipated return to form during the regular season after a year of personal and professional travail. And he was forgiven because of Johnny Sylvester and the PR wizardry of Christy Walsh.

Johnny Sylvester was an eleven-year-old New Jersey boy whose banker father had used his contacts to ask the Yankees for an autographed baseball to cheer up his ailing son. Johnny had been kicked by a horse while on a family vacation in Bay Head, New Jersey. He had developed an infection—variously diagnosed as blood poisoning, a sinus infection, a spinal fusion, an infection in the skull, and osteomyelitis—and was confined to bed. Though he was never hospitalized, Johnny's condition was said to be dire; the *New York Herald Tribune* reported he had thirty minutes to live, rallying only after his father fulfilled his final request—an autographed baseball from the Babe.

Two balls arrived by airmail from St. Louis, one signed by the St. Louis Cardinals, the other by the Yankees, with Ruth's scribbled pledge: "I'll knock a homer for Wednesday's game."

Which, of course, he did: "Babe Ruth Keeps Airmail Promise of Homer for Boy Near Death."

A follow-up letter arrived from St. Louis with yet another promise from the Babe. "I will try to knock you another homer, maybe two today," he wrote.

That was the day he hit three home runs. "Yeah,

I had a good day," he said. "But don't forget, the fans had a hell of a day, too."

In the press box, Christy Walsh began a whispering campaign, telling reporters, off the record, that Ruth might just ask the Yankees for $150,000 in 1927.

Johnny made a miraculous recovery; there was no way for the Yankees to recover from Ruth's base-running blunder. The next morning Ruth and Walsh, accompanied by a *Daily News* reporter, headed for Bradley Beach to fulfill their commitment to play an exhibition game for William Truby. En route, they made a surprise visit to the Sylvesters' Essex County home, where a maid answering the door politely inquired as to their identity. "Babe Ruth to see Johnny."

The maid dutifully asked the lady of the house if he should be let in. Ruth went to Johnny's second-floor bedroom and caught the boy totally off guard. Bed-ridden and tongue-tied, but otherwise in apparent fine fettle, Johnny exclaimed, "Gosh, ain't he big!"

Ruth's house call was on the front page of the next day's *New York Times*:

DR. BABE RUTH CALLS ON HIS BOY PATIENT
HOME-RUN KING KEEPS RECEPTION WAITING WHILE
HE SEES LAD HOMERS SAVED

—NEW YORK TIMES

The *News* published a front-page photo along with its story, in which Johnny looked just fine. "Note lad's overjoyed expression," the caption said.

(The episode imbued Ruth with magical healing powers but did nothing for his famously terrible memory for names. When he ran into Johnny's uncle six months later, Ruth asked, "Now who the hell is Johnny Sylvester?")

Having raised the dead, Ruth embarked on a barnstorming and vaudeville tour of the Midwest and California during which, by Walsh's count, he made twenty-two speeches; autographed a thousand baseballs; visited three college football camps (Notre Dame, Drake, and the University of Minnesota); played golf with Pop Warner, Howard Jones, and Walter Hagen; and received instruction in how to apply stage makeup from Gloria Swanson and Bill Tilden.

On opening night in Minneapolis, he received a congratulatory telegram from Knute Rockne, drafted by Christy Walsh, which was nice but not nearly as impressive as those that had arrived at the Palace in New York in 1922 from Eddie Rickenbacker, Bennie Leonard, Buster Keaton, and Helen Keller, then on her own vaudeville tour, who all wired to say *Break a leg.*

His act consisted of a seven-minute motion picture showing him doing his best Bambino stuff and training at Artie McGovern's gym. At the end, he stepped through the screen into the footlights and delivered the words crafted for him by Arthur "Bugs" Baer, who saved his best stuff for his columns for the Hearst Syndicate ("Love is the last line in a ten-word telegram") and for the ghostwritten columns he wrote under Nick Altrock's byline for the Christy Walsh Syndicate.

Then, as scripted by Baer, Ruth would summon a handful of kids—five or so—to the stage to receive batting tips and an autographed baseball. Each was offered the opportunity to sing a song or dance or recite a bit of poetry.

The twelve-week, fourteen-city tour with the Pantages vaudeville theater chain went well. Hailed as "Bludgeoner, Writer, Actor," he went about his business painting scenery in Milwaukee, eating Thanksgiving dinner with orphans in Seattle, dressing as Peter Pan in Los Angeles, and posing as a sports editor for the *Tacoma Daily Ledger*, where he authored a ghosted column on salary negotiations with the Yankees, in which he insisted he wasn't a holdout, claimed to be in the dark about the source of the rumors that he was demanding a $100,000 or $200,000 contract, and said if baseball didn't work out he might just take up sportswriting. Or become a movie star.

The day before his last performance in Long Beach

on January 21, he signed a $30,000 deal with First National Pictures to costar with Anna Q. Nilsson in *Babe Comes Home*. His already reluctant leading lady was none too pleased when six weeks later the contract was amended to give Ruth sole star billing. Walsh got credit on the movie posters: "By arrangement with Christy Walsh."

The next morning Ruth decided to celebrate by going fishing. There were plenty of people throughout the country happy to accommodate him in his constant search for a good time. Among them was Glenn E. Thomas, owner of the biggest Studebaker dealership in Long Beach. He was a Republican, a city councilman, a Mason, an early investor in the Hancock Oil Company, and a firm believer in the power of public relations.

The first of his three shows that day, his last in Long Beach, was an afternoon matinee. Ruth figured he had plenty of time to dip a line in the water. Dressed in boots and breeches and a warm jacket, Ruth showed up at the Riverside Studebaker dealership owned by Thomas's brother Clare at 4:00 A.M. to pose for a publicity photo—"Studebaker Car Is Choice of Babe Ruth"—and to give an interview to the Riverside *Enterprise*, in which he announced the movie deal and declined to comment on the gambling scandal swirling around Ty Cobb and Rogers Hornsby. For once Commissioner Landis's wrath was aimed at someone else, and Ruth—or Walsh—was smart enough not to divert attention away from it.

Then he and Thomas took off for the Rainbow Angling Club, a fishing resort in the foothills of the San Bernardino Mountains some three hours away.

By the time brother Clare and his companion, Will H. Marsh, the automotive editor for the *Enterprise*, arrived at noon, Ruth had caught and eaten seventeen trout. "With all due deference to the prowess of the Babe on the diamond," Marsh wrote, "he has never showed more speed or capacity on the diamond than he did right there tucking away that early morning catch."

Sated, Ruth realized it was too late to make it back to the State Theatre in Long Beach for his matinee—even in a Glenn E. Thomas Studebaker. The club secretary placed a call to the Riverside airfield, a hard-pack airstrip that was home to the Cowboy Aviator, Roman Warren, to charter a flight.

Warren had made national headlines on June 13, 1926, when he flew a Thomas-Morse Scout under the sixteen-foot-high Rubidoux Bridge. The arch of the bridge was lower and smaller than that of the Arc de Triomphe in Paris, where another daredevil pilot had lost his life making the attempt.

Photographers for Pathé newsreels and local newspapers insisted on taking Warren's picture before the flight because they didn't think they'd be able to do so afterward. After flying under the bridge at 120 miles per hour with the fuselage no more than a yard above the shallow waters of the Santa Ana River, Warren told reporters his motivation was simple: "Hunger." The stunt didn't scare up any business, however—it just scared people away. They all thought he was going to fly them under the bridge.

So he was happy to fly the Babe to Long Beach and happier still to charge him $20.00—he usually got $2.50 for a flight.

Ruth arrived at the airfield in a convoy that included local police and his fishing party. He got out a flask and four silver and gold cups, put them on the running board of the Studebaker, and offered a drink all around. Warren and his line boy John Hammond declined.

"I put him in the back seat," Hammond told the Riverside *Enterprise* some years later. "He weighed about 240 pounds. He was slightly high. He skootched around a little bit in the seat, raised his elbows and poked both elbows out through the sides of the fuselage fabric. I didn't like that much. I did scold him a bit."

Hammond found some Pillsbury bags used for dish-cloths, cut them into small squares, and had the plane patched up and ready to go in fifteen minutes. Ruth's curtain call was in less than an hour. Warren said he jabbered nonstop on the thirty-five-minute flight to Long Beach.

His mood crashed upon landing. Stage manager Roy Reid greeted him in his dressing room, where Ruth was happily juggling autographed baseballs, the *Riverside Press-Telegram Press* reported, with news that he was about to be served with a warrant on charges of violating child labor laws during the late performance at the Pantages Theater in San Diego on January 14. The very vigilant and very publicity-conscious deputy state labor commissioner Stanley M. Gue had indicted him for allowing one Baby Annette Lumb, also known as Baby Annette De Kirby, age eight, to recite a poem during his act without first having obtained a permit from the commissioner of the Bureau of Labor Statistics and for having done so after the hour of 10:00 P.M.

Ruth turned himself in at the Long Beach Police Station in stage makeup and smelling of fish. He was photographed posting five hundred dollars bail in the baseball uniform he wore for his act, street shoes, and the argyle sweater he had worn to the Rainbow Angling Club. "I've only tried to give them a little bit of sunshine," he said of the children whom he invited to the stage at every performance. "I have never been so mad in my life."

Wasn't this exactly what he warned Gehrig about in Asbury Park?

Some observers thought they caught a whiff of Christy Walsh's handiwork in the proceeding, particularly after it became known that Baby Annette was a child actress who would make her big screen debut that year as Clarabelle in the Our Gang comedy, *Dog Heaven*, and her last film appearance the following year in *Mother Knows Best*. Also, the jailhouse photographer whose picture appeared in newspapers all over the country was none other than the one employed by Glenn E. Thomas.

But those skeptics didn't see Walsh's heated correspondence with Ruth's attorneys, complaining bitterly about "Mr. Goof" and his "bid for cheap notoriety." Nor did they see his written objection to the $212.18 legal fee the lawyers charged after getting the whole thing dismissed by the time Ruth left California.

Walsh did what he did best—he changed the subject. The trial date had been set for February 7, the day Ruth believed was his thirty-third birthday. This gave Walsh an idea and an opportunity. Money was pouring in even faster than Babe Ruth could spend it. Even discounting the inflated sums reported in the industry trades for his movie contract with First National Pictures and the Pantages Theater, his off-season income exceeded his 1926 $52,000 Yankee salary by $209.69. That didn't include an additional $8,000 in endorsement money itemized on Walsh's ledger sheet.

"'Ruth coined money so fast in the mid-twenties that I bought a $50,000 annuity for him and paid it off in three years,'" the columnist Joe Williams quoted Walsh in a 1949 interview. "When Babe learned that he had to make payments at regular intervals he became so angry he didn't speak to Walsh for days. Somehow the Babe had it figured out that his business manager was invading his privacy in an unseemly manner. 'I think he also resented the regularity that was involved. As you know, nothing irked him more than a routine which he was forced to respect.'"

Walsh had waged a highly unsuccessful three-year, arm-twisting campaign to get Ruth out of hock and convince him to save for the future. By February 1927, he realized it was time to resort to trickery. He convinced Ruth that it would be great PR to stage a news conference in Los Angeles on his birthday to announce that he was penalizing himself a thousand dollars for each year of misbehavior and putting it in a new trust fund with the Bank of Manhattan in New York. Then he got the presiding judge in the child labor violation case in San Diego, the *People of the State of California vs. George Herman Ruth* to postpone the trial.

On February 7, Ruth looked into the cameras and said, "Christy, I guess you have me convinced about the importance of saving a few bucks. You can penalize me a thousand dollars for each year. That'll make thirty-three thousand dollars to start with."

John B. Kennedy elaborated in *Collier's*. "To make it look real, the Babe was photographed signing the thirty-three thousand dollars over into an untouchable trust fund. The Babe later demanded his money back but found that the principal was beyond his reach forever and that he could have nothing but the interest."

Newspapers across the country trumpeted the news of a new era of fiscal responsibility. Walsh wired Frank Hilton, vice president of the Bank of Manhattan, euphorically and followed up with a triumphant letter the next day.

> *It makes me very happy indeed to enclose herewith check for Thirty-Three Thousand ($33,000) dollars as the first step toward a trust fund for Mr. Ge. H. ("Babe") Ruth.*
>
> *This is in accordance with our several past conversations and my wire from here February 6. And it concludes a campaign of nearly three years in which I have pleaded with my good friend Babe to do this important thing for his own future hap-*

piness. The difficulty has been to get him in an agreeable mood—and with the necessary cash on hand—both at the same time. I was able to engineer this by getting him to leave all receipts from his earnings this winter in my name. Exhibition baseball games, vaudeville and a motion picture have given him his most profitable winter season and the best part of the entire experience to me is that he has not spent a cent of it. I know many, many people who would not believe this!

In a separate wire, Walsh authorized Hilton to release the telegram as received in hopes of getting "full publicity value for Babe and your bank."

The deal was: all ancillary income would go into the trust while Ruth kept his Yankee salary to live on and play with—a salary that was not yet established. Ruth and the Yankees were then engaged in the Kabuki dance between players and management that passed for negotiations in the years before agents were allowed in the room. Owners lowballed players. Players threatened to quit. Empty threats were their only leverage.

As an opening gambit, the Yankees had sent a contract for $52,000, the same salary he had earned the previous three seasons, which they knew Ruth would return unsigned.

By then, Walsh had gone on the record with the sotto voce demands he had whispered in the World Series press box, telling reporters in December: "After what the Babe has done this year, he ought to be worth $150,000 on any man's ball cub."

On February 8, the day after the $33,000 press conference, Damon Runyon published a column pointing out that Ruth was wildly underpaid compared to entertainers like the Irish tenor John McCormack, who according to *Variety* was then the highest-paid performer in the United States, commanding $5,000 a night.

Joe Williams chimed in: "Ruth is cheap at $100,000."

It also helped Ruth's cause that Ty Cobb, very much on his last legs, was rumored to have received a $75,000 offer from the Senators and that former New York mayor Jimmy Walker was said to have been offered $100,000 to serve as American League president.

On February 10, Ruth told the Associated Press he wanted "$100,000 for Next Year or I'll Quit"—a story he promptly denied.

"I'm not in the market for real estate, or stock or any easy money rackets," he told the *Los Angeles Times* the next day, sounding very much like he had bought into the logic of financial prudence. "From now on what I earn I sock away where I can't even get at it myself."

Meanwhile cameras were rolling at Los Angeles's

new Wrigley Field and on the lot at First National Pictures, where a replica of part of the stadium had been constructed in case of inclement weather. A public invitation to see the Babe hit at Wrigley Field saved producers $45,000 they didn't have to pay extras when eleven thousand fans accepted the invite. Pretzel molders, ex-pugilists, barbers, and tightrope walkers in ill-fitting uniforms played the part of baseball players.

Between takes, Ruth held court in his sumptuous dressing room, reprising his threat to stay in Hollywood if the Yankees failed to meet his price—or open a baseball school for boys or a chain of gymnasiums with trainer Artie McGovern, who had been summoned to whip Ruth into shape for the season he was threatening not to play.

He ran every morning at 6:30 and worked out ostentatiously during lunch, jumping rope and playing catch with a medicine ball. McGovern kept the papers updated on Ruth's shrinking midline: 40 inches, compared with the 48½ inches it had been two years earlier. Marshall Hunt of the *Daily News* was conveniently available on the set, having been anointed a technical adviser by the Babe, to provide breathless daily updates, punctuated by the huffing and puffing of the Big Fella during his training sessions.

The cameras weren't rolling and the Babe wasn't

acting when he trudged off the set, disconsolate at having split in two the bat he used to hit three runs in Game 4 of the World Series. "Smelling salts were applied," Hunt wrote.

Ruth spent the evening of February 17 mingling with three thousand Hollywood types gathered by studio press agents to salute thirteen starlets at the annual Wampas Frolic, a glitzy affair at the new Ambassador Hotel boasting no fewer than seven orchestras and a show featuring the Mack Sennett players, the Duncan Sisters, Douglas Fairbanks, Fanny Brice, Eddie Cantor, Tom Mix, and Babe Ruth.

The next morning, Ruth sent a letter to the Yankees, written "by his ventriloquist Christy Walsh," Ed Sullivan reported in the *Evening Graphic*, asking for the $100,000 contract he had denied asking for, plus $7,700 in salary that had been held back in fines.

When Jacob Ruppert failed to reply—that was not the Yankee way—Ruth threatened to make his own letter public. "Babe Ruth to Tell All," promised the *Los Angeles Times.*

Which he did, giving the story to Hunt, who had the whole thing in the *Daily News* on February 26. Headline writers in New York adopted a more measured tone: "Stage All Set for Battle of 2,000 Centuries."

The *News* also carried an exclusive item about

Helen Ruth, who was in St. Vincent's Hospital recovering from surgery. She had been there for more than a week. The nature of her illness was not disclosed.

Bookies back east were laying 2-to-1 odds that he wouldn't get the one hundred thou.

Ruth headed back to New York on the evening of February 26, having finished shooting his last scenes at two o'clock in the morning. It was a real Hollywood send-off: he left town with a lei of flowers and "a bevy of ravishing femininity" draped about his neck—extras hired by the studio for the occasion, Hunt wrote. He also had a $30,000 option for another feature film with First National (which was never made) and a favorable verdict in *People of the State of California v. George Herman Ruth.*

The case, having been successfully delayed by his attorneys and inclement weather, had been heard just the day before. By the time Ruth entrained, Justice Claude I. Chambers had released his six-page opinion, declaring, "If this case constitutes a violation of the law, then all my thirty years of the study of law have gotten away from me."

This did not deter Deputy Commissioner Stanley M. Gue from immediately filing another complaint, dismissed with similar alacrity. It was once again safe to take American children to see Babe Ruth. Despite the verdict in Ruth's favor, and the fact that he never had to step foot in court, Walsh protested the legal fees and still had not paid them by April 5.

Walsh was barred by tradition and by the thoroughly unbalanced balance of power in the game from representing Ruth's interests at the bargaining table. "He would have liked to be present at the negotiation, as he knew something about Mr. Generous Edward Barrow's capacity for earnestness under such conditions, but no player has ever done business with the magnates through a manager, and anyway he thought he could trust this party to hold out for $100,000," Pegler wrote in a column published in the *Washington Post* on April 25.

In fact, Walsh tried to do business with the magnates, as Pegler acknowledged in a 1941 column carried by the *Post* about the absence of collective bargaining in baseball. "The management of the Yankees had made known unmistakably its determination not to set a precedent by negotiating the Babe's terms of employment through any third person and the matter was not pressed."

This would not change until Marvin Miller organized the Major League Baseball Players Association in 1965. Roger Maris wasn't even permitted to bring his brother along with him to negotiate his 1962 contract with the Yankees after breaking Ruth's home-run record the year before.

The best Walsh could do was offer the Babe a cram course in the art of negotiation. He accompanied Ruth as far as Salt Lake City. They sat in his drawing room, playacting the roles of the respective parties, a conversation re-created by Pegler.

Walsh apprised Ruth of how much money Col. Ruppert had and how valuable he was to the Yankees and the American League and the importance of getting while the getting was good. He reminded Ruth that he had just turned 33. Then they rehearsed their lines with Walsh playing the part of the Colonel:

"Now I will be Jake Ruppert and you will be Babe Ruth," Mr. Walsh said. In the final rehearsal of the scene, "You come into the office and I say to you, 'Hello, Babe; you are not looking very well. Do you think you will last through next summer?'

"Now, what are you supposed to say?"

"I am supposed to say, 'I want a three-year-contract at $100,000 or I will retire from the great national game,'" Mr. Ruth replied brightly.

"Fine," Mr. Walsh exclaimed. "Now I say, 'You must be crazy. I think I will trade you to the Red Sox.' And what do you say?"

"I say, 'All right, then, there is no sense of our talking any more, so good-bye, Jack.'"

If they came at the Babe with anything about his debt to baseball, the Babe was to remind them of the seasons when he filled the ballparks all around the league for $25,000 and $52,000. If they brought out any statistics to show that a $100,000 salary would leave them no profits, he was to suggest an accounting of the exhibition games in the spring and on the open dates during the summer, for several years, and remind them of the exhibition games which they scheduled for this year.

The Babe is the only member of the ball club who is obliged by contract to appear in the exhibition games and this, of course, means that the promoters want Babe Ruth, not the New York Yankees.

While they talked, Artie McGovern dictated a letter to the *Brooklyn Eagle*, reporting that Ruth had achieved his ideal weight—222 pounds. They had been working out in the baggage car. Nonetheless, by the time Ruth reached New York on March 2 he had gained four pounds.

Marshall Hunt wired his story to New York, predicting that Ruth would not get the hoped-for two-year, hundred-thousand-dollar-a-year deal, and adjourned to the dining car, where he ran into Captain Joe Patterson, who had been in Hollywood on business. Patterson asked whether the Babe might be induced to come to his compartment for a chat. Nothing long, mind you; the captain was tired, but he wanted to meet the man who helped build his paper's circulation and put it in the black. Patterson said he would brush the front of his shirt when he wanted to end the interview. He never gave the signal.

Ruth was less loquacious during a layover in Chicago, explaining to reporters he was saving all his chat for Colonel Ruppert. Edward Burns of the *Chicago Tribune* suspected a different reason for his reticence: "he now thinks, talks and writes at space rates."

Arriving in New York, he went straight to McGovern's gym half a block from Grand Central Terminal, held court for reporters for forty-five minutes, and agreed to invest fifteen thousand dollars in the establishment as part of a plan for a chain of physical culture schools, described by Joe Williams as those "new health palaces where tired businessmen go to have his valves reground and his motor tuned." Nothing ever came of that.

Then, he called St. Vincent's Hospital to inquire about Helen. Dan Parker of the *Daily Mirror* recorded the tender scene in Helen's room when the Babe finally showed up at the hospital: "her pale, thin arms uplifted from her sick bed to engulf the man mountain who rushed to meet them" as "the big movie star and home-run man dropped a few honest tears on his wife's face."

The reunion was brief. Leaving the hospital forty-five minutes after he arrived, Parker wrote, "Babe scowled when some tactless reporter asked him if he and his wife were to be divorced. 'That old story is still going the rounds,' snapped Babe. 'There's nothing to it. But I wish the scandal mongers would let a man enjoy a little privacy in his family affairs.'"

Then he headed uptown for his meeting with the Colonel, which would last ten minutes longer than his visit with his wife.

Most headlines hailed the negotiation as a success: Ruth had come away with a three-year contract for $70,000 a year, the largest in baseball history. One newspaper ran a chart describing everything Ruth could buy for that money: "Every Day Ruth Earns a Trip to Europe. Every Week Ruth Earns a New Automobile. Every Month Ruth Earns a New Home. Every

Season Ruth Earns Enough to Support 20 Families Like This."

The last claim was superimposed over a photograph of a family with thirteen children.

Walsh was less enthused. In fact, he was disconsolate. "He had circulated propaganda about a demand for $150,000, figuring that left Ruth a trading margin of $50,000, which had found publication all over the United States," Pegler wrote in his April 25, 1927, column in the *Post*. "And a few days later," Walsh told him in a subsequent interview, "I picked up a paper and read something like this: 'Babe Ruth walked into the Yankee offices at the brewery today, grabbed a fountain pen out of Jake Ruppert's hand, signed a contract for three years at $70,000 and walked out saying he was well pleased with the terms and expected to have a great season.'"

Pegler called Ruth "the world's worst trader" and described Walsh's dismay at the Babe's failure to learn his lessons. "Mr. Walsh's disgust over the news that his fellow had quickly succumbed to the suasion of Edward Generous Barrow and signed for $70,000 a year was so poignant that he has not even mentioned that matter to the Babe since then."

The upshot was this: "In a five-minute interview Ruth was talked down to $70,000. This was a retreat of $5,000 a minute on a one-year basis or $18,000 a minute on the three-year contract, which the Babe eventually signed."

Or, as Parker put it, "He came. He saw. He compromised."

Ruth must have had second thoughts about the deal, too, telling Jack Lawrence of the *New York American* it was "a trifling raise."

He also predicted he would have his best season ever.

III

The game in Asbury Park started forty-five minutes late and ended three innings early. In the first inning, Ruth hit a 2-and-1 pitch into Deal Lake. No sooner had the ball splashed down than a boy in a canoe went overboard in search of it. He appeared on the field, dripping wet, shortly thereafter to procure Ruth's signature on his soggy souvenir.

It was a game worthy of a Mack Sennett movie. The Giants scored one run on an inside-the-park home run when a boy made off with the baseball. Two sure outs on foul pops behind home plate were lost when the catcher's progress was impeded by the two boys located between his legs.

Ruth was on first base in the fourth inning when

another boy, determined to allow his hero to advance safely to second, pounced on a passed ball with the catcher in hot pursuit. Ruth, who was halfway to third base, retreated to second in the interest of good sportsmanship.

Gehrig ended the game with a home run in the sixth inning, the *Times* reported, when he hit the last of thirty-six available baseballs into the lake.

The aggrieved parties were still arguing when Ruth and Gehrig ran for their 5:30 P.M. train.

By then, it was clear to everyone, including Joseph Lyons, the executive secretary of the school board who was holding the gate receipts, that there wasn't nearly enough to satisfy Grieco's judgment, cover expenses (including $350 to be shared by the Brooklyn Royal Giants and the other players on Ruth's team), repay Donahay, and make sure the school district got its 10 percent cut. So Lyons refused to relinquish the money: the total receipts came to $2,300.00—$1,500.00 less than expenses.

When a meeting on October 20 failed to produce a settlement, Sheriff Johnson brought suit in the New Jersey Chancery Court to recover Grieco's $466. The Board of Education argued that Donahay automatically became the promoter when he financed the game and that the receipts, such as they were, belonged to him, not Truby. Someone had to get the short end of the stick.

The litigation continued for a year. Finally, in an opinion released on October 13, 1928, the court ruled that the Good Samaritan Donahay had allowed "his business judgment to be overwhelmed by his enthusiasm."

In short, funds were too short to reimburse him. However, Donahay had been reelected to another five-year term as surrogate with twice the number of votes he received in the 1922 election.

Chapter 6

October 13–14 / Aboard the Manhattan Limited to Lima

RUTH AND GEHRIG WIN HEARTS OF
CHILDREN BY GENIAL SMILES

—*LIMA NEWS* (OHIO)

REPORTER SEES BABE, LOU;
FORGETS SCORE

—THE GIRL REPORTER, *LIMA MORNING STAR* (OHIO)
AND REPUBLICAN-GAZETTE

I

The dining-car waiters aboard the Manhattan Limited en route to Chicago (with stops in Newark, North Philadelphia, Pittsburgh, and Lima, Ohio) had spent an hour that week in Columbus in the Pennsylvania Railroad's newly opened Experimental Kitchen, a replica dining car in which they were taught the fine art of arranging silver, hoisting trays, and folding linens. Each man was required to spend three hours a week in school, one just prior to departure.

No amount of training could have prepared them for the spectacle of Babe Ruth and his "eats." Baked ham in cider sauce was on the menu that night, garnished with pineapple fritters, baked apples, and candied sweet potatoes—a new menu for the railroad perfected in the Experimental Kitchen. Ruth ordered triple portions of the best they had and a quart of fruit juice, into which he poured a fifth of bootleg gin. Then he drank the whole thing. With a chaser of bicarb, no doubt—a jug of which he kept in his locker at Yankee Stadium for postgame indigestion, prompting, sportswriter James Kahn observed, a belch that caused "all the loose water in the showers" to come down.

By 1927, his appetites had been amply documented, somewhat curbed, occasionally exaggerated, and generally regarded with a degree of awe usually reserved for the Seven Wonders of the World. Ford Frick testified to breakfasts of eighteen-egg omelets with six pieces of toast and three slices of ham. Room service on tour was known to require two waiters and three trays.

By the time they got to San Francisco after two weeks on the road and Ruth heaved himself on the scale, he weighed 230 pounds. "That's a lot of weight," he said.

His unslakable appetite was generally attributed to impoverished beginnings in the Ruth home, a misconception he never discussed or corrected. Food was plentiful in George Sr.'s saloons, where two generations of women fed traveling salesmen hearty meals of heavy German food. But George Jr. didn't live there. He lived at St. Mary's, where the Xaverian Brothers struggled to feed their flock on the eighty dollars per boy allotted by the city and state each year. That, the school's annual report noted, came out to six cents per child per meal.

At St. Mary's the boys ate in silence, interrupted only by the scraping of their utensils on tin plates. An offender was made to stand in front of the dining hall for the duration of the meal, then whipped, though not severely, one boy said; the public humiliation was far more painful.

They had gruel for breakfast and bread and soup for lunch and dinner. They had a single pat of butter on Fridays, and meat once a week, on Sundays—three hot dogs with their midday meal and three slices of baloney for dinner.

Is it any wonder that he gorged himself on hot dogs?

II

Life at St. Mary's was orderly and regimented: up at 6:00 A.M. to wash and dress for Mass and breakfast; classes (vocational or academic) from breakfast until 10:00; recess from 10:00 to 10:30; and another hour of classes until dinner and free time, which lasted from 11:30 until 1:30 P.M. Then classes again until 3:15, followed by Christian doctrine, required for Catholics only. After that, free time in the yard until supper at 6:00. The boys were outside in every season and every sort of weather except rain. The constant exposure to sun made George Ruth's swarthy skin even darker. Lights out was at 8:15, after three Hail Marys and a devotion read aloud by one of the brothers.

Until 1922, formal education at St. Mary's ended after eighth grade, at which point the boys picked a trade with which they would make their way in the world. They learned farming and floral arranging; shoemaking and tailoring; steam fitting, woodworking, glazing, electrical engineering, and plumbing; bookbinding, bookkeeping, and typing. They rolled cigars and knitted stockings and made all their own underwear. They did the laundry, milked the cows, and cultivated the vegetable garden. They'd even run pipe to a reservoir fed by a natural spring when additional land was acquired in 1885.

In 1902, a brush and broom shop was added, which was replaced by a toy factory in 1908 and then by a shirt factory, which by George Ruth's last year at St. Mary's employed seventy-five boys and was one of the school's most profitable enterprises.

George Ruth's first job was with the maintenance crew. Then he graduated to the Low City tailor shop on the second floor of the Manual Training building, and from there to the High City tailor shop on the floor above, where he learned to sew collars on work shirts sold to the Oppenheim, Obeindorf & Co. shirt factory—he earned six cents apiece. He would always have an appreciation for a well-turned collar and fix his own when dissatisfied with the tailoring of so-called experts.

The High City tailors also had the happy task of outfitting senior boys upon their release. "They were taken to the tailor shops at St. Mary's and were measured for suits," recalled Brother Arcadius. "They would describe how they felt like a million dollars, getting all this tailor-made stuff."

But of all the in-house enterprises, the print shop was the most lucrative and essential, producing annual calendars, the collected works of the school's super-intendent, the weekly school newspaper—*St. Mary's World*, which became the *Saturday Evening Star* and later the *Little Flower*—and glossy annual reports pre-pared for state and city officials and benefactors that detailed the school's good works and chronic debt.

The 1902 annual report included photos of senior boys milling about the Big Yard in ties, jackets, and sus-penders, all made in-house (usually they wore overalls); dogs and cows mingling in a meadow; dining-room tables set with soup bowls; and chalkboards inscribed with multiplication tables—6's, 7's, and 8's. There were two photographs of the newly planted greenhouses and four-color drawings of them in bloom.

A drought in the spring of 1902 had cut the number of bushels of wheat produced by the farm in half but allowed the brothers to charge fifteen cents more than the year before. They were always quick to tip off the local press to their industry—a bumper crop of pota-toes in 1911 merited local headlines.

But by the end of 1902, St. Mary's was $32,863.36 in debt, despite $20,000 appropriated by the city and $15,000 by the state. The 22 brothers who served the school and its 453 boys earned $12.50 a month. "Some dreaded the thought of being sent there when they were young," said Brother Arcadius. "As with any boarding school, you're on duty around the clock."

Need would always exceed funding; students would invariably exceed the available space. By 1908, there were 3,000 children being cared for at Catholic institutions in Baltimore by 500 members of various religious orders. Brother Paul, who became superintendent in 1907, complained bitterly about parents who failed to pay promised tuition. By the following year, the school was so overcrowded that there were 130 boys sleeping in dorm rooms meant to house 90. The brothers were forced to place beds in dorm hallways. "For fear of fire or disturbance among so many boys in one room at a time, we keep a watchman in each room all night," Brother Paul told the *Baltimore Sun*. "He walks from one end to the other every minute. In case of danger he could flood the place with light in an instant."

Until 1912, when the boys constructed a stone wall around the perimeter of the school with rock hewed from the property, the only barrier to freedom was constructed of wire, wood, and hedge. The back acreage dipped down into the woods at the tree line, where a small stream wound its way into Maiden Run and then into the Lower Gwynns Falls.

Uprisings and breakouts always attracted the attention of the local press, perhaps because they were so infrequent. Between 1902 and 1909, the school recorded only 252 "parole violators." In May 1908, the *Sun* reported: "Two discontented boys attacked a watchman Wednesday night in an attempt to incite an uprising, but the other boys seized them and notified the brothers."

Two months later, the *Sun* noted another incident. "Charles Gardiner, 13, who escaped from St. Mary's Industrial School Wednesday, was captured yesterday morning by Baltimore and Ohio Railroad detectives. . . . Everything is quiet at the school and no further trouble is expected. The boys were given a good lecture."

In the school's early years, discipline was harsh and corporal. When former inmate Al Jolson brought his wife to see the school in 1948, he was astonished to find the front gate open, biographer Herbert G. Goldman wrote. "It was always shut when I was here. I remember bars all around. Once I hit a boy on the stairs, coming down from chapel. They put me in solitary. That's bad enough. But to look out the window—and watch the others playing—well, honey, I screamed and hollered until I ran a temperature. So they had to let me out."

By the time George Ruth arrived, the cells were gone and the penal uniforms had been eliminated. But straps were still in evidence when Ruth brought Yankee teammates around for a visit in 1923. He acknowledged he got his discipline the old-fashioned way.

When he ran away, he sought refuge at the home of his aunt Annie and uncle Milton and cousin Milton Jr., who still lived on South Woodyear Street. Patrolman Birmingham or one of Baltimore City's new attendance officers would come and get him. "George jumped out of bed and he ran out that back door, right into the cop's arms," Milton Brundige told reporters on the Babe's one hundredth birthday.

Birmingham's great-granddaughter Mary Tormollan recalled her grandmother's stories about Officer Birmingham's rescue missions. "She said Grandpop went out to get George Ruth and take him back to the St. Mary's Industrial School because he was safer there. That's how she put it: 'He's safer there and he'll learn more there because it's a school.'

"I said, 'A school or just a home?'

"She said, 'No, it's someplace he can live, and it's a school.'"

Visitors were welcome on the first Sunday of every month. His cousin Milton remembered taking picnics to St. Mary's when they went to visit. His sister, Mamie, recalled, "Mother and I used to go out there once in a while" and bring "goodies he couldn't get otherwise."

He liked chewing gum and anything sweet—pears, peaches, bananas. "On visiting day, we had a certain place to go," she told Mike Gibbons of the Babe Ruth Birthplace and Museum. "We met in this big hall with a lot of chairs. Pick your chair and sit down. Then Babe was notified his parents were here and we'd all get together. Had to stay in the hall until time was up. Then the bell would ring, and we had to go."

With Katie Ruth's legal standing within the family precarious and her health deteriorating because of tuberculosis, her visits became less frequent. George Sr. never visited at all. Once Ruth's classmate Louis "Fats" Leisman confided that he hadn't seen his mother in two years. Replied Ruth: "You're lucky, Fats. It's been ten years since I have seen my father."

Another lonely Sunday, Ruth told his pal: "I guess I'm too big and ugly for anyone to come see me. Maybe next time."

That time, Leisman reported in his 1956 memoir, *I Was with Babe Ruth at St. Mary's*, never came.

Most inmates stayed at St. Mary's no longer than two years. The youngest of them were five years old; the oldest were released upon reaching the age of majority at twenty-one.

William Pindell, who was trained as a printer, succeeded at the trade for which he had been prepared. Others, like Brother Thomas More Page, who later became provincial general of the order, chose a life of service; Brother Arcadius served with six former St. Mary's students. Some were unredeemable; others, like William's brother Harvey, never recovered from the stigma and pain of abandonment. After his release, his family never saw him again.

Meyers Christner, a Pennsylvania boy who had no use for book learning, spent six months at St. Mary's when he was twelve years old. He slept two beds from George Ruth and was his catcher for the Third Dormitory Team, as he told reporters in 1929 when he was known as K.O., the heavyweight contender with a punch second only to Jack Dempsey's. His stay ended abruptly when he threatened to run away, and his father took him out of the school.

His battery mate George Ruth was an exception and an exemplar. Except for a brief and unsuccessful stay in 1913 at the St. James Home for Boys, a halfway house in downtown Baltimore where Ruth proved incapable of managing the limited freedom it afforded, he became, de facto, a lifer.

"Welcome back, Nigger Lips!" the boys cried upon his return, Leisman reported.

By then, he was so much bigger than his peers that visitors presumed he was a member of the staff. He embraced that role. He bought candy from the canteen for younger boys who had no money for treats. He fashioned baseballs for them out of heavy cord and black tape and warmed their small hands in his big paws on raw recess afternoons. He took the rap when a younger boy broke a laundry window. In Leisman's words, "He made life a little more livable when life seemed unbearable."

The brothers did everything they could to prepare their charges for life on the outside. They even sponsored dances for senior boys approaching parole. But, Brother Arcadius said, "The family element was not there. They were like prisoners."

"Was it grim?" said Brother Peter Donohue, who served at St. Mary's during the summer when other brothers went on retreat. "Some people had that impression. My impression was: this was their home. They went to school; they played sports. I might be prejudiced but I thought the brothers were substitute parents."

For George Ruth, that person was Brother Matthias, Big Matt, known in the Big Yard as "the Boss."

"He sensed something in Daddy that needed to be loved," Julia Ruth Stevens said.

III

Martin Leo Boutilier was born in 1872 in Cape Breton, an island off the eastern shore of mainland Nova Scotia. He was a descendant of French peasants who arrived in Nova Scotia in 1752, and one of twelve children born to his parents—of which nine survived. They lived in a small windblown community called Lingan, three miles from Glace Bay, facing out to sea. Life was cold, poor, and insular.

Cape Breton was coal-mining country. Many of the local men, including Martin's father—listed in census records first as an engineer, then as a mechanic, and sometimes a deckhand on ships bound for Boston— worked for one of the eight coal companies operating in industrial Cape Breton.

Martin's closest childhood friend was Frank McGillivary, who was born at the next farm over. They grew up together, went to school together, and played Lingan ball together, an iteration of baseball that involved throwing a ball with one hand and hitting it with the other—a technique Martin would perfect on the Big Yard at St. Mary's, where word was he batted one-handed because he once hurt a kid fielder when he hit with two hands.

Martin's father was a convert to Catholicism and enthusiastic in his faith. Eventually his overzealousness cost him his job in the mines, family member Jean Mor says. In 1881, when Martin was nine years old, Joseph moved his brood to Boston and settled in a neighborhood near the future site of Logan Airport. Two of Joseph's sons became Boston policemen; another son became a fireman. No doubt he was pleased that two of his other sons, Martin and his older brother Thomas, consecrated themselves to the Xaverian Order.

Upon professing his faith, Martin took the name Matthias, derived from the Hebrew *Mattathias*, meaning "gift of Yahweh." He arrived at St. Mary's in 1894 and was granted full admission to the Congregation of the Brothers of St. Francis Xavier (CFX) in June 1895. In his black cassock, with the Sacred Heart of Jesus sewn into the chest of his vestments, Matthias was a formidable figure and grew more so with each generation of boys. He was listed in his official Church biography as six foot four and 225 pounds, but he grew in myth to be six foot six and perhaps 300 pounds.

Big Matt, chief of discipline, dorm prefect, and assistant athletic director, was large enough that the door to his six-and-a-half-foot-square sleeping quarters had to be hung on the outside of the doorjamb to accommodate the length of his extra-long bed.

Brother Thomas More Page, who was known as

Melvin Page when he attended St. Mary's, long after Ruth's parole, testified to Brother Matthias's outsized authority. While on retreat at Mount Saint Joseph's, a Xaverian high school in Carrollton, Maryland, Brother Matthias received an urgent call from Brother Paul: a riot was brewing among the older boys in the Big Yard. He was needed on campus immediately. "When the boys saw Matthias at the head of the steps overlooking the yard, they immediately dispersed without saying a word," Brother Thomas More wrote.

Matthias possessed a receding chin hidden by his clerical collar, sloping shoulders, and "a boy's heart hidden beneath his cassock," as described by the *Baltimore Sun*. A 1919 official report submitted to the St. Mary's school board said he was of "pleasing manner and impressed us that he was one of the boys entering in all things, education, play and work with them."

The *Boston Evening Transcript* ascribed to him "a shambling gait, and a quiet and diffident manner." He never needed to raise his voice.

Electricity was his hobby. Baseball was his passion. On Sunday evenings after supper, Brother Matt provided the entertainment for five hundred boys by hitting fungoes (with his right hand only) that fell "like snowflakes over the entire yard," Brother Thomas More wrote.

As disciplinarian in an overcrowded school full of dis-
enfranchised boys, Matthias had charge of a multitude of
young souls. According to Westbrook Pegler's 1920 con-
fabulation, he singled out Little George on his first night
at St. Mary's, proffering a lifeline in the form of a bat: "I
made the Colts, the smallest ball team in the institution,
as catcher, and it was only a couple of days later that I
stepped up to the plate with the bases full, measured a
nice groove ball and socked it over the center fielder's
head for the first home run of my career."

In his playing days, Ruth would credit Brother Matt
for his pigeon-toed gait and his uppercut swing—saying
he was born as a hitter the first time he saw Matthias hit
a ball. In his dying days, Ruth would credit him with
"teaching me how to play ball—and how to think."

He called Brother Matthias "the greatest man I've
ever known."

Pegler's account omitted the role others played
in Ruth's development: Brother Herman, the director of athletics, under whom St. Mary's won its first
city championship in 1897, and Brother Albin, an
Englishman, who played first base on many of the
teams he coached. "I've heard older brothers say
Brother Herman was the real discoverer of Babe Ruth
when he was a new kid standing off to the side, shy,"
Brother Arcadius recalled. "But he always stayed out

of the limelight instead of claiming any fame to Babe Ruth. Of course, many brothers at St. Mary's would say they taught Babe Ruth even though they weren't born yet."

Baseball was more than a diversion at St. Mary's. It was an organizing principle: dorm played dorm, floor played floor; and shop played shop. It was also a form of crowd control, a way to channel a surfeit of glands and hormones. In 1909, the school fielded twenty-eight uniformed baseball teams; three thousand spectators showed up for one home game that year. The brothers created a de facto farm system with a four-team league—the Red Sox, White Sox, Cubs, and Giants—for the top players. When Ruth outgrew the competition on campus, the brothers allowed him to play in weekend semi-pro and amateur league games around town. By the time he was released in 1914, St. Mary's had forty-four teams in uniform.

Ruth once estimated that he played two hundred games a year at St. Mary's and he played every position—Brother Matt believed that a boy needed to be adept at everything. Ruth caught for the St. Mary's Red Sox in 1913 when they won the school championship. He was a left-handed catcher playing with a right-handed mitt, which he would take with him to the major leagues just in case. His arm was so good, so accurate, that even after dropping the glove on the ground, and switching the ball to his left hand, he still threw most everyone out.

"A bone out of joint, one of nature's misfits," is how Brother Gilbert would remember him squatting behind home plate.

He became a pitcher by accident of misbehavior. As Brother Matthias told an interviewer from the *Boston Evening Transcript* in 1935: "He was catching for me one day and the boy who was pitching was hit hard, and 'George' was laughing and making fun of him from behind the plate. So I sent him to the mound in the hope that it might be a lesson for him. Instead 'George' struck out the side and went on to become a great pitcher."

Ruth went missing the week before the first big game of his life, a contest between the privileged students of Mount Saint Joseph and the ne'er-do-wells consigned to St. Mary's. Bill Morrisette, the star right-hander for St. Joe's, who was getting a lot of attention from the *Baltimore Sun*, was scheduled to face George Ruth, the unknown lefty from St. Mary's. (Morrisette lasted parts of three seasons in the bigs, appearing in all of thirteen major-league games, and spent eleven years in the minors.)

Classes were canceled while the brothers met to discuss the crisis. Lefty High, the night watchman who manned the back gate, and Mr. Hennessey, the school's probation officer, went in search of him. He returned after three days on the lam, allegedly without coercion. Brother Matthias meted out his punishment: he had to spend all his free time standing on the road that divided the Big Yard from the Little Yard. His embarrassment was on display for all to see.

American flags draped the grandstand the day of the game. George Ruth pitched a shutout, beating St. Joe's 6–0. "Ruth, one of the 'star' slabmen allowed but one hit, that being a two-base hit. He also struck out twenty-two and issued but one pass," the school newspaper reported. "During that same game, he hit safely four times."

In his end-of-the-year report to the city and state Brother Paul noted: "One boy created a sensation by his excellent work."

Jack Dunn, owner of the Baltimore Orioles, may or may not have attended the game. How and when he learned about the prospect "out the Frederick Road" is a matter of debate. Either Brother Gilbert, the St. Joe's coach who had already lost Morrisette to the Orioles and did not want to lose another pitcher (Ford Meadows) to Dunn, tipped him off. Or he heard about Ruth from Washington Senators' pitcher Joe Engel, an alumnus of Mount St. Mary's College in Emmitsburg, who had seen Ruth pitch at the Mount. Or both. Dunn was a premiere baseball scout—he discovered big leaguers Lefty Grove and Ernie Shore. It was his business to know the local talent.

On Saturday, February 14, 1914, one week after Ruth's twentieth birthday, Dunn showed up at St. Mary's with Yankee third baseman Fritz Maisel, Brother Gilbert, and a rookie sportswriter for the *Sun* named Jesse Linthicum and asked to see Brother Matthias. Yes, he assured them, "Ruth can hit."

"Can he pitch?" Dunn asked.

"Sure, he can do anything," Brother Matt replied.

Ruth was summoned from the High City tailor shop in a pair of overalls that matched the ones Brother Matt was wearing. Dunn took him out in the Big Yard and had him throw. It didn't take him long to figure out what he had. Nor did it take long for Dunn and Brother Paul to agree on a $600 contract for the 1914 baseball season. "It was an easy matter to produce a baseball contract," Linthicum said. "But after all he was in an orphanage. He was a minor and could not sign such a contract and have it legal. So Dunn was forced to sign two contracts, a baseball contract with the Babe and he also signed a contract to become his guardian."

The brothers routinely delegated that authority to

prospective employers. That would prove helpful to the Orioles' owner later in the spring when "Jack Dunn's Baby"—a moniker acquired early in spring training in Fayetteville, North Carolina, and soon shortened to Babe!—attracted the attention of the rival Baltimore franchise in the upstart Federal League. The guardianship that enabled underage George H. Ruth Jr. to leave St. Mary's also precluded him from accepting a big-money offer from the Baltimore Terrapins without Dunn's permission—"Ruth Safe from Federal Raids," the *Scranton Truth* noted on May 28, 1914.

There was no High City tailor fitting for him. Brother Paul took him downtown to purchase clothes befitting a professional baseball player—one more indication of the status he had achieved and its importance to the institution.

A new entry was made in the St. Mary's roll book: "George Herman Ruth, discharged Feb. 27, 1914—To join the Balt. Baseball Club."

IV

Within eight months of leaving St. Mary's, George Ruth was sold to the Boston Red Sox, for whom he made his major-league debut on July 11; demoted to the Providence Grays, for whom he hit his first professional home run on September 5 at Hanlan's Point in Toronto; and met his first wife, Mary Ellen "Helen" Woodford, a waitress who served him breakfast at Landers' Coffee Shop in Boston, whom he would marry that fall.

He was not yet twenty-one. Not exactly a man of the world. His first love letter to a girl he had somehow met on Edmondson Avenue in Catonsville while at St. Mary's was ghostwritten by a young Baltimore sportswriter named Rodger Pippen, who covered St. Mary's and Orioles' spring training. Ruth later faulted the quality of his prose for the lack of a response.

His mother, Katie, was dead two years, having spent her final days living with her sister Lena around the corner from the house in which she gave birth to her son. She died at age thirty-nine in Baltimore's Municipal Tuberculosis Hospital on August 11, 1912, after being hospitalized for eleven days. Her death certificate described her as a widow. The cause of death: exhaustion and lung disease.

She was buried in an unmarked grave in the Schamberger family plot in Most Holy Redeemer Cemetery in east Baltimore. Her son was granted leave for the day to attend his mother's funeral.

Nearly a century later he was excoriated for failing to erect a headstone for his mother and neglecting her eternal soul, in a widely circulated and credited history of Ruth's childhood written by prominent Baltimore attorney Paul F. Harris, whose father had played for Mount St. Joseph's.

"Shame on the Babe," Harris thundered in *Babe Ruth: The Dark Side.*

In 2008, he arranged with the Babe Ruth Birthplace and Museum for a headstone to be erected and prayers to be said at her grave. Harris died without knowing he owed Katie's son an apology.

There were no guests at the wedding of George H. Ruth Jr. and Mary Ellen Woodford at St. Paul Catholic Church in Ellicott City, Maryland, on October 14, 1914. There was no pomp or flourish either; the only attendants were two members of the congregation, one of whom was the officiant's sister.

It is tempting to dismiss this sweet, early, impetuous act of adulthood as a doomed, youthful folly. What did he know of his bride, who served him breakfast at the coffee shop in the morning and sneaked out of her parents' house to meet him at night? What could he know about women? Or about himself? But it was also the conventional act of a young man conforming to societal norms. This was not the wild man of myth who, freed from the strictures of St. Mary's, indulged every appetite and vice. His first instinct was to construct a family, to give himself a place at the table, reclaiming the spot he willingly relinquished in Pegler's fabulist version of his childhood.

V

George Sr. remarried a year later on Christmas Day, 1915. His bride was Martha E. Sipes, twenty years his junior. She had been married before, when she was sixteen, to a Baltimore cop who made an honest woman of her only after being threatened by her brother Benjamin. The groom lost his job with the city. The marriage lasted six months.

She was living with George above his saloon at 406 West Conway in 1912 when he applied for a new liquor license at that address; when the bar was raided by police for serving liquor on Sundays; when a fire started by rats gnawing on matches in the cellar forced them to drop her nieces out of the bedroom window into the arms of waiting police; and when Katie Ruth died.

In the aftermath of all that, George Sr. quit the saloon business. He went back to what he knew: repairing lightning rods and harnesses. George Jr. was having more success in his line of work. In 1915, his first full season as a pitcher for the Red Sox, he won eighteen games and lost only eight, leading Boston to the World

Series against the Philadelphia Phillies. Deemed too young to trust in such crucial games, he made only one appearance in the Series—which the Red Sox won, four games to one—as a pinch-hitter, grounding out in the ninth inning of Game 1. But he earned a full World Series share, $3,780.25.

The brothers urged him to take an off-season job selling cars. Instead he used his money to set his father up in a swanky new saloon, which his daughter Julia later construed as evidence that he had forgiven, if not forgotten, the pain of paternal abandonment. "Daddy never held it against his father," she said. "He even went and helped out."

Ruth's Cafe was no gin joint. It occupied an enviable location at the corner of Lombard and Eutaw Streets opposite the Emerson Tower, a Baltimore landmark modeled on Florence's Palazzo Vecchio. Helen and Babe would spend the winter of 1915 living above the saloon with George and Martha.

Father and son were photographed behind the bar one evening as they awaited the holiday crowd. The cafe is decked out with Christmas balls, banners, lanterns, and tinsel dangling from the pressed-tin ceiling. A gleaming punch bowl and empty crystal glasses refract light from the bar's mahogany sheen. A patron in a crisp fedora, an African American waiter, a barman, and a dog perched on a wooden chair eyeing the raw bar fill out the tableau. A 1916 calendar advertising the saloon as "Babe Ruth's Favorite" hangs on the wall behind George Sr.'s shoulder—perhaps it was New Year's Eve.

In the photograph, the only known picture of George Sr. and Jr., their identical attire—black vests, striped shirts, and unblemished white aprons—underscores the profound similarity in face and build. But the distance between them—ten feet or more—also speaks volumes.

The father, grim, stiff, and unsmiling, looks sideways at the camera—florid even in black and white. He dominates the foreground, as stout as his son would later become, a lit cigar burning between the stubby fingers of his left hand.

George Jr. meets the camera's lens with the nonchalance acquired in public life. He is accustomed to attention and has the bonhomie his father lacks. He has already distanced himself from the old man. Two women, perhaps Helen and Martha, linger in the shadows of a darkened doorway at the far end of the bar.

They would remain shadowy figures in his life: the young wife who couldn't keep his attention, and the stepmother with whom he couldn't get along. "Babe and Martha, they fought like cats and dogs," Mamie Ruth Moberly said. "All they had to do was look at one another—they disliked each other that much—and then they were in an argument. She had spells. Sometimes she could be as nice as oh anything; other times [she was] like the devil."

Mamie had quit school after seventh grade to help out—her father's eyes were failing, she recalled. She cleaned the rooms for boarders who came through town, sometimes bringing lice with them, and fixed her mother's recipes. She left home as soon as she could, taking a job at Hutzler's, a local department store.

On January 10, 1918, Martha's brother Benjamin Sipes, who had intervened on her behalf with her first husband, was arrested in Ruth's Cafe for selling dope to an Army private stationed at Camp Meade, outside Baltimore. It was a sting operation arranged with military police after the soldier confessed that he had been buying morphine from Sipes—known as "Doc" to members of the Ruth family—since the previous October. The charges were dropped after an analysis of the alleged morphine revealed that it was a compound of sugar, starch, and salicylic acid.

Small wonder that George Ruth Sr. reacted fiercely when seven months later, on August 24, Sipes got into a heated argument in the saloon with his brother-in-law Oliver Beefelt. Beefelt was married to Martha's sister, Nellie, who had been living with George and Martha.

Beefelt, who was out on bail after being arrested for statutory rape of a sixteen-year-old girl, had quit providing for his wife. "My great Grandfather was a peddler and unscrupulous," his great-grandson Jonathan Shahan reported in an email. "He had my great-grandmother Nellie Sipes committed in 1920 mainly because she was getting in his way of life. He was getting in trouble for scalping tickets and not having licenses and so forth. . . . Nellie was distraught, and her brother Benjamin went over to have it out with Oliver. But George was running a business and didn't want that beef in his bar."

Sipes left the cafe and went across the street to buy a cigar. George Sr. intercepted him at the corner. An argument ensued and quickly escalated. Blows were exchanged. Sipes would testify that Ruth hit him twice and kicked him once without provocation before he retaliated.

"Doc didn't mean it to happen the way it did," Moberly said. "Doc hit my daddy, right there at Lombard and Eutaw. He fell off the curb. The back of his head hit a manhole cover in the street. They say his brains was just laying out when they picked him up and took him to the hospital right up the street. He never gained consciousness. They said you could tell when he was laid out in the casket. The back of his head, I guess they couldn't get it all back in place. It just didn't look normal."

Sipes was arrested and taken to the Western District police station, where he spent the night in jail. A coroner's jury exonerated him, ruling that he had acted in self-defense.

It had already been a summer of upheaval for George Jr., whose manager, Ed Barrow, was every bit his equal in size and stubbornness. They were born to contend with each other and had done so, physically and otherwise, all season, which would end five weeks early due to the war. Barrow loathed Ruth's innate insubordination as much as he had grown to depend on him. He had adamantly opposed converting Ruth into an everyday player until he needed another bat in the lineup and sent him to the outfield. "I'd be the laughingstock of baseball if I changed the best left-hander in the game into an outfielder," he said.

Then, in the summer of 1918, with baseball losing players to the draft and Boston's pitching staff in a shambles thanks to the government's "work or fight" mandate, Barrow ordered him back to the pitching mound. Ruth balked. He liked hitting home runs.

He lost his temper, quit the team—to play briefly for the Chester Ship Building Company over the July 4 holiday—decamped for his father's bar in Baltimore, then returned, compliant, as always.

He was the winning pitcher on the afternoon of August 24, beating the St. Louis Browns 3–1, and looking forward to spending Sunday, an off day, at the beach with Helen. Instead they took the train to Baltimore after receiving a telegram about George Sr.'s death that morning.

In a photograph accompanying his obituary in the *Sun*, George Sr. looks nothing like the man in the picture taken in Ruth's Cafe two and one half years earlier with his son. Gone were the fullness of face and thick dark hair they shared. He had the appearance of a man much older than his forty-seven years, hollowed out perhaps by illness or maybe just life.

The obituary ended on a jarring note that suggested there was more to the story than the writer was allowed to say: "Mrs. Ruth today denied that she had any trouble with her husband before the dispute as was reported."

He was buried in Loudon Park Cemetery with four of the children who predeceased him: Augusta (or Augustus), Anna, Gussie, and William. An imposing granite headstone identifies him as the "Beloved Husband of Martha E."

She inherited the bar and its contents, itemized in probate documents: "43 Cases Whisky, 40-Gal Whisky, 20-Gal Whisky, 40-Gal Wine, 40-Gal Gin, 3 Half Barrels Beer, 20 Cases Beer, Miscellaneous Cordials, 500 Cigars, Miscellaneous Lot of Bottle Goods, 1 Box Pretzels, 3 Cash Registers, One Player Piano, Clock, 11 Pictures, Iron Safe, 80 Rolls Toilet Paper."

In 1920, Martha married George's bartender, George Strohmann, her third husband, whom she outlived by fifty years. Upon her death in 1966, she was buried with him, leaving George Sr. alone in the ground with his dead children.

Ruth's Cafe at 38 South Eutaw Street now operates as a strip club called the Goddess Gentleman's Club.

With George Sr.'s death, twenty-three-year-old Babe Ruth became the orphan that history had deemed him to have been.

VI

His allegiance to Brother Matt and to St. Mary's never wavered. The brothers would remain a source of solace and moral authority long after George Ruth became the Babe. "I'm as proud of it as any Harvard man is proud of his school, and to get crude for a moment, I will be happy to bop anybody in the beezer who speaks ill of it," Bob Considine wrote in *The Babe Ruth Story.*

After the 1919 fire that destroyed most of the school he took Brother Simon, Brother Matthias, and the St. Mary's band on a tour of American League cities to raise money to replace their lost equipment. He loaned money to classmate "Dope" Flaherty to start a moving company. He sent flowers often to the grave of his closest pal, Tommy Padgett, after his death in March 1920 and detoured off his 1921 barnstorming tour to pay his respects. They had arrived at St. Mary's together and had both pitched for the St. Mary's Red Sox. A scout from the Class D Interstate League offered them each seventy-five dollars a month to sign. Padgett took the offer and played for three years in Hornell, New York. Ruth held out for more money and when it didn't come through elected to stay at St. Mary's. After serving in the Army in World War I, Padgett took a job as a brakeman for the Allegheny Division of the Erie Railroad. He died a couple of days later after falling between cars of a moving freight train.

In coming seasons when Ruth encountered problems adhering to routine and convention, accepting the authority of manager and management, the Yankees turned to the brothers for help. "That boy needs a talking to!" Brother Paul would declare, hastening to New York.

Ruth responded with devotion, Brother Paul told the Baltimore *Sun*, rushing from the field to the clubhouse to put in a long-distance call to the brothers after setting a home-run record. In the summer of 1920, Big Matt gathered all the boys in the grandstand by home plate to read aloud the *Baltimore Sun*'s account of the Babe's great success: "Baltimore Boy Exceeds His 1919 Record by Making Two, Ball Player Gets $100,000 Movie Contract as Result of Feat." Six years later Brother Matthias showed up in the lobby of the team hotel in Chicago at the invitation of Yankee management, which had arranged for him to be invited to an international eucharistic congress, where he delivered a long lecture on the importance of avoiding a recurrence of his misadventures in 1925.

In gratitude, Ruth bought Matthias a second $5,000 Cadillac Touring Car. At his behest, the boys in the St. Mary's automobile shop cared for it like a Stradivarius. On August 17, 1927, the day Ruth hit the thirty-eighth of that season's sixty home runs, the car stalled out on the B&O tracks in Dorsey, Maryland, and was demolished by an express train, leaving only two tires intact. Ruth bought the good brother another machine.

The *Sun* was quick to report that Brothers Benedict and Matthias were Ruth's special guests at the first two games of the World Series in Pittsburgh. By then, Matthias had become intrinsic to the myth of the Babe, thanks to Westbrook Pegler. Yet within four years, Matthias dropped from public view. With the exception of the 1935 interview in the *Boston Evening Transcript*, later reprinted in the *Sporting News*, there was no mention or sighting of him; no more visits to Yankee Stadium or tickets put aside for him at World Series games.

In June 1931, he was reported to a local priest at Mount St. Joseph's near St. Mary's and then to the provincial general of the Xaverian Order for consorting with a young woman, Helen Bownes, who lived on Amberley Avenue, less than two miles from the school. Neighbors of the woman in question, members of the parish, reported the liaisons with determination and damning detail. They had seen him coming and going at all hours of the day and night for at least six months and said they recognized him from a newspaper article. They provided dates, times, and the frequency of his visits, as well as the license plate numbers of the cars he drove, one a Cadillac Touring Car.

After denials of wrongdoing and acquaintance-ship, and after again being seen at the lady's home at

3:00 A.M., Brother Matt was reassigned to St. John's Prep in Danvers, Massachusetts, and ordered by the archbishop not to return to Baltimore, his home for thirty-eight years.

The vigilant neighbors reported seeing him back on Amberley Avenue, where he spent eight to ten days with Miss Bownes between July 9 and July 27. Called to account by his superiors in August, he admitted to "keeping company early and late with the Bownes woman," to violating his vow of poverty, and to defying direct orders from the archbishop.

The final report, dated October 11, 1931, stated, "If Brother Matthias had been more amenable to discipline over a period of years, his scandalous actions might have been avoided."

Upon acknowledgment of and repentance for his sins, he was allowed to remain in the community and on staff at St. Joseph's Juniorate, a Xaverian High School for postulants in Danvers, where Brothers Arcadius Alkonis and Peter Donohue would see him walking the grounds, using a fungo bat instead of a cane, to steady himself in old age.

In Considine's *The Babe Ruth Story*, Brother Matthias dies in the mid-1930s, just as the Babe's major-league career is coming to an end—another factual error in the authorized account. Big Matt died alone in his room on October 16, 1944, at age seventy-two. Which suggests that either Ruth was out of touch with his mentor during the last years of Brother Matt's life or with the author of his own life story.

VII

Arriving fully sated in Lima, Ruth and Gehrig were greeted by a brass band and whisked away to pay visits to the Allen County Children's Home, St. Rita's Hospital, and the St. Rose School. After that, the welcoming committee took them door-to-door shaking hands until they were sore, selling them like Fuller Brush Men. Next they paraded them through downtown, such as it was, and had them preside at "the Big Baseball Party" in the Public Square, sponsored by the *Lima News*, before dropping autographed balls from the roof of a local bank. Then, thanks to the good midwestern manners of Lima's spectators, who declined to interrupt play, they played the first full nine-inning game of the tour and would be on their way to Kansas City via Chicago less than five hours later.

It was Ruth's second visit to Lima in as many years. A town in northwest Ohio known for harboring the KKK in the early twenties and for building locomotives and school buses, Lima was a place you went because so many important passenger trains went through it—the Erie, Manhattan, and Broadway Limited—en route to somewhere else. Ruth's friend Bernie Halloran, the owner of the Murphy Street ballpark, had gotten in touch before there were any games scheduled between Brooklyn and K.C., offering Ruth $5,000 to get off the train in Lima.

The year before, Ruth had played every position except right field and catcher, hitting two doubles and two home runs. In his telegram accepting Halloran's offer, he vowed to play eight positions in his encore performance so that everyone in the ballpark could get "a close squint" at him.

The home plate umpire was John Phillips, a local fireman summoned from the grandstand the year before when the original ump called too many strikes on the Babe. Fearing for the man's life, Halloran had sent Phillips home to get his blue suit and his protective equipment.

This game actually meant something to most of the players on the field, who were vying for the Allen County championship between Halloran's Lima Beans and the Celina Carp. When Ruth came to bat for the Beans in the seventh inning with a runner on first, Gehrig was on the mound for the Carp. Determined not to give the Bam anything good to hit, he threw three straight balls low and outside. Ruth turned to Phillips and ordered him to call the next two pitches strikes—no matter what.

The next pitch was also low and outside. Phillips called it a strike. The crowd booed. Phillips called the next pitch, thrown to the exact same spot, strike two. Ruth hit the 3-2 pitch over the center field fence, where Phillips swore it hit a B&O Railroad boxcar passing on the tracks outside the Murphy Street park.

Babe Ruth's Beans prevailed 9–6, thanks to his two home runs and four innings of scoreless relief pitching. Although he didn't play all eight positions, he was the winning pitcher, striking out all three batters in the top of the ninth, including Gehrig.

This did not detract in the least from the opinion of the Girl Reporter representing the *Lima Morning Star and Republican-Gazette*, who was, as Walsh envisioned, in full reportorial swoon. "Gehrig, unmarried, could make the most hard-hearted Hannah melt in his arms. Being single and so impressed with Lima's flappers, perhaps accounted for the 'losing pitching and the lack of home runs.'"

Phillips, who had the best vantage point in the ballpark, had to agree: Ruth was "all man" from the waist up, but Gehrig was "all man" from the feet up.

"By the by, sisters of beauty, Gehrig was privately

heard to remark that Lima sure had some 'warm-looking mamas,'" the Girl Reporter reported, which was something of a scoop as no one had ever heard Lou Gehrig talk about warm-looking mamas before.

She saw other qualities in "the Bambino of the diamond," who was "gracious with all the flappers who were lucky enough to meet him."

That was not the opinion of New York society matrons—like Mrs. Adler of the *New York Times* Adlers, who happily solicited his help raising money for charity, then gasped at his offhand reply: *Shit, lady, I'd do it for anybody.*

Or the hostess of a formal dinner who made the mistake of asking, "Don't you like the asparagus salad, Mr. Ruth?" only to get a disquisition on its effect on the smell of his urine.

The fact is, the Babe had come a long way since St. Mary's. Ford Frick, who had escorted him to the asparagus disaster, saw it, as did Marshall Hunt. He had learned the niceties of etiquette and acquired, as Hunt put it, "at least the veneer of a gentleman."

Like Jack Dempsey, who came from similarly challenged circumstances, the Babe had acquired important social skills, such as holding out his pinkie finger while sipping from a china cup, and to bow and say, "Charmed to meet you."

"It got so you could take either of them anywhere with greater safety than a lot of businessmen," Hunt told Jerome Holtzman. The Big Bam and the Manassa Mauler could be "civil and polite and even gallant at times."

Before taking their leave of Lima, Ohio, Ruth and Gehrig had one more civic task to perform: accepting bronze baseball statues from "two of Lima's feminine beauties," who, the *Lima News* reported, were "expected to remind the twins to return to Lima not to play baseball but to enjoy some of its hospitality."

Gehrig politely accepted his statue of a right-handed slap-hitter, choking up on his bat, and asked to have it engraved, "Hello, Mother—with my Lima friends today," and shipped home to Mom Gehrig.

Ruth received his trophy from Miss Rosemary McNeff, a seventeen-year-old high school graduate, who also presented him with an opportunity for graciousness. Her aunt Rose, a local seamstress, had made her a brand-new suit for the occasion and borrowed a high-fashion accessory, a large, dead fox that she draped just so over her niece's bosom, its snout nestled in the crevice of her cleavage and one of its tiny little feet pinned across her chest.

The Girl Reporter, who reported everything else that transpired that afternoon, did not note any remarks from the Babe after the presentation. In the picture taken before he and Gehrig hustled back to the Pennsylvania Railroad Station, his eyes are firmly on the ball he autographed for Rosemary, which is still in her family.

"What an awful break that the train left at four P.M.," sighed the Girl Reporter.

Chapter 7
October 15 / Kansas City, Missouri

**BABE RUTH AND LOU GEHRIG ARRIVE
FOR BENEFIT GAME**

NUMBERS WILL IDENTIFY PLAYERS

—*KANSAS CITY POST*

**"WHAT IS THE RACIAL ORIGIN OF
BABE RUTH?"**

—*PITTSBURGH COURIER*

I

The entourage detrained at Union Station in Kansas City, Missouri, at 10:25 A.M. They were greeted by the Boys' Pinto band; a sleek, tan-colored Cadillac sedan trimmed in blue, courtesy of the Greenlease Motor Company; and George Cauthen, photo editor of the *Kansas City Post*, who had given himself the plum assignment of following Ruth and Gehrig around town all day.

Even by Walsh's energetic standards, the schedule was ambitious, with visits to three orphanages (two white, one black), two newspapers, and one hospital in addition to a noontime parade downtown with the usual ball scramble, all before the 2:30 P.M. game at Muehlebach Field.

At the *Kansas City Star*, Ruth rolled up his shirt-sleeves, donned an editor's green eyeshade, and affected to tinker with copy. It was a favorite Walsh move, a way of rewarding—and ensuring—the loyalty of newspapers that bought Ruth's stuff. The caption under his studious mien read:

BABE RUTH EDITS STAR SPORTS PAGE.
NOTED BEHEMOTH OF BASH TOILS OVER
UNFAMILIAR TASK, SAYS PUTTING OUT A SPORTS
PAGE IS HARDER WORK THAN HE THOUGHT.
NEXT TIME HE'LL HAVE MORE RESPECT FOR
THE ENERGETIC EFFORTS OF THE GENTLEMEN
OF THE PRESS.

At the rival *Kansas City Post*, Ruth thanked assembled staffers for sponsoring that afternoon's game, a benefit for Mercy Hospital for Children, the next stop on the hectic itinerary, where they presented a $650 General Electric Monitor Top refrigerator to an assemblage of doctors, nurses, and children who gathered on the hospital steps trying to look grateful. "This is a big, fine refrigerator," Babe ad-libbed.

A residential version of the refrigerator was just coming on the market. A Kansas City appliance salesman named M. A. Glueck was responsible for the donation. He had run into Ruth in New York earlier in the fall and suggested the giveaway. "The Babe was all for it," Glueck told the newspaper years later, "and the kids were tickled to death."

Next up: the St. Vincent's Home in Leavenworth, Kansas, the Gillis Home, the Kansas City Orphan Boys' Home, and the Guardian Angel Home for Negroes—all before a scheduled luncheon at the Kansas City Athletic Club. But somewhere, somehow, between Leavenworth and downtown Kansas City, someone representing the Wheatley-Provident Hospital for Negro Children reached Ruth and asked him to make time for them.

Wheatley-Provident was the first black-owned and -operated teaching hospital in the Midwest. It was founded in 1916 by Dr. J. Edward Perry, with the help of Dr. Katherine B. Richardson, who, along with her late sister Alice, had founded Mercy Hospital. Unable to persuade Mercy's board of directors to admit black children, Richardson led a fund-raising campaign for Wheatley-Provident, securing five thousand dollars in ten days, Perry noted in a 1927 issue of the *Journal of the National Medical Association.*

At Wheatley-Provident, George Cauthen took the most important and enduring image of the day: a portrait of a sleeping baby snuggled in Babe Ruth's arms. It is a study in opposites, black and white, stark and tender: the infant, eyes closed, pressed against the bulk of Ruth's chest; while the Babe, his face turned fully toward Cauthen's lens, smiles broadly and without inhibition for his camera. The white of the baby's hospital gown vibrates against Ruth's dark brown jacket—his favorite color. The child's furrowed brow underscores Ruth's untroubled gaze. Tiny fingers splayed across his wide lapel, reaching for security the way babies do, the Babe securing the baby's bottom in one large paw.

The lead story in the *Post* made no mention of the visit except in the caption: "Although not on the original schedule, the Babe answered an urgent invitation to visit the children's ward at Wheatley-Provident hospital and missed lunch as a result. He is shown with a little Negro sufferer in his arms."

When Cauthen made up the page that night, he put that image in the center of the two-page spread.

II

The photo was available to twenty-five Hearst newspapers read each day by three million Americans, nearly 10 percent of the population, through Hearst's International News Photos. Within weeks, it appeared in two of the nation's most prominent African American newspapers—the *Chicago Defender* and New York's *Amsterdam News*.

The image was powerful, too powerful perhaps, which may explain why it could not be found in any of the white newspapers currently digitized by the Library of Congress or by those on the online databases newspapers.com and newspaperarchives.com. Nor is it surprising, given the mores of the times, that the white children photographed with Ruth and Gehrig at Mercy Hospital are named by the *Post* but not the black infant in Ruth's arms.

Major-league baseball remained a bastion of white privilege, ignoring the views expressed in a December 6, 1923, editorial in the *Sporting News*: "It matters not what branch of mankind the player sprang from with the fan, if he can deliver the goods. The Mick, the Sheeney, the Wop, the Dutch and the Chink, the Cuban, the Indian, the Jap, the so-called Anglo-Saxon—his nationality is never a matter of moment if he can pitch, or hit, or field. In organized baseball there had been no distinction raised—except tacit understanding that a player of Ethiopian descent is ineligible—the wisdom of which we will not discuss except to say by such rule some of the greatest players the game has ever known have been denied their opportunity."

The same day Ruth was photographed cuddling a sickly black child in Kansas City, the *Pittsburgh Courier* reported that commissioner Kenesaw Mountain Landis had banned white minor-league players from participating in the integrated Southern California Winter League Baseball season, scheduled to begin play the following week.

The ban carried "the threat of expulsion from organized baseball." The season was canceled.

Landis would brook no chink in the color line that had banished African American players from major-league baseball since 1887 and would remain in effect under his fiat until Branch Rickey and Jackie Robinson ended it in 1947.

Ruth had to have known that posing with the baby in the city where the Ku Klux Klan had held its national convention three years earlier would rekindle all the talk and the whispers about him and the cruel epithet that took root on the playgrounds at St. Mary's. The name, a confabulation of childhood cruelty and crude stereotype, had jumped the fence at St. Mary's and spread to other precincts where baseball was played. Benjamin Gorfein, a young Jewish boy growing up in Baltimore when Ruth was a teenager playing ball at Druid Hill Park, told his grandson that everyone knew Ruth as Nigger Lips. Nor did it die with Babe Ruth's family. "I got that when I was growing up," said Harry Pippin, a distant cousin, who bears a striking resemblance to Ruth in the shape of his face and his girth. "Boys are unmerciful."

The epithet followed him to Boston, where Red Sox teammates called him Nig, Nigger, and Tarzan, an allusion to Edgar Rice Burroughs's 1912 *Tarzan of the Apes.*

"What's this Tarzan stuff?" Ruth asked one day. "Ape? You're calling me an ape?"

In conversation, Marshall Hunt and Ed Barrow casually referred to him as the Big Baboon. "He wasn't human," his teammate Joe Dugan said. "He fell out of a tree."

He meant it kindly.

Stories spread by Red Sox teammates about his gluttony and lack of personal hygiene—toothbrushes he borrowed, underwear he eschewed, baths he didn't take, and body odor he exuded—fed a collective impression of piggishness that found expression in caricature.

Paulo Garretto's 1929 drawing for the *New York World*, loaned to the National Portrait Gallery by the Ruth family for a 2016 exhibition, turned his head into a bloated baseball, suggesting with a few sleek art deco lines a tautological truism: Ruth *was* baseball and baseball *was* Ruth. But Garretto also gave Ruth a nose as wide as the downturned corners of his mouth and nostrils as big as the pupils of his eyes—eyes squinched shut by weight and gravity—not a pretty portrait. In fact, it is porcine.

Six years later, when Ruth was voted into the Hall of Fame, the sculptor Alexander Calder created a grotesque wire figure of the man with a pig's snout and ears.

In this way, art gave expression to the sotto voce whispers and intimations that Ruth was something other than human, deviant even, a man unable to control his temper, his urges, and his appetites. Later, those whispers would be made explicit and held against him when he wanted to become a major-league manager. *How can he control others when he can't control himself?* This was the coded language of racial prejudice.

Louder voices in opposing dugouts at the Polo Grounds and Wrigley Field impugned his mother's reputation, ridiculed the breadth of his nose (broken in a fight, daughter Julia says), and the shape of his body, all that chest balancing on kindling legs. *Never seen a white man looks like that.* Press-box chatter, never elevated, devolved into predictable racial stereotype, gossip about the size of his genitals, and whispers, Fred Lieb shared with Jerome Holtzman, that Ruth had fathered a Negro child. When he ran into a fellow parolee from St. Mary's at a prizefight at Madison Square Garden, Ruth's greeting was preemptive: "Now don't call me Nigger Lips, or I'll break your arm."

So the buried one-line item in the next-to-last paragraph of Rollo Wilson's three-dot sports column in the *Pittsburgh Courier* on April 9, 1927, was as significant as it was unusual, giving voice to a possibility greeted in black neighborhoods with knowing glances and hopeful smiles and expectorated from big-league dugouts with venom and spittle. "What is Babe Ruth's racial origin?"

Wilson hid the question in a list of otherwise innocuous and seemingly random inquiries—space fillers columnists use when they're hard up for something to write. "What does the referee say when he calls the fighters together for a conference before the bell starts 'em off?" "Why does anyone run 26 miles?" "Would you call Tiger Flowers a tiger lily?" and "Why will thousands of colored baseball fans cheer Ty Cobb this year? Or will they?"

He promised "a slightly soiled press pass good at all press gates at the Sesqui to the correct guesser."

In 1927 America, there were two competing narratives about the Babe, divergent creation myths: one the white Horatio Alger myth; the other, the story of a secret brother whose words and deeds, especially involving "race players," were reported religiously in the black press:

When he supplied batting tips for readers of the Baltimore *Afro-American* on June 10, 1921, including details of his off-season training regimen: "Between seasons I keep fit by hunting, fishing, hiking, and keeping out in the open and getting as much exercise as I can."

When he was the honored guest at a benefit for the Mother AME Zion Church in Harlem in 1923, and, the *Amsterdam News* reported, he was the highest bidder on autographed balls he himself had signed.

When that same year, he refereed a boxing match between a black and white fighter, the *Chicago Defender* reported that he ended up with so much blood on his shirt that it had to be thrown away—this at a time when many white Americans wouldn't dream of drinking from the same water fountain.

When he played against Negro Leaguers in exhibition and barnstorming games, and happily shared a chaw of tobacco, these things were noticed.

When tickets went on sale for the first World Series game at Yankee Stadium in 1927, the twice-weekly Associated Negro Press (ANP) news agency in Chicago reported that second in line, arriving at 6:00 the night before, was a one-legged African American man who had hitchhiked from Washington, D.C.

When Ruth either did or did not call his shot by pointing to the outfield bleachers in Wrigley Field during Game 3 of the 1932 World Series, the ANP account and African American papers offered an alternate history: "Babe Ruth Socks a Homer for Loudmouth Latimer, Cub Rooter, Taunts of Fan in Bleachers Irks Bambino, So He Smacks One into the Bleachers, Missing His Tormentor by Three Feet."

The story did not appear in the white press until E. M. Swift wrote it for *Sports Illustrated* in 1980: "The Bleacher Bum version is that he was pointing to a black man named Amos (Loudmouth) Latimer, traveling secretary for the Chicago Negro League's Forty-seventh Street team. The story, which Loudmouth told for years afterward on Forty-seventh Street, goes that Latimer had been provoking Ruth from the centerfield bleachers by throwing lemon rinds at him and called him 'brother,' a reference Ruth had heard before because of his facial features."

Loudmouth that he was, Latimer rooted loudly for the Cubs, shouting after Ruth's first inning home run off Charlie Root, "Aw, the big bum, he ain't no good," the ANP reported. "That was just an accident. Get him a pair of crutches."

The ANP charged "the irrepressible colored bleacherite with unwittingly" bringing about the Cubs' downfall.

When the Babe came to bat in the third, he took off his cap and waved it to his tormentor in the centerfield bleachers. He also unburdened himself of a couple of choice remarks to Guy Bush, pitcher in the home dugout. . . .

Loudmouth could be heard yelping all over the field. The Babe held up one finger, signifying that it took only one swing to hit the apple.

Root shot the ball in. The Babe caught it square

on the nose and sent it more than 440 feet beyond the score board in the center-field bleachers. It missed Loudmouth by just three feet.

Among the many witnesses at Wrigley Field that day were Franklin Delano Roosevelt, the Democratic candidate for president; Chicago mayor Anton Cermak (who was assassinated four months later while riding in an open-top car with FDR); and a twelve-year-old boy named John Paul Stevens, who would become one of the longest-serving justices on the United State Supreme Court.

Stevens was sitting with his father and two brothers in box seats behind the third base line, from which he could see Ruth jawing with players in the Cubs dugout, most especially with Bush, a swarthy Mississippi boy who had lost Game 1 of the Series. Like most of the eyewitnesses, Stevens assumed the dispute was "about the Cubs being cheapskates, giving [former Yankee] Mark Koenig only a half share" of their World Series earnings.

Stevens couldn't hear the Cubs calling Ruth old and fat and far worse. Nor could he hear the Yankees yelling back, "Who are you calling a nigger? Look at your pitcher."

He was still yakking at Bush when he pointed to

the bleachers. "I always interpreted his pointing at the scoreboard as 'I'm going to knock *you* to the scoreboard,' rather than 'I'm going to hit a home run,'" Stevens said.

Ruth said nothing about intent immediately after the game; nor did most of the reporters, save Westbrook Pegler and Joe Williams. But, as the legend of the Called Shot gained currency, he was quick to take ownership of it.

You read the newspapers, don't you?

African American readers, meanwhile, were treated to a news item, courtesy of ANP, about Ruth's guest aboard the Yankee special en route to New York. Bill "Bojangles" Robinson, the tap dancer remembered chiefly for four movies he made with Shirley Temple, danced through the aisles, having bet two thousand dollars at 6-to-1 odds that the Yankees would sweep the Cubs.

Back in Manhattan, Ruth was invited to a swank dinner party with his friend and golfing partner Grantland Rice. Also in attendance: Walter Lippmann, the political commentator, and his wife, who were unaccustomed to the Babe's vernacular. When Mrs. Lippmann politely inquired about the home run, Ruth replied with newfound gusto. "After the second [censored] pitch, I point my bat at these [censored] bleachers—right where I aim to park the [censored] ball," Rice reported.

The Lippmanns quickly made their farewells.

The following summer, when the Yankees were in Pittsburgh for an exhibition game, Ruth was interviewed by the *Pittsburgh Courier* about the inaugural East-West Negro League All-Star Classic, which was played at Comiskey Park in Chicago two months after the first major-league All-Star Game was played there. "The colorfulness of Negroes in baseball and their sparkling brilliancy on the field would have a tendency to increase attendance at games," Ruth said. "The [All-Star] game in Chicago should bring out a lot of white people who are anxious to see the kind of ball that colored performers play."

The story was reprinted in the *Chicago Defender* with a large photograph of the Babe, proclaiming him "a friend of the race."

III

Ruth wasn't the only white player to barnstorm against Negro Leaguers, but he was the most important and the only one suspected of "passing." In so doing, he sanctioned the quality of play and also provided fodder for further speculation about his ethnicity among whites and blacks.

His appearances were meaningful even if the games were not. "He gave them a stage to play on," said Negro League Baseball historian John Holway, not to mention a good payday, which was no small thing.

Ruth was not yet a full-time outfielder the first time he competed against a mixed-race team at the end of the abbreviated 1918 season. He had, nonetheless, tied for the American League in home runs with eleven. After leading the Red Sox to the world championship with his pitching arm, Ruth joined the New Haven Colonials of the Eastern League, owned by future Yankee general manager George Weiss, for a game against the Cuban All-Stars from Havana.

No official statistics from his games against Negro and mixed-race teams exist. (No official records of Negro League competition were kept.) The closest thing to it is the ledger compiled by baseball historian Bill Jenkinson, author of *The Year Babe Ruth Hit 104 Home Runs*. Jenkinson has documented sixty-five at-bats in sixteen games in which Ruth batted 25 for 54 with eight strikeouts, ten walks, and eleven home runs, including the three he hit off Dick Redding in Trenton in 1927 when Cannonball was allegedly grooving his pitches. To Jenkinson, the walks and strikeouts are proof that "there was no regular 'grooving' by black pitchers" in exhibition games against Ruth.

To John Holway, the encounters—and the statistics Jenkinson has tabulated—are meaningless. "He didn't face the best players in America," Holway said. "In an integrated league, he might not have hit 60 homers and he might not have hit 714."

After Ruth retired in June 1935, he made his first New York appearance in an exhibition game at the Dyckman Oval in Harlem against the New York Cubans. Also, in the thirties he faced Satchel Paige in Chicago, a story Buck O'Neill, the gregarious and accomplished first baseman for the Kansas City Monarchs, loved to tell. In fact, he loved telling it so much, he told it a variety of different ways. "Babe hit the first pitch over the seats," O'Neill said at Hofstra University's 1995 Babe Ruth Symposium. "Satch followed him as he ran around the bases and when he got to home plate, Satch shook his hand."

In another telling, for Ken Burns's documentary *Baseball*, O'Neill added, "They stopped the game and waited, he and Satchel talking, until the kid went out, got the ball, brought it back, and Satchel had Babe Ruth autograph that ball for him."

Like others in the black community, Negro Leaguers wondered, gossiped, and made happy assumptions about his racial background. Ruth's granddaughter Linda Ruth Tosetti was introduced to Theodore Roosevelt "Double Duty" Radcliffe at the annual Hall of Fame induction weekend one year in the late 1990s. Double Duty was then the oldest living Negro Leaguer, perhaps the oldest living professional baseball player. "He said, 'Sit down, I'm gonna tell you about your granddaddy. He was a good man. People used him. He knew it, and he helped them anyway. That's a fine tribute to a man. And he used to be a friend to the Negro Leagues. He used to speak up about us. They tried to shut him up, but he wouldn't be shut up. And he used to come to my games when he could. And he used to bring a blond one for him."

Double Duty treated the rumors about Ruth as fact. "Babe Ruth was mulatto," he told *Sports Illustrated* in 2002. "He had the nose of a colored man. He grew up in that orphanage, so nobody knows what all is in him for sure, but there's black and white blood in him. We all thought it was great that he could pass for white and hit all those home runs and make all that money playing white baseball."

It was still a subject of conversation among Negro Leaguers when young Monte Irvin joined the Newark Eagles in 1938. "Some of the knowledgeable players would mention it just in passing," Irvin said before his death in 2016. "They'd say, 'Babe's got the big lips and the wide nose. Maybe that's why he was so well thought of by the Negro community and the players.' They used to say, 'I think Mrs. Ruth was dating other guys.'"

Irvin, later a member of the major league's first all-black outfield with the 1951 New York Giants, a Hall of Famer, and president of the National League, also heard stories about the size of Ruth's personal assets from former Yankee Waite Hoyt, by then a broadcaster for the Cincinnati Reds. This, too, was purported evidence of his blackness for those who trucked in stereotype. "When he went to Japan, the women in Japan couldn't handle him, so they had to send up to Northern Japan where the Russian women were to import them for him to have somebody to play with," Irvin quoted Hoyt as saying. "He was known to be heavily endowed. He complained about the little women in Japan who were too skinny. He needed some real women. So he told the Japanese authorities about it; and they sent up to Sapporo, which may be 100 miles or so more or less, to import a bevy of women to make him happy.

"Hoyt said when he would finish with one of those

women, he would light up a cigar. And when he came in the room in the morning, there were four cigars in the tray; so that meant he had sex with these girls. Then Waite said that's the way he knew how much fun he was having by counting the cigars in the ashtray."

IV

One story that did not appear in the African American press—probably because black sportswriters did not have access to white clubhouses—marks the only time on record that Ruth publicly responded to the insults and epithets. The occasion was Game 3 of the 1922 World Series against the Giants, the last time the Yankees called the Polo Grounds home. Ruth had a sore elbow, a bad Series, and unaccustomed bad press.

The Giants, under the direction of manager John McGraw, employed benchwarmer Johnny Rawlings, a boyhood schoolmate of Walsh's in Los Angeles, to hector Ruth at the plate. Rawlings was the type of ballplayer for whom the word *scrappy* was invented, a guy who would do anything to help his win team, even if it included shouting racial slurs from the home dugout in a voice loud enough to be heard on the other side of the Harlem River, where construction on Yankee Stadium was under way.

"I'll get them," Ruth told his teammate Bob Meusel after going hitless in Game 3. "In fact, I think I will right now."

With Meusel in tow, Ruth charged into the Giants' locker room to confront the slanderer. The sanctity of the clubhouse is a foundational principle of baseball etiquette, a threshold not to be crossed—as opposed, for example, to calling a man a nigger within earshot of fifty thousand people.

Frank Graham, then writing for the New York *Sun*, gave the fullest account of the episode in his 1943 book, *The New York Yankees: An Informal History.*

Rawlings, one of the heroes of the 1921 series, but now a utility infielder, was sitting in front of his locker putting on his socks. He was a little fellow. The Babe strode over to him.

"If you ever say again what you said to me out there today I'll beat your brains out. I don't care how small you are."

Rawlings grinned up at him. "What's the matter," he asked quietly, "can't you take it?"

"I can't take that."

Earl Smith, hard-boiled Giant catcher, walked over while the other players looked on in silence.

"What did he say to you, Babe?" he asked.

The Babe told him. Repeated here, it would burn a hole in the paper.

Smith shook his head. "That's nothing," he said, and walked away.

The conversation escalated, with other Giant players joining in and everybody calling everyone else a liar. Ruth almost came to blows with Frankie Frisch when he accused him of staging the act to get his name in the newspaper. It was only then that Ruth noticed a cohort of baseball writers looking on.

"Gee, fellows, I didn't know you were here. Please don't write anything about this. Please! I'm sorry I came in."

As he turned to go, he looked at Rawlings and said, "But lay off that stuff. I don't mind being called a —— or a —— but none of that personal stuff."

The Giants howled.

The story stayed secret until Graham told it in 1943 but gained no traction until Robert Creamer repeated it in his 1974 biography, *Babe*, filling in the blanks: a prick or a cocksucker.

That was the year Hank Aaron broke Ruth's lifetime home-run record—a milestone that subjected Aaron to racist invective and prompted a literary reconsideration of Ruth. Four major biographies would be published between 1973 and 1975, not to mention *No Cheering in the Pressbox*, with all its first-person recollections of the Babe.

"I've been somewhat amused this past summer reading about the trouble Hank Aaron was running into when he was chasing Ruth's record," Fred Lieb told Holtzman. "Aaron said—and it came out in the papers—that the fans were writing him abusive letters, calling him, 'nigger,' and he said that Babe Ruth was never confronted with anything like that.

"What Aaron doesn't know, and I supposed what most people don't know, is that some of Babe's teammates on the Red Sox were convinced he had Negro blood. Many of the players, when they wanted to badger him, called him 'nigger.' Ruth had Negroid features, Negroid nose, mouth, lips. But when you saw him naked, from the neck down, he was white, a good deal whiter than most men."

Lieb had been covering sports for over fifty years; his words carried a lot of weight and were widely repeated and recycled by sportswriters and biographers. Especially the stories about Ty Cobb, the son of the South, baiting Ruth about his body odor and hurling the N-word from the Detroit dugout. By 1924, the Tigers had acquired the acerbic personality of their player-manager, which was much in evidence during a testy series in Detroit that June. With the Yankees leading 10–6 in the top of the ninth inning on June 13—and New York and Boston a game ahead of Detroit in the standings—Ruth had "to duck to escape a pitch near his head," the *Times* reported. Having failed to hit him, the Tigers' aggrieved pitcher Bert Cole promptly nailed "Languid" Bob Meusel in the ribs, whose response was anything but languid. The ensuing altercation, no mere baseball rhubarb, involved two major-league rosters, all the police on duty at Navin Field, and 18,000 spectators. According to Fred Lieb, Ruth and Cobb went after each other "like two football linemen, each trying to put the other out on the play." Ruth had to be restrained by "two umpires and three or four players," Tigers' owner Frank Navin reported to league president Ban Johnson, "like an enraged tiger held at bay."

In his letter to Johnson, protesting his innocence, Ruth said only that "several sharp things were said to me, and I replied with remarks of the same sort."

Umpire Billy Evans made no mention of Ruth's role in the riot in his official report to the league, except to note that Cole had almost hit him, too. Much to the Tigers' dismay, Ruth was not punished. Cole and Meusel were suspended indefinitely.

Lieb told Jerome Holtzman a story he had heard about Cobb refusing to share a cabin at a Georgia hunting lodge with Ruth, saying, "I won't sleep with a Nigger," which gained wide circulation after the publication of *No Cheering in the Press Box*. He also told Holtzman, from the neck down, Ruth was "as white and a good deal whiter than most men."

(Though Ruth and Cobb collaborated in a series of charity golf matches to raise money for the USO during World War II, Cobb's resentment was still in full flower in letters addressed to Christy Walsh years after Ruth's death.)

Every ten years or so, the stories would resurface, sometimes in most unexpected fashion. In 1984, during previews for the very brief run of the off-Broadway play *The Babe*, Max Gail, the star of the one-man show, appeared on a radio call-in show hosted by an African American sportscaster. "On the show, a guy said there was a story that Babe Ruth was actually a black brother," Gail recalled. "I said a lot of black people knew people who were passing."

A day or two later, he received a telephone call from a woman who said, "Mr. Gail, my name is Dorothy Ruth Pirone and I have a bone to pick with you. I hear you're out there telling people my father's a black man."

Then she said, "I just wondered how you'd feel—I have children and grandchildren—how you'd feel if someone said your parent was black?"

Gail replied, "They probably will, because my wife is black."

In fact, Dorothy's youngest daughter, Linda, had questioned her mother about her grandfather's skin color and been told his swarthy complexion was the result of how much time he spent outside at St. Mary's. So one day when an African American couple greeted her by saying, "You can't be Babe Ruth's granddaughter—you're not black," she had a ready reply. "He was German and suntanned."

In May 2001, Spike Lee dedicated his inaugural sports column in *Gotham* magazine to the subject of Ruth's race. After rehashing Ty Cobb's slurs, he suggested that perhaps it was time to dig up the Babe and test his DNA. As quickly as he made the suggestion, Lee assured his readers that would never happen, allowing Hank Aaron to explain why: "They are not going to dig up the Babe. They don't want that revealed, that there could be an ounce of black blood in him."

Lee's column set off a flurry of renewed speculation and opinion. Clarence Page, columnist for the *Chicago Tribune*, and a prominent voice in the African American community, brought new perspective to the old tale, pointing out Ruth's quandary: "Even if there were no hard evidence that he was black, how was Ruth to come up with hard evidence that he wasn't? You can't prove a negative, as the old saying goes. Gee, imagine how the Babe must have felt," Page wrote. "Whether he was a black man or not, he was getting abused like one."

His daughter Julia came to believe, as she said her father did, that racial bias was the decisive factor in his banishment from baseball and the unwillingness to hire him as a manager. "Judge Landis was absolutely against blacks," she said. "He knew that if Daddy was a manager, Daddy would have had blacks on the team. He felt they were discriminating against him, Judge Landis in particular, because he had absolutely no objection to blacks in baseball."

It isn't necessary to elevate him to the rank of a civil rights pioneer in order to imagine how it must have felt to be the object of racial invective. Nor is it necessary to dig up his corpse, as Spike Lee proposed, to appreciate why the answer to the question would have special significance in the African American community.

In the interest of history, Jan McNamee, Mamie Ruth's granddaughter, his closest proven biological relative, agreed to have her DNA tested. A saliva sample analyzed by CeCe Moore, of the DNA Detectives, a consultant for the PBS series *Finding Your Roots*, *Genealogy Roadshow*, and *ABC News*, concluded that her test sample showed no evidence of African "admixture" in her DNA.

It follows, Moore said, that if Ruth's biological parents were who they were believed to be, Ruth had no "significant amount of African admixture" in his DNA.

No test is required—or sufficient—to measure the quotient of delight in the faces of the African American fans photographed leaning out of a rickety spring training ballpark in the South, hands reaching for the sweaty Babe, taking his ease by the right field fence, just out of their reach. Or the concern in the eyes of the well-heeled Washington, D.C., fans in their white straw boaters consigned to the black section of Griffith Stadium on July 5, 1924, when the Babe knocked himself unconscious running into the concrete parapet. A fat white cop raised his arm toward the men peering over the wall to see, an officious and peremptory reminder that blacks were not permitted on the field. The Babe was out cold for a whole five minutes but stayed in the game.

There is no photographic evidence of his visit to a crippled black man in Chicago one Friday afternoon in November 1927, just an address scribbled on a pad in the hotel suite he was sharing with Lou Gehrig. They were expected at the Palmer House that evening for the annual All America Football dinner hosted by Christy Walsh to promote the new rivalry between Notre Dame and USC and the big game that weekend at Soldier Field. They had promised to show up in team colors. When, late in the afternoon, Ruth was still AWOL, Gehrig went in search of him.

"He rode out to the address—in the black belt on the mid-South Side," John B. Kennedy wrote. "He located Ruth in a dingy bedroom of a Negro tenement telling a beaming little colored cripple just how the Yankees won the World Series."

V

Because of the added visit to Wheatley-Provident Hospital and a promotional appearance the Babe had tacked on to his already overscheduled day, he was running late for the game at Muehlebach Field. Because it was one of the first tour dates announced, it was also one of the best publicized and best attended. Zack Wheat, the future Hall of Famer who had just concluded the last of his nineteen years in the major leagues, was there, as was Pat Collins, the Yankee catcher, with whom Ruth and Gehrig would sneak out of the ballpark after the game—"Just try and find us," Ruth teased. (One place they weren't found was Lawrence, Kansas, at the annual Dad's Day banquet at Kansas University, which they had promised to attend. They sent their regrets.)

Tickets were sold at fifty-four stores. A local railroad advertised a special excursion fare from Chillicothe for the game—$2.50 round-trip. Fifteen patrolmen were required to direct traffic and find parking spaces for two thousand cars arriving at the ballpark.

The Buddies Friend club transported fifty residents of a veterans' hospital, guests of the *Post*, who were admitted free, along with fifty children from the Gillis Home and the Kansas City Orphan Boys' Home. Ruth donated another fifty tickets to children from the St. Vincent's Home and the Guardian Angel Home for Negroes, who arrived early in a caravan of Army trucks from Fort Leavenworth. They had busied themselves at the concession stands while waiting for Ruth and Gehrig. By the time they appeared for batting practice, the *Post* reported, "the youthful worshippers were so full of peanuts, soda pop and hot dogs about all they had for the two sluggers was a glassy stare."

The paper estimated the crowd as "9,900 conscious spectators, weakly backed by 100 peanuts and pop foundered orphans."

Newsreel cameras from Pathé and Paramount filmed

highlights of the game, which would be screened the next night at local movie theaters for those who'd been unable to attend.

It was an Indian summer day, with a glorious, golden sun, lasting longer than the season normally allowed. The paper's unidentified scribe wondered whether Ruth's power extended to turning back the clock. "Babe Ruth, the fair fans idol, envy of fallen arches—the answer to Boyville's prayer—loveable boyish Babe" autographed two hundred baseballs before the game and convinced "the kind, generous old sun" to hang around until the game was over.

Gehrig was admired for his dimples and his physique. "Men looked at him and wondered where their waist line had gone; wished the old muscles hadn't gotten so tight and that they had been a little fairer with Mother Nature in her efforts to keep them human. For Gehrig, clear eyed, fair of face and clean limbed, showed himself to be a worthy model for any male."

His inside-the-park home run on a ball that stuck in the sod at the base of the right-field wall and popped straight up was a challenge to the Babe. Of course, he was up to it. Gauntlets were his specialty.

He hit a towering shot that sailed over a hundred stomachaches and the right field wall, bounding off the pavement on one bounce into the hands of an African

American boy balanced on a billboard "heavily laden with spectators at the corner of Twenty-First Street and Brooklyn Avenue."

The boy maintained his equilibrium on his perch and clung to the ball.

Chapter 8
October 16 / Omaha

BABE RUTH HEN WINS EGG RECORD
LAID ONE A DAY TILL SCORE OF 173 MADE HER
WORLD CHAMPION
—*NEW YORK TIMES*

AN OMAHA SCHOOL GIRL IS MISSING
POLICE FIRST HEAR OF IT WHEN MOTHER'S AD SEEN
IN PAPER—TWO BABE RUTHS MEET SUNDAY
—*LINCOLN EVENING JOURNAL*

I

The summit between the Babes was hastily arranged on October 11, the day the aviary cham-

pion laid her world-record-breaking 166th consecutive egg. Lady Norfolk, a single-comb white Leghorn chicken weighing in at 4¾ pounds at the beginning of the National Egg Layers' Association contest in November 1926, had laid an egg a day every day since April 29, two weeks after Ruth hit the first of his sixty home runs. She was a 307 chicken, meaning her mother had produced 307 eggs in a lifetime of laying them. Her paternal grandmother was a 275 hen.

She came from a good family.

Her owner, A. R. Landers, proprietor of the Allan Landers Commercial Egg Farm in Norfolk, Nebraska, was a baseball fan and, more to the point, a Yankee fan, of whom his son Jack would later say, "He threw a mean ball."

Landers, a college man, got his start with eighteen pullets and an eighty-dollar stake from his father-in-law, Doc Campbell, an old-time practitioner who made house calls in his buggy, with a hot brick to keep his feet warm in the snow. By October 1927, Landers had twenty-five hundred high-producing layers, working round the clock, and a ten-thousand-egg incubator where the future champion was hatched. The eight-month-old pullet had not yet laid a single egg when Landers went to his chicken coop and spent an hour among fifty of his finest cod-liver-oil-fed, blood-tested birds, to decide which to enter in the egg-laying contest taking place in Omaha that year. "I picked out this particular chicken because she was alert, quick, working all the time and"—like the Babe himself—"eating everything in sight."

She had, in fact, worked her fingernails to the bone, what with her industrious digging and scratching in order to keep fit, which was more than you could say for the Big Fella.

Lady Norfolk, as the bird had come to be known in deference to the Norfolk Chamber of Commerce, quickly distinguished herself among the 255 contestants representing thirty-two states at the American Milling Company henhouse. The makers of the high-octane Sucrene Egg Mash that had stimulated her to production—"heavily laden with protein, meat scraps, wheat flower middlings, finely ground oats, corn meal, wheat standard middlings, wheat standard bran and salt"—were moved to rename her Lady Amco of Norfolk.

By September, when she eclipsed the American record held by Lady Lindy, who had laid 149 eggs in 1926, the comparison with Ruth became inevitable. After all, he had had a good month, too. Wire services began issuing bulletins about Lady Babe's daily progress. Like Ruth, Landers declared, "She represents perfect co-ordination of the bodily functions, the nervous system and the mind."

And so, despite the objections of her hometown newspaper, Lady Amco of Norfolk became Lady Amco of Norfolk, the Babe Ruth of Layers. "She isn't Babe Ruth as the United Press persists in calling her," an October 17 article in the *Norfolk Daily News* protested. "She isn't Lady Amco as the *Omaha Bee* accommodatingly calls her in order to give a little free advertising to an Omaha product. She's Lady *Norfolk*."

Squawks of protest were also heard from Colorado, where a white Leghorn hen named Lady Skyline was said to be 45 eggs ahead of Lady Amco—but that competition wasn't officially sanctioned. Claimants from Vancouver and Scotland also cried foul. Word came from Australia that a chicken down under had laid 165 sanctioned eggs. No matter, Lady Amco kept batting them out.

The world-record-breaking egg, known as the Coolidge egg, was laid at 10:35 A.M. on Tuesday, October 11. Amco immediately put out a press release announcing that the Coolidge egg would be flown by airmail to the White House and the next one to New York for the other Babe. Then, deus ex machina, that very afternoon came word that Ruth would be appearing in Omaha later that week in a hastily arranged exhibition game.

George A. Danforth, superintendent of the competition, examined the bird and pronounced her good to go, ensuring a highly publicized and heavily marketed tête-à-tête between the two "Record Busters."

The Coolidge egg departed Omaha as planned on that Tuesday evening from the same airport Charles Lindbergh used in his days as a barnstorming airmail pilot. Lindbergh's landmark transatlantic flight had proved to be a boon for private aviation. Less than a month later, Charles A. Levine, a New York businessman, became the first passenger to cross the Atlantic by airplane. Two months after that, the United States Post Office turned over all airmail service in the country to private contractors. And a month after that, American Railway Express began air cargo express operations, delivering packages coast-to-coast in thirty-two hours. The Associated Press was one of its first clients, sending a package of news photographs from New York to Chicago.

The Coolidge egg left Omaha on a Boeing B-40 airmail plane en route to Chicago, where it changed planes for a National Air Transport flight to New York. Oddly, the country's first airmail route, established in

1918 between New York and Washington, had recently been discontinued. Which meant that when the egg got to New York, it had to catch a train to the nation's capital, arriving late on the afternoon of October 13, two days after it was laid, and just as the president returned from the annual observance of Founder's Day at the Carnegie Institute in Pittsburgh.

"Here was a story of a non-stop egg coming to a stop against a palate of such a nature that everyone would want to read about it," the United Press declared. "The egg arrived. But it reached the White House in the mail last night after all the reporters had gone home and the man named Smith, who opens the White House packages, could distinguish nothing about the package to show it contained the egg.

"Smith deferred opening the packet until the morning. And when he untied the package it was too late to include the egg in Mr. Coolidge's breakfast.

"Smith went, therefore, to the White House egg basket. He gingerly put Babe Ruth's championship egg in it where Mrs. Coolidge or the White House cook would be sure to find it."

Unfortunately, by lunchtime, the regular White House egg man had added a dozen plebeian Potomac eggs to the basket and none of the president's many advisers could say which was which. Also, the wire services had begun to express concern about "just how long an un-iced and uneaten egg will be a good egg."

By then, reporters had begun putting words in the bird's mouth, quoting an indignant and defiant chicken from Omaha: "I'm going to keep on laying until my illustrious namesake gets here." The little white Leghorn went on to say that she was sure that the Babe would not be "so choice in what he eats as Mr. Coolidge in that he thinks that one of my eggs won't keep three days without ice."

The summit at the henhouse was recorded by newsreel cameras and still photographers and slavishly reported by three wire services, the *Omaha World-Herald* and *Omaha Morning Bee*, the *Lincoln Evening Journal*, as well as the *New York Times*, which published a two-column profile of the bird accompanied by a photo of Landers and his prizewinning fowl. Egg-laying competitions were serious business—and big business for the National Egg Layers' Association, not to mention feed manufacturers like the American Milling Company and Nebraska farmers, then ranked fourteenth in the nation behind big egg-producing states like Missouri and Texas.

Harold Chenoweth, a Nebraska filmmaker who made industrial films—one-reelers, they were called—and who worked on retainer for Paramount News, shot the footage, bringing along his four-year-old son, Bob, for the momentous occasion. Decades later Bob would find his father's footage moldering in his sister's garage and have it painstakingly restored with help from UCLA film school. Of the hundreds of hours of film Bob donated to the University of Nebraska, twenty-eight seconds of the meeting of the Babes survive.

It shows a quiescent bird, spent perhaps by the effort of having just laid her 171st egg in as many days, lying quietly in Danforth's arms, blithely ignoring the crowd of Amco officials, reporters, and well-wishers, including one four-year-old boy in knickers and a newsboy cap sneaking into the frame.

The lady even showed a little leg.

Then came the handoff. With Chenoweth's camera grinding away, Danforth presented the Babe to the Babe. Immediately, the lady got her back up. Apparently, it ruffled her feathers to be used as a promotional prop. Ruth appeared equally ruffled by what one reporter described as "her sudden dash for liberty."

"Whoa," Ruth exclaimed, as she made a break for it. "There she goes." Only his quick reflexes and athletic dexterity prevented a tragedy. Handlers ascribed her nerves to the large number of visitors.

"One a day for 171 days!" Ruth added, when she

was back safely in his arms. "Gosh, how I wish I could do as well!"

II

This was no ordinary meeting between man and bird. In modern parlance, it was a media event, and a triumph of what is now called synergy. In 1927, synergy was a medical term employed to describe the cooperative interaction between organs. The industry—and the language—of public relations was still in its infancy then, incubating in Manhattan under the stewardship of Ivy Lee, Bruce Barton, and Edward Bernays, the founding fathers of PR, and the most celebrated of the city's five thousand "Merchants of Glory" counted by the *New Yorker* in 1926.

In the fall of 1927 everyone was in the thrall of propaganda, a word that had not acquired a pejorative connotation. Everyone who could afford a "propagandist" or "builder-upper" hired one. Everyone else was reading about them in Bruce Barton's number one bestseller, *The Man Nobody Knows*, a retelling of the life of Jesus Christ as the first super-salesmen leading his twelve apostles into "a kingdom of heaven" where nobody needed to know what they wanted. The book sold seven hundred thousand copies between 1925 and 1927 and earned Barton an invitation from Cecil B. DeMille to act as a consultant on Hollywood's first biblical spectacular, *King of Kings.*

There was no one better to be tied to in the fall of 1927 than Babe Ruth. Arriving in Kansas City, Ruth might have seen in a local paper the "Exploit-O-Grams" column reprinted from the *Film Daily* touting the success of the MGM exploiter who had arranged for Lillian Gish, star of the new film *Annie Laurie,* to donate box seats for the game at Muehlebach Field to twenty-five local orphans.

Ruth probably hadn't seen the story in the May 1927 issue of *Studebaker Wheel* magazine detailing his January fishing trip with Glenn E. Thomas, the Long Beach, California, car dealer who had brought along his publicist and cameraman on their excursion to the Rainbow Angling Club.

The interconnectedness of things was becoming more literal every day: wires and cables and track, electrical grids and radio frequencies, highways and tunnels, regularly scheduled airline flights and airmail delivery routes were bringing everything and everyone into a new kind of proximity, uniting the United States in ways never before possible.

A parallel system of opportunistic connectivity, benefiting a multiplicity of interests, was also proliferating. That was the motivation behind the meet-and-greet at the Omaha henhouse. All the clucking, pecking, and flapping of wings by 255 participating pullets could not obscure the tour de force of modern marketing in the photo taken of the Babes with AMCO spelled out in big letters over Ruth's shoulder, and the *NY* on his jacket, and the bird clucking what some interpreted as approval.

The business of public relations is as old as the urge to profit and to win. What was new in 1927 was the marriage between mass production and the mass distribution of goods and mass communication and mass psychology—a union employed on behalf of the Big Sell. Walsh had arrived in New York as a young advertising man just as the machinery of the wartime economy was being reinvented to serve consumers. And just as the original Mad Men were demonstrating how to manufacture desire for whatever or whomever they had been hired to sell.

These Merchants of Glory were the answer to the rhetorical question Bernays posed in his 1928 book, *Propaganda*: "Who are the men, who, without our realizing it, give us our ideas, tell us whom to admire and whom to despise, what to believe about the ownership of public utilities, about the tariff, about the price of rubber, about the Dawes Plan, about immigration; who tell us how our houses should be designed, what furniture we should put into them, what menus we should serve on our table, what kind of shirts we must wear, what sports we should indulge in, what plays we should see, what charities we should support, what pictures we should admire, what slang we should affect, what jokes we should laugh at?"

Ivy Lee, a former journalist who remade John D. Rockefeller as a philanthropist, imposed decorum on the messy business of hucksterism with his 1906 "Declaration of Principles," which stressed the need for "accuracy, authenticity and interest" in public relations. He also wrote what is widely considered the first press release when he persuaded Pennsylvania Railroad officials to release a factual account of that year's wreck at Gap, Pennsylvania, rather than try to suppress the facts, as was the custom.

Bruce Barton, the Congregational pastor's son, infused salesmanship with spirituality and wholesomeness, creating the mythic housewife Betty Crocker for General Mills, and "the silent majority" for Calvin Coolidge.

Bernays, who honed his skills on behalf of the U.S. war effort as a member of the Creel Committee, was the philosopher king of promotion. The nephew of Sigmund Freud, he appropriated his uncle's theories about unconscious desires and put them to work in the service of his clients. Bernays understood that a direct appeal was not enough to make consumers buy what they had never needed and didn't know they desired. And so he put psychoanalytic principles to work for Henry Ford, Thomas Edison, Enrico Caruso, Sergei Diaghilev and the Ballets Russes, Ivory Soap, A. G. Spalding & Bros., and the United States Brewers' Association, which hired him after the repeal of Prohibition to improve the image of German brewers, including Jacob Ruppert.

His methods were agnostic. The same techniques and sales pitches worked equally for fatty foods, presidential candidates who looked—as Alice Longworth Roosevelt said of Coolidge—like he'd been "weaned on a pickle," and physical culturists like *Evening Graphic* publisher Bernarr Macfadden, who'd had the poor judgment to advocate sex for pleasure rather than procreation.

Bernays pioneered the use of celebrity pitchmen, a term that entered the lexicon in 1926, when he put Charlie Chaplin in advertisements for Dodge Sixes— new 6-cylinder-model cars. He created panels of experts, the precursor of the modern catchphrase "nine out of ten doctors say," to testify to the bona fides of cigarettes and beer, and organized foundations that identified his clients with the public good.

Bernays also mastered the art of staged productions he called "overt acts"—the media events of today. He served up the first pancake breakfast at the White House for Coolidge and members of the Ziegfeld Follies, prompting the *Times* to observe: "President Nearly Laughs."

The most notorious of his gala productions was the smoke-in he organized during the 1929 Easter Parade on Manhattan's Fifth Avenue, when he armed a cadre of women with Lucky Strike cigarettes he called "Torches of Freedom." Every smoke ring they blew into the crowd was a declaration of independence and an argument for their right to smoke in public. High above their heads, a pilot spelled out "Smoke Lucky Strikes" in skywriting. A taboo evanesced in the skies over Manhattan and a new market opened.

Bernays had little use for exercise and once claimed his only experience in participatory sports was as a golf caddy at the Lake George Golf Club in 1901. But after *Time* magazine dismissed the *Evening Graphic* as "the most abnormal sheet in U. S. journalism" in February 1927, ridiculing its publisher as "BodyLove" Macfadden, his disquieted editorial board summoned Bernays.

He moved swiftly. First, he nixed Macfadden's plan for a nationwide tour of a nude statue of his twelve-year-old-daughter, which he had envisioned "as an example of what adherence to high standards in physical culture in parents could produce in off spring," urging instead establishment of a foundation to promote a national curriculum for physical education. Then, in lieu of a proposed barefoot hike from the Macfadden Building at Sixty-fifth Street to City Hall to "demonstrate how healthy living preserved the vigor of a 59-year-old man," Bernays sent Macfadden to London to address the House of Commons. His speech, hailed on the front-page of the *Evening Graphic*, was picked up by wire services and other dailies.

Upon his return, Macfadden was received at Gracie Mansion and on Capitol Hill, not as a kook but as the senior statesman of fitness. It was a classic demonstration of the Bernays system for "injecting news into an event that the public relations counsel creates for public appearance"—and for generating free advertising.

Their alliance lasted just long enough for Bernays to collect twelve thousand dollars and to conclude that his client was "unfathomable." Nonetheless, when he published a list of the fourteen most influential opinion makers in the country, he included Macfadden along with baseball commissioner Kenesaw Mountain Landis.

Christy Walsh was watching. He didn't subscribe to Bernays's highfalutin terminology; as he told an audience of potential 1939 World's Fair sponsors a decade later: "We were known as press agents until someone started using fancy titles like 'Public Relations counselor.'" But he borrowed liberally and overtly from Bernays's methodology. What else would you call that stunt he pulled in July 1926, when he stationed the Babe on a dusty runway beneath an airplane flying a hundred miles an hour dropping baseballs at his head, if not an "overt act"?

When Walsh wanted to help elect the Catholic governor of New York president in 1928, he paraded a chorus line from Murderers' Row carrying "Yankees for Al Smith" signs around major-league ballparks, bought radio time for a national address by Ruth, and stationed him atop a skyscraper in a dark suit and bowler with a campaign pin stuck in his lapel and a stogie protruding from his mouth. The photo left the unfortunate impression that Ruth was endorsing a gangster for president. He would steer clear of politics for the next sixteen years.

Walsh loaned Ruth's name generously, but not indiscriminately, to Madison Avenue's new celebrity endorsement campaign. He understood that if Ruth was going to sell shoes and caps and sweaters to kids, he had to be able to sell the Babe as a champion of children, which wasn't difficult given the genuine affinity between them. But it didn't hurt when Ruth became a national spokesman and fund-raiser for Father Flanagan's campaign to prevent "profiteering in homeless boys" in 1926 (an association Walsh conceived of after Ruth got himself in a legal jam in Michigan by fishing out of season). A visit to Boys Town, just outside Omaha, was scheduled between the confab at the henhouse and the exhibition game later that afternoon.

Many of the homes, hospitals, and orphanages that Ruth visited, including Boys Town, made sure to mention that Ruth was an orphan in their fund-raising campaigns, thereby perpetuating an untruth that he had long since given up trying to disprove but also forging a sympathetic bond between him and the institutions he visited. "Johnnie 'the Gloom-Killer,'" the newest and youngest host on Father Flanagan's radio station, WOW, invoked the Babe's example in his follow-up broadcast. "The Babe told us, 'When you leave this Home and make some money, help support it. Our Home burned down in Baltimore and I worked hard to raise about three million dollars to build the new Home.'"

As the public grew wise to the ways of marketing manipulation, however, the ubiquity of the photographs of Ruth posing with lost, orphaned, and abandoned children gave rise to a new kind of cynicism and the suspicion that the visits were "arranged solely for the publicity they afforded him," Frank Graham wrote in his history of the Yankees. "After a while, hurt by the charge that they were but publicity dodges"—an assertion uniformly denied by Graham and other writers who covered Ruth regularly—"he exacted promises from his friends among the newspapermen not to mention them and these promises always were kept."

III

Lady Amco did not know it, but she, too, was in debt to Edward Bernays. The Beech-Nut Packing Company, purveyors of everything from chewing gum to pork products, had hired him in 1925 to increase the American appetite for bacon. Until then, America had gotten by on a cup of coffee, a piece of toast, and maybe a glass of juice for breakfast. Bernays asked physician Dr. A. L. Goldwater whether a heavier breakfast might be beneficial to the workingmen of America. Knowing which way his toast was buttered, the doctor confirmed Bernays's suspicion and agreed to consult five thousand of his closest doctor friends, most of whom concurred, thus allowing Bernays to claim they had made a scientific study of the matter. The demand for bacon—and eggs—soared.

Just that week, the White House forwarded a menu to industrialist R. M. Melon in advance of a morning meeting at his home in Pittsburgh, notifying the chef that the president required "the breakfast standby of America"—bacon and eggs. (Lou Gehrig would refuse to leave his hotel room in Sioux City until he'd had his fill of the same.)

Thus, upon receiving Lady Amco's 171st egg, the Babe eyed the assembled newsreel cameras and newspaper reporters and declared, "Looks like breakfast to me!"

To his grave disappointment, there was no bacon. The Cudahy Packing Company of Sioux City stepped into the breach two days later, presenting him with a personalized ham—his name spelled out in cloves. "So Now Babe Ruth Can Have Ham and Eggs," read the ensuing headline.

(Less than a decade later, the Babe's ad men would employ the same strategy in cartoon strips created by Quaker Oats to accompany his endorsement of Puffed Wheat and Puffed Rice, quoting a prominent nutritionist who testified to the wonders of dry cereal.

"AMAZING BUT TRUE. MORE THAN DOUBLE THE FOOD-ENERGY OF EGGS, EVEN MORE BODY-BUILDING PROTEIN THAN BACON.")

By the time Ruth and Gehrig arrived at Omaha's Western League Park, Babe's egg had been sent downtown to a local artist, who inscribed it: "From the Queen of Hens to the King of Swats." Or "From the Queen of Eggs to the King of Hitters." It depended on which newspaper you read. The egg was then packed in a jewelry box and tied with a ribbon and delivered to home plate for the formal presentation.

The best amateur baseball talent in Omaha, teams representing the Omaha Printing Company, winners of the Saturday League, and the Brown Park Merchants, winners of the Sunday League, had been scheduled to play for the city championship that afternoon. Instead they found themselves sharing the day and the bench with Babe Ruth, whom seventeen-year-old Francis O'Donnell, the Prints' batboy and occasional utility player, pronounced "as common as anyone in the dugout."

A compliment.

When Ruth stepped to the plate for his first at-bat, the game was interrupted for the presentation of the ceremonial egg. With Landers at his side, H. L. McLaughlin, Nebraska's secretary of agriculture, launched into a speech extolling the virtues of clean chickens. "The Norfolk hen, I suppose, has breeding, but there is no mystery about her diet or her care," he said, seizing the opportunity to urge Nebraska farmers to clean up their chicken coops. "She was given no dope, just plain food but kept very clean in clean surroundings. What her owner has done others may do. Dirt and filth is what is holding back Nebraska poultry in the markets of the east. They breed disease."

Amco officials, who were heavily invested in promoting what its mash could do for the lagging state egg industry—including a two-page ad in the souvenir scorecard—couldn't have been happy with his remarks.

When the game resumed, Ruth and Gehrig took turns playing first base and pitching to each other. Ruth hit two home runs, one of which, O'Donnell told his sons later, he called. "He pointed to center field. Just like in the movies."

Ruth went to the pitching mound in the seventh inning and struck out four of the batters he faced, among them Johnny Rosenblatt, the youngest player on the field, who led off in the ninth, and Gehrig, who didn't fare any better. So after Ruth struck him out to end the game, Ruth just kept pitching until Gehrig finally got ahold of one, thereby delaying the first pitch of the city championship game to the point that it had to be called on account of darkness.

Meanwhile, back at the henhouse, Amco handlers were beginning the delicate process of "breaking" Lady Babe from her high-protein feed, upping the percentage of carbohydrates from 10 to 20 percent and lowering her protein by inverse proportion. "She could have continued until she laid 300 or more eggs if we continued to feed her proteins but in doing so she might have killed herself," Danforth told reporters. "We did it for her own sake."

(This was an allusion to the unfortunate death of the 1926 champion Lady Lindy, who laid 149 eggs in as many days and succumbed two hours after her final effort.)

Landers told reporters that Lady Babe, who had lost three-quarters of a pound during her championship season, would quit laying before "she layed herself to death." She quit two days later after delivering an under-par 173rd egg. She was too valuable for breeding purposes to be sacrificed for the few extra eggs she might lay. He expected her to produce thirty pullets worth $100 to $155 each and twenty cockerels worth $50 to $100 each, he told the New York Times—an $8,250 profit off a $2 hen. Little wonder he had turned down a $3,000 offer. He planned to breed her in the spring with a cock he promised to name Buster Gehrig.

The photo of the "Two Record Busters" traveled to sixteen states, appearing in thirty newspapers in a single day. Other papers printed a drawing of the Babe clutching his namesake alongside Joe Williams's syndicated "Nut Cracker" column: "That picture of Babe Ruth holding the Omaha chicken named after him indicates that his barnstorming tour is having splendid results."

No doubt it helped sell tickets to upcoming games in San Francisco and Santa Barbara, two of the cities where the photo appeared. But more important, it promoted the image of a wholesome Babe, clucking with pleasure at the feathery bundle in his arms. The wire service caption reminded readers: "He is a bit of a farmer in the off-season."

Walsh wasn't about to object to the outdated tidbit of information, which helpfully reinforced the image he had been cultivating of Babe Ruth as a gentleman farmer and family man—a life he had briefly led at Walsh's behest in a highly publicized reclamation effort in the fall of 1922.

This was as good as money in the bank. More valuable than the twenty-five-hundred-dollar guarantee (plus 50 percent of the gate) Walsh had been promised by promoters J. J. Isaacson, recreation director for the city of Omaha, and Johnny "Dynamo" Dennison, the czar of the municipal baseball league (and nephew of a local political fixer and crime boss).

Only seven hundred fans turned out for that one. Newspapers estimated there were five thousand people at League Park five years later; Dennison reckoned the count was more like seven or eight thousand, which at a dollar a head was good money for a couple of hours of work.

Among those in attendance were two local lovelies who caught Ruth's eye, Dennison related to the *Omaha World-Herald* years later. "He told me, 'Every day the girls are looking better.'"

He spotted a couple of good-looking girls in the grandstand and told me to give them the key to his room at the Fontanelle. He said I should tell them to leave in the seventh inning, and that he would meet them later.

Well, the priest at Immaculate Conception Church asked me if I thought I could get Babe to stop at the school. I think they were laying a cornerstone. The Babe said he'd be glad to.

He went to the school after the game and said a

few words. The kids just climbed all over him and started asking for autographs. He said he couldn't stay; he had to catch a train.

Hell, he just wanted to get back to the hotel.

Whatever or whoever was waiting for him at the hotel never became public—thanks, no doubt, to the ever-vigilant Christy Walsh. Unfortunately, he hadn't been on retainer during the 1920 tour of Cuba when Ruth was fleeced out of somewhere between $60,000 and $130,000 by gamblers and con men—the amount depended on which magazine exclusive you believed—and had to be bailed out by the missus.

And he wasn't yet fully in charge when Ruth, who had doubled his income by barnstorming in 1919 and 1920, signed a contract to do so again in defiance of Commissioner Kenesaw Mountain Landis in 1921. The contract called for him to play exhibition games in New York State, Pennsylvania, and Oklahoma from October 16 to November 1 for a guarantee of a thousand dollars each, followed by a sixteen-week vaudeville tour on the B. F. Keith vaudeville circuit.

A loosely enforced ban prohibiting players from World Series teams from such tours had been on the books since 1911. Landis reiterated his intention to enforce the arcane prohibition when he took office in January 1921 and again in the clubhouse after the Yankees clinched the pennant. "Well, I'm notifying you that I am going to violate the rule and I don't care what you do about it," Ruth declared.

With that, he walked—or barnstormed—into a legal ambush. It was a test case of the authority of the new commissioner, who began his imperial reign only after being granted unilateral powers over the game. He could summon witnesses, order the production of documents, and impose penalties, just as he did from the federal bench. He had insisted on keeping his seat on the court when he assumed his new role. As a result, he continued to issue judicial opinions while meting out punishment to the eight White Sox players who allegedly conspired to throw the 1919 World Series.

Eager as Landis was to consolidate his power—particularly over his rival, American League president Ban Johnson—he had another reason to make an example of Ruth. Landis had been formally censured by the American Bar Association at the beginning of September for refusing to give up his $42,000-a-year federal judgeship. On October 20, in the midst of the Ruth imbroglio, a congressman from Brooklyn announced he was introducing legislation barring judges from holding any other paying position, the third congressional attempt to dislodge Landis from the bench.

The more Landis railed against Ruth—calling his conduct "mutinous defiance," and thundering, "Who the hell does that big ape think he is?"—the more he was able to divert attention from his own compromised position. (He resigned from the bench on February 18, 1922, waiting just long enough to give the illusion that he wasn't quitting under fire.)

Ruth responded to Landis's fulminations with logic and a blithe disregard for his authority. He ignored a summons from the commissioner the night the series ended and set off for Buffalo at midnight with Yankee teammates Bob Meusel and Bill Piercy despite the threat of suspension. Landis generally enjoyed the support of the press, publicly and privately, for staring down a national idol. Jay Jerome Williams, superintendent of the Consolidated Press Association, wrote from San Francisco: "So glad you've stood your ground on the Babe Ruth-Meusel suspension. That's great stuff. It shows that whether on the bench or off of it when you say a thing you mean it. (Of course, we knew this to be the case but I reckon there were some natural born detracts and 's-o-b's' that figured otherwise.)"

Landis also received covert intelligence from Yankee co-owner Colonel Tillinghast L'Hommedieu Huston, who sent an especially unctuous letter informing him of Ban Johnson's complicity in the effort to impeach him.

"I would feel a delicacy in working on this matter while the Ruth case is up before you for adjudication did I not know that it would not influence you in the slightest degree," Cap Huston wrote. "I want you to know that you are placed under no obligation whatever. I am working from purely selfish incentives."

Indeed. His motives had everything to do with Ruth's stunning 1921 season—59 home runs, 168 RBI, and a .378 batting average—and the $224,234,200 (in 2016 dollars) that he generated for the Yankees from home, away, and exhibition games. Currying favor with Landis by sabotaging Johnson was the Yankees' way of pleading for their pocketbook.

Walsh, who was already exploring endorsement deals for a line of boys' clothing for 1922, needed a compliant Babe, a wholesome Babe, to sell to manufacturers. Walsh wired Huston to suggest enlisting New York City's sports editors to communicate their disapproval of the tour. Huston arranged for W. S. Farnsworth of the *New York American* and W. J. Macbeth of the *New York Tribune* to meet Ruth in Jamestown, New York, where he agreed to quit the tour if the commissioner indemnified him against punishment, which was a nonstarter. He also asked Huston to meet him in Scranton.

When Huston arrived, Ruth told him he was in bed and blithely kept his boss waiting for an hour in the lobby of the Hotel Casey before capitulating to reason— also the weather, crowds, and notices had been lousy. Huston wrote to Landis immediately: "He agreed to abandon his trip because, he said, he had been made to realize by Messrs. Farnsworth and Macbeth (and he gave this as his sole reason for quitting) that the New York club was the principal (and possibly the only) sufferer in the matter."

After sharing the good news, Huston wrote a couple of mollifying checks to local promoters of the canceled games.

Landis took the case under advisement; Ruth took to the boards with an old-time vaudeville song-and-dance man, Wellington Cross, who crooned "Along Came Ruth" by way of an introduction. A few lame Landis jokes were added during a tryout in Mount Vernon, New York, before the opening in Boston on November 7. Politically tone-deaf tour manager Harry Weber solicited a congratulatory telegram from the commissioner, which failed to materialize.

Ruth had come down with a bad case of laryngitis in Mount Vernon, which may or may not have made any difference in his delivery. He gamely croaked his way through his solo, "Little by Little, Bit by Bit," reminding the critic from the *Boston Post* that as a member of a Red Sox quartet no one was quite sure if Ruth was a tenor or a bass. A reviewer for the International News Service observed, "You just knew he'd like to get his hands on the guy who wrote the song."

Helen Ruth fretted over her hubby from a box in the B. F. Keith's Theatre. Helen was most often seen in those days waving from the grandstand at the Polo Grounds. She made occasional predictions—one hundred home runs in 1921!—and occasional wifely pronouncements: "Clouting Home Runs Good for Appetite." She offered even more occasional insights into their relationship. "Babe says there's two sides to his head. One of them is for baseball and the other is for me. And I love baseball enough to divide anyway."

Margery Lee, a society reporter for the *Boston Telegram*, sat behind her at the opening performance, noting the jeweled hands that played nervously with her beaded purse, the brown eyes that never left the Babe's throat, and her refusal to laugh at a single joke. Lee was kind enough not to mention the hat she wore, which resembled the back end of a turkey. Perhaps it was one of the twenty-five chapeaux, the *Boston Globe* reported, that she had had purchased for $840 the year before.

Lee was rewarded with a marital scoop: "Babe Ruth in Danger of Being Kidnapped—Mrs. Babe Threatens to Take Him Away from Public to Farm":

"Honey-dear, does it hurt terribly?" she cooed. "Does his sweet little voice hurt him?"

"Rats, it's all right," says Babe, in a raspy squeak. "What's a little sore throat to a big husky man? And suppose I do lose my voice? I'll never be a singer anyway, and I could always go in the movies."

"Oh, I'll be so glad when I can have my hubby all to myself," Mrs. Babe Ruth said. "He's such a busy man. I feel as if he only belonged to me when no one else happened to want him. Some day people are going to find that I've kidnapped my own husband and have run away some place with him where we can lead a simple life away from grandstands, and managers and photographers and all the annoying things that clutter up our life.

"You know what I'd like to do?" she said with a sudden sparkle in her mischievous eyes. "I'd like to slip away to a little farmhouse in the hills, where we could have a little garden and Honey could rest and play with me. We could fish and go on tramps together and have a glorious time."

Meanwhile, the Babe was confessing to a peculiar strain of stage fright.

"There's something about women that scare me to death. I'm not afraid of any man on earth but almost any little scrap of woman can knock the nerve out of me. Gee, they have a way of looking at you that makes my knees turn to butter and my tongue forget the English language.

"Women are so little, and there's such a lot of complicated fussiness about them, I mean their fluffy little clothes and bewildering hats, that are entirely beyond me. A vaudeville audience of women is about 60 times harder to face than all the baseball fans in the world. Gosh, I never knew what stage fright was 'til I looked over the footlights and saw two little flappers staring at me from the front row."

Perhaps what really scared him was his wife's vision of happiness. Because, Lee wrote, "he added, sort of confidential-like, 'It's funny 'cause I certainly do like the little darlings.'"

The tour proceeded from Boston to the Palace Theatre in New York, where Ruth was greeted with a standing-room-only crowd and a one-minute ovation when he took the stage. Then Chicago, Washington, Philly, Pittsburgh, Detroit, Cincy—major-league cities—and lots of bush-league towns, too. In Helen's absence, Ruth toured the country living large. He granted interviews from a pink silk chaise longue in Washington and hosted one of his humdingers in his suite at Chicago's Congress Hotel. As he rushed to the theater one evening, he instructed the hotel's wine agent, a fellow named Joe, to fill the closet in his suite with booze. "Joe filled it up," Marshall Hunt told Ruth's biographer Kal Wagenheim. "Babe did a double-take at the bill when he got back. It's $4,000. The closet was as big as an ordinary sleeping room! An adjustment was reached there."

While in Chicago, Ruth's pal Rogers Hornsby, the great infielder for the St. Louis Cardinals, paid a call. "Somehow Rogers got ahold of a big thing that looked like a cow's drinking trough," Hunt said. "It was round and about two feet deep, made out of galvanized sheet metal. They filled that with hot water. Then all these dames came. Rogers sent them into another room to dress in these costumes that he had made for them. So they came out looking beautiful, and they all had to get in the tub. They were made out of paper and loosely glued together; so, the second they got in the tub, all this came off.

"Rogers didn't smoke or drink, but he was a very good picker of dames."

Though he filed stories about Ruth almost every day, Hunt never did find an occasion to write that one for the *Daily News*. Nor did he ever mention their spring training excursions into the countryside in search of farms offering "the chicken and daughter" combination dinner.

Landis took his sweet time deciding Ruth's punishment. His office was inundated with petitions and letters on Ruth's behalf from fans who liked that Ruth was bigger than the game. Preacher Billy Sunday, the former ballplayer, said Ruth was only as foolish as the rule he had violated and advocated fining him the amount he had earned on the barnstorming tour. Cap Huston and the Yankees begged for leniency, invoking Ruth's lack of advantages at the "Reformatory Institution" in Baltimore, the adulation that had "enlarged his cranium," and his "sincere, if hazy, idea that he was a crusader and was helping the ball players by his daring."

Huston also proposed that the rule be changed in the interests of baseball.

When Landis issued his ruling on December 5, banning Ruth and Meusel until May 20, 1922 (one quarter of the season), and relieving each of his $3,362.26 share of the World Series loot, the Yankees were secretly relieved—especially because Ruth was allowed to participate fully in spring training and the lucrative exhibition games the Yankees staged as they made their way north.

Participate fully he did. Spring training was defined by a single headline: "Yankees Training on Scotch."

On March 10, he signed a three-year contract with the Yankees for $52,000 a year—a figure that appealed to him because he always wanted to be able to say he earned "a grand a week." Notably omitted from the deal was the bonus clause that had paid him $50 for each of his fifty-nine home runs in 1921.

Helen posed for the newspapers clutching the signed document like an ancient scroll and wearing another remarkable fascinator—this one resembled an opulent porcupine. Babe bristled at the criticism that followed the signing, which unlike that of most baseball contracts was highly publicized. He hardly sounded like a simpleton in stating the case for a ballplayer's right to earn an unfettered living. In this, he had both a firm grasp of his own worth and ownership's unfair and unilateral control of the game. "It isn't right to call me or any ballplayer an ingrate because we ask for more money. Sure I want more, all I'm entitled to. The time of a ballplayer is short. He must get his money in a few years or lose out. Listen, a man who works for another man is not going to be paid any more than he's worth. You can bet on that. A man ought to get all he can earn. A man who knows he's making money for other people ought to get some of the profit he brings in. Don't make any difference if it's baseball or a bank or a vaudeville show. It's a business, I tell you. There ain't no sentiment to it. Forget that stuff."

The Yankees tried to protect their interests by inserting a hilariously unenforceable morals clause in the new contract, widely believed to be the first in professional sports and widely believed to have been inspired by language in a 1921 contract between Universal Studios and Fatty Arbuckle, then on trial for rape and manslaughter.

It is understood and agreed by and between the parties hereto that the regulation above set forth, numbered "2" shall be construed to mean among other things, that the player shall at all times during the training and playing season of the term of this contract and any renewals thereof refrain entirely from the use of intoxicating liquors and that he shall not during the training and playing season in each year stay up later than 1 o'clock A.M. on any day without the permission and consent of the Club's manager.

Legislating the libido of the man roommates called "the noisiest fucker in North America" was nonnegotiable. "I'll promise to go easier on drinking and to get to bed earlier, but not for you, fifty thousand dollars, or two hundred and fifty thousand dollars will I give up women," sportswriter Fred Lieb quoted him as saying. "They're too much fun."

On opening day of the season at Griffith Stadium in the nation's capital, Ruth, looking especially dapper in civilian clothes, was conspicuously photographed hobnobbing with the commander in chief by the presidential box. He watched the game from the grandstand with Ban Johnson and Cap Huston and opined in his next ghostwritten column that the Yankees would have won had he been playing the sun field.

The vengeful patriarch of major-league baseball was not among the luminaries mentioned in the *New York Times* account of President Warren Harding's day at the ballpark.

Yankee fans stormed the ticket offices at the Polo Grounds in anticipation of Ruth's return on May 20,

1922. He was received like Ulysses, lauded and feted with plunder—floral tributes, a silver bat, and a silver loving cup filled with dirt, dug by Brother Matthias's own two hands from the area around home plate at St. Mary's.

He was also greeted by three sign-carrying representatives of the Babe Ruth Shoe Company, which had pledged twenty-four pairs of shoes to the orphans of St. Mary's upon Ruth's return, and ten additional pairs on the occasion of his first home run.

He had signed two new five-year endorsement deals to merchandise goods in his name, one with Rosenwasser Bros. Inc. for shoes and leggings, for which he was to receive 1 percent of net sales each year, and the other with the Manhattan Knitting Mills to produce sweaters for men and "he-boys," advertised in the *New York Times* that morning as "a whale of a hit for boys, $4.00." Ruth earned a dollar per dozen sold.

Walsh wasn't worried about whether boys wanted to look and dress like Ruth. As his step-grandson Frank Merritt would observe, "Every boy by definition is misunderstood; so, of course they would identify with Babe Ruth as this bad boy." Walsh needed him to act like someone their parents would pay for their sons to look like—at least until they outgrew their first pair of Babe Ruth shoes.

Within five days, Ruth threw dirt on umpire George Hildebrand when he called him out trying to stretch a single into a double and charged into the stands to confront hecklers—actions that cost him his team captaincy, a $200 fine, and a one-day suspension. On June 19 in Cleveland, he charged in from left field, cursing and kicking umpire Bill Dinneen, and, worse, calling him "yellow." This violation of baseball's eccentric and unwritten code of honor was a slur so damnable that Ban Johnson wrote Ruth a letter questioning his breeding and fitness to play in the American League.

The next day in the Indians' dugout players had to intercede between the combatants. Ruth's punishment, as reported at the time, was a five-day suspension (three for kicking, two for cursing, none for questioning the umpire's mettle) and a $1,502.85 American League fine. Not reported at the time was an additional $9,017 fine imposed by the Yankees.

Yankee management responded by hiring a private detective named Jimmy Kelly to follow Ruth and his fellow merrymakers on the Yankees' upcoming road trip through the Midwest. Kelly wasn't above a little entrapment. He plied the players with so much booze in St. Louis that they begged him to join them in Chicago, where he arranged a trip to a Joliet brewery and suggested a group photo be taken, copies of which he got each of the duped revelers to sign. The incriminating photos made their way up the chain of command to Landis, who arrived in Boston to deliver some fire and brimstone along with additional fines.

The Yankees kept the private dicks on retainer through the rest of the season, paying the Burns Detective Agency $2,650.03 in total, according to team ledgers at the Hall of Fame. The last payment in October bore the explanation of $259.50 for a "Ruth matter." By season's end, Ruth had been suspended four times for a total of forty-four days and had been fined $10,719.95 of his $52,000 salary.

September arrived with a welcome, if puzzling, addition and distraction. The Yankees were in Cleveland when sixteen-month-old Dorothy Helen Ruth made her public debut in New York: "The Secret Is Out—Babe's a Father." The announcement was awkward inasmuch as her parents couldn't agree on the facts of her birth or provide a convincing explanation of where she had been since the blessed event. Babe told reporters that she was born on February 21, 1921, at Presbyterian Hospital in New York. Helen said she was born on June 7, 1921, at St. Vincent's Hospital. Her hubby had confused the baby's birthday with his own, she said. *You know how he is.*

(Found among Helen's personal effects at the time of her death was a certificate of baptism for a child born February 11, 1921, the Associated Press reported.)

The divergent accounts led to immediate, published speculation about Dorothy's parentage. Both parents heatedly denied she was adopted. "I should know, shouldn't I?" Helen said. She had been seen wheeling a baby carriage outside the Ansonia in New York and during spring training but had said nothing publicly, she claimed, because Dorothy was born prematurely, a small, sickly child, and Babe feared being teased about her size.

(Dorothy's youngest daughter, Linda Ruth Tosetti, said her mother weighed five pounds at birth and was born with rickets. Helen said she weighed three and a half pounds and was in an incubator. In her memoir, Dorothy claimed that her nursemaid told her she weighed two pounds and was "so ugly she used to put a net over the carriage, so no one would see me.")

Speculation did not abate. Things just didn't add up. There was no mention of a child in Margery Lee's *Boston Telegram* story from November 1921. Nor was there any mention of a child in May 1922, when Helen had surgery at St. Vincent's Hospital in New York, described as "slightly more serious" than the tonsillectomy her husband underwent at the same time. Hugh

Fullerton reported in the *Chicago Tribune* that Helen had suffered two previous miscarriages, which matches Julia Ruth's understanding of events.

On September 26, a photo of a chubby baby in a white silk organza dress clutching a toy wooden bat was released to the newspapers. She had unruly hair and melancholy eyes. The story proved a welcome albeit brief respite from a season of turmoil. But unknowns and uncertainties would become the defining factors in Dorothy Ruth's sad life.

IV

Walsh's efforts at damage control began in earnest late in the fall of 1922. Ruth needed and wanted the money he had been fined. On November 13, he agreed to an amended version of his three-year contract. In exchange for a return of his money, Ruth accepted a stricter (though equally unenforceable) morals clause and a payout system that allowed the Yankees to withhold half his monthly salary until the end of each season as a guarantor of good behavior.

The amended contract prohibited him from indulging in intoxicating liquors and staying up after 1:00 A.M. "whether in the playing season or not." What's more, "any action or misbehavior" that rendered him unable to perform gave the Yankees the right to terminate the contract and keep the withheld salary—what lawyers call "potential liquidated damages."

The fine fiscal hand of Christy Walsh was evident in the new arrangement, an allowance giving Ruth a single monthly payment of $4,333.33. Left to his own devices he spent it all. He was always running short. That danger was made patent the day after he signed the addendum, when his attorney was notified of a threatened lawsuit by an aggrieved Manhattan shopgirl named Dolores Dixon, who claimed she was expecting a Little Babe and wanted fifty thousand dollars for her trouble and her silence.

Walsh met with Babe and Helen at their apartment to broach his idea for a program of rehabilitation, starting with a public mea culpa to be staged at the November 20 dinner of the New York chapter of the Baseball Writers' Association of America. With Helen's encouragement and Babe's grudging consent, Walsh set about planning an event at the Elks Club, guaranteed to garner the maximum public exposure for the humbling of the Babe. Walsh called it the "Back to the Farm" dinner. He considered it the turning point of Ruth's career.

All the top sportswriters and sports editors in New York attended, not to mention Cap Huston. Standing in the center of the head table amid a heap of alfalfa and root vegetables was a stuffed heifer, a reminder of Ruth's wild ride ten days earlier aboard a famously ill-tempered 2,400-pound New Jersey bull named King Jess—and his wild season. Ruth received a paper shovel as a gift, a not-too-subtle reminder of the depth and nature of the hole he had dug for himself.

The ground rules allowed the gentlemen of the press free rein to question Ruth on any subject. They gave him a good going-over. Then the featured speaker, Gentleman Jimmy Walker, the future mayor of New York, beseeched the Babe never again to disappoint the "dirty-faced kids" of New York. "Will you not, for the kids of America, solemnly promise to mend your ways?"

Ruth tearfully and solemnly pledged reform. Raising a glass to the assembled writers, he vowed: "Fellows, you've told me the truth. Now, I'm going to tell you something true. I'm going to take this one drink with you to show there's no hard feelings—and this will be the last drink for me until the end of next season—October 1923."

He vowed to go back to the farm he told the *Times* he had purchased in the spring in Sudbury, Massachusetts. (Documents from the Middlesex County Registry of Deeds record a single purchase from John McCrillis in June 1923.) There would be chickens to feed, wood to chop, pit bulls to raise, and plenty of photo opportunities.

"Quite an act," Hunt recalled.

Two years after she had daydreamed aloud to a reporter about slipping away to a little farmhouse in the hills, Helen Ruth believed she was about to get her wish.

Chapter 9

October 17 / Aboard the Rock Island Line to Des Moines

"RUTH POSES IN OVERALLS,
THEN COLLECTS $3000"
—ASSOCIATED PRESS

"WELL, I AIN'T EATIN' YOUR DAMNED
CANDY BAR ANYMORE!"
—BABE RUTH, ON THE BABY RUTH CANDY BAR

I

As Babe Ruth headed for Des Moines with three thousand dollars in his pocket from a quickie photo shoot in Kansas City and a two-day-old unrefrigerated egg, twenty-four freight cars loaded with

Baby Ruth candy bars hit the rails in Chicago, traveling deluxe in Baby Ruth refrigerator cars making their maiden voyage on behalf of America's sweet tooth.

"No longer will our candy bars associate with machinery, soap, canned goods, and other ordinary freight," declared Otto Y. Schnering, president of the Curtiss Candy Company, in announcing the purchase of an additional two hundred dedicated freight cars necessitated by the annual production of one billion Baby Ruth bars. Which, he happily reported, totaled 15 percent of all the candy bars—and 12 percent of all chocolate-covered confections—consumed by the American public. "Our plan is to have one thousand of these cars in operation in the near future."

Most everyone in the country—from radio disc jockeys to stock boys to baseball fans mailing Baby Ruth wrappers to the Babe for his signature to Ruth's own caddy—accepted as fact that the Ruth in question was him. "Yah, sar, you're de man daf makes dem candy bars," his caddy replied one day when asked by a sports columnist if he recognized the man whose clubs he was carrying. "I eats one of 'dem every morning."

Everyone but Schnering, who maintained in contravention of logic and public belief that his candy bar was named for Baby Ruth Cleveland, the long-dead daughter of President Grover Cleveland who succumbed to diphtheria at the age of twelve in 1904—fifteen years before the first Baby Ruth bar appeared on American store shelves. The name had "a smile in it," Schnering said.

While Schnering was ostentatiously counting his blessings and the $1 million Baby Ruth generated each month, Christy Walsh was preparing for his deposition in the ongoing litigation between the Curtiss Candy Company and the George H. Ruth Candy Company, formed in 1925 in a belated attempt to take a bite out of Schnering's sales—litigation that would eat up a substantial portion of the next six years. Meanwhile, Ruth was cashing in any way he could.

While in Kansas City, he had dashed off to an impromptu photo shoot for the H. D. Lee Mercantile Company, maker of Lee jeans (née cowboy pants) and its new line of buttonless men's (and boys') workwear featuring the newest technology: the zipper. Lee had just announced the winner of a fifty-state naming contest for a new line of Union-Alls featuring the new technology, a marketing strategy that offered cash prizes of $1,000—$250 to the winner—as an inducement to come on down to your local store and try on a pair! The winning entry, courtesy of George M. Mock of Seattle: Whizit!

Who better to promote the unheard-of speed afforded by the Whizit than the Babe, who spent a lot of time getting in and out of baseball uniforms and other suits of clothes?

The pit stop produced a national advertising campaign with print ads in *Liberty* magazine, among other outlets, featuring Ruth and a young boy named Sonny Bowles standing by a Model T, car crank in hand, with his dress shirt peeking out from the collar of his Union-All and a well-shod foot perched on the running board. "Well, who wouldn't?" wrote columnist Joe Williams when news broke of the Babe's latest gambit.

Such were the spoils of fame in 1927: bigger than ever and smaller than they ought to have been. The parameters of celebrity were changing as fast as the Babe got in and out of his Whizit. While he was testifying to the efficacy of the zipper—"as much speed as there is on a Walter Johnson fastball"—attorneys for the George H. Ruth Candy Company were trying and failing to prove in patent court the patent injustice of their case against the Candy King of Chicago.

Ruth was famous in a way that no one had ever been famous before. Famous in a way the law had never envisioned. The patent court had no way to make him whole. In short, Ruth was penalized for his originality. It would take thirty years for jurisprudence to catch up with him.

II

Thanks to Ruth, Damon Runyon, who knew a thing or two about dice games, cardsharps, and horse players, was no longer the only sports scribe filling white space with talk about money. Just that week a syndicated sports filler ran in hundreds of newspapers across the country: "Babe Ruth receives $92 an hour. This is based on five hours a day."

His visit to Boys Town prompted this calculation in the *Lincoln Star*: "Babe Ruth now earns more in one year than it takes to care annually for 200 homeless boys in Father Flanagan's boys' home."

While his Yankee salary continued to generate envy and debate on the sports pages, the *Wall Street Journal* took an unprecedented look at what Walsh liked to call his "by-product money." "He scores homers by allowing his name to be printed on boys' underwear, caps and shoes," the *Journal* reported. "He gathers in royalties from manufacturers of all kinds of soft drinks and holiday souvenirs.

"No figures are kept, or at least made public, of the Babe's total income."

In fact, Walsh kept meticulous accounts of the income he generated for Ruth, down to the penny, less his commission. The ledger he prepared at the end of their contractual relationship in May 1938 documented every dollar Ruth earned through his management, Walsh wrote in an accompanying letter to the Babe.

The year-by-year accounting does not include contracts Ruth signed prior to their relationship, or those for vaudeville and barnstorming tours managed by others in 1920–21 and in 1923. Nor does it include an untold number of endorsement deals Ruth negotiated for himself, such as the Whizit. It's impossible to know just how much the document underreports the income generated through his fame.

One figure stands out in neon sizzle from the rest. In 1927, Ruth earned $73,247 in by-product money, $3,247 more than his Yankee salary, making him undoubtedly the first professional athlete to earn as much or more off the field as on it. According to Michael Haupert, professor of economics at the University of Wisconsin–La Crosse and the executive director of the Economic History Association, Ruth's take-home pay that year was the equivalent of $26 million in today's purchasing dollars.

Chump change compared with the incomes of today's top earners. According to Opendorse, the athlete-marketing platform established in 2012, Roger Federer was 2017's top athlete endorser, with $60 million in off-the-court income. Twenty-two major leaguers made the list of the top 100 in 2017, but the best of them, Buster Posey of the San Francisco Giants, was ranked forty-eighth, with only $4 million in endorsement income.

Ruth earned $13,000 from endorsements in 1927, which doesn't sound like much except that it was then twice the average major-league salary. (In modern dollars, it would buy, for example, 177,323 Baby Ruth bars.) By addressing the subject of Ruth's financial portfolio, the editors of the *Journal* were acknowledging a new phenomenon in the American marketplace. He was the prototype for the modern athletic pitchman: Joe DiMaggio for Mr. Coffee, OJ for Avis, and Peyton Manning for everything. Everyone, except the Curtiss Candy Company, wanted to be associated with him.

III

It was the decade of the "new consumptionism," Samuel Strauss declared in a cautionary essay titled "Things Are in the Saddle," published by the *Atlantic Monthly* in 1924. World War I had primed American industry for the mass production of consumer goods. The Highway Act of 1921 spurred the growth of interstate trucking and facilitated the delivery of those goods. The electrification of factories and households—in concert with aggressive advertising campaigns and increased disposable income—stimulated a national spending spree. By the end of the twenties, nearly half the American population had purchased automobiles, radios, refrigerators, and vacuum cleaners. Consumer credit made it easy to buy on time. Chain stores and mail-order houses proliferated.

Ruth was a model citizen in the Country of More—the perfect spokesman not just for things but for an entire era. "Talk about a consumer!" said George Lois, guru of the sixties creative revolution on Madison Avenue.

He had the name—the Babe!—and name recognition forty years before a Long Island company began measuring it in 1964. He remains "the name-ly-est guy in the world," in the words of Henry Schafer, executive vice president of Marketing Evaluations.

He was—and is—instantly recognizable. "He had a face that looked like the clay moved," in the words of Lois, who was famous for, among other things, putting Mickey Mantle to work on behalf of the children's cereal Maypo in the 1960s.

Ty Cobb, who did all right for himself, investing in and shilling for Coca-Cola, sneered at Ruth's bona fides as a spokesman—"Ruth endorses whorehouses by word of mouth," he told biographer Al Stump. But businessmen did not share his skepticism.

Babe Ruth wasn't baseball's first huckster. Hall of Famer George Wright of the Boston Red Sox posed for Red Stockings Cigars in 1874. Cap Anson and Buck Ewing promoted E. & J. Burke Pale Ale and Extra Stout brews in 1888. Honus Wagner touted the "vim and vigor" of cocaine-infused Coca-Cola in 1908.

Giants manager John McGraw endorsed Colgate's Ribbon Dental Cream and brought a dentist to spring training. Ty Cobb and Walter Johnson showed up in a 1914 Royal Tailors catalog, promoting a line of Hart, Schnaffer and Marx clothing for boys. Ruth would appear in the 1921–22 edition advertising clothes for Big Fellas with his measurements included: "Babe Ruth Pays No Tax On His Size."

Ruth quickly became baseball's most profligate and indiscriminate pitchman. On one November day in Boston in 1921, he shilled for Dr. Reed's Cushion Shoes; the Talbot Company; Wolf's clothier; S. J. Beckwith & Co. hardware; the Horace Partridge Co., purveyor of sporting goods; the Donovan Car Co., a Studebaker dealership which had provided his transportation in Boston; the Grafonola Co., a manufacturer of phonographs; and Richardson's cigar shop. The *Boston Post* ran a helpful schedule of his appearances in the morning paper under the headline: "Babe Ruth Appears in Boston in a New Role."

Over the course of his career he deployed his mug on behalf of a stunning array of consumer goods: Mrs. Sherlock's Home Made Bread, Puffed Wheat, Puffed Rice, and Muffets Whole Wheat Biscuits; Bambino Cola and RedRock Cola; Babe Ruth Big League Chewing Gum, Sport Kings Gum, Babe Ruth Fro-joy Ice Cream for Sealtest ("with Youth Units"), Babe Ruth Home Runs, Chocolate Covered Ice Cream Baseballs, and Girl Scout cookies; Bambino High Grade Burley Rolled Cut Smoking Tobacco (1½-ounce tin 10 cents, 3 for 25 cents); Babe Ruth Pinch-Hit Tobacco; Kaywoodie pipe tobacco; Old Gold Cigarettes ("Presenting BABE RUTH in the Blindfold cigarette test") and Raleigh Cigarettes ("NOW! MEDICAL SCIENCE OFFERS PROOF POSITIVE! No Other Leading Cigarette Is Safer to Smoke! No Other Gives You LESS NICOTINE, LESS THROAT IRRITANTS"). With the lucrative exception of the contract with Quaker Oats, none of these deals were negotiated by Walsh or tallied in his ledger.

He endorsed Murphy-Rich Soap and, although he rarely shaved himself, Barbasol shaving cream—"an errorless shave and hits 1,000 in smoothness, comfort, speed."

Also: a celluloid "Babe" Ruth Baseball Scorer, available with coupons in the *New York American* and the *Washington Times*, among other newspapers; Babe Ruth's Baseball Game marketed by Milton Bradley; Remington Hi-Skor .22 rifles and ammunition; and a 29-inch Babe Ruth doll (available in Red Sox and Yankee colors) from the Sterling Doll Company that resembled a demented Howdy Doody with blue eyes, plucked eyebrows, dimples, and a serious overbite.

He endorsed cars as quickly as he wrecked them, promoting Cadillacs in New York, Packards in Boston, and Reos in St. Louis. Elsewhere he preferred Auburns, Studebakers, Chevrolets, and Chryslers. It depended on which dealership was providing a car for his use. (He endorsed Nash cars after he retired.)

Under Walsh's management, he became a more discriminating endorser, adopting what has become the modern model of affiliating himself with only one company in each product category. Walsh put him in conservative and predictable deals for Louisville Slugger bats and "Big League Gloves" for A. J. Reach. Between 1927 and 1938, he earned $26,381.59 from A. G. Spalding & Bros., the sporting goods manufacturer, for a full line of baseball equipment that came with instructional manuals and "Babe Ruth's Questions and Answers Booklet," produced by none other than Edward Bernays, making a brief foray into sports promotion.

There were book deals and movie deals—a 1928 primer, *Babe Ruth's Own Book of Baseball*, for which he received a thousand-dollar advance, and *Play Ball with Babe Ruth*, a series of five instructional movie shorts released by "Christy Walsh All America Sport Reels" in 1932: *Fancy Curves, Just Pals, Over the Fence, Perfect Control*, and *Slide, Babe, Slide*, which brought in another $5,625.

"Walsh was a visionary, ahead of his time," declared Leigh Steinberg, the Christy Walsh of the eighties. "He understood branding and product categories. This sort of thing hadn't been done since P. T. Barnum."

Ruth's longest association was with the McLoughlin Manufacturing Company, makers of Babe Ruth All America Athletic Underwear and Underwear for Boys—"*The* Right Underwear for Boys Who Want to Hit Home-Runs." Five decades before Baltimore Orioles pitcher Jim Palmer scandalized Western civilization by posing in a bikini brief for Jockey, Walsh recruited Ruth's teammates Joe Dugan, Myles Thomas, Lou Gehrig, and Earle Combs to show a little leg in the Yankee locker room in their one-piece Babe Ruth union suits. It wasn't exactly a sexy look—especially with Combs sporting black socks and garters—but it was unheard of.

The deal yielded more attention than cash: $13,443.09 between 1926 and 1938. But Walsh understood that in marketing, one thing leads to another, in this case a deal for Babe Ruth Longjohns made by Jockey in the 1940s. Ruth, who had been known to eschew underwear, winter and summer (*Collier's* reported), became adept at slipping mentions of his skivvies into routine news coverage. Thus, the breathless dispatch out of San Francisco: "Babe Ruth has a crush on (leave the room, Willie!) cream silk undies."

He had persuaded McLoughlin to manufacture a silk version of the cotton underwear sold under his name just for him.

He wasn't shy about making appearances on behalf of his undergarments either. One day in Chicago, teammate Waite Hoyt recalled, the advertising director for a big department store phoned Ruth at his hotel, requesting his presence at the underwear counter. "Ruth said: 'I can't say anything without consulting my business manager. You'll have to call him in New York. No. No. I'll tell you now, it's gonna cost you a thousand dollars an hour.'

"There was a sudden stupefied click and the conversation was over. But in twenty minutes the phone rang again. Same man. Ruth was paid the shocking sum of one thousand dollars an hour to stand next to a pile of underwear."

IV

The product with which he is most identified is also the one from which he never earned a nickel—America's first nickel candy bar, that gooey confection of nougat, chocolate, peanuts, and gall.

The history of Baby Ruth and the Babe is murky and not at all sweet. The Curtiss Candy Company was not the only commercial enterprise to profit from a presumed association with Ruth. Walsh, who had never made use of the legal education he acquired to please his father, spent so much time putting out legal brush fires for the Babe, he could hardly be expected to keep up with all the various and nefarious attempts to cash in on Ruth's name, too. When Ruth's vaudeville tour visited Vancouver in December 1926, Duplex Sales Limited, the local distributor of Auburn and Pierce-Arrow automobiles, offered him use of an Auburn 8-88 Roadster. Ruth wired his regrets, saying the theater manager had made other arrangements.

"Always happy to have Auburn for use," he added politely. "I favor it over other cars."

The dealership promptly took out an ad for the Auburn Roadster in the *Vancouver Sun*: "What Babe Ruth Drives When He Has His Choice."

When he arrived in San Diego a month later, he was photographed—between vaudeville shows—standing arm in arm with real estate developers James Love and W. J. Touhey, who were then selling building lots in a new development at Windsor Hills on Mount Nebo with magisterial views of the city below. The photo was published in the *San Diego Sun* along with a headlined story: "Babe Ruth Buys Lot in Windsor Hills. Panorama from Point Aery Charms Athlete, Will Hold for Investment Value." According to the caption, "Ruth grabbed five minutes between acts to purchase" the lot.

By then, Ruth had promised Walsh, in writing, not to purchase any real estate without prior approval. Perhaps they offered him a lot—Walsh said later that Ruth turned down offers of beaches, battlefields, farms, and manors. Probably the developers showed him the view and paid him to say it was swell. (An advertisement in the *San Diego Union* on January 9 quotes him as saying, "I clipped this from Love & Touhey's Windsor Hills ad because It's the Way I Saw It.") There is no deed in his name in the San Diego recorder's office; nor was any such property mentioned in his will. But locals still swear he owned a piece of the view.

As much as Ruth made by exploiting his name and image, what was truly noteworthy was how much others made off him. Enterprising businessmen, with deep pockets and good lawyers, appropriated his name, betting he'd never find out about it or knowing there was nothing legally he could do about it.

Bambino Pinto Beans from Mingo, Kansas? Big Hit Babe Ruth candy from Oconto, Wisconsin? Who'd ever heard of those?

But nothing was as infuriating as the case of the Baby Ruth candy bar.

For the better part of the two years, since Ruth and Walsh had decided to get in on the nut roll action—agreeing to license his name in December 1925 to produce Ruth's Home Run bar to compete with the fifty to sixty similar confections already on the market—Walsh had been exhorting, cajoling, hectoring, and pestering executives and attorneys for the George H. Ruth Candy Company with marketing ideas, legal strategies, advertising campaigns, and, finally, pleas to be released from the contract. Although Walsh and Ruth were stockholders—Walsh had been named a director and the Babe a vice president with 5 percent royalties on sales—their relationship with the company was tenuous to say the least.

They had negotiated the deal with Louis Glick, a candy manufacturer from Cleveland, who had approached them with the idea, in hopes of capitalizing on Baby Ruth's notoriety, according to Curtiss's attorneys. (Among them was Sylvester J. Liddy, the father of G. Gordon Liddy, who organized the burglary at the Democratic Party headquarters at the Watergate for Richard Nixon.)

The Home Run bars were manufactured in Glick's factories. William F. Eckhardt, his former employee, was named secretary and treasurer of the company. Though Eckhardt stated under oath that Glick had no role or interest in the company, it was to Glick that Walsh directed many of his appeals. The candyman dismissed Walsh's suggestions as a matter of course and eventually ignored him altogether.

The trouble began when the company sought trademark protection for "Ruth's Home Run" bar and "Babe Ruth's Own Candy" in June 1926. Curtiss immediately filed an objection, claiming the Home Run bar unfairly infringed on *its* trademark, causing irreparable harm given its financial investment in the production and promotion of the Baby Ruth bar.

Walsh embarked on a public relations campaign to gin up sympathy for the Babe, placing stories with friendly reporters in New York dailies. "Some months ago, a manufacturer brought out a confection bearing the magic name of Ruth," George Daley wrote in the *New York World*. "It sold well. As the Babe is big and generous so was this lump of sweetness big and generous. But there was nothing in it for the Babe, although many fans bought it with the idea that he had something to do with its making. This manufacturer scoffed at Ruth's contention that his name was being bootlegged and pirated. There was nothing George Herman could do about it. George Herman figured he might as well get some of it. He's trying. What next? Most anything can happen in these highly commercialized days."

Walsh quickly realized that he had met his match in Otto Schnering, who was working as a piano salesman when he formed the Curtiss Candy Company in 1916 with four employees, a secondhand stove, and a five-gallon kettle in a rented space above a plumbing shop. He named the company after his mother in an effort to deflect anti-German bias.

Chicago was not just the Windy City. It was also the candy capital of the country, the birthplace of Wrigley's Gum (and the family that owned the Chicago Cubs), Cracker Jack, and the Oh Henry! bar. Schnering made

Polar Bars, Jolly Jacks, Marsh-O-Nut Dipps, Honey Comb Chips, and the Kandy Kake bar—more pastry than candy bar. But he needed a name product in order to make a name for Otto Schnering.

In 1919, just as Babe Ruth was giving Boston an intimation of the fullness of his powers, Otto reformulated the former Kandy Kake into the Baby Ruth and began telling poignant tales of Baby Ruth Cleveland's visit to the factory that manufactured the bar in her honor—a convenient transposition of time and place for marketing purposes that would have required the reincarnation of the president's daughter.

He put Baby Ruth's name on circus elephants, barns, racehorses, billboards, hot-air balloons, gum, and a company hydroplane that he piloted to victory in midwestern regattas and packed with miniature candy bars attached to rice-paper parachutes, a sweet payload dropped over county fairs and picnics. "Airplanes to Drop Candy; Hog-Callers to Yodel." These stunts became so popular that Schnering hired barnstorming pilots to carry out similar missions in some forty states. One of them took along a twelve-year-old boy named Paul Tibbets to drop candy on the Hialeah Race Track in Florida in 1927. He fell in love with flying that day. Some twenty years later he would drop the A-bomb on Hiroshima.

A graduate of the University of Chicago, Schnering strafed editorial offices with press releases: "Love of Candy Makes Huge Lion Purr Like a Pet Kitten." "Daily Production of Baby Ruth Bars Requires Services of 4,700 Milk Cows and 45,000,000 Pounds of Peanuts." "Special Car of Baby Ruth Candy to Leave for Pacific Coast." Said twelve-car train loaded with 2,618,400 bars, weighing over 400,000 pounds, "if laid back-to-back would make a giant Baby Ruth bar 165 miles long."

He solicited expert testimonials from nutritionists and physicians and secured one from the Dallas Public Schools and another, later, from the doctor who cared for the Dionne quintuplets. He declared Baby Ruth to be "rich in dextrose," allowing him to market it as "an energy bar" and a "complete luncheon for 5¢." Admiral Richard Byrd was said to have packed a thousand Baby Ruth bars for his expedition to the South Pole.

All this went without any apparent challenge or remark from Ruth or his representatives, a fatal delay in trademark litigation, until they rolled out the first Ruth's Home Run bars in April 1926, which differed from the Baby Ruth bars primarily in packaging. "CAUTION: Absolutely none genuine without the photograph and official signature of 'Babe' Ruth himself."

What exactly transpired between Ruth and the Curtiss Candy Company—and for that matter between Ruth and other candy manufacturers—prior to signing the agreement to create the George H. Ruth Candy Company is unclear. Who, if anyone, was in a position to challenge the Curtiss trademark in a timely manner on Ruth's behalf is also uncertain. What is clear is the law. Or more precisely, the lack of law protecting the rights of celebrities in 1927.

V

The right to privacy, protecting against misappropriation of name and likeness, was established as a legal principle at the turn of the century. In 1902, a Rochester, New York, teenager named Abigail Roberson sued the Rochester Folding Box Company for using her picture on twenty-five thousand posters advertising "Flour of the Family"—allegedly causing such severe nervous shock that she was confined to bed. She lost the case but won the war. The New York Court of Appeals overturned the lower court by a 4–3 vote, ruling that the advertisement did not violate "a sacred right of privacy." But the New York State Legislature overruled the court a year later and created that right, prohibiting the use of a person's name or likeness for the purposes of advertising or trade without prior written consent.

But Babe Ruth wasn't interested in being private. He was interested in getting paid for being public. There was no law on the books that could help him, no precedents to cite.

Two cases that came close to being on point involved newsreels, one from 1913 concerning a ship's captain whose likeness was used in a fictionalized account of a shipwreck. The second case involved Ruth himself. In June 1920, he signed a $50,000 contract for his first feature film, *Headin' Home*. He got $15,000 up front and got stiffed on the rest when the producers went belly-up. He carried the useless check around for years as a sight gag. But it was also a caution and reminder of how unprotected his interests were in matters of law.

While he was busy filming *Headin' Home* in Haverstraw, New York, Educational Films was busy splicing together newsreel footage taken at the Polo Grounds to sell a series of "instructional films" entitled *Babe Ruth in Over the Fence* and *How Babe Ruth Makes a Home Run*.

Ruth sued, asking for $1 million in damages, claiming that using the footage without his consent violated his civil rights. In prepared testimony, Ruth declared his intention to "capitalize my baseball ability and reputation throughout the country as a baseball player to the utmost degree" and argued that the unsanctioned films would cause him "irreparable loss."

The judge granted a temporary restraining order but ruled against him a month later, saying civil rights law did not apply, and that Ruth's image and actions were newsworthy and therefore a worthy subject for the films.

The defendants celebrated their victory by countersuing for $250,000 for defamation of character and accused Ruth of legal posturing calculated to provide "the King of Swat oodles of free space, not only in the trade press, but in the dailies as well."

Both suits were dropped when the appellate court agreed with the trial judge.

So the limitations for legal remedies should have been clear when attorneys for the George H. Ruth Candy Company challenged Curtiss in patent court, the only avenue available to them. Their case was doomed before it began, as Curtiss's lead attorney, Victor Cutting, explained in a tart letter to Walsh, "Mr. Ruth having permitted the Curtiss Candy Company, without objection, to develop the name 'Baby Ruth' to its present value."

In other words, it was Ruth's fault for not acting sooner.

Ruth's daughter Julia faulted Walsh for failing to trademark her father's name. Given the astonishing sums generated by nearly a century of nickel candy bar sales, her feelings are understandable. But they also reflect a misunderstanding of federal trademark law, under which only trademarks attached to goods or services are granted protection. Without a product, a name is not a registerable trademark.

Moreover, it's not clear that Walsh had the authority to challenge Curtiss early enough to have made a difference. In 1921, Schnering was already heavily promoting the brand; Walsh was working under a one-year contract with Ruth that pertained only to syndicated columns.

However, there is some evidence that Curtiss reached out to Ruth or to his representatives early on in the development of the product. Found among Walsh's papers at the time of his death was a proposal for a Baby Ruth Candy Bar, signed by Walsh and Ruth, and a large mock-up of the product, according to his step-grandson Frank Merritt.

John Kenfield, a vice president of Curtiss during the formative years of the Baby Ruth bar, who later became an acclaimed tennis coach at the University of North Carolina, stated in his official university biography that he contacted Ruth about licensing his name as a new moniker for the existing Kandy Kake but that Ruth demanded more money than Curtiss could pay at the time. According to Kenfield, he then suggested Baby Ruth as an alternative name.

Joe Williams told a similar story in his obituary for Christy Walsh. "Walsh demanded a percentage of gross sales. The manufacturer decided a Baby Ruth bar would sell as well as a Babe Ruth bar. Result: Ruth and Walsh were left twiddling their thumbs."

None of this was introduced in the case against Curtiss, which might have been embarrassing, but would have gone a long way to disproving the specious claims of honoring the memory of Baby Ruth Cleveland.

Depositions began March 4, 1927, the day after Ruth reached a new deal with the Yankees. Schnering was also in New York, giving a bravura performance on behalf of Baby Ruth, testifying that the candy bar was trademarked and introduced to the market "about the year 1919"—November 1919 to be precise. In fact, according to government records, Curtiss didn't apply for a trademark until 1923 though the application cited 1921 as the year of first usage. Lawyers for the George H. Ruth Candy Company either did not know about those documents or chose not to submit them.

Schnering conceded there was financial value in

the felicitous association with Babe Ruth but refused to posit a guess at the percentage on the grounds that Ruth wasn't such a big deal in 1919. "Not over twenty percent?" demanded the lawyer. "Fifteen?

"Not so much," Schnering replied.

That was Ruth's last year with the Boston Red Sox and the first year he demonstrated his offensive prowess, leading the American League in runs (103), RBI (113), and home runs (29).

"There was a suggestion, at the time, that Babe Ruth, however not a big figure at the time as he later developed to be, might have possibilities of developing in such a way as to help our merchandising of our bar Baby Ruth," Schnering allowed.

Cutting did not pursue that line of questioning either.

In legal terms, the case for potential damage to Otto's baby was strong. Of particular interest to the patent court judge was Schnering's testimony that Curtiss had spent more than $3,629,000 publicizing and developing Baby Ruth. As evidence that "Ruth's Home Run" bar was confusingly similar to the Baby Ruth bar, Schnering cited candy wrappers he had received from young boys asking for Ruth's autograph.

Initially, sales of Ruth's Home Run bars were promising: $50,000 a month or more, Eckhardt, the company secretary, said in his deposition. If so, Ruth never saw anything like that. He earned five thousand from the doomed confection in 1927, the most he would ever make from it.

Three weeks after Schnering's deposition, Walsh wrote an indignant letter to Glick in Cleveland, declaring the whole operation a "flop," and a "piker proposition doing business on a shoe-string basis." He complained bitterly that sales had "dwindled to a miserable mark" because of a lack of advertising. "It makes no difference whether you are selling newspaper features or candy you have GOT TO ADVERTISE."

To which Glick replied there was no point in advertising as long as the case remained unsettled. Moreover, he added, the fate of the enterprise had been compromised from the outset by the failure of Ruth and Walsh to disclose a previous attempt to compete with Curtiss under another corporate name, Babe Ruth Candy Company. (Advertisements for a Babe Ruth candy did appear in midwestern newspapers in 1924 and 1925 prior to the development of the Ruth's Home Run Bar.)

When Glick stopped replying to Walsh's entreaties, he turned to his personal attorney for advice, confiding, in May, his concern that the failure of the company will be "detrimental to the commercial value of Babe Ruth's name and reputation."

In short: he was worried about Ruth's brand. Still, he didn't pull the plug. "Babe is just as disgusted as I am. While both of us are really anxious to drop the thing, still I don't want to cut off my nose to spite my face and may be sorry afterwards."

By June, Walsh was ready to throw in the towel, writing to ask for a cancellation of the contract. However, that became impossible when neither Glick nor Cutting replied.

In August, Walsh received a copy of the August 1927 issue of *Chicago Topics* magazine from a friend featuring an article titled "Otto's Baby Ruth," in which Schnering blithely admitted that the brainstorm for the candy bar came to him while attending a baseball game. "Why not, I thought, make a candy bar that would combine ingredients and flavors which were the favorites of the American public?" Schnering was quoted as saying. "This idea is more than a mere platitude, everyone will agree. Or else why the tremendous success of the product?"

Why, indeed?

Walsh figured he had finally gotten the goods on Otto.

"These people are certainly getting away with murder in glaring fashion," Walsh railed in a letter to Cutting.

Incredulity was not a party to the case.

Walsh succeeded in reading a portion of the article into the record during his deposition on November 21–22, 1927. Legally, it was beside the point. On January 28, 1930, the George H. Ruth Candy Company's request for trademark protection was denied. A notice of appeal was filed two months later. Ruth's profits that year totaled $120.

By the time the Court of Customs and Patent Appeals upheld the original decision on May 27, 1931, denying trademark protection on the grounds that "Ruth's Home Run" was confusingly and unfairly similar to "Baby Ruth," the Home Run bar had disappeared from the shelves. Curtiss and all the successor ownership companies would continue to promote and profit from that confusion and the public identification with Ruth for nearly a century.

"Well, I ain't eatin' your damned candy bar anymore!" Ruth said.

Fourteen months after the decision, Ruth hit the Called Shot in Game 3 of the 1932 World Series at Wrigley Field. The ball landed more or less metaphorically in Otto Schnering's backyard. In short order, Schnering mounted an illuminated "Baby Ruth" sign on the roof of an apartment building on Sheffield Avenue, just above the grandstand where Charlie Root's pitch came to a stop. The location proved fortuitous when the Cubs began to televise their home games in the 1940s—the sign was in the line of sight of the ground-level camera behind home plate. The neon taunt remained in place until the 1970s.

"Ruth's attorneys were never able to argue the merits of the case or enter evidence of all the ways Curtiss profited from the presumption of his participation," explained Kevin Goering, an expert in sports litigation and the right of publicity. "This manifest injustice was a comedy of errors on the part of his lawyers, the courts and the undeveloped state of the law in 1926. The right of publicity should have been born right then."

With the passage of the Lanham Act twenty years later, federal trademark law was expanded dramatically, prohibiting the use of trademarks like Baby Ruth that cause a likelihood of consumer confusion. "There is overwhelming evidence that the public identified the candy bar with the baseball player, not with its manufacturer," in Goering's opinion. "Today, Ruth would undoubtedly have been able to obtain a cancellation of Curtiss's trademark, giving him the ability to sell his own candy bar. Even his delay in asserting his rights would probably not have been fatal. Schnering's lack of credibility was apparent. No jury then or now would believe his tale about President Cleveland's daughter given the timing. This evidence of bad faith would be another reason for canceling the trademark, especially under modern trademark law."

The courts did not recognize celebrity as an exclusive property right until 1953. The ruling emerged out of an argument over baseball cards. Topps Chewing Gum, Inc., which until then had maintained complete dominion over the trading card industry, brought suit against Haelan Laboratories, Inc., parent company of the Fleer Corporation when it challenged the happy monopoly by offering major-league baseball players a better deal for the use of their names and likeness.

In his landmark ruling, Judge Jerome Frank of New York's Second Circuit Court of Appeals not only recognized the right of publicity—acknowledging that a person's likeness was an asset—but asserted that it was a property right that can be assigned to a third party or agent for exploitation. "It is common knowledge that many prominent persons (especially actors and ballplayers), far from having their feelings bruised through public exposure of their likeness, would feel sorely deprived if they no longer received money for authorizing advertisements," Frank wrote, revolutionizing an entire area of law.

The decision has benefited every professional athlete and every two-bit Tinseltown celeb since. But it was too late for the Babe. His will, rewritten seven days before his death, did not designate or anticipate the importance of royalty or licensing rights, which Claire Ruth bestowed on a New Jersey Little League when she gave them permission to rename themselves the Babe Ruth League, Inc. in 1954.

That left his daughters, Dorothy and Julia, and the Babe Foundation, established in 1947, with their hands tied when the import of Judge Frank's ruling reached the marketplace. Ten years after Claire Ruth's death in 1976, Dorothy and Julia hired the Curtis Management Group, an Indiana company formed to protect the interests of dead celebrities, to do right by the Babe.

They cut a deal with the Babe Ruth League, giving the family two-thirds of any money generated by CMG through licensing. They registered "Babe Ruth" as a trademark for use in paper products such as writing paper, playing cards, and envelopes, and jointly sued Macmillan Publishers when three photographs of the Babe were used in a 1988 calendar. They lost. The Second Circuit Court of Appeals in New York ruled it wasn't a trademark case because no consumer was likely to believe that Ruth had authorized the calendar from the grave. And there was no violation of the right of publicity because, unlike tangible property rights, this one couldn't be inherited.

Ironically, New York State, the first jurisdiction to recognize the right of publicity, is one of the last without a right of "descendability." The right of publicity remains an unsettled and contentious area of the law, evolving along with the technology that has extended the marketing life span of the reanimated dead, among them Babe Ruth, whose buff avatar appeared in a 2013 advertisement for Jockey briefs.

There was plenty of life left in the Babe as an endorser of authorized products, CMG found. At first the dollars were minimal but welcome, Julia told *Sports Illustrated* in 1995, perhaps five thousand dollars a year. Then, in a coordinated blitz calculated to take advantage of his hundredth birthday in 1995, CMG put his name on everything from beer steins to debit cards, mouse pads, nonalcoholic wine, and a talking picture frame. Julia told the magazine she received between "fifty thousand and seventy-five thousand dollars," that year. "Just my part."

Actually, that number is conservative, said his granddaughter Donna Analovitch. The Babe continued to generate hundreds of thousands of dollars a year for the next decade. "He's the man who never stops giving," she said.

After Otto Schnering's death in 1953, the Curtiss Candy Company sold the Baby Ruth brand to Standard Brands, which sold it to Nabisco, which sold it to Nestlé, each of which continued to embrace the mythology of Baby Ruth Cleveland. As part of the big birthday celebration, however, Nestlé, which acquired the brand in 1989, licensed his name and likeness for a TV campaign that, a CMG executive said then, would make "the Babe-to-Baby Ruth bond explicit."

But when he offered the mild observation that the Babe had strengthened Baby Ruth sales—as Schnering conceded in 1927—Nestlé cried foul. In an impassioned letter to another Chicago institution, Dear Abby, a Nestlé spokeswoman—while calling the official Baby Ruth origin story "folklore"—adamantly rejected the notion that Babe Ruth enhanced the Baby Ruth brand. Perhaps, she said, citing Nestlé's TV commercial, Baby Ruth was "the secret weapon responsible for the Babe's success."

Evidently, she was unaware that Ruth had sworn off the candy bars after losing the case in patent court. She attached a letter from Julia, which Dear Abby also printed, politely noting another reason for her father's success—"his generosity and sincere appreciation of his fans."

Not to mention eye-hand coordination, muscle mass, and audacity.

In 2002, Nestlé celebrated the seventy-fifth anniversary of Ruth's sixtieth home run—as well as the beginning of a new baseball season—by announcing that "Baby Ruth, 'America's baby,' embraces its heritage and association with baseball"—in other words, embracing the Babe's merchandising clout without actually embracing him.

Four years later, on June 6, 2006, Baby Ruth was designated the Official Candy Bar of Major League Baseball. The three-year agreement between Nestlé and Major League Baseball expired in 2008 and was not renewed. A decade later, Nestlé USA quit the candy business, selling off all its sweets, including Baby Ruth, to the European food conglomerate Ferrero for $2.8 billion in cash.

Chapter 10
October 18 / Sioux City

**5,000 S.C. FANS SEE BABE RUTH
HIT A HOMER**
KINGS OF SWAT DISPLAY WARES
GEHRIG FAILS IN GAME BUT GETS TRIO IN PRACTICE
—*SIOUX CITY JOURNAL*

**"BABE" KNOWS WHERE TO READ
SPORT NEWS**
—*SIOUX CITY JOURNAL*

I

The genteel gathering in the backyard of the Donohue residence at 3723 Jackson Street in the North

Side neighborhood of Sioux City on the afternoon of October 18 looked like any other garden party except for the absence of libations and the presence of two men in baseball uniforms and a pony named Molly.

Before the game scheduled for that afternoon, John "Jiggs" Donohue, cattleman and sports promoter, had brought Ruth and Gehrig home to meet the family: his wife, Jo, and her sister, Ursula, both in cloche hats popular with the flappers back east, and his posse of boys, the oldest, Jimmie and Phil, in full buckaroo regalia—plaid shirts, kerchiefs, billowing chaps, and cowboy hats—and Jack and Kenny in short pants and knee socks. The four-month-old twins, Tommy and Joanne, were inside fast asleep.

Dudley Scott, owner of two movie theaters in Lemars, some twenty-six miles away, was recording the event with a 16mm camera that he sometimes used to shoot shorts he ran in advance of the main feature. He panned the crowd, capturing the guests milling under a canopy of trees: the two women wearing their Sunday best on a Monday afternoon; the men all in three-piece suits except Christy Walsh, in his trademark double-breasted gabardine, gnawing on a wad of gum. He doffed his hat for the camera but didn't stop chewing.

Young Phil, aboard Molly, a lovely piebald pinto

with a crooked blaze on her nose, backed her hindquarters into Dudley Scott's lens. His mother, heels sinking into the sod, pointed to the camera and gave Molly's rump an encouraging shove. Phil turned her around and whipped her onto her hind legs, showing off for the Babe. It looked for a minute like Phil meant to lasso himself a hero. Ruth ducked out of range of Phil's rope, raising his hands in self-defense.

Next thing you knew: he grabbed Phil's cowboy hat and mashed it down on his own large head. Phil was lucky he didn't smash the crown the way he did the straw panamas of God knows how many unsuspecting gentlemen. *Dontcha know not to wear a panama after Labor Day?* (Ruth also liked water balloons, whoopee cushions, and hunting frogs with a light attached to the end of his rifle.)

Babe grinned, the boy grinned back. A knowing look was exchanged. A deal brokered. Phil slid off his mount. And suddenly Ruth's big right foot was in the stirrup and he was hoisting himself into the center of attention. Molly canted slightly under his weight, then righted herself brightly as he settled into the saddle, while Phil and his brother Jimmy stood by, stroking Molly's nose and hoping for the best.

Once, twice, three times he bounced up and down, trying to get comfortable. Molly staggered. Gehrig stood at her left flank, with two-year-old Kenny in his arms, a buttress against the Babe's girth.

Dudley Scott got it all: Gehrig grinning so broadly at the sheer contagious joy of Ruth's impulsivity that it looked like his dimples might drill through his cheeks. This was the Babe at his best, serving the two masters whose authority he never defied: the need to please and the need to be seen.

Sixty-five years later a snippet of film from that afternoon showed up in two HBO documentaries produced by George Roy, *When It Was a Game 2* and *Babe Ruth*. A decade later, R. C. Raycraft, a filmmaker whose parents own the 3rd Sunday Market in Bloomington, Illinois, met an antiques dealer there who said he had home movies of Ruth and Gehrig to sell. Knowing that less than an hour of unrehearsed Ruth footage survived him, Raycraft bought the eight reels of 16mm film. On the seventh reel, spliced into aerial footage of Iowa farmland and Nebraska football games, Raycraft discovered 2:22 minutes of film shot in the Donohues' backyard. A typed summary provided the date and the name of the cinematographer.

Raycraft tracked down members of the Donohue family, who were puzzled by his find since they had assumed the only copy was the one stored in cousin Michael's basement. He shared a bit of the footage with a reporter from the *New York Times*, who shared it with Ruth's daughter Julia and her son, Tom. For two minutes, the man she still calls Daddy came alive, the catalytic force of his personality leaping from the screen.

Raycraft hired a lip-reader to try to put words to the action. He was especially interested in those addressed to Scott when he turned the camera on the Babe for an especially tight close-up. The grin was usurped by pursed lips and a deeply furrowed brow. It seemed that all the light had gone out of his eyes.

"Turn that fucking thing off," was the lip-reader's interpretation.

II

It was the era of silence. As far as most of the country was concerned, Ruth was as he appeared, a playful man-child; a family man, father of six-year-old Dorothy, who had been seen in widely disseminated photographs horsing around with her daddy at Fenway Park, feeding chickens at their farm in Sudbury, and most recently during Games 3 and 4 of the World Series at Yankee Stadium, where he hit home runs just for her.

Until August 1925, Ruth had no fear of anyone saying otherwise. New York scribes, wise to Ruth's ways with women and his relationship with a former show-girl named Claire Hodgson, rarely mentioned Helen in their copy anymore—unless she had been hospitalized again, having another breakdown or surgery for another undisclosed illness.

But out-of-town writers queried him about her whereabouts. Arriving on the West Coast three days later, Ruth told Jack M'Donald of the *San Francisco Call*: "No, I didn't bring the wife out on this tour. Any woman who would try and travel as far and often as we have would have been dead long ago."

M'Donald dutifully reported: "Ruth is a dutiful husband, called Mrs. Ruth, who is in New York, from his suite at the Whitcomb and chatted the dollars away."

He even vowed to give up his annual hunting and fishing forays for the pleasures of the familial hearth. "I'm content to sit around by the fireside in New York with the wife and kid."

By then, Babe and Helen had been legally separated for more than two years.

Christy Walsh had worked very hard to keep the state of their union as quiet as an idyllic winter scene inside a child's snow globe. He had confected for Babe and Helen and Dorothy a Currier & Ives tableau of family life in the off-season of 1922, packing them off to the homestead in Massachusetts. The old Perry Farm was known to locals as a party house, the town historian said.

Sudbury was a miniaturist's vision of a perfect New England town. Henry David Thoreau had walked its woods and knew its freshwater ponds as well as the Babe knew its watering holes from his days with the Red Sox. Twenty-nine miles from the Fens, Sudbury was close enough to be accessible and distant enough to afford cover for ballplayers who partied in lakeside cottages, and for members of the Jewish mafia, who used them as hideouts during Prohibition.

Babe and Helen had spent the winter of 1917–18 in a small, sparsely furnished fishing camp on the banks of Willis Pond. Ruth called the place, loaned to him for life by its owner Bill Joyce, Ihatetoquitit. The one-room cottage was just twenty feet by fifty feet, and featured fold-down cots, a Franklin stove, Japanese lanterns, flags from all the nations of the world except Germany, and an upright piano that would become the holy grail of the Curse of the Bambino.

Boston Globe baseball writer Melville E. Webb Jr. trekked through the snow that winter to report on the domestic bliss of Ruth's country life, giving ample space to the Bunyonesque feats of the ax-wielding left-hander—a twenty-four-game winner in 1917 with thirty-five complete games in thirty-eight starts—who hauled half a birch tree to the cabin on his shoulder as easily as a hickory bat.

As much as he may have hated to quit the place, it was not a suitable family home. So when they returned to Sudbury four years later, it was to a colonial farmhouse at 558 Dutton Road. Built in 1800, it was one of the oldest homes in the area, and set on 190 acres, with a millpond stocked with pickerel, a wood, a swamp, a pasture, an icehouse, a chicken house, and a cedar-shingle barn large enough to accommodate four horses and twelve cars.

Ruth left his mark on the pine floorboards of the Gathering Room, where he dropped cigar ashes—a selling point for future real estate brokers, who made sure to include the "Historic 'Babe Ruth' cigar marks" in their sales brochures. The Babe made himself comfortable by selling off all the valuable antiques and hammering bats and balls into the walls. He called the place "Home Plate Farm."

Again reporters trekked through bucolic snowdrifts to witness the domestication of the Babe. They dutifully recounted the piles of wood he chopped, the pickerel he caught, the pranks he played, only some of which made it into print, and the schedule he kept, which involved spending as little time as possible in Sudbury.

When Edward M. Thierry, reporting for the Scripps-owned Newspaper Enterprise Association, arrived three days before Christmas, Ruth explained that he went down to Manhattan every Monday through Thursday in his $9,600 limousine, making the two-hundred-mile trip in five and a half hours, which made the week go faster and the simple life less lonely. He had installed a special 55-gallon gas tank in the Packard so he could make the trip without having to stop on the way.

A *Globe* photographer arrived one day hoping to catch Ruth in the process of withdrawing a really big fish from a hole in the ice. Short on time and patience in the cold, the enterprising photographer asked to borrow an already dead, very much frozen 22-inch pickerel caught earlier in the day by another fisherman, which they hooked to Ruth's line and dropped through the ice. "When Babe pulled it out and held it up it looked as though it was thrashing about, all crooked," the town historian reported. "It made a good picture."

Marshall Hunt of the *Daily News* arrived unannounced one day, having detrained in a blizzard in the middle of nowhere. He was lucky to hitch a ride to the Ruth place from the local undertaker, whose services he might otherwise have required. He found the Babe home alone in his pajamas making breakfast.

Ruth performed his favorite parlor trick, involving another piano and the family cat. "He put a cat on a rocking chair," Hunt recalled. "When the cat went to sleep, Babe opened the window nearby, discharged a shotgun out the window, and this cat made a magnificent leap, hit the floor once and up on top of the piano where he lit his landing gear out and, naturally, there were a few scratches.

"I said, 'What kind of cat is this if you can play the same miserable trick on him?'

"He said, 'I don't know how long it's gonna last; maybe this is the last.'"

Helen was absent that day, as she so often was, and Ruth offered no explanation for her whereabouts. Even in this idyllic respite, she was an afterthought.

Helen Woodford Ruth was a mysterious and ultimately tragic figure in Ruth's life, an unfinished woman who married too young and died too early to become fully fledged. She was seen primarily through a camera lens—in brief flares of flash powder—and through a scrim of misinformation, some of it supplied by her young husband. He wrote El Paso, Texas, as her birthplace on a 1920 passport application when in fact Mary Ellen Woodford was a child of an Irish Catholic family, born in Boston on October 20, 1896. Westbrook Pegler recycled that falsehood in his August 1920 newspaper serial, adding that she was a student studying in Boston when they met.

Even their wedding date became the subject of dispute. A widely reprinted wire-service story published the week of Helen's death claimed they had been married in a double ceremony in Boston with friends in late 1914, not in Ellicott City, Maryland, where their marriage certificate remains on exhibit under glass at St. Paul Catholic Church. (No documentation for a Boston marriage could be found in Massachusetts or the Boston city archives.)

For young George Ruth, the impulsive culmination of the whirlwind courtship was as much a pledge of conformity as it was to fidelity, neither of which he would be able to sustain. Their lives and ambitions would diverge as widely as their accounts of Dorothy's birth.

"The Doomed Marriage of George Herman Ruth & Helen Woodford"—as it is described in the church brochure—was a turbulent union pockmarked by car wrecks, infidelities, and loss.

On the day Dorothy was introduced to the public, Helen told the *New York Sunday News* that they had lost three children, and pointed to their photographs, displayed on the mantelpiece of their Ansonia apartment. Neither their births nor their deaths had ever been publicly acknowledged. The *News* checked New York City records and found no births listed for the Ruths between 1920 and 1922.

The only documented birth for George Ruth and Helen Woodford in Massachusetts records was a stillbirth on November 19, 1916, which was just a month before newspapers reported that she had been thrown from a car while joyriding with her husband in Boston. The accounts did not specify the month or date of the accident, which was first reported by the *Baltimore Sun* in December.

Boston police had notified George Ruth Sr. by telegram, and he told the paper she had been pitched from the car, suffering serious internal injuries requiring hospitalization. The following day, the *Chicago Daily Tribune* reported that Helen was "in a delicate condition" at the time of the crash.

Neighbors in Sudbury were not sure what to make of the missus. In the early days, when the Ruths lived in the Ihatetoquitit cabin, she was known to play a good game of whist and to be generous with milk and cookies for local children who came wanting to play with the Babe. She was a more remote figure when they resided at Home Plate Farm.

"I am not sure that I can express my feelings toward Mrs. Ruth," Forrest D. Bradshaw told Ruth's biographer Marshall Smelser in a March 10, 1972, letter. "What dealings I had with her were very pleasant. She seemed to me that she was married to someone that she had to live with and had to be at his beck and call. She was much smaller than he was. She acted more like a servant or slave than a wife. I don't know that Babe would have known how to treat a wife."

Bradshaw ran the local grocery store, where Ruth once bought all the out-of-date gourmet goods he had displayed in the front window that no right-thinking New Englander would have paid a nickel for—and spent $60 for the lot of it!

He routinely bought two slices of top-of-the-round steak cut three inches thick for himself and hamburger for Helen and the chauffeur. "I think that his wife was afraid of him because there was never any argument, in the store, at least," Bradshaw wrote. "She would sort of hold back and let him have his way. It was seldom that they came to the store together. When she came in it was mostly because the chauffeur had brought her down. I don't recall that I ever saw her drive.

"My wife thinks that her hair was auburn. She was small, as I recall, about 5 ft 6., medium build, say about 130 lbs. about 25, not beautiful, possibly attractive. Serious and brooding. I think Catholic, democrat, frugal, a girl that seemed to be lost."

Bradshaw thought Ruth was very much attached to Dorothy, who would remember the years at Home Plate Farm as the happiest of her young life. She had her father to herself, and a nursemaid named Fanny, whom she called Mommy. (Later, long after Helen's death, Fanny confided that Helen "couldn't stand the pressure and loneliness of my dad being away so often," Dorothy said in her memoir, and started to drink and take pills, but Dorothy was blissfully unaware at the time.)

The winters, when he was there most often, were beautiful, with lots of snow. There were ninety chickens in the new henhouse, a horse, a cow, and two pigs. She had a terrier named Lollipop. Her daddy raised and bred white English pit bulls. But then Lollipop drowned in the ice pond and Daddy left, heading south three weeks early to take the baths in Hot Springs, Arkansas, and hit some golf balls in preparation for serious training.

Boarding the train in New York on February 16, Farmer Ruth pronounced himself a changed man, telling the *Hartford Times*, "When I came down from frozen little Sudbury, Massachusetts, I left two things behind: the old limousine with the brass-buttoned, gold braided atmosphere it created last season and, get this, TWENTY-ONE pounds of flesh."

And now it seems that everybody is more interested in my stomach than my home runs. Even up there in that little Massachusetts town youngsters would ask about my weight and the day I left, the garage owner waited three hours for me to come by. When I did, he pulled out a tape measure and asked me to stand still while a wager was being decided.

The measurement was two inches less than he had wagered, and so it cost him $20. I learned afterward that the fellow who won had visited my farm every day to see if I was actually chopping wood and working hard. I proved my reduced weight pretty well to the experts up there in Sudbury.

His waist, Ruth bragged, had shrunk from 45 inches to a perfect 39 inches.

Mert Haskell, a young man who grew up on the farm next to Ruth's, and with whom he had a good relationship, later told the *Sudbury Town Crier* that he had wielded the ax on the Babe's behalf. "I'd do all the work and he'd sit there and drink beer and talk to me."

III

The rehabilitation of the Babe lasted not much more than a month. In March, he was sued by his bookie for welching on a $7,700 gambling debt, and Dolores Dixon, the Manhattan shopgirl, made good on her threat to go public with the story of her pregnancy. Her hopes for a private settlement dashed, she sold a six-part series to a newspaper syndicate detailing the summer fling that ended with an alleged assault aboard a fishing boat off Long Island.

The March 14 headlines were as damning as Ruth was adamant in his condemnation of them: "Nineteen-Year-Old Girl Alleges Babe Is Cause of Her Impending Motherhood—Ruth Wires Attorney to Fight the Case."

Phil Payne, managing editor of the *New York Daily News*, got Marshall Hunt on the phone in New Orleans and ordered him to confront Ruth. This was a first for Hunt, who thought his boss was a busybody with poor editorial judgment. "We were doing so much with Ruth," he said. "I didn't want to damage anything."

It was also the first and last public allegation of the sort made against the Bambino. Given his liberal reputation with women, this is surprising, even to relatives—his grandson, Tom Stevens, wonders if the Babe was sterile.

Dorothy had a similar thought: If the Babe was so promiscuous, "Why don't I have all these brothers and sisters popping up?"

(Asked why she and Babe never had any children, Claire Ruth told one family member, "It just didn't happen.")

Hunt knocked on Ruth's door, reluctantly and apologetically. "He wasn't mad at me, but he was kind of surprised that I barged up to his room that night and wanted to know these things," Hunt told Kal Wagenheim. "But I did explain that the office wanted it. In fact, I said Phil Payne, the managing editor, kind of put the heat on me for the first time ever.

"Well, he didn't invite me into the room, and we stalled around there, and finally he said, 'I don't want to say anything.'

"'Well,' I said, 'that's okay with me, Babe.'

"I immediately went back to my room and called up the office. I guess I talked with Payne. He seemed to think I should have milked the Babe, but he didn't understand my end of it then. But he did later.

"I asked the Babe if he knew Dolores Dixon. He didn't bat an eye and said, 'No, I don't know any dame named Dolores Dixon.'

"I said, 'Take it easy now, Babe. Better think twice. Do you know her or not?'

"He said, 'God damn it, I don't know her.'"

Helen was with him when the story broke and stuck by him. Ruth summoned the Yankee writers to his suite, where they found him rocking the baby to sleep. "Nothing but a holdup game," he said.

Ruth's salary, and the money he earned outside the game, made him not only the highest-paid baseball player ever, but also the first worth blackmailing. He declared his intention to fight Dixon in court and ordered his lawyer, Hyman Bushel, to hire a private detective.

He was less solvent than his extravagances made him appear. He was still in the hole from the losses in Cuba and $9,000 in fines in 1922. Although the Yankees had refunded $415.80 for his tonsillectomy in 1922, laid out $620.51 to the sheriff of New York City for a judgment against Ruth involving the Automobile Association in May, and refunded another $1,500 fine, Ruth had still had to take a $5,000 advance on his 1923 salary in June and borrow $5,000 against his syndicate earnings in the fall to pay legal fees. The private eye was hard on her tail when Dixon's lawyers finally filed their lawsuit on April 17. Yankee Stadium opened the next day.

Other teams had Fields and Parks and Yards and Grounds. The Babe required something grander. *The*

Yankee Stadium, as it was known until the late fifties, was a great concrete-and-copper coliseum, whose antecedents were in ancient Greece and Rome. It rose out of raw earth and vacant lots on the east bank of the Harlem River in just 284 days.

The purchase of ten acres of shanty- and rubble-strewn landfill belonging to the William Waldorf Astor estate was announced on February 6, 1921. It had been the site of a Revolutionary War–era farm, a silent movie studio where cowboy pictures were made, and a lumberyard. A rusty sign for Mancuso's Manufacturers was leaning against a ramshackle fence on the property when the deal was announced. A trickle of a stream, Cromwell's Creek, ran 125 feet below. The floodplain and mud flats had been filled with Manhattan schist dug up when railroad tunnels were built below the Grand Concourse in 1905.

"Goatville," John McGraw called it dismissively.

The Yankees did not disclose how much they paid the Astor estate. But according to team minutes dated March 1, 1921, the team paid $550,000 for the lot and $15,000 plus interest for two smaller parcels at the unpaved corner of River Avenue and 161st Street. According to Yankee accounting books, the cost of 11.6 acres in Goatville was $792,000. The location, Ruppert noted, had the advantage of being sixteen minutes from Grand Central by subway, and taunting distance from the Polo Grounds.

The Stadium was designed to inspire awe and built to accommodate Ruth's left-handed power. The lopsided playing field tapered to just 275 feet down the left and right field lines that first year but was lengthened just a bit the following season. The original blueprints called for battlements to be installed above the third deck, but that proved too expensive even for the Yankees, who spent $2.5 million on their swanky new joint. Ruppert praised Cap Huston, a former Army engineer who supervised the project, for keeping the costs down, and promptly bought him out of his half of the team a month after opening day, a deal that had been announced the previous December.

A 15-foot-deep scalloped copper frieze hovering 109 feet above the playing field would have to suffice as an architectural signifier of monumentality, which the *American Architect* dismissed as "rather idiotic."

It was a thoroughly modern facility with eight restrooms for men and eight for women (tastefully furnished with wicker chairs and dressing tables), and a 15-foot-deep brick-lined vault buried beneath second base housing electrical wiring, and telephone and telegraph equipment, so that a boxing ring and press area could function in the infield. It was constructed with 800 tons of rebar, 2,300 tons of mechanical steel, 950,000 feet of lumber, and one million brass screws, which held their own until a misguided modernization in 1974–75 did away with the elegant rotunda and archetypal frieze.

Star-spangled bunting draped the Stadium's boxes for opening day on April 18, 1923. New York governor Al Smith threw out the first pitch at least ten times in order to accommodate all the photographers. John Philip Sousa led the Yankees and the Red Sox to the flagpole in deep center field and conducted the 7th Regiment Band in a pregame concert from left field. The place was so vast, twice the size of any other ballpark, that the music sounded to a *New York Post* scribe sitting upstairs in the press box as if he were hearing a Fifth Avenue parade from a building a block away.

"I'd give a year of my life if I can hit a home run in the first game in this new park," the Babe said.

And so he did—the 198th of his career. The Red Sox outfielder backed up the hill in right field thinking, hoping, pretending he had a chance to catch the ball. When Ruth stepped on home plate, delicately for such a large man, the roar could be heard across the Harlem River in the Polo Grounds. "It would have been a home run in the Sahara Desert," wrote the *New York World*'s Heywood Broun.

The announced attendance was 74,217, an astonishing number given that the Yankee Stadium had only 62,000 seats.

Fred Lieb dubbed it "The House That Ruth Built."

Just like that, Dolores Dixon's baby was relegated to fine print. Five days later, she recanted. The lawsuit was dropped when Ruth's attorney produced a witness ready to testify that the whole thing was a scam.

The Yankees arrived in Washington for their first visit to Griffith Stadium just as Ruth's friend Jim Barton began an out-of-town run of his new show before its Broadway opening. It was called *In the Moonlight* then but would be renamed *Dew Drop Inn* by the time they got to the Great White Way. On Broadway, Barton would be best remembered for his role in *Tobacco Road*. In Yankee lore, he is best remembered for asking Claire Hodgson, a bit player in the company, but a very pretty girl, if she liked baseball. Why, yes, she replied, Ty Cobb was a client of her lawyer father back home in Athens, Georgia. In one of the several iterations told over the years about meeting her future husband, Claire said Barton extended an invitation to accompany him to the ball game, where he made an introduction to the Great Bambino.

Born Clara Mae Merritt, she had fled a failed early marriage for the footlights of New York. Claire was gorgeous and sassy and talked back, the way other women, Helen specifically, wouldn't or couldn't.

At not quite age fifteen, she had eloped with Frank Hodgson, the richest, most eligible bachelor in Athens, a gentleman caller more than twice her age. "She went off to marry him and left her schoolbooks behind the door as if she was going to school," her daughter Julia Ruth Stevens said. "She and my biological father went off to get married and then she went off to school. That afternoon, he came to pick her up and my grandmother said, 'Frank Hodgson, I told you I never wanted to see you again around this house.'

"He said, 'Ma'am, I came to pick up my wife.'

"That stopped my grandmother."

Julia was born on July 17, 1916. "He was all right up until I was born," she said. "I came along and he started spending his nights at the Elks club. She said, 'I've had enough of this.'"

In fact, Claire filed for divorce on June 3, 1919, charging Hodgson with habitual drunkenness, which he admitted, and verbal and physical abuse. According to the divorce petition, "He struck and beat her with his fists so forcibly as to bruise and discolor her face," precipitating their immediate separation in the fall of 1917. The divorce was granted by jury trial on July 9, 1920. She received sole custody of Julia and three hundred dollars in alimony. She was granted permission by the court to remarry; he was not.

She left for New York with a hundred-dollar loan from a sympathetic member of the Hodgson family and a letter of introduction to Howard Chandler Christy— the bon vivant illustrator with an eye for a choice bit of calico. In the city of reinvention, Clara Mae introduced herself as Claire, a glamorous young widow of the South. "Mother was a dish," Julia Ruth said. "So she went to the door with me. . . . He said, 'Good, God, don't tell me it's another one of mine.'

"She told him she just wanted a job. He said, 'Well, come right in and let me take a look at you.'

"He used her as a model. She had a friend who was on the stage and she told her, 'They're having a casting call tomorrow, why don't you go and see if they can use you?'

"She went to the casting call and they picked her for the chorus line. Some people have said she was with the Ziegfeld Follies. Mother was very petite. The Ziegfeld girls were big girls."

On a visit to Athens in 1922, Claire told her home-town paper that Christy helped her land a job with the Follies in 1918 and had arranged for her to pose as Lady Liberty for a Third Liberty Loan Drive poster drawn by Harrison Fisher. She described herself as "a three-or-four-line actress," appearing in two movies, *Fools First* and *Rough and Ready*, in parts so small her name didn't appear in the credits. She got a mention as an extra in the 1919 show *The Magic Melody* on Broadway and had toured the country in the road company of the Broadway hit *Tangerine*.

She was modeling in early April 1923—perched on the shoulders of a male model—in silk hose and heels while applying a coat of paint to a boat called *The Pollywog*. By the beginning of May, she was auditioning for the role of a lifetime as the future Mrs. Babe Ruth.

Which was much better than languishing in the ensemble of *Dew Drop Inn*, a play remembered chiefly for Jim Barton's debut in blackface. Either Barton invited her and a girlfriend along to a party that night at the Babe's hotel suite (the story Claire Ruth told in 1974) or the Babe sent the hunchbacked team mascot Eddie Bennett to the theater the next afternoon with an invite to the soiree. Either way she went after extracting a promise that she could bring a girlfriend along.

Babe told her the place would be lousy with people, which it was—most of whom didn't know him and all of whom seemed intent on making sure his glass stayed full. She told him he drank too much.

First dame ever to tell him that.

He said she reminded him of Miller Huggins.

"I think the party would have gone on all night but around midnight I asked the bartenders to stop serving drinks," she told the *Buffalo Evening News* in 1974. "I asked the bartenders to quit serving. I explained to everyone that the Babe had to get his sleep for the game the next day and suggested that the partygoers leave."

A ballsy move from a tagalong chorus girl.

He said, "May I call on you in New York?"

And, according to her daughter, Julia, "She thought about it and said, 'You may.'"

From then on—when he wasn't on the road with the Yankees and she wasn't on the road with the show—Ruth's big maroon Packard was often spotted near the apartment she shared with her mother, Julia, and her two uncles at 219 West Eightieth Street.

Claire's mother, Carrie Lou Merritt, was the disciplinarian. "Mean," Julia said. "She did all the spanking."

But she didn't say a word to her daughter about keeping company with a married man. "And if she did,

Mother didn't pay attention," Julia said. "And Daddy didn't care. He was separated."

Helen and Dorothy remained sequestered in Sudbury.

IV

Nineteen twenty-four was supposed to be the year of maturation. He was twenty-nine years old. "He's beginning to grow up now," manager Miller Huggins declared a month into the regular season.

Huggins spoke too soon. Or, it might be argued, not soon enough.

Two weeks after Huggins issued his happy prognostication, Yankee general manager Ed Barrow wrote an urgent appeal to Commissioner Landis asking him to intervene on behalf of the club. Ruth was gambling on the ponies again. The Yankees had paid $209.50 in May to the detective agency that followed him.

"We have been told that Ruth and several other Yankee players are 'playing the races' again," Barrow wrote. "The chief offender, of course, is Ruth. The others are merely 'piking' along in a small way on 'tips' that Ruth has been receiving.

"The betting has not been done openly, therefore,

we have been unable to take any action in the matter. Manager Huggins has had Ruth 'on the carpet' a couple of times but the player denied that he had done anything more than make an occasional small bet. Mr. Huggins is convinced, however, that Ruth has made and lost some large bets this spring. He has won some bets too, but most of them have gone against him."

What was needed, Barrow said, was "a good stiff letter" from the commissioner telling Ruth "if he doesn't cut it out you'll take 'drastic action'"—something stern enough to "scare him into stopping before he gets in too deep. The poor big simpleton hasn't saved a dollar out of all the money he has made, and will in all probability wind up his baseball career flat broke."

Letters of reproach and denial were exchanged with appropriate and unenforceable promises of reform. Ruth was not the leading man in the June 13 melee on the field in Detroit, but the mere possibility of his suspension merited a headline in the *New York Times*.

At the first whiff off misbehavior, Christy Walsh sprang into action. His efforts at imposing discipline, fiscal and otherwise, were flagging. There was no sending Ruth back to the farm or its woodshed in the middle of the season. And no one, it seemed, could make him salute and take orders either. But Walsh could at least align him with forces that did.

Ruth had not served, nor had he been drafted into the Army, during World War I. As a married man, he was exempt from military service. He had, however, been the subject of an FBI investigation, an early lesson in the privilege and sting of notoriety. In October 1917, George A. Anderson, the United States attorney in Boston, received an anonymous tip that Ruth was a draft dodger. The matter was referred to the director of Military Enrollment and then on to the FBI, with Anderson's request "that the investigation be made in a quiet way owing to the prominence of Mr. Ruth."

A case was opened: "In re: George H. Ruth, alias Babe Ruth—Alleged Slacker."

FBI agents visited his father's saloon in Baltimore and reported back: "Ruth not registered in Baltimore. Information received from cafe he is supposed to own that his home is in Boston."

The investigation was then turned over to a volunteer operative in Boston, who located his draft number. It had been a bum tip; the investigation was closed. But a paper trail had been created and the dossier remained on file, available to Landis in 1921 when he ordered his assistant to investigate Ruth's service record as part of the barnstorming fiasco.

Three years later, with Ruth's sullied reputation

again under review by the commissioner, Walsh devised a preemptive strategy that established Ruth as a friend of law and order and an adjunct to military discipline—an association that would protect him should the file ever become public or his service questioned.

Everyone knew Ruth never followed orders. So Walsh decided to clothe him in the vestments of obedience and patriotism. In April 1924, he arranged a meeting at the home of General John J. Pershing, with whom he had begun the largely one-sided correspondence during his tenure in the Army Motor Pool. He suggested using Ruth as a recruiter for Pershing's summer Citizens' Training Camps.

This, Pershing agreed, was a pretty good idea.

He was scheduled to address a dinner in New York in May with a thousand former Army officers in attendance. Back in his Manhattan office, Walsh wrote to the general with his latest brainstorm, putting Ruth forward as an after-dinner speaker. Granted, he wasn't an orator, Walsh wrote, but had spoken at "similar occasions with credit." He felt sure that Ruth would respond positively to a personal appeal from the general.

Pershing politely demurred, saying he preferred to save Ruth for a more auspicious occasion.

The next day, May 13, Ruth's byline column in the *New York American* offered a sales pitch for the Citizens' Training Camps, encouraging boys ages seventeen to twenty-four to join up for what he described as spring training for soldiers. He provided an address for potential candidates, suggesting they mark their envelopes "application through Babe Ruth."

A week later he enlisted in the 104th Field Artillery of the National Guard at high noon in Times Square, taking the oath of allegiance in a three-piece suit beside a gun carriage. Police reserves had to be called in to handle the mob.

When the Yankees arrived in Washington a week after that, Private Ruth, in a hastily tailored uniform, reported for duty at the War Office, smartly saluting his commanding officer, General John J. Pershing. He went 3 for 8 in a doubleheader later that afternoon at Griffith Stadium.

In gratitude, Walsh sent the general a desk blotter in the shape of a baseball, autographed by Babe Ruth, John McGraw, Miller Huggins, and Nick Altrock, with a note expressing his hope that it would facilitate the writing of the general's war memoir.

"A unique souvenir," Pershing called it.

From then on, Walsh never missed an opportunity to put Ruth in uniform. He addressed cadets at a Citizens' Training Camp, caught baseballs dropped from the roof of the George M. Cohan Theatre in Times Square to benefit a fund for the widows and orphans of New York City policemen killed in the line of duty, practiced his marksmanship under the tutelage of Medal of Honor winner Samuel Woodfill, signed up with the New York City Police Auxiliary, and conducted military drills in June 1927 on Governors Island with little boys armed with wooden bats.

As hoped, the displays of discipline distracted attention from his misbehavior, which didn't seem to detract from his performance at all in 1924. He was splendid, leading the major leagues in batting average, slugging percentage, and on-base percentage in the American League. The Yankees, who finished second two games behind the Washington Senators, never got around to disciplining him.

Huggins assured Mark Roth, the team's traveling secretary, that he would find the right time and place to address Ruth's chronic tardiness and impertinence. But then Ruth would hit another two home runs and the manager would lose the initiative. "Now?" Roth said, nudging Huggins in a Chicago elevator as Ruth headed out for a night on the town.

"Shut up," Huggins replied.

Another time, also in Chicago, Huggins hovered by the clubhouse door, vowing to confront Ruth when he breezed in late yet again. But then, seeing the room enlivened by his arrival, Huggins hesitated. "You going to speak to him?" Roth said.

"Sure," Huggins replied.

And he did.

He said, "Hiya, Babe."

V

It takes a lot of agility for a big man to get off a small horse without looking silly, which may explain why Dudley Scott's camera was turned off when Ruth alighted from the pony Molly that afternoon in Sioux City. A still photo of the moment, sold by International Newsreel, caught the anguished look on his face when he realized his predicament. The photo, accompanied by a pithy caption—"Ride 'Em, Big Boy, Ride 'Em!"— showed up in the *New York American* and the *New York Evening Journal*, and in two of the cities they had yet to visit. Editors elaborated at will. In the *Evening Journal*, "Babe wanted to ride the pony, but the pony wouldn't stand for it." In the *San Francisco Examiner*, the reluctant Babe was coaxed into the saddle by the Donohue boys. "Babe feared his weight would be too much for the little horse, but he was assured the pony was 'tough.' We don't know whether the photographer tricked this picture, but Ruth really looks bigger than the pony."

This was the predicament of the size of his fame: every gesture, grimace, and offhand remark could catch up with him. For someone described by *New York Times* reporter John Drebinger as "the most uninhibited man" he'd ever met, learning discretion was not just difficult, it was antithetical to his entire being. But he was trying.

Claire was cooperatively mum. Even if she got wind of the gossip that reached the smallest-circulation dailies like the *Town Talk* of Alexandria, Louisiana, in early 1927, there was nothing she could do or say about it. "Babe Ruth, batting his eyelashes before Hollywood movie cameras, says he prefers blonds. We thought it was bonds. The Babe is batting a thousand for popularity honors. He plays right field at a dinner party almost every night."

As for Helen, she was like disappearing ink. After his visit to her in the hospital in March on the day he returned from California, there was no mention of her in any of the papers, no follow-up on her condition or her whereabouts. She was subsumed by the cacophony of loud headlines generated by news of the three-year contract he had signed for 1927–29. At season's end she made the obligatory wifely appearance at the World Series with Dorothy and then disappeared again.

And so, apparently, Walsh felt confident enough to

allow John B. Kennedy to tag along on the barnstorming tour. That fall, he was also working on a football story for *Collier's,* "The Halfback of Notre Dame," which gave him an entrée to Rockne and Walsh. The Rock liked the article enough to make Kennedy his de facto ghostwriter. His eight-part series for the magazine, published in 1930, would be hastily assembled as a posthumous autobiography when the Notre Dame coach died in an airplane crash in 1931.

Walsh could count on Kennedy to craft a credulous story, which was timed to run with the opening of the new baseball season. He called it "Innocents Abroad," and cast Ruth as a wise elder, tutoring innocent Lou on the pitfalls of dames and fame. "The Babe led Gehrig in avoiding all but the necessary lionizing," Kennedy wrote, "and ladies in waiting were completely out of luck."

When one such lady, professing a "personal friendship," reached Ruth on the phone in their hotel suite in Omaha, Kennedy dutifully recounted Ruth's refusal to take her call, not once but twice, putting her off by putting her on the line with Gehrig, whom he called his social secretary. "'See Lou,' Ruth moralized. 'You've got to be careful who you talk with and what you say.'"

Chapter 11
October 19 / Denver

"MY FRIEND, YOU NEVER LEAVE
WHITE SPACE. YOU ALWAYS FILL IT."
—DAMON RUNYON TO WALLY PIPP ON THE DAY HE TOOK
HIMSELF OUT OF THE YANKEE LINEUP BECAUSE
OF A HEADACHE

"VENI, VIDI, VICI"
—OTTO FLOTO, *DENVER POST*

I

Otto Floto, sports editor of the *Denver Post*, made
himself at home in the suite he had reserved for
Ruth and Gehrig at the Brown Palace Hotel. Floto,

who was hired on at the *Post* because one of the paper's owners liked the sound of his name, was on familiar terms with Ruth, who had wired ahead to ask a favor. "Please have dining car steward lay in supply of buffalo meat. I want to give Lou a thrill and a good feed."

Floto's sports section provided a reliable home for Ruth's column, and the *Post*, as sponsor of the game at Merchants Park, was an enthusiastic cheerleader for Walsh's Symphony of Swat. In one pregame puff piece, Floto reprinted verbatim correspondence from Joe Bihler in Walsh's New York office demanding "GOOD BASEBALLS"—"the finest grade, most expensive baseballs—in other words, the Spalding National league or the Reach American league ball." (Both endorsed by Ruth.)

The failure of either of the Bustin' Twins to hit a home run in Des Moines had resulted in poor reviews, with the *Des Moines Register* calling the game "a baseball atrocity," which Walsh attributed to inferior baseballs and overindulging at a pheasant dinner hosted by Gehrig's fraternity brothers.

Floto dutifully reported Walsh's promise of a rivalry between Ruth and Gehrig "just as intense as was the rivalry of the Yanks and the Pittsburghs in the recent World's Series."

Having appointed himself flack and consort for the

day, Floto greeted the party at Union Station, where three thousand people, including tribal elders bearing ceremonial headdresses, awaited, then escorted them to their hotel, where he recorded a scene of tender friendship and harmony "such as grows up only between few men."

Floto was a barely literate drunk who loved three-syllable words but eschewed punctuation, according to one of his successors, Woody Paige. He wrote about fights he secretly promoted, claimed to have discovered Jack Dempsey, giving him leave to announce himself on the section masthead as "dean of boxing writers," brawled with the legendary Wild West gunman turned sportswriter Bat Masterson, married a bareback rider performing in the eponymously named "Floto Dog and Pony Show" (funded by the *Post*), and hired a young local writer by the name of Alfred (Damon) Runyon to ghostwrite his columns.

In short, he fit Paul Gallico's retrospective assessment of his former colleagues in the fun and games department: "One grade above the office cat."

Floto knew Walsh and Ruth well enough to have been granted an audience with the pajama-clad King of Swat on the roof deck of St. Vincent's Hospital when he was recuperating from surgery in May 1925. His former assistant, Gene Fowler, was one of Walsh's most trusted spooks. No doubt Floto took Ruth's inscription on the obligatory photo—"To my friend, Otto Floto"—to heart and would not have seen anything wrong with documenting the friendship in print.

When the Yankees headed south in the spring of 1927 without the Babe, who was then still holding out for a hundred thousand dollars a year, Floto, who had a fondness for Big Top similes, opined that this was like "the circus coming to town without its clowns." He put forth the novel suggestion that the owners of the other seven American League teams contribute twenty-five thousand to Ruth's salary.

Far be it from Otto Floto to commit journalism on the day Ruth and Gehrig came to town. He solemnly recounted the jig Lou danced upon reaching their hotel and reading the telegram bearing the news that his mother had finally been released from the hospital. And the moisture in Babe's eyes as he whispered, "You know, every town we go into, immediately on arrival he writes to his mother and what a wonderful thing it is to have a mother at his age. You know, I was unfortunate enough to lose my mother when I was a mere tot in Baltimore."

Otto Floto reliably reported the misstatement of fact, true only in Ruth's heart. After all, Floto wrote, it was a privilege to be with him.

II

Sportswriting in the age of jazz journalism was "a low form of art," said Stanley Woodward, the venerated sports editor of the *New York Herald Tribune*. You couldn't get much lower than Otto Floto, who was a one-man circus of ballyhoo.

This in no way made Otto exceptional. Today's conflicts of interest were yesterday's norms: the "sugaring" of writers—paying money under the table to guarantee coverage of events or personalities—was a given; press releases were routinely printed as copy; beat writers traveled and ate on the team's dime; reporters for afternoon papers moonlighted for morning papers, padding their bank accounts while bringing a certain sameness to the coverage of the day's events.

Not everyone in the business bowed to the status quo. Protests by the Baseball Writers' Association of America about the proliferation of ghostwriting since its debut at the 1911 World Series had been lodged with the baseball commissioner. It was one of the practices responsible for the establishment of the American Society of News Editors (ASNE) and its code of journalistic ethics in 1922.

Sportswriters in the golden era committed as many sins against language as they did against journalistic propriety. Contrary to the received wisdom, purple prose wasn't invented in the press box at Yankee Stadium. "Weighty openings and grand declarations often / Have one or two purple patches tacked on, that gleam / Far and wide," the Roman poet Horace wrote in *Ars Poetica* in give or take 19 BC.

Stanley Walker, editor of the New York City *Herald-Tribune*, was responsible for the linguistic division of sportswriters into two camps: "gee whiz" and "aw nuts." The golden era was heavy on gee whiz, and Grantland Rice, an erudite practitioner of press box poesy, was its poet laureate. He was also the most widely syndicated and imitated sportswriter in the country, best remembered for his 1908 homage to the alumni of Vanderbilt football: "For when the one Great Scorer comes to write against your name, / He marks—not that you won or lost—but how you played the Game."

Rice was unequivocal about his mandate: "When a sportswriter stops making heroes out of athletes, it's time to get out of the business."

For Rice, Ruth was the Crown Prince of Verdun. For Paul Gallico, he was the American Porthos. For Otto Floto, he was the Julius Caesar of home-run hitters, who provided "the big music, the blare of trumpets and the crash of cymbals stuff."

They wrote from above, literally, filing dramatic set

pieces from the remove of the press box without descending to the level of conversation or inquiry. Gallico said he covered sports as parable, contests between good and evil, not, say, the Yankees versus the Pirates. As the boxing writer Larry Merchant once told *New York Times* columnist Robert Lipsyte, "If sportswriters back then had asked questions, we would know whether Babe Ruth really pointed to the stands before his home run in the 1932 World Series."

Occupying the other end of the press box were the "aw nuts" reformers also known as knockers, led by the curmudgeonly Westbrook Pegler, W. O. McGeehan (the only writer, Walsh said, to rebuff his offer to join his staff of ghosts), and McGeehan's former editor Heywood Broun, who once informed his staff that if a "reporter finds out that a baseball player struck out with the bases loaded because he was out on a beer party the night before the game, that's the story I want."

Reporters who filed for morning papers had no time to ask questions; those who wrote for afternoon dailies had the leisure to look for "color" but never quoted anyone the way they actually talked.

That left an open field for Walsh's ghosts. Ford Frick, who channeled the Babe for the better part of ten years, never expressed any conflict about the conflict of interest at the center of his dual career: not in private correspondence (now on file at the Hall of Fame), nor in any of his newspaper work, nor in any of the many articles written about him after he became baseball commissioner. In a single aside in his 1973 autobiography, he mentioned "doing a little ghosting for Jedgie." He cast his lot with the mediums and never looked back. "It's easy to be a debunker," he said. "But why do it? That's the thing I can't understand."

III

It began with a gurgle, then a cramp, then a pain so acute that it felled him as he did his roadwork in Hot Springs, Arkansas, in the spring of 1925.

In retrospect, the "bellyache heard round the world" in April 1925 would prove a turning point for both Ruth and the writers who covered him. The story became a season-long feeding frenzy, a steady diet of column inches about Ruthian excess.

The gastric crisis was inevitable. Inevitable because everything about him had become overstated: the meals, beer, pounds, spending, and even the linguistic entitlements. He had begun speaking of himself in the third person, a disease that has become endemic to the modern locker room. "The Babe can't disappoint his fans," he declaimed the day before he passed out in Asheville, North Carolina, as the Yankees headed north from spring training.

And it was "heard round the world," in McGeehan's felicitous phrase, because of the proliferation of New York City tabloids and because of the echo chamber created by the evolving mass media. The coverage was as feverish as the Babe when it all caught up with him.

Ruth had shown up in Hot Springs for what would prove to be the last Babe Boil more zaftig than ever, weighing in at 256 pounds. The Yankees had always sanctioned these pre-spring-training trips. In fact, Marshall Hunt later confessed to having been a party to Ruth's contract negotiation in a Hot Springs hot tub, offering advice to both sides, and witnessing the Babe signing while stark naked and sopping wet.

Soaking and sweating and then soaking some more, he lost thirty pounds in less than a month. Weakened by "too rapid a reduction in fat," as the *Evening Graphic* put it, he collapsed one day in acute pain while running the hills outside town. He nonetheless found the energy to entertain "two damsels who may or may not have been professionals of one kind or another," the *Daily Mirror* observed.

The Yankees had moved their spring training camp from New Orleans to St. Petersburg that year. Nothing went right from the moment he got to Florida. There were alligators in the outfield. He broke a finger on his left hand making a catch. And then Helen and Dorothy showed up.

The marriage was foundering and had been for some time. Reporters had overheard Babe and Helen quarreling in New Orleans in 1923 when she stood by him throughout the Dolores Dixon debacle. "I wish you would blow back home," Ruth told her. "You certainly cramp my style."

He was on his best behavior two years later in St. Pete while Helen and Dorothy were around but broke loose as soon as they left. He went on a bender with Steve O'Neill, one of the four baseball-playing O'Neill brothers he knew from Scranton, who became a regular playmate when he joined the Yankees in 1925. And, Ruth played day and night despite increasing chills, a chest cold, stomach cramps, and a fever. Arriving in Asheville on April 7 after a long and winding train trip through the Great Smoky Mountains, he collapsed in the station waiting room and announced he wanted to go home.

"He was right in front of me," Marshall Hunt told Kal Wagenheim. "He collapsed in Steve O'Neill's arms. He fell against a steam radiator there and then down on the floor. Ford Frick was with him. I said to Ford, 'I don't think he's faking this time.'"

Hunt borrowed a camera and "got a beautiful shot of him propped up in bed, took it down and gave it to a Pullman porter. The paper had it the next day all over pg. 1."

He was said to be suffering from boils, flu, and indigestion brought on by an onslaught of hot dogs. The *New York Evening Journal* published a photo with twelve numbered franks superimposed on his belly.

The Yankees insisted he stay behind and installed scout Paul Krichell as his minder and personal shopper. The only nightclothes he could find were size 42—six sizes too small—and pink. Word reached the Big Apple that the "King's Pajamas" had to be split down the back in order to fit, qualifying him for his debut in the new *New Yorker* magazine. He was "The Talk of the Town."

When he finally headed north, a missed connection in Salisbury, Maryland, meant that he failed to arrive in Washington at the appointed time. News flashed around the world to London, where one newspaper pronounced him dead. The obituary made note of his recent abdication of a belt in favor of braces, a concession to his expanding girth.

He wired Helen: "Meet me. The report that I am dead is a lie. Love."

En route to New York, he rallied, and availed himself of a light breakfast of bacon and eggs, juice, toast, coffee, and four porterhouse steaks, according to the newly vigilant *New Yorker*. He collapsed again, this time in the washroom, hitting his head against the basin of the sink as the train approached Manhattan on the afternoon of April 9. Somehow Krichell and the train's private detective got his unconscious bulk back into his berth.

Bulletins were issued; editions were held; headlines blared: "Ruth Shakes Off Coma," "Babe's Doctor Denies Brain Injury," "Relapse Followed Fried Potatoes for Breakfast."

Helen and a friend arrived with Walsh to meet his train at Pennsylvania Station. The scene resembled something out of a Harold Lloyd comedy except for the severity of his condition. The first ambulance broke down. A congregation of press, police, and other interested parties gathered, including Rube Marquard and Jesse Barnes, heading north with the Boston Braves. They were turned away from his train car when they asked to pay their respects. Ruth was still unconscious.

Another ambulance was called. The window in his sleeping compartment had to be removed in order to accommodate the Babe-laden stretcher. Finally, at 2:30 P.M., he was lifted through the window, taken down in the baggage elevator, and loaded into the ambulance, where he went into convulsions.

Six attendants were required to hold him down.

Sedatives were administered. Helen and Walsh accompanied him in the ambulance for a silent-movie ride downtown. The vehicle's "bell" had failed, making it one of the few times Ruth went anywhere anonymously.

Damon Runyon wrote in the *American*: "The 'Big Bam' just about beat a long throw from old Death, the outfielder in Life's game. He slid in safe over the home plate of hospital rest and medical attention."

At St. Vincent's Hospital, Walsh barred everyone from his room except Helen, Dorothy, and Ed Barrow. Even Jake Ruppert was kept at bay. Ruth rallied on a diet of poached eggs but continued to run a fever. A week after he arrived, the Yankee team doctor Edward King informed the press that Ruth had developed an intestinal abscess and would undergo surgery on April 17.

Overnight the most accessible public personage in the United States became the least available. All updates on his condition would henceforth come from the Yankees, or from his doctors with the team's approval, which meant little if any information would be forthcoming about the diagnosis or the procedure beyond its duration (twenty minutes) and its success (it was successful).

That morning Jack Conway had reported in the *New York Daily Mirror* that Ruth's condition resembled "a fistula." The editors crowned the story with an ominous headline: "Feeling Grows That Babe Is Critically Ill."

(A fistula is an opening that allows gastric fluids to be discharged through the lining of the stomach, intestines, or colon, which can result from genetic diseases such as Crohn's disease. According to Doris Keil-Shamieh, a distant cousin on Ruth's father's side of the family, inflammatory bowel disease, including Crohn's, runs in her family.)

The indolent sporting press propelled itself into a state of high dudgeon.

Paul Gallico demanded that the Yankees allow one pool reporter to see Ruth once every day, warning that ink-starved wretches would inevitably start smelling rats, speculating about sinister causes and doubting "the communiqués that the Yankee offices have issued."

This was a first. Reporters were accustomed to believing what they were told, not reporting what they were told not to, and having complete access to

Ruth. They besieged Barrow for details, who let it be known, off the record, that a social disease—not ballpark wieners—was the source of the infection. Even if Barrow's diagnosis was accurate, Ruth would hardly have qualified as the first or last baseball player to contract such an ailment. More to the point, the diagnosis doesn't match the cure. Surgery has never been a typical treatment for syphilis or gonorrhea. Claire Ruth, in her 1959 memoir, *The Babe and I,* posited yet another cause, which she said was too delicate to name at the time—a torn groin muscle.

Whatever the diagnosis, Gallico wrote in his 1938 valedictory *Farewell to Sport,* the most remarkable feature of Ruth's illness was the sympathy pains experienced by the vox populi: "A baseball player lay close to death and an entire nation held its breath, worried and fretted, and bought every edition of the newspapers to read the bulletins as though the life of a personal friend or a member of the family were at stake."

Doctors prescribed a liquid diet and solitary confinement. Hard to say which was the greater deprivation. No telegrams, no telephone calls, no visitors, Ruth complained to sports editors in a note blaming his unaccustomed silence and the absence of his promised columns on "hospital censorship." It was published beside his first column upon his return to his literary labors:

a cri de coeur on behalf of fat people, who hurt just as much as skinny ones in encounters with a surgeon's blade.

Nonetheless, he improved.

Then, at 5:00 P.M. on the afternoon of April 24, at the entrance to St. Vincent's Hospital, while in conversation with Dr. King, Helen Ruth collapsed.

This was no swoon. This was a crack-up. Wire service stories spread the news with bells and clatter in newsrooms across the country. "Mrs. Babe Ruth Suffers Complete Nervous Breakdown."

She was admitted "in a nervous condition, brought on by worry over her husband's illness," King informed reporters.

No one questioned the official explanation.

She was confined to a room in the same wing of the hospital as her hubby and may or may not have seen his June "as told to" published in the *Evening Graphic*, in which he said, among other things: "It's rather funny but the truth is that a home run is the nearest I ever got to a home. I have never known the pleasures of a home, a real home with the care and love of a mother."

It could not have improved her condition.

He was released on May 25. His six-week stay in the hospital cost the Yankees $1,107.03 and the American

League pennant. He returned to the lineup on June 1. It was something of an omen when, in the fourth inning, he was thrown out trying to score from first base on a double by Bob Meusel. He landed on home plate like a seal on a sandbar at low tide.

IV

The summer of 1925 was a sulky, desultory time for Ruth and the Yankees. The dark mood in the clubhouse was understandable. Languishing in the standings, the Yankees would finish seventh in the American League. Ruth's mood was harder to comprehend: antic and manic, he ate and drank his way through June, July, and August, defying common sense and managerial dictates with a vengeance that was as selfish as it was self-destructive.

When Brother Paul, superintendent of St. Mary's, saw Ruth in Washington during the first week of June, the Babe confided that his legs swelled every afternoon and ached every night. Brother Paul advised him to sit out the rest of the season. When Big Matt had dinner with the Babe in New York shortly before the Yankees left for a fifteen-game road trip on August 14, "he found him still worried about his physical condition but hopeful," Brother Paul told the *Baltimore Evening Sun,* and "apparently in the best of spirits." Or so Matthias said.

Yankee management was not so guileless.

The inevitable and belated confrontation occurred when he showed up late for a game against the Browns in St. Louis on August 29 after staying out all night. "Don't bother getting dressed, Babe," Huggins said. "You're not playing today."

BABE RUTH OUSTED; $5,000 FINE
—*NEW YORK SUNDAY NEWS*

He was suspended indefinitely, prompting questions in 24-point type about whether he had a future with the Yankees, and giving Joe Patterson, the publisher of the *News,* an opening to run the story every baseball writer in New York had been sitting on since Ruth's car had been spotted nightly parked outside Claire Hodgson's West Side apartment.

Today's scoops were the chum of press-box gossip—but nothing more—for yesterday's sportswriters who, paradoxically, knew their subjects far better and wrote far less than their modern counterparts; today, reporters are expected to divine their inner thoughts while kept at a galactic remove by media-relations staffers who dole out access like carbohydrates.

The writers who covered the Babe with centripetal force didn't want to risk their entrée, as Marshall Hunt patiently explained to his managing editor after the Dolores Dixon affair. And as Richards Vidmer, of the *Times*, told Jerome Holtzman, he didn't want to hurt anyone. (Later, as a reporter for the *Herald-Tribune*, he would keep Lou Gehrig's ALS diagnosis to himself.)

Maybe, too, they didn't want anyone to know how much fun they were having. So the best stories went untold.

Like the night Vidmer found ten message slips from the Babe under his hotel room door telling him to come on up for a nightcap—or twelve. Vidmer pointed out he was still hungover from the previous evening. "Well, goddammit, last night we killed a bottle of scotch between us and I had two home runs today," Ruth replied.

Or the time Ruth asked an elderly woman on the porch of a Hot Springs Hotel whether beer made her urine sudsy. "God, you gotta watch your talk, Babe," admonished one of the reporters within earshot. To which Ruth replied: "Oh, for Christ sake. I used the word 'urinate' didn't I?"

The time he was chased stark naked through a train car by a woman, equally naked and armed with a knife, who was said to be the wife of a state legislator. In legend, Babe had told her she was the only one.

The time a good-looking woman with a baby under her arm ventured close enough to the Yankee train for the Babe to give her a once-over. "Better get away from here, lady, or I'll put one in the other arm."

The time he arrived in St. Louis and instructed the cabdriver to take him to the House of the Good Shepherd, a favorite destination in the red-light district, and the request was bellowed from the taxi line up and down the sidewalk for all to hear.

The time in St. Petersburg, Florida, he disappeared into the woods with a voluptuous redhead, a member of a chorus line performing for the city's dignitaries and their wives. Emerging hand in hand some twenty minutes later, Ruth and friend took their places among the invited guests. "Some were giggling inside," Hunt told Kal Wagenheim. "Some were so shocked they couldn't talk."

Occasionally, during late-night spring training fishing trips arranged by Hunt, Ruth would remember to ask, "You're not writing this, are you?"

To which Hunt would reply: "Good God, when are you gonna learn? Off hours, Babe, off hours."

Everything was off the record—unless Ruth went overboard. Sure enough, one night he did. Hunt wrote that story and sent a copy to general manager Ed Barrow, who was on the phone at 9:00 the next morning, screaming.

"Let's get this straight," Hunt told him. "He's fishing on his own. I'm fishing. We just happen to be together in a boat."

"Did you invite him?"

"I invited him, yes. But I'm not responsible for him falling in."

"Well for God's sake, knock it off for a while, will you?" Barrow said. "We're not over spring training and we gotta get that Big Baboon back to New York in one piece."

The era of protection came crashing to an end on August 31, 1925, when Patterson lifted the de facto embargo on reporting about Ruth's mistress, Claire Hodgson, and splashed her heavily painted kisser on the front page of New York's biggest-circulation newspaper.

The photo was sent to the *Chicago Tribune* and the *Los Angeles Times* via Telepix. Overnight, Claire's slim, elegant silhouette—with a swath of alabaster décolletage visible at the collarbone and pert lips pursed in a slight pout—was everywhere. You could almost smell the Bellagio perfume that she preferred—and that Babe sometimes used in lieu of cologne—leaping from the page.

Hers was the face that launched a thousand headlines. The ménage à Ruth took New York City's fifteen dailies and approximately 3,625,922 readers hostage for a week. "Slightly more than 82,000 words written over four days" or "four times the amount in 'Much Ado About Nothing,'" the *New Yorker* reported in its September 19 issue.

The magazine's fact-checkers credited the *Evening Journal* with 10,350 words, closely followed by the *Telegram* and the *Times* with 9,000 words each, not including, according to Paul Gallico's jovial estimate, 396,578,298,400 editorials.

And that was just in New York.

By linking Huggins's condemnation of Ruth's "off-the-field misconduct" to his previously unreported relationship with Claire, a baseball story about a .266 hitter quickly became something much bigger and much more modern: "Fandom Tip Links Babe's New Woes with Family Rift."

The first shot across the bow was a blind item in the *News* on August 30 in which "the Babe was asked about a fair fan, whom fans in the neighborhood of St.

Petersburg, Fla., last winter noticed as being one of his most fervent admirers. He flushed brick red and seemed highly embarrassed."

He was also asked "about a reported quarrel at a Boston hotel, when Mrs. Ruth packed her trunks and told the wife of another player she was 'through.'"

The next day Patterson upped the ante, naming Claire as "the fair fan" and planting her picture on page 1. Julia remembered returning from an outing with her mother and the camera flash in the vestibule of their apartment at 315 West Seventy-ninth Street. "They had it in the *Daily News* the next day. I can't remember how they put it: 'Babe's new girlfriend' or something."

Claire was something, all right, alternately and alliteratively described as an "ardent admirer," a "fervent admirer," a "pretty admirer," a "fair friend and admirer," a "party hostess," "the merry widow," "the rich widow," "the lady in the case," and "the party of the second part."

Ruth made the front page in Chicago when he impulsively cashed in the train ticket the Yankees had purchased for New York and headed north instead to plead his case with Commissioner Landis, who was out of town and unlikely to have provided a sympathetic ear.

The *Tribune*'s headline was far more daring and damning than any in the New York papers: "BABE RUTH, MAD, DENIES ORGIES."

Ruth admitted to having stayed out all night—with "friends"—in Cleveland, Chicago, and St. Louis, but only once in each city. Perhaps he didn't realize the Yankees had their private eye on his tail. He parried the allegations and issued ultimatums, turning his ire on his manager—"It's him or me!" Huggins was incompetent and worse, a .210 hitter.

In fact, Huggins hit .265 during thirteen years in the National League and once led the league in on-base percentage. He was "a scrawny little man, touched by baseball genius," Frank Graham wrote. No matter. Ruth swore he would never play for him again.

"Let Ruth quit," Huggins, Barrow, and Ruppert replied in resounding unison.

"Ruth, bah!" said a teammate in St. Louis.

In Chicago, Ruth had plenty to say: "He has been laying for a chance to get me and I gave it to him by staying out until 3:30 A.M. on Saturday in St. Louis," Ruth told the *Tribune*. "As for the drinking charge, he's a liar."

By way of explanation Ruth pointed out: "Anyway, it was too hot to sleep in St. Louis."

"Why that fine is a joke," he continued. "They don't

give bootleggers $5,000 and men get out of murder charges for less. I haven't killed anybody.

"They think I haven't been hitting 'em because I have been dissipating. I know why I have fallen off. For one thing, I tried to play before I was fully recovered from my recent illness. I was out so long that I needed a regular training trip to put me in trim. A man can't jump from a hospital cot and into a baseball uniform and hit .350."

The *Tribune* also offered the first plausible explanation for Helen Ruth's nervous breakdown in April. "Mrs. Hodgson in her solicitude for Ruth's health is said to have called on Babe at the hospital during the latter's recent illness. Mrs. Ruth also was a patient in the hospital at the same time."

The dam broke, propriety drowned in a flood of innuendo and pent-up reportage. Hearst's *Daily Mirror* brazenly trumpeted new details of the "mystery diagnosis" that landed Ruth in St. Vincent's Hospital in April: "The secret could not be kept, however, from Mrs. Ruth, who is reported to have in the shape of doctors' reports material for successful prosecution of a divorce action."

Helen, who had been regularly briefing reporters by telephone between Broadway shows and denying reports that she intended to sue for separate maintenance, took to her bed at the Concourse Plaza Hotel overlooking Yankee Stadium. She was said to be suffering from another, albeit partial, nervous breakdown and an infection of the ring finger on her left hand, injured when she tried to remove her wedding and engagement rings.

"These pictures have put Mrs. Ruth on her sickbed," her husband fumed, as he boarded the 20th Century Limited and headed home to face the little woman.

Paper by paper, edition by edition, detail by detail, the story ballooned. The elevator man in Claire's building cataloged his frequent visits. The druggist at the Concourse Plaza testified to Ruth's preference for a denatured alcohol easily distilled into gin. The president of the American League divulged Ruth's failure to respond to a July summons to account for his behavior, saying, "Guess he was too busy writing syndicate articles."

Little birdies keeping the *News* in the know reported Claire's presence in a front-row box at the Stadium, "from which she has observed nearly every game this season."

The *New York Journal* added more juicy details: "Huggins knew of her and told him to spend less time in social pursuits. He had visited her apartment before the western trip, and she had been in Hot Springs at the same resort last spring."

The hoopla and hysteria were punctuated with occasional pleas for perspective. From Frank Wallace in the *New York Evening Post*: "His is a big soul made bigger by our applause. And a big soul needs room to roam. Smaller souls might well close their eyes at times like these and let these big souls roam; else they stifle and die and lose the thing that makes them big."

From Heywood Broun in the *New York World*: "The present moral indignation about his conduct is the phase of the controversy I can't abide. . . . It isn't the long hours but the short hits to which they object."

From Christy Walsh, nothing. He was neither seen nor heard. His only apparent role was to assemble a voluminous clip file documenting the humbling of the Babe, each story meticulously delineated by thick, red crayon.

Ruth arrived at Grand Central Terminal at 10:40 A.M. on September 1 and was met on the platform by two porters—who carried his portable phonograph and suitcase filled with nine pairs of white flannel trousers—and a Catholic priest, Father Edward J. Quinn, newly ordained and serving at the Augustinian Academy on Staten Island.

As they trudged out of the subterranean darkness into the starry vaulted light of the terminal's main concourse, thousands of New Yorkers "cheered till the very girders rang with the echo," the *Evening Journal* reported.

The beleaguered Babe straightened his worsted shoulders and smiled.

Part pastor, part bouncer, part spokesman, Quinn cut a swath through the throng. His most urgent task was to get Ruth to shut his mouth. "The way this thing has been handled is very much to be regretted," he told the *New York Telegram*. "All the good things which Ruth has done have not been mentioned. All the trash that could be dug up has been thrown into his face by some of the newspapers. All that Ruth did for St. Mary's and Catholic Church charities and for orphans never will be known to the public. But I know it and I am here to defend him."

With that Quinn joined the upright cadre of men who seemed to appear whenever Ruth was most in need of uprightness. Unlike Jack Dunn—who had "almost been a mother to me," Ruth had said in June—and Brother Matthias and Christy Walsh, each of whom had some legal or institutional history with the Babe, Quinn materialized out of nowhere. He was identified the next morning as "a friend from St. Mary's," "a

friend of the couple," and "a lifelong friend and counselor of the player," whose task in New York, Fred Lieb
wrote in the *New York Telegram*, was to "bring Ruth
to his senses."

Quinn's family in Jessup, Pennsylvania, told the
Scranton Times he was Ruth's "spiritual advisor" and
an old family friend.

Almost immediately came a dispatch from Baltimore: "Ruth's Action Depresses St. Mary's School
Boys," and the announcement that Brother Paul was en
route to New York to impress upon the Babe the effect
of his conduct on the boys when they heard their hero
had fallen from grace.

Quinn was only five years Ruth's senior—far too
young to have served at St. Mary's during Ruth's tenure. Quinn was an intellectual, not an incorrigible, with
a BA from Villanova College and an MA from Catholic University. As a boy growing up in baseball-mad
Lackawanna County, he was a delegate to the Catholic
Total Abstinence Union Baseball League Convention,
along with Mike McNally from neighboring Minooka.
Later, Minooka Mike—Ruth's teammate with the Red
Sox and then the Yankees—introduced the Babe to the
pleasures of Lackawanna Valley, including its many
bars and ballplayers. Perhaps he also introduced him
to Quinn.

Outside Grand Central, on Vanderbilt Avenue, Quinn ushered the penitent into a pink-striped taxi-cab, which was held up in traffic by a thicket of camera shutters and reporters occupying "a large procession of machines, as in a politician's entourage," the *American* said.

"Come up to the hotel later, boys," Ruth called out. "Maybe I'll have something to say then."

The convoy lit out for friendly territory—Helen Ruth's five-room suite at the Concourse Plaza. It was a swanky joint, completed in 1923 after Ruth made the Bronx swank enough to matter. The lobby was thick with more reporters and one process server—Ruth's chauffeur had been in an accident earlier that week. "He shoved his way through the scribes, sent the process server flying over a nearby desk and stamped to his rooms alone, like an injured child," teammate Waite Hoyt said later.

Reporters trailed him all the way to the bedroom door and watched as he sat himself down on the side of his wife's bed. "Oh, Babe! How glad I am to see you," she said, throwing her arms around him, unmindful of her injured finger and the newspapermen who filled the open doorway. Ruth blubbered and "made a strange noise like a little boy who has been forgiven," the *American* reported.

The priest closed the door, sequestering himself with the couple. None of the reporters could have missed the symbolism: the Babe following the Church in the person of Father Quinn, returning to his spiritual and marital home. Turned out he was more than a pastoral adviser—he was a marriage counselor, too, as Lieb reported, having "recently patched up the marital differences between the Babe and his wife and brought about a reconciliation" no one previously acknowledged was necessary.

Lieb also reported that Father Quinn had been in close touch with the Yankees, acting as a liaison between the front office and its wayward son.

After a tactful pause, the gentlemen of the press asked to have a word with Mrs. Ruth and a photo. Behind closed doors, the penitent husband could be heard making the request in "a loud contralto voice," the *New York Evening Post* reported.

Tearfully, she relented. "The little woman was fetching despite her indisposition," the *Post* continued. "Her auburn hair lay loose on her pillow. Her face was pale but pretty. Her third finger on her left hand was bandaged. It had been infected, she explained.

"One newspaperman professed to see something symbolic in this. He was jubilant when Mrs. Ruth confirmed his suspicions by saying that her wedding and engagement rings had had to be filed off the swollen number but that she had had them repaired and would put them back on as soon as the swelling subsides."

A series of photos documented the "tender" reconciliation: Babe, head in hands, weeping; Helen, hands raised, railing and pleading, "Why do you bring all this trouble upon those who care the most? Think about Dot."

The photographers suggested something more intimate. Ever compliant, Ruth buried his head in her bosom. Their tears mingled on her crisp white sheets. "The Babe sobbed aloud and comforted the missus with affectionate pats," the *Washington Post* reported. "The scene was so obviously sincere and so moving that reporters and photographers in Mrs. Ruth's room, completely forgotten for the moment by the Babe and his wife, backed into corners or silently from the room, overcome with embarrassment."

As promised, Ruth had something to say, a revelation of sorts to share with the press. "'My wife's the only gal,' he declared in the *American*. 'I never knew she was so sensitive before when other women were mentioned.'"

No one asked about the white gauze bandage wrapped around her left wrist. But the interview had to be cut short when Helen complained of feeling faint and collapsed.

Also, Ruth had an appointment at Jacob Ruppert's brewery at Ninety-second Street and Third Avenue in Yorkville, where he was expected to perform further acts of contrition.

That was all staged, according to granddaughter Linda Ruth Tosetti.

Before heading downtown, Ruth mugged for Fox Movietone cameramen on the windy roof deck of the hotel, grinning and brushing his hair from his brow with the vast emptiness of Yankee Stadium looming over his shoulder.

Meanwhile, across town on the Upper West Side, "the party of the second part" went into seclusion. Heavily veiled, Claire Hodgson quit her apartment in a limousine, with its shades drawn, for a month in the Bahamas.

The furor did not disappear with her.

On September 2, the *Evening Graphic* published a first-person tell-all in which the Babe humbly confessed the American public's love for him. The *New York American* identified two particular devotees: Bee Palmer, the "Shimmy Queen," and Miss Rose Davis of Maxine Elliott's Theatre. And the *Washington Post* reported: "It was definitely learned today that [Mrs. Ruth] commissioned a New Rochelle attorney with offices in New York to prepare papers to be served on Ruth in a separate maintenance action."

What the press did not know—or did not report—was that a separation agreement had already been signed on August 4, 1925, in Richmond County, otherwise known as Staten Island, a favorite jurisdiction for celebrities wishing to keep legal proceedings on the q.t. Walter Winchell, the gossip columnist who preferred not to be the subject of gossip columns, filed for divorce in Staten Island.

The agreement called for Helen to receive four annual payments, beginning in October 1925, of $20,000, $30,000, $25,000 and $20,000. In addition, she was to receive $100 a week until the first payment was made; she would also receive their property in Pasadena, Florida, and the farm in Sudbury; a Packard; and Dorothy.

The agreement was witnessed by E. J. Quinn, the same E. J. Quinn identified in press accounts as having effectuated a reconciliation. Presumably this was not one of his customary priestly functions.

Quinn himself was something of an enigma. A solemn young man with preponderant eyebrows, a high forehead, and owlish black spectacles, who smoked cigars and burned holes in his habit with the ashes, he liked the ponies and he liked his drink. He gave the benediction at the New York State Democratic Party convention in 1932 and returned to Villanova as procurator in the 1950s. "He was kind of a wild man, very like Babe Ruth," recalled Father George Riley, who served with Quinn later in his priestly career.

According to family members and other members of the order who served with him, Quinn, who died in 1967, never acknowledged his relationship with Ruth; nor have any of Ruth's closest surviving relatives heard of him. Whether this was a belated nod to clerical privilege or a function of estrangement or perhaps embarrassment is impossible to say. But he was a trusted figure at a critical juncture in Ruth's life and posed a significant challenge to Walsh's eminent domain.

Babe Ruth repented. He broke all records repenting, Bill McGeehan wrote. And then he apologized. He apologized to Ruppert, to Barrow, to Huggins. And then he apologized again. Runyon called it an apology for hitting .260.

He went straight to the Stadium after making his amends at Ruppert's brewery and was cheered by everyone except his manager, who refused to see him and refused to reinstate him, allowing the story to percolate for another five days while Ruth was buffeted by the ill winds of unaccustomed public animus. The leisurely exercise of managerial justice was made possible only by the Yankees' dismal record, for which Ruth bore a goodly portion of the blame.

Prohibited from joining his teammates for batting practice, he took his bows from a grandstand box with Ruppert and Quinn close by. He offered to pitch every fifth day upon his return in addition to playing the outfield. Huggins was unmoved. After the game, Ruth drove the priest back to Staten Island, which remained his religious posting until 1932.

Huggins finally relented on September 5 after announcing he was paroling Ruth to the custody of his wife. The anointed "night watchman" fled to Sudbury as soon as practicable.

Ruth returned from exile on September 7, the same day he learned that his English bull terrier, Dot, had run wild on the farm in Sudbury and killed a neighbor's pedigreed cow, resulting in another lawsuit that would cost another five thousand dollars. He hated the place, he told reporters, hated winter farming, and was planning to sell and build something in Florida. He hit safely in nine straight games—batting .346 with 10 home runs and 30 RBI in the last three weeks of the season.

Joe Patterson's decision to treat Babe Ruth like news prompted a public display of soul-searching, chest beating, and chutzpah in New York City sports pages. He had made patsies out of every Yankee writer who had hidden what he knew out of custom and habit, which is to say everyone. He had exposed a raw nerve that ran through the coverage of every "gee whiz" columnist who had elevated Ruth to saintliness. While Ruth dangled in sackcloth, the biggest names in New York sportswriting publicly wrestled with—and debated—their role. Were they cheerleaders or journalists?

"How Great Is the Responsibility of Baseball Writers, If Any, in Player's Plight?" asked Dan Daniel in his column in the *New York Telegram*.

Plenty, replied Broun, in the *World.* "Babe Ruth never went about and requested baseball writers to doll him up as an ideal for growing boys. The reporters did that on their own responsibility. Now that the crash has come they ought to take the consequences and not try and shoulder the burden off on the shoulders of Ruth."

Embarrassed and defensive, Daniel called out those among the sweaty literati who accepted filthy lucre from ghostwriting syndicates as if they were the only culprits: "It is not true that baseball writers have held up Ruth as an ideal for growing boys. Can anybody produce a story written by anybody not connected with the Ruth syndicate in which the Babe is pictured as a mental and moral ideal?"

In his indignation, Daniel neglected to mention his own past efforts at ghostwriting. In fact, "the unholy union," as *Detroit News* managing editor Malcolm Bingay called it, was so pervasive that by the time Walsh closed up shop in 1937, he estimated that he had paid thirty-seven ghosts $100,000 for copy that filled 5,641 solid pages of newspaper type (worth $3 million in free advertising for the big leagues at prevailing advertising rates, by his calculations).

Editors like Shirley Povich of the *Washington Post*, who couldn't afford to buy Walsh's airy impersonations, resorted to cheeky headlines to try to sell readers on actual journalism. "Charles Lindbergh, Vice President Charles G. Dawes, Aimee Semple McPherson, and Others Will Not Cover the World Series for the *Post*," he wrote in advance of the 1924 World Series between the Senators and the Giants. "The Baseball Classic Will Be Covered by Baseball Writers. Reach for a *Post* instead of a Ghost."

Ruth, who "covered" fifteen consecutive World Series for the Christy Walsh Syndicate—and once threw a newspaper out of a hotel window after seeing the poor play his column had received, according to a syndicate dispatch—wasn't in his assigned seat at Griffith Stadium the following year when the series between the Pittsburgh Pirates and the Washington Senators shifted to the nation's capital. As Povich told it, Ruth had been sent to the hospital with acute appendicitis. His ghost was also missing in action. Walsh, who never did any writing unless a ghost was sick or drunk, sized up the situation, bellowed into a telephone, "Get me an operator," and began to dictate, Povich said. "Washington, D.C., by Babe Ruth, paragraph, quote. 'As I lie here, in Washington's Emergency Hospital . . .'"

Povich misremembered some of the particulars. Ruth was not in a Washington hospital; he did not have appendicitis. He had what the *Post* described as an infection high on his left leg, causing him to limp badly, which physicians thought might be the reoccurrence of the abscesses he suffered in the spring. They importuned him to return to New York for treatment. Dire headlines—"Ruth Quits Series"—followed him home, declaring further surgery was in the offing. Instead he treated the leg with ice packs at home and improved enough to leave five days later for a little moose hunting in Maine and New Brunswick, Canada. In the *Post*, an unnamed staff writer, who sounded a lot like Povich, bemoaned the loss of Ruth's bons mots: "162 union writers and 29 players, umpires and wives and children of players experting on the series have altruistically agreed in the emergency to put forth special efforts to fill the aching void."

Walsh possessed the Irishman's gift for blarney and the adman's knack for selling baloney as truth. In his worldview, ghostwriting was a venerable, solemn, and honorable craft, no different than speechwriting for pols or the disciples—no one believed that Matthew wrote the Gospel of Matthew, did they?

That's what he told Alva Johnston in the *New Yorker* in 1935. His defense was as ingenious as it was disingenuous. He claimed the moral high ground on the theory that Ruth's columns were authentically unauthentic. "I wouldn't insult the intelligence of the public by claiming they write their own stuff," Walsh said. An inexperienced ghost makes the mistake of trying to write the way his celebrity talks. "This is an error. He ought to write the way the public thinks his celebrity talks."

Ruth's columns, which ran in Hearst papers across the country and in the two Hearst flagship papers in New York, the *Evening Journal* and the *American*, sounded exactly like him—if you believed that "bunk" was the only four-letter word in his vocabulary. They ranged from insipid to innocuous. One early effort presented a "Glossary of Terms in Daily Use by Ball Players but Not Readily Understood by Fans," including

"Giving It the Old College Try" and "Barber—Name Applied to Person Who Talks a Great Deal," which explained the stropping motion Ruth and Gehrig employed throughout the 1927 tour when a windy guest overstayed his welcome.

But content was never really the point. The *ur-narrative* was no different than today's ghostwritten Twitter feeds or the first-person postings on Derek Jeter's "The Players' Tribune." The bylined columns Walsh peddled sold the illusion that Ruth was knowable, that he was speaking directly to the man in the stands, or the boy on the street corner waiting for the afternoon paper to arrive. Banal as they might have been, they played an indispensable part in shaping Ruth's image, while casting a roseate glow over the golden age of sports. They built a reservoir of good feeling and, ironically, trust that came in handy in moments of crisis, while adding nearly $160,000 to his bank account between 1921 and 1936.

Even in the giddy ghosting days of 1927, there were intimations the system couldn't last. Jack Dempsey's October testimony in a lawsuit against his former manager (and Walsh client), Jack Kearns—in which he contended that he couldn't be called to account for statements in his columns because he hadn't read any of them—drew the reproach of a nationally syndicated literary critic in the October issue of the *Bookman*. "The Bookman's Notes" column outed the ghosts of Dempsey, Ruth, Lindbergh, Queen Marie of Romania, Henry Ford, Paul Whiteman, Helena Rubinstein, and Aimee Semple McPherson.

Privately, Walsh railed against bookish types who looked down on the business that he had perfected. Denied membership in a club of publishing elites in 1925 despite the patronage of Hendrik Willem van Loon, Walsh vented in a reply to him that "some of the little Kikes who publish books for a living are not nearly so low in the order of social welfare as a Syndicate Man."

Ford Frick, who was one of the Syndicate Man's two highest earners—accumulating ten thousand dollars from his ghosting gig—hit a new low in September 1925, when he wrote a first-person column for the *Evening Journal* declaring that he had "no brief" for the Babe while taking the Yankees to task for having one set of rules for the Big Fella and another for everyone else. A few days later, under Ruth's byline, he crafted a mea culpa written to coincide with the Babe's reinstatement. It was a tour de force. Ruth fell on his rhetorical sword, confessing all, taking full responsibility, even accepting the manager's prerogative to ask him to bunt.

So serious was he about reform that for the first time in eight years he was going to forgo a lucrative off-season. He had turned down a fifteen-thousand-dollar offer to play in Japan three months earlier, and now, as an act of penance, he had rejected seven thousand dollars for a series of games in Canada.

With the exception of one brief December wire dispatch datelined Sudbury, Massachusetts, in which Helen denied she was seeking a divorce, no one followed up on the separation agreement; no one followed the money. The Babe cleaned up his act. He learned, as Paul Gallico wrote in *Farewell to Sport*, what "every celebrity in the United States must learn—to perform his peccadillos in strict privacy if possible. Formerly Ruth had perpetrated his right out in public."

When Ruth retired in the depths of the Depression, there were no more stories to write about inflated baseball salaries. During the war, readers wanted and needed their sports and their sportswriters to entertain and divert—the reason President Roosevelt insisted that major-league baseball, even in its diluted state, soldier on. The *Herald-Tribune*'s sports editor, Stanley Woodward, quit "the toy department" to cover the war. Upon his return, he created what most believe to have been the best sports section in newspaper history at the *Tribune*, where "godding up" ballplayers was not tolerated.

Sportswriting would not fully emerge from its journalistic coma until 1957, when Mickey Mantle and a band of marauding Yankee revelers tangled with a bowling team from Washington Heights at the Copacabana. The scoop belonged to *New York Post* gossip columnist Leonard Lyons, who was making his rounds of Manhattan nightspots when fisticuffs were exchanged. But the story would be turned over to a new generation of sportswriters known as the Chipmunks, for whom questioning authority was a generational prerogative. The sports pages would never be the same.

In the absence of further scrutiny in the fall of 1925, Walsh delved into his usual bag of tricks. On September 24, Ruth was sworn in as a lieutenant in the New York City Police Reserves. The papers were bemused. "Sultan, lieutenant, private—it's complicated," opined the *New York World*.

He was escorted to police headquarters by Lieutenant James Dunedin of the Reserves, booking agent for the Keith vaudeville circuit, which put things in perspective. At his swearing-in, he was presented with "badges, clubs and other symbols of authority," the New York *Sun* reported, including a shiny silver whistle. He was also fingerprinted before being assigned to the recreation division of the Reserves.

Meanwhile, Walsh arranged for another mea culpa, this time in *Collier's*—"Babe Ruth—I have been a Babe and a Boob," which appeared on October 31, 1925, the same day he was to make his first payment to Helen. He owned up to five hundred thousand dollars in losses through gambling, partying, lawsuits, blackmail, and general excess. "I was going to be the exception, the popular hero who could do as he pleased," Ruth declared. "But all those people were right. . . . I've got to face the fact and admit I've been the sappiest of saps."

Ruth vowed to return to the woods, to shed the wise guys and the avoirdupois. But the monetary losses were most pressing. He didn't have enough money to pay Helen. And when he found himself short of funds in March 1926 he turned to Walsh for a $4,000 loan.

Walsh was as tight with money as Ruth was profligate. He still deposited ten dollars a month in the bank account he opened when he graduated from college, which he would leave to his son, Christy Jr., in his will, with the admonition that he do the same. But he was more than happy to make this loan, which gave him the leverage he needed to assume complete control of Ruth's finances. He stated his terms in early March 1926 and minced no words. His wife was in the last months of a difficult pregnancy. His father was dying. His patience with Ruth, expressed in exasperated letters to Frank Hilton at the Bank of Manhattan, was fraying.

In his absence, Ruth had turned to others for guidance and advice, giving Father Quinn equal authority over financial matters, as he made clear in a June 3, 1926, letter to Walsh:

Dear Christy:

This will more fully explain my telegram of March 19th, at the time you advanced Four Thousand ($4,000.00) Dollars to me. I accepted that amount on the terms of your letter of March 16th, 1926, as follows:

(1) I agree that I not invest any money in real estate, or in any other manner for a period of ten years from this date, without the approval of Father E.J. Quinn and yourself.

(2) I further agree that I will not borrow on or in any way use the insurance money which is now to my credit in the Equitable Life Assurance Society, for a period of ten years from date—except with the approval of Father Quinn and yourself.

(3) In addition to this, I agree to let you retain One Half (½) of my share from the profits on

"RUTH'S HOMERUN" candy to be invested by you in securities or other high grade, conservative investments for me. Any securities you purchase must be with our joint approval and I will not sell them or transfer them or borrow money on them for a period of ten (10) years, from this date without the approval of Father E.J. Quinn and yourself.

In a copy of the letter found in Walsh's files after his death, Quinn's name was struck from each paragraph. Ruth and Walsh initialed their consent to the change. With that okay, Walsh assumed unilateral control over Ruth's financial life.

Eight months later, Ruth opened the irrevocable trust account at the Bank of Manhattan with the $33,000 check that Walsh tricked him into signing, which brought forth a spate of good press praising Ruth's financial probity and self-restraint.

But Walsh knew that Ruth could no longer count on the gentle treatment to which he had become accustomed. Patterson had put him on notice: he had to behave, or at least learn how to fake it. Skepticism now informed assumptions about his future as a ballplayer too. By the end of the 1925 season, many writers thought—and wrote—that Ruth was on the "down grade," as McGeehan put it, and "possibly through."

In lowering expectations, they inadvertently set the stage for a miraculous reincarnation.

Ever resourceful, Walsh cast Ruth as a nouveau Bernarr Macfadden, selling newspapers on a complete package of dietary and illustrated exercises from the Babe. (He recommended a lot of soft-boiled eggs in the morning and hot fruit juice with dinner.) Then he got Knute Rockne to endorse a mail-order exercise regimen—"Babe Ruth's Complete Course"—which came with an autographed bat to use with stretching exercises. "You know how easy it is for a fellow to get out of shape," the Babe declared in the advertising copy that appeared in *Collier's*. "I do. Believe me, men, I know. My batting average dropped, too—just because I let myself go to pot, physically. But I came back. You can, too!"

V

The day the Bams played in Denver, chapter 1 in the syndicated thirty-part life story of twenty-five-year-old Henry Louis Gehrig appeared in the *San Francisco Examiner*. The Yankees' chiseled first baseman revealed that he had been called "fatty" in his youth and that boys in his Upper Manhattan neighborhood "threw the ball wide to me just to get a good laugh when I started to waddle after it."

The game at Merchants Park had to be called in the ninth inning due to a predictable lack of good-quality baseballs—three of which had exited the park thanks to the Babe—and an overnight train departing at 6:30 P.M. that would take them through the Rockies to Ogden, Utah, ten miles east of the Great Salt Lake.

Al Warden, sports editor of the *Ogden Standard-Examiner*, who did a lot of business with the Christy Walsh Syndicate, met them at Union Station, a railroad hub where they were to transfer to the Southern Pacific Railroad for the second leg of the trip to Northern California. Warden had dug up a couple of local VIPs and a movie star no one had ever heard of and whisked them away for a half-hour tour of the six-mile-long Ogden Canyon. Ruth pronounced it marvelous. Gehrig was disappointed by the absence of cowboys and Indians.

They received an invitation to return in November for a hunting expedition, an offer Ruth said they would consider as plans for additional "picture work" in Hollywood had been canceled. The option that Walsh had negotiated with First National Pictures for a second feature film would never be picked up.

Instead, they went to Chicago for the big game between the Fighting Irish and the Trojans of USC on November 26. Walsh dragooned them into appearing in full football regalia at the pregame banquet he hosted at the Palmer House, where Ruth, in Notre Dame pants that refused to tie around his middle, addressed Knute Rockne, Tad Jones, Pop Warner, and the crème de la crème of American football writers, assembled fans, and boosters.

"It's a pleasure and inspiration," he boomed into a microphone, "to have a fellow like Gehrig as a runner-up in the home-run race. Lou's a great first baseman. And he protects his father and mother."

Encouraged by a vociferous round of applause, Ruth plunged ahead, praising Gehrig's pleasant smile and his qualities as a son and a roommate while Gehrig looked on sheepishly in his USC uniform. "He doesn't snore, and he could sleep on a meat hook. And—he protects his mother and father."

Someone pulled on the sleeve of his jersey and whispered, "You said that once."

"Lay off," he barked, and the microphone caught it. "I'm making this speech."

Nobody read that story in the morning paper.

Chapter 12
October 21–22 / Bay Area

**RUTH, GEHRIG ON KGO TONIGHT
WITH SANTORO**
POST-ENQUIRER ARRANGES FOR RADIO INTERVIEWS
OF GREAT HOME-RUN HITTERS
—*OAKLAND POST-ENQUIRER*

SOCKOLOGY MADE EASY
—*SAN FRANCISCO CALL*

I

On Friday morning, October 21—some twenty-four hours after crossing the Continental Divide—Ruth, Gehrig, and Walsh made a brief stop in Sacramento, California, birthplace of the transcontinental railroad, en route to the Bay Area. Abe Kemp of the *San Francisco Examiner* boarded the train, found them filling up a compartment in car number 19, and sat down for a chat on the art and science of hitting home runs.

"I couldn't explain the secret of it to you if I wanted to," said Ruth.

"Gosh," blushed Gehrig, "if the judge (that is what Lou calls his pal) can't tell you, I certainly can't."

"A lot of it is in the eye," said Ruth.

"And the swing," offered Gehrig.

"You must have good eyes, then," we said.

"Sure," admitted Ruth, "but a lot of times, I never see the ball. That's right: look at me funny, but I tell you, lots of times when I sense the ball is coming in a certain place, I just close my eyes and swing."

"How did you feel when you made that sixtieth home run?" we ventured.

"You don't think I burst into tears, did you?"

Into the breach stepped Gehrig. "The judge was sure tickled, but I'll bet there wasn't a happier man in the ball park than I was."

"I don't know what is responsible for a streak of home runs," Ruth said. "But I know this, a man can't worry and hit home runs."

J. E. Doyle of the *Oakland Post-Enquirer* boarded the train in Benicia and joined the conversation. While Gehrig took a turn driving the locomotive and tooting its whistle, Ruth continued the colloquy. "Do you think you will break your record next year?" Kemp asked.

"I'm going to try hard to," Ruth replied. "That is only natural, but let's talk about something else."

Nobody wanted to talk about anything else. Not when Frank "Lefty" O'Doul, Ruth's former teammate, met their train at the pier in Oakland. Not when Mayor "Sunny" Jim Rolph and his chief of police met them at the Ferry Building in San Francisco. Not when they arrived at the Hotel Whitcomb, which briefly served as City Hall after the 1906 earthquake, with its gilded lobby filled with rare Janesero wood paneling, marble columns, inlaid ceilings, Austrian crystal chandeliers, a cornucopia of Tiffany glass, and well-heeled admirers.

Not on Saturday morning when they distributed one thousand autographed baseballs and handkerchiefs to boys and girls gathered at the Knights of Columbus Hall. Not when they played the first of three games in the Bay Area at Recreation Park that afternoon. Not when they ascended to the Whitcomb's Roof Garden for a Saturday-night dinner dance advertised in the morning *Chronicle*: it cost $1.50 to get on their dance card. Babe was a mighty fine hoofer if he did say so himself, which he did, telling a reporter from Los Angeles that he had worked as a ballroom professional.

And surely not during a forty-five-minute radio interview with KGO broadcaster Al Santoro, sports editor of the *Oakland Post-Enquirer*, which Walsh had shoehorned into the brief respite between the 2:45 P.M. game and the dinner dance.

"Their appearance marks another scoop for the *Post-Enquirer*," the paper bragged in its Saturday edition. "Thanks to arrangements made by this paper thousands have heard the voices of many celebrities including Harold 'Red' Grange, Jack Dempsey, James J. Corbett, Gertrude Ederle, Helen Wills, and others.

"Ruth and Gehrig will stand before the KGO microphones tonight at 6:30 P.M. Their athletic prowess astounded the nation. Add to that their personality, their clean living and their excellent speaking voices and you have everything you need to make a radio attraction. Santoro will do his regular show at 7:15 P.M."

(The *Examiner* also boasted an interview with the Bustin' Twins at 7:00 P.M. on its station KYA from the

Clift Hotel. "The Babe is getting to be quite a radio talker," Abe Kemp wrote in advance of the show, but the paper didn't advertise the show or offer details from the interview.)

KGO broadcast out of a state-of-the-art facility in Oakland. It was one of seven affiliates linked by 1,709 miles of AT&T cable six months earlier, when NBC created the Orange Network to serve the Pacific Coast, and was one of three GE stations designed to cover the entire country.

Because of the dinner dance, the interview was instead conducted in a converted second-floor hotel room at the Whitcomb, the former studio of KFRC, the official station of the *San Francisco Bulletin*, which broadcast from the hotel until 1925, using an L-shaped transmitter on the roof suspended between two hundred-foot ship's masts.

A photograph memorialized the occasion: Ruth and Gehrig in dinner attire, holding either end of a Louisville slugger, and talking into a microphone perched atop a carved wooden lamp stand, an accommodation devised in the early days of radio to mitigate "mike fright."

Ruth knew all about that. He was one of Harold Arlin's first celebrity interviews on Pittsburgh radio station KDKA, which also broadcast the first national election returns and the first major-league baseball game, with Arlin at the mike (a converted telephone receiver), on August 5, 1921. A month earlier, when the Yankees were in town for an exhibition game against the Pirates, Arlin had provided Ruth with a prepared script for what was almost certainly his first radio interview. But Ruth went mute when the microphone went live. Arlin grabbed the script and read, "This is Babe Ruth," while Ruth leaned against a wall smoking a cigar. For days afterward, Ruth received kudos on his smooth delivery.

Ruth fared better six months later when he went on WWJ in Detroit, the first commercial station in the nation, to promote his vaudeville show: "Just let me say that it's a great pleasure to talk with you through the ether. . . . And by the way—I'm singing this week at the Temple. Come and hear me. There are always plenty of doctors on hand."

He would never acquire the practiced, honeyed delivery that Christy Walsh mastered for the college football interview shows he hosted and as a narrator of sports films, but his voice was surprising nonetheless. Stilted as it could be, Ruth's voice was deeper and more polished than the guttersnipe listeners expected, and carried unexpected authority and authenticity. The mistakes made him real.

What made Santoro's interview unusual was the fact that it was unscripted and "a three-cornered air talk." His paper was part of the Hearst chain and carried Ruth's columns. Walsh had brought Ruth to the newsroom during his 1924 visit to the coast for one of his "editor-for-a-day" gigs; the paper recycled three-year-old photographs in advance of the 1927 interview, showing Ruth poring over copy with the dapper, mustachioed sports editor with a radio voice. He had been to Santoro's home for one of his famous Sunday spaghetti dinners where the guests included athletes, sportswriters, and bums off the street.

Like everyone else, Santoro wanted to talk to the Babe about home runs. He elicited what passed for headline news: "Ruth Challenges World to Break His Record, Ruth Believes His Mark of 60 Homers Will Always Stand"—a prophecy that remained fact until Roger Maris hit 61 homers in 162 games in 1961.

"When I get up to the plate I just swing, that's all," Ruth told Santoro. "If it goes out of the lot, hooray. I've added another home run to my string. I don't take much stock in this place-hit talk."

Ruth also credited Gehrig, batting fourth in the lineup behind him, with providing the protection and the impetus for his late-season power surge.

Gehrig deflected the praise and demurred when

asked if he expected to equal the 47 home runs he hit in 1927. "I will be in there offering at the good ones (maybe some bad ones)," he said, "but I can't promise I'll get as many as I did this year or even come close."

Santoro devoted the lead of his Monday column to his big interview, which no one else in town reported, and ran an unsigned news story on his section page beside a photo of the happy trio, with an effusively self-congratulatory caption claiming they "aired everything but a baseball scandal. No umpire ever got the talking to that 'Iron Mike' got Saturday night."

Santoro wrote: "Mr. B. Ruth and Mr. L. Gehrig, King and Prince of Swat, respectively, do an Alphonse and Gaston. Each credits the other for what he is today—Ruth home-run record holder, Gehrig most valuable man to his team in the American league. Gehrig praises Mr. Ruth for personal instruction in the art of lifting the ball out of the lot, and Ruth says that his protégé's consistency with the willow put him in such fear of his title that it spurred him on to a new home-run record, 60 for a season.

"It may be modesty when Ruth says he doesn't believe it likely that he will duplicate his feat of 1927, but it sounds considerably like a challenge to the Gehrigs and others, who may wrench their backs with a good old college try. Ruth believes his mark of 60 will stand."

Sadly, that's all that remains of the landmark interview.

II

The third installment in the thirty-part life story of Lou Gehrig, titled "FOLLOWING THE BABE," appeared in the *San Francisco Examiner* the day he and Ruth arrived in town. The chapter recounted his first visit to Yankee Stadium when he was still Columbia Lou and his first close-up look at the Babe.

> When I saw the way he swung, watched the perfect rhythm and timing, and saw how he managed to get his full weight back of the blow without hitching or losing any of his smoothness, I made up my mind that there was the one man to pattern after. I learned a lot from Babe Ruth in that one day. And I'm still learning. Talk all you please about Cobb and Speaker and the rest of the great hitters. The Babe is in a class by himself.
>
> When I reported for practice the next day I changed my whole batting style with [Columbia coach Andy] Coakley helping me. Before that I had been a "choke" hitter, as they call a fellow who holds the bat up toward the middle. Now I started

gripping my bat at the end and taking a full arm cut. "You've got great shoulders and great driving power," Coakley used to tell me. "If you can learn to take a full swing you ought to be able to hit for plenty of extra bases."

That sounded like Gehrig as far as anyone knew, given how infrequently players, especially shy Lou, were quoted. But Ed Neil of the AP had gotten him talking that afternoon in Asbury Park. Among other things, what made the interview so compelling was the unaccustomed authenticity of his unimproved speech.

"The Babe is a freak," Gehrig told him. "He's the greatest player, the greatest hitter, in the history of the game, but he's a freak just the same. Look at the way he swings, legs, body, arms, shoulders, even his ears go with the bat. No one else can do that."

Like Gehrig, Ruth divided the world into "choke" hitters and "swing" hitters. Ty Cobb, who would get his four thousandth hit on July 18 that season, was the best of the former; Ruth was the prototype of the latter. "The choke hitter was all right," Ruth would say later, damning him with faint praise. "But he couldn't give you much of a thrill."

Having created that expectation, he understood it was his job to fulfill it. During the 1946 World Series, the St. Louis Cardinals employed a then radical defensive shift to foil Ted Williams, packing the right side of the infield and leaving the left virtually unprotected. "They did that to me in the American League one year," Ruth told Frank Graham. "I coulda hit .600 that year slicing singles to left."

"Why didn't you?" Graham asked.

"That wasn't what the fans came out to see."

Home runs were a fact of life before Babe Ruth. But they were infrequent, rarely decisive, often inside-the-park or short fence jobs, not totemic occasions. The high-water mark in nineteenth-century baseball was in 1894 when twelve teams conspired to hit 629 home runs. Over the next twenty-five years, home-run totals waxed and waned as Ty Cobb's brand of "smart" baseball asserted itself.

No one hit more than 12 home runs in 1916, 1917, or 1918, when the major-league total was 235, the lowest in thirty-six years. That season, the year before Ruth's first offensive detonation, the major-league average was 14.7 home runs per team, or one every 9.5 games, .116 per game. Only .2 percent of the United States population witnessed one of those 235 events—11 of which were contributed by Babe Ruth, who also surrendered one as a starting pitcher for the Red Sox. According to economics professor Michael Haupert, a person was more likely to know one of the 177 American survivors of the sinking of the *Titanic* than to see a home run hit in 1918.

Thanks to the Babe, by 1927, the number (922) and frequency (.373 per game) of home runs had tripled and the experience of power had become if not commonplace then at least a reasonable expectation for the 5.2 percent of the U.S. population that saw a home run hit that year and for countless others who experienced the reverberations over the radio. That's 36.3 times as many witnesses as in 1918.

Ruth's power was the consequence of reflex and eyesight, coordination and strength, but also personality. Each of his 714 career home runs was the act of a man who defied expectation and authority at every turn. He may not have set out to revolutionize baseball when he learned to hit at St. Mary's Industrial School but there was intentionality in his insistence upon playing the game his way.

Did he change the game because he could or because he wanted to? It's a question Bill James, another baseball revolutionary, has wrestled with for years. His conclusion is unequivocal.

"I would argue that defiance of authority is THE central idea of Babe Ruth's life, and the secret of his success," he said. "It was mostly a cheerful, agreeable defiance of authority, but I argue that if you pick ANY story about Babe Ruth—any of the thousands of Babe Ruth stories—and look at it, what it really is, is Babe Ruth's way of saying that 'the rules don't apply to Babe Ruth.' Dangling a manager off the back of a moving train, whether it actually happened or not, is Babe Ruth saying that the rules don't apply to Babe Ruth.

"And his success as a player absolutely came directly from that. The belief of the time was that hitting long fly balls was a sucker's game, because for every long fly ball that made the fences, there would be twenty that were outs. You tell Babe Ruth he can't do something; he's going to show you that he can. Some people have suggested that he was 'allowed' to do this only because he was a pitcher. He wasn't 'allowed' to do anything; you just could not tell him what to do. He was determined to become an outfielder because people told him that he couldn't. That was who he was; giving him rules or instructions or directions just made him angry."

In Ruth's day, the language of baseball was simple. He liked to say he felt "hitterish." Or better yet, "homerish"—his word of choice while waiting impatiently for Charles Lindbergh to arrive at the Stadium on June 16, 1927. "My left ear itches," Ruth said. "That's a sure sign."

The umpire delayed the first pitch as long as he could, twenty-five minutes, which was not nearly long enough for Ruth, who hit his twenty-second homer with a poor swing off poor Tom Zachary in the bottom of the first inning. "I held off as long as I could but it had to come," Ruth told reporters later. "When you get one of those things in your system it's bound to come out."

Biomechanics and kinetics, weight transfers and loading mechanisms, would not enter baseball's vocabulary for decades. Nobody analyzed what the Babe did, they just marveled at it. And what he did was so novel and the way he did it was so biomechanically efficient that few contemporary observers had the ability to describe it.

To wit: Otto Floto in the *Denver Post*. "He has mastered the knack of making his bat meet the ball at the psychological moment."

Shirley Povich at the *Washington Post* was an exception, providing elegant eyewitness testimony to the chaos Ruth wrought on the national pastime. "Every pitcher who faced him would have the memory of Babe Ruth stationing himself in the batter's box, standing a bit behind home plate, his feet close together, toes turned in somewhat," Povich wrote in 1995. "The bat on his shoulder was twitching a bit as if eagerly awaiting the pitch that Babe liked. The picture he presented was that of a menace looking down the pitcher's throat."

His hands bunched together at the end of the bat looked big enough to strangle it. But he kept the little finger of his bottom hand on the knob, not because his hands were big, but to facilitate the follow-through on his swing—it was a pinkie guidance system.

"When he did uncoil that swing it was easy to see where the power came from," Povich continued. "In addition to the hands and wrists that brought the bat flying off his shoulder, the Babe also got the big power from an almost imperceptible lunge that brought into play his hips and derriere, all of it adding up to a gorgeous piece of timing that sent the pitch streaking."

Most striking of all, Povich told *Sports Illustrated* in 1998, "There was no violence in the stroke. He put everything into it, but he never looked like was extending himself."

Scientists began trying to explain this phenomenon in 1920, with Professor A. L. Hodges, "the Well-Known Physicist," taking the first hack in a syndicated newspaper story that appeared, among other places, in the *Richmond Times-Dispatch* under the headline: "Science Explains 'Babe' Ruth's Home Runs, Interesting

Principles of Physics and Psychology Involved in the 44 Horse-Power Swing Which Shoots the Ball Skyward at Six Miles a Minute."

Hodges concluded that over the course of a fifty-home-run season, Ruth would expend enough energy to lift a fifty-five-ton locomotive six inches off the ground.

His numbers were specious. Alan M. Nathan, the go-to guy on the physics of baseball in the modern era, deconstructed Hodges's analysis in 2011, pointing out, among other things, his failure to take into account the crucial variable of bat speed and to differentiate between the transfer of energy from the body into the bat and from the bat into the ball. The real significance of Hodges's article was the recognition that Ruth represented something entirely new, and the attempt to come to grips with it.

The following year Walsh sent Ruth to Columbia University for a battery of tests to gauge motor skills and cognitive performance and generate hype. The results, trumpeted in the October 1921 issue of *Popular Science Monthly* and on the front page of the *New York Times*, proved that he met the criteria for what sports orthopedist Stephen B. Haas has called "neuromuscular genius."

The testing was primitive, cave art compared to the high-tech, biofeedback, neural-patterning analyses employed today to decode and enhance athletic genius. Its true value lay in Walsh's creation of an irrefutable idea of the Babe. Nobody has improved on that methodology.

"Ruth Supernormal, So He Hits Homers," the *Times* declared. "Psychologists Prove Co-ordination of Eyes, Brain, Nerves and Muscle Is Virtually Perfect, 30% HIGHER THAN AVERAGE."

Among the findings: "The average man responds to stimulus of light in 180 one thousandths of a second. Ruth needs only 160 one thousandths of a second. . . . Translate the findings of the sight test into baseball if you want to see what they mean in Babe Ruth's case. They mean that a pitcher must throw a ball 20 one thousandths of a second faster to 'fool' the Babe than to 'fool' the average person."

In August 2006, *GQ* magazine asked scientists at Washington University in St. Louis to run similar tests on Albert Pujols, then with the Cardinals. To measure speed and endurance, he was asked to press a tapper with his finger as many times as possible in ten seconds; he finished in the 99th percentile, as had Ruth. In a test of bat speed—a critical factor left out of Hodges's analysis—Pujols measured 86.99 miles per hour with a 31.5-ounce bat, compared to Ruth's 75 miles per hour with the 54-ounce bat.

Which, Ruth noted, he wielded against pitchers who had at their disposal "ash cans, mud buckets and licorice pits into which they used to dip the ball before firing it up to the plate. We put everything on it but a cable to Mussolini. Often it was so discolored it was practically invisible when thrown with any great amount of speed."

Hitting got easier, he told Grantland Rice in 1930, when there were no more "sail balls, the fuzzy wuzzies, and the emery balls that used to flop in all directions and keep you guessing."

III

For an architect, space is liberty. A gift to the imagination seeking to impose form and function in unprecedented fashion. For an athlete, whose success is contingent upon the ability to replicate form that affords maximum function, space is an invitation to deviation, which is an invitation to disaster. To the yips. To messed-up mechanics and lost release points. To 0-fers and golden sombreros. To sophomore slumps that last a lifetime.

The greatest athletes are nonconformists like Babe Ruth, inventors who think outside the box with their bodies. Athletic genius—kinesthetic intelligence, as it's now called—is the ability to impose order on the human form as it moves through space, maximizing (and also taming) the idiosyncrasies of body shape and body type while summoning the muscle and the muscle memory necessary to create the most biomechanically efficient means to an end.

Only those with the highest kinesthetic IQ can remake an entire sport in their own image: Jimmy Connors at the baseline turning a return of serve into a weapon by taking the ball on the rise; Maury Wills on the base paths disrupting a pitcher's concentration with timing, daring, and speed; Bill Russell, the NBA's first great shot blocker, showing that defense wins the most important games; Bobby Orr, revolutionizing the role of NHL defensemen by making theirs an attacking position; Johnny U. distributing the ball to a plethora of receivers and making the quarterback the fulcrum of the NFL game; and Babe Ruth devising the modern power swing that transformed the national pastime.

He honed his swing the way he boned his bats. And he had the neuromuscular control—the physiological self-discipline—to repeat it again and again. That's what made him a career .342 hitter as well as baseball's sui generis slugger. There is irony and truth buried in the statistic known as OPS+, the modern metric that combines on-base percentage plus slugging—power and discipline—and adjusts the numbers according to ballpark and league allowing for a comparison of players from different eras. Ruth is the all-time major-league leader with a rating of 206, ahead of Ted Williams who is second with 190. Isn't it ironic that a man known for succumbing to so many temptations did not yield to those afforded by infinite space?

Ruth called Shoeless Joe Jackson "the greatest natural hitter I have ever seen" and said he had the "perfectest swing." Ruth had faced him from sixty feet, six inches, often enough as a pitcher—holding him to a .282 batting average and a .300 on-base percentage in 39 at-bats—to observe the way he went about his business. They played together for Reading Steel and Casting after the end of the war-shortened major-league season in the fall of 1918. Each owned a bat he called Black Betsy.

"Babe Ruth used to say that he copied my batting stance and I felt right complimented," Shoeless Joe told Furman Bisher in a 1949 interview for *Sport* magazine. "I was a left-handed hitter, and I did have an unusual stance. I used to draw a line three inches out from the plate every time I went to bat. I drew a right-angle line at the end next to the catcher and put my left foot on it exactly three inches from the plate. I kept both feet together, then took a long stride into the ball."

Comparing them in the smattering of available film clips, it is easy to see what Ruth stole and what he improvised on: feet stacked together at the rear of the batter's box, Ruth kept his left rear foot slightly behind the right and his body turned almost at a diagonal to the plate so that he was looking at the pitcher over his front shoulder.

He was so much bigger than everyone else and his body type so unusual that old-timers mistakenly labeled him "an upper-body hitter." They didn't focus on what the lower half of him was doing. Grantland Rice, in a departure from his usual poetics, described his biomechanics perfectly in a May 24, 1924, "Sportlight" column. "Ruth, by keeping his left foot well back of the right, gets an abnormal body turn as he swings into the ball. As he steps forward with his right foot his vast body turns with the swing and adds at least 20 percent more impetus than he would normally get. Through this turning movement of the body he can whip the bat through at greater speed with less effort and with less of a lunge or a lurch.

"Ruth does no swaying. It is all in the turn of the body, with his head held as anchor. In this way he can speed up the big bat he uses without putting the entire burden on hands and arms. If he had to swing a 52-ounce bat as most ball players swing a much lighter bludgeon the extra effort needed would kill all timing and rhythm. The 'Babe' worked out his own system, basing it in part upon Joe Jackson's way of batting with the right foot well advanced."

The reason for that was to increase the distance for acceleration of his hips as he turned into the ball, increasing rotation and force. Or as Ruth put it in a recently discovered 1943 interview broadcast on Armed Forces Radio: "Well, I'd always put my front foot toward the home plate and the back foot back a little bit so I'd give ya a perfect pivot."

No squishing the bug for him. Grinding your heel in the dirt, flat-footed? Slapping at the ball? He wanted to swing *right through the ball.*

"In boxing your fist usually stops when you hit a man, but it's possible to hit so hard that your fist doesn't stop," Ruth once explained. "I try to follow through the same way."

So far so good. "The harder you grip the bat the more you can swing it through the ball, and the further the ball will go," Ruth said.

Actually, Ruth was wrong about that. "My mantra is, 'The Grip Doesn't Matter,'" says Alan Nathan.

"The batter's grip plays absolutely no role in determining the ultimate fate of the ball. In fact, the hitter could let go of the bat just prior to impact and it wouldn't have any impact on the fate of the ball."

Few baseball players—Sandy Koufax and Ted Williams come to mind—are actual students of the game, conversant with the kinetic chain of events embedded in the pitching motion or the batting swing; fewer still can explain what happens when that chain breaks down.

Partly that's because the links could not be isolated or visualized until late-twentieth-century technology allowed for it. And partly that's because these motions of childhood, memorized through a million backyard iterations, move from one memory center in the brain to another, from what's called explicit memory (of people, places, and things) to implicit memory (sensory motor skills).

Muscle memory is recalled through performance, not conscious effort or even the awareness that you are drawing on memory. A 90-mile-an-hour fastball, traveling at 132 feet per second, gives a hitter .4 second to decide whether it's a ball or a strike and whether to swing at it. That doesn't leave a lot of time for thought. So hitters rely less on the slower, decision-making part of the brain and employ more of their "subconscious motor cortex," as Jason Ochart, the head batting instructor at Driveline Baseball in Kent, Washington, puts it. "Like Yogi said, 'You can't think and hit at the same time.'"

In fact, research has shown that athletes who are compelled to articulate what they do, do it worse. That's why so many hitters rely on batting coaches to supply language and explanations, especially when things go awry.

The Babe may not have been a "smart hitter," but he understood intuitively what his body was doing. And he explained himself in language and with concepts that are strikingly modern. "I swing right from the hips," he noted in a 1932 instructional film. "Note that my weight is on my left foot and as I start to swing my weight *shifts* to my right foot."

No one else in baseball history so thoroughly mastered the principles of momentum and leverage as he did from either end of a pitch, an asset when he made the transition from starting pitcher to everyday player. As a pitcher Ruth had the advantage of a hill to work with; as a hitter, starting from flat ground and stasis, he had to create momentum by turning his body into a pendulum. This deceptively simple act is actually an intricate biomechanical task requiring the coordinated mobilization of virtually every muscle in the body in less than a second.

"Imagine a little flatbed truck going down the street," Jim Lefebvre, the 1965 Rookie of the Year, tells hitters trying to comprehend the physics of a baseball swing. "On the back of that is a merry-go-round. On top of that is a Ferris wheel. So those three entities, those three motions, have to blend together. The truck is your stride. Once I slam my brakes on—when I put my front foot down—what's going to happen? Everything goes forward and initiates what, the hip rotation. That's the merry-go-round. And as the hips start to rotate, the barrel of the bat follows that form of energy. That's where the Ferris wheel comes in."

Every swing requires an ignition switch, one of the elements of batting style, which is idiosyncratic, as opposed to technique, which is universal. Stride, no stride, hands high, hands low, that's all style, as Mike "Super Jew" Epstein used to tell his hitting students at Epstein Hitting. "But if a good technique doesn't conform to the laws of physics, then you're essentially rolling a boulder uphill."

Ruth's trigger mechanism was a hand pump, moving his hands from his chin almost to his waist, a technique also employed by Barry Bonds and Chris Davis, who discovered the similarity while studying film with *Sports Illustrated* reporter Tom Verducci in August of his breakout season in the major leagues.

Today that's called preloading and it facilitates a faster, better contraction of the muscles in the arms and the trunk. As biomechanical gurus now know, and as Ruth intuited, power comes from the contraction of muscle, stretched to a breaking point, that snaps forward with propulsive force when released. Batting coaches with Chris Davis's previous team, the Texas Rangers, told him he'd never be able to hit that way. Then he led the major leagues with fifty home runs for the Baltimore Orioles.

The pumping motion initiated the complex sequence of motions that composed Ruth's swing. What modern coaches call "syncing up the upper and lower half," Ruth called "a harmony of action," the biomechanical process of generating the leverage required to create torque and lift. As he rocked back, shifting his considerable weight onto his left foot, he was pile-driving energy into the earth. But the earth didn't move—not even for Babe Ruth. The energy reversed course, traveling up the kinetic chain from his lower legs to his thighs through his trunk, shoulders, and arms, and eventually into the bat and ball.

He twisted his upper and lower body in opposite directions until his body was stretched taut. Then, in rapid succession: his feet came square with the plate, and he took a menacing stride toward the mound as if to reclaim what was formerly his, while shifting all his accumulated power and leverage back to front. His stride was long—far longer than allowed for by the miles per hour of modern pitching. "Give him a 30-ounce bat and he would be fine," Ochart says.

His upper body rotated with such force his lower body twisted like a double helix, his back left shoulder pivoting until it was parallel with his firm front leg. And he did it while keeping his head down and still. No small task, albeit an essential one that placed inordinate stress on the muscles of the neck and shoulders. "You're essentially keeping your eyes as still as possible while absolute chaos is happening underneath you," Ochart says.

Which explains this July 26, 1923, wire-service bulletin: "Babe Ruth Swings So Hard at Ball He Strains Neck."

Rick Schu, assistant hitting coach for the San Francisco Giants, couldn't help but notice the resemblance to Bryce Harper, another force of nature, when he coached the Washington Nationals. Just to be sure, he put clips of the two of them side by side on his computer monitor: he watched their bats uncoiling through the strike zone around the axis formed by their stiff front leg and their rear foot coming off the ground, signaling the transfer of weight was complete. When they made contact with the ball, their bats were in the exact same position.

Photographers crouched along the first base line in anticipation of the next Ruthian blow captured those moments of exquisite contact with their old-fashioned equipment: chest forward and chin up, Ruth hurled himself down the base line as if running for the elevated train that stopped just outside the Stadium. That mincing gait everyone described when he circled the bases—that was his home-run trot. He ran hard, and slid hard, when he had to.

As for telling Abe Kemp in the train compartment heading for Oakland, "Lots of times I just close my eyes and swing," it turns out this is just another example of how far ahead of the game and all its experts Ruth was. It would take another sixty years for science to demonstrate what he already knew.

The results were published in a 1984 study in *American Scientist* called "Why Can't Batters Keep Their Eye on the Ball?" After testing athletes who could track the ball until it was 5.5 feet from the plate, authors Terry Bahill and Tom LaRitz concluded, "The best imaginable athlete could not track the ball closer than 5 ft from the plate, at which point it is moving three times faster than the fastest human could track."

Which means, in Ochart's words, when "the ball enters this dark area, your swing is already on its path."

If, as claimed, Ted Williams was able to see the collision of his bat and the ball—and the smoke signals generated by it—the authors contended, "it could only be possible if he made an anticipatory saccade that put his eye ahead of the ball and then let the ball catch up to his eye."

Which sounds an awful lot like what Ruth meant when he told Kemp lots of times he sensed "the ball was coming in a certain place" and swung.

A 2016 Japanese study of college baseball hitters titled "Contribution of Visual Information about Ball Trajectory to Baseball Hitting Accuracy" confirmed Ruth's conclusion that no useful information is gained by a batter in the last third of a pitch's sixty-foot, six-inch journey to home plate, so you might as well close your eyes and swing.

Unlike today's visually primed hitters armed with video available for review before, during, and after games, Ruth had only his visual acuity, recall, and a few fleeting, flickering film clips to document his form. Rudimentary and grainy as they are, the footage that survives, culled from the library of Major League Baseball Productions, by Preston Peavy of Peavy Baseball, testifies to his exquisite athleticism.

Watch him move his feet, adjusting his stance in the batter's box, trying this and that—sometimes even crossing his front foot *over* the back one in order to accentuate his weight shift; other times, literally walking into the pitch. "Watch where he walks *through* a pitch, where he actually moves his feet in the batter's box," Schu said.

Probably he was trying to time whatever junk those early-twentieth-century hurlers were throwing. Whatever the reason, his technique remains an exemplar and a teaching tool for Schu and Lefebvre, trying to help players who are "dead in their lower half" regain rhythm and timing that has been coached out of them. "When I say, 'Do the Babe Ruth drill,' they all know exactly what it is," Lefebvre says.

Ochart does it, too, but he calls it the Happy Gilmore Drill. "He didn't follow any rules," Ochart says. "Of course, there weren't any rules to follow. It was like dancing, art really."

He had no fear of failing, only of being ignored, and no need to be like anyone else. He conformed to one thing only—the kinetic ideal. He may not have invented the crack of the bat but he altered the acoustics of the game. He created the syncopation of modern baseball—and inspired its soundtrack: from Ronald Reagan's wood-block re-creations on WHO in Des Moines to Red Barber's gentle home-run call from the catbird seat ("Going, going, gone!") to the booms that punctuated eighties TV highlight packages. Buck O'Neill, the future Negro League Hall of Famer for the Kansas City Monarchs, heard the future as a young boy, shagging balls outside a spring training game in Sarasota, Florida. It was a sound he had never heard before, the full muster of weight and leverage brought to bear on a big-league baseball. He wouldn't hear anything like it again until the sound of Josh Gibson's bat meeting a ball in a head-on crash at Griffith Stadium lured him out of the locker room in his jockstrap.

Balls hit by Ruth looked different, too. "They were like homing pigeons," his teammate Lefty Gomez once said. "The ball would leave the bat, pause briefly, suddenly gain its bearings, then take off for the stands."

For an instant, the ball defied the laws of gravity and was free. He knew that kind of liberty. Free since childhood from the constraints and conventions that governed everyone else, he was granted autonomy to define himself.

Why not soar?

He viewed every called strike, every swing and a miss, not as an impediment but as a prelude to the next home run. He swung the bat the way he lived his unexpected life—like a boy with nothing to lose. "I swing big with everything I've got. I hit big or I miss big."

And in so doing he changed the trajectory of America's game.

Chapter 13
October 23 / Bay Area II

**HOME-RUN KING AND RUNNER-UP
DO STUFF HERE**
—SAN FRANCISCO CHRONICLE

**BABE RUTH, "SULTAN" OF SWAT ARTIST,
JUST A BIG "KID" WITH ZEST FOR PLAY**
—SAN FRANCISCO CALL

I

Two San Francisco boys, Rinaldo Ardizoia, known as Rugger, and Jack Stuart, known as Whitey, awoke on Sunday morning with the same American ambition: to see the Great Bambino hit a home run.

They had little in common except for the opportunity the day presented. Jack had status, thanks to his father, a city cop who moonlighted for the San Francisco Seals. Rugger had moxie, a quality acquired through independence and derived from the name of the president's preferred soft drink. Jack knew baseball; Rugger knew his way around town. But they had everything in common with the millions of boys—thousands in the Bay Area heading for the ballpark—who would hang from rough-hewn outfield fences trying to catch a glimpse of the Babe, and maybe even catch his eye; who darted across infield dirt to attach themselves to his arms, legs, bat, so he had no choice but to carry them home; who joined forces to hold him hostage in a sea of knickers and bandit caps. Boys for whom, as big as the Babe seemed to them on that Sunday, he would only grow bigger in meaning and memory.

Rugger was two years old when he and his mother, Annunziata, arrived in New York aboard the S.S. *Colombo* on December 6, 1921, from Oleggio, a small town in northwest Italy. His father had emigrated a year earlier, having gotten a job in a Port Costa brickyard. By the time Rinaldo was six, his mother was dead from double pneumonia. His father, Carlo, was working six days a week—"eight hours a day, almost ten hours coming and going"—boiling animal by-products into glue in a factory in a windblown part of the city known as Butchertown, where decades later someone had the misbegotten notion to build a ballpark. "I lived by myself since I was six," he would say.

He spent his days in a park across the street from their home at 145 Arkansas Street watching the big boys play baseball at Jackson Playground. Some of them would go on to play in the Pacific Coast League; a few, Eddie Joost and Walt Judnich, would even make it to the bigs. They called him Rugger in admiration for the ruggedness he showed ducking through the thistles that surrounded the park.

He took Joseph as his middle name upon confirmation and took his meals at the Connecticut Yankee, a neighborhood joint owned by the Salvotti brothers, who didn't need encouragement to look after a motherless boy.

Jack Franklin Stuart was eight years old, the son of Harry F. Stuart, a special officer attached to the Southern District of the San Francisco Police and to the city's first bloodhounds, King and Lady. Harry and his boss, George Merchant, who trained the dogs to track the scent of missing children and miscreants, preferred the more dignified Scottish term sleuthhounds. "Just don't call them meathounds," Merchant told the press.

Harry loved hunting and baseball and worked as a security guard at Rec Park. It was a wreck of a place—an old wooden ballpark swaddled between Fourteenth and Fifteenth Streets on the north and south, and Valencia and Guerrero Streets on the east and west in the Mission District. It was a snug fit, 250 feet or so down the right field line, beloved by lefty sluggers. And it was a raucous place to watch a ball game. Especially in the Booze Cage, a field-level enclosure behind home plate where, before Prohibition, seventy-five cents bought a seat, a ham-and-cheese sandwich, and two beers or a shot of booze. The Eighteenth Amendment was *federal* law; it did not apply in the Booze Cage: Harry F. Stuart looked the other way if patrons chose to bring their own flasks.

Thanks to his connections and largesse, his son Whitey was named batboy for the Seals in 1927 and would keep the job through the 1930 season. On Sunday, October 23, it was his job to serve the Babe.

II

The Bay Area went to bed on Saturday night swathed in thick coastal fog as it so often did, and awoke that Sunday morning to news that the outward-bound steamer *Coos Bay*, loaded with lumber and a crew of thirty, had run aground at Mile Rock at the Golden

Gate. Overnight radio airwaves had been cleared for emergency transmissions. The city was still draped in mist as Rugger Ardizoia and an older friend from the playground made their way from Potrero Hill, a working-class neighborhood on the eastern side of the peninsula, insulated from fog and chill and tourists, to the Ferry Building at the foot of Market Street.

Christy Walsh had scheduled a Sunday doubleheader for Ruth and Gehrig, which by local custom called for one game to be played on either side of San Francisco Bay. The morning game was called for 10:00 A.M. in Emeryville, a small town snuggled between Oakland and Berkeley, home of the 1927 Pacific Coast League champion Oakland Oaks. The afternoon game would be played at Recreation Park, home of the once and future champion San Francisco Seals and the also-ran Mission Reds.

The matinee would start after church let out. Sunday services at the Welsh Presbyterian Church located just beyond the center field fence had been interrupted once too often by loud home runs. By covenant, no Sunday-morning baseball was played at the Rec.

Rugger had listened to the World Series on the radio, the first carried coast to coast. He couldn't remember years later whether he heard Babe and Lou on the radio the night before with Al Santoro on KGO. He didn't know that much about the game then—he didn't start playing ball with the Catholic Youth Organization until three years later. All he knew about the Babe was that he hit home runs and had a candy bar named after him.

He was determined to see both ends of the Sunday doubleheader, never imagining that one day he'd call each of the ballparks home.

The Ferry Building, built on the Embarcadero in 1898, was still the locus of the city. It survived the 1906 earthquake—housing city refugees beneath its 660-foot skylight—with the hands on the 22-foot clock face frozen at 5:16 A.M., when the earth split in two. At peak operation, it accommodated fifty thousand travelers each day. Despite the optimistic lead story in the *Chronicle* that Sunday morning, the Bay Bridge, first proposed in 1872, was nine years from realization. The Golden Gate Bridge, that haughty feat of human artistry and engineering, would follow six months later. In October 1927, San Francisco and its residents were still living at the mercy of the tides and the fog. The steamer *Coos* was a total loss.

The Southern Pacific Railroad, with its terminus at the Oakland pier, ferried railroad cars and automobiles on steam-driven boats that served full-course meals during the eighteen-minute, 3.5-mile trip. Ridership was down, the *Oakland Tribune* reported that morning, but consumption was up—235,000 snails consumed during the previous twelve months!

The Key System, a privately held commuter rail-and-ferry system created by Francis Marion Smith, manufacturer of the cleanser 20 Mule Team Borax, made the trip three minutes faster, thanks to a pier that reached three miles into San Francisco Bay. Commuters from Oakland and Alameda were accustomed to traveling with un-showered baseball players still in uniform. J. Cal Ewing, cofounder of the Pacific Coast League, still owned the Oaks and Seals then and saw profit in promoting the Bay Area's version of New York's subway series.

The bright orange electrified Key boats, with stained-glass windows on the upper decks and inlaid tile floors, left the Ferry Building every fifteen or twenty minutes beginning at the top of the hour. They served coffee in the morning and corned beef hash and apple pie at night. On board, you could buy a shoeshine, a milkshake, or the morning paper with the recap of the Saturday game at the Rec.

Ruth hadn't done much. The quality of Bay Area competition may have had something to do with his sorry performance, though it didn't bother Gehrig. He had a double and a long home run. Even so, the headline in the morning *Chronicle* was about Ruth: "Out in Cold Where Homers Figure."

"I suppose you're going to rub it in now but go ahead and have your fun," Ruth told Gehrig after the game. "I'll get ahold of one tomorrow and when I do—"

"They'll forget that I ever hit one," Gehrig replied.

III

Disembarking in the East Bay, Rugger and his friend took the San Pablo streetcar to the corner of Fortieth Street and Park Avenue, where a ballpark had been constructed in three months during the winter of 1912–13 to celebrate the Oaks' first Pacific Coast League championship—and their last until they beat the Seals in 1927 by fourteen and a half games. The ballpark was happily situated on 495 acres once part of the homestead of town father John Emery and today is part of Pixar Animation Studios. Home plate currently resides in Pixar's parking lot.

By the twenties, the streetcar line along San Pablo Avenue had attracted lots of business to an assortment of speakeasies, racetracks, gambling parlors, brothels, and other establishments of the flesh that later prompted Alameda County district attorney Earl Warren to label Emeryville "the rottenest city on the Pacific Coast."

But the weather conditions were particularly favorable for baseball and a 120-game season. Geographically and financially independent from the big leagues, the Pacific Coast League—the third major league, as it was so often called—produced many of the game's greatest names: Joltin' Joe DiMaggio, the Splendid Splinter, the Old Perfessor, "Poosh 'Em Up" Tony Lazzeri, Frank "the Crow" Crosetti, Frank "Smead" Jolley, Arnold "Jigger" Statz, Paul "Big Poison" Waner (and his brother, Lloyd). Also, Earl Averill, Harry Heilmann, Dutch Ruether, Mickey Cochrane, and Billy Martin. In 1928, the Cleveland Indians offered to trade outfields with the Seals—San Francisco management wisely declined. A year later, the Yankees bought pitcher Vernon "Lefty" Gomez from the Seals, salvaging their season and acquiring a lifelong friend for Babe Ruth.

Oaks Park was the largest in the Pacific Coast League in dimension, with fences equal to if not farther than those in many major-league baseball stadiums, but seating capacity was only ten thousand. So when thirteen thousand people showed up by 10 A.M., half of them children, it was clear special ground rules would apply. Outfielders made up their own rules, dropping fly balls on purpose to allow kids a chance to grab a souvenir.

Rugger and his pal arrived in time to find a place

for themselves in a walkway along the third base line. They witnessed the presentation of floral pieces to Ruth and Gehrig. They heard the Big Brother Band from the Oakland Lodge of the Elks, which also entertained between innings, and observed eighty-eight-year-old Dan "the Plucky Pedestrian" O'Leary—known for walking 144 straight hours in 1875—circle the bases six times in five minutes.

The lineups featured plenty of talent: Lefty O'Doul, another pitcher turned slugger, who would twice lead the National League in hitting; just-retired Babe Pinelli, who went on to become an umpire, calling balls and strikes for Don Larsen's 1956 World Series perfect game; Gussie Suhr, who hit .279 during eleven years in the majors; Willie Kamm, the Chicago White Sox third baseman; Gordon Slade, who would play five years in the majors; Yankee shortstop Tony Lazzeri, another San Francisco boy who started in the PCL and ended in the PCL with the Seals in 1941.

The Sunday-morning lineups were further distinguished by the presence of two of Ruth's roommates, both of whom claimed authorship of one of the most quoted of Babe-isms: Ping Bodie, who played the outfield for the Bustin' Babes, and Jimmy Reese, who played second base for the Larrupin' Lous: "I didn't room with Ruth. I roomed with his suitcase."

Otherwise, the game was noteworthy for what Ruth failed to accomplish. His back was balky. His hands were bleeding. "Just try hitting for about a solid hour each day and see how sore your hands get," he said.

Wylie Wells Kelley, the official cinematographer of the *Oakland Tribune*, trained his trusty movie camera lens on the Bambino, as the paper put it in its Monday edition, capturing a succession of Ruthian pop-ups, fly-ball outs, and groundouts, and his outsized attempt to please, all of which appeared nightly that week at Oakland's Hippodrome Theater. "Failing to hit, he tried to pitch and then to satisfy the customers he jumped into the stand and led the band," Abe Kemp wrote in the *San Francisco Examiner*.

Which was situated just in front of Rugger Ardizoia, who admired the way the Babe swung his arms in time to the music just like a real conductor.

Gehrig, who drove in four runs with a homer, a triple, and a double, went to the mound in the ninth. But Oakland fans were so eager to get a look at Ruth they refused to let the last hitter bat, clambering over the fence en masse. Gehrig tossed the last ball in the air, as was the custom at Oaks Park, and fled. The game was called. The Lous won 6–3.

Rugger did not join the stampede. "Being a little guy, you could get trampled," he said.

IV

Jack "Whitey" Stuart was already in uniform when Rugger's chaperone dropped him off at the Rec for the second game of the doubleheader. "Then I was in charge of my own self," Rugger said. "I had to get around. Otherwise, what could I do?"

Jack—wearing his home white Seals uniform, the pants just reaching the knee as was the fashion, with thick, dark stirrups covering his white socks, and white baseball shoes with real spikes—arrived early with his father, who was a good friend of the Seals' manager Nick Williams. They had work to do.

Rugger *had* to get there early enough not to get caught climbing the twenty-five-foot stack of lumber that hugged the left field wall. "That's where we sneaked in," Rugger said. "We'd climb up the lumber and over the fence. I went down into the stands and got a seat."

The ballpark, built a year after the quake, was idiosyncratic even for its time. The clubhouse was in deep center field with a Camel cigarette billboard mounted on top. Beside the clubhouse stood a fifteen-foot-high woodcut figure of a bull—an advertisement for Bull Durham Tobacco. A fifty-dollar prize went to any player who hit the bull on the nose. According to the ground rules any ball coming to rest in the one-and-a-half-foot-square hole in front of the clubhouse housing the gas meter was an automatic home run.

A goat housed under the grandstands cut the grass. Two apartment buildings perched over the right field fence provided target practice for lefty sluggers. "They haven't moved the fences back at Rec Park, have they?" was Ruth's first question for Abe Kemp when he met their train.

No, Kemp said. But they had mounted a thirty-foot chicken-wire screen on top of the right field wall to add a measure of respectability to all those cheap chip-shot home runs.

"You'll like the park," Ruth assured Gehrig.

Christy Walsh was busy meeting with a delegation of city fathers from Santa Cruz who hoped to secure the last open date on the tour, Wednesday, October 26, but were outbid by deeper pockets from San Jose. News photographers jockeyed for position as Lefty O'Doul, the PCL's first Most Valuable Player, received a thousand-dollar check from Lou Gehrig, the major league's unremunerated Most Valuable Player. Ruth had requested O'Doul's presence in as many of the California games as possible. O'Doul was an old running buddy from the 1920 and 1922 Yankees who later explained their friendship to his cousin Tom this way: "Everybody liked him because he had an automobile."

Lefty also said they had a lot in common: neither was college educated, both came from working-class families, and both liked to have a good time.

When one of the photo jockeys asked Ruth for a picture, Babe summoned his batboy to join him. Maybe it was in thanks for bringing a first-aid kit to the mound when he hurt his finger while throwing batting practice, or some other bit of baseball business that Whitey had seen to in the clubhouse.

They stood shoulder (Whitey's) to waist (Babe's) on the infield grass. Ruth's ham-hock arm reached all the way around him, his ring finger extending below the boy's elbow; Jack stood stiffly with his fist clenched at his side. Two holes oddly excised from the bill of his cap let the light shine through, making him squint and exposing his nervousness. Ruth was his hugely nonchalant self, hand on hip, fingers splayed like the prongs on the end of a backhoe.

More than any other photograph taken of Ruth with children, this one gives a sense of his size and how it must have felt to be a boy standing in his shadow.

"Looming," is how Jack would describe Ruth to his daughter. "A big, looming guy."

V

In the seventh inning when the teamsters and working joes in the Booze Cage had had their fill, they opened the place up to kids who came to gawk and transact business with representatives of the daily papers who needed paperboys, like Rugger, to hawk the afternoon editions in the stands. "In those days, they used to grab you and put newspapers under your arm: 'Sell these, kid,'" Rugger said.

Boys with ambition spread out through the stands with afternoon papers to sell. Rugger's goal was to earn enough to buy the candy that would sustain him on the forty-minute walk up Potrero Hill. The paper sold for three cents. Sometimes his customers would give him a nickel and say, "Keep the change."

All that divided the players from the booze cagers was a scrim of chicken wire. It was very intimate and very profane. Women were not welcome in the eight rows of seats that stretched from third to first. You said whatever you wanted and the players said whatever they wanted back to you.

"Everybody was yelling, calling, trying to commandeer the Babe's attention," Rugger said. "'Hey Babe!' 'How you doin' there?' 'Hey Lou!' But nothing personal."

Ruth and Gehrig didn't acknowledge him. "Aw, no, too many guys are yelling. They'd be turning around all the time."

Ruth couldn't have been more than a couple of feet away from him. What Rugger noticed, right then and there, was the size of his hands. "Oh, Christ! Another half the time bigger than an ordinary man's.

"And goddamn can he hit that ball."

Ruth resumed his "murderous art" that afternoon, Kemp wrote after counting seven batting-practice home runs bombard the Welsh Church behind the center field fence.

"*Holy,*" Rugger said.

When boys in the left field stands cried out for him to hit a few their way, he did—the boy working the scoreboard caught one on a fly. During the game, he hit two home runs, one of which, Rugger said, was caught by a boy standing on the roof of one of the apartment buildings behind the chicken-wire fence in right field.

The Babes won 15–4 and he was redeemed.

After the game, Rugger went back to the Booze Cage with the money he'd made from the papers he'd sold to settle up with the newspaper dealer. On a good day, he'd end up with maybe ten, eleven cents. "Enough for a couple boxes of Zeenuts. A Zeenut with a baseball picture inside."

He was pooped after the long day and the two-mile walk home. He didn't tell his father about it. Carlo didn't speak English. "No use talking to him," Rugger said. "He didn't know what baseball was. He only cared in 1936 and 1937. I was taking home $150 a month. And he was making $20 a week."

VI

Other kids left the Rec with miniature bats and balls that Ruth threw into the stands. Jack Stuart came away with the jersey he wore, an autographed bat and ball from the Babe, and bitter memories at odds with the sentiment he would come to attach to the occasion. In June 1997 he would tell a reporter from the *Register-Pajaronian*, a not-quite daily paper in Watsonville, California, that when he asked Columbia Lou to pose with him and the Babe, Gehrig refused on the grounds that he didn't approve of Ruth's morals, which doesn't sound like something an eight-year-old batboy would know or something Gehrig would have said then, no matter how strongly he would come to feel later about Ruth's behavior.

Jack's adult children figured he had gotten some inside dope from players on the Seals' bench. He also said that when cries rose up from kids in the bleachers—"Hit it here, Babe!"—Ruth would nod and smile and mutter under his breath, "Little bastards."

Jack used the bat that Babe Ruth gave him and broke it, not the biggest loss of his childhood, which wasn't any happier than the Babe's. His mother bet the ponies and lost the family house in the Marina district. His father was killed by a shotgun blast from his own rifle on Jack's twenty-first birthday. Police ruled Harry's death an accident after finding that the trigger caught on a coat hanger in the back seat of his car, discharging the bullet that killed him. It also shattered a window in the garage, through which Jack and his mother saw him slumped across the running board. It fell to Jack to inform the police.

He joined the force and then the Army and became an investigator. He saw a lot of the world but not his own family. After he retired, he was asked to join the San Francisco Baseball Old Timers Association, an invitation-only group formed in 1941 for the express purpose of talking baseball and occasionally playing baseball, which Jack did, not particularly well, until the mid-1990s. His claim to fame was that he had once been Babe Ruth's batboy.

As he grew older, he found that the Babe still loomed over his life. When the *Register-Pajaronian* resurrected the story of his day with the Babe and reprinted the photo of them together on the field. Jack gave it to all the past presidents of the Old Timers Association, including Rugger Ardizoia. Sometimes he even signed autographs at Candlestick Park—Jack "Whitey" Stuart, Babe Ruth's batboy—and after that at Pac Bell or whatever it was called next.

When Jack died in October 1998, his death notice in the *San Francisco Chronicle* listed all the places he had served: Japan, Korea, Germany, and the Old Rec. At his wake, the jersey he wore that day was laid out in the coffin with him.

VII

Rugger Ardizoia never figured to get any closer to the Babe than he did that long, sweet day in his hometown by the San Francisco Bay. It was enough that they had baseball in common and some other things, too—they had led independent lives at a very young age.

He joined the CYO baseball league when he was old enough, played American Legion ball, and became a pitcher late, like Ruth, in his junior year at Commerce High School (striking out sixty-three batters in seven games, including two no-hitters). Like the Babe, he signed a contract when he was underage with the Mission Reds, forcing him to forgo a scholarship offer from

Stanford University that arrived after high school grad-
uation. For a time he was considered the best pitching
prospect in the PCL since Lefty Gomez. "My father
said, 'I supported you for seventeen years, now you
support me.'"

In his first professional game, he pitched five innings of no-hit ball against the Padres, including Ted
Williams, in San Diego. Then he came home to pitch
at the Rec.

In 1939–40 he pitched for the Hollywood Stars, the
Pacific Coast League franchise in Los Angeles owned
by Bob Cobb, Christy Walsh Jr.'s father-in-law, and
was good enough to be acquired by the Yankees, who
brought him to spring training in 1941—just in time
for the war to get in the way of his aspirations. It did
not occur to him to object to the draft on the grounds
that he wasn't a citizen.

He served in the Air Corps and played on the Seventh Air Force baseball team that entertained the
troops in the Pacific, including on the battlefield of Iwo
Jima, less than a week after the shooting ended. Also on
the team were a couple of other Italian boys from San
Francisco—Joe DiMaggio and Charlie Silvera. And
some other local guys who went to the majors: Walt
Judnich, Red Ruffing, and Joe Gordon.

In 1946, he returned to baseball and to Oaks Park,

where he won fifteen games for manager Casey Stengel, helping the Old Perfessor win back some of the respect he'd lost after being canned by the Boston Braves.

In the spring of 1947, he went to spring training with the Yankees again and this time he made the big club. He was a relief pitcher who threw batting practice, a mop-up man with Zelig-like timing if not a powerful arm. He was the unidentified player standing beside Joe D. in a nude locker-room photo taken in the spring of 1941, auctioned off for big money some sixty years later. Some doubted its authenticity until Rugger vouched for his privates. "Jesus, that's me," he said, after recognizing himself in the Sporting Green section of the *Chronicle*.

So it figured that he would be standing in the right spot in the Yankees dugout when Babe Ruth, hair, voice, and strength ravaged by radiation, an experimental form of chemotherapy, and the cancer it had been prescribed to kill, and swathed in a topcoat that fit him like a shroud, stumbled while trying to climb the four steps to the field that once was his.

It was April 27, 1947, Babe Ruth Day at Yankee Stadium and throughout major-league baseball. Rugger Ardizoia had been waiting a baseball lifetime for a chance to make a difference—just not this one. "I grabbed him and held him up for his people," he said.

"They came over and brought him out on the field. He gave a little speech out there. When he came back, both of his tenders held him—one on each arm—and helped him on down the stairs.

"When he fell, he said, 'Thanks a lot, kid.'

"I said, 'You're welcome, Babe.'"

Three days later, in St. Louis against the Browns with the Yankees trailing 13–4 in the seventh inning, Rugger finally got his chance to pitch in the major leagues. He survived the seventh inning. In the eighth he faced one of the guys he'd looked up to at Jackson park, Walt Judnich, who'd been with him at Iwo Jima. "I had 3 and 2 on Walt. And I said, 'What the hell? Another run's not going to hurt.' So I toot one down the middle and boom!"

Eight days later he was sold to the Stars. His major-league career was over, his pitching line complete.

One game: 9.00 ERA, 2 IP, 4 H, 2 ER, 1 HR, 1 BB, 0 SO.

The Yankees won the World Series without any help from him.

He didn't figure to get a ring or a check. But a month later, on his birthday, November 20, a card came in the mail. It had a picture of the Babe on the front, all decked out in a tuxedo, blowing out forty-nine candles on a three-tier cake at the annual Baseball Writers' dinner in New York. "Rugger, Wishing you a very Happy Birthday!"

It made no difference to him then—or in his last days, at age ninety-five, when he was the oldest living New York Yankee—that the card was signed by "The Yankee family." He had no doubt it came from the Babe. "This was on his authorization," he said firmly. "He made up the list of who to send. The way I got on a list was helping him when he stumbled."

It validated what he already knew about the Big Fella. "The Babe was a real nice guy. He never *phoofed* nobody. Y'know, flipped nobody. 'See ya later, buddy, take a hike.' He always had a good word for his teammates."

Even a Yankee for one game.

Chapter 14
October 25 / Marysville

HOLIDAY DECLARED FOR RUTH-GEHRIG

—OAKLAND TRIBUNE

TROTSKY BOOED OUT OF OFFICE

—WOODLAND DAILY DEMOCRAT

I

The town of Marysville, named for one of the surviving members of the Donner party, declared a municipal holiday when arrangements for the 10:00 A.M. game were finalized late Sunday afternoon. Closing all shops and city offices for the morning, Mayor E. J. Carlin expressed regret that he lacked the authority to dismiss the public schools, which the superintendent promptly agreed was the proper course of action.

Word of the game overshadowed all other news, including a demand by the beloved Marysville Giants for a change in league rules allowing the team to keep all future home-game receipts at Marysville Municipal Ball Park, an estimated $1,700 that year, and a wire-service story datelined Moscow informing citizens of the Sacramento Valley that Leon Trotsky had been booed off the stage at the Communist Party convention.

The addition of the Tuesday-morning game, sandwiched between a Monday-afternoon date in Stockton, ninety miles south of Marysville, and a previously scheduled Tuesday-afternoon date in Sacramento, was curious. Pure greed was the only explanation, *Stockton Record* columnist John Peri would opine, in a morning-after snit occasioned by Ruth's lackluster showing in the pregame hitting exhibition. "In trying to grab off more dates than can be conveniently handled, Manager Christy Walsh of the tour only injured the drawing power of his attraction particularly if he should plan a return engagement next year."

Peri's pique was a startling departure from the usual obsequiousness that greeted them in the local press and

more than a bit odd given Ruth's five hits that afternoon, including a home run that "kissed the moon,"
the *Record* reported.

There was a more compelling reason than a measly
thousand-dollar guarantee for the unlikely detour
north to the old gold-rush town where city fathers had
kicked in fifty dollars each toward the visit. Ruth had
been tipped off to the services of a chiropractor named
John W. Rattray, the trainer for the Marysville Giants,
who maintained an office two hundred feet from the
entrance to the Hotel Marysville, where the traveling party arrived two hours late for a banquet in their
honor scheduled to begin at 8:00 that evening.

The advertisement for the $1.25 full-course dinner
in the Marysville *Appeal-Democrat* was accompanied
by the now ubiquitous photo of the Babe with Lady
Amco of Omaha, the champion hen having been identified that morning by the United Press as Mrs. Babe
Ruth, his real wife, Helen, having disappeared from
public view after her cameo appearance at the World
Series.

A reception committee of "50 prominent citizens"
and "some 30 young Americans" began gathering at
6:30 P.M., an hour before the promised arrival of Ruth
and Gehrig. Among them was George Nicholau, an

eight-year-old newspaper boy for the *Appeal-Democrat* with twenty papers to sell and plenty of time to do it.

Marysville was a drinking town and a baseball town: tickets to the game were sold at the Brunswick, one of the many saloons along the main drag, D Street, which had broadcast World Series games as a public service. The sidewalks had filled with whoops and roars. Devotion to the game was fierce. Standing in the street talking baseball for three and a half hours, long after his bedtime, was heaven for an eight-year-old newsie who figured it was as close as he was ever going to get to Babe Ruth, what with school the next morning.

Marysville's own Hall of Famer, Harry Hooper, who advised Ed Barrow to make Ruth an outfielder in 1918 and then observed the transformation of the Babe from "a human being into something close to a god," signed a one-game contract with the Marysville Giants at the end of his career just so he could say he retired as a member of the home team. He went 2 for 4 that day.

At 10:05 P.M., Ruth stepped gingerly from the car belonging to the president of the Giants, Jack Frederick, and the stampede was on. Ruth acknowledged the crowd like a potentate and said a few words before being ushered into the hotel's banquet room, where guests awaited promised remarks about the World Series and impressions of California that would not be forthcoming. After a moment of decorous restraint, Nicholau said, the kids swarmed through the entrance and through the legs of their elders.

"Here's where the war starts," Ruth groaned as he took his seat of honor.

Immaculate in a blue suit and cravat, he seemed far more put together than Gehrig, who had on a rumpled suit, a crooked tie, and a bashful smile, "attesting to the fact that he had been asleep on the train," the *Appeal-Democrat* noted. "His hair is curlier than Ruth's."

The paper detected in Ruth a mood of tolerant boredom. "We are tired, and I've got a wrenched back, something cracked when I missed that ball today, and we'll see in the morning if it's going to come out," Ruth said. "Our tour this month has been tougher than six months on the ball field. We've slept only two nights in hotels since we left New York."

Gehrig shuffled like a schoolboy, the paper reported, when summoned to speak. "I get a kick out of Babe. I call him Babe even if he did call me Mr. Gehrig a minute ago. He is always boasting that he has had eight or nine years more experience than I have. He may be older, but he can still go more than I can. Babe entertained friends in Stockton and on the train, but I slept. They woke me up in Sacramento, so I could see that new million-dollar theater."

With that, the mayor hustled them off to bed without so much as a bite of the telegram-shaped cake the Ideal Bakery had prepared in welcome.

The King of Clout did not sleep.

He called Doc Rattray instead, spent an hour on his chiropractic table, and made an appointment to see him again at 7:30 A.M. John W. Rattray, a true Scot from the MacDonald clan, had been born in the small town of Pipestone in Manitoba, Canada. While still living north of the border, he fell off a horse, which then landed on him, injuring his hip. During his convalescence in the hospital, he met his future wife, Esther Lensgraf, a member of the first family of American chiropractic. They would relocate to Davenport, Iowa, to study together at the Palmer College of Chiropractic, along with Esther's sister and six brothers, later moving to California, seeking warm weather for his compromised hip.

They were the first chiropractors licensed by the state, opening their practice, Rattray & Rattray, in Marysville, where they acquired a reputation for setting things straight among ballplayers coming through town. One of the Sacramento Senators had referred Ruth to Doc Rattray's care.

The Rattrays and Fredericks were friends. Jack Frederick was a big muckety-muck in town and not just in baseball circles: he was a supervisor at Pacific Gas & Electric and president of the Marysville Merchant Association. He helped raise the money to bring Ruth and Gehrig to town and invited them home for breakfast the morning of the game, after Doc Rattray got the kinks out.

The Babe brought steak.

Jack's young daughter Doris, a shagger at Marysville Giants games, was told to wait on the Babe. He rewarded her with a beat-up batting practice ball he dug out of a canvas equipment bag and signed for her, she later told her son. "My mother always said that was the first time she'd ever seen a steak. She said in one sitting, he ate a steak and a loaf of bread, which, at the time, was more food than her family almost would eat in a week."

Then Jack and Doris and old Doc Icy Fingers and his son Jimmy headed for the ballpark with Babe and Lou riding shotgun, honking and waving, with young Jimmy hanging out the window, announcing who was riding in his daddy's car.

II

The little ballpark on Third and H Streets, which would blow away in a windstorm in the 1930s, exerted something like centripetal force on the morning of October 25. Though it had seating for perhaps eight hundred spectators, more than two thousand people—a third of the town's population—showed up. That didn't include an untold number of kids who crawled through a hole in the left field fence and adults from all over the valley who drove their vehicles right on up over the curb and parked behind the outfield wall.

A section of the grandstand had been set aside for children, who dutifully reported to school at the 8:00 A.M. bell only to discover that classes had been canceled. "They marched us to the ballpark rather than let us go on our own," Nicholau remembered. "They didn't want guys running all over, loose."

Like Doris Frederick, George was a ball shagger for the home team, a paying job that involved retrieving foul balls for the batboys, Vince Fasano and Bill Conlin, a future sportswriter for the *Sacramento Bee*. There were fewer balls to return than usual that day as spectators helped themselves liberally to souvenirs. George regretted not doing so himself. One of the balls Babe Ruth hit in batting practice proved unretrievable, landing in a passing boxcar headed for Oregon, making it the longest home run ever hit. At least that's what locals would tell their grandchildren.

Thanks to his exalted position with the organization, Nicholau was allowed to sit on the field near the dugout. "I was kind of getting in the way. I hoped for a 'Hi kid, how are you?' Coming back to the dugout, I got a pat on the head from Babe and Gehrig. I was damned glad to get that."

On the mound for the Larrupin' Lous was Marysville's own Clyde "Tub" Perry, the biggest, brightest, widest star in the Sacramento Valley League at a time when "the Sunday league played better baseball than some lower classifications of pro leagues," Bill Conlin would write in 1973.

Tub was twenty-two years old, married to his high school sweetheart, Alice, and the father of a baby girl, Jane, not yet two years old, and Clyde, known as Brud, who turned two months old that day. He had been pitching for the Giants since 1925. In July, the local papers reported Tub had signed with the Seals, but it was really only an invitation for a tryout. Still, it was a big deal. "Tub Signs." An earlier tryout with the Sacramento Senators had not gone as he had hoped.

Facing Ruth in the bottom of the first inning was an opportunity he did not mean to squander. This wasn't just lefty versus lefty. This was a confrontation of intentions and expectations. Perry was everything Ruth was not: rooted, earnest, purposeful, and most of all, serious about that day's game. "I didn't want to let him hit a home run, but I didn't want to walk him," he said, recalling Ruth's first inning at bat. "I aimed for the corners and worked up a three and two count."

A couple of inside pitches almost hit the Big Fella, who didn't much like the young man's attitude. Gehrig called time and walked to the mound. Tub assumed he was in for a scolding. *C'mon, let the guy hit.* Instead, Gehrig said, "Let's see you strike this bum out."

"I tried my damnedest, but I walked him," Tub remembered.

Much as the hometown folks loved Tub, they didn't much like that. "I knew they would 'Ooooh' when he was walked because they wanted Tub to let him hit one," Nicholau said. "But Tub was trying to make a name for himself. In his mind, this was a challenge to prove himself."

Ruth didn't much like it either.

There was some chitchat back and forth as he gimped his way down the first base line. *Damn farm kid made him run the bases.*

Which was the last thing he wanted to do. The way Tub's niece, Marlene Coleman Benniger, heard it, "Babe went back to the dugout and says, 'Who in the hell is that kid?'"

Get that wild man out of there before I hurt my back again.

Ruth said later he was in such a bad way Gehrig had to pick up his glove for him each time the Bustin' Babes went back onto the field.

Eddie Burt, sports editor of the *Appeal-Democrat,* and official scorekeeper, remembered to get Ruth and Gehrig to sign his scorecard at the end of the game but neglected to record Tub's complete pitching line. His century-old, pencil-drawn hieroglyphics, as idiosyncratic as any scoring system, nonetheless make clear that Ruth got his wish. They got Tub out of the game before the Babe had to face him again.

The manager brought in the starting center fielder to pitch and everyone went home happy. Tub kept his honor. Babe got his home runs: one in the seventh that flew over the center field wall, over the railroad tracks, the levee, and into the Yuba River, and a grand slam in the eighth.

George Nicholau went back to the ballyard the next morning before school and collected a couple of neglected baseballs from foul territory to show off to his classmates. And Tub's father-in-law, Bill McFarland, got a brand-new automobile courtesy of his winning ticket in a game-day raffle.

III

In January 1928, Tub Perry was rewarded with a contract with the San Francisco Seals, the perennial Pacific Coast champions who had finished second in the league that year. The team sent transportation money. But when the day came for Tub to report to spring training in Monterey, he was a no-show. He said he was never told when to report. The big-city sports columnists had a whole lot of fun with that.

In February, Tub asked for his release but the team refused; management still saw potential in his left arm. He was placed on the voluntary retired list and went back to pitching for Marysville, where he remained the local boy who might still make good, which was not a bad thing to be. He had a good year for the home team.

That fall, while the Yankees were celebrating their third consecutive pennant with a party in a Detroit hotel for which the Babe purchased a piano when the concierge failed to procure one, Tub was the starting pitcher for the Sacramento Valley League All-Stars against a team representing the San Francisco Stock Exchange in a much-anticipated series in Marysville.

Ruth's wife, Helen, did not make her customary cameo appearance that fall at the 1928 World Series. On September 10, she had been admitted to the Carney Hospital in South Boston for treatment of another nervous breakdown. She had left eight days later, declining the advice of her physicians, who urged her to seek long-term care at Dr. A. M. Ring's Sanatorium in Arlington Heights, a rest home where women were treated for hysteria.

She chose instead to go home to the six-room cottage at 47 Quincy Street that she shared with Dr. Edward H. Kinder, a Tufts-educated dentist and decorated war veteran, who practiced locally and in the Back Bay. Neighbors, bankers, and telephone operators all knew her as his wife. They were said to be a devoted couple.

The name Helen R. Kinder appeared on the deed to the house and on the mortgage taken out with the North Columbia Co-Operative Bank of Cambridge on May 31, 1927. The couple had added a downstairs sun porch and a sleeping porch adjacent to the upstairs bedrooms. His family believed they had been married in Montreal; her people said they were old family friends from South Boston.

They had enrolled a little girl introduced as their daughter, Dorothy, in a boarding school run by the nuns in Wellesley. They did not tell the child in advance why they were visiting the convent school, or that they would be leaving her there that same day. Nor did they bring her home on weekends or visit on

Sundays. She would remember "many a Sunday crying myself to sleep because no one came to see me," she said in her 1988 memoir.

Neighbors on Quincy Street noted that she received a life-size doll when she came home at Christmas. During the summer, when she was often seen around the house, she seemed to have plenty of dolls and expensive playthings.

Watertown, a small Boston suburb due west of Cambridge, is now best known as the site of the shootout between police and the Tsarnaev brothers on the evening of the Boston Marathon bombing in 2013. On Friday night, January 11, 1929, it was the site of a house fire caused by faulty electrical wiring in which a woman, identified as Mrs. Helen Kinder, died from "incineration and suffocation."

Dr. Kinder was at the Friday-night fights at the Boston Garden. Helen had declined to go because she had a cold. She hadn't seemed well since her last hospitalization, neighbors said. Dorothy would confide later in her friend Carolyn Rendon that her mother said she knew she was going to die, Rendon recalled. "She was quite sick before she burned in the fire. She was taking all kinds of medication for something."

The fire alarm was called in from Fire Box 425 at 10:04 P.M. Captain John J. Kelly of the Watertown Fire Department fought his way up the stairs, crawling on his hands and knees through smoke and flames to find a woman facedown on the bedroom floor. She was in her nightclothes, lying by the door.

News accounts reported that she died at the scene. In fact, according to the Watertown Police report, she lived for twelve hours after the alarm was called in.

She had received mouth-to-mouth resuscitation from members of a volunteer group called the Box 52 Association before doctors arrived.

Watertown Police Log, January 12, 1929, 12:15 A.M.: "She was rescued by Capt. Kelly, Hoseman Devaney and Officer Clinton. I met them on stairway and assisted her to the home of Aubrey Bichard 35 Quincy St. I sent an emergency call for a doctor and Dr's Kelly and Butler responded."

The entry did not say in what condition she spent her last hours. She was pronounced dead at 10:41 A.M. the next day, according to the police report.

Paged at the Boston Garden, Edward Kinder had made his way back to Watertown, and then to the Bichards', where he collapsed, dropping to the floor with a moan, according to neighbor Dorothy Sweed, whose father had called in the alarm. "Then he came to a bit and mustered up strength enough to go to view the burned body," she told reporters.

"She is my wife; her name is Helen Kinder," Kinder told the medical examiner, George L. West.

Plans were made to bury her on Sunday morning in the Kinder family plot in St. Joseph Cemetery in West Roxbury. A grave was dug in the reluctant winter soil.

The next morning, news of the death of the wife of the prominent Watertown dentist appeared on the front page of the *Boston Post*. A photograph of the deceased appeared on an inside page. An anonymous caller tipped off the police to the case of double identity and offered information that Helen may have been "under the influence of narcotics, and that the fire in which she died may have been of incendiary origin," as the Universal Service, a Hearst-owned news agency that served its morning papers, would report the next day.

By then, the prominent Watertown dentist had disappeared. And the fire inspector who had answered the alarm, and who had described her body as "slightly burned and probably suffocated," had concluded that the fire was caused by "overloaded electrical wires" resulting in a short circuit in the living room which had been caused by "amateur work" and "wiring spliced and taped with no solder." Nothing in two subsequent visits by state fire marshals changed that assessment. The fire had started in a first-floor partition—in the dining room, according to the initial report—and then worked its way up through the ceilings and walls to the upstairs bedroom, moving with rapidity and sufficient intensity to cut a hole in the floor large enough for a radiator to fall through. Police estimated the damage at four thousand dollars.

Babe Ruth had spent that Friday training at Artie McGovern's Manhattan gym, "his portly waistline encased in a rubber shirt," the *Times* reported. (Photographic evidence of his sweaty diligence would appear in the Sunday paper.) At City Hall that morning, Mayor Jimmy Walker had accepted on his behalf a ceremonial bat made from rare lignum vitae wood excavated in the Panama Canal Zone with a promise that he would make sure to get it to the Great Bambino.

In October, the Yankees had fashioned another World Series sweep, brushing aside the St. Louis Cardinals, prompting a raucous, sudsy, well-fed trip back to New York aboard the Yankee Special—thanks to a clothes basket full of ribs Ruth had delivered to the train. He led a conga line of celebrants through the aisles, smashing straw hats in jubilation and separating gentlemen from their shirts. Jake Ruppert was relieved of his silk brocade nightshirt. "My, that Baby Ruth is a bad boy," the Colonel said.

Crowds gathered at midwestern railroad crossings and train stations to hail the victorious Yankees. This was customary for Ruth, whose "progress through the countryside was like that of a president or a king," Frank Graham wrote. "And the Babe never failed them. He would leave his dinner or a card game, even get up out of bed, to go out on the platform and greet his admirers and shake the hands stretched up to him."

On this trip, Ruth made sure to put in a good word for Governor Al Smith, who had opposed Prohibition, was an early supporter of Sunday baseball, and was waiting for the Babe in his suite at the Biltmore Hotel upon his return to New York.

He stayed just long enough for the former governor to appoint him "the boss of the Youth of America." Walsh had planned a reprise of the 1927 barnstorming tour, which was to begin at Dexter Park three days later, before heading to upstate New York. An AP reporter reached Ruth in Watertown, New York, to inform him of the death of Jack Dunn, the owner and manager of the Baltimore Orioles, who had ransomed young George Ruth from St. Mary's Industrial School.

Ruth called him "a fine fellow and a good sportsman." He did not attend the funeral.

By January, he was back to offering opinions on things he knew about, expressing his disdain for a proposal to add a tenth hitter to the batting order to hit for the pitcher. He said it would take all the strategy out of the game.

On Saturday night, January 12, he attended a party at the Westchester home of his teammate Joe Dugan, where some time before midnight he received a telephone call informing him about Helen's death. Ruth was on a train to Boston by 1:15 A.M.

Christy Walsh was in Portland, Oregon, at the Hotel Benson, arranging syndicate bookings for the coming season, when he received a telegram from his wife, Mada, at 5:45 P.M. on January 13: "NEWSPAPERS TRYING TO LOCATE YOU OR BABE."

Wires from the *New York Daily News* and the *New York American* followed in short order.

RE DEATH OF MRS BABE RUTH REPORTS HERE THAT SHE AND BABE WERE SECRETLY DIVORCED THREE YEARS AGO AND SHE MARRIED DR E H KINDER DENTIST SECRETLY PLEASE WIRE COLLECT

IMMEDIATELY WHETHER ANY TRUTH
TO THESE REPORTS.

Editors at the *American*, trading on their relationship as longtime subscribers to Ruth's column, asked
for "any private information or angles on the case."

In the nine years Walsh had managed Ruth's career, assuming responsibility for his financial life and
his public image, nothing approached the magnitude
of Helen's death as a challenge to his public relations
skills. And none of the previous crises—not Dolores
Dixon's paternity suit, not the bellyache heard round
the world—implicated him personally and legally as
this did.

The timing was awful: to be three thousand miles
away and three time zones behind the news was a
nightmare. Unable to reach Ruth by telephone and un-
sure of all the facts, Walsh released a carefully crafted
statement, a primer in the practice of damage control
intended, in modern parlance, to "get out ahead" of the
story he knew was coming. He extolled Helen's virtues
as a wife and mother, calling her "a grand little woman."
It was a masterpiece of modern spin, preempting the
bad news he knew would soon appear in print with just
enough of the truth that no one could accuse him of

lying. But his statement was also brazenly misleading in its portrait of the Ruths' marriage.

"Despite the unconfirmed inferences printed today I can positively say Babe and his wife were not divorced. Both of them were in my New York office with me three weeks ago. We were going over personal and business matters and she was calling him 'Hon' and 'George' just as she had for years at Yankee Stadium. . . .

"I have just received a wire saying he and his wife were going next week to visit his sister in Baltimore and to spend several days there at St. Mary's Industrial School, where he got his start in life."

He was far less circumspect in an undated letter to Ruth, written after speaking with Claire Hodgson.

> *Be careful Babe. Be careful what you say and what you do. In spite of the horrible tragedy everything will work out right if you are CAREFUL in what you say and do.*
>
> *You have many well-meaning friends but remember few if any of them are properly equipped in experience and complete understanding of circumstances to guide you properly. I am asking Bihler to go to Boston so he can help you in my absence. Joe understands everything as well as I do*

and realizes fully just what might happen if you do certain things or fail to do them.

In spite of whatever may have happened in recent years Helen was your loyal supporter to the last. I know she loved you deeply Babe from many conversations I had with her and I know that your heart is very, very heavy today. You must bring Dorothy closer to you now and I am sure everything is going to work out right.

He authorized the Bank of Manhattan to provide $15,000 cash from Ruth's emergency fund to cover expenses and ordered assistant Joe Bihler to take the next train to Boston. Bihler wired Walsh to say that Ruth had told him his help wasn't needed. "Said he is getting good advice."

A fraught and sleepless Ruth was met at the Back Bay train station by Arthur J. Crowley, the son of Boston's superintendent of police, Michael H. Crowley, and a battalion of reporters. A sensational account of the meeting was carried by the Universal Service, a Hearst-owned news agency that served its morning papers. "Where is my baby? Where is my little girl, Arthur? I have got to see her. It isn't true, Arthur. It can't be true."

Crowley escorted Ruth to his usual suite at the Hotel

Brunswick, room 574, the only constant in a surreal return to the city where as a young man he first fell in love.

Though police had enough information by late Saturday night to corroborate Helen's identity, the story did not hit the papers until Monday morning. The time of her death, the delay in making the identification, and the undeveloped state of broadcast news gave Ruth time to compose himself and to approve a dignified statement composed by his lawyer that he delivered to a waiting horde of newsmen.

The four-sentence statement scribbled on hotel stationery acknowledged the separation that had been in effect since 1925. "My wife and I had not lived together for the last three years. During that time, I have seldom met her. I've done all that I can to comply with her wishes. Her death is a great shock to me."

That morning police brought two of Helen's sisters to Watertown to identify her body. "Leave the talking to the Big Boy," they said, after making the identification.

Ruth had no comment.

On orders of the Middlesex County district attorney, the funeral of the woman known as Helen Kinder was canceled just hours before it was to begin, but not soon enough to prevent the erroneous death certificate from being published on the front pages of newspapers across the country. (It also gave January 12 as the date of her death.)

A full investigation worthy of the wife of the King of Clout was opened. A second autopsy was ordered, which was complicated given that her body had already been embalmed. The undertakers brought her back to the medical examiner's office. The contents of her stomach were sent to Harvard Medical School to be examined for traces of drugs and poison.

IV

Just as Walsh feared and anticipated, the story of Helen's death proved incendiary. Rumor kindled by accusation and recrimination, fanned by competitive zeal, and fed by animus and grief burst into a conflagration of competing headlines, beginning with Monday morning's *New York Daily News*: "Mrs. Babe Ruth Dies in Love Nest Fire."

In the anguished four-day pause, while city and state fire marshals checked and rechecked the wiring at 47 Quincy Street and medical examiners checked and rechecked the cause of death, there was no end to speculation. The stories grew only more heated.

Twelve days after rounding the bases for the sixtieth time in 1927—bellowing, "Sixty! Count 'em, sixty. Let's see some other sonofabitch do that!"—and four days after carrying the New York Yankees to a World Series triumph, Babe Ruth set out for a victory lap across the American heartland with Lou Gehrig in tow. Wherever he went, he carried with him a uniquely American sense of prowess and possibility. After the crash of 1929, he carried a whole country's sense of itself on his back.

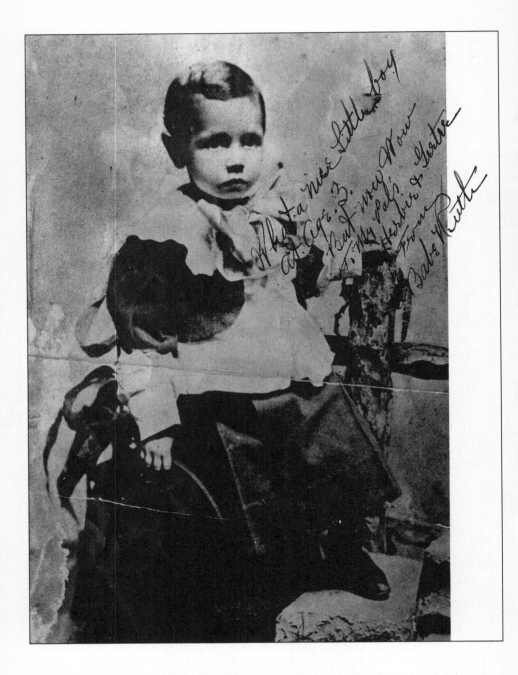

Autographing a portrait of himself as a child for friends, he wrote: "What a nice Little boy at. Age. 3. But now Wow"—flouting the rules of grammar and punctuation the way he flouted expectation and authority. But there was sadness, even at age three, in his downcast expression that no frilly collar could disguise. The professional portrait sitting gives the lie to the notion that he was an impoverished waif of the Baltimore waterfront.

THE ✦ NEWS

FINAL EDITION

NEW YORK'S PICTURE NEWSPAPER

Vol. 2. No. 21.   20 Pages   Daily Except Sunday.   New York, Tuesday, July 20, 1920.   •   2 Cents

"COLOSSUS OF SWAT"

Page 2

GEORGE "BABE" RUTH, THE BIGGEST MAN IN BASEBALL

At Polo Grounds yesterday "Babe" Ruth, left fielder for the Yankees, knocked two home runs off Dick Kerr, in the second game with the Chicago White Sox, then smashing his own and the world's records and bringing his total for the season up to thirty-one. Both hits went into the right field bleachers.

The back page was not created for Ruth, but it was created just in time for him, debuting in America's first tabloid in November 1919. He demanded space. On July 20, 1920, the day after he broke his 1919 record of twenty-nine home runs, the *Daily News* reported: "Twenty-eight thousand fans leap up screaming as Chicago pitcher Dick Kerr gives up Babe Ruth's 30th home run. Ninth inning. Strike one. Strike two. Kerr fires again, and into the bleachers goes Babe's 31st. Pandemonium. Bedlam."

If the twenties roared, it was because of newer, louder, faster ways of knowing. On September 26, 1921, Charles Farbizo's carrier pigeon was still the fastest way to update anxious fans on the East Side of New York about the Yankee game at the Polo Grounds. The pigeons would soon be an anachronism. Six weeks earlier, radio pioneer Harold Arlin called the first major league game broadcast on radio from Pittsburgh on station KDKA. A year later, the World Series was carried by WJZ in New York. By 1927, two rival radio networks, NBC and CBS, broadcast the Series from coast to coast.

Ray McNamara, automotive expert and enthusiast, was one of sports agent Christy Walsh's first clients. His "More Miles per Car" column identified him as having "Motored Farther Than Any Man in the World." This early example of cross-promotion—which played on Ruth's need for driving tips—reveals Walsh's instinct for marketing and public relations.

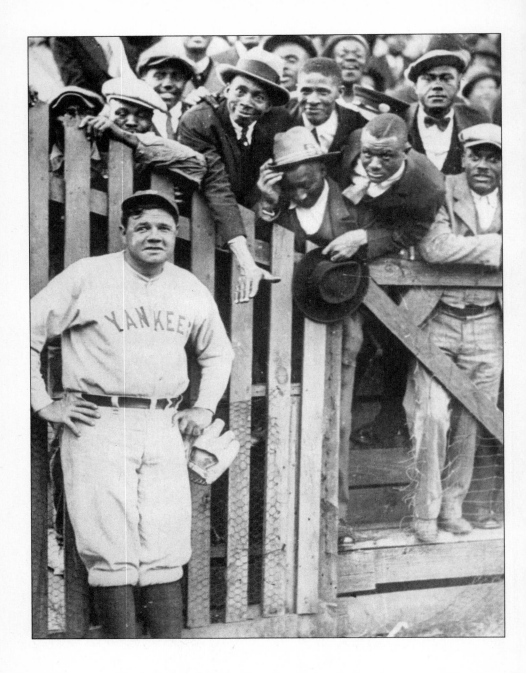

Throughout his career, Ruth contended with rumors about his racial makeup, which were embraced by many in the African American community, where he was hailed for barnstorming against Negro Leaguers, for sharing a chaw of tobacco with them, and for praising "their sparkling brilliancy on the field." When the Yankees re-signed him in 1932, albeit at a reduced salary, New York's *Amsterdam News* reported: "Harlem Is Breathing Easier Tonight."

Ruth's first, early marriage to Helen Woodford, a year after he left St. Mary's Industrial School, would end in discord and tragedy, leaving Dorothy, seen here with her parents at Home Plate Farm in Sudbury, uncertain about her parentage. But it was also an act of conformity by a man hoping for stability and normalcy in the wake of twelve years of institutional life.

While on a vaudeville tour in January 1927, San Diego sportsman and friend Carl Klindt (far left) arranged an outing on the water with local angling columnists "Doc" Gottesburen and Max Miller (far right). Sportswriters and company executives routinely found reason to entertain the Big Fella as a means of generating copy or good public relations for themselves.

(DEBBY GUMB)

At the end of his barnstorming and vaudeville tour in the winter of 1926–27, Ruth prepared for the coming season by taking his ease on the beach at the Hotel del Coronado. Here Ruth is seen doing something he rarely did: sitting still. He appears to be asleep but it's possible he was playing possum.

(AUTHOR'S PRIVATE COLLECTION)

Appreciation to Matt Gallagher for doing the best ballyhoo on our tour 1927

Babe Ruth

Lou Gehrig   *Christy Walsh*

In advance of the mother of all barnstorming tours, agent Christy Walsh (center) orchestrated a photo shoot at Yankee Stadium to publicize the upcoming "Symphony of Swat." He also arranged for smaller, pre-signed photos of Babe and Lou to be handed out at ballparks, banquets, train stations, and hotels. Wherever they went, ballyhoo followed.

LOU, BABE &
LADY AMCO.

"A Coupla Babes": that's how Ruth and his namesake, Lady Amco of Norfolk, the Babe Ruth of Layers, were described in hundreds of papers across the country. Their much-publicized meeting took place at the American Milling Company henhouse, the site of Lady Babe's triumph in the National Egg Layers' Association's annual competition. Her record-smashing total of 173 eggs in as many days was the envy of all, including Ruth, who said, "Gosh, I wish I could do as well."

In 1930, the new family Ruth created with his second wife, Claire Hodgson, became legal. On February 2, the Supreme Court of the City of New York granted an order of adoption, making nine-year-old Dorothy (second from right), the little girl Ruth had called his daughter since 1922, his legal offspring. On October 30, he adopted Claire's daughter, Julia (far left), and Claire adopted Dorothy. When they sat for this family portrait in November, they looked much happier than they had in the newspaper photos taken during the ceremony.

Thanks to his father's connections, Jack "Whitey" Stuart was Babe Ruth's batboy at Recreation Park in San Francisco on October 22–23, 1927. Ruth's hands were almost as big as Jack's head. "Looming" is how he would describe the Babe to his daughter: "a big, looming guy." When Stuart died, he was buried with the jersey he had worn for the occasion.

(CAROLE STUART TOLLEFSON)

A month after he retired in June 1935, "Admiral Ruth" appeared in Napoleonic-era military garb at the Westchester Country Club for the annual July 4 society softball game. Never was his dependence on baseball more clear than in the days after his career ended. "I'm the Admiral of the Swiss Navy," he proclaimed. Brandishing a sword for Paramount Newsreel cameras and club members sitting in lawn chairs beside a makeshift baseball diamond, he threatened to cut a ball in half before the game between teams of bachelors and husbands. While Ruth held out hope for a managing position, organized baseball would never find a place for him.

Babe Ruth celebrated his fifty-third and last birthday a day late, as he always had, on February 7, 1948, the day his mother claimed he was born. Having spent much of the winter in the hospital, he told a friend, "I haven't much further to go but I'm not going to die in here. I'm going to get out and have some fun first." He shared his birthday cake with two five-year-old boys in Florida.

Babe returned to the House That Ruth Built for a last goodbye on June 13, 1948. He had to use Bob Feller's bat, loaned to him by Eddie Robinson of the Cleveland Indians, to climb the dugout steps, gripping the shaft with both hands. He took a few feeble swings for photographers, then saluted the crowd—50,000 would-be residents of Ruthville—who had come to say farewell.

On Monday, Helen's brother Thomas, a former Boston police officer, charged foul play. "What is there to prove the house wasn't fired? What is there to prove that she wasn't murdered?"

Another Woodford brother, William, a New York attorney and former Boston city alderman, tearfully told reporters, "Helen was a good girl but she was secretive. For a long time my mother and sisters wondered what was the matter with her. But now I guess I have the key to those words she said to me: 'I have found a doctor who will give me opium tablets.'"

Press-box scuttlebutt concurred. "The boys in Boston all said Helen was with the doctor for the drugs," Marshall Hunt of the *Daily News* said later. "He could give her prescriptions."

Edward Kinder's brother insisted to the press that the couple had married two years earlier in Montreal. And the Universal Service, continuing its sensational coverage, distributed a florid dispatch from the scene of the fire. "On the front lawn today, near the ruined walls of the pretty house, among other debris from the fire, lay a badly burned caracul coat of expensive make. It bore the label of one of Boston's leading establishments and neighbors identified it as belonging to Mrs. Kinder.

"On the ground nearby, where it fell from the pocket

of the coat were the rosary beads that belonged to Mrs. Ruth. A charred doll and some other playthings of Dorothy's were scattered about, where they fell when thrown from a window by some one during the fire."

The neighbors expressed shock at the deception perpetrated in their midst and responded with neighborly pique. "Mrs. Kinder, as I knew her, was a short, good-looking but somewhat coarse woman, apparently given to a generous use of cosmetics," noted Mrs. Bichard. "She was always nicely dressed."

And then Edward Kinder turned himself in to Watertown police. During four hours of questioning, he told police that no, he and Helen had never been married and he had never said they had been—nor did he remember telling the medical examiner that Helen was his wife. No, he hadn't gone to New York. He had walked the streets of Boston fearful of the story becoming public and spent Sunday in seclusion at his father's suggestion. Yes, the Babe knew full well where his wife was staying. She had come to work for him as a housekeeper two years earlier.

Watertown's chief of police, John F. Milmore, pronounced himself satisfied with the doctor's account of events and moral conduct. Kinder promptly dropped from public view.

The pressure on Ruth to respond to the press of

events mounted throughout the day. Thanks to the good advice of counsel and his own innate sense of decency, he had maintained a degree of dignity that had eluded virtually everyone else connected to the tragedy. He had managed it largely by remaining quiet and by remaining out of sight. Now he invited twenty reporters to his suite in the Brunswick. "I'm in a hell of a fix boys," he said, his voice breaking. "This thing has licked me. The shock has been terrible. I hold nothing against my wife. She was the victim of circumstances. I still love her. I have fine memories of her."

Then, gulping for air and composure: "What I'm going to say I can say in a very few words. Please leave my wife alone. Let her stay dead."

No one, including her family, would let Helen be.

MRS. RUTH MURDERED,
HER MOTHER DECLARES
BALL PLAYER REFUSED DEMAND FOR $100,000
WITH CONTEMPLATED RENO DIVORCE
—*PALM BEACH POST*, JANUARY 15

The story, another courtesy of the Universal Service, detailed a meeting in Christy Walsh's New York office in December, attended by Helen and her youngest sister, Nora, at which Babe told her he wanted a divorce so that he could marry Claire Hodgson. Except for the resurrection of the 1925 front-page photograph by some newspapers around the country, Claire had managed to stay out of sight. And Ruth, in his mourning clothes and somber silence, had cut a sympathetic figure while Helen's reputation had been torched—as a married woman living with another man, her funeral service could not be conducted in a Catholic Church.

Nora had lived with Babe and Helen at the Ansonia in the early years of their marriage and had gotten a taste of their high life. Babe introduced her to Flo Ziegfeld and suggested she might like to join the Follies. She declined, according to her daughters, because she didn't want to run around in short skirts.

Sitting in the family parlor with her mother, waiting for the Boston medical examiner to complete his autopsy and issue a death certificate in Helen's real name, Nora told reporters about accompanying her sister on subsequent trips to New York to see the Babe play ball and getting an eyeful of Claire as well. "She was popular with the players from the way she was greeted by most of them," Nora said. "Helen pointed her out to me and remarked, rather grimly, 'That's Claire.'"

Helen had been coached by her attorney and had a ready reply when Babe informed her that he wanted a divorce, so he could give Claire's daughter, Julia, a last name, Nora said, re-creating the conversation between Helen and Babe in Walsh's office for the Universal Service reporter.

Well, Helen said to him—and Christy Walsh will tell you this is so:

"All right, I'll go to Reno and get a divorce quietly so your reputation in baseball won't be ruined but you've got to pay my expenses out there and give me one hundred thousand dollars."

And 'Babe' told her to go to hell, that he had given her enough money already.

Mrs. William Woodford, 60-year old mother of the dead woman, said she was familiar with this story and that it was all true.

"So, you see, my daughter didn't marry Dr. Kinder."

And, she added, climactically, with a fierce gleam in her ordinarily faded eyes:

"Helen never died by accident. She was done to death."

Nora also told the reporter that Ruth had chased Helen around the Sudbury farm with a loaded shotgun.

The attorney retained by the Woodfords immediately issued a statement saying that Nora was not authorized to speak on behalf of the family.

Asked to respond, Ruth again exercised unaccustomed understatement. "It isn't true. That's all I have to say about the charges at the present time."

In the same story, also carried by the *St. Louis Post-Dispatch*, Edward Kinder acknowledged that he and Helen had lived together as man and wife "off and on for almost two years."

On Wednesday, Helen's brother William threatened "red hot exposures" after Helen's funeral and declared the family's intention to fight him for custody of Dorothy.

Finally, Ruth broke his silence, his composure cracking: "Never! I'll stand for almost anything but that. You can never have Dorothy."

Meanwhile, the International News Service reported, "The child played on the snow-covered slope on the grounds of the Academy of the Assumption at Wellesley Hills, cheeks rosy and eyes twinkling."

Late in the day, the second medical examiner released his findings: no poison, no drugs, no stab wounds, no unexplained bruise on her scalp, no evidence of foul play of any kind. Helen's body was released to her family for burial.

Their claims and threats evaporated, but not their enmity and suspicion. Thomas Woodford's daughter, Jean Beswick, said her father refused to speak about Babe Ruth ever again except to say that he was a bum. "He hated him," she said.

Two of Nora's daughters, Patricia Grace and Kathy Honey, claimed that Helen lived in fear of the Babe. "When she was in a department store with my aunt Helen—she might have been 23 years old—my aunt Helen all of a sudden said, 'C'mon, quick, we gotta go, we gotta leave, we gotta leave,'" Grace said. "They went out the back way.

"Aunt Helen was in fear for her life because Babe Ruth wanted a divorce because he was carrying on with women. Of course, we were a Catholic family and she would not divorce. He was trying to get rid of her. He had these hoodlums or what have you. Those are the stories my mother told me."

Ruth arrived at the Woodford residence on West Fourth Street in the tangled South End of Boston near midnight on Wednesday, January 16, in impressive company: Police Superintendent Crowley, his son Arthur, and attorney John Feeney. The show of strength may not have been intended as such but would prove necessary. Gray-ribboned mourning crepe draped the doorway where a guard stood in the cold. "A crowd of the curious"—a new feature of the American century—filled the side streets and front stoops of Southie.

Helen's brother Thomas opened the door to the Babe and showed him to the parlor, which was overflowing with floral tributes from Yankee management and players. Nora greeted her brother-in-law with the fury of a biblical curse. "I'm sure you'll suffer more than Helen."

Petite in life, eviscerated in death, twice embalmed, and laid out in the massive bronze casket Ruth had purchased—said in press reports to have cost $1,000 or perhaps even $10,000—Helen was overwhelmed by him even in repose. He knelt at her side, clutching the coffin rail with one hand and a set of rosary beads with the other, staring into her face for a full five minutes. Moaning, sobbing, and sweating, he called her name, "Oh, oh, oh, oh, Helen."

What was it he saw in her stilled features that shook him so convulsively? Was he thinking about the sordid end of his parents' marriage? His mother's death in 1912, when she was thirty-two, just a year older than Helen?

The dashed hope for something better, something solid, had prompted their whirlwind courtship and the mad dash to the altar in the fall of 1914. The premature end of Helen's life and of their life together also signified the end of the George she knew when he was young enough to require his father's permission to marry.

He collapsed by her coffin when he tried to stand. Arthur and Michael Crowley helped him to his feet. John Feeney whispered in his ear that all the arrangements for the funeral had been made.

"What funeral?" the Babe said.

V

On the day of the fire that claimed Helen Ruth's life, Jack Frederick drove to the town of Colusa, twenty-five miles west of Marysville, where Tub Perry had accepted a job with Pacific Gas & Electric, in hopes of reclaiming the Marysville Giants pitching ace for the 1929 season. He was out of luck. Perry would lead the Colusa Prune Pickers to the 1929 Sacramento Valley League championship with a 16-2 record—and a streak of twelve straight wins. No one in league history had ever pitched better, and it earned Tub another shot with the San Francisco Seals, the team he had spurned a year earlier.

He was summoned to pitch their last game of the season in Sacramento on October 4. Tub held the Senators to five hits. "You have a million-dollar arm but need more experience," Seals manager Nick Williams told him. "We need left-handed pitchers and we need you. We will take care of the money side of it."

Lefty Gomez, an old friend from the Valley Peach League, was being scouted by the Yankees, who also liked what they saw in Tub, according to family lore. "That is when the Yankees asked him to go to New York," Tub's grandson Steve Perry said.

Tub said no. San Francisco was as far as he would go. If that far.

When spring training rolled around in 1930, Perry required "a special bodyguard in the person of Eddie 'Fat' Aflinso to personally guide him to the city," Abe Kemp wrote in the *San Francisco Examiner.* "Perry had heard so much about the pitfalls of a wicked city for innocent boys that he demanded to be chaperoned—and was. The Perry's [*sic*], which include the missus and the little one, called on Nick Williams upon his arrival and had to be reassured that good-looking pitchers—good looking in the sense of ability—do not have to fear the city traffic cops."

Manager Williams noted that Perry had added to his frame since he was first signed in the summer of 1927. "He's six feet two, weighs 210 pounds and is three feet wide."

Williams named him the starting pitcher for a pre-season game against the Prune Pickers on March 30, 1930—Tub Perry Day in Colusa. His hometown gave him a gold watch. The *San Francisco Call* declared him "a fine major league prospect."

But he wasn't. The gold watch proved to be both the highlight of his professional career and the signifier that it traditionally is—a sign that it was time to retire. He didn't pitch much that season and he didn't pitch well. The Seals decided to try him in the outfield in 1931 where, the San Francisco papers reported, "he moved with all the grace of an elephant."

He went home and pitched for the Prune Pickers in 1932 and for the Marysville Giants in 1933, the year his daughter Joanne was born. There were more kids to feed, meters to read, ducks to hunt, one-arm chin-ups to count, and one-hundred-pound sacks of beans to hoist late into the night after his day job was done. But he never quit pitching—he pitched until he was fifty-five years old. He picked off Jackie Robinson when he came through town on a fifties barnstorming tour, a quarter of a century after he faced down the Great Bambino.

On hot Sacramento Valley summer nights, when Joanne Perry Raub was growing up, she and her dad would lie on the cool kitchen floor and listen to the Senators' games on the radio with a breeze blowing through a squirrel cage rigged up as an air conditioner. "The rest of the family—some of them went outside and slept on the grass; some got in bed and suffered," Raub said. "But we stayed out there and listened to the ball game." Lying there in the cool, he told her about the day he pitched to Babe Ruth, the day he refused to cater to artifice. He said he didn't much like the Babe, though he never did say why. He thought Lou Gehrig was a fine fellow.

It remains a matter of considerable civic pride in a town where there isn't much left to be proud of—except for the roadside sign that still describes Marysville as the "Gateway to the Gold Fields"—that Babe Ruth didn't get anywhere with Tub Perry.

Tub talked about it until the day he died. "And we never got tired of hearing about it, either," Raub said.

He died in June 1971, not quite six months after his wife, Alice. The Marysville Little League Field was dedicated to him on April 16, 1977.

VI

On the morning Helen Ruth was buried in Section 10 of the old Calvary Cemetery in Mattapan, the Watertown city fire inspector visited West Junior High School and

Parochial Senior High School to warn students about the dangers of overloaded electrical wiring; he would visit East Junior High school the next day.

At the gravesite, mourners mingled with police officers, onlookers, and snowflakes; neither Edward Kinder nor Dorothy Helen Ruth was among them. The service was brief and punctuated by the wails of Helen's sisters. Head bowed, Ruth stood arm in arm with her mother, a family united only in grief.

Helen was buried atop a slight rise, just across the road from the stonecutters who later chiseled the name HELEN (WOODFORD) RUTH into a Swedish granite headstone the color of butterscotch. Her brother William was buried beside her ten years later.

The deed to the grave remains in the name of the purchaser, George Herman Ruth, as it will in perpetuity. "He was a man on fire," said cemetery foreman Bill Cuddihy, pointing the way to her final resting place one fine summer day in 2016. "You can use that."

Although her grave is rarely visited, she still receives birthday cards and digital bouquets—182 of them as of April 2018—on her page at the modern celebrity website findagrave.com, which also rates the degree of fame of the deceased. Mary Ellen (Woodford) Ruth currently ranks 3.6 on a scale of 5.

On the afternoon of the funeral, the Babe slept. Arthur Crowley issued a statement on his behalf, telling reporters that "the future of little Dorothy is in the hands of a competent attorney."

The next day, before leaving for New York, Ruth admitted, "This week has been a living hell for me—absolutely torture," he said. The Universal News service dispatch went on to describe the "one bright spot, the only one of his Boston visit," a trip to the Academy of the Assumption in Wellesley "to arrange for the future of Dorothy. He was greeted by a crowd of Academy boys with glad cries of 'Hello, Babe.' It brought a smile to his lips."

He did not take Dorothy with him to New York. Nor, apparently, did he tell her Helen was dead.

A week later, Dorothy recounted in her memoir, she was awakened in the middle of the night by two nuns who escorted her to the New York Foundling Hospital on the East Side of Manhattan. There she was delivered into the care of a hospital employee named Miss Dooley, who took her to live in Brooklyn, where she was to stay until her father came for her some months later. Miss Dooley told her that Helen had gone to heaven.

Two weeks after Helen's death, on January 29, Dorothy's father sneaked out of New York City, leaving for Florida several weeks in advance of spring training, in hopes of playing some golf and getting away from it all. But there was no getting away from it. That morning, details of Helen's will, which had been filed in probate court, were made public. She had left the bulk of her purported $50,000 estate to her "beloved charge and ward, Dorothy Helen Ruth, at one time known as Marie Harrington." (This was the name Miss Dooley told Dorothy she was to use while she lived in Brooklyn.)

The posthumous acknowledgment that Dorothy was not Helen's biological daughter opened the door to contention, speculation, and grievance, and set in motion another cascade of headlines and revelations, claims and counterclaims, that would result in a lifetime of heartache and uncertainty for Dorothy Helen Ruth.

In her will, Helen left five dollars to each of her brothers and sisters as well as her estranged husband. The news accounts listed among her assets "a cause for action for $13,000 against a resident of New York City"—presumably Babe Ruth, which was accurate although the figure was far too low.

Judson Hannigan, the Woodfords' attorney, immediately threatened to contest the will, which he hadn't read, noting that it was strange that Helen would "slight her family."

The family's attempt to break the will would prove unsuccessful. But within a week another interested party stepped forward, filing suit in New York State Supreme Court, claiming that Dorothy was born to a murderess serving twenty years at the Auburn state prison. The lawsuit was dismissed but the warden felt compelled to deny the allegation.

All of this proved too much for Helen's sister, Johanna McCarthy, who vented to the Associated Press: "Little Dorothy is the real daughter of Babe Ruth. My sister carried his secret to her grave, a brave heroine because she wanted to protect Babe and never let his friends or other members of our family know the truth.

"Mrs. Ruth was the child's foster mother. Let him tell who the mother is if he cares to do so. The mystery about Dorothy has gone far enough, and now that she is accused of being born of criminal parents we must correct this impression that Dorothy will not be stigmatized."

Which was curious, as it contradicted their attorney's written statement of two weeks earlier stating that Dorothy was neither the adopted nor biological daughter of Helen and Babe.

Walsh wrote from the West Coast, urging Ruth to make arrangements to "bring Dorothy closer." But her fate was not the most pressing issue in Walsh's view, as evidenced by a January 24 letter to Ruth he considered so sensitive he would not allow his lawyer to keep a copy of it. The subject was the December meeting in his office that Nora had attended. His letter, which does not mention divorce or a demand for $100,000, casts the financial conversation in a different context—Ruth's tardiness in meeting the terms of the 1925 separation agreement. The final installment of the promised $100,000—$25,000—had been due in October. He hadn't paid it. He had been chronically late in making the payments while building up his trust fund at the Bank of Manhattan. At the meeting, Ruth apparently gave Walsh a check to make up what he owed, as Walsh noted in his letter:

Dear Babe:

After the first shock of the terrible news from Boston the first thing I thought of was the $31,000 you gave me for Helen before I left New York. I certainly hope now that you save that entire amount and I would like to turn it over to you at once. But Babe the whole affair is so mixed up I want to be careful. I will most assuredly protect your interests as you know I have always done—but I must also protect my own interests.

As far as I'm concerned the money is yours.

But my opinion or your opinion in a time like this must take second place to the opinion at the courts. Although everything seems now to be amicably settled—between you and Helen's parents—still some of them showed themselves pretty nasty the first day or two after her death. And there is no telling what they might try to do regarding this $31,000.

They knew about your agreement with her and her sister Nora was a witness in my office when you handed me that check.

If I pay it to you now without an official order from some authorized court they might sue me. Or you. Or both of us. Of course, as long as you are alive and have the money it would be okay. But if you should die (like Rickard or anyone else) or for any other reason didn't have the 31,000 then her relatives could sue and COLLECT from me.

Even at the time I hesitated taking the money. I held the check several days before accepting and depositing same—because I disliked the responsibility of such a position. My only reason for going ahead was my friendship for both yourself and Helen.

Apparently, Walsh wanted a court order to determine whether the separation agreement was still binding and whether the money belonged to Helen's estate or to Ruth. But mostly he wanted to be rid of it. In closing, he again apologized for his absence during the period of shock and publicity and encouraged Ruth to look "to the bright side of the entire situation and the future."

Little wonder he didn't want anyone to see the letter.

VII

George Nicholau and the other children of Marysville who had marched to the old Third Street ballpark in supervised formation broke ranks and chased Ruth and Gehrig's sedan all the way back to the Hotel Marysville. As promised, the game had gone the full nine innings, unlike in bigger cities that had to settle for less. The municipal holiday declared by the town's mayor in advance of the game had lasted less than two hours.

Ruth and Gehrig set off by car for Sacramento, where they arrived to great huzzahs given their highly publicized promise to forfeit a guarantee in support of the Catholic Orphanage Building Fund. Somehow by the end of the grueling two-city doubleheader, the *Sacramento Union* reported, they had pocketed $1,000 in Marysville and $2,300 in Sacramento. Ruth hit three home runs. "I guess I did pretty good for the shape I'm in," Ruth said. "I ought to be in the hospital instead of on the ball field."

Ruth also told reporters, "I would not be in uniform if Dr. Rattray had not taken care of me"—an endorsement Rattray would use to promote his practice, bragging that he made $85,000 in seventeen days as the result. Rattray also claimed that he saw indications of Gehrig's future disease in 1927 and when he saw him again two years later.

In its morning recap of the biggest day in Marysville's history since the first riverboat steamed up the river carrying gold prospectors, the *Appeal-Democrat* described Ruth's weariness and his eagerness for the barnstorming tour to be over. "Ruth's wife and baby are waiting for him in New York, where he hopes to spend a quiet and peaceful winter after the long grind of the American League season, the World Series, and his tour of the country."

Chapter 15
October 26 / San Jose

**KIDDIES REIGN WHEN BABE HIT HOME
RUN OVER FENCE IN NINTH**

—SAN JOSE MERCURY HERALD

GIRLS WHO DROVE RUTH GOT THRILL

—SAN JOSE NEWS

I

Smoke began to fill the grandstand behind home plate just before game time. The swells in the important seats were just getting settled in them when it became apparent that it was important to leave them. Pop Warner, the Stanford coach, who was Walsh's guest and client, was there along with teammate Ping Bodie, umpire "Beans" Reardon, and G. Logan Payne, publisher of the *San Jose News*, the host and sponsor of the "King Ruth and the Crown Prince of Swatonia."

Sodality Park was an old wooden bandbox, built in 1908. It looked and felt much like other amateur ballparks of the era except that it was set among fruit orchards and canneries on land that had been donated by the men's Sodality of St. Joseph's Church. "A little burg in the prune trees," was how the Babe described the city of sixty thousand when Payne collected Ruth and Gehrig at the train station that afternoon.

They had toured the newspaper, posing in front of a *San Jose News* truck, and addressed the monthly luncheon of the Rotary and Lions Club, with Ruth telling the membership, "If we don't make good this afternoon we won't be able to look at the kiddies at all. We'll get out of town in 20 minutes. If we sock them a mile, though, we may want to hang around for an hour or so."

Then he hustled off to the newly opened Theodore Roosevelt Junior High School to warn students about the evils of smoking, arriving at Sodality Park for Dan O'Leary's speed-walking exhibition just in time to see the puffs of smoke wafting from the stands behind home plate courtesy of four boys armed with a pocketful of matches and a handful of wet grass.

Payne had set the admission price for all children under the age of fourteen at thirty-five cents—as long as they brought a note from their parents saying they were allowed to skip school that day. But that was still too rich for the Cirone brothers—Dom, Joe, Nuncie, and Bennie—who grew up in a two-room shack with a dirt floor on Bird Avenue in the Palm Haven subdivision abutting the park. Like most of the Italian immigrants who lived in the neighborhood, their parents worked in the fields picking fruit processed in the California Packing Corporation cannery that stood right behind the right field fence. That was the reason for the misshapen field. The right field wall was indented like a can of prunes that had fallen off a truck.

Later, the Cirones would move south to the town of Campbell, now the home of eBay, where they farmed their own fruit trees. But upward mobility was still years away. Dom, the oldest of the Cirone brothers, hatched a plan that would allow them to join the paying idolaters.

"You guys go behind the outfield fence and dig a hole and I'll go underneath the grandstand and light a fire," he said. "To make sure it doesn't catch, I'll put wet grass on it."

While Ruth and Gehrig were fighting the wind blowing in from right field and failing to hit any of their customary batting practice home runs, Dom, the arsonist, shimmied through the hole his brothers dug, crawled under the grandstand, and lit a fire. Nothing big, mind you, just enough to smolder and scatter the gathering crowd.

In the smoke and commotion as officials ran to put out the fire, Joe, Nuncie, and Bennie joined their older brother, and the paying customers, in the covered stands behind home plate.

The game proceeded without incident until the fifth inning, when authorities proved no match for the youths of San Jose, who surged over fences onto the field, and "fondled" the major leaguers, halting play for half an hour, according to a prim dispatch in the *San Jose News.* Lefty O'Doul was in left field, having been summoned by the Babe for some companionship. O'Doul vaulted the outfield fence to escape the attentions of his many female admirers. The superintendent of schools put down the insurrection by threatening to end the game.

In the ninth inning, Luke Williams, managing the Larrupin' Lous, known locally as the team from Consolidated Laundry, summoned a junk-throwing, camellia-growing future police officer named Earl

"Duke" Perry from shortstop to face the Babe, who had so far managed only two singles against regular pitching and a lusty wind blowing in from right field.

Unlike Tub Perry the day before in Marysville, Duke Perry was happy to serve one up for mythology. Duke was a pretty fair ballplayer at Santa Clara College but no pitcher. He gave up a leadoff single, a triple to Mario "Speeder" Duino, a local boy who was scheduled to report to the San Francisco Seals in the spring, and then walked another Santa Clara boy, Tom Randazzo, a future city councilman, pitching around him to get to Babe Ruth. It was the greatest accomplishment of his father's baseball career, Tom Jr. said later.

Joe Pizzo, Ruth's batboy that day, brought the Babe his bat, which felt as heavy as a telephone pole.

Press-box wags claimed to see a wiggle in Duke's windup and a twinkle in his eye as he "shot the ball down the grove." In the aftermath, he was declared as much a hero as Ruth for giving the Babe a chance to gratify his fans. "I motioned to Ruth to indicate where he wanted the pitch," he told the *San Jose Mercury-News* in a 1959 retrospective. "He shouted out to me, 'Anywhere around the plate.' I threw the first pitch for a called strike on the outside corner. I remember remarking to the umpire that was a dangerous spot because Ruth was liable to belt it back and knock my legs off. The second pitch was low and inside. And he really connected."

As he did, the wind died.

And the ball soared and soared and soared over the truncated right field wall, over the Guadalupe Creek that flowed around the outfield, and in some accounts, over the cannery buildings. "Clearing the fence by at least 50 yards," the *Mercury-Herald* said, it "plunked against a little house a few feet west of the city limits sign."

Young enthusiasts intercepted the Babe between second and third and hoisted him high upon their shoulders. "Before I got to third, the kids swarmed out on the field and mobbed Ruth," Randazzo said. "He never did complete the circuit."

That wasn't the story the Cirone boys told their sons and daughters and nieces and nephews. The point wasn't what they saw; the point was that they saw it. So years later, when Uncle Bennie, a prune farmer all his life, drove three hundred miles north to Mount Shasta to collect mountain water, as he often did, and saw in a gift shop in Dunsmuir a photo of four little boys peeking out from behind the pillars of an old wooden bandbox during a barnstorming game, he was sure he recognized himself and his brothers.

Look at the black eye. That had to be his brother Joe. You could never say anything bad about Italians to Joe. *Look at the cold sore on his lip. The tilt of his head.*

"Where was this picture taken?" Bennie asked.

"Babe Ruth was in Dunsmuir," came the reply, "and this is where the picture was taken."

"Well, I've never been in Dunsmuir before. How could my picture be here?"

Bennie didn't press the point. But, upon his return home, he got a copy of the negative from the *San Jose Mercury-Herald* and made prints for Dom, a military attaché with the Army; Nuncie, a butcher; and Joe, a convivial barber turned building contractor, all of whom became convinced that they were the boys in the picture and that the picture had been taken at Sodality Field.

"Let me tell you about how I saw Babe Ruth," Joe told his children, two of whom, Richard and Joe Jr., were by then prominent pediatricians in town. "If you notice, most everybody's got seats except us four little guys in the front."

Local sports bars displayed their picture on the walls of their establishments. Richard and Joe hung it in their medical office and told the story in infinite iterations to generations of San Jose children who needed to hear that moxie can triumph over a dirt-floor start.

II

Babe Ruth had more power than he knew. He had the power to create a story that defied provable fact—the distinguishing characteristic of myth—a story transporting four poor sons of immigrant parents, boys so poor they wore kerosene wicks as neckties in a family portrait, to a baseball game they couldn't possibly have attended. He had the power to convince them that they saw themselves looking over his shoulder in grainy reproductions of the original image, their features eliding with each successive reprint.

The Dunsmuir photograph, as it is known in the Ruth oeuvre, was taken on October 22, 1924, by Sponagel & Hermann/Commercial Press Photographers of San Francisco, hired by Christy Walsh to document a game scheduled at the last minute at the City Ball Park in Dunsmuir, one of the few from that era still in use today.

What made the photo unusual and valuable, according to Robert Edwards Auctions, was its perspective. Taken from the vantage point of the pitcher, it is a folk-art tableau of small-town baseball in the not-so-roaring twenties. In the background, behind the Babe, batboys and players slouch against the slatted wooden backstop, a ramshackle affair; some of its unmatched, vertical boards are coming apart. Behind them, in the grandstand, and peering over either one of the catcher's shoulders, are two boys—one in overalls with slicked-back hair, and the other with a shiner nearly obscured by a thick forelock draping his brow—both gazing intently at the man with the interlocking NY on his cap and NEW YORK spanning the great vault of his chest. Walsh had the uniforms made to look like Yankee road jerseys.

By the time Ruth and Gehrig arrived in San Jose three years later, barnstorming Yankee players were prohibited from wearing uniforms that resembled the real thing, which is why Walsh commissioned the Spalding Company to produce a limited edition of Bustin' Babe and Larrupin' Lou regalia. When the Babe gallantly presented his Bustin' Babes cap to the sweet young thing employed as a pastry chef at the Carrillo Hotel in Santa Barbara the next day, he had no idea what a rich gift he was giving.

The cap would be sold by her grandson in 2008 for $131,450 and resold five years later for $155,000, according to Chris Ivy, director of sports auctions at Heritage Auctions. To date, it is the only personal item from the 1927 tour to reach the marketplace.

The Dunsmuir photograph took on a life of its own in the Cirone family and the world of sports marketing. Donated to the Helms Athletic Foundation (now known as the LA84 Foundation) by members of Christy Walsh's family, it was reprinted and misidentified by the *San Jose Mercury-News* in 1973.

So Bennie Cirone's confusion was understandable. The grandstands in Dunsmuir and San Jose looked a lot alike, except for the wooden boards in the backstops, which ran vertically in Dunsmuir and horizontally in San Jose. In 1994, at the height of the baseball trading card mania, the Ted Williams Trading Card Company produced a colorized version of the Dunsmuir photo, offering it as the premiere card in its '94 limited-edition series. The company also made a poster version, and put the image on that year's marketing brochure, which Tony Cirone spotted in a baseball card shop in a strip mall owned by his uncle Bennie. Uncle Bennie's tenant gave each of Joe Cirone's sons a copy of the poster.

"Everybody attaches something to him," said Richard, the oldest of Joe Cirone Sr.'s sons, looking at the photograph in the light of new and unwelcome information a reporter has just delivered. "They had that story and they attached that story to the picture. I guess I should take it down . . ."

Though he and his brother Joe have retired from practice, the photo is still hanging in the pediatric office now run by Joe's son Chris. "But . . . the kid had a black eye and a cold sore. And my dad said, 'That's me.'"

III

At some point in the trajectory of fame, real life becomes apocryphal. Home runs travel in perpetuity, drafting on a perpetually willing suspension of disbelief. The temporal facts of biography no longer matter because everyone knows a person who can hit sixty home runs will live forever. It's hard to say the exact moment when Babe Ruth passed over into that other realm, though September 30, 1927, is a good guess.

By the time he arrived in San Jose on the afternoon of October 26, 1927, he had become a "legend in his lifetime," a phrasing devised by the writer Giles Lytton to describe Florence Nightingale in 1918. No one asked what that felt like—or, if someone did, recorded his reply. No one asked if he knew what he meant to the hordes of boys who would pass him down in their DNA. Or what it meant to him. Those weren't questions for locker room confab in 1927. And besides, the inquiry would have been superfluous. All you had to do was look at him to see how he basked in the white glare of attention, inhaling the bloated roar of approval that drowned out unquiet memories of his own loud childhood.

Reflection was not his wont; that would have required sitting still. Introspection was not the fashion of the time. No one wrote elegies to absent parents in the Jazz Age. In fact, according to the U.S. poet laureate Robert Pinsky, none of the great poets of Western civilization touched upon the death of a parent until the self-indulgent sixties. Why would we expect more of the Babe, who had no time or instinct for rumination?

Ruth never said much about how he felt about his celebrity, though he did march himself unbidden into Red Grange's hotel suite before a 1926 football game at the Polo Grounds to offer advice: "Don't believe anything they write about you and don't pick up too many checks."

Of course, Grange was also getting advice from his agent C. C. "Cash and Carry" Pyle, who had signed him to a professional contract in 1925 and was doing for him and for French tennis star Suzanne Lenglen what Walsh had been doing for Ruth for years.

The best evidence of his feelings on the subject is photographic. Look at his smile and his body language as five thousand boys try to press themselves into a single frame outside a ballpark in Syracuse, New York. They stand shoulder to shoulder, filling the photographer's viewfinder with their exuberance, mouths agape, caps and grins of every variety tilted this way and that, gloves and hands saluting the camera in an expression of "see me" modernity. There's one little girl, held aloft on a pair of sturdy shoulders. And one mama's boy in the front row wearing an egregious beanie and a knotted tie, craning his neck to look back at the Babe, who stands—presumably, he was standing—gridlocked in a clot of joy, head and shoulders above them all, with a gobsmacked teenager draped about his shoulders like one of Claire's fur boas, wearing his fame as jauntily as his crooked bow tie and cockeyed straw boater.

There isn't a hint of claustrophobia in his lopsided grin. The Babe, who chafed at every constraint—who according to his daughter Julia couldn't stand to have his feet tucked beneath the bedcovers—felt safe inside the frame of fame.

This was who he was raised to be in the overcrowded dormitories at St. Mary's Industrial School, where 130 boys slept, bathed, dreamed, and survived puberty in a space designed to accommodate 90 of them. One reason he loved baseball as much as he did, teammate Waite Hoyt said, was that "it projected him into a certain limelight, which was commensurate with Babe's sense of well-being."

What nobody seemed to know was who he was—how he was—when there was no frame to fill. That was true in 1914 when Jesse Linthicum, a young reporter for the *Baltimore Sun*, observed this when he accompanied Jack Dunn to St. Mary's to sign George Ruth to pitch for the Orioles in 1914. "No one ever knew the Babe real well," Linthicum told Mike Gibbons of the Babe Ruth Birthplace and Museum in the 1990s. "As a matter of fact, he didn't know other people. He always seemed sort of bewildered as far as the other fella was concerned."

Hoyt, who influenced a succession of Ruth biographers through his correspondence with *Babe* author Robert Creamer, and through his rain-delay broadcasts while a play-by-play man for the Cincinnati Reds, as well as his brief 1948 memoir, *Babe Ruth as I Knew Him*, laid it out in several letters to Creamer over a period of years: "I am almost convinced YOU WILL NEVER learn the truth on Ruth. I roomed with [Joe] Dugan. He was a good friend of Babe's. But he will see Ruth in a different light than I did. Dugan's own opinion will be one in which Dugan revels in Ruth's crudities, and so on. While I can easily recognize all of this and admit it freely, and yet there was buried in Ruth humanitarianism beyond belief—and intelligence he was never given credit for, a childish desire to be over virile, living up to credits given for his home run power—and yet a need for intimate affection and respect, and a feverish desire to play baseball, perform, act and live a life he didn't and couldn't take time to understand. . . ."

The truth about him was unknown, Hoyt said, and may be unknowable. "The guy was an enigma even to those who knew him and played with him."

IV

On the evening in May 1923 that Ruth invited Claire Hodgson to dinner in his hotel suite in Washington, he told her he thought everyone hated him and that he pretty much shared their opinion, she wrote in *The Babe and I.* It wasn't the kind of evening, or conversation, she was expecting. She thought they were having a quiet dinner, instead she found Ruth holding court in an easy chair amid a pestilence of floozies and hangers-on, ballplayers and pols eagerly refilling his glass. It was the sort of gathering Ruth garnered everywhere he went. If there wasn't a crowd, he created one, throwing humdingers in the hundred-dollar-a-night hotel suites he rented in every American League city. "A fella's gotta entertain," he liked to say.

"I never saw so many people in one suite in all my

life and the Babe later admitted that he didn't know more than half of them," Claire told the *Buffalo Evening News* in June 1974. "I knew they had crashed the party and it bothered me. But it didn't concern the Babe at all."

She thought he seemed morose and worried about his performance after the disaster of the previous season, which began with his defiance of Commissioner Landis and ended with the public scolding by Jimmy Walker at the Back to the Farm dinner organized by Christy Walsh. Maybe they were all right about him: maybe he was through.

He wasn't. That year, he would do everything right that you can do wrong on a baseball field: he batted .393, drew 170 walks, a record that would stand for almost 80 years, led the league in on-base percentage (.545) and slugging (.657), home runs (41), and runs (151); set career highs for doubles (45), plate appearances (697), innings played in the outfield (1,335); he matched his career high for steals (17), tripled 13 times, threw out 20 baserunners from the outfield, and never got suspended. He was not only the Most Valuable Player of the year; he was the most valuable player ever.

Though still married to Helen, he was making a new life with Claire. She was unlike Helen in so many ways, chief among them the fact that she never knew him as George. And, oh, she came with a crowd, a mother, a daughter, and two brothers.

"Baggage," in the words of Julia Ruth Stevens.

"My home became his," Claire would write in her memoir. "My mother was his; my daughter was his; my brothers his fishing and hunting chums"—one of whom never recovered from having been gassed during the Great War and leaped to his death from the apartment window while Babe and Claire were in Florida in 1936.

But crowds were good. He liked crowds.

Claire didn't view herself as a home-wrecker. She couldn't break up a marriage that was already broken, she often said. In the years before Helen's death, he led a bifurcated life. Church doctrine and his very public identification as a practicing Catholic, albeit one who rarely went to church, made divorce untenable. So he had the best of both worlds: on the road he continued to live large, but quietly.

In New York, he had the security of the family he had thought to begin with Helen and in Claire a worldly woman who imposed the discipline he needed and looked the other way when she had to because she had no other choice. Her apartment, where he kept his slippers under the bed, was the only one in America where his photograph could not be hung on the wall, Claire said.

In the evening, when he got home from the ball-park, he'd inquire about plans for the evening. "He'd ask Mother if anybody was coming to dinner," Julia recalled. "If she said no, he'd get into his pajamas. And we had a cook that was horrified that he would come to the dinner table in his pajamas. Never saw such a thing in her life."

Sometimes, Julia said, he wore them even when they had people over. After all, they were made of the finest Egyptian cotton.

He didn't have a lot of friends. Perhaps a half a dozen or a dozen people he really liked, whom he would call to come over for an after-dinner drink: Peter DeRose, the composer, and his ukulele-playing wife, May Singhi Breen; June and Lefty Grove; May and Tony Lazzeri; Doc Painter, the Yankees' chiro-practor, and his wife, Eleanor; Juanita Jennings Ellias and her husband, Charlie, the accountant for Yan-kee Stadium concessionaire Harry M. Stevens, also a friend of Ruth's.

"He didn't like to be alone," Julia said.

In fact, he couldn't be by himself, Claire would con-fide to family members in the years after her husband's death. When you have a childhood like his, there's a kind of loneliness that sticks with you the rest of your life, Julia believed. "That's the reason he liked to have people over to the house. He'd call and say, 'Come on over and have a drink.'

"And they always came. Nobody ever said, 'Gee, we can't.'"

V

On April 17, 1929—three months and four days after Helen's death—Babe and Claire were married before the 6:30 A.M. Mass at the Church of St. Gregory the Great on West Ninetieth Street in Manhattan. Only the timing was surprising. Ruth had rung up sixteen hundred dollars in long-distance telephone calls to Claire during spring training. The early hour, intended to foil inquiring reporters and accommodate opening day festivities at the Stadium, failed on the first score and proved unnecessary on the second. A photographer hid a flash bomb behind the altar, "strong enough to split a granite block," Westbrook Pegler wrote in the *Chicago Tribune*. And the game was rained out, allowing for a champagne breakfast in the new fourteen-room family apartment at 345 West Eighty-eighth Street, where, Red Smith wrote, the Eighteenth Amendment did not apply. Ruth showed reporters the bedroom that had been fitted out with twin beds for twelve-year-old Julia and nine-year-old Dorothy, who had not yet joined the family.

Julia, who had spent the night at a girlfriend's house, learned about it from the headline of a soggy tabloid she saw lying on the sidewalk outside her school. "Babe Ruth Wed." When she got home they could tell by her face she knew. "They said, 'Well, you must have expected that this was going to happen,'" she recalled.

He gave Claire a $7,000 diamond bracelet and, on her first day at Yankee Stadium as Mrs. Babe Ruth, a first-inning opposite field home run that sailed past her in the third base box she would occupy for the next fifty years, as it traced its unusual path into the left field stands. He tipped his cap as he rounded third and blew her a kiss.

Babe also found time on his wedding day to autograph a photograph of himself for a former mistress—"Lest you forget Many happy evenings we have spent together."

The new, reformed Babe was a gentleman.

Claire was as sophisticated and assertive as Helen was withdrawn and malleable. Helen Ruth had entertained neighborhood children in Sudbury with milk and cookies while playing an upright piano in their rented cabin on Willis Pond. Claire Ruth went to the Aeolian Hall on Fifth Avenue to procure rolls of music for the player piano that dominated the living room.

Helen told reporters in 1921 she wanted to kidnap her husband so they could take tramps in the woods; Claire wanted to reform him. She would put him on diets and on a fifty-dollar-a-week allowance, announcing to the press, "He realizes now mother knows best." She was speaking of orange juice but nobody missed her point. Asked about plans for a wedding party, Ruth had replied, "No wedding party. Parties are over."

She would limit the flash in his wardrobe and put an end to politicking after the 1928 presidential election and the embarrassing headlines that appeared when he refused to pose with Herbert Hoover. "She did not think it was good for his image to favor one man over another," according to Julia.

He didn't vote either. "Because Mother told him not to."

Or read, he told Carl Sandburg, the "Noted American Poet," as he was identified in the 1928 spring training story in the *Chicago Daily News*: "Poet Fans Babe Ruth with 750 Words." Ruth swatted away Sandburg's condescending inquiries about the great events of the day—all of which were calculated to make him appear stupid. Did he know Clarence Darrow? Yes, he had given him an autograph just the other day. What were his favorite passages in the Bible and Shakespeare? Ballplayers don't read. Not good for the eyes. Favorite author? Christy Walsh was his stock answer. Claire read aloud to him.

She traveled with the team and answered all his calls—a lot of them from women. Her presence—and her increasing control of his diet, his money, his schedule—was the source of much ridicule, especially in opposing dugouts, where what passed for small talk was unrecognizable in fashionable salons. "Your face is certainly getting fatter," Browns manager Dan Howley told Ruth on Claire's first visit to St. Louis.

"Yeah?" questioned the unsmiling Ruth, spitting a gob of tobacco juice twelve feet. "Well, I don't hit or run or slide with my face."

"Is the wife on this trip with you?"

"Sure."

"Having a hard time dodging the old phone calls?"

"Aw, go to hell."

Her mother was very jealous, no question about it, Julia said.

Fidelity is not now and was not then included among

the myriad regulations in the major-league baseball handbook. Faithful? "No," said Julia's son, Tom Stevens, "and mother doesn't think so either."

Babe Ruth remained faithful only to who he was.

VI

On February 2, 1930, the Supreme Court of the City of New York granted an order of adoption making nine-year-old Dorothy, the little girl Ruth had called his daughter since 1922, his legal offspring. In a highly unusual and highly publicized ceremony on October 30, 1930, with both girls looking on, Claire also formally adopted Dorothy, and Babe formally adopted twelve-year-old Julia.

Julia was compliant and grateful—for the name he gave her and the attention he lavished on her. He may not have been her biological father, but she regarded him as a kind of savior, particularly after the 1938 blood transfusion he provided when she had strep throat at age twenty-two.

"After they were married and Dorothy came to live with us, Mother said to Dorothy, 'You'll have to teach Julia to call him Daddy.' I got onto it after a while and then I got to the point where I couldn't say Babe."

She was still calling him Daddy on her 102nd birthday.

She called him a cupcake. He called her Butch. He fixed one-eyed eggs and fried baloney for breakfast, and he made his own green tomato relish and barbecue sauce to take along on hunting trips for venison. (She would inherit the recipes, which her grandchildren are hoping to replicate. Early attempts failed the taste test. They just didn't taste like Daddy's.)

He liked to roughhouse, wrassle on the floor. So what if they broke the crystal on the watch he'd bought her? *Don't cry. I'll get you another one.*

He took her to football games, and to Artie McGovern's gym when she needed to lose weight, arranged for her to sing on the radio, and taught her to dance like a lady. They practiced the fox-trot to the player piano in the apartment's foyer. Imagine: Babe Ruth, who eschewed underwear and borrowed a teammate's toothbrush when he came to the big leagues, believed that every proper young lady needed to know how to dance. And how to follow.

He had very definite ideas about how to raise a young lady. She had to be home by midnight. Or else. Even after she was of age. He told her: "Don't ever marry a baseball player."

So omnipresent would he become in her life that she

couldn't recall meeting him. "It seemed like he'd always been there."

Dorothy's Daddy was never there enough.

No matter how many Christmas trees they decorated, or episodes of *The Lone Ranger* they listened to or times he tossed his big raccoon coat at her to see if she could catch it, which was impossible because it weighed more than she did, Dorothy needed more.

By the time she was ransomed from Brooklyn—about two months after Babe remarried, according to her memoir—she had become a truculent child, hostile and resentful, in her words. When he introduced her to Claire as her new mother, she dismembered the doll she was brought as a present, tearing the wig from its head, the arms from its sockets, and poking its eyes out for good measure. "Claire tried to make overtures," her daughter Genevieve Herrlein said, "but she wanted no part of that."

He had rescued Julia from fatherlessness but had consigned Dorothy to it when he separated from Helen, abandoning her as he had been abandoned, leaving her in the care of an unstable parent who sent her to live among the nuns just as he had been sent to live among the brothers at St. Mary's. It was a pattern Dorothy would repeat in her life as a parent, her daughter

Genevieve Herrlein said, leaving her and her brother, Danny, in the care of the Ruths' former maid, Nora McIntyre, for a year and later placing them in a Catholic boarding school for three months while she traveled with her second husband.

"She didn't talk about Helen much," Dorothy's friend Carolyn Rendon said. "She told me her mother died in a fire. I said I was sorry. She'd say, 'Nobody loves me.'

"And I said, 'Oh I'm sure Babe—'

"And she said, 'I think Babe loves me, but he isn't around long enough to show it.'"

Nor, Rendon and others say, did he see how she was treated when he was away.

Not surprisingly, given the holes in his childhood and the lack of them in his schedule, he had neither the time nor the resolve to fill in the gaps in her history when she inquired about them. She was never told the details of Helen's death, learning about the fire after stumbling on press clippings while assembling a scrapbook about her father's career with Claire's mother. Nor would he answer questions about the identity of her biological mother, according to the family maid, saying he could not do so while Claire was still alive.

And so he bequeathed her a lifetime of bitterness and enmity, much of which found its way into the pages of a score-settling memoir, *My Dad, the Babe*, published a year before her death in 1988. She described Claire as a "mommy dearest" drunk who consigned her to the maid's quarters, a room so small she could count all the flowers on the wallpaper, and cited a litany of stepdaughter injustices: inferior schools, missed trips abroad, hand-me-down clothes, while Julia got all the latest fashions.

Of course, Dorothy didn't help, her daughter Linda said. "When they'd say, 'Stay clean for the press,' she'd go out and help a neighbor pick coal and come back black," she said.

Her wardrobe was the putative cause of the falling-out between Ruth and Gehrig. When Dorothy arrived at Mom Gehrig's house looking particularly shabby one day, Christina Gehrig complained to someone who told someone who told Claire that it was shameful the way she dressed Dorothy. Claire complained about Christina to Babe, who told Lou, who said you can't talk about my mother that way.

That was the end of the friendship.

Her efforts, and subsequent ones made by her daughters, to answer questions about her birth raised in Helen's will were thwarted by New York State law, which gave judges the right to seal the birth certificates of adoptees in 1924 and made it mandatory fourteen years later. A letter from her father to be given to her after his death, supposedly containing information about her birth, never materialized.

All of which seemed moot, she wrote, when Juanita Ellias, an old family friend, came to live with Dorothy in the last days of her life and made a deathbed confession that she was Dorothy's birth mother and the Babe was her biological father. The unsubstantiated revelation, made in conversation with Dorothy's late daughter, Ellen Hourigan, was recorded in handwritten notes provided to Chris Martens, who collaborated on Dorothy's memoir. The notes conclude: "At this time I have no proof only Juanita's word."

Definitive scientific proof may never come to light. Two of Dorothy's daughters, Donna Analovitch and Genevieve Herrlein, doubt the story and still wonder about their ancestry. Their sister Linda Ruth Tosetti is unequivocal in her belief that "I have his blood in my veins, as my mom did before me."

But one fact remains incontrovertible. Ruth's silence left room for ambiguity and doubt. He bequeathed his daughters a legacy of animosity and mistrust, which was unfortunate as they had more in common than their relationship with him. Both women lived with unknowns: Julia never knew her biological father;

Dorothy never knew for certain the identity of her father or mother. But the rifts of a splintered childhood never mended. When the Yankees observed the fortieth anniversary of his death—a year before Dorothy's own passing—Julia and Dorothy ate at separate tables and sat on opposite sides of the baseball diamond.

The schism remains. Ruth's descendants tell his story, extoll his virtues, and express their pride on separate websites: Julia's family call theirs "Babe Ruth Central, The Site That Ruth Built." Tosetti calls her webpage "The True Babe Ruth, The Official Babe Ruth Family Site."

The issue isn't money, Analovitch said. It's a far more precious commodity. "It's all about who's going to be at Cooperstown," she said. "Who benefits from the fame."

VII

After Babe Ruth climbed down from the pedestal of young shoulders that carried him halfway around the bases at Sodality Park, he and Gehrig made a break for it. For a minute, it seemed they had negotiated safe passage. But the car and driver designated to ransom them from the ballyard were nowhere to be found, and the masses converged upon them. The Cirone brothers disappeared into the crowd, unnoticed among the paying customers.

"Police and traffic officers tried to shield them but were powerless before the adoring crowds," the *Mercury-Herald* reported. "Suddenly a big closed auto containing three girls came along the street. A police whistle shrilled and the girl driver jammed on her brakes, afraid she was being arrested. Someone pulled open a door of the auto and Ruth and Gehrig were shoved in.

"Two policemen climbed on each running board and the girls were told to 'Drive ahead.'"

The young ladies did not recognize their famous passengers, which was as unusual as it was comic, a getaway scene Harold Lloyd might have written as a sequel to *Speedy* if Hollywood was making sequels in 1927. This time, with the Babe dashing *from* the ballpark, fleeing the maddening crowd with the help of law-breaking Keystone Coppers and—oh, the irony!—into the arms of improbable anonymity.

How many teenagers in America in the fall of 1927 would fail to recognize Babe Ruth? Did he get the joke? Did it please him to be unrecognizable just for an instant?

The San Jose police pushed Ruth and Gehrig into

the back seat and directed the hijacked car to take them to the posh Spanish Renaissance Sainte Claire Hotel, where they would change for dinner with Pop Warner.

"Flustered and not knowing whether they were being robbed or arrested the frightened girls drove on," the paper reported. "When they found they were rescuing the famous Babe Ruth, however, they broke into laughs of joy and showed their surprise and pleasure. It was a thrill that comes but once in a lifetime."

The girls made no comment.

Chapter 16
October 28 / San Diego

**REAL BASEBALL GAME PROVIDED AS
VEHICLE TO SHOW BABE, GEHRIG**

—SAN DIEGO EVENING TRIBUNE

**PAIR OF HOME-RUN SWATTERS DUE TO
ARRIVE IN SAN DIEGO AT NOON;
PLAN BIG RECEPTION**

—SAN DIEGO UNION

I

Before checking out of the Carrillo Hotel in Santa
Barbara, Christy Walsh sent an SOS to Knute
Rockne at Notre Dame. Needed: "four GOOD tick-

ets" in a "FRONT box" for the November 12 game at Yankee Stadium between the Fighting Irish and the Cadets of West Point for Babe and Lou. "He says the last time I got him football tickets they were ROTTEN," Walsh wrote. "He would like a FRONT box. But if the FRONT boxes are all gone he would prefer four GOOD ones in a reserved section."

He assured Rockne that the tour had been "a smashing trip all the way" but allowed that it had been taxing. "Four more games and the long grind is over," he said, which is as close as his professional ebullience ever came to wavering.

Smashing and wearing. Baggage and tempers had been lost, itineraries and judgment scrambled. Walsh had inexplicably scheduled a Friday-afternoon game in San Diego and one the following afternoon 340 miles north in Fresno, which meant spending Saturday night at a church banquet in the San Joaquin Valley instead of attending a midnight frolic at the Mayan Theater in Los Angeles with Charlie Chaplin, Bill Tilden, Joe E. Brown, et al., in advance of the Sunday game at Wrigley Field.

Walsh arranged an overnight at a Los Angeles hotel en route to San Diego, allowing for a quick how-do-ya-do with the press to gin up sales and a night in L.A. for the Babe.

The next afternoon, in San Diego, Carl Klindt, a debonair local sports fixer—promoter of amateur and semi-pro baseball games; manager of a multitude of baseball teams, including an all-star girls squad that competed on the beach in bathing suits; lifeguard at the Mission Beach Plunge pool (though he couldn't swim); booker of fishing charters, quail hunts, and duck drives; author of the *San Diego Sun*'s "Powder and Hooks" column; and all-around hail-fellow-well-met—was waiting for them on the field at City Stadium, along with five hundred lucky children who had caught balloons bearing free tickets dropped from the roof of the Union Building that morning.

Klindt was a local golden boy, one of those graceful former high school stars, not quite good enough to make a living at it. He carried himself like an athlete, leaned on a bat with the je ne sais quoi of an athlete. He was useful and charming, skills championed in the July 1920 issue of *Hardware World* magazine as a sporting goods merchant "who really knows."

In the decade before San Diego acquired a Pacific Coast League franchise, when amateurs and semi-pros competed for use of the City Stadium field on Sundays (against the wishes of local clergy), Klindt wielded his charm and resorted to threat when necessary in order to provide the city with "clean and regular baseball throughout the year." As founder of the San Diego County Managers' Baseball association, he fined teams that failed to show up for appointed games and helped to fill the stands and rosters for barnstorming tours that came through town.

His friendship with Ruth—commemorated by a thank-you note on yellow "'Babe' Ruth's coming to town!" stationery addressed to "Dear Friend Carl"— extended to rounds of golf, hunting and fishing trips, visits to local bootleggers, outings at the Hotel del Coronado, and, family lore has it, dinners at the Klindt home featuring bathtubs filled with gin.

In January 1927, during Ruth's weeklong vaudeville run at the Pantages Theater, Klindt, then employed as the manager of the athletic department at the Cycle & Arms sporting goods store, had arranged a fishing trip to the Point Loma kelp beds for the Babe, who wanted to catch a jewfish—a bottom-feeder with large lips that has since acquired the politically correct name "goliath grouper." They were accompanied by Linn Platner, a local boxing promoter, Speed Martin, a former big-league pitcher, and a school of local waterfront reporters. "We caught no jewfish," Max Miller of the *San Diego Sun* reported in his bestseller *I Cover the Waterfront*. "We caught five mackerel." He credited

Ruth with one fish. "One Strike and He's Out," his column read.

"Doc" Gottesburen, angling columnist for the *San Diego Union*, credited Miller with five mackerel, Klindt and Ruth with three each, and the Big Fella with a Big One that got away. Ruth and Klindt appeared with their catch in the April issue of *Tackle* magazine along with the particulars of the equipment Ruth used. The well-mannered Babe promptly wrote Klindt's boss, extolling his employee's virtues, and thanked Klindt separately the next day for making his week in San Diego "an extremely happy one."

By the time he returned nine months later, Ruth was happily counting more than fish. The man who once said, "I've spent a half a million dollars and I haven't the faintest idea what I've spent it on," was swimming in dough and boasting of his ambition to become a baseball magnate, telling West Coast reporters, "I have saved enough money to buy a club tomorrow." (Indeed, he could have purchased the Cleveland Indians that year for $1 million, or the Oakland Oaks of the Pacific Coast League for $175,000.)

It was a career year financially for the Babe. Between his $70,000 Yankee salary—sixty-seven times that of the average American worker—and the $73,247.34

he made in what Christy Walsh called "by-product money," Ruth earned the equivalent of $10,232,799 in 2016 dollars. And that didn't include the money accruing in his annuity accounts with the Equitable Life Assurance Company.

II

By sleight of hand and dint of luck, Walsh had engineered a stunning reversal of fortune in the eighteen months since Ruth had come to him for a $4,000 loan in March 1926. Thanks to assorted fines and misdemeanors, Ruth had been paid only $42,000 of his $52,000 1925 Yankee salary. He, in turn, had paid his estranged wife Helen only half of the $20,000 he owed her in October 1925, as stipulated by their 1925 separation agreement. And he had paid only $25,000 of the $30,000 he owed her the following October. He was in arrears $15,000 by February 1927, when Walsh trumpeted the news that Ruth had agreed to fund an irrevocable trust at the Bank of Manhattan.

By the time the trust was executed on April 26, he had upped the initial deposit from $33,000 to $40,000. In August, he socked away another $10,000—a fact Walsh publicized widely and loudly, tipping off *New York World* columnist Joe Williams and providing the bank with a spate of free publicity. He coordinated with Frank Hilton on the circulation of the Babe's own (ghostwritten) story about his new fiscally responsible self and the fiscally conservative portfolio the bank had created for him, investing his money in treasury bonds and blue-chip stocks, protecting him from the crash that manager Miller Huggins warned his players was coming.

Hilton, in turn, had commended Walsh to his banker father-in-law, Oscar M. Souden, president of the U.S. National Bank in Los Angeles, as a consummately "alert" young man.

But frugality did not come naturally to the Babe. Results came naturally to the Babe. Behind the scenes, throughout the tour, he had been hectoring Walsh about a dividend check he had expected by the first of October, the initial quarterly return on his investments. In the absence of tangible results from New York, Walsh was having no luck convincing Ruth to add to the account, according to John B. Kennedy's barnstorming travelogue.

"You're doing well on this trip, Babe, why not sock a few thousand away in your trust fund?"

The Babe bit at a cigar and replied, "Shut up."

Undeterred, Walsh persisted. "In a year or two

you'll have $100,000 in that trust fund, Babe. And that's a small estate. Lots of men who live in swell apartments on Riverside Drive and have cars and chauffeurs don't leave estates that large when they pass out."

"Don't give me a pain," Ruth replied.

Walsh could imagine all his years of financial conjuring disappearing like a cheap scarf up a magician's sleeve. He had coerced Ruth into creating the trust, using his leverage over the Babe to divert all his outside income into the account. He had built it up while allowing the debt to Helen to go unpaid and the interest to mount. Whether this was accomplished with Ruth's knowledge and approval—or hers, for that matter—is impossible to say.

He had gotten the Babe to agree to live on his Yankee salary with the incentive that he could keep the dividend checks and the interest generated by the account as play money. "Were I to insist he save what his trust fund earns there would be no fun in saving," he explained to writer Norman Beasley in *Forbes* magazine. "That is not for him."

He had enlisted Ed Barrow's help in arranging for the Yankees to pay Ruth once a month instead of biweekly starting in 1926, an enforced savings plan that remained in effect through 1933.

He had cajoled Hilton into sharing proprietary information without Ruth's knowledge that so he could keep an eye on things. Hilton had acceded to the request after reminding him of the confidential nature of the fiduciary relationship and pleading with him to keep the information in extreme confidence.

Walsh reciprocated with an introduction to Gehrig.

But Ruth was a "supremely unconscious financial wizard," as Tommy Holmes put it in the *Brooklyn Eagle*, and an impatient one.

Walsh fretted in a letter to Hilton, "He is losing some of his enthusiasm on this subject which is having a poor influence on Gehrig. . . . Personally, I fully understand the delay etc etc but no one knows better than yourself the obstacles I have had to overcome in lining Babe up in this matter."

Hilton replied with alacrity; he didn't want to lose the Babe either. A check for $643.13, the first money generated by the trust, and a suitably unctuous letter, noting that the quarterly return was higher than the projected estimate, arrived in time for Walsh to read it aloud to Ruth on the train en route back to New York. "Your example in establishing this trust fund has caused a great deal of most favorable comment on all sides."

Walsh replied: "He was well pleased and particularly delighted with the check. Money talks.

"I am hopeful to have had his promise to add $20,000 to his Trust fund at a very early date. However, since I talked to you he has showed signs of weakening. He changes his mind so much on me that I am confident I can get him to do as he promised. I wish you would please write me a letter immediately which I can show him along the lines of the enclosed copy."

Hilton followed the script calculated to inflate the Ruthian ego and trust fund, writing the next day that he was "gratified" by the Babe's decision and commending his "rare good judgment at the time of his prosperity."

He also commended Walsh's "splendid effort."

Later, in the club car, Kennedy overheard Ruth in conversation with Gehrig.

The Babe's voice rang out like an organ note. "A young guy like you," he declaimed, "should be saving his money."

"Yeh?" said Gehrig.

"Yeh," said Ruth. "You've got ten years ahead of you in the big league. Save your dough now. Start one of these trust funds and push away the jack you're making out of a racket like this. Every dollar you sock away now will be one more laugh left when your home run days are over."

Back in New York, big-city columnists dutifully composed hosannas saluting Ruth's excellent example.

In December, the promised $20,000 was added to the account: $10,000 from barnstorming tour earnings, $4,654.58 of his $12,807.59 syndicate profits, $3,000 from unnamed royalties, and $1,500 from the comedy record he and Gehrig had made for Perfect Records. The remaining $845.42 was a loan from Walsh, who had a fondness for round numbers. They looked good in press releases.

III

There are many ways to measure a man's worth.

By September 1927, according to a widely syndicated story published in, among other places, the *Baltimore Sun*, Babe Ruth was the second most valuable human being in the United States, carrying a reported $5 million in life insurance, second only to department-store magnate John Wanamaker. Ed Barrow quickly dismissed the story as "bunk," telling the *New York Times* Ruth's life was worth no more than those of Charlie Chaplin, Mary Pickford, Douglas Fairbanks, Will Rogers, Gloria Swanson, or John Barrymore, who each carried $3 million.

In denying the inflated report, Barrow actually conceded the point that Ruth was now an entertainer, an economic engine for major-league baseball, the American League, and every American League city he played in—not to mention the Yankees, his family, his agent, every barnstorming town he visited, every sporting goods store he patronized, and every brand of cigar he smoked.

The full extent of his economic clout was documented in Yankee accounting books and daily cash ledgers discovered by economist Michael Haupert in a climate-controlled storage room at the Hall of Fame in the summer of 2000. The Hall had acquired the records covering the twenty-four years of Jacob Ruppert's ownership in 1973 when a team employee offered them to the head librarian in advance of the renovation of Yankee Stadium. The team's new owner, George Steinbrenner, had deemed them unnecessary.

In the eighteen years since his discovery, Haupert has published extensive analyses of the Yankee economic juggernaut and Ruth's role in creating it. The records show how much he was paid annually and at what rate, how much he was fined, and how much he borrowed against his future salary, figures that help explain the financial hole he had created for himself. They reveal how much the Yankees spent on his medical care and on private detectives to follow him, what it cost for Helen and later Claire to travel with the team, and how much they charged for his uniforms.

In an effort to produce a complete picture of Ruth's financial worth and his worth to the team, Haupert agreed to reexamine the Yankee records in conjunction with the earnings spreadsheet Walsh prepared for Ruth in 1938 and Bank of Manhattan account documents found among Walsh's papers at the time of his death. (Those documents can be found in appendix 2, "The Babe's Portfolio.")

Ruth earned $860,913 in salary and bonuses during fifteen seasons with the Yankees. But as Haupert points out, salary tells only half of the story. "Actually, it only tells 57 percent of the story," he explains. "Christy Walsh helped Babe Ruth nearly double his income during his lifetime through endorsements and investments."

In the twenty-eight years between 1920 and Ruth's death in 1948, his total income from salary and Walsh's so-called "by-product" money was $1,511,577, or

$124,603,370 in 2016 dollars. It was an astonishment of riches compared with the earnings of the men he played with and against and all those who came before him. "But compared to what the Yankees made off him, and what athletes make today, it's chump change," Haupert says.

No matter what the Yankees paid him, he was a bargain. There was a reason they kept their books a secret.

The purchase price was $100,000—inaccurately reported by the *New York Times* in January 1920 as $125,000—to be paid to Red Sox owner Harry Frazee in four annual $25,000 installments, with 6 percent interest on three promissory notes due each November through 1922. The first $25,000 payment was made on December 6, 1919, a month before the sale was announced and three weeks before the Eighteenth Amendment became the law of the land. The brilliant brewmaster of East Ninety-third Street knew he was going to need a new source of income.

Harry Frazee was already hard up. So Ruppert agreed to loan him $300,000, guaranteed by the deed to Fenway Park, kept on file in the Suffolk County Registry of Deeds in Massachusetts.

"Frazee borrowed $300,000 at 7 percent a year, or $21,000 annually," Haupert explains. "Ruppert bought Ruth for $100,000, a total of $108,750 with interest paid over three years. But Frazee sent Ruppert a check for $21,000 in interest that first year on a $300,000 loan that was not repaid in full for thirteen years. After six years he had paid over $100,000 in interest alone, more than Ruth had cost the Yankees. And Ruppert had the deed for Fenway! In the end, it didn't cost him anything to buy Babe Ruth. He was a genius and Frazee was desperate. So the Red Sox actually paid the Yankees to take Babe Ruth."

Talk about cursed.

Yet even Ruppert could not have envisioned just how much—or just how quickly—his investment would pay off. A good albeit conservative return is 4.5 percent, Haupert says, the same return Ruth averaged on his stock portfolio throughout the Great Depression. The lowest single-season return on Ruth was 4.5 percent in 1925, the year the Babe got a tummy ache and gave the Yankees indigestion. The Yankees earned more than 100 percent of their investment in Ruth back in 1920 alone. Then he continued to pay off for fourteen more years. By 1934, the Yankees had made $1.25 million on the $100,000 investment. (Haupert calculated the return by compiling the team profits from concessions; ticket sales for home, exhibition, and away games; plus World Series revenues during Ruth's Yankees career.)

The best year was 1926, when Ruth returned 191

percent. "Except for 1925, the annual return ranged between 32 percent and 192 percent," according to Haupert's calculations. "These returns are so gaudy, they're embarrassing. In each of six different years the Yankees earned more than double Ruth's purchase price.

"To give you an idea how that investment stacks up, if Ruppert had taken that same $100,000 and, on the same day he bought Ruth, he invested in the stock market, he would have made $17,000 by the end of 1934, because his earnings would have been suppressed by the stock market crash. Had Ruppert purchased $100,000 of low-risk bonds he would have doubled his money by the end of 1934. Instead, he bought Ruth and more than doubled his money in less than two years, even after paying Ruth's salary and 6 percent interest."

Actually, Ruppert didn't pay all of his salary. As part of the sale agreement with the Red Sox, and as an inducement to Ruth, the Yankees doubled his $10,000 salary on the two remaining years of his Red Sox contract, of which Harry Frazee agreed to pay $5,000.

The raise was offset, in part, by the Yankees' take of $2,613.59 in additional spring training ticket sales his first year with the team, an indication of the draw Ruth would become and what economists call "the superstar effect"—people who came out to the ballpark just to see him. "Over the course of his Yankee career the Yankees sold $38,605 in exhibition game tickets just because of Ruth," Haupert says. "No Ruth, no $38,605."

Ruth was worth $137,975 to the Yankees in 1920, a whopping 17 percent of their total earnings that season. They rewarded him with a bonus in his 1921 contract—$50 for each home run. That was the year he hit fifty-nine, which added $2,950 to his Yankee salary. They never made that mistake again.

By 1923, Ruth was a box-office sensation, an indispensable cog in the economic powerhouse the Yankees were becoming. On the road, where visiting teams received only 20 percent of the gate, Ruth generated $42,448 for his team. At home, in the newly opened House That Ruth Built, he was responsible for 19 percent—or $132,156—of ticket sales. Those sales contributed to an additional revenue stream for Jacob Ruppert, who had bought out his partner, Tillinghast L'Hommedieu Huston, that spring. And that didn't include what he generated in concessions. As tenants in the Polo Grounds they received a flat fee of $8,000 annually. In their first year in their own ballpark, the Yankees made $94,025 on peanuts, popcorn, and Cracker Jack, an increase of 1,070 percent.

Perhaps the best illustration of the "Ruth Effect" is

provided by looking at 1925, when he played in only ninety-eight games, his fewest as a Yankee. Attendance plummeted 34 percent and revenues dropped 22.5 percent. In 1926, when a reformed and resurgent Ruth led the major leagues in home runs (47), runs scored (139), RBI (153), walks (144), on-base percentage (.516), and slugging (.737), the Yankees drew 1,027,675 spectators and their revenue jumped 72 percent to $1.6 million.

And in 1927, powered by Ruth's sixty home runs, attendance increased another 13 percent, all of which Haupert attributes to Ruth's drawing power. By the end of the year, the initial $100,000 investment in Ruth had already returned $779,075.51.

He would continue to generate showy profits for another seven years, a reality Ruppert acknowledged with the two-year, $80,000 contract for 1930–1931, which also included a clause awarding him 25 percent of the net receipts of exhibition games played during the regular season (as long as he played in at least five innings). That would remain true for as long as he remained a Yankee. Ruppert could well afford this gesture of largesse. According to Haupert's analysis, of the $3.4 million in profits the Yankees earned during Ruth's tenure, 37 percent can be directly attributed to the Babe.

By the end of Ruth's Yankee career, the team had

earned over $2 million it would not have made without him. "That's $12.6 million in net profits adjusted for inflation," Haupert maintains. "For each dollar they spent on Ruth, they made back twenty."

IV

At a meeting in Christy Walsh's office the day before Babe and Claire were married on April 17, 1929, Ruth agreed, in writing, to allow Walsh to manage the trust as he saw fit. Walsh wrote to Hilton twelve days later, informing him that it was no longer necessary to consult Ruth or apprise him of deposits and transactions. "This would prevent him from objecting as frequently as he does, feeling that he needs the money for some other purpose," Walsh explained.

He also confided his intention to bring the total in the trust to $150,000 by the end of the year, at which point he intended to step away from daily management of the account. "I hope by then he will be able to continue the good work of his own accord, because in spite of the satisfaction it gives me you can appreciate it has taken an unlimited amount of my time and energy."

Hilton replied swiftly that it was incumbent upon bank officials to notify Ruth of all transactions. Walsh's beleaguered and defensive response, more retort than reply, noted that it was 3:00 P.M. and he had just had lunch. "That is the way it goes with me every day."

He enclosed a statement from Ruth authorizing the arrangement, pointing out that the Babe had even scrawled "thanks" next to his name. "Sometimes he is less pliable than others and I would rather not discuss the matter again with him until I have reached the goal of $100,000."

If Hilton felt it necessary to copy Ruth on all future correspondence, Walsh suggested the bank send it to his office.

No doubt keeping the Babe on the financial straight and narrow was exhausting. But Walsh had other reasons to want to remove himself, given his role in funding the trust and the annuity at Equitable Life while allowing the debt to Helen to accrue.

Even before Helen's death, Ruth had begun planning for a life with Claire and Julia. According to a letter in Walsh's files, Ruth asked for the language in the trust to be amended before it was executed in April 1927, allowing him to designate a new beneficiary "in the place and stead of said DOROTHY RUTH and said next of kin of donor" after a period of five years.

Another unsigned letter in Walsh's files, drafted upon their return from the barnstorming tour in December 1927, instructed a bank attorney to "eliminate the beneficiary's names now standing" on an unnamed account or policy and "substitute with the following 'Mrs. Claire Hodgson and Julia Hodgson.'"

The changes were not implemented. The final trust document gave him the right to change beneficiaries but only by changing his will, which he did not do until the last week of his life, when he named Claire in Dorothy's stead. This gave her use of the principal during her lifetime with the remainder to be shared equally by Dorothy and Julia upon her death.

That financial windfall of 1927 enabled Walsh to put $70,000 in the trust and have enough cash left over for Ruth to write a check to Helen on October 11 for $29,000, at which point he was only $5,000 behind in the scheduled payments to her.

Another $25,000 was due in October 1928. The payment was not made. That month, Walsh added $10,000 to the trust, which, ironically, became public on the day of the fire that took Helen's life. (He had also made a $10,123 contribution to Ruth's Equitable Life insurance policy in July.) Once again, obligations to Helen came last.

At the December 1928 meeting in Walsh's office with Helen and her sister, Nora, Ruth had given him a check for $31,000 to cover the payment due two months earlier plus the interest on the overdue amount. Apparently, the check was made out to Walsh, as suggested by his letter to Ruth on January 28, 1929: "I certainly have no advantage in keeping it there in my name and want to turn it over the very second I can."

But Helen would never see the check. On July 26, 1929, six months after her death, estate attorneys reached a settlement that called for Ruth to pay the remaining $32,007.50 he owed, including interest, in two installments: $15,000 due by September 1, 1929, with the balance due the following September. Helen's lawyer held on to the Equitable Life Assurance policy purchased in 1923 as collateral and did not return it until the last payment was received. Her estate would not be settled until 1932.

The final accounting of Helen's will, reported in the *Boston Globe* on October 29, 1932, included $4,190 in jewelry relinquished by Ruth as part of the 1929 settlement—her diamond-and-platinum wedding ring, a diamond-and-platinum dinner ring, and an elaborate diamond brooch. The total value of the estate was $20,000 less than reported at the time of her death. She left $29,000 to Dorothy and $5 to each of her siblings, her mother, and her husband.

Meanwhile, Walsh continued to add money to the trust, and the Bank of Manhattan continued to invest the Babe's money. Their investment strategy was the antithesis of the Babe's approach at the plate: *I hit big or I miss big. I like to live as big as I can.* Their fiscally conservative approach would allow him to continue to live large throughout the biggest economic crisis in American history. They invested 70 percent of his money in fixed-income U.S. government and municipal bonds and 30 percent in dividend-paying blue chips, utilities, railroads—Standard Oil, Southern Pacific, Penn Power and Light, U.S. Steel, General Motors, General Electric, Standard Brands, R. J. Reynolds, Hershey, companies that long outlived the Babe. "Pretty much all, if not all, were dividend-paying stocks, which was very key because dividend stocks pay even if the stock is going down," Matthew Zaft, a financial adviser at Morgan Stanley in Washington, D.C., points out.

When the crash came, the King of Clout would not take a hit.

Unencumbered by Ruth's interference, Walsh added $3,000 to the trust on September 11, 1929, bringing the total to $97,000, and another $3,000 on October 24—otherwise known as Black Tuesday, when the Dow Jones dropped 11 percent at the opening bell, signaling the beginning of the Great Depression.

Along with the check, Walsh sent Frank Hilton a chirpy, prophetic note. "Babe does not know it is this high and I want to surprise him and reach the $100,000 by depositing the enclosed $3000. This takes a big load off my mind and I am very happy to have done this much toward protecting him from the rainy days of the future."

Four days later, when the *New York Times* lead headline read: "Stock Prices Slump $14,000,000,000 in Nation-Wide Stampede to Unload," Hilton took a moment to applaud Walsh's efforts.

"In the light of what took place last week, it would seem to me that any one [*sic*] who had taken precaution to set aside a definite sum in the hour of prosperity has much to be thankful for when an adversity such as overcame so many people in the stock market last week leaves them immune to such a catastrophe."

Walsh commemorated the occasion with a memo found in his files after his death: "Entire amount paid into Trust derived from newspaper syndicate and other revenue outside of Yankee baseball salary. Starting this date, Mr. Ruth will receive more than $5000 per year in dividends for the remainder of his life. Within (approx.) eight years, at age 43, he will have received $50,000. in dividends, one half the full amount of his investment. At age 53, Mr. Ruth will have received $100K in dividends—the entire amount of his investment."

In fact, Ruth would reach that milestone in 1941, well in advance of his fifty-third birthday.

At Walsh's urging, Ruth would continue to add large chunks of change to the account—$50,000 in 1930 and 1931. All the while, he was receiving a return on his money of close to 5 percent. "Making Babe add to the trust allowed Manhattan to buy low and it allowed them to not have to sell low," Zaft says. "As banks were failing, and stocks were dropping, it allowed them to wait and sell high. In fact, he profited on literally every sale made from July 16, 1930, through April 20, 1931."

The "corpus of Ruth's portfolio," including his Equitable Annuity, had reached "a Quarter of A Million Dollars," Hilton wrote in a letter praising the "magnificent result" Walsh had achieved and expressing his regret that Walsh felt his job was done. "Words fail me," he said.

By the end of 1935, Babe Ruth and Carl Klindt were out of work. The economy had cost Klindt his sporting goods business and the sales jobs he took afterward. He quit the business for the security of a position as a police officer with the San Diego County Sheriff's Department but lost that, too, in a departmental shake-up. By the spring of 1935, he was working part-time as a security guard at the big California Pacific International Exposition in Balboa Park near the stadium where he had brought Babe and Lou to play.

When that ended, he moved his family to an unheated cabin in the Cuyamaca mountains an hour and a half northeast of the city and began collecting K-rations from the Navy surplus store—dented, swollen cans of beans, meats, vegetables, and sardines that he would continue to hoard for the rest of his life. In 1937, he went back to work as a patrolman for the Coronado Police Department. His annual salary was less than the quarterly dividend checks Ruth received from the Bank of Manhattan.

Ruth's investment income continued to grow every year from 1935 through 1940, paying $8,000 annually until mid-1941, when interest rates declined. Only then would the trust account show its first loss—less than 1 percent. During his lifetime, the account was never worth less than the $200,000 Walsh invested for him. It had thrown off $148,000 in cash by his death in 1948.

Asked to evaluate how well Christy Walsh had looked after Babe Ruth and his money, Zaft's reply is unequivocal: "On a scale of one to ten—eleven."

Kind of like the home run the Babe hit during the pregame exhibition in San Diego, a clout so frightful, the *San Diego Tribune* said, "it almost paralyzed a cuckoo bird in a sentinel tree" beyond the left field fence.

Chapter 17
October 29 / Fresno

**HONOLULU BOYS HELP LOU GEHRIG
DEFEAT BAMBINO**
ZENIMURA, YOSHIKAWA, AND NAKAGAWA ALL
REGISTER HITS IN 15–3 WIN
—HONOLULU STAR-BULLETIN

**MORE THAN 200 ATTEND BANQUET
FOR RUTH-GEHRIG**
—FRESNO BEE

I

One week after arriving in San Francisco at the conclusion of a six-month goodwill tour of Asia with his Fresno Athletic Club, Kenichi Zenimura, all five feet, 105 pounds of him—known in the Japanese press as "positive poison to every opponent"—learned that Babe Ruth was coming to California. By the time he made his way home to meet his new four-month-old son, Howard, word was Babe and Lou would play at Fresno's Firemen's Park against an all-star team of the city's best local talent sometime in late October.

By any reasonable definition other than size, Zeni—or Ken, as he was known in the Caucasian press—was an all-star shortstop and catcher. Born in Hiroshima, raised and educated in Hawaii, Zenimura was Issei, a member of the first generation of Japanese immigrants. In 1920 he settled in Fresno, where he founded a baseball team and created a wooden stadium for it to play in next to the city dump. He was also the manager and promoter of the team, organizing trips to the Far East in 1924, 1927, and 1937. They had beaten Pacific Coast League teams in 1924, and Negro League teams in 1926–27.

Zeni had managed two all-white Fresno Twilight League teams in 1926. He had led his team of Nisei players—second-generation Japanese Americans—to a record of 42-6-2 during their tour of Japan, Korea, China, and Hawaii. The invitation had been arranged through a close family friend, Takizo Matsumoto, who

introduced the sport to Meiji University upon returning to Japan after living in Fresno for a time.

Fresno was fertile baseball ground: Frank Chance
was a native son, as were Alex Metzler, the hot young
outfielder for the Chicago White Sox, and shortstop
Lyn Lary, who would join the Yankees in 1929. There
was plenty of talent to choose from.

On October 18, managers Pete Shepherd and Gene
Jewett announced that four members of the Fresno Athletic Club, including Zenimura, would play with Ruth
and Gehrig: left fielder Harvey Iwata, catcher Fred
Yoshikawa, and center fielder John Nakagawa, known
as the Nisei Babe Ruth. Zeni immediately scheduled a
game on October 23 between his club and an all-star
team representing the Veterans of Foreign Wars to ensure they would be at their best for Ruth and Gehrig.

The starting pitchers were ringers from the Pacific
Coast League. Zeni went 3 for 5. "Now everyone was
warmed up and ready for the Ruth-Gehrig show to arrive in Fresno," the *Fresno Bee* declared.

II

Waiting at the station for Ruth and Gehrig that morning was Father John J. Crowley, aka the Desert Padre,
the pastor of Fresno's St. John's Cathedral, known for

his religious tolerance and his flair for publicity. With him was photographer Claude C. "Pop" Laval, who took perhaps a hundred thousand photographs of life in Fresno beginning in the 1900s.

Pop captured in granular detail the scene at the Southern Pacific depot: the conductor watching from the train platform above, a passenger peering through the car door, the priest casting a beneficent "mind-your-manners" glance at an unnamed boy in a tartan-plaid jacket receiving a ball from Babe Ruth, and a glum gaggle of youths looking on in envy. "Everybody in Fresno wanted to be that boy," Pop's great-granddaughter Elizabeth Laval recalled. And over the years, three would come forward presenting their bona fides, presenting a problem for local newspapers who anointed the wrong one and had to retract the story when someone else showed up with the actual jacket.

Laval, who maintains Pop's archive and has cataloged every photograph he took, says he took only two that day, both at the station. She believes there was an agreement that he would cover the arrival and that Frank Kamiyama, a prominent Japanese American photographer, would cover the game because of its significance in the Nisei community. Howard (Taizo) Toshiyuki, a pharmacist and owner of a local drugstore, brought his 16mm camera to further memorialize the occasion.

In baseball, the saying goes, the older you get, the better you used to be. That's true of virtually everyone who ever played the game, with the possible exception of Babe Ruth. Retelling the events of October 29, 1927, some thirty-five years after the fact, Kenichi Zenimura's memory of his performance had improved a bit. "The very first time up I got a single," he told the *Fresno Bee.*

In fact, he walked.

"I was very fast and took my usual big lead off first. Ruth glanced at me and said, 'Hey, son, aren't you taking too much of a lead?'

"I said, 'no.'

"He called for the pitcher to pick me off. The pitcher threw and I slid behind Ruth. He was looking around to tag me and I already was on the sack. I think this made him mad. He called for the ball again. This time he was blocking the base and he swung his arm around thinking I would slide the same way. But this time I slid through his legs, and he was looking behind. The fans cheered. Ruth said, 'If you do that to me again, I'll pick you up and use you as a bat, you runt.'"

The box score shows that Zeni walked twice and stole a base.

What it doesn't show is that the Big Fella had met his spiritual equal in Zenimura, a diminutive man who needed baseball—who relied on it to organize his day and define the boundaries of his life—every bit as much as did the Babe. They would both find a future without it impossible to tolerate.

With the help of Zeni and the Nisei players, the Lous whomped the Babes, 13–3 or 15–3, depending on which newspaper you read. Either way, they were whomped. John Nakagawa was 1 for 2 with a stolen base. Fred Yoshikawa had a double. Harvey Iwata did not get in the game.

Afterward, Frank Kamiyama gathered the four Japanese Americans beside Ruth and Gehrig for a commemorative photograph. Toshiyuki had his 16mm camera running as Kamiyama tried to herd them into place.

In the still photo, Ruth and Gehrig tower over Zeni and the others like skyscrapers on a block of tenement houses, with the Babe using his shoulder as a convenient armrest, smiles and smirks frozen in place. The footage remained buried in an attic for seven decades until family members presented it to Zeni's son, Howard, at a memorial service for his niece. He gave it to

Kerry Yo Nakagawa, a local filmmaker and author, whose uncle John was one of the Nisei.

He screened it that night on his laundry room wall, watching as the figures in the still photo camera came alive, his Uncle Johnny grinning, and Zeni clowning, pulling Gehrig into the center of the group, Lou bending a knee so as not to dwarf him too much.

"You start seeing Babe Ruth swinging, [taking] batting practice, mingling," Howard said. "He made sure my dad was in the middle. He's leaning on my dad, making fun of him. He's the great kidder, Babe Ruth. I couldn't imagine how small he was and how big Babe Ruth was. How can he compete with guys that big?"

Johnny was bigger than the others and had had to turn down a scholarship to play baseball for a Japanese university in order to help out on the family ranch in Fresno. When his nephew, Kerry, pointed to the picture on the wall and asked about the game, Johnny could say, "We were on Lou Gehrig's team and we beat Babe Ruth."

Kerry Yo Nakagawa would establish the Nisei Baseball Research Project and tell their story in a documentary and a book, *Through a Diamond: 100 Years of Japanese American Baseball*. "For Johnny, it was much like the Negro League players—his chance to show how equal they were inside the lines," he said.

For Zeni, it was also an opportunity to try to accomplish what no one else had been able to do so far: arrange a trip to Japan for Babe Ruth.

When he received copies of the still photograph taken at the game, Zenimura scribbled a handwritten note on the back of one and mailed it to his friend at Meiji University and also to Japanese newspapermen, hoping to elicit interest in promoting a tour for the Babe, who had turned down an offer of 30,000 yen from Waseda College—approximately $15,000—in 1925. (Walsh had demanded $25,000.)

"This picture was taken at Fresno when Babe Ruth and Gehrig of the New York Yankees visited us on October 29th," Zenimura wrote. "We played against them and made a wide reputation for our team. Babe Ruth is interested to visit Japan and have asked me to try and line up things in Japan so that he may be able to come to Japan with our team. I wrote to the Meiji University asking them to what extent they can offer to have Babe Ruth in Japan. I believe it will draw to have Babe Ruth in Japan.

"I am sending this picture to you so that you may have this picture in your leading page. It's my remembrance to you."

An offer was forthcoming. Again, it wasn't enough.

"I got a call from Japan to see if I could get Ruth to go to the Island and play for a $40,000 guarantee," Zenimura told the *Fresno Bee* in 1962. "I contacted Ruth and he said he would go for $60,000."

Conquering Japan was going to cost.

III

When Ruth returned to Firemen's Park in the fall of 1931, the game was played at night under newly installed lights, which Ruth declared unnatural. Zenimura and the Nisei players were pointedly not included by the organizers, an omission Zenimura's biographer, Bill Staples, attributes to rising ethnic tensions in the area stemming from the Depression.

Much had changed by then. The Yankees of Murderers' Row encountered mortality in 1929. First in the bottom of the fifth inning of the first game of a Sunday doubleheader against the Red Sox at the Stadium on May 19. There were 50,000 people in the ballpark, 9,540 of them in the uncovered outfield bleachers. Of those, 5,000—mostly young boys known as "Babe's gang"—were stationed behind him in Ruthville.

Ruth had hit his seventh home run of the year in the third inning and was due up again in the fifth. So even as the skies darkened, and rain began to fall, they held their positions, hoping he might gratify them again, but he grounded out to first.

Then: a cloudburst. The suddenness of the squall propelled them en masse toward the closest exit, down fourteen, steep, wet wooden steps constrained on either side by chicken wire and two-by-four wooden posts, a chute no more than ten feet wide.

The exact catalyst for the stampede that followed was uncertain. Someone said a woman screamed at a bolt of lightning; someone else said a boy slipped, or maybe it was a grown man. Accounts varied. "Panic Occurs in Ruthville," read the thirteenth deck of the *Times'* fifteen-deck front-page headline.

Sixty-two people were injured; two were trampled to death: sixty-year-old chauffeur Joseph Carter and seventeen-year-old Hunter College student Eleanor Price, who had brought her little brother, George, to the game. They were found at the bottom of the steps.

A patrolman, one of three hundred that converged on the scene, drew his pistol, ordering the pushing, fleeing, bellowing crowds to help him remove the chicken wire after one boy was pushed through it. A ladies' room was converted into a temporary emergency room. There were no drugs or medical supplies on hand.

The players, who had retreated to the clubhouse, and the fans seated beneath the overhangs in the covered grandstand, were oblivious until sirens began to wail and the injured began straggling onto the field. The most serious cases were taken to the Yankee locker room.

The Associated Press and the *Daily News* credited Ruth with being first to return to the field and, "using his hands as a megaphone, summoned physicians to come to the Yankee offices." The United Press reported that Price died in his arms as he stroked her brow. "Ruth Holds Head of Dying Girl Victim as Grandstand Throngs Laugh, Unaware of Tragedy," blared the headline in the *Philadelphia Inquirer*. The story mentioned that an elderly fan had collapsed in his arms and died during a barnstorming tour the previous year.

The *Daily News* called it "a tragedy of stupidity," blaming throngs of fans who had huddled at the bottom of the stairs when the rain began, waiting in case it abated or Ruth pulled off another spectacular feat, something worth hustling back up the steps in the rain to see.

The Yankees were absolved of responsibility by the Bronx District Attorney. They did not cancel their exhibition game in New Haven the next day.

Upon their return, Babe and Claire, accompanied

by Christy Walsh and a contingent of press photographers, went to Lincoln Hospital to visit the remaining convalescents, boys with broken ribs, fractured skulls, and battered faces, whose appearance compelled Claire to retire to the hospital office, where restoratives were applied. Then they paid condolence calls at the homes of the deceased. George Price, who did not yet know of his sister Eleanor's death, told Ruth she would be sore at having missed him.

Two weeks later, after hitting his tenth home run on June 1, Ruth disappeared from the Yankee lineup. His right wrist was hurting, and he had developed a heavy chest cold that threatened to turn into pneumonia. But it seemed more dire than that when Dr. Edward King, his personal physician, sent him to St. Vincent's Hospital overnight, and later acknowledged hearing a slight heart murmur. Rumors spread of a heart attack.

"Reported at various times yesterday first as desperately ill, then as dying and finally as dead, Babe Ruth, lying comfortably on a day bed in the living room of his apartment . . . chuckled at the radio bulletins" and, the *Times* said, instructed Claire to inform reporters congregating at the front door: "You tell them that I'm far from a dead one."

The next day, the invalid granted them an audience in a room the New York *Sun* compared to the rotunda of Grand Central Terminal and Versailles. He was reclining in a chaise longue in "a Paisley dressing gown of the stuff and design so beloved by our maiden great-aunts," the *Sun* opined, "over which was spread a pale violet coverlet of heavy silk. Upon his small feet were fawn-colored slippers."

Ruth informed the press that henceforth he would no longer play both games of a doubleheader or any regular season exhibition games. Also, he was going on vacation. He said he needed some time to "get my nerves in shape."

Ordered to bed for a minimum of ten days, and warned that he would have to observe certain abstentions—*no smoking, no chewing? No bending an elbow?*—Babe and Claire took off for parts undisclosed. A cottage on the Chesapeake Bay near Annapolis, it turned out, where he did some fishing and swimming. He also played croquet in Washington.

He did not return to the team until June 19, pronouncing himself fine and acting as if nothing had ever happened. But things were not fine. The team was slipping and aging and maybe a bit spooked. Manager Miller Huggins developed a bacterial infection on his cheek that began as a carbuncle, which he could not quit worrying about. Three times during the summer he missed games because of illness. He entered the hospital on September 20. Five days later he was dead.

News reached the Yankees in the bottom of the fifth inning at Fenway Park. After a moment of silence, while the flag was lowered to half-mast, they played on, with the Yankees winning in the eleventh inning by the score of 11–10. In the clubhouse, Ruth cried, as did several of his teammates. When Tom Meany reported this to a copy editor at his paper in New York, he was ordered to quit overwriting. "I can't help it," Meany replied. "They were crying."

They finished second behind the Philadelphia Athletics in 1929 and 1930 and third in 1931. The Ruth-Gehrig-led Yankees would win only one more championship, which is remembered more for the legend of the Called Shot than for Ruth's accomplishments in that World Series (preceded by a week in bed, packed in ice with a low-grade fever and suspected appendicitis.)

Perhaps this explains, at least in part, why everything after the sixtieth home run and his three-home-run game in the 1928 World Series feels almost anticlimactic—just more of the same.

Ruth became a constant in a time of national upheaval, a last repository of American bravado. No one begrudged him his eighty thou a year for 1931–32. Or minded one little bit his braggadocio when asked about making more than the president of the United States: "I had a better year."

His decline as an offensive player was hardly precipitous. In his last seven years in Yankee pinstripes, designed to make him look more svelte, his percentage of home runs per at-bat actually increased from 8.4 percent to 8.7 percent, compared with Gehrig's career percentage of 6.2 percent. His rate of RBI production also increased later in his career: from 0.84 RBI per game between 1914 and 1927 to 0.95 RBI between 1928 and 1935. (Gehrig's career value was .92 RBI per game.)

His WAR for his last seven years as a Yankee was 8.2, compared with 9.2 during his first eight years in New York. Most tellingly, according to Dave Smith, founder of Retrosheet, the online compendium of major-league statistics, his OPS+ was 195 for the later years of his career, "which is still 95 percent better than the average major leaguer."

In 1931, he had one of his finest offensive seasons, the last of six straight years in which he led the major leagues in home runs (46), along with 162 RBI and 149 runs scored. At Wrigley Field a year later, where he sabotaged a short fly ball hit to him in the outfield, the problem was clear. "My dogs ain't what they used to be."

Watching from the press box, Westbrook Pegler wrote, "As an outfielder he is pretty close to his past tense, which may mean that one year from now he will be only a pinch-hitter. He has been breaking this news to himself and the customers all year."

Whatever he had lost in reflex and mobility, he maintained in dramatic timing—hitting the first home run in the inaugural All-Star Game at Chicago's Comiskey Park in 1933. He finished that season, his twentieth in the major leagues, with 34 home runs, 104 RBI, and a .301 batting average. Pretty good for anyone else. He was thirty-nine years old. The Yankees had had enough of him.

At the end of the season, Frank Navin, the owner of the Detroit Tigers, asked for and received Jake Ruppert's (grateful) permission to speak to Ruth about becoming player-manager for the Tigers. But Christy Walsh had scheduled exhibition games in Hawaii. Ruth blithely said he'd call Navin when he got back.

By the time he got home the job had been filled by Mickey Cochrane.

In December, Walsh staged a celebratory dinner at the New York Athletic Club on the occasion of the announcement of Ruth's All America Baseball Team. He created a testimonial tabloid he called "The Daily Ghost," which included a tribute from Hendrik Willem van Loon casting Ruth as the unlikely antihero of the self-indulgent twenties:

> During the great and unglorious period of our national delusion when every man was a potential millionaire and the wisecrack was the passport to success, when nobody any longer tried to do things well or at least as well as he could which is all we can ever ask of anyone all the old standards went by the boards and all that was necessary to become a hero was a sneaky ability to "get by" with the least possible effort. It was then that you rendered us all a service for which I am among many others who still believe in human progress are profoundly grateful. For during those unfortunate years, we could still be certain of two absolute standards of values that could not possibly be challenged: the integrity of Christy Walsh and the perfection of your work on the diamond.

It read like an epitaph. Only Ruth didn't recognize it.

Desperate to be rid of their arthritic, obese albatross in the outfield, Ruppert and Barrow cut his salary to

$35,000. When that didn't discourage him, Barrow suggested he might like to manage the Yankees farm club in Newark.

Why, that's like asking Jake Ruppert to run a soda fountain, Ruth replied.

Walsh indulged his vanity, as did Claire, and later rued his bad advice, telling columnist Joe Williams that had Ruth accepted the minor-league assignment and gotten some managerial experience, Ruppert surely would have summoned him to the Bronx after another desultory season under McCarthy. "That year the Yankees were to finish second for the third straight year," Walsh said. "If I hadn't dissuaded Ruth against going to Newark I'm sure Ruppert would have called him up."

By 1934, his body was breaking down; his knees so painful, his grandson, Tom Stevens, said, he once had to ask teammate Joe Sewell for help putting on his baseball pants. He had taken some kind of painkiller and in his stupefaction had put them on backward.

His roistering days were behind him. If not quite sedate, the Babe had become at least respectably middle-aged, especially around the middle. He had made his future ambitions all too clear, all too often.

He hadn't understood why the Yankees turned to former teammate Bob Shawkey to succeed Huggins in 1930. He wasn't alone in his perplexity; that experiment didn't work. He fumed, pouted, and turned surly when former Chicago Cubs manager Joe McCarthy was hired to succeed Shawkey in 1931.

His thwarted ambitions filled hundreds of column inches in the summer of 1934. Friendly writers pointed out that the Babe had never made a mistake on the baseball field; naysayers responded that he couldn't remember anyone's name much less all those complicated signs that needed to be relayed from the dugout—like scratching your head when the batter was supposed to take a pitch.

On Saturday morning, June 25, Jhan Robbins, the boy reporter from Samuel Tilden High School in Brooklyn, boarded the train for the hour-and-a-half ride to Yankee Stadium to interview the Babe. He wasn't a Yankee fan—he was from Flatbush, after all. But he had an assignment for his school newspaper and a note from his teacher, which served as a press credential, and a brown-bag lunch his mother had tied with string. He headed for the bleachers, where he asked an usher for directions to the Yankee locker room.

The Babe was drinking a soda pop, and gulping

handfuls of salted peanuts when Jhan found his way to the clubhouse. "Have a swig," the Babe said, handing over the soda bottle.

Somehow overcoming the germophobia his mother had instilled in him, Jhan helped himself to a deep gulp of independence and recalled the sports column he'd read on the train, the sum total of which was the old saw: "How can he manage the Yankees when he can't even manage himself?"

Hoping to sound grown-up, he thought that might make a good line of questioning, and worked that one in after lobbing some initial softballs. Ruth's response was molten. "That's the trouble with you newspaper guys," Ruth roared. "You never forget the past. You never give a guy a credit for learning anything.

"Maybe I lived it up in my time; but don't forget, I did the papers a favor—I gave you plenty to write about!"

The spasm of fury directed at the high school boy—*you newspaper guys*—was as poignant as it was hilarious.

Now I've got to answer to a kid?

"I've settled down now," he said. "All I want is a chance."

It was the plaintive cry of a man whose epitaph had already been carved in a million headlines: *Just a big overgrown kid.* It was an authentic voice, not the con-fabulation of a ghostwriter. This was a man begging to be seen for who he had become and not for the image he so happily collaborated in constructing. It figures he would reveal himself most fully to a fourteen-year-old boy reporter trying to play the role of an adult, but ironic, too, that he was pleading with a child to be seen as an adult.

The Babe couldn't allow the kid to go away feeling as bruised as the banana his mother had packed for him that morning. So he made him a promise he could no longer keep. "I'll show you I still got plenty," he vowed. "I'll hit one just for you."

He didn't. But he hit a grand slam the next day, the sixteenth and last of his career.

It would take decades for Robbins to understand the complexity of the emotional transaction that had taken place between them. If Ruth was the first athlete to fully avail himself of the modern mechanisms of image making, he was also the first to feel trapped by them. *The boy who never grew up.* The idea was as fixed and as immobile as he had become in the field.

He was a national monument, something to ogle, to say you'd seen. Kids on the West Side of Manhattan, like Arnold Hano, went to the Stadium and demanded that Joe McCarthy put him back in the game after he'd been taken out for a late-inning defensive replacement—as he was seventy-nine times in 1934—though they knew the rule. *We want the Babe. We want the Babe.* "Still we were disappointed," said Hano, who became a sportswriter and twice wrote about Ruth for *Sport*. "You couldn't replace him. It was like having a godfather that we could look up to and be proud of, doing all those things nobody had never done before."

Kids like Blake Talbot, a young Missouri recruit at one of the Citizens' Military Training Camps that Ruth supported, who swelled with pride when he was selected to attend a St. Louis Browns game at Sportsman's Park and visit the Yankee locker room. "And there was the ol' Babe setting on one of the wooden benches taking his pants off and getting ready to get dressed in front of his old tin locker. His tummy was hanging over his belt."

Low over his belt.

Naked except for the burning stogie in his mouth, he talked to the kid for maybe half an hour, answered all his questions, leaning over to Gehrig to ask, "Did they give me a hit or an error on that one I mauled?"

"Gehrig said, 'An error.'

"And Babe said, 'Those SOBs. I have to put it over the fence to get a hit.'"

After hitting his 700th home run on July 13 in Detroit, he announced he was done as an everyday player. He went 0 for 3 in his last game as a Yankee on September 30. At season's end, he asked Ruppert if he was still satisfied with McCarthy as his manager. "Thoroughly," Ruppert replied.

His Yankee career was over.

The Babe made plans to set sail for Japan with Lefty O'Doul, Connie Mack, and a team of American League all-stars, among them Lou Gehrig, Jimmie Foxx, Charlie Gehringer, and Moe Berg, the catcher who would become better known as an American spy. It was then, in applying for his passport, that he discovered he was a year younger than he thought: his birth date was February 6, 1895, not February 7, 1894.

He left Vancouver on October 28 aboard the *Empress of Japan* with Claire and Julia and Lou and his wife, Eleanor (enjoying a belated honeymoon). Whatever the state of the rift between them when they embarked for Japan—and no matter how much worse it was upon their return—it did not preclude an act of generosity on Ruth's part, recalled by the *New York Times* reporter John Drebinger in an interview with Jerome Holtzman. Perhaps Ruth was trying to make things better between them. Or maybe it was just his way. "Lou never could forget he was a poor boy once and was always worried that he was going to lose his money," Drebinger said. So Ruth advanced him the $5,000 each was to receive, telling Gehrig, "When the trip is over and you get your $5,000 you can pay me."

One afternoon, Eleanor found Claire sitting by herself topside in a deck chair. A spontaneous hello, a crack in the frigid familial relations, led to a mutual understanding that the feud, instigated by Lou's mother, was silly, which led to a spontaneous invitation to join the Ruths in their stateroom to partake in "an empire of caviar and champagne," as Eleanor described it in her memoir, *My Luke and I.*

She partook for two hours while her anxious hubby (and most of the crew) searched the ship and scanned the horizon. When the iron-willed Iron Horse finally found his happily tipsy bride in the Ruths' cabin, he refused to speak to her and spurned Ruth's "Let's be pals" bear hug when he barged into the Gehrigs' stateroom later that day.

Eleanor denied subsequent rumors (circulated by her attorney, according to author Ray Robinson) that she had shared more than caviar and champagne with the Babe. Either way, the rift was irrevocable. It would remain so until July 4, 1939, when Gehrig, dying of amyotrophic lateral sclerosis, the disease that would come to bear his name, gave his "luckiest man" speech at home plate at Yankee Stadium. And Ruth, resplendent in a white suit and an open-collared shirt, wrapped him in a bear hug and whispered something that made him smile.

As their motorcade made its way from the station in Tokyo on November 2, heading east toward Frank Lloyd Wright's Imperial Hotel, a half-million Japanese lined the Ginza, shouting, "Banzai, banzai, Babe Ruth!"

The outpouring was balm to his soul. He called baseball his love game. In Japan, he found a place where baseball still loved him back. Connie Mack hailed him as a "peace promoter" on the front page of the *New York Times*, and said he looked better at the plate than he had in two years. Meanwhile, Moe Berg was photographing military installations with the help of Takizo Matsumoto.

On their way home, Babe, Claire, and Julia stopped in Manila and Singapore, as well as Bali and Java, where he pronounced himself unimpressed by the women, whom he found "too chesty and too black," according to the United Press. He rode in rickshaws and passed through the Suez Canal en route to Marseille. He skied in St. Moritz. He was disdained in Paris. "Not much of a town," he said.

He liked London better.

The more Ruth saw of the world, the more he missed the only one he knew. Two days after the Ruths disembarked in Manhattan on February 20, word reached the United States that a nationalist fanatic had stabbed the publisher of Tokyo's third-largest newspaper in retribution for his disloyalty to the homeland in sponsoring Ruth's barnstorming tour.

While the Ruths were still in Europe, Walsh had received an offer for the Babe's services from the failing 101 Ranch Wild West Show. They'd pay him $75,000—or 30 percent of the gross—to ride an elephant behind a calliope playing "Take Me Out to the Ball Game."

The only baseball offer came from Judge Emil Fuchs, owner of the Boston Braves, which looked swell compared with the alternative. The $25,000 salary included two fancy titles—vice president and assistant manager—and the glimmer of a prospect of a hope of succeeding Bill McKechnie as manager.

The Yankees gleefully granted him his unconditional release. By the time spring training camp opened, they had assigned his number 3 to a new right fielder, George Selkirk, and filled his St. Petersburg locker with kindling.

He hit a home run in his first game back in Boston as a member of the National League Braves off King Carl Hubbell, raising hopes of a miraculous reincarnation, only to spend the next two months dashing them. He went a whole month without hitting a home run and arrived in Pittsburgh in late May with a .153 batting average, two aching knees, and a shape that exceeded caricature. McKechnie had him batting third and staking out his old territory in right field on Saturday afternoon, May 25.

The Pirates pitching staff included two particularly familiar faces: his old friend and teammate Waite Hoyt, and his old tormentor from the 1932 World Series, Guy Bush. In the clubhouse before the game, according to Marshall Smelser's account, starter Red Lucas expressed qualms about facing the Babe—even this old, doddering version of him. Hoyt assured him the solution was simple: throw behind him. "One base on four balls or four bases on one ball."

Bush scoffed. Throw him sinkers, he said. He'd gotten Ruth out on sinkers in Chicago in 1932. Yes, Hoyt, pointed out, but Charlie Root had thrown him sinkers and they ended up in the center field bleachers.

In the top of the first inning, Lucas threw Ruth a

sinker and it landed in the right field stands. He was replaced by Guy Bush, who'd hurled racial invective at Ruth from the top step of the dugout in Game 3 of the 1932 Series and hit him in the arm with his best fastball in Game 4. Hard enough that Ruth wouldn't have been able to play had there been a Game 5.

There are many definitions of greatness. Surely one of them is the ability to summon the memory of it when fate, or in this case the opposing manager, offers an operatic opportunity to perform at your best one more time.

Ruth arrived at the plate with one on, one out, and a long memory. Like Lucas, Bush threw him a sinker. It, too, landed in the right field stands, though not by that much, for Ruth's second two-run home run of the afternoon.

The *Boston Globe* dismissed these less than titanic blows as being "in the manner of ordinary sluggers." But there was nothing ordinary about what followed.

Bush was still on the mound when Ruth came to bat in the seventh. Having also surrendered an RBI single to the old man in the fifth on yet another sinker, Bush reconsidered his approach. No more pussyfooting around. The Babe was getting his best stuff. But Bush's fastball came in straight and far too true, between Ruth's sagging waist and his aching knees, and caught a little too much of the plate.

A flock of *Pittsburgh Press* delivery boys and the usual neighborhood crew occupied the lower right field stands set aside every Saturday afternoon. Phil Coyne, a seventeen-year-old from the Oakland section of town located behind the ballpark, was there, as he would be many days thereafter. He would go to work as an usher two years later and continued to show Pirate fans to their seats until the end of the 2017 season, when he was ninety-nine years old. "The first two home runs we really didn't pay attention to," he said. "We just run around a lot. But the third one we paid attention to. A miracle happened and he hit it all the way over the fence."

By which he meant the eighty-six-foot-high roof of the grandstand that had been extended into right field two years earlier. "That was a good, good, ways up there."

The last home run of Ruth's career, number 714, was one of those rainbows young Arnold Hano saw so many of in the Bronx, so high they "almost scraped the top of the sky."

A bunch of kids ran after it into the hollow behind the ballpark; Phil Coyne couldn't honestly say that he was one of them. The senior usher Gus Miller was dispatched and came back with a report that the ball bounced off a roof of a house on Bouquet Street. Phil was pretty sure that wasn't true—Bouquet ran parallel to the ballpark.

As Ruth circled the bases, Bush tipped his cap. And the Babe tipped his. It was a bravura performance: 4 for 4 with 6 RBI.

He bypassed the Braves bench and headed directly for the Pittsburgh dugout, which was the only way to access the visiting clubhouse. He plopped himself down on the end of the bench beside a rookie pitcher, Mace Brown, who'd placed himself there hoping to get in Ruth's way. "Boy, that last one felt good," Ruth said.

Duffy Lewis, a former Boston teammate and now the Pirates' road secretary, pleaded with him to quit. Claire pleaded with him to quit. Walsh called from New York and ordered him to quit.

"I can't," Ruth said, explaining the commitment he had made to Judge Fuchs to appear at scheduled Babe Ruth Day events on the road trip. "I promised the old sonofabitch I'd play through the Memorial Day double-header in Philadelphia."

The thing they accused him of lacking—a sense of

responsibility—kept him going another two weeks. He never got another hit.

On Thursday, May 30, in Philadelphia, he hurt his knee trying to reach a ball hit in his direction in left field. At age forty, he was unable to move quickly enough or far enough to catch it. The ball rolled past him to the wall of the old Baker Bowl where he had played in his first World Series game. After the hitter was thrown out at the plate trying for an inside-the-park home run, Ruth stuffed his glove in his back pocket and headed for the clubhouse in deep center field.

He announced his retirement three days later.

IV

By unhappy coincidence, Ruth's acrimonious separation from the Braves came just three months after Walsh's equally acrimonious divorce from his wife, Mada. He withdrew from New York, from daily engagement in Ruth's affairs, and from daily management of the Christy Walsh Syndicate in March 1935 to attend to litigation and a protracted custody fight, which would prove to be as sordid as any story he ever suppressed involving the Babe. His wife accused him of fathering an illegitimate child; he accused her of turning his son against him. After meeting with Christy Jr. in chambers, the judge called the eleven-year-old boy "a cream puff" and coun-seled, "what he needs is a good spanking."

The timing of Walsh's removal from the scene was ironic for him, given the New Yorker's belated ap-preciation for "The Ghosting Business" he had built, expressed in an Alva Johnston profile published in November. It was just plain untimely for Ruth, who "covered" his fifteenth consecutive—and last—World Series for the Christy Walsh Syndicate that fall without Walsh at his side.

For the entirety of his adult existence, the dailiness of baseball, its rhythms and immutable schedule, had governed and organized his life. Rebel as he might, the expectations were ingrained—and reinforced by Walsh, who held him accountable by making it profit-able to do so.

Now the two great organizing principles of his life, baseball and Walsh, were gone. The distance between them was more than geographical. To some extent, that was inevitable. They had played out their string. The market for has-beens in the depths of the Depression wasn't what it is today. There was also tension between Walsh and Claire over control of the family pocket-book.

Ruth would continue to earn significant endorse-ment income from contracts Walsh had negotiated for the next three years, including those for radio shows with Sinclair Oil and Quaker Oats, and a sporting goods deal with A. G. Spalding. Those three endorsements alone generated $55,000.

Details of various endorsement contracts had been strategically leaked and often inflated over the years. But the first accurate dollar figures were reported as a consequence of a lawsuit Walsh filed against his wife stemming from their divorce, charging her with absconding with $23,931 in community property.

Newspapers that subscribed to the Christy Walsh Syndicate picked up the March 5, 1937, United Press dispatch promising "inside dope" on the endorsement game: Ruth's $25,000-a-year deal with Quaker Oats; Walsh's 50 percent take of the Babe's ghostwritten stories; and his ten-cent take on the sale of every "All-American" sweater sold by Pacific Knitting Mills because he owned the rights to the title "All American Board of Football."

When Walsh's last contract with Ruth expired on May 1, 1938, he sent a letter marking the end of their formal relationship, which he called no "ordinary friendship" and "a bond of understanding and confidence." He also prepared an itemized account of his stewardship of Ruth's affairs during "17 years of congenial and mutually profitable relations."

Walsh complained bitterly about paying alimony, legal fees, and medical bills for Christy Jr., whose health appeared more delicate to his mother than to his many physicians, but when all the legal wrangling was said and done, he told van Loon, "I do not owe a dollar to any man or any woman in the world . . . and I have a few dollars in the bank!"

In the fall of 1937, Walsh placed an advertisement in *Editor & Publisher* announcing that the Christy Walsh Syndicate had given up the ghost. With Ruth retired, Huggins and Rockne dead, and radio giving voice to a new generation of athletes, the ghostwriting business was DOA. The willing suspension of disbelief was no longer willing.

It was time to say adios to ghosts. He wrote and published the little memoir of that name in September (available by mail order for fifty cents) in which he revealed a few trade secrets, which everyone already knew, and got his name in the papers again. In October, he accepted a $10,000-a-year job as director of sports for the 1939 World's Fair in Flushing Meadows.

Three months later, he gave up his three-year fight for joint custody of his son, surrendered his parental rights, and returned to New York, bringing his mother with him. He threw her a seventy-fifth birthday party at the Hotel Roosevelt, where he assembled an unlikely a capella quartet featuring Eddie Rickenbacker, Babe Ruth, Democratic party boss James A. Farley, and Governor Al Smith.

He threw himself into work and his new New York life, crowing in a letter to van Loon, "I am 44, still able to produce a family, do not smoke or drink; swear artistically, when the occasion demands; never gamble or play cards but won $3 the first and only time I played 'Monopoly'; my temper is not uncontrollable (as was recently alleged in court) and I am not 'imperious' (as was further alleged); I have NO INTENTION OF MARRYING AGAIN, on the other hand, if a gorgeous creature, who is intelligent and congenial, comes along, my decision is subject to appeal. IMPORTANT: I have long, skinny legs, a funny looking Irish face but I am a hell of a lover!"

He changed his mind about matrimony after meeting Miss Margaret Merritt, a young hostess at the fair, his new "oh-my-goodness"—in Winchell's delicious phrase. They would "middle aisle it"—as Winchell might have said—but not until after his dear mother's death.

He created an Academy of Sports for the 1939 World's Fair, which he envisioned as a gathering spot where luminaries of the sports world—most of them former clients—would meet with fans and give athletic tutorials. He stationed the Babe on a float in the April 1938 parade through Manhattan and Queens, touting "the world of tomorrow" being built in a former ash heap.

He had been hired for his contacts in the sports world and newspaper business, but his enthusiasm for employing them irked Commander Howard A. Flanigan, chief administrative assistant to World's Fair president Grover Whalen. "It is evident throughout this report that Mr. Walsh is thinking of a 'Christy Walsh' show at the Fair and not a World's Fair show," he tutted in a memo.

Walsh fulminated in reply and threatened to quit, citing his lack of autonomy and vacation days, not to mention missed paychecks, but stayed on when Whalen granted him greater control of sports for the 1940 fair.

He continued to perform the occasional service for the Babe, but when executives at the Equitable Life Assurance Company with whom Walsh had worked to create Ruth's annuities appealed to him to intercede with Ruth because new advisers were encouraging him to take money out of the account prematurely, Walsh pointedly declined. "This has been a headache to me for many years, with no compensation (and little or no evidence of gratitude) so I don't feel like putting any more time in on the matter," he told Equitable vice president William J. Graham in a November 1938 letter.

Apparently, the headache to which he referred—and which he would disclose a decade later to a friendly Los Angeles sports columnist—was Claire Ruth's belief that he had structured the policy in order to prevent her from having access to the funds in the event of a divorce. "Claire thought Walsh had been plotting directly against her, which was not the case," the columnist wrote. "But she resented it, nevertheless. While they were friendly in ensuing years, the Babe and Christy never were as close again."

In Walsh's absence, Claire put her husband on a fifty-dollar-a-week allowance.

By the time the country emerged from the twin cataclysms of World War II and the Great Depression, the business model Walsh had created—"making the circus tent as large as possible without denigrating it to the point where people don't want to pay for the ride," as one modern agent described it—and Walsh himself had been completely forgotten.

No one would come along to take his place until George Weiss, who had succeeded Larry MacPhail as Yankee general manager, fired traveling secretary Frank Scott in 1950 for getting too close to the players. Scott then opened a business arranging side deals for the likes of Berra, Mantle, and DiMaggio, which earned him a prominent obituary in the *New York Times* in 1998, in which he was identified as "Baseball's First Player Agent."

By then, Christy Walsh had been dead and buried for forty-three years.

V

After leaving the Braves on June 2, Ruth went home and waited for the phone to ring.

It didn't.

A month after he retired, Paramount News cameras were on hand to film his return to the field of play—in a celebrity softball game at the Westchester Country Club. Decked out in Napoleonic-era naval garb, with a bicorne hat, and whiskers drawn on his cheeks, he arrived in the company of a drum major, an accordionist, and a sax player. As club members looked on from lawn chairs, Ruth affected to cut a ball in half with his sword and then when the game began swung and missed at the first pitch. His faux whiskers spread a black stain across his face as he did battle with heat and exertion.

In August, Paul Gallico brought him to Jones Beach to hit fungoes into Zach's Bay at a water circus promoted by the *Daily News*. When the tens of thousands of sunbathers gathered on the shore caught sight of him, "the crowd caught fire like a blaze running over a dry meadow," Gallico wrote. Then the Babe began hitting balls from the stage, and hundreds of children quit the beach, churning the bay into foam, in hopes of corralling one of the white orbs that traveled farther and farther as he found his rhythm. At the evening performance, he launched phosphorescent balls into the night sky for thousands more screaming adherents—some 60,000 had come to see him that day—and Gallico wondered how it was possible that he remained unemployed.

"I know no words for his despondency," Claire Ruth wrote later.

Ray Robinson, a teenage delivery boy for a neighborhood liquor store on Manhattan's West Side, who later authored a well-regarded Gehrig biography, delivered Scotch to Ruth's Riverside Drive apartment one afternoon. He found the Babe in his robe and slippers. And he got a one-dollar tip—the only tip he ever got.

Ruth went to very few ball games. The Yankees never issued him a lifetime pass to the Stadium. Ford Frick saw to it he got a pass for the National League. "It is nice to know the National League has a heart," Ruth said. He had to pay his way into American League ballparks until 1936, when both leagues created a program of passes for ten-year veterans.

That year, he was at the Polo Grounds for opening day. When the photographers found him, he was his most accommodating self: "Grin, sure I'll grin," he told the Associated Press. "What's that? You want me to look bewildered? Okay, okay, anything to please."

Then the game began and they had better things to do.

The AP referred to him as baseball's forgotten man—a new name to add to the list of out-of-date honorifics that writers summoned now only in pity.

The 1936 season ended with another Yankee World Series victory and rumors that Cap Huston was interested in purchasing the Dodgers and might want the Babe as his manager. At the Yankee victory banquet at the Commodore Hotel, Walsh arranged to have the band play "Take Me Out to the Ball Game" as Ruth entered the room and eased his passage, escorting him to the table where all the bigwigs were gathered. But the rumors came to naught. Frick, whom he'd enriched through Walsh's ghostwriting syndicate, had taken up broadcasting for WINS and championed Ruth's managerial cause: "Miller Huggins predicted that if ever Babe Ruth grew up, quit his kidding, and got serious, he'd make a whale of a manager. Babe has done just that. I'd like to see him get his chance. I think he'd be a howling success."

Upon Frick's elevation to president of the National League in 1937, however, he had a stone-cold change of heart, telling the Associated Press, "Despite all these heart-rending pieces I've been reading about what a pitiable figure he is—forced to spend his days shooting golf and moose [hunting] and following the sunshine in winter—I can't help thinking there must be many folks in a worse fix."

The night before his forty-third birthday, Ruth rounded up a bunch of reporters for an impromptu celebration. He had installed a beer spigot in the kitchen. Claire had purchased a new easy chair for his less-than-easy retirement. He told reporters gathered in the den his proudest possession was a cartoon showing his bat parting the black clouds hovering over the game after the cheating scandal of 1919.

Someone asked about his golf handicap. "Boys, if it wasn't for golf I think I'd die," he replied, according to the AP's February 6, 1937, dispatch. "God bless the man who invented golf. I'm 43 on the head. But I can't tell whether I'm just beginning to live. If it's okay with everyone, I'd just as soon be 21 again."

He divided his time between bowling (usually alone, often at the Riverside Plaza Hotel) and golf (240 rounds in 1936). The day he retired, he called his friend Granny Rice and said, "Get out your clubs, kid, I'm ready for you now."

But how many rounds can a man play for fun or for charity before his patience wears thin and an executive in the Babe's foursome who'd been berating his caddy finds himself dumped in a water hazard by the Big Fella who had nothing but time on his hands but no time for such foolishness.

He began spending time at Greenwood Lake, a resort community in Orange County, New York, where he kept a Morin Craft speedboat and, according to Dorothy, a mistress. The lake straddled the New York–New Jersey border, its shore lined with restaurants and roadhouses. He spent most of his time at Greck's Maplewood Inn on the Lake, a resort where he was treated like family.

Ruth hunted with proprietor Ted Greck Sr. and bunked in a cottage bedroom with two twin beds belonging to Ted Jr., who piloted Ruth's boat when he was too drunk to do so. He also played catch with local kids brave enough to approach him in one of the bars he favored and treated them all to ice cream. He hung out at the local firehouse and helped raise money for the ladies' auxiliary. He always came alone.

"He had sad eyes," said Sally Jo Greck, Ted Sr.'s granddaughter. "He was looking for something."

Neither she nor her brother remembers the red-headed woman called Loretta mentioned in Dorothy Ruth Pirone's memoir.

The relationship with the Greck family did not end well. Ruth and Ted Sr. liked to gamble on the ponies and would sit in the bar and listen to the races broadcast from Monticello Raceway. "The bookie, Mr. Zimmerman, would come over, and they would bet on the horses," she said. "One night he kept getting up to make a phone call. So the bookie says to my grandfather, 'There's something wrong, Teddy; he's winning too much money.'

"Ted goes, 'No, no, no, he's probably just luckier than me.'

"Lo and behold, he was getting the race results from the race they were going to bet on because there was a delay from the time it was announced on the radio. They had a falling-out at that point. They never reconciled; then shortly thereafter, he passed away."

In June 1938, the phone rang. The Dodgers wanted him—basically as a lawn jockey in the first base coaching box, but they wanted him. Also, he would play in exhibition games and bat in pregame long-distance hitting contests. In his mind, and his mind only, there was also a possibility he might succeed Burleigh Grimes as manager. He asked Walsh to handle the negotiations. He asked for $25,000 and settled for $15,000 and cried when he signed the deal.

His first day in uniform was June 19, a Sunday doubleheader. He did his job well, clapping and gesturing broadly in the first base coaching box, and helped increase Dodger attendance by two hundred thousand over the previous year. Then he got into a scrap with the ineffably scrappy Leo Durocher, the Dodgers shortstop and managerial heir apparent.

They had never liked each other—both were still sore over the watch that went missing from Ruth's locker when Durocher was with the Yankees in 1928–29, which Leo either did or did not steal, depending on who you believed. In the Yankee locker room, only Ruth was believed.

At the end of July, Durocher got even, telling a reporter that Ruth had not called for the successful hit-and-run that scored the winning run on July 27. The reporter called Ruth a "wooden Indian" in the coaching box, according to Paul Dickson's account in *Leo Durocher*. The next day in the clubhouse, Ruth demanded the opportunity to confront his accuser in front of the team. Durocher was not alone in the belief that Ruth's inability to remember signs and plays should disqualify him from higher office, an ambition the Lip viewed as an expression of Ruthian entitlement.

Durocher shoved Ruth into his locker, slapping his face repeatedly, leaving a mark beneath his right eye— Durocher said—and leaving Ruth in a crumpled heap on the floor.

A month later, at Forbes Field in Pittsburgh, with nothing left to lose, Ruth asked the club road secretary to relay a request to be activated as a pinch-hitter, a conversation overheard by a young reporter for the New York *Sun*, Herb Goren, who recounted the events in a 1985 story for the *New York Times*.

I asked him why he wanted to be a pinch-hitter.

"Well, nobody sees me now," he said. "By the time they get to the park, we're done with batting practice."

And then the Babe had this afterthought: "In a couple of days the rosters go up from 25 to 40. I wouldn't be taking anybody's job. I wouldn't want to do that. Oh, I know what the guys are saying. I wouldn't get any fat ones to hit at. I can't run. OK, if I hit one out, I don't have to run."

The request was rejected. The clubhouse fracas with Durocher became public during the World Series, dooming whatever limited prospects remained for a managerial job. *He couldn't control himself!* He walked away from his last job in major-league baseball with another black eye on his reputation.

The following spring, the May 8, 1939, issue of *Look* magazine featured a two-page photo spread devoted to baseball's deposed home-run king—"The Strange Case of Babe Ruth." The author was Christy Walsh. He found Ruth in the den of his Riverside Drive apartment dressed in a gaudy kimono and surrounded by 350 equally gaudy trophies and 150 cartoons. The Babe was at peace with his modest fortune. "They'll never have to throw a benefit for George Herman Ruth," Walsh said. "Only a month ago, he rejected an offer that would have made him wealthy ($5,000 just to sign the contract) because it involved liquor and that involved his obligation to his kid fans."

Much as he longed to be back in the old monkey suit, Walsh wrote, "he happens to be one of those-old-fashioned Americans who admits an employer has rights"—including the right not to hire him. That said, Walsh testified to Ruth's expectation that he would be back with the Dodgers in 1939. "Babe would never have signed for a 'short haul,'" he said.

It was about this time that he was spotted wandering around the upper deck in right field at the Polo Grounds, directly across the Harlem River from the House That Ruth Built, where he no longer felt welcome, much less at home.

It was a weekday afternoon. A bunch of kids from the Catholic Youth Organization and the Police Athletic League had gotten in free. One of them, Vin Scully, had walked twenty blocks from his grammar school to see his favorite player, Mel Ott. "There was a disturbance. And all the kids started going over to see what was going on. Well, curiosity killed the cat. There was the man, dressed the way you'd expect him to be, in a camel hair coat and cap. I guess it was early spring or fall. He said, 'Hold it, hold it.' He reached into his pocket and got a fistful of autographed, stamped cards, about the size of business cards with his name. He didn't want pen and paper: he didn't want ink on his coat.

"When I told that story to friends of mine, they said, 'Why was he in the Polo Grounds?' When you're eleven years old, you don't think about those things. There he was. Maybe he heard there was a bunch of kids there. Then he kind of wandered away."

It was June 1902 all over again. It wouldn't have been so painful if he hadn't made the mistake of conflating fans and family. "As much as he surrounded himself with people, I think he was alone," said his granddaughter Donna Analovitch. "He couldn't get enough of people, but I don't know if he was ever attached to anything other than his fans and the game. And I don't think he had to have it because he was an egomaniac. I think he had to have it . . . for that sense of family.

"I think Babe was a window-wisher. You look at other people's lives and you wish. You're in a car, you drive by a house, the windows are open, they're all sitting down to dinner, and you wish some more. But you don't really connect with it. And you don't ever feel like you can have it.

"Look at how he related to people. 'Hey, kid! What can I sign?' 'Hi, Ma, how are you?' 'Hi, Pop, how are you?' He really related to his fans on a level of his pals or his mom or his pop. You have all these people, but you can't be close to any of them. They're not yours; they're not your people. You get to enjoy them and then they go home to their family, their parents, siblings, wives. And there he is alone again."

When the war came and the Japanese bombed Pearl Harbor, he took it almost personally. Hadn't they loved him, mobbed him, celebrated him? The framed flag of Japan presented by the emperor—gone. The flags he'd hung in the living room—out the window. The two engraved bronze vases earned for the "Long Distance Hitting Competition" and "Most Runs Scored"—one of them he kicked across the room so hard he dented it.

And when he learned they were taking his name in vain, charging into the American lines with a battle cry, "To hell with Babe Ruth," he replied, "I hope every Jap that mentions my name gets shot—and to hell with all Japs anyway."

The *New Yorker* sent an emissary from "The Talk of the Town" to his apartment to find out how he was bearing up.

"Sort of thing you'd expect from the itty-bittys," Ruth replied hoarsely—he was nursing a scratchy throat.

"I figured at the time that they were acting *awful* friendly. Why, we arrive at Yokohama and there's one million of the little fellows lined up, bowing and cheering and carrying American flags in one hand and Jap flags in the other. We take the train to Tokio and there's another million standing around near the station, all too damned polite. We schedule a practice game at a secret hideaway and when we arrive sixty thousand Japs are there first, yelling their lungs out. We get up in the mornings and are invited to eight different breakfasts by assorted committees. We step out of the hotel room and they're jammed in the corridors and down on the street, waiting for autographs. They were lovely to us, just lovely. . . .

"I'd go to bat and they'd yell, 'Hooray, God of baseball, yee, yee, yee.' I'd dust off my pants at second and they'd roar fit to die."

The patent wistfulness dissolved in an instant of baseball realpolitik. "A bat is as about as big as a Jap, and the fact is the itty-bittys can't hit."

VI

In the second week of May 1942, three months after President Franklin D. Roosevelt signed Executive Order 9066 authorizing the internment of tens of thousands of Japanese American citizens, Kenichi Zenimura; his wife, Kiyoko; and his sons, Howard and Harvey, were sent to live in an assembly center adjacent to the site of Firemen's Park, which had been destroyed by fire in 1932. They lived in hosed-down horse stalls for five months, during which Howard celebrated his fifteenth birthday and his father built a baseball field and organized an Assembly Center baseball league.

Meanwhile, Ruth was doing his bit for the war effort, selling war bonds, playing charity golf matches against Ty Cobb to raise money for the British War Relief Society and United Service Organizations, joining other prominent German Americans in condemning "every thought and deed of Hitler and his Nazis."

On August 23, 1942, he returned to the Stadium to face Walter Johnson, the Big Train from Washington, D.C., in a hitting exhibition between ends of a double-header on behalf of the Army and Navy Fund, for which they raised more than $80,000. Johnson was fifty-four; Ruth was forty-eight. For the first time in seven years he was back in pinstripes, and fretful in anticipation, worrying about his spikes and his uniform—was it back from the dry cleaner?

Ruth hit Johnson's fifth pitch into the right field stands. Johnson, who as a Senator surrendered 7 of Ruth's 714 career home runs, kept throwing. Ruth kept swinging. Seventy thousand fans kept roaring. On the twentieth pitch, Ruth hit a ball into the upper deck that went just foul. He circled the bases anyway, doffing his cap to seventy-thousand partisans.

In October 1942, the Zenimura family was deported to the Gila River Relocation Center, constructed on Pima Indian land in the Arizona desert, some fifty miles from Phoenix. The seventeen-thousand-acre center, divided into the Butte and Canal camps, was built in part by future Yankee owner Del Webb, who had competed in the Fresno Twilight League where Zeni had served as a manager. At its peak, the camp held 13,348 prisoners—most of them from the central California valley areas of Fresno and Sacramento—making it the fourth-largest city in Arizona.

In a modern retelling of Zeni's story, a children's book called *Barbed Wire Baseball* published in 2013, the photograph of Ruth and Gehrig and Zeni taken in 1927 meant so much to him that he took it to Gila River, hanging it on the raw wood wall of the barracks as soon as he arrived.

"Oh, no." Howard shook his head. They had only one suitcase. He had to leave room for his baseball uniform, glove, and spikes. For two weeks Kenichi Zenimura refused to unpack his suitcase. Angry at the loss of his freedom, his automobile garage and dealership, his possessions, and at having burned everything he owned that he brought back from trips to Japan; depressed at being separated from his friends, who had been sent to a relocation center in Arkansas, he refused to do anything at all. And there was plenty to do. The barracks at Gila River were better built than others that had just black tar-paper roofs; they had double-roof construction and mason-board walls. But there were cracks between the floorboards, which had been raised above the unpaved desert roads. Kiyoko, who had lost a lung to tuberculosis, struggled to breathe when the wind picked up and the dust blew in. She spent days stuffing sheets in the cracks.

The temperature in July reached 109 degrees. The desert nights were cold. The Zenimuras lived in Block 28, on the edge of the Butte camp, next to the barbed-wire fence and near a pile of cast-off lumber left behind by construction crews in their haste to finish the job in four months. One night at a bonfire, Zenimura decided to build a baseball diamond there.

At first, he and his sons did all the work, cutting and burning sagebrush, cactus, and greasewood out in the desert, beyond the chain-link fence. Then other internees began to pitch in. Everyone in camp had a job—farming, cooking, working in the camouflage net factory, or building warship models. Zeni's job? "The ballpark," Howard said. "The camp was all dirt. Every so often they had to come and grade it. The scrapers that they had, the guy driving it was a Japanese guy so my dad said, 'Can you level this area for us?'"

An irrigation ditch from the camp farm ran right by the edge of Block 28. "We dug a trench at night from the irrigation canal to water the field. We diverted that wastewater into the ballpark and flooded the whole area and packed it down, let it set."

They planted castor beans for the outfield wall and Bermuda grass for the infield.

"We stole every other pole in the chain link fence to make the backstop"—burying the four-by-fours and two-by-fours in the desert at night. "The guards, they didn't come around. They were mostly on the gate. We're on the desert. There's nothing out there for fifty miles. Where we going to go?

"We dug out the dugouts and used the dirt to smooth the base paths. We picked the big rocks by hand. I threw a lot of rocks. Then we screened the pebbles."

Those were used for the dugout floors. The head dietician contributed flour to use for baselines. Empty rice bags filled with dirt doubled as bases.

They constructed a grandstand and painted and numbered the rows. They printed tickets in English and Japanese. Those who could afford the good seats were expected to pay their way; a coffee can was left at the entrance for other donations. Zeni used the money to send away for equipment to replace uniforms made out of mattress fabric.

On March 7, 1943, camp director Leroy Bennett

threw out the first pitch at Zenimura Field, in an 8–0, one-hit shutout won by Block 28.

Zenimura organized a thirty-two-team league. He placed advertisements in the newspaper seeking games against Negro League, Pacific Coast League, and California Winter League clubs. And they came. The games were covered by the *Arizona Republic*.

When the Zenimuras were released from the camp in 1945, he wrote a letter to the Gila River internees thanking them for their support and invoking the healing power of baseball: "I will be returning to Fresno and while I am there will try to make a team to play in the league in the city, [to] try to speed up the mutual feeling between the Americans and the Japanese."

Zeni continued to play and coach baseball, catching his last game at age fifty-five. At home, he never talked about the game at Firemen's Park; nor did he speak about Babe Ruth. After serving in the U.S. Army, and graduating from Fresno State University, where both were star baseball players, Howard and Harvey Zenimura moved to Japan to play professional baseball for the Hiroshima Carp. Zeni coached until his death in an automobile accident in 1968. Years later Howard found his father's treasured photographs, and the ball autographed by Babe and Lou, in the orange iron trunk labeled Fresno Athletic Club that he took to Japan in 1927. The wooden home plate, all that remains of Zenimura Stadium, went on display at the Hall of Fame in May 2017.

VII

Bishop John E. McGinley was the keynote speaker at the 7:00 P.M. banquet at the Hotel Fresno on Saturday evening, October 29, 1927. Two hundred guests, including the coaches and players from Fresno State University and St. Ignatius College, but none of the Nisei players, assembled in the lobby for what the newspaper called "pleasant music." Organized as a fund-raiser for the Monterey-Fresno-Catholic Diocesan Campaign and a testimonial to Ruth and Gehrig, McGinley saluted Ruth as an example of the Catholic doctrine of perseverance, the key to all of life's success. When Father Crowley introduced the Babe predictably as "the boy who never grew up," the paper reported that "the ovation sounded for blocks around."

Reporters did not record Ruth's response to the tired refrain or the size of the pledge he made to the campaign. In his remarks, he proudly acknowledged his debt to St. Mary's and to Brother Matthias, whom he now called "a big brother" instead of the father he never had—one indication that he had done some growing up since then. He extolled the virtues of sports especially for children who came from family difficulty, which may be the closest he ever came to acknowledging his own.

But he interrupted his remarks when he noticed a couple of young interlopers eyeing the dessert tray. "Dive into the pie," he told the kids. "There's plenty more where that come from."

Chapter 18
October 30 / Los Angeles

**RUTH WIRES HE'LL SMASH TWO
HOME RUNS OFF ROOT**

—LOS ANGELES TIMES

**SPORTS BRIEF: RUTH AND GEHRIG BACK
HOME AFTER THREE WEEKS TOUR**

**YANK HOME RUN TWINS TRAVELED
8,000 MILES**

PAIR PLAYED BEFORE 220,000, MOSTLY KIDS,
AND AUTOGRAPHED 5,000 BASEBALLS

—SCRANTON REPUBLICAN

I

"Glad you signed Root to pitch against me," Ruth cabled from Santa Barbara, it was reported in the *Los Angeles Times*. "Tell the fans for me that I'll hit two home runs off Root or be disappointed."

Root was one of the best pitchers in the National League in 1927, a twenty-six-game winner for the Chicago Cubs. "Charlie took that as an insult," the *Times* said, and had been working out in earnest, vowing to approach the exhibition game sponsored by the American Legion with the same purpose he would have brought to a World Series confrontation. "'Ruth is a great slugger, all right, but I don't believe he'll get any two home runs off me. Who can tell, maybe I'll strike out the Bambino a couple of times.'"

Arriving at Wrigley Field on Sunday afternoon was a kind of homecoming for Ruth, who had helped inaugurate the new ballpark's alternate life as a Hollywood location by filming scenes for *Babe Comes Home* there nine months earlier. The gates opened early and the stands filled quickly. The *Times* estimated 25,000 were in the house that held 20,500 without the extra seating in the roped-off outfield; the *Examiner* claimed 30,000. Hollywood was much in evidence—Douglas

Fairbanks, Mary Pickford, Clara Bow, Buster Keaton, Marion Davies, and her old man, Hearst. The Hollywood American Legion Band played. The lieutenant governor threw out the first pitch. The president of Piggly Wiggly donated one hundred baseballs for Babe and Lou to toss in a scramble after the game.

Down on the field, Ruth was greeted by a roster of familiar faces: Lefty O'Doul, making another command appearance at his behest, and a spate of local ballplayers he knew from around the major leagues: Ernie Orsatti, the former Hollywood stuntman turned Cardinal outfielder; Fred Haney, Christy Walsh's pal; Jigger Statz and "Irish" Meusel, Bob's brother, who'd played with the Brooklyn Robins that year; and Johnny Rawlings, the onetime Giants' benchwarmer who taunted him during the 1922 World Series at the Polo Grounds.

The little gem of a ballpark built by Chicago chewing-gum mogul William Wrigley as the home for his newly acquired Los Angeles Angels was deemed perfect by the *Times*. Wrigley had ordered his architect, Zachary Taylor Davis, who designed both of Chicago's major-league ballparks, to pattern it after the one then known as Cubs Park. Built of iron and steel, it cost six times the price of the original. "Wrigley's Million Dollar Palace," sportswriters called it. "The finest baseball edifice in the United States," the *Sporting News* claimed.

The red roof and Spanish-style exterior matched the homes in the surrounding neighborhood (what is now South Central Los Angeles). Palm trees hovered over the outfield wall where eventually ivy would grow. An elevator whisked spectators to an observation platform with views from mountain to ocean. A twelve-story office tower stood at the entrance to the ballpark with thirteen-foot clocks on all sides, visible to the players on the field below.

In the next four seasons, Ruth would hit another 257 home runs, leading the American League in slugging and on-base plus slugging; and had they calculated such a thing back then, he would have led in wins above replacement, too. He would help the Yankees win two more World Series, batting .625 against the Cardinals in 1928, and keep his promise by hitting two home runs off Charlie Root, albeit five years later, at the other Wrigley Field, before his time ran out.

II

When Ruth returned to Wrigley Field in 1942 to play himself in *The Pride of the Yankees*, Lou Gehrig had been dead of ALS less than a year. Eleanor Gehrig did not want Ruth to have any part of the movie, as she made clear in an exchange of uninhibited letters with Christy Walsh leading up to the shoot. She was adamant: for once the Babe was not going to upstage her Luke.

Whatever reconciliation had taken place at home plate on July 4, 1939, when Gehrig said goodbye at Yankee Stadium, did not assuage Eleanor Gehrig's feelings.

Samuel Goldwyn and Christy Walsh convinced her that Lou's story could not be told without Babe Ruth but promised he would appear only in group scenes with the other Yankees. When he signed a contract for $1,500 a day on November 2, 1941, he weighed 267 pounds. He went on a crash diet, losing fifty pounds, and landing himself in the hospital on January 2 with what doctors called a nervous condition.

He seemed in fine condition to play his former self by the time he arrived at Los Angeles's Union Station to a suitably Ruthian greeting orchestrated by Walsh: "SPECIAL SUNSHINE ORDERED FOR YOUR ARRIVAL AND UNIFORM BAND OF TWENTY LITTLE ORPHAN KIDS." Walsh also had a dozen roses for Claire and breakfast arranged at the Hotel Roosevelt with Bill Dickey, Bob Meusel, and the orphans.

He was back in his element at Wrigley Field, trading insults with his old teammates and entertaining East Coast scribes visiting the set with precise memories about how many home runs he had hit off of whom. But he was still run-down and caught pneumonia and was hospitalized in critical condition on April 2, generating lots of worried headlines and forcing the director to shoot around him.

The photogenic ballpark was almost as popular with Hollywood directors as it was with baseball sluggers: the Hollywood Stars, L.A.'s other PCL franchise, shared it with the Angels until 1939. Wrigley Field played a supporting role in fourteen feature films after *Babe Comes Home* and *Speedy* inaugurated the ballpark as a film location in 1927. Gary Cooper had delivered a rousing speech to a packed stadium for Frank Capra in *Meet John Doe* just the year before he returned to the field as Lou Gehrig.

Walsh kept Eleanor Gehrig up to date on all the latest gossip in detailed, single-spaced letters, describing the scene in the Ruths' suite on arrival.

"To give the devil his due Babe and the Great Woman acted simply swell so far. No COMPLAINTS but you ought to have heard him griping because trunks didn't arrive AT ONCE and when they did, he started looking for golf togs and boy, what a show . . . he simply poured the trunk contents all over the room and out the window. Raising hell because someone in N.Y. had failed to pack his favorite golf stuff and then after 30 minutes of that—he found the stuff right under his nose."

The state of the Ruth marriage was a topic of conversation in the make-believe clubhouse in Los Angeles and elsewhere—much to Christy's and Eleanor's glee. The family maid, Nora McIntyre, told her daughter, Dorothy Patterson, about shouting matches in the Riverside Drive apartment and one aboard a Pullman involving who gave who a social disease. Another time, as he left on a purported hunting trip, Claire looked out the back window of the apartment and saw him getting into a car with a female behind the wheel. "Call Abercrombie and Fitch," she instructed Nora. "I want some hunting clothes."

She meant to track her prey.

A week later, Walsh sent Eleanor Valentine's Day greetings and more gossip.

The Great Woman has been in virtual seclusion. But you would have absolutely expired with laughter the other day. Dickey, Meusel and Babe and I were in their dressing room which has kitchenette, ice box, shower bath etc. They were all sitting around wise cracking etc and finally Babe started talking about his "old woman." Night before he had been out with Rice, Gene Fowler, Barrymore, and a few others. He was supposed to get home at 9:30 P.M. but came in at 11:30 and you ought to hear what his "old woman" said to him. He told us, he told her if she didn't lay off, she could pack up and go home etc etc. She was griping because she is "golf" widow etc and because she is "alone all the time out here." Thurs. night we went to annual stag dinner Baseball Assoc. She raised H—— again. Anyway, Babe was ranting and threatening and telling Dickey, Meusel and me how he was going to be in charge from now on but all the time we were splitting our sides laughing and Meusel and Bill were winking at me on the side. The chances are when he went home that night he pussy-footed in with hat in hand. SPECIAL BULLETIN: Mr. Ruth officially announces that he and his "old women" now sleep in separate bedrooms!!!

III

The critical and financial success of *The Pride of the Yankees* inevitably triggered thoughts about a Babe Ruth movie, which in 1942 lacked the obvious pathos of Gehrig's life story. Walsh, who had refreshed his acquaintance with General John J. Pershing in making a deal for a 1943 Eddie Rickenbacker feature film, told Eleanor he was also busy acquiring the film rights to the life story of Yale football coach Howard Jones.

It was too soon for a Babe movie. He had to get sick first.

The forties were unkind to both men. They stayed busy and disappointed. Walsh, the staunch right-wing anti-Communist, was investigated by the FBI in 1943 on suspicion of exchanging coded messages with the lighthouse keeper at the Molokai Light Station in Hawaii, who was suspected of tracking a U.S. Naval Minecraft #30 built in 1919. Secret ink tests for code proved negative.

Walsh had recruited former clients to join what he called a "non-partisan sports committee" opposing Franklin D. Roosevelt in 1940 and wrote to Ruth soliciting his support four years later. "In other years, I know that you have hesitated to lend your name to a political committee. But, Babe, from the bottom of my heart, I tell you that the crisis is deeper than PO-LITICAL.

"The very money that you have saved in your insurance and trust funds is liable to be taken away from you very cleverly unless the present communistic trend is stopped in its tracks at the next election."

According to Walsh's nephew, Richard, Uncle Christy arranged for him to appear on a thirty-minute pre-election radio broadcast with the Babe in support of Thomas Dewey in 1944. He was just a teenager. In one of his lines, he was to complain that he had known only one president during his lifetime. There was only one problem: Ruth had lost his place in the script. "He was drunk out of his mind," Richard Walsh said. "One thing you can't be on the radio is drunk. There was a thirty-second pause before he could find in the script where he was supposed to be."

Walsh's attempt to create a new, profit-sharing sports syndicate for TV and movies, Sportswriters, Inc., went nowhere. He went all in with the actor Don Ameche in an effort to bring professional football to Los Angeles and to acquire the right for pros to compete at the Coliseum, previously the sole province of collegiate competition. As vice president of the American Football Conference and part owner of the Dons, he traveled the country, signed players, and hosted fund-raisers, all on his own dime, only to be pushed out when Ameche withdrew without warning and a new ownership group took over.

His instincts were sharp—he was prescient about the future of professional football. But he would not share in the success. After eighteen months of unpaid effort in 1944–45, during which he laid out $13,000 of his own money, it took more than two years to recoup his losses.

He had seen the future of major-league baseball on the West Coast, too, in the sellout crowd that showed up at Wrigley Field to see Babe and Lou. He said right then, "They'll come out for baseball if you give them baseball to see." And then he learned that the Ruth project he'd been unsuccessfully pitching for years had been sold out from under him. He would have no part in the making of *The Babe Ruth Story*. Negotiations for the sale of the film rights to the forthcoming Bob Considine book had been under way for some time when he learned of a prospective deal with Roy Del Ruth and Republic Pictures.

Walsh's August 31, 1946, letter to Ruth was gracious considering his deeply hurt feelings—and pocketbook. He wrote that he had long hoped to make such a picture but had been unable to interest any of the studios he had approached. Universal-International had turned it down; Twentieth Century Fox had not rejected the idea but nor had it shown any indication of accepting. "After all the years we were associated, it will be a great disappointment not to be associated in the making of your picture," he wrote, before closing with some prophetic, unheeded advice. "Make sure to get approval of the shooting script and don't tie up with any but a major studio."

When the deal with Allied Pictures was announced in July 1947, paying Ruth $150,000, one of Walsh's sportswriting allies, Oscar Ruhl, ran a sympathetic item in his column, noting that Walsh had been "knocked out of a $25,000 cut" of the action.

Ruth, too, was at loose ends. He refereed two wrestling matches in 1945, losing ten pounds in the process. He traveled to Mexico with Claire and Julia at the invitation of Jorge Pasquel, the head of the Mexican League, which led to speculation about a possible job, but there was nothing there for him either. He couldn't quite hide his enmity toward the power structure of baseball, revealing a grudge he'd been carrying since 1914 when he turned down big money from the Federal League, then vying to become a third major league, "because we were told by organized baseball that if we jumped we would be barred for life. But nobody was barred for life and I just got jobbed out of $20,000 without a thank-you from anybody."

He swallowed what remained of his pride and wrote to Larry MacPhail, now running the Yankees, and begged for the job in Newark he had rejected in 1934. MacPhail replied by mail three weeks later—always a bad sign, Babe told Claire—saying he thought there was lots of opportunity for him in organizing sandlot baseball.

Then the headaches began.

Headaches so searing, Dorothy said later, that he threatened to jump from the apartment window. He left the apartment in a wheelchair on November 26, 1946, and was taken to the French Hospital on West Thirtieth Street, where he would remain for three months.

He was first misdiagnosed with sinusitis and then with dental problems, so doctors pulled three teeth. His face swelled, his left eye shut; he lost the ability to swallow and then to speak. When an X-ray showed a mass at the base of his skull, radiation treatments were begun. His hair fell out in chunks. He had to be fed intravenously and lost eighty pounds.

Cancer had taken root in the air passages behind his nose, an area inaccessible to surgery, and it had spread from there. In December, a mass appeared in the left side of his neck. Doctors operated but were unable to remove it all. The cancer was strangling his carotid artery. They tied it off and prescribed female hormone treatments and more radiation.

It fell to Julia to address the press when he was released on February 15, 1947. She said he just wanted to go home and look out the window at the Hudson River.

That night on the radio Walter Winchell reported that Ruth had lost 125 pounds while in the hospital. Ruth was incensed and demanded a retraction. "When I die my bones will weigh more than 100 pounds," he said.

Dorothy wrote in her memoir that he was in so much pain that spring that he became addicted to morphine, an addiction she also claimed he overcame before his death, putting himself "into the hospital for drugs" and "staying clean until the very end." Even a soft-boiled egg became painful to eat. He had a butcher on Ninth Avenue grind chopped sirloin for him and took it with him on golf outings when he was well enough to play. Beer was sustenance now.

Babe and Claire made plans to go south, the way he always had in February for spring training. They stayed with his friend Ray Kilthau in Miami Beach and visited the Yankees' new spring training stadium, Al Lang Field, in St. Petersburg. He pointed to the weathered facade of the Gulf Coast Inn, which, Red Smith wrote later, had stood in "an everlasting distance beyond the outfield wall" of the old ballpark. "He remembered how he'd really got his adjectival shoulders into a swing and had knocked the indelicacy ball against the Anglo-Saxon hotel out there."

In Ruth's absence, Emory Perry, a Chicago businessman who, along with attorney Melvyn Lowenstein and executor Paul Carey, had assumed a greater role in his affairs since the rupture with Christy Walsh, wrote to baseball commissioner Happy Chandler describing Ruth as "a mighty sick boy" with "not too long a time upon this earth."

They had spoken on the telephone the day before. Perry wrote on February 21 to recapitulate the conversation so that the commissioner could share his thoughts with other baseball bigwigs: "Babe has been led to believe that the Doctors are in a quandary as to what his illness might be and have told him that it is an unusual case. This has placed him in a rather good frame of mind, which is a good thing. It would be most detrimental for him to hear over the radio or read in the papers what might actually be the truth of the matter."

Perry urged Chandler to declare opening day "Babe Ruth Day" at every major-league ballpark. While he doubted Ruth would be strong enough to attend, perhaps he'd be able to listen to the tribute on the radio. The suggestion was quickly adopted. Perry then suggested making it an annual event with proceeds going to the Babe Ruth Foundation, which would be established in May. Baseball higher-ups had no intention or interest in doing that, though several lent their names to the foundation's board.

American League and Yankee team officials conferred about Ruth's financial situation and whether some degree of support should be provided. Ed Barrow confirmed that "Ruth had been obliged to dispose of some of his principal in order to meet hospital bills etc."

Terms of the 1927 trust prohibited him from withdrawing funds from the account, other than the quarterly dividend checks he received. He had money in the bank—$107,611 in cash and $78,017 in U.S. savings bonds at the time of his death, according to an estate tax appraisal reported in the *New York Times* in 1951. (His net estate, including the trust, was $360,811 at that time.)

He also had an insurance policy worth $10,343; a motorboat; a Lincoln Continental from Ford worth $4,210; baseball memorabilia valued at $1,175; 55 Mexican pesos; and five shares in the George H. Ruth Candy Company, which had no value at all.

The Yankees and American League officials settled on giving him a $5,000 honorarium and an RCA television so that he could watch baseball.

Christy Walsh came east for Babe Ruth Day. He hadn't flown since Knute Rockne's death in an icy airplane crash over western Kansas on the last day of March 1931. The Rock had been en route to Los Angeles to do work for Studebaker and to sign the $25,000 movie deal Walsh had negotiated. In Walsh family lore, his life was spared when his train arrived late and the plane took off without him.

That's not what he wrote in his syndicated column that week, describing his attempt to warn Rockne off "his airline intentions" at dinner the night before his flight. The coach "scowled with good nature, and said, 'Aw you've got to get over that.'"

The future was in the air, Rockne said.

Acceding to his wife's plea not to fly, Walsh planned to take the train to Los Angeles, the wire services reported. He was in South Bend when word of the crash came clattering across the tickers, the news editor of the *South Bend News-Times* recalled, tearing stories off the wire machines in the newsroom until editors forcibly ejected him.

Walsh never got over Rockne's death, the first celebrity casualty in the skies. But he was at Newark Airport to meet Babe and Claire when they returned from Florida in time for Babe Ruth Day. He brought a plaque from Eddie Rickenbacker honoring Ruth's thirty-minute victory over a fifty-pound sailfish—an odd pretext for renewing a relationship that had dwindled to a cursory correspondence featuring requests for autographed photographs.

Walsh also brought his son, Christy Jr., with whom he had reconciled, to Ruth's apartment. "Christy Jr. couldn't understand why Babe didn't recognize his dad," recalled Christy Jr.'s son-in-law Matt Cwieka. "Christy Sr. said, 'It's okay.'"

The *Daily News* dug up Johnny Sylvester, the New Jersey boy whose life "Dr. Ruth" was credited with saving in 1926, and brought him to see the Babe. Sylvester was by then a Princeton graduate and worried that Ruth wouldn't recognize him.

But his concern was misplaced. It was the Big Fella who was barely recognizable. His appearance was shocking. Just a couple of days before the ceremony at the Stadium, he attended the annual Banshee luncheon at the Waldorf-Astoria with Bob Considine. "Bugs" Baer, who wrote Ruth's act for vaudeville, was the emcee. Noticing the Duke of Windsor among the gathering of fifteen hundred editors and publishers, he ad-libbed: "Hey, Duke, you're outranked. We've got some other nobility in the house. A famous king—the King of Swat."

And then he summoned Ruth to the stage to say a few words, not realizing how difficult that might be. His cheeks were sunken, almost caved in, the fullness gone from the familiar features, shoulders, chest. He held his double-breasted windowpane sports jacket close as if worried it might fall off him.

He opened his mouth to speak but his voice only cracked. He tried again. The result was no better. His hand fluttered to his chest and then to his throat. Turning away from the microphone, fighting back tears, he allowed Baer to help him back to his seat.

On his day at the Stadium, he was in better spirits and better voice, calling the umpires "three blind mice" and chuckling at his own corny joke. But his laugh became a cough and the cough didn't want to end. He said, "I never knew what sickness was until now."

The press was careful never to use the word "cancer," but the stooped, ashen figure who leaned into the microphone that afternoon, exposing the wispy steel wool remains of hair that barely covered his skull, spoke to no other diagnosis. He said that his voice felt as bad as it sounded—a death rattle carried on the Mutual Broadcasting Network and broadcast in every ballpark in the majors. His appearance led to unseemly requests, unhelpful speculation, and unwanted advice.

First thing Monday morning American League president Will Harridge sent a note of congratulations and a stack of 8-by-10 glossies for Ruth to sign when he had the time, by which Harridge meant while there was still time.

Ruth sent the Yankees a letter of heartfelt thanks.

John Rattray, the Marysville chiropractor Ruth had traveled ninety miles out of his way to see twenty years earlier, had wired the Babe in January "in a vain attempt to delay the operation that was performed to stop his headache," he wrote in a promotional brochure for his practice circulated at the time of Ruth's death.

Rattray was convinced he could have restored the Babe to full health and that he died not of cancer but as the result of nerves severed during surgery. "Of course, at that time, Babe Ruth was so famous that he was beyond personal communication," Rattray's daughter Pat Johnstone noted.

Bernarr Macfadden, the herald of the physical culture movement, would put Ruth on the cover of his magazine of the same name three months after his death, declaring that had he been "put on an exclusive grape diet he might have returned to the baseball field for many years of active service, notwithstanding his age."

Ruth chose another course. He consented to an experimental form of chemotherapy and radiation then being tested on mice at New York's Mount Sinai Hospital, where doctors reported that tumors treated with the drug "melted away." On June 29, he began receiving daily injections of Teropterin (pteroyl triglutamic acid), a developmental drug which was being used in trials with children with leukemia at Dana-Farber Hospital in Boston and on a woman with breast cancer at Harlem Hospital in New York. He was among the first patients anywhere, if not the first, to receive the combination of chemotherapy and radiation for naso-pharyngeal cancer.

Ruth knew it had rarely if ever been used on humans. He asked no questions but knew the risk. "I realized that if anything was learned about that type of treatment, whether good or bad, it would be of use in the future to the medical profession and maybe to a lot of people with my same trouble," Ruth told the ghost-writer of the autobiography he was too ill to contribute much to.

Which belies the much-repeated claim that he was oblivious to the nature of his illness. What else could he have meant when he told Connie Mack, "The termites have got me." He was dying, not stupid. "He figured it out," Julia Ruth said. "So Claire had to tell him eventually."

The improvement was dramatic. His pain abated, along with his need for narcotics. Able to eat again, he gained twenty pounds. By August, the mass in his neck and the enlarged lymph nodes had completely disappeared. In September, doctors reported the breakthrough at the International Cancer Congress in St. Louis. Ironically, Ruth made the most important news of his life as an anonymous patient in the lead story of the September 11, 1947, *Wall Street Journal*, declaring that scientists were on the verge of a cure for cancer.

The claim proved to be wildly overoptimistic, the Babe's recovery short-lived. Nonetheless, the knowledge gained from his case helped shape the combination-therapy approach that became standard treatment for the disease.

Although Teropterin is no longer used to treat naso-pharyngeal cancer, a closely related drug, Methotrexate, remains a standard treatment for a variety of other cancers, including leukemia and uterine cancer, as well as Crohn's disease and rheumatoid arthritis. The authors of a 1999 paper published in the *Laryngoscope* concluded that "Ruth had contributed as much in death as he had in life, which only adds to his immense legend."

In April, he had signed a contract with the Ford Motor Company as an evangelist for American Legion Junior Baseball. In exchange, Ford, the only company that saw fit to employ him, gave him the Lincoln and $500 for each city he visited. He would travel fifty thousand miles for them during the last two years of his life. Why did he go? Because he felt better. Because they paid him. Because he didn't know how to stop being Babe Ruth.

In November 1947, Ford hired a twenty-three-year-old former military flight nurse named Aline Maas to accompany him to Omaha to receive an award from Father Flanagan and Boys Town. It was a long way to go to be remembered. "He was withering away," Maas told the *Chicago Tribune* decades later. He was depressed, distressed, resigned. "A big puppy dog," Maas said.

All the old gratifications were gone except the ever-present cigar plugged in his mouth and the kids waiting to see him. He got off the train frequently to sign autographs. Sister Mary Bertille Geffert, a Franciscan nun at Boys Town, made him vanilla ice cream from her secret recipe to soothe his throat, which worked well enough to allow him to talk about Brother Matthias, telling the boys how Big Matt stationed Little George in a corner and threw balls at him every day until he learned to hit them in self-defense.

That evening he received the first annual Boys Town service award for the advancement of youth. All the big shots in Omaha assembled at the Paxton Hotel. Among them was Johnny Rosenblatt, who had been struck out by him in October 1927. He was then engaged in building Johnny Rosenblatt Stadium, the future home of the College World Series, and getting himself elected mayor. Rosenblatt brought along his young son, Steve, who remembered the conversation between his dad and the Babe. Rosenblatt had continued to play baseball, he told Ruth, and had faced Satchel Paige in 1935, who came down off the mound, halfway to home, to warn him, "You will never see strike three."

Which he didn't. "Struck out by Babe Ruth and Satchel Paige. How many people can say that?"

Dim as it was in the ambient light of the Art Deco mezzanine, Steve could see his father's purpose. He just wanted to make a dying man smile.

Which was also Aline Maas's purpose when she asked Ruth on the long train ride home what he considered his most important contribution to the game. His response was quick and unequivocal: "That I got baseball salaries up."

It was a widely held, though undocumented, belief, touted by his teammate Waite Hoyt: "Every big leaguer and his wife should teach their children to pray, 'God bless Mommy, God bless Daddy, and God bless Babe Ruth.'"

And by Ford Frick in 1933: "Babe instituted big salaries all the way down the line."

In January 3, 1941, *Friday* magazine, a short-lived left-wing weekly that advertised itself as "the magazine that dares to tell the truth," sent veteran sportswriter Ed Hughes to Ruth's apartment to provoke the otherwise unoccupied Bambino into politicizing the issue by linking it to his banishment from baseball. "'Why not speak out?' I prodded. 'You know you're being sidetracked because you jacked up the wages of all ball-players. What are you afraid of—offending the magnates' feelings?'"

Hughes's editors stretched Ruth's one, bland quote into a provocative headline and a three-page magazine spread: "Why the Babe Was Banned."

"I don't care about hurting the magnates' feelings. They certainly have not spared mine. But I don't want to say anything that makes me look like a bad sport. You know—on account of the kids."

The assertion that he fundamentally altered the salary structure in big-league baseball does not stand the test of time. After analyzing decades of major-league-baseball data, Michael Haupert concluded that Ruth's salary had no measurable effect on the average major-league salary, during his career or afterward. "He was an outlier," Haupert says. "The general salary trend was being driven by attendance and general salary increases during the 1920s and the effects of the Great Depression and World War II thereafter. That doesn't mean Yankee wives shouldn't have gotten down on their knees in thanks because Ruth's performance lifted the team to such a degree that it drove higher attendance, which is what fueled their higher salaries. And some of those players were making 50 percent of their salary on their World Series checks."

IV

Babe Ruth arrived in Los Angeles on May 1, 1948, with Claire, Julia, Emory Perry, and his new male nurse, Frank Dulaney, to assume his duties as technical adviser to *The Babe Ruth Story*. They were met at the station by William Bendix. There was no band of orphans, no bouquet of roses for Claire, no Christy Walsh.

Most of the movie had been shot. The trip was promotional and motivational. The book and the film made from it had given him a purpose—as well as income. That spring, he donated the original manuscript to Yale University; it was accepted on the pitcher's mound by the team captain, George Herbert Walker Bush. He attended a book party at the office of his publisher,

E. P. Dutton & Co. in New York, where Bennett Cerf and Papa Hemingway stood in line for his autograph. When his co-author, Bob Considine, asked him to sign his copy, Ruth asked him his name.

Considine had hired Fred Lieb, who had the advantage of actually knowing the Babe, to lend the oeuvre the patina of authenticity. The Hollywood script doctors undid whatever truths might have found their way into the manuscript. Ruth emerged, in the person of William Bendix, as a caricature of a caricature. Even the most credulous moviegoers would have had a hard time believing the phantasmagoric cinematic dimensions of the Called Shot, conflating it with the 1926 story of Johnny Sylvester, the allegedly dying New Jersey boy who wasn't dying, wasn't in the hospital, and certainly wasn't in Chicago as the movie script has it, with Ruth appearing at his bedside deus ex machina, promising a lifesaving home run at Wrigley Field. Thus healed, the screen version of Johnny leaps from the stands, pleading with the Babe Ruth not to retire.

Charlie Root pointedly said he refused to perpetuate a falsehood and declined the opportunity to play himself.

The movie folks took him to the studio to see the faux baseball diamond and grandstand laid out on a soundstage that passed interchangeably for Wrigley,

Fenway Park, Comiskey Park, and Yankee Stadium. Louella Parsons introduced him to Betty Grable and June Havoc, who swooned over him while Claire queried the dominatrix of hearsay about the Babe's appearance. "Don't you think he looks better? He has put on a few pounds."

They took him to San Fernando Park, a baseball field sometimes used as a Hollywood location, where the Babe tried to show Bill Bendix how to look like he was slugging the ball. Roy Del Ruth was shooting close-ups that day of the sixtieth home run and gave Bendix thirty swings. "Gosh," said Ruth after the long at-bat, the *Bakersfield Californian* reported. "I wish I could have done it that way. If you miss in Hollywood, you get 29 other chances."

And they took him to Gilmore Field to see the Hollywood Stars, the Pacific Coast League franchise owned by Bob Cobb and a pantheon of Hollywood movie stars, including Gary Cooper. Ruth was greeted with an ovation and a visit from a few of the players on the visiting Portland Bears, a Yankee farm team. It was awkward. They were young men in the thrall of full-bodied youth, eager to get on with it. They knew it was supposed to be important. But really, they just wanted to play ball. Besides, it was hard to make polite conversation with someone who couldn't talk. "They didn't want anybody talking to him for that long," said Charlie Silvera, a catcher who had been at Yankee Stadium on Babe Ruth Day. "He was frail, my goodness he was frail. He was as cheerful as he could be."

Before leaving Hollywood on May 18 on the *Santa Fe Chief*, he learned that the Yankees intended to celebrate the twenty-fifth anniversary of the Stadium on June 13 and retire number 3. He agreed to manage the 1923 team in an old-timers' exhibition game. For one day, he would be the manager of the New York Yankees.

All sixteen surviving members of the 1923 team, the Yankees' first World Championship team, were getting dressed in the new clubhouse when Ruth arrived with Emory Perry on one arm and Frank Dulaney on the other.

The teammates didn't crowd him the way the photographers did trying to get a picture of the Babe putting on the uniform for the last time. Nat Fein, a thirty-four-year-old human-interest photographer for the *Herald Tribune*, had caught the assignment, because the usual guy had called in sick. He didn't know the etiquette of the locker room or that there was etiquette in the locker room. "He pulled out the belt showing how much thinner he'd got and I wanted to make a picture then," Fein wrote in an unpublished memoir, "but they told me he's going to have all he can do to get out there—he's a very sick man—and the least bother here as possible because there's going to be a ceremony outside."

When he raised his Speed Graphic to take a picture, Anthony Camerano, an AP sports photographer, said, "Lay off him. He's got all he can do with just lasting the day."

The photographers asked for a shot of him at his old locker. The Yankees had moved their clubhouse across the diamond to the first base side before the 1946 season but had left the old lockers behind, including the big red one still stenciled in white: Babe Ruth, No. 3.

So they led him back to the old clubhouse, draped in a gabardine topcoat to ward off death's chill.

The Cleveland Indians were in town. Visiting clubs were accustomed to seeing Ruth's locker all closed up. Invariably, one of their bunch would gesture to it as they were dressing, the way first baseman Eddie Robinson had that morning, and say, *Sure could use the Big Fella today.*

The Indians were out on the field taking batting practice when Ruth arrived. He sat in a red wooden chair the color of his locker, placed incongruously on a beat-up Persian runner, legs crossed, left over right.

Fein asked if he'd mind pretending to tie his shoe. The Sultan of Swat reached a bony right hand toward his already tied left shoe. Maybe Fein didn't know he was a left-hander. Babe gazed up at him, a limp forelock draping his brow. Even his hair was drained of energy.

Robinson was sitting in the dugout with Bob Lemon and Dale Mitchell when Ruth emerged from the tunnel. Ruth still had some belly on him, Robinson thought, and pride enough not to set foot on a baseball field without spikes. But the white long-sleeved undershirt he wore under his uniform was inadequate for the day. Raw and wet and cold, it was a day to stay home in bed even if you weren't dying. Fifty thousand of Babe's people showed up anyway.

When at last they brought him into the dugout, he sat on the bench with the Indians, pulled his topcoat close with that bony right hand, and asked to see a left-handed glove, a marvel of webbing and stitching that he declared big enough to catch a basketball. He asked Mel Harder, now an Indians coach, if he remembered the day he got five hits off him in Cleveland, all to left field, and got booed by the crowd. Harder remembered.

The Yankees lined up along the first base line, caps over their hearts as if expecting the National Anthem. Ed Barrow, the old general manager, with whom Ruth had contended his entire career, embraced him at home plate. The band played "Auld Lang Syne," a tacit, melancholy acknowledgment of the estrangement between the Babe and his team. The Yankees gave him a gold pocket watch—an odd gift for a dying man. "The guys didn't know what to do," said Yogi Berra, then in his first full year with the Yankees. "We just stood and watched."

Ruth was the last player introduced, summoned into "the cauldron of sound he must have known better than any other man," as W. C. Heinz wrote in his indelible phrase.

Robinson gauged the rise of the dugout steps and reached into the bat rack for a bat. "He just looked wobbly to me," Robinson said. "I just didn't think he shouldn't be going to up to home plate without some support and maybe he should have a bat in his hand—that's what he was famous for."

The one he grabbed belonged to Bob Feller, who was in the bullpen warming up for his start.

Most of the photographers had hustled across the field to the first base side of the dugout and were kneeling on the grass near the Yankees, waiting for the Babe to climb into the cauldron. Fein hung back. "The story was 'No. 3 Bows Out,' Fein said later, the title he gave the picture, "the uniform being retired and all."

So with the band playing, he walked behind the Babe and took the picture that would earn him the 1949 Pulitzer Prize, the first awarded for sports photography.

Mel Allen's booming introduction—"Ladies and Gentlemen, George Herman Ruth"—reverberated back and forth across the diamond, creating a swell of applause that turned into a riptide, waves of sound that eddied and crested as they bounced off hard surfaces of copper filigree and swelling chests. The roar spilled out of the Stadium, filling the side streets, and the avenues, and the airwaves. Allen's voice reached into every borough of the city and into every living room and den equipped with a radio like the Philco that had kept Ruth company during so many afternoons when he sat in his leather easy chair wondering if this day would ever come.

To Ruth, at home plate, Allen whispered: "Do you want to speak?"

"I must," Ruth replied, his voice a scrape of sandpaper on wood.

No one knew in advance of the ceremony whether he'd be able to do so; they hadn't written him into the script. He steadied himself on Feller's bat and leaned into the microphones adorned with the call letters of WINS radio and WABD TV, the DuMont television station broadcasting the "Baseball Fanfare," as the daily TV listings described it.

"Ladies and gentlemen, I just want to say one thing. I am proud I hit the first home run here. God knows who will hit the last one. It is great to see the men from twenty-five years ago back here today and it makes me feel proud to be with them."

He swung Feller's bat a couple of times at home plate for photographers and cameramen. In the drama of the moment, the extraordinary span of his baseball life went unnoticed, or at least unspoken: as a teenager he pitched his first major-league game seven years before baseball debuted on radio; he left the baseball diamond with TV cameras recording his final unsteady steps.

In the visiting dugout, Robinson asked Ruth to autograph Feller's bat for him. The Babe said what he always said. "Sure."

He didn't stay for the old-timers' game. His doctors decided the day was too raw. So he never did manage the New York Yankees even for three innings.

Ruth's fate was clear to everyone, including him, when he disappeared down the dugout steps into the tunnel, out of the chill, where he was greeted by his old teammate Joe Dugan. "Joe, I'm gone," he said. "I'm gone, Joe."

In the next eleven days, he traveled to Sportsman's Park in St. Louis, where ten thousand children gathered for a baseball clinic sponsored by Ford and the American Legion; to Sioux City and Sioux Falls, where he had ridden Molly the Pony in October 1927; and to Minneapolis.

The designated representative of the boys in St. Louis was six-year-old Billy DeWitt, the son of Browns owner Bill DeWitt Sr. He was too young to realize how sick Ruth was or how bad he looked or how hard it was for him to hold the bat he was supposed to show Billy how to swing. He just knew how important he felt when people started asking for his autograph as he made his way through the stands in his St. Louis Browns uniform. "Being six, I signed, 'Billy,'" DeWitt said. "My mother said, 'You might want to add your last name.'"

Ruth received a trophy from Joe DiMaggio in honor of his work with the youth of America. He greeted the players on the Browns' bench, a bunch of baseball nobodies he treated like somebodies because, first baseman Chuck Stevens said, "We were ballplayers.

"We knew he was dying. We all knew he was a rascal and God love him."

He posed with Yogi Berra, who looked as nervous as he felt, and wished him luck in the future the Babe knew he wouldn't witness. "Found out later it was the last time Babe ever appeared in a ballpark," Berra said.

In Minneapolis, he was interviewed on the radio by an eleven-year-old blind boy sitting in his lap. "How are you, Babe?" Johnny Ross asked.

"I don't feel so good. I have a very bad throat and my head aches."

Johnny asked a bunch of other stuff about Ruth's new autobiography and who was likely to win the pennant before running out of questions. "I think both of us are out of words, Johnny," the Babe said.

Then he went home to die.

He left his room at Memorial Hospital only twice after being admitted on June 26. On July 13, he flew to Baltimore for an Interfaith Charity Game—he had promised to present an award to Paul Geppi, a boy from St. Mary's Industrial School. The organizers included the Knights of Columbus and B'nai B'rith. Sig Seidenman's father, a lodge president, called his son home from a stickball game and said, "I'm going to meet Babe Ruth at the airport. Do you want to come?"

En route they bought two baseballs at a sporting goods store. At the airfield, Ruth's sister, Mamie, was waiting for the Babe along with a photographer from the *Baltimore News-American,* who suggested that Sig and some of the other boys greet him at the top of the stairs when he arrived and needed to be helped down to the tarmac. "It was shocking," Seidenman said. "There was no TV yet. The only picture I'd ever seen of him, he was Babe Ruth—a strapping guy. This guy, his fingers were like twigs. I felt like if I'd squeezed his hand I'd have broken all his fingers."

The game was rained out but Ruth insisted on staying for the banquet, where he saw Rodger Pippen, the Baltimore sportswriter who had covered the Orioles' spring training camp in 1914, describing Babe Ruth's first professional home run as "a hit that will live in the memory of all who saw it." On the ride through the slick city streets of the hometown he had abandoned, men on street corners doffed their hats. Women waved and youngsters shouted, "It's the Babe! It's the Babe!"

A car was waiting on the tarmac at LaGuardia Airport to take him back to the hospital. He did not stop to talk to reporters.

A week later, Ruth received the last rites from Father Thomas H. Kaufman, which some members of the faith felt he didn't deserve. Kaufman, a Dominican priest from St. Catherine of Siena parish, was filling in for a priest who was on vacation. He was from Baltimore and had spent one troubled night at St. Mary's as a boy. The bond was as fortuitous as it was strong. They talked as much as Ruth's condition allowed.

Five days later, Ruth was hauled out of bed to attend the premiere of *The Babe Ruth Story* downtown at the Astor Theater. He stayed twenty minutes. He was so doped up he didn't know the movie was about him, which was just as well. Bosley Crowther of the *New York Times* dismissed the movie as "a typical debasement of human qualities in the muck of the cliché."

V

RUTH GETS ONLY DOUBLE OFF ROOT AND RED OLDHAM
—*LOS ANGELES TIMES*, OCTOBER 31, 1927

The game at Wrigley Field in Los Angeles ended with Ruth's prophecy of two home runs unfulfilled—his only hit a first inning opposite-field double off Charlie Root, who bore down on him, having taken umbrage at Ruth's showbiz braggadocio. "Root got two strikes on Ruth," the *Times* reported, "then served up an outside pitch to the Bambino. Babe calmly reached with his big bat and shoved a double down the left field line."

The two promised home runs would have to wait until they met again in Game 3 of the 1932 World Series where, Root said, if Ruth tried to show him up, pointing to the grandstand and calling his shot, he'd have "put one in his ear and knocked him on his ass."

Gehrig fared better, leading the Larrupin' Lous to a 5–2 win with two home runs. The Babe was the only pitcher who got him out all afternoon.

After the game, they climbed to the top of the stands and began hurling one hundred autographed baseballs to several times that many children gathered on the field below. Ruth had grown weary of his feet getting trampled by littler ones.

"There couldn't have been more excitement if the Twins had been tossing out gold pieces or passes to ride in Lindy's plane," the *Los Angeles Herald-Examiner* reported.

The skies were clear. The breeze was light. If the Babe had gone up higher, all the way up to the observation deck, he might have seen the mountains, the ocean, and the future he had created. He might have glimpsed the future of big-league baseball on the West Coast—even briefly at Wrigley Field—although he might have had a hard time believing it would take three decades for the pooh-bahs of baseball to see what was right there before his eyes.

In 1957 Walter O'Malley would purchase Wrigley Field and its home team, the Los Angeles Angels, as part of his master plan of moving the Dodgers out of Brooklyn. They would play at Wrigley until a suitably modern California ballpark could be completed. But the neighborhood of Spanish bungalows had declined over time and O'Malley soured on the plan, Los Angeles sportswriter Mel Durslag said later, when he got a look at a cathouse across the street.

More to the point, Wrigley had proved to be an exceedingly generous home for sluggers—its diminutive power alleys made the park play especially small. Ford Frick, who was baseball's commissioner by then, weighed in against the plan. He didn't want anyone breaking Babe's home-run record in a "cow pasture," he told the *Los Angeles Times*. But it was the perfect setting for the *Home Run Derby*, the syndicated TV series that debuted in 1959.

If the Babe had peered that far into the future, he might have seen Mickey Mantle and Willie Mays down on the field, vying for two thousand bucks in the same kind of competition he and Lou put on before every barnstorming game in quest of Walsh's Copper Cup. The same kind of competition that is now a heavily promoted prelude to every All-Star Game.

So the Dodgers ended up playing in the Olympian Los Angeles Coliseum until Dodger Stadium was completed in 1962. And, when major-league baseball finally came to Wrigley Field in 1961, it was for a single year as the home of the new American League expansion team, also called the Los Angeles Angels. Fred Haney, the third baseman for the Bustin' Babes on October 30, 1927, was the general manager.

If Ruth looked further into the future—and thirty miles south of Long Beach, where he and Gehrig were scheduled to play their final barnstorming game the next afternoon—he might have seen Scott Boras, the only sports agent in 2017 with more than $2 billion in active player contracts, in his Newport Beach office, preparing another Boras binder crammed with fifty or maybe even a hundred pages of proprietary data, generated by MIT-trained engineers. That binder would document not just the worth of a particular client but the argument for why signing that client to the $60 million to $90 million a year he figures Babe Ruth might be worth in today's $10 million to $12 million industry makes financial sense for a particular baseball owner. And Ruth might not have liked what Boras had to say.

Boras wasn't all that impressed with Walsh—because he didn't get himself in the room with the owner. In his world, you don't wait to be asked in—you barge. As a result, he said, "Ruth was never contractually rewarded as the game's greatest player. More importantly, he was never rewarded for the amount of money he generated for the league and his specific teams. Once they didn't establish that precedent, asking the player to negotiate for himself is the equivalent of someone going out on the field and to play for the player."

Babe's worth in today's market? Well, that depends. First: "You would never use what other players are paid as a method because that is unilaterally controlled by owners.

"You're talking about someone bringing a value to a multibillion-dollar regional sports network, then to a multibillion-dollar franchise, then to a league itself, that may have an impact on the league for national TV contracts."

Negotiating with the owners isn't the hard part. You simply have to explain to them why the player's worth what Boras says he is in terms of raising ticket prices, advertising revenues, concession sales, championships, and potential resale of the franchise.

The hardest negotiation is with his own client, to get him to understand that the ultimate competition is between himself and the game. "You can't let the influence of greatness erode greatness," Boras explained. "That is always the hardest dynamic for a great athlete. It's not that the game will not beat you in the end; it's how long can you beat it? Your behavior is going to limit or sustain the number of years you can beat the game. We're trying to keep the performance focus at a level where it's myopic."

Which might mean telling Babe Ruth not to grant an interview to a reporter wanting to talk about how his swing compared to Joe Jackson's, the way Boras advised his client Bryce Harper not to discuss the similarities his batting coach saw between him and the Babe.

And if instead, from his perch high above Los Angeles, Babe Ruth chose to look back, to look east, into the past with those eyes he never taxed in the dark of movie palaces—unless they were showing one of his own movies, which never failed to make him laugh—he might have seen in black and white just how far George H. Ruth Jr. had come, how much he had made of himself, for himself, and by himself.

Now that was power.

VI

The $12,000 in rain insurance Ruth purchased in advance of the tour finally paid off on Halloween when the game in Long Beach was called on account of the downpour. The town where he had been unduly arrested nine months earlier for exploiting children was still jinxed.

Glenn E. Thomas, the wealthy Studebaker dealer who had arranged a fishing outing for the Babe in January, put himself at Ruth's disposal, helping him fulfill his promise to take Gehrig hunting. Thomas staged an outing to the Farmers Gun Club in Orange County near the present site of the Los Alamitos Race Course. Again, he brought along his publicist, a professional photographer, and a cameraman, who filmed the scruffy, unshaven Babe happily lying in the dirt with his shotgun and a wreath of dead ducks.

He also filmed Ruth passed out dead drunk in his duck blind, chin collapsed on chest, thick hair matted and unkempt—much to the amusement of an old-timer sitting beside him, who can be seen in the background tippling from an imaginary cup.

The 16mm footage, spliced into a roll of home movies featuring the likes of Charles Lindbergh, remained unwatched and undisturbed until Thomas's daughter and her stepdaughter shared it with author Chris Epting in 2012. Epting dug up Thomas's account of his harrowing night in Ruth's duck blind at the Long Beach Police Historical Society: "Thomas was afraid that Ruth might accidentally shoot him. Thomas reported that on the second night of the hunt he stayed with Gehrig."

With the cameras rolling in the clear light of day,

the Babe sat still while young Lou patiently picked through his mop of unruly hair, seeking nesting critters in the Ruthian roost. One of the still images lives on as wall art in the Bass Pro wilderness shop in Rancho Cucamonga, California, and at some of the chain's other seventy-six locations in thirty-four states.

They were scheduled to board the *Santa Fe Chief* for New York on Saturday, November 5, with planned stops in Albuquerque, New Mexico; Emporia, Kansas; and Gary, Indiana. Local newspapers published their schedule in advance, promising that Ruth would detrain and greet local fans. Occasionally, as at Emporia, the schedule proved erroneous, requiring a retraction. "Today's Tragedy: Portly Pullman Passenger Nearly Mobbed."

The weather eased their departure by turning surly.

Ruth returned to Wrigley Field to visit Harold Lloyd, who was busy shooting the final scenes for *Speedy,* his last silent movie, having coaxed the best acting performance of the Babe's life a month earlier in New York.

In gratitude, Louella Parsons reported in her gossip column, Ruth had given him the bat he used to hit his sixtieth home run. Lloyd's architect was busy adding a special niche to the game room of the new $1 million estate Lloyd was building in Benedict Canyon.

The provenance of the alleged artifact was dubious

at best; comedian Joe E. Brown and reporter James E. Kahn also claimed to be in possession of the precious totem, the latter donating his Babe Ruth bat to the Hall of Fame the year it opened in 1939.

Parsons also said that Ruth was planning to return to his farm—the one he no longer owned—to begin training for the 1928 season.

Also that week, Ruth and Gehrig addressed the Wampas Club, a prominent assembly of Los Angeles PR men, on their favorite topic. "How to Hit Them and for How Much."

Walsh issued a triumphal press release summarizing the Symphony of Swat, with a crescendo of unverifiable statistics: they had traveled 8,000 miles, playing before 220,000 people and signing 5,000 baseballs. Of the twenty-one games they played in twenty cities in nine states, thirteen were broken up by fan enthusiasm. Schools were closed in three of jurisdictions. Offers for thirty-nine additional games were received from nineteen states.

Ruth led in homers but Gehrig had the better batting average—.618, 55 hits, and 13 home runs. Ruth hit .616, with 61 hits and 20 home runs. The Copper Cup was his, along with $28,281.93 he netted during the tour, according to Walsh, plus $3,000 for modeling those overalls in Kansas City. Ruth said he paid Gehrig

$9,000, more than his 1927 Yankee salary. The Bustin' Twins also shared $4,700 in "pick-up" money, Walsh reported.

Asked about his intentions for the off-season, Gehrig said he planned to play a lot of basketball. The Philadelphia Warriors of the American Basketball League immediately expressed interest in signing him.

Ruth, who had received a telegram in Fresno offering a fat sum for a vaudeville tour, turned it down cold. "It's been a rough season," he said. "I ain't going to do a thing except you know what."

The *Fresno Bee* went with a cleaner version of his remarks. "I need lots of rest," Ruth said. "I'm going to spend a lot of time hunting and fish and taking things easy."

Epilogue

I

August was the cruelest month for the Ruth family of Baltimore City: George Sr., Katie, and their youngest child, William, had all died in the eighth month of the year.

Babe's sister, Mamie, knowing she would soon be the only surviving member of the family, told her husband she was going to New York to see if she could help. There wasn't much anyone could do. Toots Shor, the bon vivant restaurateur, sent catered meals Ruth couldn't eat. Father Kaufman said he looked like "a triangle standing on its point."

On August 8, he developed bronchial pneumonia and required an oxygen tank. On August 9, he signed a

new will—misspelling his name, "Georgge," and naming Claire as chief beneficiary with Julia and Dorothy
sharing the remainder after her death. He also left
$10,000 in cash to Mamie, and $5,000 each to Claire,
Julia, and Dorothy.

By the time Mamie arrived, she told Mike Gibbons
in 1991, "I don't think he knew what he was doing or
what he was saying."

He asked to see Ford Frick, but when Frick arrived
on August 13, lacked the breath to whisper in the old
ghost's ear. Dorothy reported the arrival of the red-
headed woman from Greenwood Lake named Loretta,
who claimed to have been Ruth's girlfriend for the past
ten years. In her memoir, Dorothy said Claire gave her
$25,000 to go away when she threatened to make the
affair public.

Ten thousand telegrams and letters—including one
from the White House—arrived in two days, along
with offers for an equal number of blood donations,
which were politely declined. A bottle of pine cologne,
a gift from Betty Grable, was accepted and gratefully
acknowledged. (The Babe liked a little in his evening
bath.) He reciprocated with an autographed picture
from their visit to the set of *The Babe Ruth Story*.

On his bedside table stood a statue of St. Martin de

Porres, the patron saint of orphans and mulattoes. Born in Lima, Peru, to a Spanish nobleman and an Indian woman, de Porres had been abandoned by his father, who was ashamed of his son's swarthy complexion, a suggestive detail to those inclined to believe the rumors about Ruth's racial heritage.

But St. Martin de Porres was also the patron saint of the Knights of Columbus, the organization Ruth had joined in Boston in 1916, and which had sponsored so many of the barnstorming games. The statue had been given to him by a fellow knight.

On August 12, the hospital announced his condition was critical. Two days later, doctors began issuing hourly bulletins. On the fifteenth, Paul Carey reached Julia at the nearby hotel where she was staying with Claire, "I think you'd better get over here."

On Sunday, August 16, he managed to get out of bed and sit in a chair for twenty minutes, but his breathing was labored. His temperature continued to rise. He told Claire, "Don't come back tomorrow, because I won't be here."

Slugger rallies. Pulmonary complications. Family at bedside. Slugger sinking rapidly. Slugger failing.

The slugger had never failed at anything and he certainly wasn't going to fail at this. At 6:45 P.M., May

Breen DeRose read him a telegram. As she got ready to leave, he lurched out of bed and started across the room. "Where are you going, Babe?" the doctor asked.

"I'm going over the valley."

At 7:30 P.M., he received a final blessing. Minutes later he fell into a deep coma. He was pronounced dead at 8:01 P.M.

Father Kaufman told the flock of boys waiting beneath Ruth's window that it was a beautiful death.

The autopsy results, reported two days later in the *New York Times*, sounded anything but beautiful, revealing that the cause of death was not, as previously supposed, cancer of the larynx, but a very rare and aggressive form of nasopharyngeal cancer that had spread to his neck, his lungs, and his liver.

His granddaughter Linda offered a different opinion. "I think baseball killed him; not cancer. He had no more worth in his head."

II

August 17, 18, and 19 were undeclared days of national mourning. He now belonged to history, a point underscored by Claire's hurried, furtive attempt to hide a few of his baseball belongings from representatives of the Hall of Fame when eventually they came calling. The executors of his will, Paul Carey and Melvin Lowenstein, had decided to give all his baseball memorabilia to Cooperstown.

"Just a minute, just a minute," Julia remembered her mother saying. "I'll be right there in a minute."

She saved a loving cup trophy, his hunting cap, a white silk dress scarf, and a handful of bats stowed in a duffel bag in a closet.

His death was announced in the *Daily Mirror* in 172-point type reserved for declarations of war and peace. The *Sporting News* rushed a special section into print. Sportswriters published stories they had buried at his request like the one in the *Oakland Tribune* about a poor southern farmer who arrived at his hotel at midnight in a downpour with a horse and wagon saying his boy was sick and needed the Babe. And the Babe got out of bed and went. In another iteration, it was daytime and he took a cab.

It was the undertaker's idea to have a public viewing in the Rotunda at *the* Yankee Stadium. One thing Julia and Dorothy agreed on: neither liked the idea. Dorothy's objections were institutional—she shared Claire's bitterness toward the Yankees. "He had to die to get back in," Dorothy said.

Julia's objections were aesthetic and historical. She didn't want anyone to remember him this way. "Poor

Daddy, he looked so awful. I hated to think of all those people going by and seeing him look like that. He looked so old, so sad."

Laid out in a blue double-breasted suit and a blue-and-gold tie, with black rosary beads wound around his thick fingers, he was a shriveled husk of a man. The undertaker had done the best he could. The wispy, radiation-rotted hair had come back in dark and was slicked back to camouflage the insult of the autopsy. But as Julia recalled, "Golly gee, he was 53 years old, and he only weighed 150 pounds."

The Babe came home again with a police escort, making the trip from the Universal Funeral Chapel at Fifty-second Street and Lexington Avenue in eighteen minutes flat, the exact time it took for the cops to get him from the Mulberry Street jail to the Polo Grounds in 1921. The Yankees were out of town, in Washington for a three-game series. Pete Sheehy, the clubhouse man who went to work for the team in 1927, stayed up all night scrubbing the concrete floor with his tears.

When Babe Ruth returned to the house he built at 3:48 P.M. in an African mahogany casket lined with eggshell velvet, thousands of fans were waiting for him. The catafalque was positioned between pillars adorned with the jaunty new Yankee top hat and bat logo introduced in 1946. Urns filled with red, yellow, and white gladiolas stood at attention along with three of New York's finest. At one end of the coffin stood a six-foot crucifix and a vigil candle; at the other end a screen of potted palms and huckleberry sprays. The lid was folded back like a blanket. A spray of American Beauty roses from Dorothy rested on the closed end. Claire arranged for a grand blanket of orchids and roses and asked the Babe's fans not to send any others.

The clot of mourners hugging the Stadium wall along 158th Street parted to allow Claire, Julia, and her husband, Richard Flanders, who would be dead six months later of heart failure, entry through the press gate. Dorothy didn't accompany them to the private viewing. By then, their estrangement precluded mourning together. The hospital rewrite of Babe's will hadn't helped.

Julia wouldn't remember much about the day. "It's almost like I was sleepwalking through it," she said. "It was quiet. As quiet as you could get in New York City. And bare. Absolutely bare. There were flowers. There was light."

The gates were scheduled to open at 5:00 P.M., close at 10:00, and reopen again the next morning. Within an hour, a prayer rail and rug placed alongside the casket had to be removed. There were simply too many people who wanted to be able to say, "I saw Babe Ruth."

The procession of mourners surrounding the Stadium was rerouted so that the line cleaved at the foot of the bier, allowing the Babe's people to surround him, too.

Packed elevated trains arriving on the IRT tracks showered passengers emerging from the IND stop beneath 161st Street and River Avenue with sparks as they screeched to a halt. So many came, police announced, that at Mrs. Ruth's request the Stadium would remain open all night. An honor guard arrived at midnight to stand vigil.

Aloysius White, a twenty-six-year-old Army veteran who had lost his right leg in Italy, stood in line with a blind man and his guide dog, keeping company with a full moon. White told reporters that when he was a boy in St. Joseph's Orphanage in Poughkeepsie, Ruth took 250 of the kids to a game at the Stadium.

In the morning, charter buses arrived from Maryland, Delaware, Massachusetts, Rhode Island, and Connecticut. People came dressed for a ball game in short-sleeved shirts and shirtwaist dresses. Vendors sold hot dogs and photographs of the Babe. It was hot and humid, pennant-race weather.

A fifty-year-old woman fainted.

Mike Klepfer, a nine-year-old boy from Binghamton with a bad case of asthma and a tough-guy dad who worked on Manhattan's waterfront, arrived with his father at 10:00 A.M. It was already too late.

Every summer, Mike spent a month in the city with his father. Every morning, Mike's father gave him enough money for subway fare, a bleacher seat at Yankee Stadium, and a hot dog. Only twice did his father accompany him: on Babe Ruth Day in April 1947, when Mike saw his dad cry, and on August 18. "It took an hour to walk to the back end of the line, longer. I kept asking, 'Will we make it, Dad? Will we make it?'" Klepfer recalled. "We just inched and inched. No water, no food. You had to go all the way down the left field line and go counterclockwise around the ballpark. It was six or seven people wide all the way around the Stadium. We were six hours on line."

They never made it into the Rotunda. By 4:00 P.M. his father was out of time and patience. They quit the line and Mike would always feel that he had quit on the Babe. Which may explain why when he had the opportunity many years later, after outgrowing asthma and his career as a New York State Trooper, he befriended the next Babe Ruth—Mickey Mantle—acting as his bodyguard and confidant late in life.

George Lois, the son of a Bronx florist, who later put Mantle in TV commercials for breakfast cereal, cut school to go see the Babe. He cut the line. So he didn't wait long, an hour maybe, to get a look at him, and then wished he hadn't.

He'd delivered flowers to hundreds of funeral parlors and had seen hundreds of bodies in hundreds of coffins but he had never seen anything quite like this. A profusion of unwanted floral arrangements—one a gigantic baseball, another an approximation of crossed bats—stood at attention by his coffin. "It looked like Lenin's Tomb," Lois recalled. "It shook you up. I remember really sweating. Everything was done richly. The coffin looked like a rocket ship or something. Everything was first class. Maybe not in taste but first class."

Some boys wore sneakers and chewed gum. Some wore ties and jackets. Little League teams were summoned from the diamond in dirty uniforms to pay their respects. Newspaper photographers noticed the Negro teams especially: the Gramercy Boys Club, the Harlem Flashes, and the Harlem River Athletes.

VIPs were whisked inside. Ruth's friend Bill "Bojangles" Robinson, and Beau Jack, the boxer, with his three children. Jim Barton, who introduced Babe and Claire. Hank Greenberg and Leo Durocher, that sonofabitch. Frank Haggerty, an eleven-year-old boy from Danvers, Massachusetts, who had corresponded with Ruth in 1947, volunteering to represent him at the funeral of Brother Gilbert, the athletic director from Mount St. Joseph's, who claimed a pivotal role in the Orioles' signing of the Babe. Ruth had cabled his grateful acceptance without disclosing his dislike for the man.

Young Frank was a hot commodity at the viewing—a new angle on life's oldest story. He had dressed for the occasion in a spiffy new plaid sports coat. A host of reporters had offered to escort him. But he arrived with Brother Samuel, a member of the Xaverian Order who had the advantage of being Brother Gilbert's blood brother.

Frank had pull. He was the designated representative of the Youth of New England. He was hustled to the front of the line where somebody put a baseball in his hand and one of the photographers, all of whom knew who he was by then, said, "Why don't you brush a tear from your eye?"

So he did.

Several versions of the photograph went out on the wires with several different captions: "A Sight to Remember," and "Boy Cries Over Body of Babe Ruth."

He never actually said he'd been crying.

The calculus of grief was difficult to ascertain. The *Journal-American* estimated that sixty souls a minute filed by his casket; the New York City Police revised that figure upward to eighty a minute; the Associated Press counted two thousand an hour; the *New York Times* respectfully disagreed: six thousand, the paper of record claimed, meaning that when the gates closed at 7:35 P.M. on August 18, seventy-seven thousand had filed by Ruth's bier.

Three-year-old Harry Escobar, who came in his Yankee uniform with a black armband his father had taped around his left sleeve, filled the front page of the *Daily News*, giving a face to the tabloid's perfect headline: "Ruth's Last Gate, His Greatest."

III

Hours earlier, in Chester, Pennsylvania, an Irish police captain named Paul McKinney picked up his son in the family car and said, "C'mon, Jackie, we're going to see the Babe."

That evening in New York City, they went to see *The Babe Ruth Story*. They elbowed their way through the sodden crowd outside St. Patrick's Cathedral the next morning. There were seventy-five thousand people in the street waiting for the hearse to arrive—another sellout. McKinney found a fellow Irish cop, flashed his badge, and said, "Sergeant, I've driven all the way from Pennsylvania with my son to see the Babe."

In short order, they found themselves standing in the back of the great cathedral among the fifty-seven pallbearers whose names had been published in the morning paper—New York governor Thomas E. Dewey and New York City mayor William O'Dwyer, as well as the mayors of Boston and Baltimore; baseball commissioner Happy Chandler and league presidents Ford Frick and Will Harridge; Brother Charles from St. Mary's, Emory C. Perry, Paul Carey, and Melvin Lowenstein; Joe DiMaggio and Frank Crosetti, on leave from the team in Washington; Ed Barrow, Jack Dempsey and Bobby Jones; Bob Meusel, Earle Combs, Mark Koenig, Lefty Gomez, Waite Hoyt, Joe Dugan; Bojangles and Bill Bendix; the writers Grantland Rice, Bill Corum, Bugs Baer, Bob Considine, Fred Lieb, Joe Williams, Westbrook Pegler, Jim Kahn, Rud Rennie, Burris Jenkins, Alan L. Gould, John Kieran, Dan Daniel, Dan Parker, John Drebinger, Walter Winchell, Ed Sullivan, and Frank Graham.

All the writers had their say—biographer Marshall Smelser counted 490 columns in New York City alone. Everyone would remember Granny's line: "Game called on account of darkness. Babe Ruth is dead."

But no one wrote it better than Frank Graham. "They say he is dead but it is very hard to believe because he was so alive."

Though listed among the pallbearers, Christy Walsh stayed in Los Angeles. On the morning of the sixteenth, before the news reached the West Coast, he had written the Babe a thank-you note for three autographed baseballs he had just received. Then he sent Claire an awkward condolence note via Western Union: "There were just too many extra innings for Babe's poor overworked heart."

He organized a Mass, open to all denominations, at the Church of the Blessed Sacrament in Hollywood for the morning of the funeral. He gave an interview to the Associated Press that bore the headline: "Fun-Loving Babe Wised-Up Under Christy Walsh." And he prepared a ninety-second radio address, delivered on KECA, about the last baseballs autographed by the Babe.

"From Memorial Hospital, New York, a package arrived yesterday. Inside were baseballs for three little fellows in Los Angeles—Robert, Wayne, and Donald Billings. Each ball autographed in the old familiar hand of their hero. Even in his dying hours Babe Ruth was thinking of boys. And even before the lads could claim their sacred souvenirs, Babe Ruth had breathed his last."

He crossed out a line he'd written about Babe addressing the package himself. He appeared with the boys and their autographed baseballs in the next day's edition of the *Herald Express*, a new iteration of the newspaper that first hired him as a cartoonist in 1911.

In the years to come, Walsh stayed busy, though he had to work at it now. Staying busy was integral to his belief system. "If you want something done *now*, then *always* give the job to a *busy* man," he told his nephew Richard, time and again.

He gave interviews about the Babe; newspaper friends gave banquets in his honor when he published a 1949 follow-up to his encyclopedic 1934 history of college football, and four years later, *Baseball's Greatest Lineup*. He produced glossy annual sports calendars and got the formerly silent Harold Lloyd to speak on behalf of them. He was elected president of the Los Angeles branch of the Society of the Friendly Sons of St. Patrick, an extraordinary honor for a teetotaler, his grandson says. Cheap as he was, he was known to serve liquor stored with mothballs, causing guests to flee fund-raisers he hosted.

He continued to name his annual All-American football teams, which were increasingly eclipsed by those selected by *Look* and *Collier's* magazines. He hosted an annual breakfast for the "Morning After the Rose Bowl Society of Inquisitive Reporters and Cautious Coaches" at the second coming of Walshchateau in North Hollywood.

He was up on a ladder in the attic on the afternoon of December 29, 1955, making preparations for his annual Rose Bowl breakfast, when he suffered a fatal heart attack. He was sixty-four years old. A dinner in his honor given that evening by the Sports Ambassadors of Pasadena went on as planned, though his death had not been announced. He'd rather die than face such an onslaught of praise, his nephew said.

His old friend, the baseball lifer Fred Haney, gave what amounted to a eulogy: "Babe himself was not a well-educated man. He'd take a few drinks, run around and do a few things and it was all kept from the press. I think that was one of the greatest journalist jobs ever done and Christy never got credit for it."

Babe Ruth stopped traffic on Fifth Avenue on August 19, a gray, dismal morning brightened only by the umbrellas shielding the huddled masses lining the sidewalks of New York, seventy-five thousand strong, his second sellout in as many days. Francis Cardinal Spellman, who had witnessed and testified to the miracle of the Called Shot in Chicago, conducted the funeral Mass at St. Patrick's, with the help of forty-four priests, including Father Kaufman. Six thousand mourners attended, only half of whom were seated; the others were crammed in the aisles and chapels and open spaces at the rear of the cathedral, pressed in among the pallbearers and the casket.

Young Jack McKinney, who would become a Pennsylvania coaching legend at St. Joseph's College and later NBA coach of the year in 1981, found himself among the celebrants, wedged between Governor Dewey, Bill Bendix, and the Babe. "He had not yet been wheeled forward for the Mass," McKinney remembered. "They turned the Babe around so he was facing the altar. Then they started playing hymns."

It was a singular moment for a thirteen-year-old: to encounter death and greatness in such proximity. He and his dad didn't stick around for the Mass. They weren't dressed for that. His father gave him the signal and they made their way out of the front entrance to the cathedral.

On the way home, in the car, he turned to his father and offered the only eulogy offered that day.

"Holy smokes, the Babe."

IV

George Herman Ruth Jr. was buried in section 25 of Gate of Heaven Cemetery in Westchester County, some twenty-three miles from the Yankee Stadium, surrounded by some two hundred thousand Catholics, including a few old friends—Gentleman Jimmy Walker, who admonished him about disappointing the dirty-faced boys of America, as well as Westbrook Pegler and Bob Considine, the first and last mythologists of his life. His grave is up a slight rise, just off Cardinal Avenue, overlooking a man-made lake, the Taconic Parkway, and the railroad tracks of what used to be known as the New York Central and a trickle of the Bronx River heading for the city.

There's nothing subtle or understated about the gravesite, dwarfed as it is by a sandblasted statue in Westerly granite of Jesus blessing a young baseball player. It is engraved with the words of Cardinal Spellman: "May the Divine Spirit That Animated Babe Ruth to Win the Crucial Game of Life Inspire the Youth of America!"

Claire Ruth was buried beside him in 1976. She died of breast cancer, having refused to seek treatment because of what she saw him endure during the last years of his life. After his death, she maintained a prominent public presence at Yankee Stadium in the box set aside for her along the third base line, attending important occasions, including the October 1, 1961, game when Roger Maris broke the Babe's home run record. That day, "she might have shed a tear," Julia said. "But, like Mother used to say, 'Well, Lindbergh was the first to fly the ocean. But you never heard anything about anyone who did it later.'"

Bus tours arrive in advance of every opening day. People leave him gifts, as if trying to return a favor. Hot dogs are a favorite, some of the plastic dog toy variety. Yellow plastic carnations. Airplane bottles of Smirnoff vodka. Casino chips from the Jackpot Casino in Las Vegas. Cigars. Wedding favors. Neon green Top Flite XL golf balls. And baseballs, lots and lots of baseballs, some autographed to him on the sweet spot, some inscribed with his major-league records, some with his most famous aphorism—"Never Let the Fear of Striking Out Keep You from Playing the Game." Some of the balls have been there so long, exposed to the elements and the trampled dirt surrounding the headstone, they look like something he threw in the dead ball era.

It's hard to surprise the Babe's caretakers. They are accustomed to seeing footprints in the snow, to license plates arriving from Indiana, Arkansas, and Minnesota. Interest peaked in the days when the Curse of the Bambino still prevailed. Nuns arrived with curse-breaking cookies they baked in Boston. A Beantown radio station sent a drive-time broadcast crew—they wanted to know if they could camp out with the Babe. The trunk of their white stretch limo was filled with beer. A guy showed up in a 1920s baseball uniform with a plastic recliner prepared to spend the night.

Then, one day during the 2004 American League Championship Series, when the Yankees blew a three-game lead over the Red Sox, the section foreman noticed a beat-up car cruise to a stop on Cardinal Avenue. A guy in a white cook's apron got out, retrieved an insulated delivery bag from the trunk, and walked up the hill toward Jesus. He extricated a white, square cardboard box, still spewing steam, from the bag and placed it on the ground in front of the headstone.

It was a large New York–style pizza—none of that Chicago, deep-dish stuff for the Babe—with plenty of sausage and peppers.

The delivery boy opened the box before backing down the hill and driving away.

Acknowledgments

On October 4, 1951, as Bobby Thomson circled the bases at the Polo Grounds propelled by the Shot Heard 'Round the World, Red Smith typed these words for the *New York Herald Tribune*: "Now it is done. Now the story ends. And there is no way to tell it. The art of fiction is dead. Reality has strangled invention. Only the utterly impossible, the inexpressibly fantastic, can ever be plausible again."

I wasn't thinking about how well those words described Babe Ruth when I asked Red about them. "You know, I've seen that quoted and reprinted thousands of times and every time, I think, gosh, that's overwritten," he said blushing, the way he did. "Why didn't I just say, 'Today reality surpassed imagination?'"

The answer is, some people—the Babe, for example—and some occasions require excess. This is one of them. You can't overwrite thank-yous.

Now that it is done, now that the eight-year war to wrassle the Big Fella into submission has reached an end, it's time for the shout-outs and hosannas. I've come to believe, having spent many evenings with the Babe, that the extraordinary generosity of the 250 or so people I dug up to interview—who knew him, or knew something new about him, or knew someone else who did—and that of the colleagues who shared their research and sometimes did mine for me, was inspired by his example. I am grateful that so many of the gracious people the Babe introduced me to have become my friends.

I knew that writing this book would be different from anything I'd ever done before, like putting together a twenty-thousand-piece jigsaw puzzle. And I hate jigsaw puzzles. To everyone who helped put a piece in place or contributed one, however small, and seemingly inconsequential, I am in your debt.

First among them: Ruth's daughter Julia Ruth Stevens, her son, Tom, his wife, Anita, and son Brent; his granddaughters Donna Analovitch and Genevieve Herrlein, and Linda Ruth Tosetti. Very special thanks to the relatives I met in my neck of the woods: his grandniece Jan McNamee and cousin so-many-times removed Doris Keil-Shamieh, a fine genealogist with reportorial curiosity, Harry and Gina Pippin, and Shelby Fell Daugherty. Thank you for trusting me to tell his story.

From the Christy Walsh clan: the garrulous and generous grandson Bob Walsh and his wife, Katie, nephew Richard Walsh, step-grandchildren Kelly Merritt and Frank Merritt, and cousins Paula and Michael Messina.

From Helen Woodford Ruth's family: Lynn Woodford, Jean Beswick, Patricia Grace, Katherine Honey, Craig Woodford, Mark Saidel, and Tim Mitchell, who helped me piece together her short, sad life; and Ryan Nicholson of the Watertown, Massachusetts, fire department, who provided documents from the night of the fire that took her life.

In Baltimore: Shawn Herne, Babe Ruth Birthplace and Museum, and former curator Greg Schwalenberg, who let me swing the Babe's bat; William Greskovich of St. Agnes Hospital, and Brian Cromer, caretaker of the former St. Mary's property; Christina Callender, Dorothy Miceli Dupski, Mary Tormollan, descendants of Harry C. Birmingham; and Esther Hynson, Father Michael Roach, and Dottie Schluepner, former residents of west Baltimore. Members of the extended Ruth family: Jim and Tony Brady, Anna Maria and Noreen

Frontera, John Munion, Jonathan Shahan. And friends of the family: Carolyn Rendon, Father Gabe Costa, and Ken and Dorothy Patterson.

Sudbury: Kevin Kennedy, master upholsterer and true believer, and Charlie Barry, who shared the secret of the piano.

Omaha: Members of the Landers family, Polly Thielmeier, Jack Landers Sr. and Jr., and Jane Landers Price, who helped bring Lady Amco back to life; also, Bob Chenoweth, Pat O'Donnell, Steve Rosenblatt, and Steve Hayes.

Sioux City: Filmmaker R. C. Raycraft, who shared the story of Ruth's visit to the Donohues and footage of him clambering aboard the obdurate pony, Molly; Joanne Donohue Sanderson, and Dan Donohue.

Bay Area: Mark Macrae, Randy Stuart, Francesca Santoro, Tom O'Doul, Len Hockney, John Ward, Bill Jones, and all the guys at the San Francisco Old Timers' Baseball Association who told me about Jack "Whitey" Stuart, and Jack's daughter, Carole Tollefson, who shared her father's story and the photograph of Whitey with the Babe in his honor.

Marysville: Steve Perry, Joanne Perry Raub, Bruce Minton, Randy Newton Sr. and Jr., Patricia Johnstone, and Carolyn Ralston-Bordeaux, who welcomed me into Tub Perry's life.

San Jose: Richard, Joe, and Tony Cirone, who were kind even though I think I broke their hearts; Don Cordoni, for introducing me to them; Tom Randazzo and Joe Randazzo, Andrew Shepherd, and Diane Lechner.

San Diego: Debby Gumb, Toni McGowan, and Charles "Boomer" Turpinseed, who shared everything they knew about their grandfather Carl Klindt and made me feel like a member of the clan; Bill Swank, who knows everyone and everything about baseball in San Diego; Carolyn Neilsen-Major, Toni Stein, and Rolland Thomas, for making Glenn E. Thomas and Ruth's outings with him come alive.

Fresno: Kerry Yo Nakagawa, Howard Zenimura, and Bill Staples, who educated me about and welcomed me into the world of Kenichi Zenimura and Nisei baseball.

Greenwood Lake: Sally Jo Greck, Deems Grabowski, Steve Gross, Walter Petaluna, and Skip Hart, who re-created Babe's life among them.

Baseball guys: Yogi Berra, Monte Irvin, Phil Coyne, Mike Rizzo, Bill DeWitt, Charlie Silvera, Dick Beverage, and Babe's alter ego, C. J. Wilson.

Fanboys of long-ago summers who met or saw or mourned the Babe, some of whom I mourn now: Rugger Ardizoia, Mike Klepfer, Jack McKinney, George Morgenweck, George Nicholau, Anthony Puliatti, Sig

Seidenman, Blake Talbot, and most especially the ineffable Roger Angell and the Honorable John Paul Stevens for his personal testimony to the Called Shot.

When no living sources could be found, the information I needed was ferreted out by a cadre of librarians and archivists to whom I pledge my troth, chief among them Jeff Flannery, head of the Manuscript Reading Room at the Library of Congress, who can find anything, and Paul Janov, now retired, who found everything else. Malea Walker provided additional help.

At the New York Public Library, Tal Nadan and Rebecca Federman. Kevin Cawley at the University Archives, University of Notre Dame, where the archives of the Xaverian Brothers are housed, along with Knute Rockne's papers, including his correspondence with Christy Walsh; Nancy Pope at the National Postal Museum; Anne Thomason, archivist for the Joseph Patterson Collection at Lake Forest College; the Japanese American Historical Archives; and Lesley Martin, Chicago History Museum Research Center, Kenesaw Mountain Landis papers.

Jennifer Hafner and Owen Lourie at the Maryland State Archives, and Jennifer Fauxsmith at the Massachusetts Archives, who located the documents that allowed a peek into the history of the Ruths of Baltimore and Boston.

In cities and towns that Ruth inhabited or visited on the 1927 tour: Francis O'Neill, Maryland Historical Society; Christopher Boone, School of Sustainability, Arizona State University; Sarah E. Hinman, Leiden University, Netherlands; Jerry Williams, Baltimore Trolley Museum; Ellen Warnock, Catholic Charities, Baltimore; Mary Ann Moran-Savakinus, Lackawana Historical Society; Jonathan Gust, Villanova University; Marta Otero, Asbury Park Library; Kate Wells, Providence Library; Caleb Horton, Rhode Island State Archives; Anna Selfridge, Allen County Museum, Lima, Ohio; Lee Swanson, Sudbury Historical Society; Kara Evans, Missouri Valley Special Collections, Kansas City Public Library; Jean Svadlenak, Lee Jeans, historian; Theresa Gipson, Mercy Hospital, Kansas City; Emiel D. Cleaver, Black Archives of Mid-America; Kenneth J. LaBudde, Nichols Library, University of Missouri Kansas City; Andrea Falling, Nebraska State Historical Society; Amy C. Schindler, Criss Library at the University of Nebraska-Omaha; Benjamin L. Clark, archivist, Boys Town, Omaha; Tom Carey, San Francisco History Center, San Francisco Public Library; Catherine Mills, Archives History San Jose; Acuna Espinosa, Fresno County Public Library; Patrick Ogle, Fresno State University; and Tricia Ford, the director of my beloved summer sanctuary, the Truro Public Library.

What they couldn't find, my more than generous colleagues supplied. Leigh Montville, whose biography *The Big Bam* preceded and informed my own, shared the transcripts of interviews conducted by Jerome Holtzman. Bob Creamer offered his unique take on the Babe in the months before his death. His son, Jim Creamer, and friend Paul Ferrante shared letters and papers from Bob's precedent-setting book, including his correspondence with Waite Hoyt.

Jonathan Eig, author of *Luckiest Man*, passed on a trove of barnstorming clippings he collected in his research and invaluable insights into his subject, Lou Gehrig; Richard Sandomir, author of *The Pride of the Yankees*, shared gossipy correspondence between Eleanor Gehrig and Christy Walsh; Gregg Kaufman and R. A. Cabral, who had the notion to re-create "The Symphony of Swat," before it occurred to me to do it, shared their research and intelligence. Although writing on a similar subject, Tom Barthel took my calls and shared information. Chris Martens, the ghostwriter on Dorothy Ruth Pirone's 1988 memoir, shared her handwritten notes.

Dennis Snelling, Rob Neyer, and Jeff Passan did legwork for me. Seriously.

Ed Achorn, Jean Ardell, Dave Bohmer, Paul Dickson, Tom Friend, Arnold Hano, Terry Hersom, John

Holway, Richard Johnson, Steve Kettmann, Tim Kurkjian, Mike Lackey, Elizabeth Laval, Jon Leonoudakis, Matt Lloyd, Paula Lloyd, David A. Mark, Mike McDermott, Mark Patton, the late Ray Robinson, Vin Scully, Dan Shaughnessy, Steve Steinberg, Charley Steiner, the late Bob Wolf, and Steve Wulf all had stories to tell or tips to share and leads to follow. Bill James put it all together in the way that only he can.

Shout-outs:

For their knowledge of Brother Matthias, St. Mary's, and the Xaverian Brothers: Kathy Carmody, Francis X. McGillivary, Jean Mor, Brother Arcadius Alkonis, and Brother Peter Donohue.

For their expertise in the physics and biomechanics of hitting a baseball: Jason Ochart, Jim Lefebvre, Preston Peavy, the late Dave Vincent, and always and most especially Alan Nathan.

For their expertise in the world of sports agenting, advertising, marketing, memorabilia, and promotion: Scott Boras; Leigh Steinberg; Ken Goldin, Goldin Auctions; Pete Siegel, Gotta Have It Collectibles; J. P. Cohen, Memory Lane, Inc.; Rich Mueller, editor of *Sports Collectors Daily*; Tim Slavin at MLBPA; Fred Toulch; John Reznikoff; Jerry Della Femina; and George Lois.

For their legal, economic, and medical counsel: Lawrence Altman, Lori Andrews, Ev Ehrlich, Amy Katz, Laurence J. Lebowitz, Mary Moran, Moses Schanfield, and CeCe Moore at the DNA Detectives.

For sharing the images that illuminated Ruth in his time: Jay Gauthreaux, John Horne, Bruce Menard, Stephanie L. Stricker, Ben Weingarten, Anne Wermiel, and Wayne Wilson.

For acts of kindness and competence: Mark Rathbun, Ellen Victor, Steve Marmon, Sean Lamarre, and Brian Combs.

For being indefatigable and patient with my very disorganized self, my cohort of research assistants: darling Claire Ulak, Rachel Lesaar, Terry Tatum, and Alex Holt. Craig Dougherty, an online sleuth and genealogist, whom I met through ancestry.com, was responsible for getting the research started. If he quits his day job, I know what he should do. And JR, who doesn't think she did anything to help, did the greatest service of all. She made me realize I wasn't alone with the Babe.

For making the computer cooperate and making inaudible interviews resemble human speech: Rick Prescott, Bruce Maliken, and Marti Hagan of Word-Wizards.

For being my go-to guys: Marty Appel, Steve Fehr,

Rob Fleder, Jeff Katz, Dan "Subtitle" Okrent, John Powers, and Nick Trotta.

For being my go-to gals: anatomical goddess Amy Engelsman, front-office doyenne Harolyn Cardozo, and Janet Marie Smith, who makes baseball more beautiful every day; everyday life enablers Amy Sachs, Toni Cortellessa, and Jordana Carmel; and book group stalwarts Carole, Deborah, Kim, Madalyn, Leslie, Lynn, and Other Jane.

For making me feel at home in Cooperstown: Jim Gates, Bill Francis, Bruce Markusen, Tim Wiles, and Cassidy Lent.

For giving me a social media presence: Antonella Iannarino.

For giving me a chance: George Solomon and Mary Hadar.

For so much more than I can say, my MVPs:

Tom Shieber, senior curator at the Hall of Fame, answered every query, corrected every mistake, read every page, and never lost patience or enthusiasm for the task. Chris Ivy, director of sports auctions at Heritage Auctions, shared information from the Christy Walsh catalogs, making my understanding of the Ruth-Walsh relationship possible.

Michael Haupert, professor of economics at the University of Wisconsin–La Crosse, crunched every number and never once laughed at my lack of mathematical proficiency. This is his book as much as it is mine.

Kevin Goering, über–sports law attorney, provided expert counsel in the history of the right of publicity and did legwork in dusty storage rooms of New York City courthouses with enthusiasm verging on glee.

Bill Jenkinson, author of *The Year Babe Ruth Hit 104 Home Runs* and historian of all things Babe, made his comprehensive and painstakingly compiled ledger of Ruth's every game—regular, spring training, barnstorming, and home run—available to me. Better yet, he made himself available.

Dave Smith, sabermetrics guru and founder of Retrosheet, supplied the stats and the expertise as he has done so expertly in all three of my baseball books.

Fred Shoken, Baltimore historian and historic preservation specialist, made me my very own binder of his research into the city of Ruth's birth, census documents, family papers, and news clippings that I never would have found on my own.

David Stinson, author/sleuth of all things Baltimore, escorted me through the back alleys of the Babe's hometown, in search of clues to his past and an understanding of his formative years.

Matthew Zaft, financial adviser at Morgan Stanley

in Washington, gamely accepted five hundred pages of badly Xeroxed financial documents dating back to 1927 and made sense of them and thus made sense of the economic force the Babe became.

John Thorn, the elegant and always definitive official historian of Major League Baseball, read every word and saved my *tokhes* more times than anyone but the copy editor can count. Yes, prior to 1969: it is major-league baseball, no caps.

Carole Horn, healer, helper, editor, Renaissance woman, and reader for all things medical in the book, refused to let me look stupid.

Hans Ulrich Gumbrecht, Stanford professor of cultural history, soccer aficionado, and expert on the aesthetics of sport, shaped my thinking and approach to the subject with his discussion on the advent of stardom in *In 1926: Living on the Edge of Time*. Thanks for making me smart.

Mike Gibbons, director emeritus at the Babe Ruth Birthplace and Museum, shared invaluable tape-recorded interviews of sources no longer alive, including Ruth's sister Mamie Ruth Moberly. And he made me brave when, during our first conversation, he answered my question about which Babe book he considered definitive, by saying, "It hasn't been written yet."

For being my peeps and VIPs: Hal, Marilyn, and the

whole Weiner gang; Sid and Diana Tabak; Judith and Kosta Tsipis; Roberta Falke and Andy Levey; Rhonda Schwartz and Steve Wermiel; Kim Sammis and Jim Ulak; Bonnie Nelson Schwartz and Arlie Schardt; Leslie Harris and Peter Basch; Mary Brittingham and David Plocher; Gerri Hirshey and Mark Zwonitzer; Elissa Poteat, Brad Garrett, and Mr. Max; Alan and Terry Chebot; Mark and Lori Roux; John and Yvette Dubinsky; Dick and Caren Lobo; Norman Steinberg; Gloria Weissberg; Steven Phillips. For being my ports in the storm: Amy Katz and Irv Sher; Barbara and Alan Weinschel.

For being the best first readers any writer could imagine: Dave Kindred and Robert Pinsky. Gail Mazur—baseball muse.

For making life possible: in Washington, Ann Hess; in Truro, Jeremy Young and Maria Volpe.

For making Bette's life possible: Janno Parky; Adam and Callie Crain; Julian and Dylan Ann Ambrose, and their enablers Ivy and Michael Meeropol; Eliot and Owen Taber; Kaira von Salis, Paulo and Bruno Frias; Audrey and James Acres.

For being my main man: David Black, knight errant among literary agents, and his round table of noble jousters, led by Matt Belford. David, you are my liege.

For my boy, Nick, who bravely hefted the Babe's bat

over his seven-year-old shoulder and gave me a way to begin.

At HarperCollins, I've got what you call deep depth: art guys, cover designer Milan Bozic and book designer Bill Ruoto, who made it look so good and worked so hard doing it; PR goddess Kate D'Esmond, who made sure it got seen; marketing dude Tom Hopke, who made a dream come true. The production wizard who turned a mess into a book: David Koral, senior production editor.

Jane Cavolina made sure I didn't make too many mistakes. Beth Silfin made sure I didn't do anything dumb. Publisher Doug Jones and sales president Josh Marwell made the Babe their cause. Sarah Ried, Brooklyn's finest, and her predecessor, Erin Wicks, made my writing life as easy as it was possible for it to be. Jonathan Burnham, publisher, granted my wish.

Former editor David Hirshey brought me into the fold and out of left field when he asked me to write about Sandy Koufax in 1999. Before departing for some well-deserved beach time, he published *The Last Boy* to perfection, nurtured the embryonic *Big Fella*, and turned me over to Jennifer Barth, Mets masochist and editrix extraordinaire, who already had a full roster of big-league talent when she inherited me.

She not only made room in her all-star lineup for

me and the Babe, but she arrived on my doorstep in Birkenstocks and sunglasses with soft (editorial) hands, a keen eye for anything wide of the mark, and the chops to call me on it. She's a gamer. How lucky I am to be her player-to-be-named-later.

Appendix 1:
The Power of the Man

FULL NAME: George Herman Ruth

BORN: February 6, 1895, Baltimore, Maryland

DIED: August 16, 1948, New York, New York

Buried at Cemetery of the Gate of Heaven, Hawthorne, New York (Section 25, Lot 1115, Center of Graves 3 and 4)

FIRST GAME: July 11, 1914

FINAL GAME: May 30, 1935

BAT: Left

THROW: Left

HEIGHT: 6' 2"

WEIGHT: 215

SELECTED TO THE HALL OF FAME: 1936 (95.1%)

AWARDS: 1916 AL pitching title; 1923 AL MVP; 1924

AL Batting Title; Named outfielder on the *Sporting News* Major League All-Star Team (1926 to 1931)

EJECTIONS: 11

TRANSACTIONS: Sold by Baltimore (International) to Boston Red Sox with Ernie Shore and Ben Egan for more than $25,000 on July 9, 1914.

Sold by Boston Red Sox to New York Yankees for $100,000 on December 26, 1919.

Released by New York Yankees on February 26, 1935.

Signed by Boston Braves February 26, 1935.

H is was a less precise time. Technology had not yet enabled the instant verification of miracles, leaving room for imagination and several municipalities—and one prison—to stake a claim and plant a sign on the alleged spot where the longest ball Babe Ruth ever hit came to rest. The language of those boasts is charmingly imprecise: "longest hit with the Boston Red Sox" (Tampa, Florida, 1919); "longest confirmed linear distance" (Navin Field, Detroit, 1921); "longest actually measured" (City Point, New York, 1925); "longest home run in competitive baseball history" (Wilkes-Barre, Pennsylvania, 1926); "longest hit before a captive audience" (Sing-Sing Prison, Ossining, New York, 1929); "longest hit off major-league pitching" (St. Petersburg, Florida, 1934).

Measuring the Babe in his time—trying to pin him down—was as difficult as it was antithetical to his being. But try they did, if only in an effort to document their own incredulity. Bill Jenkinson, the author of *The Year Babe Ruth Hit 104 Home Runs*, has researched and logged eleven hundred Ruthian blows hit in regular-season, postseason, and exhibition games—and walked the path of perhaps half of them. Of Ruth's sixty home runs in 1927, Jenkinson says, twenty-eight traveled between 400 and 450 feet; seventeen traveled between 450 and 500; three others broke the 500-foot barrier. All together in 1927, counting home runs he hit in every venue, including twenty on the barnstorming tour, Ruth hit thirty more home runs than the record books credit him with, according to Jenkinson.

The Babe announced the arrival of long-distance baseball in spring training 1919. Red Sox manager Ed Barrow was still anguishing over his decision to make Ruth a full-time outfielder. On April 5 in Tampa, Ruth hit a ball against the New York Giants that soared out of the ballpark and across a racetrack before coming to rest 587 feet away. (The specificity of the account was courtesy of Mel Webb of the *Boston Globe*, who asked the right fielder where the ball landed, and then fetched a tape measure.) A Florida historical marker marks the spot as "Babe's Longest Homer."

Two years later, on July 18, 1921, at Navin Field in Detroit, where he hit sixty of his 714 career home runs—including number 700—he hit a ball that according to Jenkinson is not only the longest of his career but the longest in major-league history. The ball had an 18-mile-an-hour wind and Ruth's pent-up frustration behind it. (He had walked in four previous at-bats.) The distance from home plate to the place where the ball was last seen—exiting the ballpark where the wooden fence at the far end of the center field bleachers met concrete at the corner of Cherry and Trumbull Avenues—was 560 feet. The distance was confirmed with the aid of stadium blueprints provided by the head groundskeeper and "a sextant," the *New York Times* reported.

The zeal to tether him to numbers and geometry caught up with him at Ahrco Field at New York City's College Point in October 1925, as researcher Bruce Orser learned. In advance of the game, amateur surveyors, employees of the American Hard Rubber Company, laid out 590 feet of steel tape from home plate to the center field fence. Thus they were able to put an exact number on a ball he hit in the October 4 game—538 feet—qualifying it, Jenkinson says, as baseball's first legitimate tape measure home run.

This was mere chicken feed compared with the one

he would hit a year later in a barnstorming tour game at Artillery Park in Wilkes-Barre, Pennsylvania, two days after the end of the 1926 World Series. Ruth was playing hurt. He wasn't wearing sliding pads when he tried and failed to steal second base in the ninth inning of Game 7, a fact that became apparent to twelve-year-old John Hogarth when he and his friend Billy Clark were invited to meet the Babe in his hotel room during his campaign through Pennsylvania. "The door opened and here's Babe Ruth, sitting there in a chair in a jock strap and a sweatshirt—that's all he had on!" Hogarth recalled in an interview recorded by his son in 1995 and posted on YouTube. "He said, 'C'mere kids.' I got on his left knee and Billy Clark got on his right knee. It was oozing blood at that time."

This did not impede his swing in Wilkes-Barre. The game had to be called after six innings, due to delays caused by Ruth stopping to sign autographs. But Ruth wanted to keep hitting and challenged a local pitcher to throw his fastest pitch over the plate. The Associated Press described the result: "The ball cleared the right field fence 400 feet from the plate by more than 40 feet and was still ascending. The ball landed on the far side of the running track of a high school athletic field in Kirby Park. Officials estimated the length at 650 feet."

The City of Wilkes-Barre built a permanent display

in Kirby Park honoring the occasion. According to Jenkinson's research, Ruth said it was the longest ball he had ever hit and asked for it to be measured, which was the only time he had ever done that.

Of course, he hadn't yet been to Sing Sing. The Yankees arrived at the prison on September 5, 1929, to play the home team, known as the Black Sheep. *Sports Illustrated* described the scene in 1967: "A home run in the yard at Sing Sing is a home run almost anywhere. It is 270 feet down the left-field foul line, 440 in dead center and 340 in right. A thick 30-foot-high stone wall, topped by three watchtowers, encloses the outfield."

The game was played before what the *New York Times* called 1,500 "more or less permanent residents," who saw the last of his three home runs carry high over the wall, past the center field guardhouse and across the New York Central railroad tracks that bisected the prison, finally returning to earth some 600 feet away. "Gee, I wish I was riding out of here on that one!" exclaimed the Black Sheep shortstop, who still had ten years to go on a twenty-five-year stretch.

Contemporaneous accounts estimated that the ball traveled 620 feet, but it was never measured. The *Times* called it "the longest non-stop flight of an object or person leaving Sing Sing."

In gratitude, the inmates made him a double-hinged

cedar chest with a pair of inlaid baseball diamonds on the top labeled "Nat. League" and "Am. League." It was sold by members of the Ruth family for $23,395 in January 2017.

The fifty-year revolution to remake baseball in the image of mathematicians continues unabated despite the 2004 warning of Paterfamilias Bill James that "the fog of data" was becoming an impediment to enlightenment.

Nearly fifteen years later, James et al. remain committed to the quest of developing a single statistic that can measure the value of an individual player to his team in such a way that his achievements can be compared with the living and the dead, no matter what era they played in, what position they manned, or what ballpark they called home. This remains the holy grail of sabermetrics.

What is clear a half century into the search is how well Babe Ruth fares in all the formulations. The Batting-Fielding Wins (BFW) metric included in Retrosheet's career record was devised by Pete Palmer, also the father of the now standard On Base + Slugging (OPS) statistic. While working overtime in Raytheon's computer lab during the 1960s, Palmer created a system of linear weights, assigning a value to each of the seven possible outcomes of an at-bat. This became the foundation for his Total Player Rankings published in *The Hidden Game of Baseball* in 1984. BFW attributes to each player the number of wins over (or under) the number an average player would contribute in his place. Ruth ranks second behind Barry Bonds in this formula.

James was still working as a security guard at the Stokely Van Camp pork and beans factory when he created the formula for Runs Created using the equation for "total bases" that F. C. Lane began compiling for *Baseball Magazine* in Ruth's time. (Ruth had 457 total bases in 1921.) In 2002, James unveiled a new metric called Win Shares, an extrapolation of Runs Created, which, he wrote, "are in essence Wins Created." Unlike the other überstats, Win Shares is tied to actual team wins. So, if the Yankees win 100 games, there are 300 Win Shares available to Yankee players, which are then distributed to players, each according to his contribution in a victory.

Ruth ranks first with 752 Win Shares, followed by Ty Cobb with 722.

Wins Above Replacement (WAR), today's most commonly cited metric, calculates the number of wins a player contributes to his team above the number the team would be expected to win if he was substituted with a replacement-level player. Ruth ranks first overall among all major-league players (pitchers and batters) with 182.5 WAR, followed by Cy Young with 168.5. According to Baseballreference.com, Ruth is also second among position players with 162.1, just behind Bonds.

Clay Davenport, a meteorologist for the National Oceanic and Atmospheric Administration, and longtime statistician for *Baseball Prospectus*, spent more than a decade working on a system that converts the fancy new statistics back into the familiar Black Ink stats—the boldfaced league leaders—recognizable to the average fan. He calls them DTs—Davenport Translations—a comparison of how a given player did against the average player in his era and how he would have fared against the average player of 2000. Ruth's career totals in translation look like this: .319 BA, 972 HR, 1991 BB, 2120 RBI, SLG .714. Davenport then translated those projected totals into an Equivalent Average (EqA) of .362, and Equivalent Runs (EqR), his estimation of Runs Created.

As always in the pursuit of objectivity, there are caveats, best articulated by John Thorn, Palmer's coauthor, who is now the official historian of Major League Baseball. "Ruth's dominance was not only the measure of Ruth; it was also, in part, the measure of the competition he faced," Thorn said. "A colossus may so far outdistance his peers as to create records that are unapproachable for all time. But Ruth faced pitchers who threw complete games about half the time (today it is one in a hundred) and thus faced the same delivery through four to six plate appearances. He saw relievers only when starting pitchers were beaten into submission, and unlike today these pitchers were second-raters. Ruth never had to hit at night; never faced a slider or a split-fingered fastball; rarely faced a pitcher who would throw a breaking ball when behind in the count; and so on.

"Ruth never hit against an African American or dark-hued Latino pitchers, at least in the big leagues. If men of color had played in his day, many white players would have lost their positions and the average level of play would have risen.

"Ruth may have been better than any anyone ever was or will be; however, it defies reason to claim that Ruth's opposition was as strong as that faced by Bryce Harper or Mike Trout."

STANDARD CAREER RECORD

AB	R	H	BA	HR	RBI	SB	On-base%	SLG.	OPS
8,399	2,174	2,873	.342	714	2,214	123	.474	.690	1.164

SABERMETRICS CAREER RECORD

WAR	BFW	WS	EqA	OPS+
183.7 (1)	114.8 (2)	726 (1)	.362	206

LIFETIME BATTING RECORDS:

1ST SLUGGING: .690

1ST OPS: 1.164

1ST OPS+: 206 (OPS adjusted by ballpark and era)

2ND RBI: 2214

2ND ON BASE %: .474

2ND RUNS CREATED: 2,718

3RD HOME RUNS: 714

3RD BASES ON BALLS: 2,062

4TH RUNS SCORED: 2,174

4TH EXTRA-BASE HITS: 1,356

7TH TOTAL BASES: 5,793

10TH BATTING AVERAGE: .342

LIFETIME PITCHING RECORDS:

W-L RECORD: 94-46

W-L %: .671, 12th all-time (minimum of 1,000 innings pitched)

ERA: 2.28, 17th all-time

BEST SEASON: 1916, 23–12, 170 strikeouts, 1.75 ERA (league leader), 23 complete games; also led the league in games started (40), shutouts (9)

MOST COMPLETE GAMES IN AL 1917: 35

WORLD SERIES: 3–0, 0.87 ERA, 2 complete games, 1 shutout. His record for 29⅔ consecutive scoreless innings stood for forty-two years. Pitched 14 innings in Game 2 of 1916 World Series, beating the Brooklyn Robins 2–1.

BATTING RECORD

Year	Team	G	AB	R	H	2B	3B	HR	RBI	BB
1914	BOS A	5	10	1	2	1	0	0	0	0
1915	BOS A	42	92	16	29	10	1	4	20	9
1916	BOS A	67	136	18	37	5	3	3	16	10
1917	BOS A	52	123	14	40	6	3	2	14	12
1918	BOS A	95	317	50	95	26	11	11	61	58
1919	BOS A	130	432	103	139	34	12	29	113	101
1920	NY A	142	458	158	172	36	9	54	135	150
1921	NY A	152	540	177	204	44	16	59	168	145
1922	NY A	110	406	94	128	24	8	35	96	84
1923	NY A	152	522	151	205	45	13	41	130	170
1924	NY A	153	529	143	200	39	7	46	124	142
1925	NY A	98	359	61	104	12	2	25	67	59
1926	NY A	152	495	139	184	30	5	47	153	144
1927	NY A	151	540	158	192	29	8	60	165	137
1928	NY A	154	536	163	173	29	8	54	146	137
1929	NY A	135	499	121	172	26	6	46	154	72

1930	NY A	145	518	150	186	28	9	49	153	136
1931	NY A	145	534	149	199	31	3	46	162	128
1932	NY A	133	457	120	156	13	5	41	137	130
1933	NY A	137	459	97	138	21	3	34	104	114
1934	NY A	125	365	78	105	17	4	22	84	104
1935	BOS N	28	72	13	13	0	0	6	12	20
Total NL (1 Year)		28	72	13	13	0	0	6	12	20
Total AL (21 Years)		2475	8327	2161	2860	506	136	708	2202	2042
Total (22 Years)		2503	8399	2174	2873	506	136	714	2214	2062

BATTING RECORD (cont.)

Year	IBB	SO	HBP	SH	SB	CS	AVG	OBP	SLG	BFW
1914		4	0	0	0	0	.200	.200	.300	0.0
1915		23	0	2	0	0	.315	.376	.576	0.0
1916		23	0	4	0		.272	.322	.419	0.0
1917		18	0	7	0		.325	.385	.472	0.0
1918		58	2	3	6		.300	.411	.555	3.6
1919		58	6	3	7		.322	.456	.657	7.4
1920		80	3	5	14	14	.376	.532	.847	9.4
1921		81	4	4	17	13	.378	.512	.846	9.6
1922	14i	80	1	4	2	5	.315	.434	.672	3.8
1923		93	4	3	17	21	.393	.545	.764	10.8
1924		81	4	6	9	13	.378	.513	.739	8.9
1925	1i	68	2	6	2	4	.290	.393	.543	1.8
1926	9i	76	3	10	11	9	.372	.516	.737	8.6
1927	3	89	0	14	7	6	.356	.486	.772	9.2
1928	8i	87	3	8	4	5	.323	.463	.709	7.1
1929	3i	60	3	13	5	3	.345	.430	.697	5.0

1930	8i	61	1	21	10	10	.359	.493	.732	7.6
1931	4i	51	1	0	5	4	.373	.495	.700	7.8
1932	4i	62	2	0	2	2	.341	.489	.661	6.4
1933	3i	90	2	0	4	5	.301	.442	.582	4.6
1934	0i	63	2	0	1	3	.288	.448	.537	3.1
1935	0i	24	0	0	0	0	.181	.359	.431	0.1
Total NL (1 Year)	0i	24	0	0	0˙	0	.181	.359	.431	0.1
Total AL (21 Years)	57i	1306	43	113	123	117i	.343	.475	.692	114.7
Total (22 Years)	57i	1330	43	113	123	117i	.342	.474	.690	114.8

i = incomplete

Source: David W. Smith, Retrosheet: Babe Ruth; http://www.retrosheet.org/boxesetc/R/Pruthbl01.htm

WORLD SERIES BATTING RECORD

Year	Team	G	AB	R	H	2B	3B	HR	RBI	BB
1915	BOS A	1	1	0	0	0	0	0	0	0
1916	BOS A	1	5	0	0	0	0	0	1	0
1918	BOS A	3	5	0	1	0	1	0	2	0
1921	NY A	6	16	3	5	0	0	1	4	5
1922	NY A	5	17	1	2	1	0	0	1	2
1923	NY A	6	19	8	7	1	1	3	3	8
1926	NY A	7	20	6	6	0	0	4	5	11
1927	NY A	4	15	4	6	0	0	2	7	2
1928	NY A	4	16	9	10	3	0	3	4	1
1932	NY A	4	15	6	5	0	0	2	6	4
Total (10 Years)		41	129	37	42	5	2	15	33	33

Year	IBB	SO	HBP	SH	SF	SB	CS	AVG	OBP	SLG
1915	0	0	0	0	0	0	0	.000	.000	.000
1916	0	2	0	0	0	0	0	.000	.000	.000
1918	0	2	0	1	0	0	0	.200	.200	.600
1921	0	8	0	0	0	2	1	.313	.476	.500
1922	0	3	1	1	0	0	1	.118	.250	.176
1923	0	6	0	0	0	0	0	.368	.556	1.000
1926	1	2	0	0	0	1	1	.300	.548	.900
1927	1	2	0	1	0	1	0	.400	.471	.800
1928	0	2	0	0	0	0	0	.625	.647	1.375
1932	0	3	1	0	0	0	0	.333	.500	.733
Total (10 Years)	2	30	2	3	0	4	3	.326	.470	.744

Source: David W. Smith, Retrosheet: Babe Ruth; http://www.retrosheet.org/boxesetc/R/Pruthbl01.htm

PITCHING RECORD

Year	Team	G	GS	CG	SHO	GF	SV	IP	H	BFP	HR	R	ER
1914	BOS A	4	3	1	0	0	0	23	21	96	1	12	10
1915	BOS A	32	28	16	1	3	0	217.2	166	874	3	80	59
1916	BOS A	44	40	23	9	3	1	323.2	230	1272	0	83	63
1917	BOS A	41	38	35	6	3	2	326.1	244	1277	2	93	73
1918	BOS A	20	19	18	1	0	0	166.1	125	660	1	51	41
1919	BOS A	17	15	12	0	2	1	133.1	148	570	2	59	44
1920	NY A	1	1	0	0	0	0	4	3	17	0	4	2
1921	NY A	2	1	0	0	1	0	9	14	49	1	10	9
1930	NY A	1	1	1	0	0	0	9	11	39	0	3	3
1933	NY A	1	1	1	0	0	0	9	12	42	0	5	5
Total		163	147	107	17	12	4	1221.1	974	4896	10	400	309

Year	BB	IB	SO	SH	WP	HBP	BK	2B	3B	W	L	ERA	RS	PW
1914	7		3	2	0	0	0	2i	0i	2	1	3.91	5.67	-0.3
1915	85		112	14i	9	6	1	11i	3i	18	8	2.44	5.21	2.8
1916	118		170	23i	3	8	1	17i	3i	23	12	1.75	3.97	5.7
1917	108		128	31i	5	11	0	39i	7i	24	13	2.01	3.68	4.9
1918	49		40	25	3	2	1	18i	3i	13	7	2.22	4.00	2.9
1919	58		30	24i	5	2	1	26i	3i	9	5	2.97	3.80	1.4
1920	2		0	0	0	0	0			1	0	4.50	14.00	-0.1
1921	9		2	0	0	0	0			2	0	9.00	13.00	-0.6
1930	2	0	3	1	0	0	0	1	1	1	0	3.00	9.00	0.3
1933	3	0	0	0	0	0	0	1	0	1	0	5.00	6.00	0.0
Total	441	0	488	120	25	29	4	115	20	94	46	2.28	4.33	17.0

i = incomplete

Source: David W. Smith, Retrosheet: Babe Ruth; http://www.retrosheet.org/boxesetc/R/Pruthbl01.htm

WORLD SERIES PITCHING RECORD

Year	Team	G	GS	CG	SHO	GF	SV	IP	H	BFP	HR	R	ER
1916	BOS A	1	1	1	0	0	0	14	6	48	1	1	1
1918	BOS A	2	2	1	1	0	0	17	13	68	0	2	2
Total (2 Years)		3	3	2	1	0	0	31	19	116	1	3	3

Year	BB	IB	SO	SH	SF	WP	HBP	BK	2B	3B	W	L	ERA	RS
1916	3	0	4	2	0	0	0	0	1	0	1	0	0.64	2.00
1918	7	0	4	1	0	1	1	0	0	0	2	0	1.06	2.00
Total (2 Years)	10	0	8	3	0	1	1	0	1	0	3	0	0.87	2.00

Source: David W. Smith, Retrosheet: Babe Ruth; http://www.retrosheet.org/boxesetc/R/Pruthb101.htm

Appendix 2:
The Babe's Portfolio

In 1927, Babe Ruth became the first professional baseball player to earn as much money off the field as on it and the template for every modern millionaire and multimillionaire celebrity athlete. His agent, Christy Walsh, the first of his kind, created a blueprint for a business that would become synonymous with the catchphrase from the 1996 movie *Jerry Maguire*: "Show me the money."

Here's how they did it.

Employing equal measures of persuasion and coercion, Walsh convinced Ruth to open a trust fund at the Bank of Manhattan in February 1927 and to deposit all of his nonbaseball income into the account. When their contractual relationship ended in May 1938, Walsh summarized Ruth's earnings under his management in a letter and accounting sheet (see pages 783-786, 789). Economist Michael Haupert translated those figures, and Ruth's annual Yankee salary, into 2016 dollars. Matthew Zaft, a financial adviser with Morgan Stanley in Washington, D.C., examined trust documents, bank statements, and income reports in Walsh's files in an effort to determine just how well Ruth was advised, how well the trust performed before and after the Great Depression, and how wealthy Ruth was compared with the average American.

PAID TO GEORGE H. RUTH BY CHRISTY WALSH APRIL 15, 1921—MAY 1, 1938, INCLUSIVE

Year	Syndicate	Spalding	Mc-Loughlin MFG. CO. (Under-wear)	Candy	Vaude-ville	Barn-storm	Adolph Kastor (Knife)	Diamond Point Pen
1921	4,246.90	—	—	—	—	—	—	—
1922	7,985.12	—	—	—	—	—	—	—
1923	11,509.29	—	—	—	—	—	—	—
1924	13,092.91	—	—	—	1,250.00	19,019.45	—	—
1925	13,218.85	—	—	—	—	—	—	—
1926	12,607.46	—	1,250.00	4,914.08	18,640.97	11,080.99	—	—
1927	12,807.59	3,235.25	2,250.00	576.61	—	28,281.93	—	—
1928	13,735.96	5,459.12	1,463.69	774.55	—	15,954.91	—	—
1929	20,484.76	5,781.98	2,195.45	—	—	1,694.98	—	—
1930	15,189.74	3,336.51	1,749.56	120.00	—	4,195.81	341.83	—
1931	13,131.73	2,076.00	988.88	—	—	10,887.09	308.16	—
1932	8,714.84	1,703.12	1,890.52	—	—	—	117.04	—

1933	4,892.13	517.37	187.25	—	—	—	37.52	—
1934	3,108.95	1,600.07	366.49	—	—	—	4.35	1,125.00
1935	1,200.44	1,061.70	416.52	—	—	2,911.91	—	232.80
1936	1,070.00	778.11	213.27	—	—	—	2.77	167.61
1937	33.52	588.07	327.03	—	—	—	—	—
1938	—	244.29	144.43	—	—	—	—	—
Total	157,030.19	26,381.59	13,443.09	6,385.24	19,890.97	94,027.07	811.65	1,525.41

Esso	Quaker Oats	Sinclair Oil	Radio Miscel-laneous	Benrus Watch	Milton Bradley (Game)	Moving Pictures	Putnam "Babe Ruth's Own Book"	Miscel-laneous	Total Across
—	—	—	—	—	—	—	—		4,246.90
—	—	—	—	—	—	—	—	—	7,985.12
—	—	—	—	—	—	—	—	—	11,509.29
—	—	—	—	—	—	—	—	—	33,362.36
—	—	—	—	—	—	—	—	—	13,218.85
—	—	—	—	—	—	—	—	1,750.00	50,243.50
—	—	—	—	500.00	—	22,488.46	—	3,107.50	73,247.34
—	—	—	1,500.00	—	975.00	—	1,000.00	3,370.00	44,233.23
—	—	—	1,500.00	—	—	—	—	2,567.50	34,224.67
—	—	—	1,875.00	—	—	—	183.37	1,975.00	28,966.82
—	—	—	—	—	1.66	5,625.00	23.36	325.00	33,366.88
—	—	—	—	—	64.77	—	—	1,498.75	13,989.04

										Total
—	—	1,125.00	—	37.67	—	—	8,567.79	15,364.73		
12,375.00	38,625.00	—	—	187.50	29.55	—	—	589.00	58,010.89	
—	18,750.00	—	1,478.68	614.32	—	—	—	724.55	27,390.92	
—	5,412.50	—	750.00	—	—	—	—	675.00	9,069.26	
—	—	14,625.00	1,860.00/ 15.00	—	—	—	—	370.00/ 5.00	17,823.62	
—	—	—	—	—	—	—	—	750.00	1,138.65	
12,375.00	62,787.50	14,625.00	10,103.68	1,301.82	1,108.65	28,113.46	1,206.73	26,275.09	477,392.07	Total Payments to Mr. Ruth (921-1938): $477,392.07

RUTH'S TOTAL EARNINGS FROM YANKEES AND OUTSIDE INCOME UNDER CHRISTY WALSH MANAGEMENT

This table shows how much Babe Ruth earned each year in salary and outside income with the dollars translated into today's purchasing power.

Year	Salary	Contracted Salary, Adjusted for Inflation (Value in 2016 Dollars)	Total Endorsement Income	Endorsement Income, Adjusted for Inflation (Value in 2016 Dollars)	Salary Plus Endorsement Income	Salary Plus Endorsement Income, Adjusted for Inflation (Value in 2016 Dollars)
1920	$20,000	$4,180,000			$20,000	$4,180,000
1921	$20,000	$5,020,000	$4,246.90	$1,065,972	$24,247	$6,085,972
1922	$52,000	$13,052,000	$7,985.12	$2,004,265	$59,985	$15,056,265
1923	$52,000	$11,232,000	$11,509.29	$2,486,007	$63,509	$13,718,007
1924	$52,000	$11,024,000	$33,362.36	$7,072,820	$85,362	$18,096,820
1925	$52,000	$10,608,000	$13,218.85	$2,696,645	$65,219	$13,304,645
1926	$52,000	$9,880,000	$50,243.50	$9,546,265	$102,244	$19,426,265
1927	$70,000	$13,510,000	$73,247.34	$14,136,737	$143,247	$27,646,737

Year						
1928	$70,000	$13,230,000	$44,233.23	$8,360,080	$114,233	$21,590,080
1929	$70,000	$12,460,000	$34,224.67	$6,091,991	$104,225	$18,551,991
1930	$80,000	$16,160,000	$28,966.82	$5,851,298	$108,967	$22,011,298
1931	$80,000	$19,280,000	$33,366.88	$8,041,418	$113,367	$27,321,418
1932	$75,000	$23,475,000	$13,989.04	$4,378,570	$88,989	$27,853,570
1933	$52,000	$16,952,000	$15,364.73	$5,008,902	$67,365	$21,960,902
1934	$35,000	$9,765,000	$58,010.89	$16,185,038	$93,011	$25,950,038
1935	$7186*		$27,390.92	$6,875,121	$34,577	$6,875,121
1936			$9,069.26	$1,986,168	$9,069	$1,986,168
1937			$17,823.62	$3,564,724	$17,824	$3,564,724
1938			$1,138.72	$242,547	$1,139	$242,547

Inflation-adjusted salary using relative share of GDP (https://www.measuringworth.com/).

* Ruth signed a three-year $25,000 contract with the Boston Braves in 1935. This is what he would have received before being released on June 2.

Source: Michael Haupert, Professor of Economics, University of Wisconsin–La Crosse

CHRISTY WALSH MANAGEMENT
SPORTS · MOTION PICTURES · RADIO

ESTABLISHED 1921   347 FIFTH AVENUE
NEW YORK

May 1, 1938

Mr. George H. "Babe" Ruth
173 Riverside Drive
New York City

Dear Babe:

The fact that after 17 years of congenial and mutually profitable relations our written contract expires today, will not alter our friendship and willingness to be of mutual assistance, so far as I am concerned. The good fortune and even more so, the occasional disappointments and set-backs which we have experienced together, have created a bond of understanding and confidence that would not come out of an ordinary friendship. And yet with the expiration of our formal agreement, it is my pleasant duty to render you an "accounting of my stewardship" – a final report of the past seventeen (17) years, results derived by reason of your personality and peerless baseball record, combined with my efforts.

The accompanying figures will show that I have paid to you, either by direct remittance or otherwise by your request – approximately a half million dollars – to be exact $477,392.07.

These figures are taken from our records, which records, as always, are available to you for confirmation or reference.

Some of the money you received through me was due to ideas I created and executed, while some of the enterprises may have developed without my assistance – for anybody with a reasonable amount of intelligence and a maximum amount of energy, should have produced profits during the peak years of your career.

But on one point I do claim a little special distinction and a great deal of personal satisfaction – the founding and completion of both your trust fund and annuity, in the combined amount of $250,000.00. This, Babe, means a lot to me because it is based on sentiment. It was the most practical and lasting way in which I could demonstrate my friendship. You have done too much for baseball and have given too many people thrills and happiness to ever have you face uncertainty in the years to come. New sources of revenue may develop for you and I hope they will, but this portion of your past earnings, derived outside of your baseball income, is a positive guarantee of comfort, security and self-respect for the rest of your days.

We need no further contract. No matter where I am or what the circumstance, I will regard you as I have in the past and I sincerely hope that the sentiment is mutual.

Wishing you many years of good health and happiness, I remain, as always,

Your friend,

Christy

When the trust was executed in April 1927, Ruth deposited $40,000 in the account, thanks to the windfall of outside income he earned in 1926–27. By November 1928, the amount had doubled to $80,000 ($1.1 million in 2016 dollars). Most of the investments made on his behalf were made in 1928, prior to the crash of October 1929. Of sixteen investments made during this period, only three came after the crash, according to Zaft's review of the account, yet the trust produced more income than the previous year.

INVESTMENTS PURCHASED BY YEAR

PDF Year (Period Covered)	Investments
1928 (April 26, 1927– November 20, 1928)	$85,660.00
1930 (November 20, 1928– April 25, 1930)	$24,791 .91
1931 (April 26, 1930–April 25, 1931)	$101,196.30
1932 (April 26 1931–April 25, 1932)	$49,012.50

The bank invested 70 percent of Ruth's money in fixed-income U.S. and municipal bonds and 30 percent in dividend-paying blue-chip stocks, which yielded a net income of $4,099.41 in 1927–28. He also earned $240 from his bonds ($3,349.25 today), generating a total income that first year of $4,659.13. By November 1928, his investments were worth $85,660.00.

His dividends increased steadily, save for a slight decrease on November 2, 1928, about which Walsh complained. After that, they rebounded, reaching a peak of $2,470.87 on May 1, 1934. Every year from 1931 to 1941, he received quarterly payments of about $2,000 ($30,000 to $34,000 today) from his investments.

Although the percentage on his return dwindled each year during the Great Depression, the trust continued to grow after October 1929, producing increased income each year until 1941.

ALL INCOME COLLECTED FROM INVESTMENTS

PDF Year (Period Covered)	All Income Collected	Percent Change
1928 (April 26, 1927–November 20,1928)	$4,659.13	N/A
1930 (November 20, 1928–April 25, 1930)	$6,176.48	32.6%
1931 (April 26, 1930–April 25, 1931)	$7,667.09	24.1%
1932 (April 26, 1931–April 25, 1932)	$9,051.09	18.1%

Ruth continued to build the trust throughout the first three quarters of 1929, sometimes adding to the account twice a month. After depositing $3,000 on October 24, the first day of the crash, he added nothing more until July 1930. But while ordinary Americans were standing in breadlines in 1930 and 1931, Ruth added $100,000 to his trust. The final $1,000 deposit was made on September 2, 1931, bringing the total value of the account to $200,000, or about $3.3 million today. By that time, Ruth had received $88,932.87 in dividends from the trust.

He earned money on every sale made on his behalf between July 16, 1930, and April 20, 1931, a net increase of $693.58 (about $10,300 today). Also, his stocks were heavily dependent on dividends, and dividends fell only 11 percent during the Great Depression. By April 25, 1932, the value of the inventory in his account had reached $200,980.02, generating $10,102.55 in income, an increase of $2,435.46 over the previous year.

TOTAL CONTRIBUTED TO TRUST SINCE INCEPTION, WITH ESTIMATED ANNUAL INCOME

PDF Year (Period Covered)	Value	Estimated Annual Income
1928 (April 26, 1927–November 20, 1928)	$80,240.00	$4,255.80
1930 (November 20, 1928–April 25, 1930)	$100,240.00	$5,244.00
1931 (April 26, 1930–April 25, 1931)	$155,928.02	$7,965.00
1932 (April 26, 1931–April 25, 1932)	$200,928.00	$10,102.55

The income statements from 1941 to 1944 show how and when Ruth began to feel the impact of the Great

Depression, slight as it might have been for him. His 100 shares in Standard Brands were paying a dividend of only $10. But his shares in the Chesapeake & Ohio Railway and Consumers Power Company delivered seven times as much. The Bank of Manhattan sold off his holdings in the American Can Company and RJ Reynolds Tobacco, which decreased 33 percent and 43 percent, respectively, in 1943, and also sold 75 percent of his shares in Standard Brands in 1944.

Those losses were offset to some extent by investments in Standard Oil and Texas Gulf Sulphur Company, which continued to pay the same dividends as before, and the First National Bank Boston, which increased its dividend. But his quarterly dividend checks decreased to $1,700. When Walsh wrote to the Bank of Manhattan to protest the loss of income, a vice president felt compelled to remind him of "the prevailing economic conditions." The quarterly dividend checks remained at that level at least through 1944, at which point Walsh stopped receiving information from the bank at Ruth's direction.

Ruth campaigned relentlessly on behalf of U.S. War Bonds. In May 1941, the bank sold off some of his U.S. Treasury Bonds to finance the purchase of over $17,000 (approximately $300,000) of U.S. Savings Bonds, Series G, or war bonds. In January 1942, the sale of Pennsylvania Power and Light Company securities financed the purchase of another $11,000 in war bonds.

Over the course of the next several years, the trust, which was funded through dividend and interest payments, remained constant. The balance never fell below $200,000, enough to provide Ruth with his quarterly checks.

STATEMENT OF SECURITIES HELD: TOTAL VALUE

Year	Value	Percent Change
1941	$100,395.00	N/A
1942	$102,445.00	2.0%
1943	$101,783.75	−0.6%
1944	$101,094.75	−0.7%

"Not only did the Babe Ruth Trust not lose money during the stock market crash of 1929, but it continued to grow all the way up until 1942," Zaft said. "Even at that point, the equity portion of the trust lost less than 1 percent between 1942–43 and 1943–44. This was due to careful management and a good balance of both individual U.S. Treasury Bonds along with stocks in quality, dividend-paying blue-chip companies. Christy Walsh's commitment to having the Babe continue to contribute to the trust even during these troubling economic times (including a deposit on Black Monday) allowed for the purchase of additional securities at low points. Throughout the 1930s sales of stock were executed in a very timely fashion, yielding net gains on the portfolio each year. The trust provided Mr. Ruth with a consistent stream of income all the way up until mid-1941, when prevailing interest rates declined. Whoever was managing the trust deserves immense credit."

HISTORY OF BABE RUTH TRUST FUND, BANK OF MANHATTAN TRUST CO. NEW YORK
AMOUNT: $200,000.00
STARTED FEBRUARY 24, 1927

Paid to Trust Fund		Dividends Received from Trust Fund to February 1, 1940			
		No.	Date Received	Amount	Covering Quarter Up To
Feb. 14, 1927	33,000.00	0	Nov. 3, 1927	643.13	Nov. 1, 1927
Apr. 26, 1927	7,000.00	2	Feb. 3, 1928	900.00	Feb. 1, 1928
Aug. 8, 1927	10,000.00	3	May 2, 1928	900.00	May 1, 1928
Dec. 7, 1927	20,000.00	4	Aug. 2, 1928	900.00	Aug. 1, 1928
Nov. 13, 1928	10,000.00	5	Nov. 2, 1928	500.00	Nov. 1, 1928
Apr. 29, 1929	2,500.00	6	Apr. 27, 1929	1,000.00	Feb. 1, 1929
May 2, 1929	1,000.00	7	May 2, 1929	1,000.00	May 1, 1929
May 16, 1929	3,500.00	8	Aug. 7, 1929	1,000.00	Aug. 1, 1929
Jun. 11, 1929	3,000.00				

Jul. 9, 1929	1,000.00	9	Nov. 4, 1929	1,000.00	Nov. 1, 1929
Jul. 23, 1929	2,000.00	10	Feb. 10, 1930	1,045.00	Feb. 1, 1930
Aug. 12, 1929	1,500.00	11	May 2, 1930	1,200.00	May 1, 1930
Sept. 4, 1929	1,500.00	12	Aug. 2, 1930	1,400.00	Aug. 1, 1930
Sept. 9, 1929	1,000.00	13	Direct to B.R.	1,650.00	Nov. 1, 1930
Oct. 24, 1929	3,000.00	14	Direct to B.R.	1,900.00	Feb. 1, 1931
Jul. 2, 1930	15,000.00	15	Direct to B.R.	2,000.00	May 1, 1931
Aug. 22, 1930	5,000.00	16	Direct to B.R.	2,000.00	Aug. 1, 1931
Sept. 29, 1930	20,000.00	17	Direct to B.R.	2,000.00	Nov. 1, 1931
Nov. 17, 1930	10,000.00	18	Direct to B.R.	2,000.00	Feb. 1, 1932
Jan. 12, 1931	5,000.00	19	Direct to B.R.	2,000.00	May 1, 1932
May 6, 1931	5,000.00	20	Direct to B.R.	2,250.00	Aug. 1, 1932
Jun. 3, 1931	15,000.00	21	Direct to B.R.	2,250.00	Nov. 1, 1932
Jun. 10, 1931	5,000.00	22	Direct to B.R.	2,250.00	Feb. 1, 1933
Jul. 16, 1931	10,000.00	23	Direct to B.R.	2,470.57	May 1, 1933
Sept. 2, 1931	10,000.00	24	Direct to B.R.	2,000.00	Aug. 1, 1933
		25	Direct to B.R.	2,000.00	Nov. 1, 1933
Total		26	Direct to B.R.	2,000.00	Feb. 1, 1934

HISTORY OF BABE RUTH TRUST FUND, BANK OF MANHATTAN TRUST CO. NEW YORK (cont.)

200,000.00	27	Direct to B.R.	2,673.67	May 1, 1934
	28	Direct to B.R.	2,000.00	Aug. 1, 1934
	29	Direct to B.R.	2,000.00	Nov. 1, 1934
	30	Direct to B.R.	2,000.00	Feb. 1, 1935
	31	Direct to B.R.	2,000.00	May 1, 1935
	32	Direct to B.R.	2,000.00	Aug. 1, 1935
	33	Direct to B.R.	2,000.00	Nov. 1, 1935
	34	Direct to B.R.	2,000.00	Feb. 1, 1936
	35	Direct to B.R.	2,000.00	May 1, 1936
	36	Direct to B.R.	2,000.00	Aug. 1, 1936
	37	Direct to B.R.	2,000.00	Nov. 1, 1936
	38	Direct to B.R.	2,000.00	Feb. 1, 1937
	39	Direct to B.R.	2,000.00	May 1, 1937
	40	Direct to B.R.	2,000.00	Aug. 1, 1937
	41	Direct to B.R.	2,000.00	Nov. 1, 1937
	42	Direct to B.R.	2,000.00	Feb. 1, 1938
	43	Direct to B.R.	2,000.00	May 1, 1938

44	Direct to B.R.	2,000.00	Aug. 1, 1938
45	Direct to B.R.	2,000.00	Nov. 1, 1938
46	Direct to B.R.	2,000.00	Feb. 1, 1939
47	Direct to B.R.	2,000.00	May 1, 1939
48	Direct to B.R.	2,000.00	Aug. 1, 1939
49	Direct to B.R.	2,000.00	Nov. 1, 1939
50	Direct to B.R.	2,000.00	Feb. 1, 1940
51	Direct to B.R.	2,000.00	May 1, 1940
52	Direct to B.R.	2,000.00	Aug. 1, 1940
53	Direct to B.R.	2,000.00	Nov. 1, 1940
	Total	94,932.87	

Bank documents, reports, and correspondence from the Christy Walsh Collection Catalog, volumes 2–3, courtesy of Heritage Auctions/HA.

Total earnings table courtesy of Michael Haupert, professor of economics at the University of Wisconsin–La Crosse.

Financial analysis courtesy of Matthew Zaft, a financial adviser with Morgan Stanley in Washington, D.C. He was assisted by Joseph Naness, a student at Johns Hopkins University.

Author's Note and Sources

Twenty-six years ago, I decided to write a novel about Babe Ruth. It wasn't an original idea. Heywood Broun beat me to it, creating the first fictive Babe in a 1923 novel called *The Sun Field*. Even then the Babe seemed too big for fact.

I never got past chapter one. One thing led to another, including biographies of Sandy Koufax and Mickey Mantle. Finally, in the summer of 2011, I went to North Conway, New Hampshire, to visit Babe Ruth's daughter Julia Ruth Stevens, who at the age of ninety-six still called her father Daddy. I figured if I was ever going to make good on my promise to myself I'd better get going.

One thing I knew for sure: I was *not* going to write a biography of the Babe. An all-star roster of sportswriters and historians—beginning with Dan Daniel and Tom Meany, followed by Robert Creamer, Ken Sobol, Robert Smith, Kal Wagenheim, Marshall Smelser, and Leigh Montville—had already done an admirable job of that. They had the advantage of knowing the Babe, or covering him, of interviewing teammates and opponents, and his closest friends and family. What more was there to say? And, more to the point, who was left to say it? Most of the people on a biographer's interview wish list were dead. And no one at the Babe Ruth Birthplace and Museum had contact information for his extended family, most of whom didn't know each other or much of their familial history. No one had ever constructed a complete family tree. (At the celebration of his one hundredth birthday, museum officials set out a table with a sign-in sheet for family members, in hopes of filling in the gaps, but it was stolen during the party.)

There was also the issue of primary source material. The Babe wasn't Lyndon Johnson, who left behind enough material for Robert Caro's five volumes of biography, or John Adams, who conducted a twenty-year correspondence with one of America's most literate first ladies. Primarily Babe Ruth wrote his signature. That's always been a quandary for practitioners of sports biography, which existed for the better part of the twentieth century as a literary subgenre dominated by what Mickey Mantle called "all that Jack Armstrong shit."

Finding a new George would be like recovering the upright piano stuck in the muck at the bottom of Sudbury's Willis Pond—the one Bostonians believed to be at the heart of the Curse of the Bambino, a spell that cast New England into eighty-six years of darkness after he was sold to New York. Retelling his life in fiction wouldn't demand dredging up any new facts.

And yet as I immersed myself in the Ruth oeuvre in advance of meeting Julia, I found myself troubled by the facts or, more precisely, the lack of them—and how little seemed to be known about the Babe as a babe. It was as if his life began on June 13, 1902, the day he arrived at St. Mary's.

A passing comment from Julia, mentioned in the nicest possible way, changed everything. Babe Ruth's parents had separated when he was eleven years old. Divorced, in fact.

She didn't realize the import of the revelation. "Well," she said, "I just thought everyone knew!"

No one knew. Babe Ruth made sure no one knew. Although he made repeated and ineffective attempts to correct the misimpression that he was an orphan, he never went further, eschewing every opportunity to tell the truth about his parents' marriage. Not once, in any of the thousands of interviews or ghostwritten columns under his byline, did he set the record straight. And why would he? The facts were ugly. Who'd want to talk about that?

Julia's revelation provided the key to unlocking the mystery of her father's childhood—the missing boy in the Babe Ruth story—and a narrative that was surely as compelling as fiction. As Jimmy Breslin once said of him, "he was more than real." The more I dug, the more real he became.

There was a new story to tell, after all. And, as it turned out, there was a new way to get at it.

The presumed disadvantage of writing about Ruth at such a remove proved to be an advantage. In the years since Montville published the last major Ruth biography, *The Big Bam*, in 2006, the digitization of state birth, death, marital, and census records, as well as the availability of newspaper archives searchable by name, provided access to material beyond the reach of previous biographers. As Smelser, a history professor at the University of Notre Dame, noted in his 1975 Ruth biography, there was almost no "archival" material available when he researched his book.

Little wonder then that when I asked Bob Creamer, author of *Babe*, one of four major biographies published in 1974, and the first serious attempt to chip away at the veil of hagiography, if he knew about the divorce, he said, no, he hadn't done much with the childhood. He would have had to scour every 1906 edition of the *Baltimore Sun* to find the story of the Ruth divorce that I accessed with one click of a mouse. No doubt, as more of the past goes digital, histories, including this one, will be rewritten over and over again.

Those online resources were augmented by extensive interviews with his surviving family members, as well as records accessed through the Maryland State Archives, the Massachusetts Archives, and the Babe Ruth Birthplace and Museum, and others accessed at www.ancestry.com and www.geneaologybank.com. The current zeal to connect with and document the past, facilitated by those websites, led me to additional members of the Ruth and Woodford families and connected me with a slew of savvy amateur genealogists and cyber sleuths.

Fleshing out the character of Christy Walsh, the man behind the Big Fella, was easier than I expected, thanks in part to his facility for promoting himself as well as his clients. His 1937 self-published memoir, *Adios to Ghosts*, which appeared in serial form in the *Sporting News* in January 1938, was invaluable not just for the facts he shared about the Christy Walsh Syndicate but for the insights it offered into how he thought and operated.

But the key was the acquisition of a mother lode of previously unexamined documents—letters, bank statements, check stubs, legal papers—contained in four auction catalogs assembled by Heritage Auctions for its 2010 Christy Walsh sale. The unpaginated volumes, created for marketing purposes, weren't offered as part of the auction. But that trove of material, inherited by Walsh's step-grandchildren, was generously made available to me by Chris Ivy, Director of Sports Auctions for HA, and by step-granddaughter Kelly Merritt. She also gave me recordings of Walsh's speeches, radio broadcasts, and interviews with the Babe, not to mention Irvin Berlin's song, "Along Came Ruth," with the special baseball lyrics penned by Walsh. Interviews with Kelly, her brother Frank; Walsh's nephew, Richard; and especially his grandson, Bob, gave me a feel for the man that no documents could convey.

The 24/7 coverage of Ruth, inaugurated by the *New York Daily News*, was a godsend. I relied extensively on reporting in the *News*, the *New York Times*, and ten long-gone New York dailies; also, the *Boston Globe*, the *Baltimore Sun*, the *Chicago Tribune*, the *Washington Post*, and the *Los Angeles Times*. G. H. Fleming's

Murderers' Row, a retelling of the 1927 season through daily news stories from New York's best sportswriters, provided a trove of material culled from otherwise difficult-to-find resources.

Thanks to the Baseball Index, which lists just about everything ever written about Babe Ruth, I was able to locate pertinent stories in the archives of *Baseball America*, *Baseball Digest*, *Liberty* magazine, *Literary Digest*, and the *Sporting News*; through the *Sports Illustrated* vault, I was able to find everything the magazine had published about him. I also reviewed *Radio Digest*, *Variety*, and the *New Yorker*, whose coverage included a 2002 piece by Roger Angell titled "Babe Ruth: My Teammate, My Lover," a satirical same-sex love letter addressed to "my bambino." (In response to the publication, Angell told me, "several people in sports said, 'I didn't know that.' I said, 'It's a joke!'")

Those news accounts were supplemented by the Ruth archive at the National Baseball of Fame, whose librarians allowed me to copy their entire collection of clippings and documents. The Christy Walsh scrapbooks, recently digitized by the HOF staff, re-creating the barnstorming tours he organized, and the coverage he generated, were indispensable.

Equally important for color and detail was the local coverage of Ruth's visits to each of the cities on the

1927 tour, accessed through www.newspapers.com, www.newspaperarchives.com, www.proquest.com, and www.newsbank.com, and through the kindness of librarians and historians at local collections and historical societies. Other resources included the Xaverian Brothers Records at University of Notre Dame Archives. Notre Dame also supplied eighty-eight letters between Christy Walsh and Knute Rockne in the athletic director's records. I drew additionally upon the Joseph Medill Patterson Papers at Lake Forest College; the Kenesaw Mountain Landis archive at the Chicago History Museum; and the Library of Congress, for both General John J. Pershing's papers and those of Edward L. Bernays, not to mention all the "By Babe Ruth" columns from 1921 to 1922.

At the New York Public Library, I consulted Jacob Ruppert's papers as well as the library's holdings from the 1939–40 New York World's Fair, which include all of Walsh's correspondence as director of sports publicity. The Bill Shannon Biographical Dictionary of New York Sports at the New York Historical Society was extremely helpful as was the "Bioproject," a compendium of baseball biographies found online at www.SABR.org.

Information about train travel in 1927 came from Chris Baer at the Hagley Museum in Wilmington,

Delaware, which maintains a collection of old train schedules and from train aficionados David Splitt and P. K. Hannah.

For information about the value and sale of Ruth memorabilia, I relied on Rich Mueller, editor of *Sports Collectors Daily*; Pete Siegel of Gotta Have It Collectibles; and www.pricerealized.com, a database of sports memorabilia sold in the United States. As of March 3, 2018, 13,733 Ruth items had been sold, of which 121 sold for more than $100,000 apiece.

I realized early on that this book would require granular reporting. I set about collecting shards of information, like the small pieces of tile in a large mosaic, hoping they would add up to a coherent picture of the man.

My own 250 interviews were augmented by 25 interviews conducted by Mike Gibbons for the Babe Ruth Museum in the 1990s, and by Kal Wagenheim's interviews with *Daily News* reporter Marshall Hunt, whom Ruth called his shadow. By donating their research materials to the A. Bartlett Giamatti Research Center at the Hall of Fame, Wagenheim and the late Marshall Smelser made my task considerably easier. The transcripts of Jerome Holtzman's interviews for *No Cheering in the Pressbox: Recollections Personal and Professional by Eighteen Veteran American*

Sportswriters were generously passed on to me by Leigh Montville. Bob Creamer's son, Jim, shared his father's correspondence with Ruth's teammate Waite Hoyt. Chris Martens, co-author of Dorothy Pirone's 1988 memoir, sent copies of the notes she had provided for his use.

Three previous accounts of the 1927 barnstorming tour were indispensable: John B. Kennedy's article, "Innocents Abroad," published in the April 14, 1928, issue of *Collier's* magazine, provided color, dialogue, and details from the tour. R. Gregg Kaufman's podcast, "Symphony of Swat," accessed on iTunes, and R. A. Cabral's *Barnstormin' Across America: The Bustin' Babes and Larrupin' Lous*, published online in September 2013, were useful guides. (Rick Cabral also shared taped recordings of interviews he conducted for his book.)

Babe Ruth's career statistics were provided by Retrosheet, the online compendium of baseball data, and vetted by Retrosheet founder David Smith and Major League Baseball historian John Thorn. Bill Jenkinson allowed me to copy his lovingly and meticulously compiled ledger documenting Ruth's every game, home run, and barnstorming tour—an incomparable resource.

Michael Haupert, a professor at the University of Wisconsin–La Crosse, who discovered seventy previously unexamined Yankee account books and daily ledgers at the Hall of Fame in 2000, combined his research on the economics of the team and Babe Ruth with the Christy Walsh accounting ledger I uncovered to produce a complete picture of the Babe's financial clout.

In order to be able to imagine Ruth in his time, I reviewed thousands of images—a select few of which appear in the book—shared by Wayne Wilson at LA84, Ben Weingarten/Weingarten's Vintage, Heritage Auctions, John Horne at the Hall of Fame, Bruce Menard at BeeSmile, Jay Gauthreaux, the Babe Ruth Museum, and the Xaverian Brothers U.S.A.

To immerse myself in Ruth's time, I read with pleasure a lot of F. Scott Fitzgerald and H. L. Mencken; Broun's *The Sun Field*; Dennis Lehane's *The Given Day*, set in Boston during the Red Summer of 1919, Ruth's last year with the Red Sox; and David Stuart's *The Babe Ruth Deception*, set in his early days in New York; as well as Thomas Mallon's 2004 novel, *Bandbox*, set in a twenties newsroom. Also Ring Lardner's *You Know Me, Al*, Damon Runyon's *The Best of Damon Runyon*, Paul Gallico's *Farewell to Sport* and *The Golden People*, Fred Lieb's *Baseball as I Have Known It*, Red Smith's *Out of the Red*, Bill Shannon and George Kalinsky's *The Ballparks*, and the biography and collected works of Grantland Rice.

To better understand the era that Ruth dominated, I read Kevin Jackson's *Constellation of Genius: 1922—Modernism Year One*, Robert Gordon's *The Rise and Fall of American Growth: The U.S. Standard of Living Since the Civil War*, Donald L. Miller's *Supreme City: How Jazz Age Manhattan Gave Birth to Modern America*, Ann Douglas's *Terrible Honesty: Mongrel Manhattan in the 1920s*, Hans Ulrich Gumbrecht's *In 1926: Living at the Edge of Time*, and my prized 1927 first edition of Will Irwin's *Highlights of Manhattan* with E. H. Suydam's gorgeous illustrations of my hometown.

A selected list of the primary resources I consulted appears in the bibliography that follows the notes. Below, more specifically, are the sources that were most instrumental in the writing of individual chapters.

INTRODUCTION

Interviews: Chris Davis, Mike Gibbons, Sally Prugh, Mark Rathbun, Cal Ripken, Tom Robbins, Ray Robinson, Greg Schwalenberg, Julia Ruth Stevens, C. J. Wilson, and Steve Wulf.

I first interviewed Julia Ruth Stevens in August 2011 for a *Grantland* story, "Being Babe Ruth's Daughter" (January 3, 2012). She spent another three days with me at her son's home in Henderson, Nevada, in May 2013 in hopes that I would convey "Babe Ruth, the man." Her invaluable observations and memories about growing up with the Babe suffuse this book.

Jhan Robbin's 1963 *Sport* magazine story, "The Time Babe Ruth Hit One for Me," reprinted in *The Best of Sport 1946–1971*, was augmented by interviews with his widow, Sally Prugh, and son, Tom Robbins.

Mike Gibbons and Greg Schwalenberg shared the story about Chris Davis's encounter with Ruth's bat. Davis elaborated on his comments in the August 26, 2013, *Sports Illustrated* cover story about his Ruthian turnaround, "Unlocking the Power and Mystery of Chris Davis."

After using the Babe's bathtub for ten years to store baseball bats, Steve Wulf decided it rightfully belonged in the Ruth family, not in his garage. He rented a U-Haul truck and delivered it to the home of Ruth's granddaughter, Linda Ruth Tosetti, who called the next day to inform him that the date stamped on the underside of the tub post-dated Ruth's time in Sudbury. He went back the next day to collect the tub that Ruth never bathed in. It is now a very large flowerpot. "I should have taken the toilet," he says now.

PROLOGUE: JUNE 13, 1902, BALTIMORE

Interviews: Christina Callender, Dorothy Miceli Dupski, Francis O'Neill, and Mary C. Tormollan.

I am indebted to Fred Shoken for sharing a trove of census reports, Sanborn insurance maps, news clippings, and photographs from the period. (That information is also posted on his own website (www .BabeRuth100). I am equally indebted to David Bennett Stinson, and his website, deadballbaseball.com, through whom I met descendants of boys who attended St. Mary's during Ruth's time there. He also made introductions to Jean Mor, a member of Brother Matthias's family, and to Francis X. McGillivary, whose grandfather was Martin Boutilier's closest friend in Lingan. Caretaker Brian Cromer escorted us through the building where Ruth learned how to make shirts and showed us architectural plans for the campus, including the reclamation of the field on which Ruth played. (See "A Fight to Save the House That Built Ruth" in the May 17, 2010, *New York Times*, and Stinson's April 1, 2016, blog entry, "The Mystery of the Stone Building at the St. Mary's Industrial School for Boys Site," at www.davidstinsonauthor.com.)

Maps, deeds, and real estate documents pertaining to St. Mary's were provided by William Greskovich and Bill Monk at St. Rita's Hospital, which owns the property. Jerry Williams at the Baltimore Trolley Museum supplemented information I found in Michael R. Farrell's 1973 book, *Who Made All Our Streetcars Go? The Story of Rail Transit in Baltimore*, enabling me to envision the trip Ruth took in 1902.

To educate myself on the history and growth of the city, particularly west Baltimore, I relied on: Francis O'Neill at the Maryland Historical Society; John Thomas Schart's 1891 *History of Baltimore City and County, from the Earliest Period to the Present Day: Including Biographical Sketches of Their Representative Men*; Clayton Colton Hall's 1912 *Baltimore: Its History and Its People*; the 2014 edition of the *WPA Guide to Maryland: The Old Line State*; Dorsey and Dilts's *A Guide to Baltimore Architecture*; and *America's Great Road: The Impact of the Baltimore & Ohio Railroad on the Baltimore Region*.

I found statistics on population growth, the racial and the ethnic composition of the city, and the growth of slums during successive waves of immigration in "Deconstructing the Slums of Baltimore" by Garrett Power, reprinted in *From Mobtown to Charm City*, published by the Maryland Historical Society in 2002. Five areas were designated as slums by the city labor commissioner in 1900, including the area "beyond

Camden Station in Pigtown," where the Ruth family made its various homes.

I accessed Maryland legislation and a trove of other historical documents in the state archives at www.msa .maryland.com. Among them: "Baltimore City, Maryland, Historical Chronology 1900-1999"; "Maryland Manual Online: A Guide to Maryland and Its Government"; and a history of the Gwynns Falls watershed in the eighteenth and nineteenth centuries, "Baltimore City and County Mills," which described the formerly pastoral land on which St. Mary's and the Wilkens "hair mines" were built. For an understanding of how industry sullied the land, I relied on the "Gwynns Falls Watershed Ecological Resource Atlas."

For background on the development of the area, I relied on materials from the Carrollton Ridge Neighborhood Association and extensive coverage in the *Baltimore Sun*, especially a May 25, 1924, story, "Do You Know the Street on Which You Live? Wilkens Avenue. Historic and Religious Shrines Adjoin Thoroughfare Named for Donor of Ground."

The item about the arrest of Mary Custis Lee is from WETA's Washington, D.C., history blog, Boundary Stones.

Photographs of the Camden Yards neighborhood and west Baltimore as it was in Ruth's youth were found at the B & O Railroad museum in Baltimore. St. Mary's annual reports were accessed at the Enoch Pratt Free Library in Baltimore, where I also immersed myself in the collected works of H. L. Mencken. Vince Fitzpatrick, curator of the collection, found every mention of Ruth, baseball, and west Baltimore in Mencken's vast oeuvre, materials that informed my description of the sights and smells of his hometown. The allusion to the Wilkens hair factory and the smell of the harbor in summer appears on page 70 in *Happy Days*, published in 1940. The description of the language of the arrabers and the polite term for Baltimore outhouses comes from *The American Language, Supplement II*, pages 162–63. The quotation about "dirt pedagogy" is from *Newspaper Days: 1899–1906*, page 151.

While I was fact-checking another part of Ruth's childhood, Rodger H. Pippen's 1947 story in the *Baltimore News-Post* about Patrolman Harry C. Birmingham popped up on my computer screen—an act of the cyber-gods: "80-year-Old Ex-Cop Remembers Babe Ruth as a Boy." His great-granddaughter Mary C. Tormollan and other family members confirmed the account. Newspaper clippings about his career and his relationship with the Ruths were supplied by his family, Shoken, and O'Neill.

These sources were also drawn on in writing chapters 2, 4, and 6.

CHAPTER 1: OCTOBER 10, PROVIDENCE

Interviews: Ed Achorn, P. T. Conley, Dan Daley, Carole Dooley, Elaine Regine, and Julia Ruth Stevens.

Daily newspaper coverage in the *Providence Journal* and the *Providence Evening Bulletin* was supplemented by interviews with local baseball aficionados P. T. Conley and Dan Daley. Carole Dooley, Judge Dooley's daughter-in-law, shared a limited-edition book about the judge, *Quiet Little Man*, written by Boswell Johnson and published by Turf and Sport Digest in 1987.

For background on Peter Laudati, the Steam Roller, Kinsley Park, and the Cyclodrome, I relied on his daughter Elaine Regine and consulted the following sources: http://artinruins.com; a 2005 story posted on www.profootballhof.com, "NFL's First Night Game"; and John Hogrogian's 1980 post on www.profootball researchers.org, *The Coffin Corner*: "The Steam Roller"; as well as Laudati's obituary in the *Providence Journal* and *Evening Bulletin* from September 15, 1977.

Though Jack Dempsey fought at Kinsley Park in 1922, the field got only three mentions in the *Providence Journal*, the first on November 13, 1925, when it was leased for baseball, and the last on November 16, 1933, when it was demolished. The *Journal* provided ample coverage of Ruth's tenure with the Providence Grays, including Arnold Bailey's February 6, 1995, story, "The Babe's 100th Anniversary, Providence Saw the Early Babe," and Brian MacPherson's August 9, 2014, story, "Babe Ruth a Hit in R.I. before He Became a Baseball Legend."

I found the interview with Mike Gazella, recorded on June 6, 1978, by Nick Cullop, in the collection of the Cleveland Public Library. Bill Nack's August 8, 1998, story in *Sports Illustrated*, "The Colossus," re-creating Ruth's march to sixty home runs, supplemented the details I found in the daily coverage of New York City newspapers. The description of the accident outside Philadelphia and Charley O'Leary's hat is from Robert Creamer's *Babe: The Legend Comes to Life.*

The background on Albert "Truly" Warner comes from a variety of sources, including a September 8, 2017, post at www.philly.com, "A Philadelphian Who Knew How Sports Gets in—and on—Our Heads." Julia Ruth Stevens supplied the information on the floral tributes awaiting her father after he hit the sixtieth home run.

Ford Frick's role in creating the myth of the quaking Pirates was described in Louis Effrat's *New York*

Times interview with Pie Traynor published on October 5, 1960.

Background on Jean Bedini, "the Turnip Catcher," also known as the "Ziegfeld of Burlesque," came from the Jean Bedini Archive at www.Travalance.com, the *Oakland Tribune*, the *Washington Herald*, and the *Washington Times*, which featured this headline on November 4, 1915: "Jean Bedini Fails to Catch Turnip; Tears Mouth: Wife Falls in Swoon." Reviews and descriptions of "Cock-a-Doodle-Doo" were found in *Variety*, the *Providence Journal*, and the *Pittsburgh Press*. See also his obituary in the *New York Times* on November 9, 1956, "Jean Bedini, 85, Produced Revues, Organizer of Vaudeville and Burlesque Shows Dies—Helped Future Stars."

Ring Lardner memorialized Ruth's ankles in the March 18, 1929, issue of *Collier's* magazine, calling them "the envy of many a Broadway chorus girl."

CHAPTER 2: OCTOBER 10, ABOARD THE NEW YORK CENTRAL TO MANHATTAN

Interviews: Christopher Boone, Jim Brady, Tony Brady, Kathy Carmody, Shelby Fell Daugherty, Guy Drebing, Jack Dunn III, Anna Maria and Noreen Frontera, Sarah E. Hinman, Esther Hynson, Doris Keil-Shamieh, Jean

Klus, Jan McNamee, John Munion, Harry and Gina Pippin, John Ridgeway, Father Michael Roach, Dotty Schluepner, Jonathan Shahan, and Ellen Warnock.

Re-creating family life in the Ruth household would have been impossible without access to a 1991 tape-recorded interview with Mamie Ruth Moberly, conducted by Mike Gibbons for the Babe Ruth Birthplace and Museum. Quotations from that interview appear throughout the book.

Moberly was generous with her recollections even as they faded, contributing to stories too numerous to count. Among the most helpful were the following: "Childhood Memories of the Babe," *Orioles Gazette*, June 4, 1993; "The Babe's Best Girl, Ruth's Sister Remembers His Playfulness—and His Warmth," *Philadelphia Daily News*, April 16, 1992; "Mary Ruth Moberly, Babe's Sister," *People* magazine, September 16, 1985; "Babe's Sister Will Gaze Out on a Field of Dreams," *Baltimore Sun*, April 5, 1992. Her 1972 letter to Marshall Smelser, author of *The Life That Ruth Built: A Biography* was among the papers he donated to the Hall of Fame.

In 2010, when I began researching Ruth's roots, there was no reliable family tree, as evidenced by the conflicting information on the many Ruth family trees posted on Ancestry.com by family and fans. I am indebted to Shelby Fell Daugherty, Doris Keil-Shamieh, and Jan McNamee for the spadework they did on my behalf piecing together their family history in Baltimore. Druscilla J. Null's 2017 article for the *Maryland Genealogical Society Journal*, "My Father Was of German Extraction: Babe Ruth's Ruth/Rudt Ancestors," confirmed much of what we had been able to assemble and added crucial details to my understanding of the Ruth family in Baltimore.

Dougherty shared Ruth's baptismal record and other family documents she located at St. Mary's Seminary in Baltimore. Father Michael Roach, former priest at St. Peter the Apostle, where George Jr. was baptized, described tensions in the Ruth marriage over religious differences.

Birth, death, and divorce records for the Ruth family were accessed through the Maryland State Archives. The case file in the divorce of George and Katie Ruth contained all police reports, filings, depositions, and briefs, as well as both of the confessions George Sr. extracted from his bartender George Sowers, in two different hands.

An updated version of Westbrook Pegler's ghost-written serial, edited by William R. Cobb, was released as a book in 2011 under the title *Playing the Game: My Early Years in Baseball*. Another literary endeavor attributed to Ruth, a children's book called *The Home-Run King, or How Pep Pindar Won His Title*, was also published in 1920.

Loudon Park Cemetery provided diagrams and interment records for the Ruth children buried in the family plot. The death certificate for George and Katie's last child, William, identified the place of his death: the Thomas Wilson Sanitarium for the Sick Children of Baltimore. For further reading on the facility and the lack of pasteurized milk in Baltimore at the turn of the century, see the *American Journal of Nursing* (April 1904) posted at www.jstor.org and *The Town: A Civic Journal* (April 2016).

Professors Christopher Boone at Arizona State University and Sarah E. Hinman at Leiden University in the Netherlands elaborated in separate interviews on their published work, *History of Public Health for the City of Baltimore: 1880–1920.* Hinson cited the lack of a comprehensive sewage system in Baltimore as a contributing factor in the high infant mortality rate, which had decreased from 25 percent in the 1880s to about 10 percent by 1900; the mortality rate in the Ruth family was higher than that of the city at large.

Among literally hundreds of stories published about Ruth's birthplace, two stand out for their color and detail about the neighborhood in 1895: John Schulian's

August 8, 1981, story for *The Sporting News*, "Babe Ruth's Shrine Draws Few Visitors"; and David Simons's January 2, 1983, story in the Sunday *Sun*, "Ruth Fans Go to Bat for Museum Funds."

The suspect time line for Ruth's commitment to St. Mary's appears on pages 2–3 in Ruth's authorized autobiography, *The Babe Ruth Story*, by Babe Ruth and Bob Considine. It is restated on page 42 of *The Babe and I*, written by Mrs. Babe Ruth with Bill Slocum.

In re-creating the working-class neighborhood where Ruth lived until age six, I relied on former residents Esther Hyson and Dotty Schluepner, who provided invaluable color and detail about daily life on Woodyear Street. Mencken's description of the playing field near Woodyear Street—now the Carroll Park public golf course—and being chased from it by ruffians who lived by the B & O railroad shops appears on page 229 in *Happy Days* in "Records of an Athlete."

Even Mencken's memory was fallible. In *Mencken on Mencken*, in the chapter "Memories of a Long Life," he describes the Union Saloon at the corner of Paca and Baltimore Streets kept by Babe's father, whom he had conflated with another German saloon keeper named Louis W. Ruths, according to Francis O'Neill at the Maryland Historical Society.

CHAPTER 3: OCTOBER 11, TRENTON

Interviews: Scott Boras, Casey Close, Jerry Della Femina, John Holway, Bill Jenkinson, George Lois, Michael and Paula Messina, Leigh Steinberg, Richard Walsh, Bob and Katie Walsh.

The opening anecdote about the ladies of the night who accompanied Ruth to Penn Station is from page 1 of Ken Sobol's *Babe Ruth & the American Dream*.

In addition to daily coverage in the *Trenton State Gazette*, the *Trenton Evening Times*, and the *New York Times*, I was aided by R. Gregg Kaufman's research and his October 24, 2002, article in the *Trenton Times*, "In 1927, the Babe Hammered Three in Trenton." Author Steve Kettmann, the ghostwriter for Joe Plumeri's grandfather, provided the background on how Joe Plumeri Sr. and Charles Giasco wooed Ruth and Gehrig to Trenton.

Ruth's cogent statement on behalf of the rights of ballplayers is from the *New York Times*, October 18, 1921.

For a man who had been largely forgotten and rarely acknowledged, Christy Walsh proved an easy subject to report. He was a PR guy and made sure to get his own name in the paper, frequently, starting with an October 7, 1916, item in *The Fourth Estate: A Newspaper for the Makers of Newspapers and Investors in Advertising.* His professional comings and goings, personal triumphs and travails, were documented in dispatches in *Advertising & Selling, Editor & Publisher, The Fourth Estate,* and then in a succession of Bay Area and Detroit dailies that sold his sports cartoons and stories. His hometown paper, the *Los Angeles Times,* recognized him as "a local boy who made good," in a February 1, 1924, column titled "Observations by the Innocent Bystander, W.M.H."

More substantial profiles followed: Joe Williams's July 29, 1927, encomium in the *New York Telegram,* "A Close-Up of Christy Walsh: The Man Behind Mr. Babe Ruth," which also ran under a different headline in the *Pittsburgh Press*; L. H. Gregory's January 14, 1929, puff piece in the *Morning Oregonian,* "Gregory's Sport Gossip, $130,000 Saved for Babe Ruth by Christy"; Norman Beasley's October 1, 1929, piece in *Forbes,* "What Babe Ruth Does with His Money." Most essential, reliable, informative, and hilarious was Alva Johnston's November 23, 1935, profile in the *New Yorker,* "The Ghosting Business." Its only notable flaw is the timing of publication, which came as Walsh's ghosting syndicate was near its end.

According to Robert Acosta, producer of a failed

1984 off-Broadway play, *The Babe*, who read correspondence between Walsh and his son, supplied by Christy Walsh Jr., "there was a fight between Babe Ruth and Christy Walsh about him representing Lou Gehrig. He wasn't getting all the attention." That correspondence was also the source for Walsh's comments about the agenting business.

Ruth's death produced a spate of favorable publicity for Walsh, much of it written by his friends in the press, vouchsafing his role in the Babe's financial prosperity, including a widely disseminated Associated Press dispatch headlined "Ruth Had to Learn Dollar Value, Fun-Loving Babe 'Wised Up' Under Christy Walsh." Very little was written about him in the four decades after his death. Richard Miller resurrected him in a March 5, 1999, story for *Sports Collectors Digest*: "Babe Ruth's 'Ghost' Put Words in Athletes' Mouths, Walsh Took Care of Ruth While Managing Syndicate of Writers." A far more in-depth treatment, "Babe Ruth's Ghostwriter," written by Robert Messenger, was posted to the www.ozTypewriter.blogspot.com on March 4, 2015. Mark Ahrens's August. 4, 2010, post on the now defunct website www.booksonbaseball .com, "Christy Walsh—Baseball's First Agent," was especially useful as it led me to Walsh's nephew, Richard, who introduced me to his grandson, Bob. Whatever information I couldn't find in print was supplied by Walsh's extended family.

Walsh's most extensive writing about himself and his business can be found in his previously mentioned self-published memoir, *Adios to Ghosts.* All the figures I've used regarding syndicate sales and profits come from his book. Ruth's yearly earnings from ghostwriting are in the accounting ledger Walsh prepared in May 1938 at the end of their contractual relationship. That ledger appears in appendix 2.

Walsh also wrote a valedictory for the syndicate man in the November 6, 1937, edition of *Editor & Publisher*, the journal in which he had announced the formation of the Christy Walsh Syndicate in 1921: "Ghost Writing Not Dead but Lacks Novelty, Christy Walsh Says That Too Many Papers, Not Too Few, Killed It . . . Sees Revival." This was wishful thinking. He contributed a self-mocking biographical sketch, "That Old Feeling," to the *Roaring Lions Magazine* of Loyola University, which was then excerpted in *The De Andrein*, an alumni newsletter published by his alma mater "Old St. Vincent's" in March 1938.

Grandson Bob Walsh and his wife, Katie, described life at Walshchateau and Walsh's courtship of the Babe. Nephew Richard Walsh provided the alternative version of events. Matt Cwieka, Christy Walsh Jr.'s son-in-law, detailed Walsh's financial dependence on his father-in-law. Walsh's correspondence with General John J. Pershing was discovered by archivist Jeffrey Flannery in the Pershing archives at the Library of Congress.

For the history of tabloid journalism and the *New York Daily News*, I read the following: Megan McKinney's *The Magnificent Medills: America's Royal Family of Journalism During a Century of Turbulent Splendor*; John Arthur Chapman's *Tell It to Sweeney: The Informal History of the New York Daily News*; Leo McGivena's *The News: The First Fifty Years of New York's Picture Newspaper*; Simon Michael Bessie's *Jazz Journalism*; John D. Sevens's *Sensationalism and the New York Press*; Michael Shapiro's "The Paper Chase: For Tabloid King Emile Gauvreau It Took a Lifetime to Slow Down," in the *Columbia Journalism Review*; "The President's Bible," *Time* magazine, August 15, 1927; and Jack Anderson's profile of Joseph Medill Patterson in the August 13, 1938, issue of the *New Yorker*, "Vox Populi II," which discounts the legend of the meeting on the battlefield, maintaining the cousins met in Paris after the Armistice. I also relied on the correspondence I found in the papers of Joseph Patterson at Lake Forest College.

The statistics on daily newspaper circulation in the

United States are from N. W. Ayer & Son's 1927 *Annual Directory of Newspapers and Periodicals*. The New York City daily and Sunday circulation figures were gathered by Rebecca Federman, electronic resources coordinator at the New York Public Library, who reviewed circulation figures for each of the newspapers in the library's collection. (She also supplied back issues of the *New York Daily News* sports page beginning in 1919.) The figures on the increase in daily sports coverage and readership are from Francis C. Richter's *The History and Records of Base Ball: The American Nation's Chief Sport*, cited in Robert McChesney's chapter "Media Made Sport: A History of Sports Coverage in the United States" in *Media, Sports, & Society*, and from pages 116–17 in Stevens.

While John B. Kennedy's April 1928 article for *Collier's* provided essential details and dialogue for many of the chapters in this book, it is clear that Kennedy was not present until midway through the tour and may have written some portions based on secondhand accounts. He includes some anecdotes from Ruth's 1926 barnstorming tour and there are a few errors in his version of the 1927 itinerary. That fall, he was also reporting a Notre Dame football story for *Collier's*, which gave him access to Walsh and Rockne.

Kennedy protested vigorously, to no avail, when he received no credit on the book version of his eight-part 1930 series on Rockne, published by Bobbs-Merrill after the coach's death, thereby breaking the cardinal rule of ghostdom. He became better known for his work as a radio broadcaster. Hailed by *Time* magazine as the "Voice of the People" in the February 6, 1939, issue of the magazine, he would receive a star on the Hollywood Walk of Fame.

Marshall Hunt's observations and memories about the growth of the *Daily News* and sports writing are from two sources: Wagenheim's taped interviews at the Hall of Fame, as well as the transcripts and published version of his interview with Jerome Holtzman for *No Cheering in the Press Box.*

The description of the *New York Evening Graphic* as "the most abnormal sheet in U.S. journalism," and the pejorative "BodyLove" Macfadden were found in the February 7, 1927, issue of *Time.* Within six weeks of its first press run, Macfadden's rag had been banned by the New York Public Library.

Lorena A. "Hick" Hickok, remembered in history chiefly for what was described as her "intimate friendship" with first lady Eleanor Roosevelt, was a groundbreaking female journalist. As a writer for the

Minneapolis Tribune, where she was often known as the "girl reporter," she also covered a "secret" Minneapolis Gophers football practice, using her professed ignorance of the game to get a foot in the door at a "rehearsal" before a big game with the Wisconsin Badgers, according to a January 18, 2018, post on the paper's website. By 1927, she had moved to New York to write for the New York *Mirror* and then the Associated Press, covering the Lindbergh kidnapping and FDR's 1932 campaign for the presidency. She quit the job and moved into the White House when the conflict of interest became untenable.

For background on the evolution of sports photography, I read Gail Buckland's *Who Shot Sports: A Photographic History, 1843 to the Present* and Jack Price's *News Pictures.*

For background on Ruth and Dick Redding, I relied extensively on the research of Bill Jenkinson, as well as John Holway's article in the SABR Research Journals Archive, "The Cannonball," and an in-depth profile published by the Center for Negro League Baseball Research in 2013, "Forgotten Heroes: Dick 'Cannonball' Redding," by Layton Revel and Luis Munoz.

For background on the sports-agenting business I relied on extensive interviews with Scott Boras and

Leigh Steinberg and read "Sports Agents—History and Law" on the Sportslaw website, as well as Gay Talese's October 1, 1961, article for the *New York Times Sunday Magazine*, "Diamonds Are a Boy's Best Friend; If a baseball star has what it takes—including the help of a business agent named Frank Scott—he can make a wad of money endorsing anything from pants to peanut butter."

I also watched the movie inspired by Steinberg's life, *Jerry Maguire*, several times.

Dan Parker recorded the scene at Helen's hospital room in the March 3 *New York Mirror*: "Helen's pale, thin arms were uplifted from her sick bed to engulf the man mountain who rushed to meet them. The big movie star and home-run man dropped a few honest tears on his wife's face, and if there was a movie camera on hand it would have recorded one of the most unaffected love scenes on record.

"Babe scowled, on leaving the hospital, when some tactless reporter asked him if he and his wife were to be divorced.

"'That old story is still going the rounds,' snapped Babe. 'There's nothing to it. But I wish the scandal mongers would let a man enjoy a little privacy in his family affairs.'"

CHAPTER 4: OCTOBER 12, CITYLINE

Interviews: Brother Arcadius Alkonis, Brother Peter Donohue, Hans Ulrich Gumbrecht, Arnold Hano, Anthony Puliatti, Vin Scully, Julia Ruth Stevens, and Anthony Swick.

I am indebted to Tom Barthel, author of *Baseball's Peerless Semipros: The Brooklyn Bushwicks of Dexter Park* and *Babe Ruth Is Coming to Your Town, Post-Season Barnstorming Games, 1914–1935*, for his excellent reporting and generosity in discussing his research with me.

I supplemented what I learned from him with information about Dexter Park, found at www.our brooklynballparks.com, and www.Brooklynology .org, the site of the Brooklyn Public Library; in articles posted to the website "Times Newsweekly Your Neighborhood the Way It Was" (http://timesnews weekly.com), and most especially Jane and Douglas Jacobs's excellent history published in SABR's *Baseball Research Journal* in 2000.

For background on Maxie Rosner and the Bushwicks of Brooklyn I drew from "Maxie Rosner, The Bushwick Goon," which ran in the *Jewish Post* on April 27, 1945, and "Bushwicks Paid Best, but Money Was Nothing to Talk about for the Semi-Pros," published by the *Ridgewood Times* and *Times News-weekly* on May 5, 2016.

The life and death of Dexter the horse were well covered in the *New York Times*, as was the evolution of the racetrack from pastoral Eden to a public park known for pigeon-shooting competitions to the home of the best semi-pro baseball team in New York and the Brooklyn Royal Giants from 1905 to 1913 and again, under Nat Strong from 1923 to 1927.

To immerse myself in the development of celebrity culture I read the following:

Leo Braudy's *The Frenzy of Renown: Fame and Its History*; Ann Douglas's *Terrible Honesty: Mongrel Manhattan in the 1920s*; Neal Gabler's *Winchell: Gossip, Power, and the Culture of Celebrity*; Donald L. Miller's *Supreme City: How Jazz Age Manhattan Gave Birth to Modern America*; Karen Sternheimer's *Celebrity Culture and the American Dream: Stardom and Social Mobility*; Warren Susman's *Culture as History*; Jules Tygiel's *Past Time: Baseball as History*; and Patrick Trimble's March 1996 contribution to the *Colby Quarterly*, "Babe Ruth: The Media Construction of a 1920's Sport Personality." I was especially influenced by Gumbrecht's chapter on "Stars" and Christy Walsh's use of a new kind of imagery; by Douglas's discussion of the upheaval and intersection in technology and marketing; and by Braudy's introduction, as well as the chapters "Above It All: Lindbergh and Hemingway" and "Democratic Theater and the Natural Performer."

For the revolution in technology and mass media, I read as much as possible from contemporaneous sources in order to get a sense of the wonder and excitement of the times. A few examples: "Our New Screen Grid Distance Getter, The Last Word in Sensitive Radio Sets," which ran in *Popular Science* in September 1929 (the issue also featured a story predicting "80 Miles on a Gallon by 1939"); "Now—You Can Receive Radio Pictures," from the October 1927 issue of *Radio Broadcast*; Calvin Coolidge's Address at the Opening Meeting of the International Radiotelegraph Conference in Washington, D.C., on October 4, 1927 (accessed online at the website of the American Presidency Project); "Newsreel Theater," which appeared in *Time* magazine's November 18, 1929, issue; and "Wire Transmission of Photos Made Practical by Telepix Machine," a page-one story in the January 2, 1925, edition of the *Chicago Tribune*.

Additional sources included the AT&T website, which provides an excellent time line of its technological advances; "The History of Movie Newsreels," retrieved from http://www.moviefanfare.com; "Behind the Dial" at www.radiostratosphere.com; *Time* magazine's January 1, 2015, article, "Celebrating 80 Years of Associated

Press' Wirephoto"; "Radio Competition with News-papers," accessed at CQ Researcher archives; "And Now a Word from Our Sponsor: Early Radio Announcers" from *Radio and Television Museum News*; Jules Tygiel's chapter "New Ways of Knowing" in *Past Time: Base-ball as History*, and James Walker's *Crack of the Bat: A History of Baseball on the Radio*.

Heywood Broun was first to fictionalize the Babe but novelist James T. Farrell, who was nineteen years old when he saw Ruth leaving Comiskey Park sur-rounded by "a crowd of over one hundred kids," de-scribed the scene in *My Baseball Diary*: "Wearing a blue suit and a gray cap, there was an expression of be-wilderment on his moon face. He said nothing, rolled with the kids and the strange, hysterical and noisy little mob slowly moved on to the exit gate with Ruth in the center of it. More kids rushed to the edge of the crowd and they, also, pushed and shoved. Ruth swayed from side to side, his shoulders bending one way, and then the other. As they all swirled to the gate, Ruth nar-rowly escaped being shoved into mustard, which had been spilled from an overturned barrel."

As a young boy, Anthony Puliatti accompanied his father and a troop of Italian-speaking New Jersey con-struction workers—taking a day off from building the Empire State Building—to see the Great Bambino. He remembered his acute embarrassment at the homemade sausage sandwiches and wine they brought to Yankee Stadium and how drunk they got on the idea of becoming fully American.

Arnold Hano shared his memories of attending Ruth's last pitched game on the final day of the 1933 season, a complete-game victory in which he gave up twelve hits and three walks but also hit a home run. "Two or three days later, I saw him crossing Broadway with his wife and daughter and said, 'Babe, I saw you pitch the other day,'" Hano recalled. "He beamed at me. I said, 'How come you didn't strike anyone out?' He laughed and said, 'I wanted those eight palookas to earn their keep.'"

CHAPTER 5: OCTOBER 13, ASBURY PARK

Interviews: Carl Conger, Carolyn Major-Neilson, Karen Conger Scott, Toni Stein, and Tom Willman.

The *New York Times* lavished attention on events in Asbury Park with full game coverage and a four-deck headline that told the entire story of the day: "36 BASEBALLS LOST ENDING RUTH GAME, Game Supply Gone When Gehrig Homer Drops into the Lake—Babe Nearly Mobbed, RUTH DEMANDS CASH FIRST, Makes Sure of $2,500

After Park of Gate Is Attached—Hits Homer, Winning at Asbury Park, 8–5."

This was the last of the barnstorming games the paper covered in detail, but not the last dispatch it published. Walsh importuned John Kieran to weigh in with an October 15 column. Other New York dailies, including the *Brooklyn Eagle* and the *New York Herald*, followed suit.

Local New Jersey papers, including the *Asbury Park Evening Press*, published Ed Neil's interview in full and continuing coverage of the legal tussle over the gate receipts. The decision in *Harry N. Johnson, Sheriff of the County of Monmouth, Complainant, v. Joseph Lyons et al., Defendants,* in the Court of Chancery, handed down on October 13, 1928, was accessed at www.Casetext.com.

In addition to the daily newspaper coverage of the miracle at Johnny Sylvester's bedside, I read Charles A. Poekel's *Babe & the Kid: The Legendary Story of Babe Ruth and Johnny Sylvester* and Paul Gallico's hyperbolic account on page 37 in *Farewell to Sport*: ". . . it was God himself who walked into the room, straight from His glittering throne, God dressed in a camel's hair polo coat and flat camel's hair cap, God with a flat nose and little piggy eyes and a big grin, and a fat, black cigar sticking out of the side of it."

Sylvester's autographed ball sold for a quarter of a million dollars in 2014.

Despite the inflated dollar figures bandied about in newspapers about Ruth's contract with First National Studios for *Babe Comes Home*, the contract called for him to receive $30,000, as stated in a letter of agreement between Walsh and the studio, which I found in the Christy Walsh catalogs. (His net was $22,488.46.)

Tom Willman, a former editorial writer for the Riverside *Enterprise*, volunteered his story about Roman Warren as well as earlier coverage of the daredevil pilot in the newspaper.

Marshall Hunt's daily coverage in the *Daily News* from the set of *Babe Comes Home* was as funny as it was invaluable. His elaboration on the events of that spring is from three sources: the transcript of his interview with Holtzman, the published account of that interview, and Wagenheim's tape-recorded interviews at the Hall of Fame. The last is also the source for the meeting between Captain Joe Patterson and Babe Ruth en route to New York.

The account of the $33,000 press conference is from Kennedy in *Collier's*. Walsh's correspondence with the Bank of Manhattan is from the Christy Walsh catalog. Westbrook Pegler first addressed the issue of Ruth's salary negotiation in two columns: "Babe Ruth Now an Industry and Has Acquired Manager," which ran in the *Washington Post* on February 11, 1927, and "Ruth Jealous of Offer to Walker," from the April 25, 1927, edition of the same paper, in which he offered his first re-creation of the dialogue on the train. Pegler revisited the issue on October 1, 1941, in his "Fair Enough" column in the *Post,* on the subject of collective bargaining and why it had no business in baseball (see chapter 11 note).

I am indebted to San Diego baseball historian William Swank for providing the legal documents in the case against Ruth for violating child labor laws (retrieved in 2004 from the San Diego Historical Society). They reveal just how much of a lightning rod Ruth's celebrity had become by February 1927 and also Christy Walsh's reluctance to pay legal bills, a recurring theme in his letters.

Stanley Gue's grandchildren, Carl E. Conger and Karen Conger Scott, provided detail on the career of their eccentric, leftist grandfather and his zealous prosecution of the Babe. A true believer in his youth, Gue had a late-in-life political conversion when called to testify by the House Committee on Un-American Activities about communist activity in San Diego.

As for William Truby's invitation to "Come See Babe Ruth Hit One 450 Feet into the Lake," it was pure marketing. The high school field at Asbury Park is one of three sites on the tour still in use today; the others are at Santa Barbara High School and Balboa Stadium in San Diego. The concrete stands in Asbury Park remain intact. Using Google Earth images of the Asbury Park field in its present configuration and a postcard from the Ticknor Brothers Postcard Collection at the Boston Public Library, baseball physicist and professor emeritus at the University of Illinois Alan Nathan calculated the distance from home plate down the foul lines to Deal Lake as only 355 feet and about 395 feet to straightaway center field. "Of course, we don't know how far beyond the shoreline the ball traveled," Nathan said. "But even at about four hundred feet, it was not a big deal, at least by today's standards—except to everyone in attendance."

Ed Neil quit the fun-and-games department to become a foreign correspondent the same year Babe Ruth quit baseball. His travels took him to Ethiopia to cover the Italian invasion, to Palestine to document an Arab uprising, to London to witness the coronation of King George VI, and to a town named Caudé in the midst of the Spanish Civil War, to cover the insurgent forces led by General Francisco Franco for the Associated Press. He and four other reporters were huddled in a car caught between the lines when an artillery shell hit their vehicle on December 31, 1937. Neil finished the story he had been writing in the car and died two days later. The only survivor was Harold A. Philby of the *Times of London*, who, in the tradition of war correspondents, sent Neil's copy to the AP. He later became infamous as Kim Philby, the British agent who spied for the Soviet Union. Ruth was named in Neil's obituary as one of his many friends.

CHAPTER 6: OCTOBER 13–14, ABOARD THE MANHATTAN LIMITED TO LIMA

Interviews: Brother Arcadius Alkonis, Kathy Carmody, Gerald Cohen, Father Gabe Costa, Brian Cromer, Carolyn Reed Detrick, Teresa Diehl, Brother Peter Donohue, Doris Kiel-Shamieh, Mike Lackey, Jean Mor, Francis X. McGillivary, Jan McNamee, Harry and Gina Pippin, Jonathan Shahan, David Stinson, Linda Ruth Tosetti, and Mary Tormollan.

The description of the fare available aboard the train came from "Pennsylvania Railroad Information Bulletin," which was published in September 1927, and included two pertinent stories: "Dining Car Workers of This Railroad Go to School" and "A Dissertation upon Roast Pig." The description of what Ruth imbibed on board the train comes from page 6 in Sobol.

Details about the hectic day in Lima were found in the *Allen County Reporter*, which was published by the Allen County Historical Society in 1995, and featured photographs of Halloran Park and other highlights about their visit. Raymond A. Shuck's stories, "When the Broadway Limited Stopped in Lima: An Ohio Town Embraces the Babe," and "Babe's in Tourland: How Babe Ruth Was Well-Suited for Barnstorming," can be found in *Baseball and the Sultan of Swat, Babe Ruth at 100*, a compendium of essays written for the 1995 Hofstra University Symposium held in honor of Ruth's centenary.

I am indebted to Mike Lackey, former sportswriter for the *Lima News*, who arranged for an item to be placed in the paper soliciting information for the book, which resulted in invaluable interviews with Carolyn Detrick, whose uncle umpired the game, and Teresa Diehl, whose mother presented the trophy to Ruth.

In the section of the chapter devoted to Ruth's life at St. Mary's and the brothers who served there, I relied extensively on Cyril M. Witte's PhD dissertation, submitted to the University of Notre Dame Department of Education in August 1955, "A History of Saint Mary's Industrial School for Boys of the City of Baltimore, 1866–1950." It was a godsend.

To supplement his account of daily life in the institution, the growth of the campus, and its early history, I examined the annual reports prepared for state and city officials in the Enoch Pratt Free Library, and the archives of the *Baltimore Sun*, which routinely covered doings at the school. The 1906 annual report noted that sixty-six head of cattle, averaging 1,800 pounds, had been shipped to Scotland. That same year, the state allocated $50,000 to build a separate dormitory for minims, with a gym on the first floor, as well as a new building for teaching the trades in which George Ruth learned to make a proper collar.

I'm especially grateful to Kevin Cawley and the staff at the University of Notre Dame, who photocopied the entire St. Mary's file in the archives of the Xaverian Order, which included religious histories for each of the brothers at the school. The file for Brother Matthias, Martin Boutilier, included the reports of his fall from grace and his removal from St. Mary's.

Brother Arcadius Alkonis, archivist at St. John's Preparatory School in Danvers, Massachusetts, where Matthias spent the remainder of his life, provided essential background on the Xaverian Order and the men who served in it. In addition to sharing his personal memories, he provided otherwise impossible-to-find newspaper articles in the religious press, among them Tom Sheehan's column in the *Church World* from

April 4, 1992: "Xaverian Brothers Influenced Babe Ruth's Early Life," with biographical information on Brother Matthias. He also introduced me to Brother Peter Donohue, who served at St. Mary's.

I also relied on Paul F. Harris's account of Ruth's early life, *Babe Ruth: The Dark Side,* and Lewis Leisman's thirty-six-page pamphlet, *I Was with Babe Ruth at St. Mary's,* found in the archives at the Babe Ruth Museum. Harris's reporting in 1995 was impressive; he found and reproduced previously unseen childhood documents. But in the absence of the full story of the family's dissolution, he came to a harsh and judgmental conclusion. Leisman became an unlikely witness for Alger Hiss in the McCarthy-era prosecution of him as a Communist spy.

Brother Gilbert's memoir, *Young Babe Ruth: His Early Life and Baseball Career, from the Memoirs of a Xaverian Brother,* was helpful in reconstructing the not-yet-Babe's baseball career at St. Mary's and was certainly far more reliable than Westbrook Pegler's 1920 fantasy, or *Babe Ruth's Own Book of Baseball,* ghostwritten by Ford Frick (as he belatedly admitted to *Sports Illustrated* in an April 9, 1962, profile), which offered few observations on life that Ruth would have recognized as his own.

The details about the culinary fare at St. Mary's are

from pages ix–x in Brother John Joseph Sterne's fore-word to *Young Babe Ruth*.

Jesse Linthicum's recollections were recorded for an April 27, 1948, Baltimore radio show that was shared by Mike Gibbons.

An April 12, 1928, story in the *Sun* sheds light on Ruth's ongoing relationship with the brothers at St. Mary's: "Brother Paul Takes a Larger Field, New Xaverian Superior." The account of Tommy Padgett's death is in his obituary in the Olean, New York, *Times Herald* from March 16, 1920, "Well Known Ballplayer Meets Death." The description of his friendship with Ruth, of the baseball offer Ruth turned down, and of his visit to the cemetery is from the *Boston Daily Globe*, October 21, 1921, "Ruth Weeps at Grave of Chum."

According to Julia Ruth Stevens, George Jr. was given leave to attend the funeral of his mother, about whom Paul Harris would later write that he had "never seen or heard of a woman more neglected." An account in the February 6, 2008, *Baltimore Sun*, "A Buried Past, 96 Years Later, Katie Ruth's Grave to Be Marked," described the efforts of Harris and the Babe Ruth Museum to rectify her son's alleged dereliction of duty, which culminated in a five-minute service held the following summer in heat so scorching that elderly mourners stayed in their cars. Father Gabriel Costa, a mathematics professor at West Point and baseball analytics guru, blessed the newly erected rose granite headstone with holy water, read from John 6:53–58, recited the Lord's Prayer, and gave the blessing asking the Almighty to "cast out all evil."

The date of George Ruth Sr.'s marriage to Martha Sipes was found in Druscilla Null's "My Father Was of German Extraction." The description of "the big to do in the saloon" was drawn from Mamie Moberly's aforementioned story in *People*.

An original print of the photograph of George Sr. and Jr. behind the bar in Ruth's Café, with the photographer's credit visible in the lower right-hand corner, V. Velzis Studios, was sold by Robert Edwards Auctions for $39,000 on May 5, 2018.

The fight in the bar that resulted in George Sr.'s death in August 1918 got big play in the Baltimore papers—"Fight Ends in Death," reported the Sunday, August 26, 1918, edition of the *Sun*—as did the arrest and subsequent acquittal of Benjamin Sipes. George Sr. was prominent enough, or his son was, to merit a front-page obituary and an accompanying photograph. No one in the press appeared to connect the fight to a small item that had appeared in the *Sun* on January 11, "Sold Soldier Dope IS CHARGE, Benjamin A. Sipes Arrest."

The sorry details of George Sr.'s death are from Mamie Ruth Moberly's 1991 interview with Mike Gibbons.

CHAPTER 7: OCTOBER 15, KANSAS CITY, MISSOURI

Interviews: Ray Cauthen, Max Gail, John Holway, Monte Irvin, Bill Jenkinson, CeCe Moore, Harry Pippin, John Resnikoff, John Paul Stevens, and Linda Ruth Tosetti.

I first heard the rumors about Ruth "passing" from my father, a water boy for the 1927 New York football Giants, who had heard them from his father. Speculation about Ruth's ethnicity has never fully abated.

Bill Jenkinson alerted me to the April 9, 1927, column by W. Rollo Wilson in the *Pittsburgh Courier*, which as far as I can tell is the first time such speculation made it into print. Frank Graham divulged the altercation in the Giants' locker room at the Polo Grounds in the *New York Yankees: An Informal History*, pages 85–87. Creamer re-created the scene on pages 269–70 in *Babe*; he quoted Louis Leisman's account of racial taunting at St. Mary's on page 38, where he also related the story of Ruth's preemptive greeting of a schoolmate at Madison Square Garden in 1930; on page 185, he elaborated on the Red Sox racial taunting. Fred Lieb's interview with Holtzman on page 54 of *No Cheering* provided further details. See Charles Leerhsen's *Ty Cobb: A Terrible Beauty* for a reconsideration of Cobb's racism.

I am indebted to John Holway for the wisdom and perspective he shared in our conversation and in two stories posted at www.baseballguru.com, "The Myth of Ruth" and "Barry and the Babe."

The *Sporting News* editorial about the color line in baseball was published on December 6, 1923.

Spike Lee's column in the May 2001 issue of *Gotham* spawned a new round of speculation and rejoinder in the press, including Daniel Okrent's May 7, 2001, column in *Sports Illustrated*, "Background Check, Was Babe Ruth Black? More Important, Should We Care?" and Clarence Page's May 17, 2001, syndicated column for the *Chicago Tribune*, "Was Babe Ruth Black? And Why It Matters," which was widely reprinted.

Historian Lawrence Hogan, who has written extensively on the history of the Negro Leagues, shared his essay at www.BestThinking.com, "Babe Ruth Was a Negro Leaguer!?" which included many clippings from the African American press.

Bill Jenkinson traced Ruth's engagement with the African American community and "mixed-race and race players" in an essay posted at his website in 2009 and updated in 2016, "Babe Ruth and the Issue of Race."

I found the Associated Negro Press account of Game 3 at Wrigley Field in the archives of Black Newspapers at the Library of Congress; E. M. Swift retold the story in his 1980 history of Wrigley Field for *Sports Illustrated*, "One Place That Hasn't Seen the Light."

Hendrik Willem van Loon's interview with the United Press, "Noted Writer Discusses Ku Klux Klan, Kreisler, Art and Babe Ruth in Interview," appeared in the *Pittsburgh Press* on October 15, 1927. For general background on the Ku Klux Klan in 1927, I read the *Literary Digest* from that period. For history on the Ku Klux Klan and its competition against an All-Black Baseball Team in Wichita, see the March 26, 2012, post "Baseball History, Only a Game, WBUR, May 26, 2012," and subsequent stories at www.kansasreporting blog.com. (The Klan Nine also played the Hebrew All-Star Nines in Washington, D.C., on Labor Day, September 1, 1926, as reported in the *Washington Post*. One of the players on the victorious Hebrew squad was Abe Povich, whose brother, Shirley, was sports editor at the *Post*.)

For Ruth's dislike for underwear, see Arthur Robinson in *Collier's*, September 20, 1924; for details on his unsanitary habits, see Ken Sobol's *Babe Ruth &*

the American Dream, pages 62–63. Creamer, on pages 19–20, quotes the owner of the toothbrush as saying the story was untrue. However, another former roommate, Charlie Deal of the Boston Braves, told stories of Ruth's inclination for spitting chewing tobacco across their small apartment while sitting on the toilet.

Background on Wheatley-Provident Hospital, the first such facility for African American children in the Midwest, is from the *Journal of the National Medical Association*, "The Pediatric Department of Wheatley-Provident Hospital, Kansas City, Missouri." Background about Ruth's visits to Mercy Hospital for Children, including the follow-up story about the donation of the Monitor Top refrigerator, was provided by the Miller Nichols Library at the University of Missouri–Kansas City.

Background on photographer George Cauthen was not hard to find, considering how often he made news. On March 6, 1931, he was punched in open court by a lawyer and former U.S. senator after photographing his client, Mrs. Myrtle Bennett, who was on trial for shooting her husband during a hand of bridge. (She was acquitted the next day.) Other exploits are described in Jack Price's history of photojournalism, *News Pictures*, including Cauthen's "shot-by-shot" coverage of a gun battle between a posse of lawmen and three escaped convicts who had abducted Leavenworth warden Thomas B. White. In August 1934, the AP reported that Cauthen took a gun off a robber who had attacked him in his car in Adrian, Missouri. (The .38 Smith and Wesson is now in the collection of the J. M. Davis Gun Museum in Claremont, Oklahoma.) By 1938, Cauthen had quit the newspaper, disappearing from the pages of the *Journal* and memory, and had a new job working as a photographer for an Oklahoma homicide-suicide squad.

His photograph from Wheatley-Provident is preserved in the Christy Walsh scrapbooks at Cooperstown and in digitized images of pages from the *Chicago Defender* and the *New York Amsterdam News.* The original negative could not be found.

The banquet at the Palmer House, hosted by Christy Walsh prior to the Southern Cal–Notre Dame game, was attended by all the important football writers in Chicago and the Midwest, and many from New York. "Grid Tutors to Speak by Radio Before Big Tilt," the *Lincoln Evening Journal* reported. Though the speeches by Rockne and the other coaches were broadcast, neither Ruth's disappearance that afternoon nor his drunken remarks were reported until Kennedy's April 1928 piece in *Collier's.*

CHAPTER 8: OCTOBER 16, OMAHA

Interviews: Anne Bernays, Bob Chenoweth, Steve Hayes, Jack Landers, Pat O'Donnell, Nancy Pope, Jane Landers Price, Steve Rosenblatt, Jean Svadlenak, Polly Thielmeier, Linda Ruth Tosetti, and Fred Toulch.

Writing this chapter was easy and fun, given the mirthful saturation coverage accorded Lady Amco in the *Omaha World Herald*, the *Omaha Bee*, the *Lincoln Evening Journal*, the *Norfolk Daily News*, three wire services, and a full profile in the *New York Times*. Arthur Brisbane, the majordomo for the Hearst Syndicate, weighed in with a column that ran in, among other places, the Manitowoc, Wisconsin, *Herald-Times* on October 19: "It would surprise the idol of America to know that such a hen as Lady Norfolk is more important to the country than all its baseball players."

The only story I couldn't find for her was an obituary. I was aided immeasurably by the surviving children of the chicken breeder A. R. Landers—Polly Thielmeier, Jane Price, and Jack Landers—and by Bob Chenoweth, whose father, Harold, filmed the meeting at the henhouse. Bob Chenoweth enlisted the aid of the UCLA film school in restoring his father's footage, which he donated to the University of Nebraska–Omaha and which was made available to me by archivist Amy

Schindler at the Criss Library. Information about air-mail service in the United States in the fall of 1927 and the harrowing journey of the record-breaking egg from Omaha to the White House came from Nancy Pope, archivist at the United States Postal Museum.

In the section devoted to Omaha baseball, I relied on Devon Niebling and Thomas Hyde's *Baseball in Omaha*; Judy Horan's 2015 article on "Western League Park," available at www.omahamagazine.com; and interviews with Steve Hayes, the CEO of Omaha Print Company, and Pat O'Donnell and Steve Rosenblatt, whose fathers played in the game.

To educate myself on the emerging industry of public relations and marketing, I read the following: Morris Markey's "Reporter at Large, Merchants of Glory" in the August 28, 1926, issue of the *New Yorker*; Calvin Coolidge's October 26, 1926, address before the American Association of Advertising Agencies in Washington, D.C., which I found online at Gerhard Peters and John T. Woolley's American presidency project; Bruce Barton's novel, *The Man Nobody Knows*; the writings of Ivy Lee, and Edward L. Bernays's *Propaganda, Crystallizing Public Opinion*, and *Biography of an Idea*; as well as Larry Tye's biography, *The Father of Spin: Edward L. Bernays and the Birth of Public Relations*.

Among Bernays's papers at the Library of Congress, I found his typescript notes describing his relationship with Bernarr Macfadden, correspondence with his cranky uncle Sigmund complaining about royalties, and a list of the press releases he prepared for Jacob Ruppert and the United States Brewers Association, one quoting "a leading doctor of a Tennessee hospital" on the medicinal benefits of beer and another attesting to its unexplored uses in cooking: "Beer Imparts New Flavor to Vegetable Salad." Walsh's speech tweaking Bernays and the World's Fair memo connecting them were found in the Christy Walsh files in the New York Public Library's Fair archives.

Benjamin Clark at Boys Town provided clippings and photographs of Ruth's visits to the institution as well as the account of "Johnnie-the-Gloom-Killer's" broadcast following Ruth's 1927 visit—"Johnnie Tells Radio Audience About Babe Ruth"—in *Father Flanagan's Boys' Home Journal*, November 1927. Frank Graham testified to the sincerity of Ruth's good works on pages 210–11 in *The New York Yankees*.

The background on the Dennison family is from "The Gray Wolf: Tom Dennison of Omaha" in *Nebraska History* magazine. Johnny Dennison's account of "The Day the Babe and Lou Were in Omaha" by

Michael Kelly appeared in the October 16, 1977, *Omaha World-Herald*.

Accounts of Ruth's gambling losses during his 1920 visit to Cuba were reported by Arthur Robinson in *Collier's*, September 20, 1924. He elaborated in a July 31, 1926, *New Yorker* profile, "The Babe," writing that Ruth had been forced to cancel his passage home because he owed $65,000. But Helen, who had saved enough money to buy apartment houses in Boston without Ruth's knowledge, bailed him out. In the 1922 *American Weekly* series, author Mrs. Margaret Hill, identified as the "Queen of the Underworld," quotes Ruth as telling Helen, "I'm cleaned out, busted, broke. I've lost $95,000 besides $35,000 that I won the first day."

T. L. Huston's correspondence with Landis is housed in the Ruth archive at the Hall of Fame. The letter from Jerome Williams commending Landis can be found in the Kenesaw Mountain Landis archives. For additional background on the fight with Ruth and the commissioner's judicial career, I read "The Jurisprudence of Judge Kenesaw Mountain Landis" by Shayna M. Sigman, *Marquette Sports Law Review* (2005); and David Pietrusza's *Judge and Jury: The Life and Times of Judge Kenesaw Mountain Landis*. The assertion that

Huston paid off promoters of the canceled games appears on page 98 in Ruth and Considine.

The dollar amount he generated for the Yankees in 1921 is based on an economic analysis of the Yankee accounting books and daily team ledgers at the National Baseball Hall of Fame compiled by economist Michael Haupert.

Hunt's stories about Ruth's 1921–22 barnstorming tour and the "Back to the Farm Dinner" are from Wagenheim. I found Margery Lee's account of the opening performance in Boston in the Christy Walsh scrapbooks in Cooperstown. *Variety*, which reported Ruth's weekly salary as $2,500 for twenty weeks, provided extensive coverage of the tour, including the opening-night telegram he received from Helen Keller, then touring in her own vaudeville show on the Orpheum Circuit, and less than satisfactory receipts resulting in the firing of the original piano player.

I first saw the morals clause inserted in Ruth's 1922 contract at the home of Jay Baker, a collector who had purchased the original agreement. It is widely available online. (See "Behave, Bambino: Ruth's 1922 Contract at Auction," *Sports Collectors Daily*, May 18, 2015.) I also read about the issue in a 2015 article in Marquette University School of Law's *Current Ethical Issues in*

Sports Law, "Morals Clauses in Sports Contracts: A Look at the Past and Future Use of Morals Clauses in Player Contracts and Sponsorship/Endorsement Agreements" by Scott A. Andresen.

"Yankees Training on Scotch" can be found on page 74 in Graham's *The History of the New York Yankees.* The account of the private eye hired to follow Ruth et al. is also in Graham, pages 76–80. The fees the Yankees paid for their services are from the daily ledgers in Cooperstown.

A. R. Landers never raised another champion chicken. He raised rabbits for food for his family after leaving Nebraska. After his sudden death in December 1967 on a trip back home to Norfolk, his wife, Dorothy, who had worked the farm alongside him, wrote a family history, "A Grandmother Remembers," for her grandchildren, which provided the only account of their brief fling with fame: "My father had a large chicken farm and your granddaddy managed it. We raised high egg-producing chickens, trap nested and kept records on each hen. Had to grade eggs each hour," she wrote with typical midwestern understatement. "There was a lot to do and to learn."

CHAPTER 9: OCTOBER 17, ABOARD THE ROCK ISLAND LINE TO DES MOINES

Interviews: Donna Analovitch, Jerry Della Femina, Kevin Goering, Michael Haupert, Genevieve Herrlein, George Lois, Leigh Steinberg, and Julia Ruth Stevens.

Jean Svadlenak, official historian for Lee Jeans, documented Ruth's participation in the Whizit campaign of 1927–28 and the distribution of $1,000 in prize money and provided copies of the original photograph of Ruth in his Union-Alls as well as a scan of the advertisement that ran in *Liberty* magazine comparing the speed of the Whizit to a Walter Johnson fastball. She could not confirm Ruth's reported $3,000 fee, which Walsh later disparaged as "purported"— probably because he didn't arrange the endorsement— in a November 1927 deposition pertaining to the Baby Ruth bar.

The case file in *George H. Ruth Candy Co., Inc. v. Curtiss Candy Co., Inc.*—including all briefs, depositions, and appeals before the United States Court of Customs and Patent Appeals on May 14, 1931, and the decision handed down on May 27, 1931—was acquired from the United States Custom and Patent Court archive in Kansas. Walsh's correspondence with company officials and their attorneys, including the angry reply from Louis Glick, dated April 23, 1927, accusing Walsh and Ruth of having been dishonest in their initial negotiations, is from the Christy Walsh catalogs.

Attorney Kevin Goering, an expert in sports law and the right of publicity, not only schooled me in courthouse legal history but gathered all the related cases: *Roberson v. Rochester Folding Box Co.*; *George H. Ruth Candy Co. v. Curtiss Candy Co.*; *O'Brien v. Pabst Sales Co.*; *Haelen Laboratories v. Topps Chewing Gum*; *Pirone v. Macmillan Incorporated.* He also dug out of the mothballs Ruth's testimony in *Ruth v. Educational Films.* Although August 20 was an off-day for the Yankees, the statement was "read in support of Motion." The subsequent lawsuit was reported in the *Times* on September 16.

For background on the evolution of the law and the Baby Ruth controversy, I read Samantha Chmelik's in-depth profile of Otto Y. Schnering, posted on the online site immigrantentrepreneurship.org; Timothy C. Williams, "The Right of Publicity: You Can't Take It with You," *Pepperdine Law Review*, May 15, 1984; "When the Babe Struck Out, Protecting the Name and Likeness of the Baseball Icon Under Trademark Law," a paper presented by attorney Sharlene McEvoy at the 1995 Hofstra University conference on Ruth's one hundredth birthday; and Charles A. Poekel Jr.'s presentation at the 2010 Cooperstown symposium, "Babe Ruth vs. Baby Ruth: The Quest for a Candy Bar."

Among the most useful of the daily news stories were: "Candy Makers Know Value of a Brand Name," *Chicago Tribune,* December 9, 1951; "Court Rules Ruth Name Is Private, Image Is Not," *Los Angeles Times,* January 31, 1990; "A Babe Ruth Myth Is Stirred Up Again," *New York Times,* April 7, 2002; "Baseball Adopts a Candy, Whatever It's Named For," *New York Times,* June 6, 2006.

John Kenfield's recollections about his employment at the Curtiss Candy Co. and discussions with Ruth about the candy bar came from the University of North Carolina's 2002 men's tennis media guide.

Coverage of the Baby Ruth candy drops was profuse. Additional details came from Jeff Wells's article "The Day Baby Ruths Rained Down on Pittsburgh," published on www.mentalfloss.com on October 19, 2015. The role of the candy drops in the fate of *Enola Gay* pilot, Paul W. Tibbets Jr., was confirmed by his November 2, 2007, obituary in the *New York Times.*

The figures on Ruth's endorsement income are from the Christy Walsh catalogs (see appendix 2). George H. Ruth Candy Co. lawyers might have had a stronger case had they produced as evidence the earliest Baltimore newspaper accounts of his career in which he was known as Baby Ruth.

He suffered another promotional setback in 1931. In an effort to cash in on his reputation for sartorial splendor, he lent his name to an ill-timed venture in upscale men's accessories—hats, ties, and belts—called "Babe Ruth's Shop for Men," which opened on Broadway with much fanfare in September 1930 and went belly-up seven months later. Once again, Ruth ended up in litigation over the use of his name when the creditors who took over the remaining inventory tried to market the resulting enterprise as Babe Ruth's failure.

The resurgence in Ruth's marketing clout in the mid-1990s was thoroughly documented in Jeffrey Marx's February 6, 1996, story for *Sports Illustrated*, "It's a Babe-O-Nanza, on the Eve of Ruth's 100th Birthday, Curtis Management Has Reason to Cheer." By agreement, all endorsement income was split three ways, with a third going to the Babe Ruth League, a third to Julia Ruth Stevens, and a third split further by Dorothy's five children. According to daughters Donna Analovitch and Genevieve Herrlein, the income was considerable, even after Curtis Management took a 40 percent commission.

His name continued to have value in the marketplace. Julia was on hand at the ESPN Zone in New

York on October 20, 2003, when the Donruss trading card company began cutting one-inch squares from a game-worn 1925 uniform, with the intent of inserting 2,100 such pieces into packs of baseball cards. (The company had purchased the uniform at auction the year before for $264,210.) Although the revenue has dwindled, Analovitch says, it has not dried up entirely.

In 1946, Ruth gamely lent his name and his girth to Jockey, the men's underwear company, in an advertisement for "Babe Ruth Longjohns" with the tag line "There Is Only One Babe Ruth, There Is Only One Jockey."

In 2013, Jockey came calling again. The advertising mavens dressed a Babe Ruth avatar in modern undies for a relaunch of the brand. The campaign was called "Supporting Greatness." They stuck Ruth's head, shoulders, and arms on top of a twenty-first-century lower body with an eight-pack he never had, in underwear he never wore, and added this message: "Babe Ruth's Durable Jockey Underwear Supported His Greatness. His Bat Helped Too. But We Don't Sell Bats." (See Tim Nudd's August 26, 2014, story at www .adweek.com.)

The TV campaign, highlighting astronaut Buzz Aldrin, with General George S. Patton and Babe Ruth in supporting roles, obscured an ironic truth. Celebrity pitchmen are no longer a safe bet for advertisers. "Every single advertiser quakes before they hire anybody," explained Jerry Della Femina, the Madman of Madison Avenue who created Joe Isuzu and the Meow Mix theme. "I once wanted to use Martha Stewart as a spokesman. They said, 'What if she gets in trouble?'

"I said, 'She's not going to get in trouble.'

"Two years later she was in jail."

In death, Ruth became what he never was in life—unassailable.

CHAPTER 10: OCTOBER 18, SIOUX CITY

Interviews: Dan Donohue, Carole Horn, R. C. Raycraft, Joanne Loughlin Sanderson, Julia Ruth Stevens, Tom Stevens, Lee Swanson, and Linda Ruth Tosetti.

R. C. Raycraft, filmmaker and flea-picker extraordinaire, made this chapter possible. In March 2011, he shared the story of his acquisition of the footage of Ruth's visit to the Donohue family home, along with some of the footage, with the *New York Times*; this resulted in three stories: "Film Shows Babe Ruth, at Leisure and Up Close," on March 22, 2011; and two stories on March 25, "Memory and Mystery for Family in Ruth Film" and "A Man Remembers Meeting the Babe," featuring an interview with Phil Donohue, the boy with the wicked lasso.

The space allotted to the story is an indication of how rare it is to see the Babe on film, especially film of this quality, which was shot by Dudley Scott, who owned two movie theaters and was president of a company that made motion cameras.

Joanne Loughlin Sanderson, the youngest of the surviving Donohue children, said the family was puzzled by the use of part of the footage in two 1990s HBO documentaries, *When It Was a Game 2* and *Babe Ruth*. The family assumed it had the only copy. Sanderson sent me copies of all the newspaper clippings she had, as well as a photograph taken that day showing her brothers with Ruth and Gehrig and the pony, Molly.

Raycraft shared the entire sequence with me, allowing me to see the Babe's exuberance close-up and the profound alteration in his mien when he no longer wanted to be photographed.

The *Sioux City Journal* published its own account, "Lost & Found: Fresh Film of Ruth, Gehrig in Sioux City Resurfaces," on March 29, 2011. I am indebted to Terry Hersom, sports editor of the *Journal,* not only for sending me the paper's entire clip file on Ruth's visits to the city but for writing a column soliciting help for my re-creation of the 1927 game. That resulted in interviews with Pat O'Donnell and Steve Rosenblatt, whose fathers were on the field that day, as well as Phil Donohue's son, Dan, and daughter Joanne, who was featured in the Cherokee *Chronicle Times* on April 11, 2011, "Cherokee Woman's Family Hosted Sports Legends, Ruth, Gehrig, Louis, Dempsey Visited Sioux City Home."

In the section about Ruth's life in Sudbury, I relied on Smelser's correspondence with former Sudbury town historian Francis Bradshaw, current town historian Lee Swanson, and the Middlesex County Registry of Deeds. According to county records, Ruth did not purchase the property until June 1923. Marshall Hunt's anecdotes about Ruth's pranks and the journalistic fallout from the Dolores Dixon affair are from Wagenheim.

Dixon did not completely disappear from the printed page. On August 5, 1923, the *Pittsburgh Press* ran a two-page spread with Dixon prominently featured in a fur coat: "How the Wolves of the Underworld Entrap Their Victims, Rather Startling Revelations of the Methods of the New York Blackmailers to Squeeze Large Sums from Prominent Men Who Cannot Afford to Be Involved in Public Scandal." Ruth was quoted at length and in high dudgeon: "A girl who has a jail record accused me of doing some serious things and sued me in court. A lot of people advised me to hush the affair up, but I didn't do what she said I did and I decided to fight it. I had been trimmed by some crooks before. I had an opportunity to settle this girl's case, but I spent twice as much proving I was innocent than it would have cost me to settle."

The dollar amounts for Ruth's fines, advances, and medical expenses are itemized in the Yankees daily ledgers in Cooperstown.

Background on the construction of Yankee Stadium comes from multiple sources: daily coverage in the *Times*; minutes of Yankees board meetings in Jacob Ruppert's papers at the New York Public Library, in which executives agreed to pay $550,000 for ten acres from the Astor estate, plus $15,000 for two adjacent lots owned by Peter Braschoss and his wife ($10,000 of which was financed at 5.5 percent interest); a transcript of an August 5, 1938, radio interview with Ruppert, which puts the figure at $600,000 plus $2.5 million in construction costs. The Yankees accounting books examined by Michael Haupert placed the cost of 11.6 acres in Goatville at $792,000.

Equally helpful was a review in the November 7, 1923, issue of the *American Architect*. While extolling the toilet arrangements, the reviewer, an architect from Portland, Oregon, despaired of the sight lines and the short porch in right field. Clearly, he didn't understand that the dimensions were tailored for Ruth's left-handed swing: form followed function. I also drew on "The Ballpark and the City: Yankee Stadium's Renovation," published in *New York Affairs* in 1983.

Nicholas F. Cotton, public and media affairs manager for the Fulton County Clerk of the Superior and Magistrate Court, provided documents from Claire's divorce from Frank Hodgson. Notice of the divorce was published in the *Atlanta Constitution* on July 10, 1920. The correspondence between the Yankees front office and Landis regarding Ruth's betting is in the Ruth archive at the Hall of Fame.

Huggins's conversation with Mark Roth about disciplining Ruth is on page 145 in Graham, pages 102–4 in Tom Meany's *Babe Ruth*, and page 280 in Creamer.

The carny quality of the barnstorming tour was in evidence at Stockyards Park in Sioux City when a young boy standing behind a rope along the third baseline darted under it to greet Ruth at home plate after a home run. Ruth shooed concerned police away—"Officers, leave that kid alone," he said, according to a letter the boy, Hy Albeck, later wrote to the Hall of Fame. "I said I wanted to take his picture and he posed for me. He then said, 'anything else' and I asked him to call

Lou over, so I could take his picture. After I took Lou's picture, he said, 'anything else.' So, I asked him to call Lou out of the dugout, so I could take their picture together. Babe then said, 'anything else.' I said I wanted their autographs, so I walked between them to the dugout where they signed my autograph book.'"

And, then he ran all the way home—as did batboy Phil Donohue, who made off with six autographed baseballs. His trove dwindled over time—he gave one away; four others were lost by his children on fields of play, until only one remained. By then Phil had fourteen grandchildren, his son Dan said. He sold the ball because he couldn't decide whom to give it to. It fetched $13,000 at Guernsey's 1999 New York auction when Mark McGwire's seventieth home run ball sold for $3 million.

CHAPTER 11: OCTOBER 19, DENVER

Interviews: Jean Beswick, Father Eugene DelConte, Patricia Grace, Katherine Honey, Bernie and Nancy and John Kennedy, Robert Lipsyte, Ellen Maher, Father Jim Martinez, Tim Mitchell, Father George Riley, Father James Spenard, Julia Ruth Stevens, Linda Ruth Tosetti, Craig Woodford, and Steve Wulf.

After all the huzzahs and hallelujah headlines greeting Ruth and Gehrig, it was refreshing to read the unadorned coverage from Des Moines. "Ruth and Lou Gehrig Disappoint Local Fans," was the headline in the *Des Moines Evening Tribune* on October 18, 1928. The game story in the *Des Moines Register* was blunter, calling it "a baseball atrocity," an estimation buried on the jump page.

In researching the evolution of sportswriting from cheerleading to journalism, I immersed myself in Stanley Woodward's primer, *Sports Page*, and his subsequent memoir, *Paper Tiger: An Old Sportswriter's Reminiscences of People, Newspapers, War, and Work*; Jimmy Breslin's *Damon Runyon, A Life*; Charles Fountain's *Sportswriter: The Life and Times of Grantland Rice*; Ford Frick's *Games, Asterisks, and People: Memoirs of a Lucky Fan*; Paul Gallico's *Golden People* and *Farewell to Sport*; and all of the interviews with reporters who knew and covered Ruth in *No Cheering in the Press Box*. Woody Paige's description of Otto Floto appeared in his June 16, 2007, farewell column in the *Denver Post*. Former *Post* staff writer Terry Frei described Damon Runyon's brief but colorful tenure in Floto's sports department, when he was still known as Alfred, in a July 24, 2000, story, "A Legend from Pueblo to the Big Apple." Hired in 1905, Runyon was fired in 1906, allegedly because a prostitute was found typing a story in the newsroom on his behalf while he was indisposed.

For a beautifully written take on the press box in the Golden Era, and the standoff between the adherents of "aw nuts" and "gee whiz" sportswriting, read the chapter titled "Young Men of Manhattan," pages 275–86 in *Farewell to Sport*, and Woodward's chapter, "Aw Nuts and Gee Whiz," pages 60–68 in *Sports Page*. The allusion to sportswriting as a "low form of art" is on page ix.

My education in ghostwriting began with the instructional tips in *The Editor*, February 25, 1920, "The Ghost Writer and His Story," followed by the collected works of Westbrook Pegler on the sins of Christy Walsh and his ilk: "Spooks in the Press-Box, A Compassionate Look at the Troubled Lives of Our Literary Ghosts," *Liberty* magazine, February 8, 1930; "Some Points About Incomes of Authors," written for the *Augusta Chronicle* on November 12, 1946, now available online at http://ourgame.mlblogs.com; and "Babe Ruth's Stab at Literature—a la Ghost," written for the King Features Syndicate in 1948.

Walsh got lots of ink after Ruth's death. Typical of the stories was Joe Williams's column, "Christy Walsh, Old Ghost Man, Talks of Ruth." After Walsh's death, Williams revisited the subject in a January 5, 1956, column for the *New York World-Telegram,* "Christy Walsh Ran a Stable of Ghosts." The article about ghostwriting appeared on page 185 of the October 1927 edition of *The Bookman: A Review of Books and Life* in a section called "A Bookman's Notes."

John Carvalho's 2007 presentation to the Newspaper Division of the Association for Education in Journalism and Mass Communications, "Haunted by the Babe, Baseball Commissioner Ford Frick's Newspaper Columns About Babe Ruth," was especially insightful.

The editorial in *Editor & Publisher* condemning the practice, "The Public Be—?" appeared in the magazine on September 8, 1923.

For Christy Walsh and the rise of tabloid journalism, see the sources listed for chapter 3.

The deluge of daily news stories documenting the surgery and scandal of 1925 provided the perfect demonstration of the evolution of the sports page. I read the coverage in every New York City paper as well as that in Washington, Boston, Chicago, and Los Angeles. The cumulative effect was to reinforce the truth of Gallico's retrospective observation that the biggest story of the year was that so many cared about the fate of a baseball player. W. O. McGeehan's columns in the *Tribune* were memorable—especially "The Age of Incredulity" and "A Demigod Has Indigestion" in which he famously dubbed Ruth "our own national exaggeration." Dan Daniel's September 3 thumb-sucker in the *New York Telegram* on the role of sportswriters, "Babe Ruth and the Scribes," was as pointed as it was defensive and pointed the way forward for sports journalism.

The *New Yorker* chimed in on April 25 with the first of approximately 130 Ruthian mentions and full-length stories in a "Talk of the Town" item called, "The King's Pajamas." He would merit its attention in three of four September 1925 issues, including Morris Markey's trenchant analysis in "The Current Press" of the mother lode of press attention Ruth received.

Richards Vidmer's story about the baby at the train window is on pages 106–7 in *No Cheering*. Marshall Hunt's anecdotes about the dinner party, the conversation on the porch, and the disappearing act in Florida are from the Wagenheim tapes at the Hall of Fame. Ruth's cruel dismissal of Helen during spring training is on page 282 in Creamer.

Ruth's visits from Brother Paul and Brother Matthias were reported in the August 31 edition of the *Baltimore Evening Sun*.

The anecdotes about the sudsy urine, the shared bottle of scotch, the whorehouse in St. Louis, and the baby at the train window are from Holtzman's interviews with Hunt, Wagenheim, and Vidmer. Marshall

Hunt's story about Ruth's disappearance into the woods is from Wagenheim.

The front page of the final edition of the August 31 *Daily News* was revolutionary in its makeup and content. The headline "Ruth's Misconduct Defense" was stripped across the top of the page in huge block letters. The Pacific & Atlantic photograph of Claire occupied the lower right corner, giving extra weight to the image and the caption: "Babe's Plea. While Babe Ruth was in Chicago last night seeking reconsideration of order banning him from baseball, interest here centered on Claire Hodgson (above), one of his fair friends. Meanwhile, Mrs. Ruth denies serious misunderstanding with Babe over friendships of his feminine admirers."

Claire's svelte figure filled the front page the next day, too: "Ruth's Party Hostess Flees."

Ruth pledged reform, reminding interviewers and readers of his column that he had come back to win the Most Valuable Player award in 1923 after being written off in some quarters after the 1922 season. He kept his promise to go back to the woods—on a hunting trip with a gang of major leaguers, leaving just days after the wire services declared he would need more surgery because of a recurrence of his stomach abscess. Oddly, the wire services also quoted Helen Ruth, who apparently reemerged in the days after the World Series, as saying that his condition was related to a leg injury he had suffered at the end of the season. It is difficult to know what to make of the report, which also suggested that she and Babe hosted the hunting party at Home Plate Farm in Sudbury. Whether they had reunited for public appearances or had a more complex separation than the legal papers suggest is impossible to know.

Gallico's description of the reformed Babe is from page 50 in *Farewell to Sport*.

In an effort to establish Ruth's relationship with Father Edward J. Quinn, the priest who shepherded him from Grand Central Terminal to Helen's bedside, and who was alternatively described as a longtime friend of the couple or Ruth's friend from St. Mary's, I contacted four priests who served with him, as well as four members of his family. None of them had ever heard of his relationship with Ruth, which raises the question whether he was recruited for the task by Walsh, who was curiously absent throughout the crisis.

Walsh protected the identity of the scribes in his "All-Star Ghost Line-up" until the *Sporting News* serialized his memoir, *Adios to Ghosts*, in January 1938. Then he named names, thirty-seven of them: Bozeman Bulger and Ford Frick had written for Miller Huggins; Frick, Bill Slocum, and Frank Graham for Lou Gehrig; a slew of writers, including, on occasion his assistant

Joe Bihler, Arthur Robinson, Joe Gordon, and Robert Harron, all wrote for Ruth. Frick and Slocum were the mainstays. Slocum was his preferred muse. "He writes more like me than anyone else I know," Ruth said. He couldn't remember Frick's name.

Typical of the skepticism Ruth faced after the 1925 season was Hugh S. Fullerton's May 1, 1926, story in *Liberty* magazine, "Can Ruth Come Back? Baseball's Bad Boy Presents the Season's Snappiest Speculation." Walsh's strategy to counter the scuttlebutt is evident in the August 1926 piece he placed in Bernarr Macfadden's *Physical Culture* magazine, "Babe Ruth Brought Back by Physical Culture, by Art McGovern, the Man Who Brought Him Back, as Told to Edwin A. Goewey"—seven pages with the tale of the tape measurements and photos of the Babe in revealing work-out gear. Taking no chances, Walsh would place a similar story under McGovern's byline in the April 9, 1927, issue of *Literary Digest*, "Salvaging the Wreck of Babe Ruth." But some newspapers were no longer satisfied with photo-op images of the Babe wrestling, stretching and catching a medicine ball. The Binghamton, New York, *Sun-Bulletin* demanded pictures of his head hitting the pillow at 10:30 P.M. There is no record in Walsh's account ledger for "Babe Ruth's Complete Course" of exercise. Perhaps that had something to do with the cost buried in fine print in the advertising copy: a $1 deposit and $11 due upon delivery.

CHAPTER 12: OCTOBER 21–22, BAY AREA

Interviews: Roger Angell, Chris Davis, Arnold Hano, Michael Haupert, Bill James, Jim Lefebvre, Jordan Muraskin, Jason Ochart, Ray Robinson, Francesca Santoro, Rick Schu, and Vin Scully.

The uneasy accommodation of the national pastime— and Ruth himself—to the radio age is beautifully rendered in James Walker's *Crack of the Bat*. Ruth's debut as a radio personality was retold by Harold Arlin in an April 5, 1969, interview with Ted Patterson in the *Sporting News*.

I could not have written this chapter without the input of the batting gurus who helped translate the language of biomechanics and physics into English—Jim Lefebvre, Rick Schu, Jason Ochart, Jordan Muraskin. But most of all, I am indebted to Bill James for reaffirming my core belief that Ruth's power was as much a consequence of personality as it was testimony to physical and biomechanical skill—in short, it was a concerted effort by one of America's greatest rule breakers. "I remember a discussion I had about Ruth during the steroids era, that somebody insisted that Ruth would never have used steroids," James told me. "I remember thinking, 'Jesus Christ, this person doesn't know ANYTHING about Babe Ruth.'"

He elaborated on this theme in a January 20, 2014, story for *Slate*, "Life, Liberty, and Breaking the Rules: In Defense of Babe Ruth, Barry Bonds, Jaywalkers, and All Other Scofflaws That Make America Great."

Furman Bisher's 1949 interview with Shoeless Joe Jackson for *Sport* magazine was accessed online at www.blackbetsy.com, "Shoeless Joe Jackson's Virtual Hall of Fame."

For a modern, annotated critique of Hodges's July 18, 1920, story in the Richmond *Times-Dispatch*, see Alan Nathan's analysis at www.baseball.physics .illinois.edu. The findings of A. Terry Bahill and Tom LaRitz about the perceptual abilities and inabilities of hitters were published in the May–June 1994 issue of *American Scientist*, "Why Can't Batters Keep Their Eyes on the Ball: A Laboratory Study of Batters Tracking a Fastball Shows the Limitations of Some Hoary Baseball Axioms." The *New York Times* ran a story on their research on June 12, 1984, "Take Your Eye off the Ball, Scientist Coaches Sluggers."

I was lucky to find and to interview a hardy band of

baseball aficionados who are old enough to have seen Ruth play and eloquent enough to be able to describe him, chief among them Roger Angell, Arnold Hano, Vin Scully, and the late Ray Robinson. A deep dive into contemporaneous accounts of his hitting technique revealed only two writers that studied and described his form as he waited for a pitch he liked: Grantland Rice and Shirley Povich.

What he liked was fastballs— "I just loved them," he said in a recently discovered thirteen-minute interview recorded by Joe Hasel for Armed Services Radio in 1943. The recording was found in storage at his high school alma mater, Cheshire Academy in Connecticut, and reported for NPR by Diane Orson on February 22, 2018.

Undoubtedly, the greatest PR coup of Christy Walsh's career was the testing he arranged at Columbia University in 1921 that landed Ruth on the front page of the *Times* on September 11, 1921. Hugh S. Fullerton's full 1921 account in *Popular Science Monthly*, "Why Babe Ruth Is the Greatest Home-Run Hitter," was accessed from their online archive.

GQ's attempt to replicate the tests with Albert Pujols was published in the August 22, 2006, issue, "St. Louis Cardinals Slugger Pujols Gets Ruth Test at Washington University."

CHAPTER 13: OCTOBER 23, BAY AREA II

Interviews: Rugger Ardizoia, Dick Beverage, Bill Jones, Mark Macrae, John McCarthy, Tom O'Doul, Randy Stuart, and Carole and Thomas Tollefson.

This chapter was a pleasure to write, thanks to the late Rugger Ardizoia and the family of the late Jack "Whitey" Stuart. Bill Jones, past president of the San Francisco Baseball Old Timers Association, deserves credit for tipping me off to the story of Jack Stuart, grabbing a tinny, cheesy microphone from the current president at the dinner I attended in San Francisco and bellowing into the mike, "Jack Whitey Stuart! Jack Whitey Stuart!" Jones described Stuart's wake and the jersey laid out in his coffin. Jack's daughter, Carole Tollefson, remembered her father's description of the Babe as a "big, looming guy." His son, Randy Stuart, remembered his disappointment in Ruth.

Mark Macrae, Rugger's friend and frequent companion during the last years of his life, was as stunned as I was to learn that Rugger had attended both games on that Sunday by the San Francisco Bay. Mark thought he had heard all of Rugger's best stories.

Dick Beverage, the founder and president emeritus of the Pacific Coast League Historical Society (PCLHS), schooled me in the history of the league and put me in touch with Gus Suhr Jr., Chuck Brown, and other invaluable sources. Tom O'Doul took me to lunch at Lefty's bar before it closed in 2017 and filled me in on the relationship between Ruth and O'Doul.

CHAPTER 14: OCTOBER 25, MARYSVILLE

Interviews: Marlene Coleman Benniger, Jean Beswick, Frank Bichard, Ken Goldin, Patricia Grace, Kathy Honey, Patricia Johnstone, Bruce Minton, Randy Newton Sr. and Randy Newton Jr., George Nicholau, Ryan Nicholson, Jerry Paine, Steve Perry, Joanne Perry Raub, Carolyn Rendon, Bob Stassi, and Craig Woodford.

In writing this chapter, I was greatly assisted by Tub Perry's family, and the Sutter County Historical Society, which assembled a roundtable of Marysville citizens with knowledge of the game and Tub's career. Joanne Raub, Tub's daughter, and grandsons Steve Perry and Bruce Minton made Tub come alive again. Joanne copied her father's scrapbook for me. Steve introduced me to George Nicholau, ball shagger and batboy for the Marysville Giants. Like Rugger, whom I met on the same trip, he was manna from heaven.

The Perrys connected me with Randall Newton Sr. and Randall Newton Jr., descendants of Jack Frederick and his daughter, Doris, who told me their mother's stories about Ruth bringing steak to breakfast. The Perry family also put me in touch with John Rattray's daughter, Patricia Johnstone, who shared the history of her chiropractic family.

Ed Burt's scorecard sold for $7,500—"light" in industry argot—said Ken Goldin of Goldin Auctions, who auctioned it in 2016.

Telling the difficult story of Ruth's first marriage was made immeasurably easier by members of Helen Woodford Ruth's family—Jean Beswick, Patricia Grace and Kathy Honey, and Craig Woodford—who added perspective and depth to the story of her life and death. Ryan Nicholson of the Watertown Fire Department made an invaluable contribution by scouring the town archives for the fire and police department records, which had not been examined since Helen's death.

Details about the attempt by a local volunteer group, the Box 52 Association, to revive Helen are from the January 17, 1929, issue of the Watertown community newspaper.

The tragedy set off a competitive feeding frenzy between Boston and New York newspapers and rival news services—Universal, INS, AP, UP—to ferret out every awful detail of her death, including unsourced charges of murder and drug abuse. Those accounts plus the crucial January 14 and January 29 letters from Walsh to Ruth—and the trove of telegrams and press releases contained in the Christy Walsh catalogs—gave the story new context and helped provide an understanding of the charges made by her family in the aftermath of her death.

The catalogs also included a copy of the August 4, 1925, separation agreement, previously disclosed in Dorothy Ruth Pirone's 1988 memoir, *My Dad, the Babe: Growing Up with an American Hero*, written with Chris Martens.

Walsh's handwritten calculations of how much Ruth owed in arrears, copies of the voided checks, and all the subsequent correspondence with her estate attorney, James Conlin, pertaining to the settlement of her estate as well as the final disposition of the case, cast the story in an entirely new and not particularly flattering light.

CHAPTER 15: OCTOBER 26, SAN JOSE

Interviews: Donna Analovitch, Don Cardoni, Joseph and Richard and Tony Cirone, Genevieve Herrlein, Chris Ivy, Diane Lechner, Marla Duino Lenz, Dorothy and Ken Patterson, Richard Pinard, Robert Pinsky, Carolyn Rendon, Andrew Shepherd, Julia Ruth Stevens, Tom Stevens, and Linda Ruth Tosetti.

Two San Jose families—the Cirones and the Randazzos—made this chapter possible. Joseph, Richard, and Tony Cirone shared the story of their grandfather's eventful day at the ballpark. Tom and Joe Randazzo shared the story of their father's experience playing in the game, the highlight of his baseball career.

In addition to the coverage in the rival daily newspapers, I relied on the following retrospective accounts: "The Day the Babe Connected Here," in the October 18, 1959, *San Jose Mercury-News*, featuring an interview with Tom Randazzo Sr. and Mario Duino; "When the Babe Came to San Jose," also in the *Mercury-News*, on September 14, 1975; a November 19, 1974, interview with Duke Perry in the *Santa Clara Sun*; and an October 26, 1987, *Los Angeles Times* piece, "When Giants Walked the Land in California, Barnstorming with Gehrig and the Babe."

Marla Duino Lenz, "Speeder" Duino's niece, and daughter of the longtime sports editor of the local paper, provided portions of his unpublished diary, including descriptions of the game. Richard Pinard shared the story of his father's participation in the game. At age sixteen, he was the youngest player on the field. But he got edged out of the photograph taken with the Babe by a bunch of younger kids.

With the help of librarians at the San Jose Public Library and a 2010 "San Jose City Planning Study" commissioned to evaluate the land where the ballpark once stood, I was able to unscramble the confusion between Sodality Park and the field at Dunsmuir, which looked remarkably alike. An original print of the Dunsmuir photograph, in which Bennie Cirone thought he recognized himself and his brothers, was sold by Robert Edwards Auctions in 2013. Expected to sell for $500 to $1,000, the photo fetched $1,659. Despite the revelation that the boys pictured in the grandstand behind the plate in Dunsmuir are not his relatives, it remains the centerpiece of the altar Tony Cirone built for his memorabilia collection.

The interview with Jesse Linthicum was shared by Mike Gibbons. Waite Hoyt's letters were shared by Robert Creamer's son, Jim. Carl Sandburg's condescending spring training interview with Ruth, "Sandburg, Poet, Fans Ruth with 750 Words," which enraged Westbrook Pegler, appeared in the *Chicago Daily News, Tampa Bay Times,* and elsewhere on March 27, 1928. Robert Pinsky, a kinder poet, and son of a catcher for the New Jersey Aces, provided much-needed perspective.

Harry T. Brundidge's May 23, 1929, story in the *St. Louis Star and Times,* written just a month after Ruth's marriage to Claire, declared him a new man: "Babe

Ruth, King of Swat and Bad Boy of Baseball, Is Bad Boy No Longer." More significant than the declaration of reformation was Ruth's heated insistence that he was neither an orphan nor a bad kid. The ineffectiveness of his plea was evident in the stories that followed, particularly those written while he was dying. For example, the widely circulated magazine story, "The Babe Ruth You Never Knew" in the July 1947 issue of *Sport*, promised a new Babe but delivered the same old saws.

Julia Ruth Stevens was happy to share the account of her happy childhood and the gratitude she felt at being adopted by Babe Ruth. The account of Dorothy Ruth's troubled childhood is the product of multiple interviews with three of her daughters and her best friend from her teenage years, Carolyn Rendon, as well as her 1988 memoir and the raw notes she provided for her ghostwriter to use. According to Dorothy's daughter, Donna Analovitch, she reconciled with her stepmother before Claire Ruth's death in 1976.

The sad chasm in experience and sisterly affection on view at the Yankee Stadium observance of the fortieth anniversary of Ruth's death was reported by Harvey Araton in the *New York Daily News* on August 17, 1988.

The Bustin' Babes cap bestowed upon the young pastry chef in Santa Barbara was sold by her grandson in 2008 for $131,450 and resold five years later for $155,000, according to Chris Ivy, of Heritage Auctions. To date, it is the only personal item from the 1927 tour to reach the marketplace. Duke Perry's autographed ball sold for $5,530 in 2010. The inscribed portrait, graded PSA 9—almost mint—that Ruth sent to a former mistress on the day he married Claire sold for nearly $15,000 in 2007, according to a posting at www .bidami.com, a now defunct website. Which is why Ivy considers him "the gold standard" in the memorabilia business, a "blue-chip stock."

CHAPTER 16: OCTOBER 28, SAN DIEGO

Interviews: Debby Gumb, Michael Haupert, Toni McGowan, Bill Swank, Charles Turpinseed, Carla Walker, and Boomer Walling.

I am indebted to Carl Klindt's grandchildren Debby Gumb, Toni McGowan, and Boomer Walling for inviting me into their homes and their confidence in telling the story of his life. They provided letters, newspaper clippings, photographs from family albums, and an introduction to Carl's daughter Carla, now deceased. Carl's letter to a newspaper friend summarizing his career was particularly helpful if not entirely accurate. His assertion that he played in the game with Ruth and

Gehrig was not borne out by the box score; nor was his name found in accounts of Ruth's prior visits to San Diego. I am indebted to Bill Swank, author of two books on the history of baseball in San Diego, for ferreting out all the old game stories and for escorting me to the ballpark where Babe and Lou posed with Klindt prior to the game.

"Doc" Gottesburen's January 16, 1927, story for the *San Diego Union* provided most of the color and detail about Ruth's fishing expedition. Max Miller, in his fishing column in the San Diego *Sun,* and later in his bestselling memoir, *I Cover the Waterfront,* was less generous in his praise for Ruth as an angler. The headline on his story read: "One Strike and He's Out."

Walsh's letter to Knute Rockne is from the archives at the University of Notre Dame.

The dialogue between Walsh and Ruth on the subject of money is from Kennedy in *Collier's.*

All the financial records used in the chapter—including Walsh's handwritten notes documenting Ruth's indebtedness to his wife, his correspondence with the Bank of Manhattan, and with Helen's estate attorney as well as court documents pertaining to the settlement of the case—were found among his papers at the time of his death. Those documents, along with photos and other ephemera, were reproduced in auction catalogs by Heritage Auctions in Dallas. Copies of those catalogs were shared with me by Kelly Merritt and Chris Ivy.

Additional supporting documents, including copies of voided checks to Helen, were supplied by J. P. Cohen at Memory Lane Inc., a dealer in vintage cards and collectibles, who had purchased some of the lots from the Christy Walsh auction.

Matthew Zaft, a financial analyst at Morgan Stanley in Washington, D.C., analyzed the bank records and earning reports to assess how well Ruth's money was invested and how well his portfolio survived the Great Depression (see appendix 2).

The figures for Ruth's off-the-field income come from the ledger Walsh prepared for him in May 1938, which was among the papers reproduced in the Christy Walsh catalogs (see appendix 2).

In order to provide perspective on the extent of Ruth's wealth in 1927 and how it compared with that of the average American worker and average major leaguer, Haupert translated the dollar figures on Walsh's ledger into 2016 dollars representing Ruth's purchasing power in the present day (see appendix 2).

Free agency, established in 1975, which gave players leverage in contract negotiations, and Major League Baseball's eight-year $12.4 billion television rights deal, which went into effect in 2014, make a comparison between Ruth's salary, when he was baseball's highest earner, and today's best-paid player, Clayton Kershaw, economically irrelevant. "In 2015, Clayton Kershaw signed a seven-year contract with the Los Angeles Dodgers that guaranteed him an average salary of $30,714,286—919 times the salary of the average American worker—an amount that makes sense only in light of the MLB TV deal and the Dodgers' twenty-five-year $8.35 billion deal with Time-Warner," Haupert said. "A more relevant comparison is how well he was paid compared to his peers."

His three-year, $52,000-a-year contract, signed in 1922, represented a seismic shift in baseball economics not only because it was a multiyear deal but also because it was twice as much as any player had ever been paid before. In 1921, Ty Cobb earned $25,000, which at the time was the most any player had ever been paid. Ruth's salary was also 10.5 times higher than the average MLB player salary.

"Babe Ruth was the highest-paid baseball player in the major leagues for thirteen consecutive years from 1922 until he left the Yankees after 1934," according to Michael Haupert. "No player in history before or since has been the highest-paid player for even half that long. In eight of those seasons he earned more than ten times what the average player earned and in five of those seasons the second-highest-paid player earned less than half what Ruth earned. It wasn't until 1998 that another major league player would outearn the league average salary by more than Ruth did."

Another measure of Ruth's value to the Yankees was the $100,000 they invested in four life insurance policies in 1932, reported in team minutes dated March 2, in the Yankees files at the New York Public Library.

As Ruth's career faded and syndicate sales declined, Walsh turned to commercial radio to maintain a public presence and generate new income—advertising revenues increased from $18.7 in 1929 to more than $80 million by the end of the 1930s. The Ford Motor Company's $100,000 sponsorship of the 1934 World Series was a watershed moment for baseball and advertising. Why not get Ruth some? Walsh negotiated a 1934 deal with Sinclair Oil for the Esso-sponsored "Babe Ruth Boys Club," which was to run for thirteen weeks three times a week at 6:00 P.M. on NBC's Blue Network. Charter members were promised club pins and cards, and a weekly Babe Ruth newspaper loaded with tantalizing contest offers—balls, gloves, trips to spring training—and coupons to be redeemed by their parents at their local Esso station. Half a million kids had joined up by the time the government declared the program illegal, a violation of the code of fair competition outlined for the petroleum industry in the National Recovery Act.

"Sorry, kids," said the Babe, who nonetheless received $12,375.

Walsh then turned to Quaker Oats, which proved to be a safer and more lucrative sponsor, paying Ruth $62,787.50 over the next three years. The makers of Puffed Wheat and Puffed Rice created their own Babe Ruth Boys Club and another radio program that ran for thirteen weeks, beginning on April 16, 1934. Quaker Oats distributed "Ask Me" buttons to go with a Babe Ruth "Ask Me" game of baseball facts, printed four-color newspaper advertisements designed to look like Babe Ruth comic strips, and offered prizes in exchange for box tops—books and badges and a girl's beret. By the end of the run he had received one million letters and 850,000 box tops.

Quaker Oats also produced a series of fifteen-minute fictional parables called "The Adventures of Babe Ruth" in which the King of Clout was transmogrified into a King of Altruism: an all-knowing, all-forgiving, crime-solving amateur psychologist and ethicist, who pinch-hits for his dying ghostwriter in an episode called "Harry the Hat," risking a slump by staying up all night to write the column. It's unlikely any of his young listeners would have gotten the irony of that particular plot. (The series was revived by the United States Navy after Ruth's death.)

The transition to the era of live radio was not always a smooth one. Lou Gehrig was selected by Post Huskies to go head-to-head with Wheaties in 1930. In his inaugural appearance on *Ripley's Believe It or Not* on NBC—Bob Ripley was an old pal of Walsh's as well as his client—Gehrig was asked, "What do you have every morning, Lou?" To which he replied unequivocally, "A heaping bowl of Wheaties." Embarrassed at the flub, Gehrig offered to return his hundred-dollar endorsement fee. Post refused. Four years later, Wheaties made an honest man of him by putting him and Jimmie Foxx on the cereal box.

The personal-services contracts Ruth signed with Christy Walsh Management were conspicuously absent from the documents included in the auction catalogs. Nor was there any mention of the percentage Walsh took in any of the documents or correspondence. However, some of the deals he negotiated for Ruth, including one with Spalding, continued to generate money, albeit in decreasing amounts, after the end of their contractual relationship. On May 11, 1942, Walsh wrote to Ruth enclosing a check for "his 75% share of the annual profits" from Spalding—a measly $256.00.

Detailed accounting sheets for 1934 appear to confirm that Walsh took a 25 percent cut of Ruth's endorsement income. The accounting sheet lists total receipts for the year as $48,544.44 and the amount paid to Ruth as $36,708.32, or approximately 75 percent of the gross.

According to Haupert's calculations, if Walsh received 25 percent on every deal enumerated in the ledger, he would have earned $159,130 through his representation of Ruth, which translates into $13,253,335 in 2016 dollars.

CHAPTER 17: OCTOBER 29, FRESNO

Interviews: Donna Analovitch, Phil Coyne, William DeWitt Jr., Deems Grabowski, Sally Jo Greck, Steve Gross, Skip Hart, Genevieve Herrlein, Elizabeth Laval, Paula Lloyd, Kerry Yo Nakagawa, Tom O'Doul, Walter Petaluma, Ray Robinson, Vin Scully, Bill Staples Jr., Tom Stevens, Blake Talbot, and Howard Zenimura.

In this chapter, I relied extensively on the memories, memorabilia, and most especially the honesty and kindness of Kenichi Zenimura's son, Howard, and Kerry Yo Nakagawa, founder of the Nisei Baseball Research Project, who shared family photos and footage from the game at Firemen's Park. Howard set me straight on the myth that his father packed the photograph taken at Firemen's Park in his one suitcase when the family was sent to Gila River.

Zeni's biographer, Bill Staples, and Masaki Yoshikatsu, curator at the Hankyu Culture Foundation, made it possible for me to access the correspondence with Takizo Matsumoto at Meiji University, with whom Zenimura had tried to negotiate a deal for Babe Ruth to visit Japan.

Stories in the *Christian Science Monitor*, "How One Japanese-American Runner Took on Babe Ruth" from May 6, 1997, and the *Fresno Bee*, "Zenimura: Dean of the Diamond" from August 2, 1970, helped me gain a further understanding of the man who rarely spoke about the game at Firemen's Park.

In addition to daily coverage in the *Fresno Bee* and *Fresno Republican*, reporting on the Saturday-night banquet was found in the *Central California News*, a one-time publication of the Monterey-Fresno Archdiocese, November 19, 1927, and *The Tidings*, *Monterey-Fresno Diocesan News*, November 4, 1927. For background on toastmaster Father Crowley, see Joan Brooks's *Desert Padre: The Life and Writings of Father John H. Crowley 1891–1940*.

Ruth's statement that he needed time "to get his nerves back in shape" is from page 400 in Smelser. Tom

Meany's response to his copy editor is from page 347 in Creamer.

Kelly Merritt shared Hendrik van Loon's 1933 tribute to the Babe, written initially as a personal letter to Ruth. She also allowed me access to Walsh's correspondence with his divorce lawyer, and with his friend and client van Loon, in which he complained bitterly about legal fees, the cost of maintenance of Christy Jr., and the pain of relinquishing custody of him. Little wonder, with headlines like these: "Walsh Gives Up His Unmanly Son" (*New York Post*, January 18, 1938) and "Walsh Yields 'Cream Puff' Boy to His Ex" (*New York Mirror*, February 2, 1938). Those letters offered an unguarded and unsanitized glimpse of Walsh, including a casual anti-Semitism all too common at the time—in one letter, he remarked on the increased number of Jews and skyscrapers he observed upon returning to New York after a winter in Los Angeles.

The movie he filmed for his mother's seventy-fifth birthday and the unlikely quartet of crooners he assembled to sing to her—Eddie Rickenbacker, James A. Farley, Governor Al Smith, and Babe Ruth—was screened for me by Richard Walsh, who provided additional insights into the family and into his own career. Among other things, he invented a vibrator shaped like a clamshell and operated one of the first video dating services in the United States.

In reconstructing the last days of Ruth's career, I was immensely aided by interviews with Bill DeWitt, Skip Hart, George Morgenweck, George Nicholau, Walter Petaluma, and Blake Talbot, each of whom met him or saw him play during that period of his life. Jhan Robbins's family filled in details of his visit to the Stadium in 1934. Conversations with Sally Jo Greck and Deems Grabowski, whose family owned Ruth's favorite hangout in Greenwood Lake, were also helpful. Hart and Petaluma, young boys when Ruth frequented the area, remembered how the bravest among them would summon him from a saloon to play ball and were then delighted when he bought everyone ice cream before returning to other pleasures.

The conversation in the Pittsburgh clubhouse prior to Ruth's three–home run game at Forbes Field can be found in Smelser on pages 504–5.

Phil Coyne had hoped to continue as an usher at PNC Park in 2018 for what would have been his eighty-second year with the Pirates but finally bowed to age. "I'm sad," he said. "I tried to make it to one hundred, but I just couldn't make it."

The episode with Lou Gehrig during the voyage to Japan in the fall of 1934 was documented by Jonathan Eig in his biography of Gehrig, *Luckiest Man*, pages 189–91, and in Eleanor Gehrig's memoir, *My Luke and I.* John Drebinger's story about Ruth's loan to Gehrig is from an unpublished portion of his interview with Holtzman.

Walsh's exchange of letters with the vice president at the Equitable Life Assurance Company in 1938 is from the Christy Walsh catalogs. After Ruth's death, he kept track of Claire's doings, clipping juicy headlines from New York tabs about her alleged relationship with a society polo player, among them this undated gem from the *New York Daily News*: ". . . The 31-year-old polo-playing socialite, linked romantically with Mrs. Babe Ruth, was arrested on Peeping Tom complaint brought by two UN interpreters. Story on page 4."

Ruth may have reinvented the game, but attendance figures do not support his cherished belief that he brought fans back to the park after the scandal of the Black Sox. "Legend is not fact," said major league historian John Thorn. "The scandal broke in late September 1920, so Ruth saved baseball from what? Attendance figures for major league baseball in 1919, 1920, 1921, respectively: 6.53 million (during a 140-game season); 9.12 million; and 8.61 million. White Sox attendance *did* drop off the table, though, from 833,000 in 1920 to 544,000 in 1921. This accounted almost entirely for the decline in American League attendance in 1921, while the National League held steady."

The story about the itty-bitty ones appeared in the March 18, 1944, issue of the *New Yorker*.

Background on the Gila River Relocation Center was provided by a 2012 National Historic Landmarks Theme Study produced for the National Park Service, "Japanese Americans in World War II." Gila River was considered a showplace and was selected for a visit by Eleanor Roosevelt in April 1943. The first lady's visit to the Butte Camp did not make much of an impression on Howard Zenimura. He and his friends were too busy playing baseball.

The enrichment of future Yankees owner Del Webb through the construction of military facilities and Japanese American detention camps during World War II is documented in "Confinement and Ethnicity: An Overview of World War II Japanese American Relocation Sites," at https://www.amazon .com/Confinement-Ethnicity-Overview-Japanese -Relocation/dp/029598156, and a September 8, 1985, investigation in the *Arizona Republic*. According to Bill Staples's biography of Kenichi Zenimura, Webb received contracts from the War Relocation Authority to build the Poston Relocation Center as well as a portion of the housing at Gila River (see page 117).

Home plate from Zenimura Field, which is all that remains of the ballpark that Zeni and his family created, is now on display at the National Baseball Hall of Fame. The wooden artifact, made out of scrap lumber abandoned by construction workers, bears witness to all the baseball spikes that landed upon it, as well as the rusty nails used to hold it together.

More about this can be found in Staples's May 22, 2017, article posted on the *Gila River Indian News* website, "Home Plate from Japanese-American Concentration Camp on Display in Baseball Hall of Fame," and in Alex Coffey's story, "A Field of Dreams in the Arizona Desert," accessed at www.baseballhall .org. Home plate was found buried in the dirt near an olive grove by the family of a former internee. Stubborn desert weeds were growing in the cracks of the wood.

CHAPTER 18: OCTOBER 30, LOS ANGELES

Interviews: Yogi Berra, Scott Boras, Bobby Brown, Matt Cwieka, William DeWitt Jr., Chris Epting, Jean Johnstone, Carolyn Neilson-Major, Mary C. Moran, David Nieves, Tom O'Doul, Ken and Dorothy Patterson, Eddie Robinson, Steve Rosenblatt, Sig Seidenman, Charlie Silvera, Toni Stein, Leigh Steinberg, Chuck Stevens, Julia

Ruth Stevens, Lynne Thomas, Rolland Thomas, Bob Walsh, Katie Walsh, and Richard Walsh.

The significance of the size of the crowd as a barometer for future growth of major-league baseball was much noted in the press. Bob Ray, who covered the game for the *Los Angeles Times*, cited it in his game story. Paul Lowry's November 7 "Rabbit Punches" column in the *Times* pointed out that even with a top ticket priced at $1.50, sales had reached $40,000. Proof that L.A. would support big-league sports and, as Bill McGeehan wrote in the *Herald Tribune*, sufficient to convince the "magnates . . . at last that the barnstorming trips really help to swell future gate receipts."

The presence of Hollywood celebs at Wrigley Field, found on page 24 in Sobol, presaged the star-power always in evidence at Dodger Stadium—even if they do come late and leave early.

James Gordon's 2011 description of "Los Angeles' Wrigley Field: 'The Finest Edifice in the United States,'" published in *National Pastime* magazine, helped me re-create the scene at the park, as did Lawrence Ritter's *Lost Ballparks* and Bill Shannon's *The Ballparks*.

Richard Sandomir elaborated on the estrangement between Ruth and Gehrig in his 2017 book, *The Pride of the Yankees: Lou Gehrig, Gary Cooper, and the*

Making of a Classic, and Eleanor Gehrig's unsuccessful campaign to exclude the Babe from the movie, quoting her as saying, among other things, that Ruth was drunk at her husband's funeral.

Sandomir and Eig shared the correspondence between Christy Walsh and Eleanor Gehrig. Other details about tensions in the Ruths' marriage were described by Dorothy Patterson, daughter of the family maid, and her husband, Ken; Dorothy Ruth Pirone elaborated at length in her memoir.

As Ruth left the French Hospital, neighbors leaned out of windows in buildings across the street to see his condition. They wouldn't have been able to see him wrapped in a blanket in the limousine for the short ride home. The anecdote about Walter Winchell's broadcast that evening stating that Ruth had lost 125 pounds in the hospital is from page 197 in *The Babe and I* by Mrs. Babe Ruth.

Three years after Bill DeWitt Jr. met Babe Ruth on the field in Sportsman's Park, Eddie Gaedel, the three-foot, seven-inch pinch-hitter, wore his uniform when the Browns' new owner Bill Veeck sent him up to the plate to pinch-hit for leadoff man Frank Saucier.

Information about the FBI investigation of Christy Walsh was acquired through a Freedom of Information Act request. Documents, itemized receipts, and correspondence relating to his thwarted bid to establish an NFL franchise at the Los Angeles Coliseum were in the Christy Walsh catalogs.

Walsh acknowledged that he intended to meet Rockne in Los Angeles on April 3—four days after the fatal flight he was allegedly supposed to make—in a radio address broadcast at Notre Dame on April 4. The transcript was included in the May 1931 edition of "The Notre Dame Alumnus" devoted to Rockne found in the Notre Dame Archives. His encomium was titled "Happy Landings."

Richard Walsh gleefully recounted his radio appearance with Babe Ruth. Some eighty years after the fact, some of the details about the occasion were fuzzy, including the exact date and station on which the joint interview was broadcast. On election eve in 1944, Ruth was photographed at an election night rally, standing behind Republican nominee Thomas E. Dewey.

Dan Daniel reported the story of the Newark managing job in a June 12, 1946, story in the *Sporting News*, "Turn-Down as Newark Pilot Aired." Francis Coe's description of Ruth's appearance at the Banshee Luncheon for AP Sports Features was carried by the *Palm Beach Post* on April 27, 1947.

Emory Perry's 1947 correspondence with baseball commissioner Happy Chandler and 1948 correspon-

dence with Ford Frick were found in the Ruth files at
the National Baseball Hall of Fame, where I also found
the September 19, 2000, letter from Aline Maas, the
nurse who accompanied Ruth on his travels for Ford in
the fall of 1947.

Mary C. Moran, an attorney specializing in trusts
and estates, currently director of planned giving at Massachusetts General Hospital, shared documents from
the final settlement of Ruth's estate in 1954 and Dorothy
Ruth Pirone's lawsuit against his trustees, as well as an
invaluable explanation of them. Further details came
from her August 1, 2009, article in *Trusts & Estates,
the Journal of Wealth Management for Estate-Planning
Professionals*, "Babe Ruth Hit Home Runs, but His
Foundation Struck Out."

Carole Horn, MD, reviewed the following articles
from medical journals concerning Ruth's treatment and
disease: Brian L. Hutchings, "The Synthesis of Pteroyl
& Glutamylglutamic Acid," published by the International Union Against Cancer (UICC), 1947; "Pterins
for Malignant Disease," in the *Lancet*, January, 31,
1948; Nadim B. Bikhazi et al., "Babe Ruth's Illness and
Its Impact on Medical History," in the *Laryngoscope*,
January 1999; W. J. Maloney, "The Medical Legacy
of George Herman Babe Ruth," January 22, 2011. She
also reviewed coverage by William L. Lawrence in

the *New York Times*, "Ruth Never Knew of Cancer Malady," August 17, 1948, and "Details Are Given of Ruth's Illness, Fatal Cancer Started in Spot Inaccessible to Surgery, Hospital Autopsy Shows," August 18, 1948; and "Could Babe Ruth Have Been Saved?" which appeared in the November 1948 issue of *Physical Culture* magazine.

Former *New York Times* medical reporter Lawrence K. Altman, MD, reviewed with me his two articles concerning Ruth's health: "Stored Blood: A Research Treasure," from August 18, 1987, and "The Babe's Other Record: Cancer Pioneer, a Pioneer in Chemotherapy," published December 29, 1998.

Additional details about his illness came from Dorothy Ruth Pirone's memoir and the notes she gave to Chris Martens. Macfadden's postmortem on Ruth's treatment appeared in the November 1948 edition of *Physical Culture*.

W. C. Heinz's description of Ruth's last appearance at Yankee Stadium is in *What a Time It Was: The Best of W. C. Heinz on Sports*. Additional details about Nat Fein's career were provided by David Nieves, curator and administrator of his estate. After winning the Pulitzer Prize for the photograph he titled "No. 3 Bows Out," Fein remained with the *New York Herald Tribune* until it folded in 1966. According to Nieves, the

New York Times declined to hire him because of his age. He spent the rest of his career doing aerial photography for a utility company.

Julia Ruth's family sold the gold watch he received that day for $650,108 in 2014.

Footage of Ruth and Gehrig on the hunting trip with Glenn E. Thomas was graciously provided by his step-granddaughter Carolyn Major-Neilson and Chris Epting, who first wrote about it in an August 15, 2012, story for the *Los Angeles Times*, "In the Pipeline: Local Babe Ruth Footage Unearthed." Additional details and photographs were shared by Thomas's granddaughter Toni Stein.

The anecdote about Ruth's plans for the winter of 1927 is from Sobol, page 24, and the *Fresno Bee* of October 29, 1927.

Eddie Robinson, now the oldest living major leaguer, kept the bat Ruth autographed for him for three decades, displaying it first in his Baltimore restaurant and then in his home in Texas. (Bob Feller, to whom the bat belonged, protested in true baseball fashion: *I wuz robbed.*)

One day decades later, Robinson decided to find out what the thing was worth and called Barry Halper, the über–Yankee collector (since deceased), to feel him out. Not wanting to sound too interested, Halper asked what he wanted for it. Robinson figured he'd ask for the moon—$10,000. He'd have happily settled for half that.

The check was in the mail the next day.

Years later Halper sold the bat for $107,000 to Upper Deck, the baseball trading card company, which gave it away in a sweepstakes contest to a retired truck driver, who couldn't afford to pay the taxes on it.

Feller and a consortium of supporters purchased the bat for $95,000 and installed it in Feller's museum in Van Meter, Iowa, in an oversize protective test tube that hung from the ceiling, in front of the grinning image of Chief Wahoo, former mascot of the Cleveland Indians. When the museum closed in 2014, four years after Feller's death, the bat was transferred to the town hall, and then in April 2015 to the Bob Feller exhibit at Progressive Stadium in Cleveland, where, needless to say, Babe Ruth never hit a home run.

The bat from the Joe E. Brown collection, which he said Ruth used to hit the sixtieth home run, was sold on May 18, 2018, by Heritage Auctions for $660,000. Tom Shieber, senior curator at the Hall of Fame, remains confident that the real thing is in Cooperstown.

Ruth's rewritten will, which became the subject of litigation between Dorothy and his estate, was stolen from his probate file in the New York Surrogate's

Court and sold to a memorabilia collector for $30,000, according to documents in Ruth's FBI file obtained through a Freedom of Information Act request. An unsigned copy of the will was sold for $1,067 by Robert Edwards Auctions in 2012.

EPILOGUE

Interviews: Mike Klepfer, George Lois, Jack McKinney, Kelly Merritt, Andrew Nagle, Julia Ruth Stevens, Linda Ruth Tosetti, and Richard Walsh.

The interview with Mamie Ruth Moberly was conducted by Mike Gibbons for the Babe Ruth Birthplace and Museum; she added further details in the 1985 *People* feature.

Details about the scene in Ruth's hospital room and his relationship with Loretta are on page 191 in Pirone and Martens. The detail about the statue of St. Martin de Porres at Ruth's deathbed and Father Kauffman's description of his condition are found on page 540 in Smelser.

Frank Haggerty's account of the tears he didn't shed appeared in the February 6, 1988, edition of the *Baltimore Sun*: "Missing Pieces of the Legend Museum: in 1947 Frank Haggerty Stood in for the Babe. Today, He Shares His Memories."

Jack McKinney filled in details of the day he spent with his father at Ruth's funeral, first mentioned in his 2005 memoir, *Tales from the St. Joseph's Hardwood*. Walsh's thank-you note to the Babe was provided by Kelly Merritt. She also shared a recording of the banquet that took place the day Walsh died, from which I excerpted Fred Haney's remarks. Walsh's eulogy for Ruth and his radio address are from the Christy Walsh catalogs.

The story about the pizza delivered to the Babe in 2004 was told to me by Andrew E. Nagle, associate manager of the Trustees of St. Patrick's Cathedral, which manages Gate of Heaven Cemetery. The pizza was left overnight in front of Ruth's grave. When the section foreman returned the next morning, only a slice or two remained.

SELECTED BIBLIOGRAPHY

Adams, Mark. *Mr. America: How Muscular Millionaire Bernarr Macfadden Transformed the Nation Through Sex, Salad, and the Ultimate Starvation Diet*. New York: HarperCollins, 2009.

Alexander, Charles. *John McGraw: A Giant in His Time*. South Orange, NJ: Summer Game Books, 2014.

Appel, Marty. *Pinstripe Empire: The New York Yankees from Before the Babe to After the Boss.* New York: Bloomsbury, 2012.

Barthel, Thomas. *Babe Ruth Is Coming to Your Town: Post-Season Barnstorming Games, 1914–1935.* Amazon Digital Services LLC, 2013.

——. *Baseball's Peerless Semi Pros, The Brooklyn Bushwicks of Dexter Park.* Haworth, NJ: St. Johann Press, 2009.

Barton, Bruce. *The Man Nobody Knows.* Lewis Press, 2013.

Bernays, Edward L. *Biography of an Idea: The Founding Principles of Public Relations.* New York: Simon & Schuster, 1965.

——. *Crystallizing Public Opinion.* New York: Boni and Liveright, 1923.

——. *Propaganda.* Brooklyn, NY: Ig Publishing, 2005. Reprint.

Bessie, Simon Michael. *Jazz Journalism: The Story of the Tabloid Newspapers.* New York: E. P. Dutton, 1938.

Bohn, Michael K. *Heroes & Ballyhoo: How the Golden Age of the 1920s Transformed American Sports.* Washington, DC: Potomac Books, Inc., 2009.

B&O Railroad Museum Education Department. *America's Great Road: The Impact of the Baltimore*

& *Ohio Railroad on the Baltimore Region.* Baltimore: B&O Railroad Museum, 1995.

Braudy, Leo. *The Frenzy of Renown: Fame and Its History.* New York: Vintage Books, 1997. Reprint.

Breslin, Jimmy. *Damon Runyon, A Life.* Boston: Ticknor & Fields, 1991.

Brooks, Joan. *Desert Padre: The Life and Writings of Father John H. Crowley 1891–1940.* Desert Hot Springs, CA: Mesquite Press, 1997.

Broun, Heywood. *The Sun Field: A Novel.* Weston, CT: Rvive Books, 2008. Reprint.

Bryson, Bill. *One Summer: America, 1927.* New York: Anchor, 2014.

Buckland, Gail. *Who Shot Sports: A Photographic History, 1843 to the Present.* New York: Alfred A. Knopf, 2016.

Cabral, Rick. *Barnstormin' Across America: The Bustin' Babes and Larrupin' Lous.* Self-published, 2013.

Chapman, John Arthur. *Tell It to Sweeny: The Informal History of the New York Daily News.* Westport, CT.: Greenwood Press Publishers, 1961.

Creamer, Robert W. *Babe: The Legend Comes to Life.* New York: Simon & Schuster, 1974.

Daniel, Daniel M., and Babe Ruth. *Babe Ruth: The*

Idol of the American Boy. Racine, WI: Whitman Publishing Company, 1930.

Della Femina, Jerry. *From Those Wonderful Folks Who Brought You Pearl Harbor: Front-Line Dispatches from the Advertising War.* New York: Simon & Schuster, 1970.

Dickson, Paul. *Leo Durocher, Baseball's Prodigal Son,* New York: Bloomsbury USA, 2017.

Dorsey, John, and James D. Dilts. *A Guide to Baltimore Architecture.* Centreville, MD: Tidewater Publishers, 1997.

Douglas, Ann. *Terrible Honesty: Mongrel Manhattan in the 1920s.* New York: Farrar, Straus, and Giroux, 1995.

Eig, Jonathan. *Luckiest Man: The Life and Death of Lou Gehrig.* New York: Simon & Schuster, 2005.

Epting, Chris. *Roadside Baseball: Uncovering Hidden Treasures from Our National Pastime.* St. Louis, MO: Sporting News Books, 2003.

Farrell, James T. *My Baseball Diary: A Famed American Author Recalls the Wonderful World of Baseball . . . Yesterday and Today.* New York: A. S. Barnes and Company, 1957.

Federal Writers' Project. *The WPA Guide to Mary-*

land: *The Old Line State*. San Antonio, TX: Trinity University Press, 2014.

Fleming, G. H. *Murderers' Row*. New York: William Morrow, 1985.

Fitzgerald, F. Scott. "My Lost City." In *My Lost City: Personal Essays, 1920–1940*. Edited by James L.W. West III. Cambridge, UK: Cambridge University Press, 2014.

Fountain, Charles. *Sportswriter: The Life and Times of Grantland Rice*. New York: Oxford University Press, 1993.

Frick, Ford. *Games, Asterisks, and People: Memoirs of a Lucky Fan*. New York: Crown Publishers, 1973.

Gabler, Neal. *Winchell: Gossip, Power and the Culture of Celebrity*. New York: Vintage Books, 1994. Reprint.

Gallico, Paul. *Farewell to Sport*. New York: Alfred A. Knopf, 1938.

———. *The Golden People*. Garden City, NY: Doubleday, 1965.

Gehrig, Eleanor, and Joseph Durso. *My Luke and I*. New York: Thomas Y. Crowell Co., 1976.

Gershman, Michael. *Diamonds: The Evolution of the Ballpark from Elysian Fields to Camden Yards*. Boston: Houghton Mifflin Company, 1993.

Goldman, Herbert S. *Jolson: The Legend Comes to Life.* London: Oxford University Press, 1988.

Haupert, Michael. "Babe Ruth: Better Than the Dow Jones." *Outside the Lines* (Spring 2008).

———. "A Century of Success: The Founding of the Yankee Dynasty." *Outside the Lines* 21, no. 1 (Spring 2015), 20–23.

———. "The Sultan of Swag: Babe Ruth as a Financial Investment." *Baseball Research Journal* 44, no. 2, (Fall 2015).

Haupert, Michael, and Ken Winter. "Yankee Profits and Promise: The Purchase of Babe Ruth and the Building of Yankee Stadium." In *The Cooperstown Symposium on Baseball and American Culture 2009–2010.* Edited by William Simons. Jefferson, NC: McFarland & Co., 2003.

Heinz, W. C. "Down Memory Lane with the Babe." In *What a Time It Was: The Best of W. C. Heinz on Sports.* Edited by Jeff MacGregor. New York: Da Capo Press, 2001.

Hofstra University. *The Conference, Baseball and the "Sultan of Swat."* Audio recordings, 1995.

Holtzman, Jerome, ed. *No Cheering in the Press Box: Recollections—Personal & Professional—by Eighteen Veteran American Sportswriters.* New

York, Chicago, and San Francisco: Holt, Rinehart and Winston, 1974.

Honig, Donald. *Classic Baseball Photographs 1869–1947.* New York: Smithmark Publishers, 1994.

Hoyt, Waite. *Babe Ruth as I Knew Him.* New York: Dell, 1948.

Irwin, Will, and E. H. Suydam, illustrator. *Highlights of Manhattan, New York and London. New York:* The Century Co., 1927.

Jackson, Kevin. *Constellation of Genius: 1922—Modernism Year One.* New York: Farrar, Straus, and Giroux, 2013.

Jenkinson, Bill. *The Year Babe Ruth Hit 104 Home Runs: Recrowning Baseball's Greatest Slugger.* New York: Carroll & Graf Publishers, 2007.

Kaufman, Gregg. *Symphony of Swat.* Podcast episodes 1–18. Accessed at iTunes, September 2008–January 2009.

Lamb, Chris. *Conspiracy of Silence: Sportswriters and the Long Campaign to Desegregate Baseball.* Lincoln and London: University of Nebraska Press, 2012.

Lee, Ivy. *Publicity: Some of the Things It Is and Is Not.* New York: Industries Publishing Co., 1925.

Leerhsen, Charles. *Ty Cobb: A Terrible Beauty.* New York: Simon & Schuster, 2016.

Lehane, Dennis. *The Given Day*. New York: William Morrow, 2009.

Leisman, Louis J. *I Was with Babe Ruth at St. Mary's: Louis J. Leisman of Aberdeen, Maryland, Tells of Childhood with the Immortal Babe Ruth*. Aberdeen, MD: Self-published, 1956.

Lieb, Fred. *Baseball as I Have Known It*. Lincoln and London: University of Nebraska Press, 1977.

Liebling, A. J. *The Press*. New York: Pantheon Books, 1975.

Lipsyte, Robert, and Peter Levine. *Idols of the Game: A Sporting History of the American Century*. Atlanta, GA: Turner Publishing, 1995.

Lois, George. *The Art of Advertising: George Lois on Mass Communication*. New York: Harry Abrams, 1977.

Macfadden, Bernarr. *The Walking Cure: Pep and Power from Walking—How to Cure Disease by Walking*. New York: Macfadden Publications, 1924.

Macht, Norman L. *Babe Ruth*. New York: Chelsea House Publishers, 1991.

McCarthy, Kevin M. *Babe Ruth in Florida*. Vero Beach, FL: Inkslingers Press, 2012.

McChesney, Robert A. "Media Made Sport: A History of Sports Coverage in the United States." In *Media*,

Sports, & Society. Edited by Lawrence A. Wenner. Newbury Park, CA: Sage Publications, 1989.

McGivena, Leo E., et al. *The News: The First Fifty Years of New York's Picture Newspaper.* New York: News Syndicate Co., Inc., 1969.

McKinney, Megan. *The Magnificent Medills: America's Royal Family of Journalism During a Century of Turbulent Splendor.* New York: HarperCollins, 2011.

Meadow, Charles T. *Ink into Bits: A Web of Converging Media.* Lanham, MD, and London: Scarecrow Press, 1998.

Meany, Tom. *Babe Ruth: The Big Moments of the Big Fellow.* New York: Grosset & Dunlap Publishers, 1951.

Mencken, H. L. *Happy Days.* New York: Alfred A. Knopf, 1940.

Mencken, H. L., and S. T. Joshi, eds. *Mencken on Mencken: A New Collection of Autobiographical Writings.* Baton Rouge, LA: Louisiana State University Press, 2010.

Mercurio, John A. *Babe Ruth's Incredible Records and the 44 Players Who Broke Them.* New York: S.P.I. Books, 1993.

Miller, Donald L. *Supreme City: How Jazz Age Man-*

hattan Gave Birth to Modern America. New York: Simon & Schuster, 2014.

Miller, Ernestine. *The Babe Book: Baseball's Greatest Legend Remembered*. Kansas City, MO: Andrews McMeel Publishing, 2000.

Montville, Leigh. *The Big Bam: The Life and Times of Babe Ruth*. New York: Doubleday, 2006.

Mosedale, John. *The Greatest of All: The 1927 New York Yankees*. New York: Dial Press, 1974.

Nakagawa, Kerry Yo. *Japanese American Baseball in California: A History*. Charleston, SC: History Press, 2014.

Nicholau, George Edison. *An Ordinary Man: An Extraordinary Life, a Sole Survivor with True Grit*. Sacramento, CA: I Street Press, 2013.

Niebling, Devon M., and Thomas Hyde. *Baseball in Omaha*. Charleston, SC: Arcadia Publishing, 2004.

Nieves, David. *The Fein Story Behind the Pictures: A Revealing Look at the Famous Images of Pulitzer Prize Photographer Nat Fein*. West Nyack, NY: Nat Fein Collection, Inc., 2008.

Okrent, Daniel. *Last Call: The Rise and Fall of Prohibition*. New York: Scribner, 2010.

Okrent, Daniel, and Harris Lewine, eds. *The Ultimate Baseball Book*. Boston: Houghton Mifflin, 1979.

Peterson, Robert. *Only the Ball Was White: A History of Legendary Black Players and All-Black Professional Teams.* New York and Oxford: Oxford University Press, 1970.

Pietrusza, David. *Judge and Jury: The Life and Times of Judge Kenesaw Mountain Landis.* South Bend, IN: Diamond Communications, Inc., 1998.

Pirone, Dorothy Ruth, and Chris Martens. *My Dad, the Babe: Growing Up with an American Hero.* Boston: Quinlan Press, 1988.

Poekel, Charles A. *Babe & the Kid: The Legendary Story of Babe Ruth and Johnny Sylvester.* Charleston, SC: History Press, 2007.

———. "Babe Ruth vs. Baby Ruth: The Quest for a Candy Bar." In *Cooperstown Symposium on Baseball and American Culture 2009–2010.* Edited by William Simons. Jefferson, NC: McFarland & Company, 2010.

Powers, John, and Ron Driscoll. *Fenway Park: A Salute to the Coolest, Cruelest, Longest-Running Major League Ballpark in America.* Philadelphia, PA: Running Press, 2012.

Price, Jack. *News Pictures.* New York: Round Table Press, 1937.

Ritter, Lawrence S. *Lost Ballparks: A Celebration of Baseball's Legendary Fields.* New York: Viking Studio Books, 1992.

Ritter, Lawrence S., and Mark Rucker. *The Babe: A Life in Pictures.* Boston: Ticknor & Fields, 1988.

———. *The Babe: The Game That Ruth Built.* New York: Total Sports, 1997.

Robbins, Jhan. "The Time Babe Ruth Hit One for Me." In *The Best of Sport, 1946–1971.* Edited by Al Silverman. New York: Viking Press, 1971.

Robinson, Ray, and Christopher Jennison. *Yankee Stadium: 75 Years of Drama, Glamour, and Glory.* New York: Penguin Studio, 1998.

Runyon, Damon. *The Best of Damon Runyon.* New York: Hart Publishing Company, 1966.

Ruth, Babe. *Playing the Game: My Early Years in Baseball.* Edited by William R Cobb. Mineola, NY: Dover Publications, 2011.

Ruth, Babe, and Bob Considine. *The Babe Ruth Story.* New York: Penguin Books, 1992. Reprint.

Ruth, Babe, et al. *How It Feels to Be a Has-Been by Babe Ruth, and Other Essays from Baseball Greats in Their Own Words.* Rye, NY: Liberty Library Ebooks, 2013.

Ruth, George Herman. *Babe Ruth's Own Book of Baseball.* 2nd edition. Lincoln: University of Nebraska Press, 1992. Reprint.

Ruth, George Herman "Babe." *The Home-Run King, or How Pep Pindar Won His Title.* Whitefish, MT: Kessinger Publishing, 2005. Reprint.

Ruth, Mrs. Babe, and Bill Slocum. *The Babe and I: This Intimate Story of America's Greatest Sports Hero—by the Woman Who Loved Him.* Englewood Cliffs, NJ: Prentice-Hall, 1959.

Sandomir, Richard. *The Pride of the Yankees: Lou Gehrig, Gary Cooper, and the Making of a Classic.* New York: Hachette Books, 2017.

Sarnoff, Gary A. *The First Yankees Dynasty: Babe Ruth, Miller Huggins, and the Bronx Bombers of the 1920s.* Jefferson, NC: McFarland & Co., 2014.

Schart, John Thomas. *History of Baltimore City and County, from the Earliest Period to the Present Day: Including Biographical Sketches of Their Representative Men.* Baltimore, MD: Regional Publishing Company, 1971. Accessed through Google Books.

Schuck, Raymond I. "Babe's in Tourland: How Babe Ruth Was Well-Suited for Barnstorming." In *Baseball and the Sultan of Swat: Babe Ruth at 100.* Edited by Robert N. Keane. New York: AMS Press, 1995.

———. "When the Broadway Limited Stopped in Lima: An Ohio Town Embraces the Babe." In *Baseball and the Sultan of Swat: Babe Ruth at 100.* Edited by Robert N. Keane. New York: AMS Press, 1995.

Shannon, Bill, and George Kalinsky. *The Ballparks.* New York: Hawthorn Books, 1975.

Shaughnessy, Dan. *The Curse of the Bambino*, New York: Dutton, 1990.

Sherman, Ed. *Babe Ruth's Called Shot: The Myth and Mystery of Baseball's Greatest Home Run*. Guilford, CT: Lyons Press, 2014.

Smelser, Marshall. *The Life That Ruth Built: A Biography*. New York: Quadrangle, 1975.

Smith, Red. "The Babe." In *Out of the Red*. New York: Alfred A. Knopf, 1950.

———. "Babe Ruth: One of a Kind." In *The Red Smith Reader*. Edited by Dave Anderson. New York: Random House, 1982.

Smith, Robert. *Babe Ruth's America: A Warm and Rollicking Portrait of the Babe and His Times*. New York: Thomas Y. Crowell Company, 1974.

Sobol, Ken. *Babe Ruth & the American Dream*. New York: Random House, 1974.

Sperber, Murray. *Shake Down the Thunder: The Creation of Notre Dame Football*. Bloomington, IN: Indiana University Press, 1992. Reprint.

Staples, Bill, Jr. *Kenichi Zeninura, Japanese American Baseball Pioneer*. Jefferson, NC: McFarland & Co., 2011.

Steinberg, Steve, and Lyle Spatz. *The Colonel and Hug: The Partnership That Transformed the New York*

Yankees. Lincoln: University of Nebraska Press, 2015.

Sternheimer, Karen. *Celebrity Culture and the American Dream: Stardom and Social Mobility.* New York: Routledge, 2011.

Stevens, John D. *Sensationalism and the New York Press.* New York: Columbia University Press, 1991.

Stevens, Julia Ruth, and Bill Gilbert. *Babe Ruth: Remembering the Bambino in Stories, Photos & Memorabilia.* New York: Stewart, Tabori & Chang, 2008.

Sullivan, Neil J. *The Diamond in the Bronx: Yankee Stadium and the Politics of New York.* New York: Oxford University Press, 2001.

Surdam, David George, and Michael J. Haupert. *The Age of Ruth and Landis: The Economics of Baseball during the Roaring Twenties.* Lincoln: University of Nebraska Press, 2018.

Susman, Warren. *Culture as History: The Transformation of American Society in the Twentieth Century.* Washington, DC: Smithsonian Books, 2003. Reprint.

Swank, Bill, and the San Diego Historical Society. *Baseball in San Diego: From the Plaza to the Padres.* Charleston SC: Arcadia Publishing, 2005.

Tofel, Richard. *Home Run Revolution: Babe Ruth in His Time, 1919–20*. Amazon Digital Services, 2015.

Trachtenberg, Leo. *The Wonder Team: The True Story of the Incomparable 1927 New York Yankees*. Bowling Green, OH: Bowling Green State University Popular Press, 1995.

Tye, Larry. *The Father of Spin: Edward L. Bernays and the Birth of Public Relations*. New York: Picador, 2002. Reprint.

Tygiel, Jules. *Past Time: Baseball as History*. New York: Oxford University Press, 2000.

Ultan, Lloyd, and Gary Hermalyn. *The Bronx in the Innocent Years 1890–1925*. Bronx, NY: Bronx County Historical Society, 1991.

Vancil, Mark, and Alfred Santasiere III. *The Official Retrospective: Yankee Stadium*. New York: Pocket Books, 2008.

Wagenheim, Kal. *Babe Ruth: His Life and Legend*. New York: Praeger Publishers, 1974.

Walker, James R. *Crack of the Bat: A History of Baseball on the Radio*. Lincoln: University of Nebraska Press, 2015.

Walsh, Christy. *Adios to Ghosts*. New York: Zinsmith, 1937.

Weintraub, Robert. *The House That Ruth Built: A*

New Stadium, the First Yankees Championship, and the Redemption of 1923. Little, Brown and Company, 2011.

White, E. B. *Here Is New York.* New York: Little Bookroom, 1999. Reprint.

Witte, Cyril M. "A History of Saint Mary's Industrial School for Boys of the City of Baltimore, 1866–1950." Dissertation submitted to the Graduate School of the University of Notre Dame, Department of Education, August 1955.

Wood, Allan. *Babe Ruth and the 1918 Red Sox.* Lincoln, NE: Writers Club Press, 2000.

Woodward, Stanley. *Paper Tiger: An Old Sportswriter's Reminiscences of People, Newspapers, War, and Work.* Lincoln: University of Nebraska Press, 2007, Reprint.

———. *Sports Page.* New York: Glenwood Press Publishers, 1968.

About the Author

JANE LEAVY, an award-winning former sportswriter and feature writer for the *Washington Post*, is the author of the acclaimed bestselling biographies *Sandy Koufax: A Lefty's Legacy* and *The Last Boy: Mickey Mantle and the End of America's Childhood*, and the comic novel *Squeeze Play*. She lives in Washington, D.C., and Truro, Massachusetts.

HARPER LUXE

THE NEW LUXURY IN READING

We hope you enjoyed reading
our new, comfortable print size and found it
an experience you would like to repeat.

Well — you're in luck!

HarperLuxe offers the finest in fiction and
nonfiction books in this same larger print size and
paperback format. Light and easy to read, HarperLuxe
paperbacks are for book lovers who want to see
what they are reading without the strain.

For a full listing of titles and
new releases to come, please visit our website:

www.HarperLuxe.com